THE BROADCAST JOURNALISM HANDBOOK

SECOND EDITION

GARY HUDSON & SARAH ROWLANDS

Routledge
Taylor & Francis Group

LONDON AND NEW YORK

First edition published in 2007 by Pearson Education Ltd
Second edition published 2012

Published 2014 by Routledge
2 Park Square, Milton Park, Abingdon, Oxon OX14 4RN
711 Third Avenue, New York, NY, 10017, USA

Routledge is an imprint of the Taylor & Francis Group, an informa business

British Library Cataloguing-in-Publication Data
A catalogue record for this book is available from the British Library

Library of Congress Cataloging-in-Publication Data
Hudson, Gary, 1956-
  The broadcast journalism handbook / Gary Hudson & Sarah Rowlands. -- 2nd ed.
        p. cm. -- (Longman practical journalism series)
  Includes bibliographical references and index.
  Previously published as: Broadcast journalism : handbook / Gary Hudson & Sarah Rowlands. 2007.
   ISBN 978-1-4082-4521-7 (pbk.)
   1. Broadcast journalism. I. Rowlands, Sarah. II. Hudson, Gary, 1956- Broadcast journalism. 2007. III. Title.
   PH4784.B75H83 2012
   070.1'95--dc23

                                                            2012008744

ISBN-13: 978-1-408-24521-7 (pbk)

Typeset in 10/12.5pt Minion by 35

CONTENTS

LONGMAN PRACTICAL JOURNALISM SERIES

The Broadcast Journalism Handbook, 2nd Edition – Gary Hudson and Sarah Rowlands
ISBN 9781405824347

Design for Media – Di Hand and Steve Middleditch
ISBN 9781405873666 (coming July 2012)

Journalism Ethics and Regulation, 3rd Edition – Chris Frost
ISBN 9781408244685

Law for Journalists, 3rd Edition – Frances Quinn
ISBN 9781408254141

The Online Journalism Handbook: Skills to Survive and Thrive in the Digital Age – Paul Bradshaw and Liisa Rohumaa
ISBN 9781405873406

The 21st Century Journalism Handbook – Tim Holmes, Sara Hadwin and Glyn Mottershead
ISBN 9781405846325 (coming July 2012)

FOREWORD

How do you learn to broadcast? I've never worked out the answer to that question. When I was a teenager, engrossed in the idea of being on the radio because of a fleeting visit I'd paid to Capital at the age of twelve, I thought you needed a Physics O Level. That would give me an understanding of the way a transmitter worked, I reckoned; what caused feedback; why speakers have magnets.

'Nonsense' said a friend. 'You don't need to know any of that.'

So I bought a book instead. In those days, there was only one book. I remember the title as *Being a DJ* by Emperor Roscoe. A great read it was too – all about how to avoid losing records on your way to a gig. Presenters were gods when I was young. They did not write books. DJs did not talk about how to broadcast. Maybe nobody did.

Spool on a few decades. London is making a claim to be the media capital of the world, and now your digital dial shows up, not only Capital, but a score of other stations. The TV has 250 channels! The media hoover up thousands and thousands of young and aspiring journalists, presenters, producers and technicians (now with Physics GCSE). There is now, more than ever, a need for a book that does quite a bit more than Rosco could, that takes up deep into the jungle of politics, ethics and the law. Well, here it is.

Good luck.

Jeremy Vine

Closer Look boxes focus on key topics or issues in more detail.

Remember boxes highlight the key points at the end of each section – a quick summary and revision aid.

Case Studies look at particular scenarios in broadcast journalism in more detail.

Tip boxes give advice on key techniques and practices in broadcast journalism.

Thinkpiece boxes encourage the reader to consider some of the issues central to working as an informed broadcast journalist.

End of chapter sections suggest **Further Reading** and **Web Links** to help you to explore the topic in more depth.

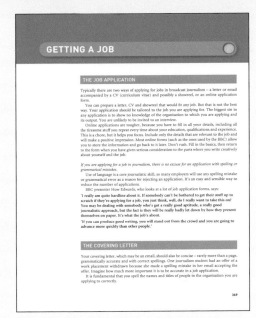

The Essential Guide section provides advice on getting a job, the law, and other tools the broadcast journalist needs.

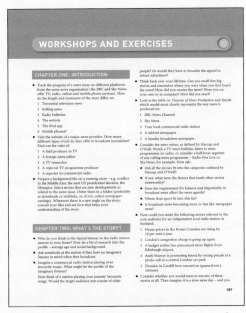

Workshops and Exercises give the opportunity to practise key skills.

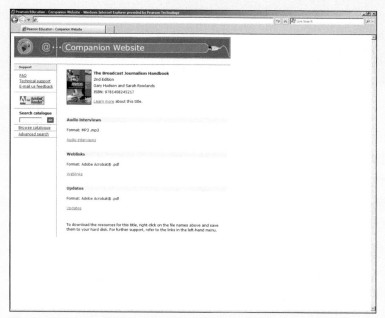

The accompanying **DVD** explains and demonstrates radio and television recording techniques.

The **Companion Website** is the place to go for audio interviews with experts and for updates on the latest developments in broadcasting.

Go to: www.routledge.com/9781408245217

AUTHORS' ACKNOWLEDGEMENTS

The second edition of this book is a product of several years of reaction from professional broadcasters, expert feedback from educators and accrediting bodies, and innumerable conversations with colleagues and students. The contributors, whether named in these pages or not, know who they are and we thank you all.

We are again grateful to the many professionals who welcomed us into their workplaces and homes, and also to the students and teachers who gave such a warm reception to the first edition, making it the leading text in its field. Our thanks too to all at Pearson for their faith in a project that has always been a more costly proposition than most books about journalism.

When we conducted our initial research, many professionals suggested that broadcast journalism was changing so rapidly that the book risked being outdated very quickly. Their fears proved largely unfounded. For this edition, we have taken a particular interest in interactive technologies and social media, and the relationship of professional journalists with their audiences. Six years on and it's clear that most of the changes in working practice have come through evolution not revolution. The old principles of good journalism remain; new technologies enhance rather than replace the old; and, contrary to the fashionable notion of some in the blogosphere, we're not all journalists yet.

Gary Hudson
Sarah Rowlands
April 2012

PUBLISHER'S ACKNOWLEDGEMENTS

We are grateful to the following for permission to reproduce copyright material:

Screenshots

Screenshot on page 8 from BBC Six O'clock News, reprinted by permission of BBC Worldwide Limited; Screenshots on pages 283, 286 Microsoft screenshot frame reprinted with permission from Microsoft Corporation; Screenshot on page 157 from William Wright's interview with Jamie Oliver, http://news.bbc.co.uk/lincolnshire/content/articles/2006/06/01/jamie_oliver_feature.shtml, reprinted by permission of BBC Worldwide Limited; Screenshot on page 283 from RadioMan® Quick Edit Pro, with permission from Jutel Oy; Screenshot on page 286 from Avid Express DV, courtesy of Avid Technology, Inc; Screenshots on page 303 from Curious World Map images, www.curious-software.com, reprinted by permission of Vizrt Ltd; Screenshot on page 304 from 3-D Graphics from senior graphics designer Sue Keeling at the BBC's Mailbox studio, reprinted by permission of BBC Worldwide Limited; Screenshot on page 360 from BBC News at bbc.co.uk/news, reprinted by permission of BBC News Interactive.

Picture credits

Horace Wetton (Staffordshire University): 110.

Text

Extracts on pages 59–60, page 86, page 166, page 350 from BBC Editorial Guidelines, reproduced by kind permission of the BBC; Extract on pages 168–169 from *Guidelines for MPS staff on dealing with media reporters, press photographers and television crews*, produced by the Directorate of Public Affairs © 2006 Metropolitan Police Authority, reprinted by permission of Metropolitan Police Service; Extract on pages 168–169 from *Staffordshire Police Guidelines for Police-Press Relations*, Pocket Guide for Officers, produced by Staffordshire Police Media Unit, with permission from Staffordshire Police Headquarters; Extract on pages 227–228 from The INSI Safety Code, www.newssafety.com/safety/index.htm © International News Safety Institute; Case Study 9.3 from Laurence Lee's report from Russia prior to the presidential elections of 2004, broadcast on Sky News, reprinted by permission of BSkyB Ltd; Case Study 11.1 from Rachel Harvey's report on the Indonesian earthquake, broadcast on BBC Radio 4 18:00 bulletin, 31 May 2006, reproduced by kind permission of the BBC and Rachel Harvey.

In some instances we have been unable to trace the owners of copyright material, and we would appreciate any information that would enable us to do so.

PARTONE THE JOB

CHAPTERONE
INTRODUCTION

WHY BROADCAST JOURNALISM MATTERS

We live in an age of information overload and instant gratification. News bulletins and programmes that used to be available only on television and radio sets are now available on your phone or computer. News reports that were once presented to viewers and listeners only at certain times of day in a running order decided by editors and producers now appear on social networks, blogs, micro-blogs, email alerts and specialist websites, whenever you want them. We thought about calling this book *Download it to Your Fridge* – except it wouldn't have shown up on a Google search for broadcast journalism. But even if your fridge is not web-savvy, you are probably as likely to learn a breaking news story on Twitter as on the radio, and as liable to watch a TV news report on YouTube as on the evening news at home. Despite all these innovations, almost all the most reliable, authoritative and accurate news content is still produced by broadcast journalists.

Technological developments in news – such as cheap video production and the opportunity for anyone to share information on the Web – did not spell the end of journalism, nor mark the death of the news story, as one senior editor suggested. Instead they place a higher premium on a quality to which all professional journalists must now aspire – trust. Without trust, journalism is worthless; with it, journalism stands above the maelstrom of competing online voices and continues to perform its role of informing and explaining. This is one of the lessons of a decade that has seen historic change in the journalistic world.

Andrew Marr, the TV and radio presenter, and a former national newspaper editor at the *Independent*, said in the 2006 Hugh Cudlipp lecture (named after the great editor of the *Daily Mirror* in the 1950s and 1960s) that we are witnessing 'the replacement of a largely written culture – the Gutenberg-Caxton culture, if you like – by a culture largely composed of spoken words and moving images'. Marr said the change was happening because of 'the convergence of television and the Internet delivered to tiny portable screens':

'All kids download film clips and television clips; they quite like the newspaper that is delivered to the front door, but they find it increasingly weird. They find it old-fashioned and nostalgic. They are used to manipulating pictures themselves on computer screens.

'We've all observed how television and even newspapers are adapting the aesthetic and the style of broadband Internet culture. Digital television has the red button, the drop-down menu, the familiarity of moving images in one part of the screen, words in another part of the screen, and perhaps a moving banner at the bottom as well.'

Never before have so many people had access to the means of producing video and audio content that was once the preserve of professional broadcasters. The media has become more fragmented – and interactive. News and ideas are no longer delivered from the top down – from an empowered elite to comparatively passive consumers. Everyone can comment on and engage in the news-making process; news production is less of a lecture and more of a conversation.

But we're not – as some have claimed – all journalists now. The idea of the 'citizen journalist' flourished as the Web enabled people to contribute words and pictures to audiences worldwide without them being scrutinised first or mediated by professionals. But not everybody wanted to be 'journalists' in the traditional sense. Instead, plenty of people were able to contribute to and comment on the coverage of events and issues that affected or interested them. Connectivity and participation have led to 'networked journalism' – a blend of online and traditional, professional and amateur, full-time and part-time media. The new media landscape has added value to all journalism, with professional journalists playing a key role in striving to maintain standards of accuracy and authority and where necessary acting as facilitators of the new ways of engaging with events.

Most of the World Wide Web's content has tiny audiences. Andy Warhol's idea that everyone will be famous for 15 minutes has been modified by the idea that anyone can be famous for 15 people (a phrase, incidentally, that was coined in 1991 by Momus, a Scottish punk techno artist, talking about the fragmentation of the music industry). The digital revolution means almost anyone can produce a video report and put it on a website for anyone to view. It's a great way to spread opinion and information, but it should not be confused with journalism.

Nick Pollard, the head of Sky News for ten years, explains:

'You shouldn't mistake the advance of technology for journalism. It's not. All it does is allow you to get stuff on air quicker, perhaps in better quality and more cheaply, in a way that you just couldn't possibly years or decades earlier, but you still have to have people who understand what the story is, and ideally who've been around the block a bit and can put it in context.'

His successor John Ryley sums up how that affects their output: 'People need to view Sky News as a brand that offers dynamic news content on television, radio and the Internet across a variety of platforms, however and wherever they want it.'

Journalism is gathering, writing and publishing news and factual information. How that information is gathered and published – in print or electronically – changes with the times. But there's no sign in the modern media landscape that there will be any less demand for professional journalists. Instead, the number of outlets for the work of broadcast journalists has multiplied. The economics of the commercial news media – and a worldwide recession – meant a reduction in the number of people employed in traditional newsrooms at the end of the first decade of the twenty-first century. But there were more opportunities for freelances and those on short-term contracts. And a new entrepreneurial journalism emerged, with self-employed multi-skilled operators micro-blogging and contributing words and electronic content to mainstream media. Andrew Marr describes journalism as 'the industrialisation of gossip'. The industry is global and the need for traditional journalism skills is still expanding in China, India and much of Africa. These are exciting times.

Remember

- We live in a culture of spoken words and moving images
- The media has become increasingly fragmented
- The advance of technology is not journalism
- Journalists gather and publish news and information.

Millions of people – many of them the same people who will access occasional online content or put their own work on the Web – still want professionally produced news content. They want journalists to interpret the world around them and tell them what's going on, because they don't have time in their busy lives to work it out for themselves. That is why the role of the broadcast journalist is more important than ever. It's why the traditional skills of the journalist – engaging with people (either face to face or remotely), uncovering information, interpreting it, and presenting what is truthful and relevant to as many people as possible – are more valuable than ever.

Journalists . . . have to gather, check and order facts. They weigh arguments. They make judgements. And they tell stories.

Presenters, reporters and correspondents are supported by researchers, producers and editors. There are many jobs in broadcast journalism other than broadcasting.

The professionals are no longer the gatekeepers – the only people who have access to the means of distributing news. But they have become the arbiters, the ethical guides and the role models for the many amateurs using the new technology. Journalists have to be authoritative content providers and collectors for the multiplicity of delivery platforms available for news and factual information. They have to deliver compelling information to engage audiences. They have to gather, check and order facts. They weigh arguments. They make judgements. And they tell stories.

Story telling is at the heart of good journalism. The stories journalists tell are true stories, not fantasy. Journalists present factual information in a way that audiences can relate to and understand. They do it in an ethical, moral and legal framework.

To suggest that bloggers and video diarists, or people who take video shots of news events, are replacing broadcast journalists is like suggesting anyone with a pen can write like Shakespeare or Dickens. The technology of story telling should not be confused with the art of story telling.

The growth of so-called 'citizen journalists' – people putting their own news online – was a challenge to professional broadcast journalists. But access to a microphone or camera crew has never been the defining characteristic of a professional broadcast journalist.

BBC radio producer Chris Vallance, who created a weekly radio feature for BBC Five Live, using podcasts and blogs from around the world, says being a journalist is not about qualifications: 'There's probably a mindset, an attitude and a commitment to a certain set of practices that makes you a journalist.'

By engaging with people on social networks, Chris was able to generate content and ideas for programmes. He developed a community of sources online:

'It's about communicating with people – getting to know them. Journalists used to spend a lot of time in the pub developing sources and contacts. Maybe this is a less fun way of doing that, but it's certainly more productive. If people know you and trust you, they're more likely to want to be engaged in the finished product.'

The American TV producer Michael Rosenblum, who has trained thousands of people in video journalism, including hundreds of BBC staff, has a broad view of what makes a journalist:

'Anybody who's a cameraman is a journalist. Anybody who came to work for the BBC is a journalist. This notion of separating journalists from craft people is entirely specious and a misnomer.

'Most of what you see on most news organisations is incomprehensible pap, filled with facts sometimes – sometimes not – but generally it has very little to do with journalism.'

Rosenblum says multi-skilling is the only way ahead, and established broadcasters with only one skill – traditional journalism – are in a fight for their lives:

'There's a whole wave of people out there who are young, bright, creative, willing to work for nothing, and can do this with their eyes closed, slam it together and make it really cool. They can sample music through MP3 off the Internet, use a lot of graphics. They make stuff you really want to watch, and at the end of the day they will win out. It's do or die.'

So multi-skilling is essential for *all* journalists. But what makes a *good* broadcast journalist is probably easier to define. Getting to the truth of a story and telling it in a way that engages wide audiences – within ethical and legal guidelines – will always be more important than mastering the latest technology. The professional journalist will want to learn the technical requirements of each new development as it supersedes the last. But the core story telling and writing skills never become redundant. They apply across all platforms.

It's a cliché of journalism that you're only as good as your last story. But it's not true. Yes, you should always try to deliver a performance better than your last. Over time, however, you develop a reputation that is about more than your performance on a given day. A commitment to reliability and accuracy will be recognised by your peers and potential employers. These qualities distinguish the professional from the enthusiastic amateur.

Andrew Marr says these are good times to be a journalist:

'It's time to reassert the need for verbal clarity and to champion good writing. We are in a strong position to do it. We are in a democratic culture of a kind we haven't had before. At a time when journalism seems to be growing a little stronger again we have comparative freedom of speech. Only the means of delivery is in doubt and that is a second-order matter.'

The BBC Director-General Mark Thompson, speaking in 2006 about the corporation's Creative Future plan, said:

'The BBC should no longer think of itself as a broadcaster of TV and radio and some new media on the side. We should aim to deliver public service content to our audiences in whatever media and on whatever device makes sense for them, whether they are at home or on the move.'

Senior editors in broadcasting organisations – and people teaching broadcast journalism in colleges and universities – will remember a 1972 hit by Slade, 'Mama Weer All Crazee Now'. The quirky spelling wasn't obvious to radio listeners – they were hearing rather than reading the title. Nowadays, even radio journalists have to know how to spell correctly, because they will have to re-version their work for online audiences. Today's broadcast journalist provides content for many different platforms. Mama, we're all content providers now.

Remember

- Story telling is at the heart of good journalism
- Journalists make judgements based on professional experience
- All journalists are content providers

There are two essentials. Be fair and be right. And if you want a third one – be bold. It's the job of all journalists to be fair and be right, but be bold too and don't be manipulated.

Greg Dyke, former BBC Director-General

THE PLEASURES AND PITFALLS

Michael Buerk, the veteran BBC reporter and newsreader, introduced himself on a celebrity edition of *University Challenge* as 'sometimes described as a "distinguished journalist", one of the great oxymorons of our time'. Journalists do not have a good reputation, often appearing just above estate agents and politicians when opinion polls ask 'Who do you trust?' But when the same polls are more specific, it becomes clear that tabloid newspaper journalists are the most distrusted, and broadcasters, in particular newsreaders, are well regarded by their audience.

British broadcasting, with its statutory requirement for balance and impartiality, has won the trust of a large part of its audience. And it seduces many of those who work in it.

BBC TV and radio presenter Anita Anand says: 'There is something so charming and immediate and honest about radio. It's the voice. It's the story, and it's hopefully the truth if you do it properly.'

Many are attracted to the job from an early age. BBC Radio Two's Jeremy Vine, who has also presented *Panorama*, *Newsnight*, *The Politics Show* and the swingometer on election specials on TV, says:

'I was intoxicated with the idea of radio when I walked into Capital Radio at the age of twelve and saw Roger Scott sitting in a tiny studio talking to all these people, and I just thought that looks amazing – this is magical. Gradually, as I went through my teenage years, I thought being a DJ is a bit of a kid's thing to do, so I went for journalism.'

Vine's advice to young people:

'When you're studying, just think broadly, read broadly, because the whole business of being in a profession is a narrowing experience. We meet fewer and fewer people; we do a very small number of things. So the wider we can keep our minds at a young age the better.'

Jeremy Vine of BBC Radio Two and TV: 'I just thought that looks amazing. This is magical.'

His BBC colleague George Alagiah grew up steeped in the values of the BBC World Service:

'I grew up in Africa to the strains of BBC News, and being clipped round the earhole by my dad if we were making a noise, because it was a kind of revered half-hour. Then when I was a foreign correspondent, literally the guns would fall silent in Africa around seven o'clock when *Focus on Africa* came on. Rebel leaders on both sides would tune in and try to work out what the hell was going on.'

Alagiah's former co-presenter on the Six O'Clock News, Natasha Kaplinsky, is frequently asked how she got to 'be on the telly'. She says:

'Anybody who just wants to be on the telly would be rooted out pretty early on, because it just doesn't work like that. You have to be completely, firmly immersed in journalism to survive five minutes in a regional newsroom let alone a highly competitive national one.'

She has sympathy with anyone trying to get their first job in broadcast journalism:

'My main message is not to give up. The people who will survive in this industry are the people that won't give up because they'll have so many rejection letters. I literally have a file, and I keep it under my bed and I keep it there as a reminder, for one reason. When I've had a rubbish day, just to remind myself how difficult it was to get the jobs, and how easily they go, and how many people can fill your shoes and probably do your job a lot better than you can do it.

George Alagiah on the BBC *Six O'Clock News*

'It is so hard to break in, but if you accept rejection first off, frankly, you know what? You shouldn't be in the business. If you are absolutely determined to not let "No" be an answer, that's what makes a good journalist.'

Among the joys of journalism are travel and meeting people. Laurence Lee, who's worked for the BBC, Sky News and Al Jazeera, visited thirteen countries across Eastern Europe and Asia during his two and a half years as Sky News's Moscow correspondent: 'I just think I'm really lucky. You'd never go to any of these places unless you were completely mad – countries nobody's ever heard of. It's really interesting and I'm getting paid for this.'

His colleague at Sky News Ian Woods echoes that thought:

'The biggest attraction of my job is that somebody else is paying for me to see the world. That's something to tell your grandchildren.

'The world is shrinking. We can go to all sorts of exotic places on holiday, but nobody goes to Iraq or Afghanistan unless they're going to kill people or going to report on people killing people.

'I like the idea of being a foreign firefighter. There's always a buzz when you get sent on a breaking story. I get excited by spending a couple of weeks in a country I've never been to before.'

THE NEWSMAKERS

We all talk about events and people that 'make the news'. But the real newsmakers are journalists. They set the news agenda. In the language of social scientists they 'frame' the news. They determine how audiences will perceive issues and stories. They portray groups in society in certain ways.

Broadcast journalists, in particular, present information in a way they believe will appeal to the widest possible demographic. They do this to maintain and increase the number of viewers and listeners for their output, because they operate in a competitive commercial environment. Stations dependent on advertising need to maintain the appeal to advertisers; publicly funded broadcasters (in the UK the BBC) need to justify their public funding (the licence fee). In doing this, they inadvertently write for 'the majority'. And so the dominant view in society is well represented in news coverage. Minority views are sidelined, and often silenced. People with opinions outside the political discourse typified by the adversarial party-political parliamentary system are underrepresented. In this way, the concept of 'balance' in reporting has come to mean a balance between differing views that reflect an assumption of the mainstream divide in public opinion. But balance suggests a set of scales and the idea that two opposing views should be weighed against each other. Many debates have more than two sides – and all those sides may not have equal validity. The global warming debate is an example of this: the BBC decided to treat with caution voices dissenting from the overwhelming body of scientific opinion and evidence that human activity is contributing to long-term climate change. It would have been easy to give both 'sides' equal prominence.

Because journalists usually opt for preferred sources of news (the so-called primary definers) the idea that broadcast news is politically impartial (as required by UK law) is questionable. 'Spin doctors' and PR agents play their part to try to influence news coverage. Resisting the influence of 'spin' often means falling into the trap of responding to the agenda set by the spinners.

There is also a bias in the choice of contributors to news programmes. Researchers in the journalism department at London's City University said in early 2011 that far more men than women were interviewed on radio and TV, and when women were seen they were more likely to be 'victims or vox-pops' than selected for their expertise. City's Lis Howell, a former senior TV executive, said this happened despite the best efforts of researchers, particularly in BBC local radio, who tried to invite more women on to programmes.

Journalists need to be aware that a truly objective account is rarely possible. The search for 'truth' is a worthy one. But selecting stories for inclusion in a news bulletin means making a value judgement that excludes other stories; adopting the objective position of the 'outsider' risks criticism that you approach the story from the assumptions of your own background.

Journalists need to be aware of these critical observations. They need to acknowledge that 'dominant values' – the conventions of global capitalism and traditional ideas of race, religion and gender – are not the only way to interpret events. News *is* constructed, but not necessarily because a dominant set of values must be followed. The modern broadcast journalist has access to more views and voices than ever before in history, through traditional and new media. It is an opportunity to challenge convention and develop new audiences for news, and to engage with those audiences as contributors and commentators. Most of the public, with access to an increasing number of platforms of information, still value the signposting and judgement professional journalism can provide.

ESSENTIAL SKILLS

It can be argued that the most basic journalistic skills are writing and story telling. But the modern multi-media journalist has to learn a lot of technology along the way to do the job well.

Although we've heard from former Sky News boss Nick Pollard that technology should not be confused with journalism, a straw poll of workers on Sky News Interactive found that they were using 23 different software programs to get content on air or online. Their deputy editor, Adam Harding, said nobody can expect to be an expert in all these programs, but you need to be good at a number of them to do the job. So the modern broadcast journalist has to be a 'jack of all trades, and master of some'.

Helen Boaden, the Director of BBC News, sums up what those 'trades' should be:

'You're hoping that someone will come with basic law, basic writing skills, particularly for broadcasting, how to ask a question properly and ideally some skills around the technology. But actually what you're asking for as much as that is a kind of mindset. You want curiosity. You want the capacity to challenge, to see stories laterally, to ask difficult questions of everybody. You want people who are interested in the people they're likely to be interviewing but also the issues of the wider world.'

Kevin Bakhurst, Controller of the BBC News Channel, emphasises the starting point for all aspiring journalists:

'An interest in news and current affairs – and not a sudden interest! I do think it's important that people take a long-standing interest and watch TV programmes, listen to the radio, use online and read the papers.

Helen Boaden, Director, BBC News, with the authors

'It is actually increasingly difficult to get people who have a real general knowledge of news and current affairs. I do find that quite worrying and disappointing. I know people are young, but you start asking people in their early twenties about the Callaghan government and even Margaret Thatcher's first government. I've done interviews with people who've been applying for jobs in the newsroom, and they didn't even know who Callaghan was. I wasn't alive during Macmillan, and certainly don't remember any of that, but I know who he was, who was in his government and what the big issues were of the day.

'A lot of the most successful journalists have had a very long interest [in news and current affairs] and have got a good hinterland.'

He says attitude is important. You should enjoy the job:

'It is a genuinely interesting, often exciting, stimulating job. There are so many people who'd like to come and work here. If you don't enjoy it, leave and someone else will come and work here who would enjoy it.

'When people in the newsroom are up for it, excited and confident, that translates directly on to screen.'

Deborah Turness, the Editor of ITV News, also stresses the importance of 'hinterland':

'I always prefer to have people coming to ITV News who have got hinterland, and who have done interesting things in their lives, and who probably haven't just come out of college. Those people are transparent in their vapidity. They've been nowhere, they've done nothing . . . Bring something else to the party. Have you travelled round

Kevin Bakhurst of the BBC: 'Picture power and story-telling with packages are really important.'

Deborah Turness, Editor, ITV News

Kirsty Young: 'Get your on-air miles.'

the world on a unicycle? Have you launched a charity, or do you speak languages, or have you got great passions in your life? Because I think there's a danger that we're creating a whole generation of identikit journalists, who think it is enough to get that degree and then they're going to be a TV star somehow. For me there is greater value placed on writing skills than ever before, and visual creativity.'

Most experienced professionals emphasise the value of starting in local radio. TV and radio presenter Kirsty Young talks of getting your 'on-air miles' – the experience of being on air frequently so that you are comfortable in front of a mic. She recommends starting in hospital or student radio and moving on to local radio.

Rachel Burden of BBC Radio Five Live says: 'I don't think anything substitutes for working in a local environment and having to knock on doors, and dig around for stories. For your credibility as a journalist, that's massively important.'

Helen Boaden expands on that theme:

'Local radio reporting is fantastically valuable. It's like newspaper reporting once was (and still is in some places). You learn the basics. You learn to ask the right basic questions; you learn to handle yourself in a lot of very different and sometimes difficult situations; you learn to talk to people on the phone; you learn to get into people's houses in a subtle and careful way without being exploitative; and you learn law and writing. You'll come with some of that from college, but actually this is where you get to practise it. And you learn from people who've done it before, and who've done it very well.

'It's about being hard working, connecting to the team, sticking up for yourself where you can, and being confident – knowing what you know and, as importantly, knowing what you don't know and being prepared to ask for help. It's important to realise that most people don't mind. So there's a sort of slight humility – knowing what you don't know and trying to do something about it.'

Broadcast journalists work to tight deadlines. Precise time keeping is essential to the point of obsession. John Sergeant, a senior political correspondent with the BBC and then political editor with ITV News, says:

'It's extremely important to make sure you stick to time. It's one of the things that becomes obsessive for a broadcast journalist in ordinary life. It's amazing how people are invited to a party, and if they're broadcasters they'll turn up on time, and find it very difficult to have people turning up five or ten minutes late. It does become an obsession and it ought to. Broadcasters who don't keep to time don't stay in their jobs.'

Many broadcast journalists are used to working long hours, travelling to foreign locations, working throughout the day, barely sleeping, grabbing food when it's available, and not having a day off until the story is over. At home, too, people make sacrifices to gain experience and get on. Natasha Kaplinsky commuted from London to Southampton to present the regional evening news before landing a job at Sky News.

Remember

- Writing and story telling are core skills in journalism
- You need to be a 'jack of all trades and master of some'
- You should have a long-term interest in news and current affairs
- 'On-air miles' help you become comfortable in front of the mic
- Precise time-keeping is essential
- Expect to work long hours

AMBITION

You will need ambition and determination to succeed in broadcast journalism. That should be coupled with a consuming interest in news and current affairs.

Huw Edwards, presenter of the BBC's *News at Ten*, says: 'It's a very difficult area to get into. I'm not sure why lots of people try to get into journalism. Lots of them don't seem to have an interest in actual journalism – it's wanting to be on television, to be on radio or to be performing.'

Shelagh Fogarty, best known as a presenter on BBC Radio Five Live, says she never had a great drive to be a presenter, but she was always interested in news:

'I didn't give a great deal of thought to what job I wanted to do until I was near the end of university [she studied foreign languages]. But I'd always been interested in news. I met an old school friend recently. She said: "You once gave up watching the news for Lent." So I must have been a right news junkie even then! I think I was, because my family's very news oriented, very political, into watching politics and that kind of thing.'

Deborah Turness, of ITV News, says she looks for that kind of enthusiasm: 'I'm looking for people who've got more than just a knowledge of how to do process journalism. I'm looking for people who have got a lively mind, who are inquiring, who have strong opinions and passions – who actually feel the news.'

Frank Gardner says a lot of obstacles were placed in his way before he got a BBC job as a foreign correspondent.

He was told he was too late to enter journalism at 33, that he hadn't been through the graduate training system and that his voice was too posh to be on national television:

'A lot of people at the BBC were very unimaginative when I said I wanted to be a foreign correspondent. They're so blinkered, and the only way to break that is to go out and do it yourself. If necessary, borrow the money, get out there and do it. If the BBC hadn't offered me some freelance shifts [in 1995] I would have gone to Afghanistan with a cameraman, carried his bags for him, paid my own way, seen how he'd done his job and perhaps sold a few stories for print, on the back of that. And that's the way to do it. Just tag on to people.'

The then-unknown Natasha Kaplinsky tagged on to Jill Dando, who was the presenter of the news, *Crimewatch* and the *Holiday* programme. Kaplinsky had been signing on and trying to gain as much work experience as possible. She says:

'I just wrote to Jill and said, "Look, please can you help. I don't know how to get into the industry." And she said, "Come and meet me for a cup of tea," which I did. She was unbelievably elegant. I'd given her a showreel which I'd done, and she was very kind and gave me some constructive criticism, and then she introduced me to her agent and somebody else and that kind of started things off for me.'

The BBC's Anita Anand says:

'Don't sit on your bottom wishing you could be in the industry. Do something. I was working in local newspapers from the age of 14. I worked at the *West Essex Guardian and Gazette*, and I cleared paper jams out of photocopiers, just so I could be around people who were working and see what it was like. You have to love it. It's a hard slog. It's such a boring thing and I used to hate it when old farts used to tell me in newsrooms that you have to pay your dues, but they're right. You have to learn everything from the ground up.'

Huw Edwards, presenter of BBC's *Ten O'Clock News*

Shelagh Fogarty, presenter on BBC Radio Five Live

BBC Security Correspondent Frank Gardner: 'Just tag on to people.'

Juliette Ferrington, a sports reporter with BBC Radio Five Live, who's covered World Cups and the Olympic Games, says you can only succeed if you learn to cope with rejection: 'I was told I'd never be a broadcaster by a BBC local radio station. They just didn't rate me.'

She also had to deal with being a woman in the mostly male world of professional sport and sports reporting. Interviewing footballers presented particular problems:

'They'd try and trip you up. It was a challenge. "See if we can get her on the offside rule, or who our next opponent is or what position I play." It was a learning experience, but once I got through that it was fine and they treated me as maybe a little bit special and they liked me being around.'

Comments about women and the offside rule were to prove the downfall of Sky Sports' Richard Keys and Andy Gray. Their off-air remarks about a female assistant referee led to Gray's sacking and Keys' resignation in January 2011. Ferrington's remarks suggest she regularly encountered casual sexism early in her career. She says a lot of women succeed in television because of the way they look:

'In radio it's ten times harder, because you don't see faces, you don't see pictures, you've got to describe what you're doing, and it's bloody hard work. You need a lot of grit and determination and a thick skin.

'It's a piranha pool. There are not many female sports broadcasters on radio, but you're competing with the men as well.'

Remember

- You will need determination and persistence to succeed
- Tag on to people – learn from experience
- Don't be afraid to start at the bottom and work your way up

THE FREELANCE MENTALITY

Many outlets will employ journalists on a freelance basis or on short-term contracts. Freelances are paid for what they do on a day-to-day basis – either for a particular story or for a day's work at a time. Contract workers may be engaged by a programme for a week or a few months. The job-for-life is almost a thing of the past in current affairs journalism. Ask most journalists about the 'freelance mentality', and they'll say it means never being able to say no. This requires a particular dedication from those who chose the lifestyle, but the versatility of the work on offer means life is often exciting, never dull and often richly rewarded.

Many freelances have a policy of never turning work down. You might not get asked again. Paul Ross, whose career spans serious journalism, local radio presenting and TV light entertainment, has an answerphone message that says: 'I'll do it!' Ross is affable and popular with everyone he works with. A successful freelance can't afford to upset anyone.

Steve Lee, a sports reporter who's worked for most of the major TV networks, might work for a BBC network sports programme, regional ITV and Sky Sports all in the same week. He's not a star name, but he's a trusted professional, respected for his contacts and knowledge of his subject. He says it's not a matter of never switching off. It's just about keeping your wits about you:

'You're always aware of what's going on. You look at the fixtures at the weekend to know what's coming up in the next week. When you visit a town you buy the local paper. You buy the regional papers too. And then a lot of it is reactive day to day.

'Most of my work is in sport, but I read the front pages as well as the back pages. I love the excitement of turning on the radio in the morning and finding out what's happened overnight. I'm fascinated by what's going on in the world. I have been since I was a teenager.

'You develop your contacts over the years and you keep in touch with those contacts and keep adding new ones.'

Natasha Kaplinsky underlines the value of keeping up your contacts. She worked for personalities such as Esther Rantzen and Ruby Wax when she was on the BBC's production panel – a kind of typing pool: 'These people come back into your life at various points. Keeping in touch with people is very important.'

Remember

- Never turn work down
- Don't upset anyone
- Develop contacts

DIVERSITY

Broadcast journalism recruits from all sections of society. You only have to watch your TV screen to realise that it is a microcosm of multi-ethnic Britain. But therein lies the problem. The on-screen talent does not reflect the industry as a whole.

Few people in senior editorial and management positions in the industry are from ethnic minorities. The BBC and commercial television have a good record of recruiting from minority groups. Commercial radio does not.

This was highlighted by Trevor Phillips, the Chair of the Equality and Human Rights Commission, a former presenter and a television executive. At the Race in the Media Awards in June 2006, he said:

'Yes, staff in broadcast organisations are more representative of modern Britain, but the change doesn't go very high in the food chain, and it hasn't penetrated the top management or the boardrooms.

'It hasn't significantly stretched to national radio where actually your colour shouldn't matter. One major radio station, I have been told, cannot count a single non-white presenter amongst its regular voices. In print, especially locally and regionally, the preferred flavour is still vanilla. The fact is that none of this will change by itself.

'Eight years ago, Sir William Macpherson added the term "institutional racism" to our media lexicon. Today, we face an added challenge – deep, institutional complacency.'

The BBC Director-General Greg Dyke coined the phrase 'hideously white' to describe the corporation. He made the comment after a management Christmas lunch in 2000. He said: 'As I looked around I thought, "We've got a real problem here." There were 80-odd people there and only one person who wasn't white.'

Dyke wasn't in office long enough to oversee major cultural change, but his successor Mark Thompson summed up the BBC's commitment to diversity in a keynote speech in June 2004. He said they planned to 'foster audience understanding of differences of ethnicity, faith, gender, sexuality, age and ability or disability, by accurately and sensitively reflecting modern Britain's diversity across our programmes and opening up the BBC itself to talent from every community'.

Anita Bhalla OBE, who became the BBC Head of Political and Community Affairs for the English Regions, said that when she joined the corporation in 1987 she had to cope with a male-dominated newsroom culture that was hard to penetrate.

She shares Trevor Phillips' (and Dyke's) concern about the lack of executives from minorities:

'While the BBC is not "hideously white" any longer and there are more opportunities, there are still issues. We have managed to get an on-screen presence with presenters and reporters from black and ethnic minorities.

'We are also getting more people into the organisation, but we are still not getting enough people into key executive, editorial and managerial posts. This is something we need to work harder at. There is a school of thought which suggests that given enough time it will happen naturally, but when? Perhaps we need to be a lot more proactive in nurturing talent.'

In the meantime, the involvement of people like Bhalla as reporters and correspondents has helped build trust in minority communities. She says: 'When I joined the BBC, its reputation in black and Asian communities was nil. As a correspondent I had to do a lot of footwork before people started ringing me and coming to us with stories. I had to prove I could deliver and get stuff on air.'

Disability is not a bar to working in broadcast journalism, sometimes at the highest level. BBC Disability Affairs Correspondent, Peter White, has been blind since birth. He has worked in local and network broadcasting for over 40 years. He says:

'Don't let anybody say it's impossible for you to work in broadcasting. Most of the problems are not technical, they're human.

'You are only ever discriminated against by people who are no good at their jobs. People who are insecure don't like the idea that disabled people can do their jobs as well as they can.

'Broadcasting is about telling stories in an engaging and exciting way, and you have to convince people that you are the right person to do the job. If they have the right attitude then the technical problems won't be a problem.'

Disability legislation has made it unlawful to discriminate against disabled people, but White warns: 'We may have legislation and pompous statements about mentors, but people don't have the time these days to help. There's a bad life–work balance. You have to want to do it more than other people want to stop you.'

Remember

- Broadcast journalism is a career open to all sections of society
- Ethnic minorities are underrepresented in senior editorial positions
- Broadcasters have been accused of institutional complacency
- Disability should not prevent you getting a job in broadcast journalism

TRAINING COURSES

In the last decade of the twentieth century broadcast journalism training moved from being almost exclusively in-house within the larger broadcast organisations to being delivered in higher education. Recruitment is no longer exclusively from print journalism (the traditional route), but often direct from colleges and universities.

The bigger broadcasters still offer bursaries for people on selected university training courses and have graduate training programmes. The BBC set up its own virtual College of Journalism in 2005. It is for BBC staff and is not an alternative to higher education courses, but its huge array of online learning tools are an invaluable aid to all trainee journalists. You can visit **www.bbc.co.uk/journalism** for everything from video master-classes by senior network correspondents to interactive online lessons in grammar and news writing.

The Broadcast Journalism Training Council (funded by broadcasters such as the BBC, Sky News, ITV, Reuters and the independent radio contractors and by training courses) accredits dozens of courses around the UK. BJTC accreditation is a benchmark of quality, guaranteeing a high level of practical content, including a regular number of 'newsdays' when you will replicate newsroom practice, working in teams to produce your own bulletins and even rolling-news programmes.

You may want to apply for an undergraduate Broadcast Journalism or Multi-media Journalism course and study for three years. Or you can take another subject you are inter-ested in at undergraduate level and move on to a one-year Postgraduate (MA) Broadcast Journalism course. There are specialist Online and Sports Broadcast Journalism courses at some institutions.

Details of undergraduate courses are available through UCAS, the university applica-tions body, and on university websites. A list of courses can be found on the BJTC website (**www.bjtc.org.uk**).

The traditional newspaper training body the NCTJ (National Council for the Training of Journalists) also accredits courses in journalism with multi-media content and it has developed exams in Videojournalism for the Web and Broadcast Journalism, which students must pay to enter. Its standards in these disciplines are less demanding than on specialist broadcast courses.

The BBC presenter George Alagiah says:

'People write to me and ask me what degree should I take, and I don't think what you study matters. The one-year postgraduate course is worth doing, but I don't think there's any particular degree that prepares you for journalism more than any other.'

That view is backed by BBC News Channel controller Kevin Bakhurst:

'You don't need to do a journalism degree to do journalism. If you want to do journalism fine, but I'll certainly give equal weight to people who've done other subjects. I often think people who've done a language degree or a science degree are a rounded person, and they will come and contribute a lot.'

BBC Security Correspondent Frank Gardner studied Arabic and it helped in a first career in merchant banking:

'What I learned after graduating is that Arabic on its own is not much use. You have to combine it with an actual skill such as being qualified in insurance, accountancy, photography, journalism, or whatever. You've got to have a core skill.'

He switched to broadcast journalism at the age of 33:

'I wanted adventure. I wasn't completely new to journalism. I'd been writing articles for magazines and newspapers on a freelance basis since I was 24. I knew how to write but I was completely new to broadcast journalism, so I found out what courses were available – just short one- and two-week courses in TV and radio production – so I understood, or thought I did, how to put together a radio package, a combination of your voice and sound effects, and I did a filming course which, unfortunately, I didn't remember enough of.

'I managed to talk my way into a Latvian women's prison – the first journalist to be allowed in. It was atrocious conditions. There were all these tough, shaven-headed, tattooed women there, broken teeth. There was no hot water, the winter was coming and there was no heating. They were having babies, born in the prison. It was really rough. But I didn't know what I was doing with the camera at the time, and I completely squandered this great opportunity. After that I resolved to learn how to do it.'

Huw Edwards, who's involved in training at the BBC and has been an external examiner on university courses at Cardiff, has this advice to students wanting to study broadcast journalism:

Wanting to 'be on the telly' is not a good enough reason for entering broadcast journalism.

'You will do yourselves an enormous favour if you question yourself quite rigorously as to why you think this is a good course for you to take. Why do you want to be in this kind of area of work? Is it because you're influenced by friends? Is it because you quite fancy being on telly? All sorts of things. And the earlier you go through that process of self-analysis the better it is. The thing you really want to do may, quite frankly, be something you're not really suited to.'

He explains why wanting to 'be on telly' is not a good enough reason for entering broadcast journalism:

'There were eight of us on my BBC training course years ago. All eight of us wanted to broadcast and perform. I'm the only one who's broadcasting. The other seven, I have to say, are far more powerful than me. They're all executives. There was no question on the course: everyone wanted to be on television; everyone wanted to be on camera. That was the attraction. But one by one they all quite correctly came to the view that they weren't properly geared to that. They were actually much better at the production and much better behind the scenes.'

If, unlike Huw Edwards' contemporaries, you have a passion for being a creative power away from the microphone there may be numerous opportunities that open up while your counterparts are struggling to be broadcasters.

The better university courses will include work placements in a broadcast newsroom. BJTC courses have formal arrangements for placements with the major broadcasters. These placements are a chance to make a good impression, to network and make contacts. They can lead to jobs. Mark Austin of ITV News has good advice:

'Young trainees, if they come here, have just got to be prepared to get on with it. Pick up the phone, make calls, and realise that news stories can be got by anybody. It's that enthusiasm you really look for in someone, and an ability to write, which sounds obvious, but it's amazing how few people that come into this business can write. There's a very big difference between writing for newspapers and writing for television.

'You get a lot of people who come in here and don't really give the impression that they are passionately interested in journalism. If you've got that and an

Coming to work at ITN or Sky or the BBC is a huge opportunity for someone who's young and could make their mark.

inquiring mind and an understanding of current affairs and the determination to get on and do things on your own when you're in here, then coming to work at ITN or Sky or the BBC is a huge opportunity for someone who's young and could make their mark just breaking one story or helping to break one story, or doing particularly well on one story. There's nothing to stop you doing that. Someone who can appreciate that will do very well.'

Remember

- There are dozens of broadcast journalism training courses
- Look for BJTC accreditation
- You don't necessarily need a broadcast journalism degree to enter the business
- Many people prefer to take a fast-track one-year postgraduate course after studying a different subject at undergraduate level
- Work placements are a chance to make a good impression with potential employers

CAREER OPPORTUNITIES

How do you knock on the door of opportunity and make sure you get an answer?

The answer is persistence and determination. No two people at the top of broadcast journalism will tell the same story about how they achieved success. But nobody who ever made it will deny that they were persistent, and didn't take no for an answer.

FURTHER READING

Branston, Gill and Stafford, Roy (2006) *The Media Student's Book*, London: Routledge. A comprehensive look at media theory and practice.

Marr, Andrew (2004) *My Trade*, London: Macmillan. Part history/part autobiography – journalism explained by a leading modern practitioner in newspapers and broadcasting.

Randall, David (2000) *The Universal Journalist*, London: Pluto Press. What journalists do and how to do it.

Ray, Vin (2003) *The Television News Handbook*, London: Macmillan. A brilliant hands-on guide to success in TV journalism – including how to get through job interviews.

WEB LINKS

www.bjtc.org.uk The website of The Broadcast Journalism Training Council, listing all its accredited courses in the UK.

www.bbc.co.uk/journalism A superb online resource, with a range of practical learning tools and expert advice from senior BBC correspondents and editors.

CHAPTER TWO
WHAT'S THE STORY?

'**WHAT'S** the story?' That's what a news editor asks a reporter offering a new item for the bulletins. And the reporter will try to respond as concisely as possible, 'selling' the story to the editor. They judge the story against a set of news values – the criteria by which all stories are measured, though often subconsciously.

Finding and telling stories are fundamental to journalism. They are the arts that distinguish the bulletin writer from the gossip in the launderette and the professional content provider from the rambling blogger.

We'll also look at different types of story, and how each should be tackled. We'll consider conventions in broadcast reporting. Why do TV and radio not follow the same agenda as newspapers? And has online news bridged the gap between print and broadcast media?

Along the way we'll try to answer that trickiest of questions, 'What is news?'

WHO DECIDES WHAT IS NEWSWORTHY?

There's a belief among old-school hacks that there's such a thing as a 'nose' for news. They know what a story is and they don't need somebody from outside – particularly somebody who's 'not a proper journalist' – coming along and telling them the stories they should be covering. This elitist view showed in the early resistance of newspapers to embrace the huge advantages the Web offered as a tool for gathering and spreading news. But it's not new. Those dismissed as not knowing what they're talking about have included TV executives, radio station managers and almost certainly any member of the public who had the temerity to phone in. Even TV presenters were not immune: a senior news correspondent was heard observing of a presenter: 'He wouldn't know a story if it hit him on the head wrapped round a house brick!'

There's also a view, from sociologists, that agreed news values are passed on from one group of mostly white, mostly middle-class men to other groups of mostly white, mostly middle-class men, who create programmes according to their own tastes and judgements and then impose them on the audience. The journalists are telling the public: 'We know what you want.'

Maybe there's not much difference between these two models. The only real difference is that the academics have analysed what the journalists do; the journalists didn't bother to analyse what they were doing because they convinced themselves it was instinctive.

In reality neither version does full credit to the way the modern news agenda is drawn up. The news is an interactive process with comment and input from audiences. User-generated content (UGC) is such an important part of the mix that a popular YouTube video is as likely to influence the content of a news programme as a government announcement.

Traditional ideas of 'newsworthiness' – the qualities that make a story worth telling – are based on the news values we outline below. They derive from newspaper practice, and the conventions of radio and TV news. These values include concepts of relevance, immediacy and an appreciation of the diversity of modern culture, and therefore of modern audiences.

The practical implications of this are straightforward. If you know your audience, and what they want, you can answer questions like these. Does the story excite you? Do you want to know more? Will your friends and family – and your audience – want to hear about it?

> Deborah Turness: 'Every single news item that we do should perform some kind of emotional function . . .

Deborah Turness, the Editor of ITV News, says: 'Every single news item that we do should perform some kind of emotional function. So it either absolutely clarifies something and makes the penny drop; it reassures; it explains; perhaps it shocks; perhaps it inspires fear; or perhaps makes you laugh. Perhaps it's delivering some consumer information that makes your life easier to live, or you are informed by it and you might base your decisions on that. There has to be a reason for every story to be in our running order.'

KNOW YOUR AUDIENCE

What the audience wants – or has come to expect – is the biggest factor in determining whether an item is suitable for a particular programme. You need to know what the audience expects. So you will need to know who they are. Many local radio stations invent typical listeners.

1 *The Local Radio Group*, with more than two dozen stations reaching nearly a million listeners a week, imagined their typical listener as Jane, a married mother of two children, in her mid-30s. Jane watches more ITV than BBC, and reads the *Daily Mail*. Because of her children

she is interested in health and education stories. The Jane in Winchester and Macclesfield is more likely to be better off than the Jane in Darlington or Portsmouth (all towns where the group had stations).

2 *BBC local radio* imagined a middle-aged couple, Sue and Dave. He's self-employed; she's a school secretary. They are on their second marriages and have grown-up children. They are saving for a conservatory – or a holiday in Australia.

The average age of the audience for BBC Local Radio is over 55, according to the corporation's own research. The average age of people working in BBC Local Radio is 30, which means most members of staff have to tune in to the values and expectations of their parents' generation.

3 *Heart FM* told staff their audience was mainly women, home owning, intelligent, professional, interested in soaps, gossip, showbiz and up for a laugh at weekends. They read tabloid papers and 'brain-drain fodder' like *Heat* magazine and *TV Quick*. Some have settled down with children; others are Bridget Jones types. They aspire to escape, be it on holidays or just a night out.

4 *Century FM* in the north-east of England – later *Real Radio* – called their target listener Debbie – but they warned their staff not to become too 'Debbie-centric', particularly as one of their most popular programmes was a football phone-in.

Market research refines the data. Statistics have shown that 'main shoppers' – what used to be called housewives – tune in to commercial radio for an average of 15 hours a week; business people for 12 hours. Commercial radio accounts for 69 per cent of the listening of 4–15 year olds – an average of nine hours a week.

Most independent local radio (ILR) stations have a younger audience profile – more under-30s and more women than their rivals. So an ILR station with a target audience of young to middle-aged women won't report stories about elderly people unless they can make them relevant to their own audience – 'Is your granny going to be feeling the cold this winter . . . ?'

Remember

- Learn who makes up your audience
- Work out what they want to know
- Make stories relevant to your audience.

Increasing your audience

Whoever makes up your audience now, you'll want to increase it. Every TV programme, every radio station and every website wants to grow its audience wherever possible. Commercial stations need bigger audiences to prove more attractive to advertisers. The BBC needs viewers, listeners and web users to justify the licence fee.

Growing an audience is about more than just numbers; it is about getting the right audience. People in the wealthier socio-economic groups (the ABC1s) are more appealing to advertisers because they have more disposable income to spend on consumer goods.

> **Growing an audience is about more than just numbers; it is about getting the right audience.**

Advertisers also like young audiences, because they are more likely to change brands or be receptive to new ideas than older people, who are more set in their ways. Channel Four has a higher proportion of young affluent ABC1s in its audience than ITV1 and its revenues reflect this. Another success in attracting the 'right' audience is BBC Radio Four's *Today* programme. It is not the most-listened-to breakfast show, but it is listened to by opinion formers and decision makers in government.

Word of mouth is a good way to increase audiences. 'Talkability' is a word coined to express how much the content of a station is being discussed at work, in the pub, the supermarket or at the bus stop. UTV Radio invites its journalists to ask which stories pass 'the Bingo Hall Test' – which one will their core listeners be chatting about when they go out at night.

Even a station with a minority target audience is in the business of broadcasting – not narrowcasting.

LOCALNESS

In local radio, one of the biggest factors in deciding the importance of a story and its place in the running order is localness. 'This is a local station for local people', as a character in BBC TV's *The League of Gentlemen* might have put it. This leads to the localising of national and international stories: 'Local man feared missing in tsunami.'

Localness is hugely important in attracting audiences and keeping them loyal. Audience focus is at the core of all successful broadcasting, and sometimes leads to uniquely local programming. On 11 February 2011, after two and a half weeks of anti-government protests by hundreds of thousands of people on the streets of Cairo and other major cities, Egypt's President Hosni Mubarak stepped down after 30 years in power. World leaders hailed it as a 'historic change'. But on BBC Radio Stoke the story was second in the running order. Instead – and within only a couple of hours of the announcement from Egypt – they led the drive-time show with tributes to Sam Plank, a much-loved radio presenter whose death from cancer had dominated their output all day. Plank was barely known outside the Potteries, where he was, according to most of those interviewed, 'a legend'. The coverage of his death continued for nearly half an hour before the station moved on to the next item – the local sports round-up.

Remember

- All channels want to increase their audience
- Write stories so they will be talked about
- 'Localise' stories if you can.

See Workshops and Exercises

PUBLIC SERVICE COMMITMENTS

Many UK broadcasters have statutory commitments to public service broadcasting (PSB) – programmes that are for the public benefit rather than commercial gain. All the terrestrial TV stations (BBC1, BBC2, ITV1, Channels Four (S4C in Wales) and Five) have a public service remit, as do the BBC's digital TV channels and BBC radio. The minimum amount of local speech content on independent radio stations (including news) is set out in their licence from the regulator Ofcom.

The PSB requirement includes a commitment to covering a diversity of interests and tastes, including minority interests. In the case of S4C, there is a commitment to the national identity and community of Wales.

Notions of public service inform the way news is covered. Broadcasters present what they believe to be in the public interest as well as what is of interest to the public.

WHO SETS THE NEWS AGENDA?

The audience may be the ultimate judge of news content – they'll switch off if they don't like what they hear – but they don't decide what is newsworthy. Some groups in society have more say in what is broadcast than others.

The education charity the Sutton Trust, which aims to provide educational opportunities for people from non-privileged backgrounds, reported in June 2006 that more than half Britain's top journalists went to private schools. A further third went to grammar schools. One danger of this is that senior journalists might be out of touch with their audience's concerns.

Theories of News Production

The Big Brother model (Manipulative)	The Dominant View model (Hegemonic)	The Audience Knows Best model (Pluralist)
The mass media are controlled by the owners of broadcasting and the press. This model is based on the Marxist position, which divides society into capitalists and the proletariat.	One set of ideas dominates society – what we call 'common sense'. The media consider these ideas normal and true.	There is a plurality of media outlets, each offering different perspectives to different audiences.
The media owners manipulate the audience. They tell them what they want them to know.	The news agenda is set by journalists and editors trained according to a shared set of values – largely because they are recruited from the same section of society – historically, white, middle-class and male. They pass on their values to new recruits, whatever their backgrounds.	The audience gets what it wants. And if it doesn't like it, it can look somewhere else.
They get news from official sources and diary events: the government, the church, royalty and capitalist press agencies, which all but monopolise the news agenda. They promote big business and capitalist interests.	News comes mostly from official and diary sources, because they are considered reliable and have the resources to offer information quickly.	News comes from a variety of sources: all the *official* ones, but also journalists' contacts and investigative reporting, 'ordinary' people contacting news organisations with their grievances, 'stringers' other than the main news agencies, pressure groups and 'axe-grinders'.
Conscious bias in the system means the rich get richer and powerful people get more powerful. Social conventions are reinforced. The notion of 'common sense' is a cultural concept that impinges on the selection of stories.	Most news organisations are based in London, so metropolitan (London) bias occurs because of the constraints of time, money and technical resources.	Broadcast organisations try to report the news impartially. Any bias is determined by what the audience wants, and one set of views is usually balanced by an opposing set of views.

See Workshops and Exercises

There has been a lot of academic study of the relationship between journalists and their sources. Some cultural critics argue that dominant groups in society such as politicians and the police are 'primary definers' of events. They set the parameters for discussion, and journalists are 'secondary definers', passing on the interpretations of the elite groups. Tony Harcup says in *Journalism: Principles and Practice* (2004): 'The question of power relations between journalists and sources has been explored at length by academics while journalists have been more concerned with the practicalities of getting the story.'

We shall look at the many ways of getting the story. But, first, have a look at the simplified theoretical models of how news is spread.

WHAT MAKES A STORY WORTH COVERING?

Broadcasters no longer slavishly follow the news agenda set by newspapers. Our bulletins would be out of date as soon as they appeared if we did. The Independent Television Commission (whose role is now performed by the regulator Ofcom) found in a 1998 survey that more than 70 per cent of the UK population relied on television as their main source of national and international news. But that dominance is challenged by online news. In the US, the Washington-based Pew Research Center found that the Internet overtook newspapers as a news source for most people in 2008, and in 2011 they reported online sources had overtaken TV for people under 30.

In 2006, a survey for the BBC and Reuters, the news agency, found national television in the UK was trusted by 86 per cent of people compared with 75 per cent who trusted national newspapers.

The most trusted specific news brand in Britain was BBC News, mentioned by 32 per cent, compared with 3 per cent for the *Daily Mail* and 2 per cent each for *The Times* and *Daily Telegraph*.

Nonetheless, broadcasters are still in debt to the news values established by the print media. They form the basis for a lot – but not all – of the judgements made in broadcast newsrooms.

THINKPIECE TEN NEWS VALUES (BASED ON A SURVEY OF NEWSPAPERS)

The following is a list of the types of stories that conform to the traditional news values of modern newspapers. Consider it in the light of the typical news agenda of broadcasters.

Tony Harcup and Deirdre O'Neill studied nearly 1300 cuttings from 'page leads' in newspapers and published a list of ten categories that describe what is selected as 'news':

- **The power elite**
  Stories concerning powerful individuals, organisations or institutions

- **Celebrity**
  Stories concerning people who are already famous

- **Entertainment**
  Stories concerning sex, showbusiness, human interest, animals, an unfolding drama, or offering opportunities for humorous treatment, entertaining photographs or witty headlines

- **Surprise**
  Stories with an element of surprise/and or contrast

- **Bad news**
  Stories with negative overtones such as conflict or tragedy

- **Good news**
  Stories with positive overtones such as rescues and cures

- **Magnitude**
  Stories perceived as sufficiently significant either in the numbers of people involved or in potential impact

- **Relevance**
  Stories about issues, groups and nations perceived to be relevant to the audience

- **Follow-ups**
  Stories about subjects already in the news

- **Newspaper agenda**
  Stories that set or fit the news organisation's own agenda

  Harcup, T. and O'Neill, D. (2001) 'What is News? Galtung and Ruge Revisited',
Journalism Studies, 2(2): 261–80.

'Galtung and Ruge' were, and are, widely cited in academic studies of news media. Norwegians Johan Galtung and Mari Ruge, who published their research in 1965, were concerned with how overseas events were reported – or not – in newspapers in Norway. Tony Harcup and Deirdre O'Neill, who have both been working journalists and academics in the UK, set out to find out whether the Norwegians' list of values applied to British national newspapers at the end of the twentieth century. They approached it from a different angle: 'Their concern was with events and how they did or did not become news. Our concern has been with published news items and what may or may not have led to their selection.'

Not surprisingly, given their very different approach, Harcup and O'Neill concluded: 'The much-cited Galtung and Ruge list of news values should be regarded as open to question rather than recited as if written on a tablet of stone: the same critical scepticism should also be applied, of course, to the set of contemporary news values we propose.'

Importantly for broadcasters, Harcup and O'Neill say: 'It would be illuminating to compare our findings with the categorisation of news values, operating at local, regional and international levels; in broadcasting and online media as well as print; to explore changes over time; and to take the process further through interviews with working journalists.'

This book doesn't set out to redefine news values for broadcasters, though it does contain many examples of the criteria they apply, and it does include plenty of comment from working journalists.

See Workshops and Exercises

A CLOSER LOOK

NEWS – SOME DEFINITIONS

'When a dog bites a man, that is not news, but when a man bites a dog, that is news.'

Charles A. Dana, nineteenth-century editor of the *New York Sun*

'News is something somebody somewhere wants to suppress; all the rest is advertising.'

Lord Northcliffe, nineteenth-/twentieth-century newspaper proprietor

'News is the first rough draft of history.'

Ben Bradlee, Executive Editor, *Washington Post*

'News is what a chap who doesn't care much about anything wants to read. And it's only news until he's read it. After that it's dead.'

The hack reporter Corker in Evelyn Waugh's *Scoop*

'News is anything that makes a reader say "Gee whiz!"'

Arthur MacEwen, editor of the *San Francisco Examiner*

'It's stuff I care about, and stuff I want to pass on.'

Anonymous, quoted in the *Guardian*, 19 June 2006

NEW VALUES FOR BROADCASTERS

When a reporter is asked 'What's the story?', he or she will have a rough idea of how the item will sound or what pictures will be needed. But in a busy newsroom the editor or producer wants a swift response, so the answer will probably be a one-sentence summary. Most journalists agree that the best stories are those that have a combination of several of the following elements, although they don't formally tick them off when they're asked.

Relevance

The relevance of a story to the audience is a result of both its cultural impact and its political importance. If petrol taxes go up in the budget, that's a political decision that affects the finances of all drivers, and the families of all drivers, which means almost everybody. In the long term rising fuel costs might change people's driving habits, affecting all road users, which means almost everybody. According to the balance of contemporary scientific opinion, levels of fossil fuel consumption are changing the global climate, which definitely affects everybody. By these criteria this is a big story.

On the other hand a reduction in corporation tax for small businesses would interest the proprietors, employees and suppliers of small businesses, but not other people. The importance of the tax cut might need to be explained in terms of how it will boost the economy and create job opportunities. It does have relevance to a wider audience, but it's a harder story to sell.

The trial of Michael Jackson for alleged child abuse, his death in 2009, and the decision to try his personal doctor for manslaughter had no impact at all on the audience's pockets – except perhaps in their decision whether or not to buy any more Michael Jackson albums. But they were massive stories because of their enormous cultural resonance. Almost everybody has heard Michael Jackson's music and his records can be found in almost every household. He'd been the biggest pop star on the planet. And in an age where celebrity culture dominates the tabloid agenda, and even the mundane details of the lives of minor television personalities sell newspapers, these were the tragic last chapters in the life story of a global star in crisis. The separate allegations of child abuse and later manslaughter were serious in their own right, but more than that the court proceedings opened the doors on one of the most bizarre lifestyles ever reported.

Jackson's story has relevance because it informs our relationship with those around us. It is a form of social currency: something everybody is talking about. Bluntly, it is good gossip.

If the relevance of a story is not clear to the audience, you need to tell them why it matters: like explaining the role of small businesses in the economy.

Remember

- Ask how a story impacts on the audience
- Explain why stories matter
- Value 'good gossip'.

See Workshops and Exercises

Interest

News has to be interesting. Anything that takes up valuable air-time on radio or television, or even space on a website, should be of interest to the audience.

If a story interests you, the journalist, it should interest the audience. You need to detach your personal interests from your professional judgement. News judgement is one of the most valued qualities in any journalist.

Should what interests an audience also entertain them? Rupert Murdoch built the biggest news organisation in the world. He became more powerful than any twentieth-century press baron. And he said of his global empire: 'We are in the entertainment business.'

News as entertainment

So where do news and entertainment meet? Is something news just because it is new and entertaining? Clearly newspapers, which have lost their role as providers of fresh news, have to offer entertainment (and analysis) as an alternative to traditional news. Tabloid papers unashamedly run many stories simply because they are entertaining. The sex lives of soap stars are not traditional news. The broadcast news agenda is defined more by the public service ethos of the need to 'inform, educate and entertain'.

Telling stories in an entertaining way is not the same as choosing entertainment over information – and certainly not the same as 'infotainment', a term frequently used as a criticism by those accusing the media of 'dumbing down'. There are stories that we call 'human interest' – stories about people. And there are other stories where we show their impact on one person or group of people to make them relevant to other people. An entertaining treatment can make a complicated story interesting and accessible. 'Worthy but dull' remains a damning indictment of any report.

THINKPIECE

THINKPIECE — THE PUBLIC INTEREST V. INTERESTING TO THE PUBLIC

The 'public interest' is a very different idea from simply being 'of interest to the public', as judges and politicians are quick to point out to journalists. Lurid stories about the private lives of celebrities may be of interest to lots of people, but their publication is rarely in the public interest.

The public interest is an important legal concept – the justification for the publication of material of social importance even when it infringes other legal rights of individuals or organisations. That is why the Ofcom Code allows secret filming or recording to be used by investigative journalists when 'there is prima facie evidence of a story in the public interest'.

In 2000, a judge ruled that a BBC *Panorama* programme was in the 'public interest'. 'Who Bombed Omagh?' was about the 1998 atrocity in which 29 people died, and it named the suspects. The Northern Ireland Human Rights Commission tried on the day of the programme to stop its broadcast, because it would be a breach of the human rights of nearly everybody involved – the police, the suspects, the survivors and the relatives of the dead – and the show was condemned as a 'trial by media'. Ninety minutes before transmission, Mr Justice Kerr accepted the BBC's argument that a ban would mean no prima facie evidence of criminal conduct should ever be exposed in public for fear of prejudicing something or someone. That would have put an end to newspapers and broadcasters exposing corruption. Similar public interest arguments won *Panorama* the right to show 'The Corruption of Racing', an exposé of alleged horse race fixing, two years later.

There is also a public interest test in the Communications Act of 2003 after extensive lobbying by pressure groups and the Labour peer and film producer Lord Puttnam. This means viewers and listeners have to be treated as citizens as well as consumers of commercial services.

A public interest test is developing too in libel cases. After the *Sunday Times* accused the Irish Prime Minister Albert Reynolds of misleading the Irish parliament, he sued. The paper lost the case, but for the first time judges ruled that the media had a duty to inform the public and engage in public discussion of matters of public interest. This is known as the 'Reynolds defence' and, as more media organisations use it in court, their duty to the public is being more closely defined by the judges.

It is important that broadcast journalists are aware of the debate about public interest and the legal precedents being set in the courts. It is equally important that we know how to interest an audience and engage them in often complicated issues.

Shock value

The very 'newness' of something – its shock value – can make something news. Rarely has an event had such an impact on the British public as the death of Diana, Princess of Wales. It was shocking to wake up on a summer Sunday morning in 1997 and discover that one of the most famous women in the world had died in a car crash; so shocking that many of us spent the rest of the day in front of our televisions.

Diana's funeral attracted a TV audience of many millions worldwide. The funerals of ordinary people caught up in extraordinary events also feature on news programmes. In April 2006 in Leek, Staffordshire, TV cameras were out in force for the funerals of three children killed in an explosion at their home. The funeral of a man who died in the same incident – their mother's boyfriend – was also covered. It was a domestic tragedy that shocked a rural community. The news media transmitted the shock to a wider audience, and the audience shared the mourning at the funeral. The initial event was clearly shocking. Does that make the funerals newsworthy? Is the coverage an intrusion into private grief or can it be justified as a tribute to those who died? Where there is a continuing police investigation, after a murder for example, reporting a funeral can keep the story – and any appeal for witnesses – alive.

Drama

Some stories grab audiences simply because they are so dramatic. Real life can have plot twists worthy of the best novels and plays. Look at the events in the life of MP, novelist, mayoral candidate, adulterer, perjurer and convict Lord Archer – every episode could have come straight from a soap opera, complete with cliffhanging 'will-he-won't-he' endings.

> **'How would you tell it to your mates in the pub?' 'Can you explain this to the receptionist at the gym?'**

The English novelist and essayist G. K. Chesterton famously said: 'Journalism largely consists of saying "Lord Jones dead" to people who never knew Lord Jones was alive.' It begs the question, would people have been interested to know who Lord Jones was if we'd told them? If Lord Jones had a life similar to Lord Archer's, we probably would.

When encouraging journalists to write in a conversational style, editors will often suggest: 'How would you tell it to your mates in the pub?' or 'Can you explain this to the receptionist at the gym?' It's also worth asking: 'Would your mates in the pub or the receptionist at the gym be interested in this?'

Remember

- News has to be interesting – to you and the audience
- News can be presented in an entertaining way
- Shock value and drama are important elements in choosing stories.

Pictures

In television and online, the level of interest is often determined by the pictures available. The drama of floods in Boscastle in 2004 was captured in home video footage later shown around the world. Exceptional rainfall caused two rivers to overflow their banks. Cars and trees were swept down the main street. Later, the footage from helicopters as people were lifted to safety from rooftops added to the spectacle.

Great pictures – from your own camera crews, from the emergency services, or from people with their own video on cameras and phones – can turn an ordinary story into exciting television.

People will talk about great pictures. The biggest stories are remembered through powerful images: smoke billowing from the World Trade Center on 11 September 2001; a lone protester in front of a tank in Beijing's Tiananmen Square in 1989; Zinedine Zidane's head-butt in the 2006 World Cup Final. And smaller stories can become more memorable if pictures are available: an air-sea rescue; a factory fire; a spectacular goal.

Remember

- Great pictures can turn an everyday story into a memorable one.

When ITV News asked viewers to vote for 'The Shot that Shook the World' as part of the 50th anniversary celebrations of independent television in the UK in 2005, the poll showed how public perceptions of what is newsworthy are affected by time and distance. This was the result of the vote for the best news pictures in 50 years:

1 The second aeroplane hitting the World Trade Center, 2001

2 Man landing on the moon, 1969

3 Tsunami, 2004

4 President Kennedy assassinated, 1963

5 England's World Cup win, 1966

6 The death of Princess Diana, 1997

7 Ethiopian Famine, 1984

8 Tiananmen Square protests, 1989

9 Liverpool's Champions League comeback, 2005

10 The fall of the Berlin Wall, 1989

Most commentators would agree that the running order would be very different if the poll had been taken in another country or at another time. Diana's death might well have topped a UK poll in late 1997. England's World Cup win would be unlikely to feature in any other nation's top ten. And in any other year or any other country, Liverpool's comeback, remarkable though it was, would probably not have featured at all. There's a sporting chance Manchester United's Champions League Final comeback might have been mentioned if the vote had taken place in 1999.

The moon landing would almost certainly have topped any poll of the late twentieth century. Is 9/11 a more significant event? Journalists – and ITV viewers – would be better off leaving that judgement to historians.

Immediacy

News has to be new. When it is no longer new, it's not news.

It is stating the obvious – but news has to be new. When it is no longer new, it's not news.

They don't even wrap fish and chips in yesterday's newspapers any more. But at least newspapers have the virtue of being available to read again if you need to refer back to them.

Much time and effort is expended in newsrooms bringing stories up to date and finding new angles to make them as immediate as possible. An editor will dismiss a story that has already been reported elsewhere as a 'history lesson'. But sometimes a story that has appeared elsewhere is so important that it can't be dismissed lightly. In these instances reporters will search for a new 'nose' or 'peg' to give the story 'new legs'. Don't worry about the mixing of metaphors in the last sentence: just remember that the job is about giving people up-to-date information. Tell them something they don't already know.

Broadcast news is of the moment or it is nothing. That's one reason why so much emphasis is placed these days on reporting live from wherever the news is happening. If you can't go live, then you have to tell the very latest on a story.

What counts as 'new'?

Journalism is about more than just reporting events. So, what happened may not be new, but the information must be. Terrorists know this. They will release a video of a suicide bomber's last message weeks after the bombing, or even on the anniversary of the event. It revives the story. Anniversaries of major events can be the 'peg' (or reason) for running any story.

Often facts emerge about events many months or even years after the events themselves, or details come to light that make a previously unreported event newsworthy. For example, the former prime minister John Major became newsworthy again when ex-MP Edwina Currie revealed they'd had an affair.

There are formal inquiries into events which also make them news again:

● **Court cases** give an opportunity to relate information that has previously been out of the public domain. It is a principle of the law (both the law in Scotland and the law in the rest of the UK, which have many differences) that reporting restrictions apply until a case reaches trial, so that a jury is not unfairly influenced (see the Law section at the back of this book). This means there's a chance for the whole story to be told when the case is heard. Once it is told in open court, in front of either the magistrates or a judge and jury, the story can be reported. The bonus for reporters is that accurate, contemporaneous court reporting is covered by absolute privilege in law. In other words, contentious and other-wise potentially libellous material can be included without fear of legal redress. What you are not allowed to do in the UK is to record and broadcast proceedings in magistrates' and crown courts. It is also unlawful to take pictures within the precincts of the court – and that word 'precincts' is defined by the magistrate or judge, not by you as a reporter. It could include the steps of the court, the street or a lawn outside: the very places where camera crews want to put their tripods.

A CLOSER LOOK

REPORTING RESTRICTIONS

The law on contempt of court is designed to allow defendants a fair trial. The idea is that a jury should only hear the evidence in court, rather than through the newspapers or on a TV or radio bulletin.

Restrictions apply as soon as a case is active. This means when a person has been arrested; a warrant for arrest or a summons has been issued; or a person has been charged orally.

At a preliminary hearing in a magistrates' court of a case that's likely to go to crown court and be tried by a jury, reporters are only allowed to report the bare details of the case. These include the name, age, address and occupation of the accused and witnesses, the charges, bail conditions, and the time and place to which proceedings are adjourned. You can name the lawyers in the case and whether legal aid was granted. The Magistrates' Court Act 1980 sets out these reporting restrictions. They can be lifted at the request of the defence. The guiding principle behind the 1980 Act is that anything that might later be presented as evidence before a jury cannot be reported at preliminary hearings because it might prejudice the jury's deliberations.

- **Inquests** are another forum where new facts – often about tragic deaths – come to light. An inquest is held whenever someone dies in unusual or suspicious circumstances. The opening of an inquest will hear evidence of the identity of the deceased and the cause of death. How they died is determined later, at a full hearing after the police and investigating agencies have gathered all the available evidence. In most cases a coroner sitting alone will record a verdict. Occasionally a jury is needed to hear the evidence and return a verdict. Misadventure, unlawful killing, suicide and accidental death verdicts usually mean there is a story to tell. Death by natural causes does not normally provide good copy, unless there were circumstances causing wide public interest – the death of a celebrity, for example. An open verdict means there is still cause for doubt. A 'narrative' verdict tells the story of what happened.

  Coroners also hold inquests into treasure trove – to determine the ownership of hidden or lost valuables. These hearings are rare, but almost always make fascinating copy.
- **Accident and planning inquiry reports** are also sources of new stories about old events. Formal hearings (into major accidents, such as plane crashes, or plans to build motorways or redevelop town centres) are followed by the release of a report, usually months later. The hearing and the outcome will be reported separately, meaning there are several chances to tell the story.

Just occasionally a story is so remarkable it doesn't matter that it has grown a few whiskers. Britain's news media reported, to most people's astonishment, on 6 July 2005 that a teenage sleepwalker had been rescued after being found asleep on the arm of a 130 ft crane. Incredibly she had climbed the crane and crossed a narrow beam before curling up on top of a concrete counterweight. The story had no relevance to listeners, other than that it was an amazing tale. The fact that it had happened 11 days earlier did not stop its being news on the day it came to public notice.

What's new? A check list

The criteria for judging what is new (rather than what is news) are clear:

- Is the story being told for the first time?
- Is new information being made public?
- Has the story changed?
- Are key people talking for the first time?
- Are there new sound clips or moving pictures?

If the answer to *any* of the above is 'yes', then you have a new story.

Remember

- News has to include new information
- The event itself need not be new.

Keeping it fresh

For broadcast journalists, yesterday's news – most of what appears in newspapers – is not news. But sometimes yesterday's news is so big that it demands to be retold for a fresh audience. Typically this applies when a story happens late in the day, and only makes the late bulletins. In radio, breakfast is the biggest audience, so the station wants to be able to retell the story to the largest available number of listeners the next morning.

> For broadcast journalists, yesterday's news – most of what appears in newspapers – is not news.

Moving a story on is an important skill. Updates are the most obvious way of doing so. New information gives the story a new lead. When a new line is available it is fairly straight-forward to use that as the top of the story for future bulletins. Occasionally there is little new information, but it is still vital to give the audience news in a way that sounds immediate.

Different treatments can also make a story sound fresh. In bulletins, you might start with a copy story, then use a voicer, an interview clip or a wrap in later bulletins.

In news programmes, stories can be treated in different ways too. You might send a links vehicle (radio car or satellite truck) to a location for live interviews, or invite people into the studio for a discussion. On a crime story, you might want to talk to a victim of crime or an expert on criminal behaviour.

TIP BOX

UPDATING – TECHNIQUES

The simple way to update a story is to ask, after an event, what happens next? Usually the answer is fairly straightforward.

After a road accident the police investigate it. So 'Two people have died in a road accident' becomes, for the next day's bulletins: 'Police are investigating a road accident in which two people died.'

After an election result, the parties assess the consequences of victory or defeat. So, 'The Conservatives have won the most seats in the General Election but do not have an overall majority' becomes, in later bulletins: 'The Liberal Democrats are in talks with Labour about a power-sharing agreement.' And other events follow: 'The Conservatives and Liberal Democrats are to form an historic coalition.'

The day after violent clashes in London between the police and students demonstrating against university tuition fees, the story became: 'Dozens of protesters are due to appear in court this morning.'

'Liverpool have come from three goals down to become champions of Europe' became, the next day: 'Huge crowds are expected in the streets of Liverpool for the return of football's European Champions.'

Many local radio stations will deliberately withhold information to use as a fresh line for later bulletins. Veteran local radio broadcaster Stuart Linnell OBE used to stretch one interview with Coventry City's football manager across at least three days of Mercia Sound's output. It is difficult to make your material sound fresh these days, if viewers of Sky Sports News have already heard the same soccer boss saying the same thing two days earlier.

Nonetheless, a guide issued by the radio company the Wireless Group to its journalists recommended that interviews should be long enough to take several cuts out to update bulletins and for overnights. When the story is not being reported widely elsewhere this is sound advice.

When you're listening to the radio, you expect different things at different times of day. First thing in the morning you probably want a digest of the day's news, a summary of what's happened overnight, anything exciting from the morning's newspapers, and what's going to be happening during the day. If you're on your way to work, you'll want travel information too. But by the end of the rush-hour, or 'morning drive-time' as radio schedulers call it, you'll probably have relaxed into wanting to be entertained or informed in a less frenetic form. You won't want information you have already heard.

A lunchtime audience will expect a summary of the events of the day so far and a look ahead to what's likely to happen during the rest of the day. Courts sit in the morning, but not before ten, and early sessions can often be taken up with legal argument. But by lunchtime there is usually something to report. The House of Commons' business is conducted mostly in the afternoon and evening, so parliamentary stories generally break after midday. The weekly Prime Minister's Questions – always a source of a headline or two – begins at noon and runs for half an hour – ideal for lunchtime bulletins. By mid-afternoon, parliamentary announcements will have been made. Reaction is gathered, either from the floor of the House, using clips from the parliamentary broadcasting service shared by all broadcasters, or in interviews. These are conducted outside, usually on College Green, the stretch of lawn opposite the public entrance to the Commons, or in Millbank, where the broadcasters have their offices.

By the end of the working day, during the evening drive-time, the second highest number of listeners during the radio day will be expecting a round-up of the day's events. Traditionally television news bulletins are scheduled at a time when they can be watched by people who have just returned home at the end of the working day (*BBC News at Six* for example) and then late in an evening's viewing (*News at Ten*).

> **Now that people have news on tap . . . the traditional bulletin may be under threat.**

Online news and rolling news stations have changed the audience's expectations. The idea of an 'appointment to view' may still be popular in many households, but people are used to having news on tap – and being able to filter the kind of news they receive – so the traditional bulletin may be under threat. We no longer have to make a conscious decision to look for news. Online and mobile phone services will deliver it to us.

Audiences at different times of the day have different expectations. You need to update stories, look for new angles and keep your output fresh. Sometimes you can withhold information to use later in the day or the next morning.

Remember

- Updating stories to keep them fresh is an important journalistic skill
- In local radio, exclusive information can be withheld to freshen up later bulletins
- Audiences expect the latest.

Controversy

It's hard to believe today, but the BBC – when it was still the British Broadcasting Company and not a Corporation – was prohibited from broadcasting 'controversial' material. Today controversy is one of the most obvious values contributing to newsworthiness. Many 'rows' are created by journalists seeking an angle for a story, but there is still a place for genuine political debate.

The news agencies that compiled the first radio bulletins were acknowledged on air. In the early 1920s, the BBC did not want to be seen as a provider of information in its own right. Indeed, so timid was the national broadcaster that they did not air news bulletins until after 7 in the evening. The news agencies had done a deal with the newspaper proprietors, who did not want to see their sales damaged. It's no wonder that Marxist analysts reckon the news agenda is determined by a controlling economic elite.

Even more remarkable to those of us used to a diet of 24-hour news, a BBC announcer on Good Friday 1930 told the nation: 'There is no news tonight.' That wasn't the only time that happened. Three-quarters of a century later, the *Guardian* newspaper could joke in an ad for its web services: 'Isn't it amazing that the amount of news that happens in the world every day always just exactly fits the newspaper?'

Much modern news content is controversy generated by journalists. They invite comment on issues from politicians or people already in the news, and then report their comments as a new story. Politicians and other opinion formers vie to be quoted in this way. In 2005, in the days leading up to the parliamentary vote on a bill to detain terrorist suspects without trial for up to 90 days, the Prime Minister, Tony Blair, the Metropolitan Police Commissioner, Sir Ian Blair, and the Home Secretary, Charles Clarke, seemed to be competing to see who could make the latest statement on the issue and so lead the bulletins.

> **Responsible journalists will be wary of presenting every new statement on an issue as if it were a dramatic development.**

Responsible journalists will be wary of presenting every new statement on an issue as if it were a dramatic development. But a balanced presentation of the arguments can involve focusing on different viewpoints in different bulletins.

Remember

- Controversy is an important factor in public debate
- Some controversy is a product of the way journalists select information rather than a true reflection of events.

Proximity

Controversy on its own is not enough unless the story fits other news criteria. It has to be relevant and interesting to the audience. Another factor that might make it relevant is proximity – or closeness to home. This is different from localness, which we'll discuss later. It's a concept that is defined by people's perception of themselves and how they fit into the world around them.

In the Second World War, television broadcasts were suspended and the British nation relied on BBC radio for the most immediate information about the progress of the war. The reputation of the BBC for authoritative news coverage was established during this time. Since then, many more wars have been reported but they were always overseas events. During the Second World War, British civilians were at risk. There can be no greater demonstration of the proximity of news to the audience; national security, and more specifically the very life and death of the listeners, was at stake. When the IRA bombed targets in England from the 1970s onwards, similar considerations affected the coverage. The success of terrorism is measured politically not in terms of lives taken, but in its effect on public opinion through the news media.

The coverage of subsequent wars – particularly those in the Falklands, Iraq and Afghanistan – focused on the involvement of British troops: sons, daughters, brothers, sisters, fathers, mothers and lovers of those watching at home. Meanwhile numerous wars in Africa have been largely unreported in the British media, because of the lack of British involvement.

A senior executive of ABC in the United States, Av Westin, used to ask these questions to decide what was newsworthy:

- Is my world safe?
- Are my city and home safe?
- If my wife, children and loved ones are safe, then what has happened in the past 24 hours to shock them, amuse them or make them better off than they were?

A more flippant version of the same idea – that the closer to home news happens, the more important it is – is found in the so-called McLurg's Law. There are various versions, though none should be taken seriously by modern journalists. The British one used to run along the lines of one dead Briton is worth five dead Frenchmen, 20 dead Egyptians, 500 dead Indians and 1000 dead Chinese. It is the kind of attitude that led to *The Times* newspaper headline 'Small Earthquake in Chile – not many dead.' It was a joke – but a sick one.

Some listeners to Radio Five Live were disappointed by the high level of coverage given to the death of 12 miners in an underground explosion in West Virginia in January 2006. One email (read out on air) said: 'The US is not the centre of the universe. Where was the in-depth coverage the last time this happened in China or South Africa?' Another said: 'It's bad enough having US news rammed down our throats every day. Why is it that British and American lives are more valuable than anybody else's?' A caller to Victoria Derbyshire's morning phone-in said the coverage reflected modern news values. Simon, a former teacher of American history in the US, now living in Cambridgeshire, said: 'Where communications are good and where the media are situated, you are going to get more coverage. The closer it is to home the more likely it is to be covered – you know – "Earthquake in south-east Asia, Cambridgeshire man survives." That's one of the truisms of news.'

A story may be more important to some members of the audience than others. The safety of home and family are the first concerns of almost everyone. A story on the other side of the world can impact on that safety.

Remember

- Audiences consider their own and their family's security to be of prime importance
- The geographical location of news organisations and their crews can distort news coverage.

See Workshops and Exercises

CASE STUDY 2.1   PAKISTAN EARTHQUAKE

When a genuinely horrific earthquake occurred in the Kashmir region in October 2005, it failed to make the front-page lead on any of the next day's national Sunday newspapers. One critic, a Labour peer, remarked that the newspapers seemed to think England qualifying for football's World Cup (which happened on the same day) was more important than the devastation in Pakistan. Not for the first time, broadcasters saved the reputation of the British media with extensive coverage that brought home not only the horrors of events in the earthquake zone but also the impact on people at home. Thousands of British Asians had relatives in the affected area. The BBC reported that 70,000 people in Bradford had links to the earthquake zone; a man in Swindon lost 17 members of his family; and there were British people who had lost up to 600 members of their extended family. Correspondent Mark Easton reported from Luton that among the town's Kashmiri community hardly any family was unaffected. Rozina Sini of radio's Asian Network told BBC News 24 that all their listeners knew someone in the region, and many were desperate both to find out more about the casualties and to offer help.

As a result, many people went to airports immediately to fly out to Islamabad. Such was the clamour to assist the rescue operation that charities and official rescue agencies appealed for people to stay at home, fearing they would hamper the relief effort.

Localness

In its 'news mission statement', the commercial radio company UTV Radio (formerly the Wireless Group) insisted that at least one of the top three stories in any bulletin should be local, with 70 per cent local content in breakfast bulletins . . . 'more if you can with localised national stories. The more local people/places mentioned in your bulletin, the more "talkability" the station gets'.

> **The idea is to win the trust and respect of your listeners.**

Radio editors talk too about 'owning your patch'. The idea is to win the trust and respect of your listeners. You are the one who tells them if schools are closed when it snows, if roads are blocked or if power is down.

Local radio stations will aim to provide an 'addictive service of vital news and information people can use in their everyday lives', but it's often the filler stories – a missing parrot, for example – that get people talking. Cuts to commercial radio budgets have made the aims outlined above less achievable – but the value of local news in winning audiences is just as true.

Localness is what makes local radio – and local TV – distinctive.

Remember

- Make sure local stories are near the top of the bulletin
- Own your patch.

A CLOSER LOOK

LOCAL STORIES WITHIN THE BIGGER PICTURE

Events that have no significance internationally can be hugely important to national or local audiences. The closer to home, the more newsworthy it is. Britain's first toll motorway, the Birmingham Northern Relief Road, later named the M6 Toll, was the result of an important transport policy decision in the 1990s, aimed at reducing traffic congestion by using private sector finance. It was a significant political debate – and therefore a national story – as the road went from planning application to public inquiry. But to those living along the route the political dimension was overshadowed by a local environmental story. Large swathes of agricultural land were being covered in concrete. Peaceful demonstrations and lobbying of politicians followed, reported mostly by local and regional rather than national media. Then protestors occupied woodland and a house due for demolition on the route; the conflict with bailiffs and police brought wider attention to the problem – with mostly regional but some national coverage.

Now the road has been operating for some years, a rise in tolls is news to its users, but is unlikely to be reported much beyond the pages of the *Birmingham Mail*, or the bulletins of Radio WM and BRMB. The M6 Toll enters the national debate only when other toll roads are proposed, and critics can point to the failure of Britain's first toll motorway to attract the levels of traffic that were predicted by its supporters.

What's the angle?

The angle is the approach a journalist takes to a story. Spotting different angles helps focus on the best way to tell a story. Sometimes there are several equally valid approaches, which means you can use these different angles in separate online stories or freshen up the coverage across a series of bulletins without necessarily relying on new information.

A question editors ask soon after deciding to cover a story is: 'What's the angle?' Some stories are straightforward: Princess dies in car crash; terrorists kill thousands by flying planes into New York landmark; tsunami kills more than a quarter of a million people.

Other stories are more complicated and can be subject to any number of interpretations. Sometimes that means journalists get it wrong. In September 2005 there was panic buying at Britain's petrol stations. Long queues formed and many pumps ran dry. The chaos was a direct result of media hype – journalists predicting that a shortage was likely because demonstrators were going to blockade supplies from oil terminals in protest at rising prices. In fact, the protesters, who turned out only in very small numbers, had already promised they would not disrupt supplies, and the government had announced it had contingency plans if they did. But newsdesks responded on the basis of previous protests in 2000 that had cut off petrol deliveries. In 2005, broadcasters and newspapers misled the public by sloppy journalism.

New angles

Usually a fresh angle, or new *top line*, is obvious; it is the latest development. It is common practice though to save secondary or less important information to use later, to provide a new 'nose' in the absence of new developments. In a breaking story – one that is developing through the day – new angles emerge as events occur.

The breaking story may become a *running story* – one that develops over the following days, months, weeks and years. Journalists need to stay abreast of running stories. Expertise in a big running story can even help you get a better job, if you've built up contacts that make you a valuable catch for a rival news organisation.

Journalists should always ask *the five* Ws – *who, what, where, when, why* – and sometimes how. *What* has happened is almost always the most important thing to report: a plane crash, a political argument, an election result, a royal marriage, a sports result. Often the 'who' gives the story its significance, but we still want to know what they've done: Prince Harry has announced his engagement; Bob Geldof is planning another global rock concert; Murray is out of Wimbledon.

Who is involved is important even if they're not famous – people want stories about other people. Unless they're well known, you wouldn't use their name in the top line, but you would use a brief description: 'A middle-aged woman has been caught on YouTube dumping a cat in a wheelie bin.'

As the story changes, the newest information usually comes first. This is the new 'nose' for the story – the new angle.

CASE STUDY 2.2	NEW ANGLES – A TIMELINE

Can you remember where you were on 11 September 2001? Many people heard that a plane had crashed into the World Trade Center in New York. To start with, that was the story. That was the angle. It happened at 8.46 a.m. local time.

9.02 a.m. A second plane crashes. *New angle.*

The twin towers are alight. *Newer angle.*

9.17 a.m. The Federal Aviation Authority shuts down all New York City area airports. *Newest angle.*

9.30 a.m. US President George W. Bush, at a school in Florida, speaks of 'an apparent terrorist attack' and 'a national tragedy'. *Another new angle.*

People are trapped on the upper floors and some are jumping to their deaths. *Newer angle.*

9.37 a.m. American Airlines Flight 77 hits the Pentagon. *Newest angle.*

9.59 a.m. The South Tower of the World Trade Center collapses. *Another new angle.*

10.28 a.m. The North Tower of the World Trade Center collapses. *Newer angle.*

10. 48 a.m. The police confirm the crash of a large plane in Pennsylvania. *Newest angle.*

And so it continued, hour after harrowing hour. The loss of fire crews, the death toll, the political fallout, the 'war on terror', Afghanistan, Iraq. Events that shaped the early part of the twenty-first century. All new angles on the biggest story in a generation.

Local angles

> **Citizen journalists – people caught up in events – can be useful, particularly if they have video or audio material.**

Big national and international stories generate local angles. Local radio stations look for victims or, better still, survivors of global catastrophes, and for local people caught up in world events. This is where citizen journalists – people caught up in events – can be useful, particularly if they have video or audio material. Their blogs and podcasts can be a source for broadcasters and mainstream news websites.

The tsunami of Boxing Day 2004 generated hundreds of local stories. There were victims' families to talk to, survivors' tales to hear and widespread charity fund-raising efforts, many of them newsworthy in their own right because of their sheer inventiveness.

As we explained earlier, the Pakistan earthquake of 2005 had a huge impact on Kashmiri families in England, many of whom had relatives who were involved. There's almost always a local angle on a really big story: for example, on 11 September 2001 the regional ITV service Central News South went into the centre of Oxford looking for reaction from American tourists and students.

But beware of tagging a local story on to a national one for the sake of it. The attempt to broaden the appeal of the local event may achieve the opposite effect. It can make something that should be included on its own merit look trivial by comparison with the national event. Here's an example from BBC *Midlands Today*:

In less than 48 hours we'll know if London has been successful in its bid to hold the 2012 Olympic Games. At the same time over one thousand of the world's young sporting stars will be arriving in the Midlands for the International Children's Games.

BBC *Midlands Today*, 4 July 2005

This approach seems rather patronising, and undersells a good local story.

Remember

- Journalists always look for a new angle
- Local angles can make a national story relevant to a local audience.

The role of local combatants in overseas wars always provides copy and story ideas. These can be expanded into longer features.

The BBC in the Midlands took advantage of a facility trip to visit soldiers of the Staffordshire Regiment preparing for the Gulf War of 1991 to produce a documentary, 'The Gulf Between', featuring local soldiers in the desert and their families, both at home in the UK and at the regiment's German base in Fallingbostel. After the war, some of the same people were revisited in a second documentary, 'After the Gulf', which included a young soldier's first sight of his child born while he was at war, and his wedding. The programme included the return to their base in Germany of two pilots held hostage in Iraq. One of them was native to the Midlands.

Regional news

As well as considering the news values of individual stories, the producers of bulletins on regional radio stations and regional TV have to consider how their programmes reflect the region they serve. News does not happen to order. So, stories may be dropped simply because there are already other stronger stories from the same part of the patch.

Mike Henfield, a former local radio managing director, says a frequent instruction at a station in the north-west of England was: 'We haven't had a story from Preston for weeks – drop that Liverpool protest story.'

Regional television was based on the areas covered by the analogue transmitters. Commercial pressures mean independent TV has cut back on many of its regional opt-out programmes. In the digital age, programmes based on regions may be an anachronism. Tim Burke, the Community Content Editor of the BBC's Local TV Pilot in 2006, put it succinctly: 'Most people couldn't give two figs about what happens in Shropshire if they live in Cheltenham, and vice versa.'

> 'Most people couldn't give two figs about what happens in Shropshire if they live in Cheltenham, and vice versa.'

The revival of government support for local TV in the second decade of the twenty-first century suggested Cheltenham people might not have to suffer Shropshire news much longer but, for now, regional considerations are all part of the 'news mix' – the choice of stories for a programme.

Remember

- Covering a region may mean dropping stories from one place in favour of another.

The news mix

Most journalists acknowledge a difference between *hard* and *soft* stories, but few will agree just where the line between the two lies. Critics of contemporary journalism often remark that there's too much bad news. In the 1990s, TV newsreader Martyn Lewis publicly declared there should be more good news – and was far from universally applauded by his colleagues. The following comment from James Naughtie on the *Today* programme in 2005 was a slip of the tongue rather than a statement of the BBC's core values:

'There's news coming in from Russia of a gun battle that's said to be taking place between police and armed men in Nalchik, which is the regional capital of Kabardino-Balkaria. One report from the French news agency, and it's pretty unconfirmed, says armed men entered a school. We don't know any more at the moment, but if it turns out to be something pretty awful, we will let you know.'

You might ask whether audiences really do prefer to hear about things that are 'pretty awful'? It's arguably a graver mistake than Naughtie's celebrated Spoonerism when introducing Jeremy Hunt, the Culture Secretary in December 2010.

Hard news

Hard stories are those with importance, significance and relevance to the audience. Almost always they are told as and when they break, so they can also be said to have immediacy. It is almost unthinkable to have a news bulletin without hard stories. Types of hard stories include events (war, conflict, disaster, emergencies, crime); international, domestic and local politics; and public affairs (health, education, housing, transport, the environment).

Events

Some events are of such immediate significance that no one would dispute their news value: September 11, war in Iraq, Britain's first coalition government since the Second World War.

The significance of outbreaks of BSE and foot-and-mouth-disease in Britain took longer to emerge. The potential tragedy of 33 Chilean miners trapped more than 600 metres underground turned to triumph 69 days later when they emerged from a rescue shaft alive and well. The dramatic rescue was a bigger story – covered live by news channels globally in October 2010 – than the loss of 33 lives in a South American mine would ever have been.

Trends in crime have a political dimension and therefore fall within the hard news agenda. And some serious crimes make it into national bulletins. But many crime and emergency stories fulfil the same role as soft stories. They don't impact on the social or political agenda, but they do interest the audience on an emotional level: a multiple murder within a family; a child rescued from a pothole. The Soham murders of schoolgirls Holly Wells and Jessica Chapman in August 2002 had emotional and political repercussions. The crime was shocking. The investigation into police checks on school staff had implications for parents everywhere.

Politics and public affairs

People may be cynical about politicians and apathetic about the political process, but policy decisions by government affect people's wealth, welfare and the way they conduct their lives.

Broadcasters are required by law to be impartial and balanced. This law does not apply to independent news websites or to print journalists, who are often required by their papers to take sides and campaign actively for one party or another. The rules on the time allocated to party political opinion on radio and TV are particularly strict at election times. A stopwatch will be applied to the output to ensure fair play – although nobody judges the quality of the politicians' comments except the voters.

According to the Ofcom Broadcasting Code, due impartiality may be achieved during a programme or over a series of programmes taken as a whole.

Political debate is a mainstay of news bulletins. But there has been a growing recognition among news organisations that top-down politics – reporting the minutiae of political debate – does not engage the audience. Political issues have to be popularised and humanised. Otherwise most people won't watch them. Broadcasters get criticised for reducing politics to the conflict between personalities. But often that is the best way to introduce the arguments.

Political issues have to be popularised and humanised for most people to want to watch them.

Mick Temple, a professor of journalism and politics at Staffordshire University, argues, in praise of 'dumbing down', that those of the population generally uninterested in formal politics – the majority – need at the very least to be informed about basic issues. He says engaging and entertaining political coverage can encourage further examination of the issues at a more informed level.

In news reporting, when a matter of public policy can be illustrated with a real-life example – somebody's personal experience – it is usually considered a better way of telling the story than simply using soundbites of politicians. As an American publisher put it, journalists cannot congratulate themselves on having got at the facts impartially by quoting at length from two uninformed idiots on opposing sides of an issue.

Remember

- Hard stories make up most of the content of news bulletins
- Political stories need to be popularised
- There are laws about political balance in broadcasting.

Soft news

Soft stories do not usually have a direct impact on people's day-to-day lives. But they are, in the words of US newspaperman Arthur McEwen, what make the reader go 'Gee whiz!' They include *human interest* stories, like the sleepwalking girl found on top of a crane, animal stories, sport; and, finally, the *'and finally . . .'*.

Human interest

Human interest is a broad term that barely does justice to the range of stories it covers. Stories have to be about people or to affect people to be of interest. So, almost all stories could be classified as human interest. But the term usually refers to emotional stories about people or lighter, quirkier stories about human beings – and animals. These stories may offer little more than 'bread and circuses' to the audience, but the editor who ignores them risks losing viewers or listeners. That means the audience for so-called 'serious' stories will be much smaller. Human interest stories are an essential part of the news mix.

Human interest stories are an essential part of the news mix.

Celebrities

The word 'celebrity' has become devalued in recent years. There are two types of celebrity nowadays: the 'elite' celebrities with whose fame no one could disagree, and the 'vogue' celebrities famous for the moment but soon to be forgotten. Elite celebrities include presidents, prime ministers and world statesmen, such as John F. Kennedy, Margaret Thatcher and Nelson Mandela. Musical figures from Mozart to Frank Sinatra and Bruce Springsteen are also part of an elite. The vogue celebs are often created by the media that reports on them. They are 'famous for being famous'. Katie Price springs to mind. Bienvenida Buck and Antonia de Sancha do not – but they were once heavily reported on, particularly in newspapers.

Celebrity stories, mostly of 'vogue' celebrities, fill so much space in the tabloids it's hard to find hard news. The *News of the World* became Britain's biggest-selling paper with a steamy mix of sex and scandal. Broadcast news has always occupied a higher moral ground, from the Reithian values of the early BBC – the Scots Presbyterian approach of the first

Director-General Lord Reith – to today's carefully regulated multi-channel environment. Arguments about 'dumbing down' and 'tabloidisation' are familiar territory to media commentators. Whatever the trend, the huge audiences attracted by network broadcasting – far bigger than any newspaper's sales – mean that broadcast news is a popular medium. That means it has to offer coverage of popular culture. Broadcast journalists need to be aware of the latest movies, the best-selling music, the stars created by reality TV and the plotlines in *Coronation Street* and *EastEnders*.

Pop and movie stars feature heavily in news stories. How newsworthy they are depends on their star quality – that elusive combination of charisma and mystique. The presence of a big name is usually enough to justify coverage on local and regional bulletins.

Royals

Royal stories also fall into the human interest category. The survival of Britain's constitutional monarchy has been assisted by favourable press coverage. Queen Victoria projected her image as a dutiful widow through the British newspapers and was apparently popular in an age sandwiched between the French and Russian revolutions, when royals were put to death. The influential press barons of the late nineteenth and early twentieth centuries used their newspapers to support the Establishment, including the monarchy. The Abdication Crisis of 1936 went unreported in the British press until it became inevitable that Edward VIII would relinquish the throne over his love for the American divorcee Wallis Simpson.

Nowadays the press can be highly critical, particularly of the younger royals. Broadcasters are traditionally less censorious, and they are criticised by newspaper editors when they follow up stories in the papers they might otherwise have ignored. So, it was the *Sun* that sent an undercover reporter into Sandhurst military college where Prince Harry was being trained for life as an army officer. The 'security breach' was covered by all the broadcasters, as was the story that appeared first in newspapers of the young prince wearing Nazi uniform to a fancy dress party. But the announcement of Prince William and Kate Middleton's wedding attracted almost universally positive coverage from all sections of the media.

> Celebrities need the media to maintain their status – whether that's measured in box-office receipts, album sales or avoiding the guillotine.

The royals and other celebrities need the media to maintain their status – whether that's measured in box-office receipts, album sales or avoiding the guillotine. So, they will collude with newspapers and broadcasters to secure favourable coverage. The prime exponent of this was the late Diana, Princess of Wales, who frequently tipped off tabloid reporters and dramatically aired her marital difficulties in a *Panorama* interview.

Children

The involvement of children in a story always makes it more newsworthy. Most adults are horrified by any injustice done to children, and are shocked by the corruption of innocence. Whenever children are caught up in tragedy or disaster, the story can be upsetting but compelling.

Television images of starving children have inspired international fund-raising campaigns – the most famous being Bob Geldof's Band Aid/Live Aid charity in 1984–5, which raised £150 million for famine relief in Ethiopia.

More health stories about children are covered than those that affect the elderly. Children are seen as being more appealing to audiences.

The appeal of children in news extends to stories of children's achievements – child prodigies, children involved in charity fund raising, children's success in school exams. The annual debate about whether exams are getting easier is always accompanied by shots of youngsters hugging as they learn their results.

Animals

Animal stories have always been popular with viewers and listeners. The Tamworth Two – two pigs who 'escaped' from an abattoir in 1998 – captivated viewers for days before they were recaptured . . . and sent to live out their days in an animal sanctuary. One of them died in 2010 – and that was considered newsworthy 12 years on!

The use of animal stories was lampooned in the title of a cult comedy series about a TV newsroom, *Drop the Dead Donkey*. And in newsrooms, the 'skateboarding duck' became a generic term for a great animal story. The original duck in question, Herbie, appeared on the BBC's early evening current affairs show *Nationwide* in the 1970s. Such was his fame that the *Mail on Sunday* felt it was of sufficient importance to report some 30 years later that – horror of horrors – the trick had been achieved by *nailing* the duck to the skateboard. The newspaper report – splashed across half a page – was untrue, as anyone who had seen the original footage of the duck jumping on and off the skateboard could have told them. Letters of correction duly appeared in the newspaper, from the duck's owner Jacqueline Randall and the retired *Nationwide* reporter Alan Towers.

Why are animal stories popular? You might as well ask why the British are described as 'a nation of animal lovers'. Animals are cute, cuddly, scary, funny and entertaining. All human life is there.

Remember

- Human interest stories attract audiences
- Celebrity news is an accepted part of the news mix
- Animal stories are always popular.

Sport – and why it's important

Do you read the back pages of the newspaper first? If you don't, you'll know somebody who does. For many people, sports stories are the most important thing on the news.

If you never read the back pages, you might want to kiss goodbye to a career in broadcasting.

If you never read the back pages, you might want to kiss goodbye to a career in journalism. It may sound harsh, but no one can expect to stay long in the job if they don't understand sport. In a local radio or regional television newsroom, you may be the only news writer on shift in the evening when the late football or cricket results come in. You'll have to write those results for a late evening bulletin or for breakfast news the next day. Online duties may include compiling results, league tables, cup draws and lists of other statistics – and writing copy to accompany them and finding pictures to illustrate the story. It's a good training ground, where speed and accuracy are vital: Sky News Foreign Affairs Correspondent Ian Woods started his career as a student compiling late sports results at Mercia Sound, the ILR station in Coventry.

A CLOSER LOOK

MAKING A FOOL OF YOURSELF

Misinterpreting sports news makes you look foolish, because so many of the audience are passionate about it. Rick Thompson was editing a national television news programme when the newsreader said England's opening batsman had been dismissed 'One-B-W'. He says she was rapped on the pads later.

The significance of sport to the community was one of the factors stressed by the London bid team that won the 2012 Olympic Games for Britain.

The TUC and the CBI (the 'voices' of trade unions and employers respectively) issued pleas to British companies to allow workers to keep in touch with the test match score during the crucial climax to cricket's 2005 Ashes series.

The veteran broadcaster, legendary interviewer and sometime sportswriter Michael Parkinson summed up the appeal of sport in his *Daily Telegraph* column shortly after that England Ashes victory: 'The importance of sport is that it doesn't matter, except as an antidote to things that do.'

A CLOSER LOOK

BRITAIN'S FIRST SPORTS NEWS CHANNEL

Sport's appeal is reflected in the success of Sky Sports News. The channel was set up after Rupert Murdoch's Sky Television bought up a huge swathe of sports rights, revolutionising the way sport was viewed on UK television. The range of live sport available to viewers increased exponentially – as did the cost of watching it. Sky's impressive roster of live sport meant there was also a growing library of highlights to exploit. Those highlights could be shown on the Sky News channel, and there was also enough to provide raw material for a stand-alone sports news channel. Sky Sports News would serve as a promotional tool for the premium-cost sports channels and for pay-per-view events. Even with the cost of employing presenters and reporters, it virtually paid for itself.

As a business model it was inspired. As a response to audience demand, it has more than justified itself, regularly attracting more viewers than the 'senior' service Sky News.

Remember

- Sports news matters to a large proportion of the audience
- Ignorance of sport will find you out.

. . . and finally

The phrase 'and finally' has become such a cliché of broadcasting that it is rarely used other than ironically. But a well-rounded bulletin on all but the hardest news day will almost always end on a lighter note. The 'and finally' will usually be a human interest story, treated with humour. Greg Dyke, when he was Director-General of the BBC, warned journalists to leave comedy to comedians. Nonetheless, a strong tradition has developed, particularly in regional TV news, of reporters offering a wry and affectionate look at life's eccentricities. The style was set by great names in broadcasting such as Fyfe Robertson and Alan Whicker on the BBC's *Tonight* in the early days of TV magazine programmes more than half a century ago, and was continued by regional reporters on news magazines. John Swallow on *Central News* and John Yates on BBC *Midlands Today* earned the affection of Midlands viewers across three decades. Chas Watkin, now a senior BBC regional executive, says: 'When I was growing up, my sister and I used to watch the ITV programme just waiting for John Swallow's piece to come on.'

Chris Tarrant says that when he was 'interviewing nutters' as a reporter on *ATV Today* he had found his broadcasting home. It led to an illustrious career via *Tiswas* to *Who Wants to be a Millionaire?*

- A well-crafted bulletin will finish on a high – usually a quirky or lighter story.

Who decides what to cover?

With so many types of story fighting for a place in news programmes, who decides what makes the cut? That depends on the news organisation, of course. But whether the decision is to be made by the editor of the day at the BBC *News at Ten* or the early reporter on shift at Signal One radio in Stoke-on-Trent, the stories are subject to the process of copy tasting.

Copy tasting

At its simplest, copy tasting involves assessing stories, or copy, as they come into a newsroom and deciding whether they are worth running. That can be as simple as the on-shift reporter taking the story straight off the wires and reading it on air in the next bulletin. Or it can mean the intake editor in a larger organisation passing the story to a researcher or reporter to investigate further.

Often your efforts will come to nought. Not because the story didn't stand up. But simply because bigger stories happened.

Larger newsrooms split the roles of intake and output. That can mean a story will be accepted by the intake desk, and time will be spent on it, only for the output editor or programme producer to decide they don't want to run it. Producers still talk of stories being 'spiked', the old newspaper term for sticking typed copy on a spike on the desk. Other stories will be developed as standbys, just in case bigger stories don't make it to air.

Newcomers to a broadcast newsroom find it hard to accept, but often your efforts will come to nought. Not because the story didn't stand up. But simply because bigger stories happened, and there was not enough room in the programme. Writing up the web version can seem like second-best, though it shouldn't – you may yet reach a bigger audience than anything in a broadcast programme.

- All stories are subject to copy tasting
- Some stories will be dropped for lack of space.

CONCLUSION

We've seen in this chapter the factors that determine if a story is worth telling. Most news organisations still choose stories according to traditional criteria. But there is a growing emphasis in news on allowing witnesses to tell their own stories, and on interactivity, audience response and enabling people to use new technologies to engage in the news-making process.

We'll move on to explain how to find stories worth telling – the traditional and modern sources of news – and how to tell them, across all media.

In the digital age, where the availability of news is limited only by the imagination of software designers, any webmaster will tell you that content is king. In news broadcasting, content almost always means the story.

FURTHER READING

Harcup, Tony (2004) *Journalism: Principles and Practice*, London: Sage. An innovative split-page layout makes this a unique blend of theory and practice.

Randall, David (2000) *The Universal Journalist*, London: Pluto Press. Strong on how to find good stories.

WEB LINKS

www.nationalstudent.tv/docs/BestPractices.Westin.pdf An online book from US experts about best practice in newsgathering – worth a look.

CHAPTERTHREE
FINDING THE NEWS

In this chapter, we'll look at:

- The traditional news sources, including the roles of reporters and their contacts, calls and voice-banks, press releases, pressure groups, staged events, agencies and freelances, wire services, and monitoring other media.

- How these sources fit into the news-gathering operation.

- The role of *social media*: how to research stories using online and mobile sources; find people who can provide content, including interviews, pictures and packages; and use social networks to promote your own news outlet, whether you're part of a newsroom team or freelance.

- The production process in a newsroom, and the importance of teamwork.

- How the information gathered from different news sources finds its way into the newsroom diary – the most important tool for running a day-to-day news operation.

Where does news come from?

MOST broadcast reporters are fed up with being asked the question: 'Where does the news come from?' It's definitely the question asked most often by any first-time visitor to a newsroom.

The answer is simple: news is everywhere. The answer is also complicated: there are dozens of sources of news – many of them tried and tested over years of newsroom practice; others unexpected; some the product of new technologies; still more probably yet to be discovered, as the means of disseminating information multiply in the digital age.

All journalists need to know the main sources of news.

We'll begin with the best way of finding original stories – those that are known as off-diary.

NEWS SOURCES

Contacts

Most reporters recognise that the best way of finding new and exclusive stories is through personal contacts, people who've become reliable sources of news and information. All journalists keep a contacts book. It is usually laid out alphabetically and contains names, addresses, phone numbers and email addresses of anyone who might be a source of news.

Who might they be? Well, almost anyone, from politicians and captains of industry to market traders, pub landlords, policemen and members of voluntary organisations. A contacts book might include a particularly chatty milkman or waiter, or local church leaders.

The contacts book has always been as much a part of the reporter's toolkit as a pen and notebook. Today, your electronic contacts on social networks such as Facebook and Twitter are just as valuable, and they can be even more vital when it comes to breaking news. As primary sources of news and expert comment, instant messages on social networks have revolutionised newsgathering. They're no longer social networks at all: they're business networks for journalists and a host of other professionals.

Organise your contacts

As a back-up against the loss or theft of your treasured iPhone or BlackBerry, or your computer crashing, you should store your contacts in more than one place. The traditional book (possibly loose leaf like a Filofax) is still a good idea and quick to access. Cross-reference the entries. You need to be able to find people easily, according to their expertise and the stories in which they've been involved.

Make sure your name and your own contact details are clearly marked on your contacts book. You may wish to offer a reward if it is lost.

A CLOSER LOOK

A GOOD IDEA FROM THE PAST

Weekly newspapers used to allow reporters out on 'district calls' at least one afternoon a week, to chat to people in a neighbourhood and to call on community leaders in the hunt for stories. These calls generated original, off-diary material. The BBC had a similar policy when it introduced specialist correspondents into regional newsrooms during the 1990s. They were 'ring-fenced' from the demands of contributing to day-to-day news. They could work their contacts and come up with exclusive stories.

Some BBC local radio stations have revived this idea of 'district calls' with 'no email' weeks – when reporters shun their most familiar form of communication and take to the streets in search of stories, armed only with a microphone and recorder. These special days have produced some original journalism. But it only works if you have enough staff to send out 'on spec'. Most commercial radio stations do not.

F. J. Mansfield wrote in *The Complete Journalist* (1944) that the good reporter 'can, according to a familiar saying, find at least two good stories during a twopenny bus ride'. You can work out how long ago he said that from just how far you would get on a bus today for tuppence (less than a penny in 'new' money). But the principle holds good today. One freelance working in the Midlands reckons he never pays for a holiday, because every time he goes away (to destinations all over the world) he comes across a story or two which he then sells, covering the costs of the family trip. If anybody has a 'nose for news', then he does.

Mixing the professional and the personal

> **The best journalists are never off duty. Regular contacts become good friends.**

The best journalists are never off duty. Regular contacts become good friends. And friends become good contacts. Separating the professional from the social relationship is not as difficult as it might appear. Good contacts know what you do for a living. They recognise when information might be valuable. Equally, no sensible reporter would jeopardise the relationship with a contact, or a friend, by treating them unfairly.

Maintaining contacts is the same as maintaining any relationship. Keep in touch, online and on the phone, socialise when possible, and remember to give and take. Some information is best kept private in return for trust.

Some contacts offer information anonymously. It may need to be checked with other sources before it can be broadcast. Others will be only too willing to be interviewed as an on-air source. And some will be public relations (PR) people, or press officers, whose job it is to contact the press on behalf of a commercial client. PR people may not sound like great contacts. After all, it is their job to give you – and everybody else – stories. Their company or client may want them to apply 'spin' to the information they give you. But a trusting relationship can lead to a steady flow of inside information about major businesses or local authorities, often in the form of an exclusive.

Sometimes, as with any other friendship or business deal, the relationship may break down. Roy Greenslade wrote in the *Guardian* how he'd been friends with Jonathan King, who became known to the tabloids as a 'paedophile pop pervert'. Greenslade was assistant editor of the *Sun* when King wrote a column for the paper, and he'd appeared on King's radio shows. But after the former pop star was jailed for offences against teenage boys, Greenslade said he felt duped by King, who'd repeatedly told him he was innocent. He refused to answer King's letters and emails.

Martin Brunt was recruited from the *Sunday Mirror* when Sky News started. He's the station's crime correspondent, and says the value of contacts can never be underestimated:

> **'Contacts are the most important thing. It's a simple question of . . . never throwing away a phone number.'**

'Contacts are the most important thing. It's not complicated or very clever. It's a simple question of doing what I learned in newspapers; talking to people, never throwing away a phone number, going to see people and ringing them up from time to time.'

'It's not sitting in cellar bars getting drunk with coppers. You still do that a little bit but it's not like crime reporters used to work, where you lived in the press room at Scotland Yard, and slept there, and a policeman would come down at three in the morning with a story.'

Most radio newsrooms don't do enough to keep track of contributors to the rest of their station's output. A database of their interests and expertise is an invaluable newsgathering tool. Even phone-in callers can provide news content. Just be aware that under the Data Protection Act people's details shouldn't be used without their permission.

Contacts on social networks are even easier to maintain than those you meet face to face. Using your status updates wisely lets people know what you're up to, and reminds them that you're a professional journalist. If you can maintain their trust, they'll probably come to you when they have a story worth telling. But don't put frivolous or offensive comments in the public domain if you want to be taken seriously.

Press officers are potential contacts. They'll be the source of many stories. But it is also important to recognise the different roles of journalists and PR people.

Columnist Cristina Odone, writing in the *Guardian* in April 2006, responded to a PR professional's assertion that there was a 'moral equivalence' between the two professions:

Journalists are in the business of exposing the truth, PRs are in the business of twisting it. Journalists want nothing more than to strip away the protective layers with which the powerful camouflage their objectives or their achievements; PRs are paid by the powerful to prevent precisely this. So, no, there is no moral equivalence between journalism and PR.

In his book, *Flat Earth News* (2008), reporter Nick Davies wrote of the distortion and propaganda in news reporting resulting from a combination of PR and cost cutting by news organisations. He argued that unreliable, and even dishonest, sources were going largely unchecked because of the reduction in newsroom staffing levels. Supporting that view, a study by researchers at Cardiff University found that the majority of the home news coverage of British newspapers (typically 60–70 per cent) was the result of press releases, PR and agency copy rather than original journalism. The term 'churnalism' (credited to a BBC reporter, Waseem Zakir) describes the process in which press releases and wire stories are processed by newsroom staff and churned out with little or no checking.

Social media

Social media have become primary sources: not just for breaking news, where someone on the scene of an event tells the world about it with a micro-blog comment or a status update on their homepage; but also for developments in running stories in the world of politics, celebrity and sport. The first pictures of an airliner that made an emergency landing on New York's Hudson river; video of anti-government protests across the Middle East; the identities of celebrities taking out superinjunctions to try to gag the press – all of these were stories which began or grew massively on Twitter. When Japan was hit by its biggest recorded earthquake in March 2011 there were a thousand tweets a minute coming out of Tokyo.

As a journalist, you need to subscribe to as many social networks as possible and to monitor their output. You can filter the content with search words. So, if you are working for a radio station in Perthshire in Scotland, you might enter local place names such as Pitlochry, Aberfeldy and Blairgowrie alongside the obvious Perth, Perthshire and Scotland; geographical features like the River Tay and Loch Leven; historical references like Mary Queen of Scots and the Black Watch regiment, and words that could throw up stories about the area's visitor attractions such as angling, golf and whisky (the area has many distilleries, including Scotland's oldest and smallest). A site like Twitterfall will allow you to see stories on all these topics as they appear. You can even put an address in the geolocation panel and see what anyone in the designated area is tweeting about, although this is only of use as a newsgathering tool when a major breaking news event triggers a wave of tweets – as did the Japanese earthquake example above. Otherwise, you will be swamped with trivia from people's everyday lives: the trend for sharing banalities with online 'friends' means the humdrum far outweighs the newsworthy on all these sites.

You can use social networks to find information about – and pictures of – people in the news. There are often tribute pages to those killed in tragic circumstances. But beware of breach of copyright and the ethical considerations of using information which was posted with an expectation that it would not be broadcast beyond a comparatively small circle of family and friends. You also need to be aware of the need to verify any information you are taking from social media sources, and to check that pictures are what they purport to be. This applies as much to unsolicited video of a street demonstration in an Arab country as it does to stills of a teenage car crash victim in Swansea. The BBC Editorial Guidelines contain specific advice about using content from social media.

If you maintain an active presence on social networks – tweeting regularly, for example – you will build a band of followers. They can become a source of stories, or provide strong examples of people affected by stories. You can localise a national story by appealing for any-one affected by it to come forward. You might be looking for someone caught in a foreign conflict or users of a swimming pool closed by council spending cuts. The BBC Technology Correspondent Rory Cellan-Jones became 'hooked' on Twitter after initially thinking he was too old for social networking. Now it is an important source of ideas and contacts. He jokes too that it is a tool for 'ruthless self-promotion' – which is possibly of even more use to someone building a career than to a successful BBC reporter.

Another valuable journalistic tool that social networks help deliver is crowdsourcing. This is a form of network or citizen journalism. Just as data-mining programs help reporters search complicated sets of figures for significant trends, so people in a social network – or people responding to your appeal online or on air – can help you look at huge amounts of information very quickly and pick out possible stories, with each person needing to look at just a small part of the whole. Your job is then to collate and assess what they've found. This happened when the state of Alaska released 24,000 emails from the office of former Governor Sarah Palin in June 2011. Some journalists – and all her political opponents – hoped there'd be evidence of misconduct or at least foolish behaviour among the routine communications. At least three major news organisations recruited volunteers from their audience to trawl through the masses of material. On that occasion, they found little of genuine public interest.

Remember

- Anyone can become a good contact
- Stay in touch with your contacts – cultivate them
- Never throw away a phone number
- Monitor social media feeds
- Promote yourself on social media
- Use people on social networks to help gather news.

Routine calls

Every newsroom carries out routine check calls to the emergency services: police, fire, ambulance, coastguard. A radio station might make them every hour; TV might make them before each bulletin with just enough time to spare to write the story and send camera crews if needed.

The calls are often carried out by junior members of staff, which is probably a false economy given how important the result can be. A warm telephone manner and incisive, but never rude, questioning used to be the keys to unlocking information from occasionally reticent control room personnel. Nowadays police and fire services are more likely to offer the

There's no substitute for talking to a real person.

increasing number of news organisations a recorded message service – the voice-bank. This is essentially second best. There's no substitute for talking to a real person. Even when a police inspector is restricted for operational reasons from giving too much information about, for example, a fatal stabbing, other facts will come from other sources – the ambulance service, perhaps, or social networks – and a more detailed story can be written.

The information on voice-banks can be limited and the journalist relies on police or fire service personnel, usually in a press office rather than an operational officer, to update the information. Follow-up calls will be directed through a press officer, rather than straight to the senior officers in charge of an incident. Police press officers in particular can now control an important part of the news agenda – crime stories.

The use of voice-banks and press officers underlines the increased importance to the emergency services of managing their relationship with the media. It also means old-fashioned – and new technology – contacts with serving staff in those services are even more important for journalists. The reporter who has a trusting relationship with senior detectives can steal a march on his or her rivals.

Some police forces have embraced social media, with officers giving regular Twitter updates on the incidents they attend. Police in Birmingham and Manchester experimented with tweeting every call in a 24-hour period. It showed how busy they were, and gave leads to numerous stories. And talking of leads, Smithy, a West Midlands Police Labrador, trained to sniff out blood and human remains, was probably the first police dog to tweet as well as bark.

Remember

- Call regularly
- Never assume recorded information is up to date – or complete
- Always try to speak to a real person
- Adopt a friendly telephone manner and develop a rapport with the person on the other end of the line
- Remember that the calls are just the start of the news-gathering process
- Sign up to the social network feeds of the police and other emergency services.

Freelances and agencies

Freelance reporters, either self-employed or working for agencies, are an important source of news copy and story tip-offs for most news organisations. These 'stringers' or correspondents, will cover court cases, for example, when broadcasters can't afford to send their own reporters. The origin of the word 'stringer' is obscure. The *Oxford English Dictionary* suggests it may be because they string words together.

Freelance photographers provide 'stills' (photographs) of people in the news to TV stations. These may be photos they have taken themselves or 'pick-ups', pictures they have collected from family members. Freelances who also work for the print media are unlikely to sell their best or exclusive stories to broadcast newsrooms because newspapers and magazines pay considerably more. Some paparazzi – unregulated freelances who typically stalk celebrities – take video as well as stills, but their pictures are unlikely to be used by broadcast newsrooms, not least because their methods are often in breach of the broadcast codes.

Many people working for broadcasters are themselves freelance, of course, but they won't be asked to come back for another shift if they start selling the story they're working on to an immediate rival.

Wire services

National and international news stories come into newsrooms on 'the wires'. They are called 'wires' because they used to be teleprinter services; now they are delivered by the Internet or satellite. The information available includes everything from share prices to racing results, and the full range of news and sports stories. There are diary subscription services too that provide advance notice of news events – with contact numbers for reporters to get in touch with PR agencies and press offices.

The main UK news agency is the Press Association (PA). Associated Press (AP) is a US equivalent. Reuters is an international name in news gathering and has a division specialising in electronic news media, as do Associated Press Television News (APTN) and United Press International (UPI).

> **In a live broadcast, the wire service may be credited as the source of information if it is not confirmed by another source.**

These are services that broadcast organisations subscribe to; they are paying for information, pictures and sound. There was a time when newsrooms trusted the wires implicitly. PA was considered the ultimate arbiter of truth. Nowadays wire services are not revered in the same way. In a live broadcast, the wire service may be credited as the source of information if it is not confirmed by another source. A conscientious journalist will check information whenever possible. Two sources are always better than one.

TIP BOX

Remember that freelance agencies and wire services are not just working for you – everybody else will have the same information, unless you pay to keep it exclusive.

Press releases

Every newsroom receives a steady supply of press releases, mostly electronically but occasionally in the post. Releases come from pressure groups, politicians, government and community organisations, sports clubs – in fact, anyone who has a story to tell.

Each contains a potential news story. Whether the story is worth telling depends on the judgement of copy-tasters (see Chapter 2) and intake desks. Not all will be worth following up.

Many are just thinly veiled attempts to gain free advertising. Some will provide filler material or short copy stories. Others will be the starting point for investigations or will provide big stories in their own right. Press releases always include contact details and usually offer the chance to speak to people the organisation is 'putting up' for interview. A press release is, by its nature, only one side of the story. Following up a press release may mean challenging the information it contains and approaching people whose views oppose those of its writers. This is an essential part of balanced and impartial journalism. It would be a naive lobbyist who did not recognise this. The rise of 'churnalism' (see Thinkpiece, page 51) suggests not enough reporters challenge what the lobbyists tell them.

Many news releases will be subject to an **embargo**. This is a request that the news is not published or broadcast until a certain date and time: e.g. 'embargoed until 0001 hrs, Friday 28 July'. It helps forward planning. The news organisation is able to gather information and conduct interviews ready for publication. It ensures the story is released on all media at the same time. No one gets the exclusive. Embargoes have no weight in law, but they are almost always worth observing. *To break an embargo is to risk losing the trust of whoever provided the information.* The embargoes on the New Year's and Queen's Birthday Honours Lists and the content of the Queen's Christmas message are almost always observed. But embargoes can be used to manipulate news media, and editors often argue that they should run the story early. If one organisation breaks an embargo, the gloves are off and others will follow.

Electronic press releases

Some organisations use new technology for their media releases. Video news releases – containing footage and interviews to enable journalists to cover a story without leaving the office – might seem a good idea. Pressure groups use them to get their message across. There are also EPKs – electronic press kits – often used to promote film releases. They will contain clips from the movie and interviews with the stars – Hollywood 'A-listers' who are never likely to visit your neck of the woods.

Most news organisations are rightly suspicious of using third-party material to tell a story.

But most news organisations are rightly suspicious of using third-party material to tell a story. To do so surrenders editorial control. The Hollywood stars won't answer the questions you want to ask; they'll just talk about their film role. And the campaigner is unlikely to be responding to the challenges you would make if you were face to face over a microphone. Agencies that supply this sort of material are offering a service to commercial clients, who see it as an alternative to paying for advertising. As we've mentioned, it's important to verify footage from any third-party source, but a decision to use it becomes much more difficult when you know the source has a political or commercial agenda.

Agency interviews for radio should only be used when it suits you.

Agency interviews for radio should only be used when it suits you. If they want their material used, manipulate them to your advantage. Insist that the interview includes local content.

Video from a pressure group will normally only be used with a strong on-screen disclaimer explaining where the pictures have come from. That's because the broadcaster cannot guarantee they present an unbalanced view of events.

Video from a pressure group will normally only be used with a strong on-screen disclaimer.

Some video footage is so graphic you will want to use it anyway. But you must tell the audience its source. The environmental pressure group Greenpeace now insists that journalists on their payroll write impartially as if they were working for an independent news gatherer. In January 2006 Greenpeace vessels clashed with Japanese whalers in the southern oceans off Antarctica, and the dramatic pictures were shown worldwide. It would have been hugely expensive for broadcasters to follow the Greenpeace ships as they tried to find the whalers in hostile seas. But there was footage freely available – from Greenpeace's own video crews. Broadcasters could present the political arguments about whaling by using the Greenpeace footage and conducting their own interviews to create a balanced report.

Remember

- Maintain your objectivity when considering press releases
- Avoid 'churnalism' – the processing of press releases without challenging them
- Beware of 'spin' – there might be a better story they don't want you to hear
- Tell the audience if audio or video does not come from your own organisation.

LIVING WITHOUT PRESS RELEASES

Is it possible for newsrooms to operate without press releases and a steady flow of emails from pressure groups and regular contacts? Undoubtedly, yes, as experiments in BBC local radio have proved.

Radio WM, in the West Midlands, banned press releases and email for a week. Only the news editor and bulletin editor were allowed access to them. Radio Cambridgeshire went a step further, banning press releases and email in a 'non-rota' week. All the usual shift patterns – except those of programme presenters and newsreaders – were scrapped.

Stuart Ratcliffe, one of the journalists in the Cambridgeshire trial, says:

'The producers and reporters just went out and we did some fantastic stuff. All our microphones, all our radio cars were out. It was exhausting, because we were never sure if we had enough, but it worked.

'After that, from what we'd learned, we rejigged all our rota patterns. There was a whole reappraisal of the way we worked.'

Sue Owen, the Managing Editor of Radio Stoke, says it's harder work than relying on press releases, but stations running these experiments get more and better stories than if their staff are desk bound:

'They get more original stories and meet more normal people – more people that aren't the "voices on sticks" we use all the time.

'We've had some of the best stories by saying, "Grab your Nagra [a portable recorder] and go out and find your story".'

Sue Owen, Manager of BBC Radio Stoke

News conferences

Press conferences are set-piece events staged by organisations wanting to make news. These days they're also known as news conferences or media conferences because they are open to all media, not just the press. Journalists often call them *pressers*. They range from government announcements and lobbying by pressure groups to opportunities to interview celebrities and sports stars.

Football clubs will call a news or media conference every time they sign a new player or appoint a new manager. But it is rare indeed for a club to announce at a news conference that they have sacked their manager. This illustrates the problem with news conferences. They are controlled by whoever stages them. Access is restricted to invited members of the media. But as long as everybody gets equal access to all the interviewees, the conferences are at least fair to all news organisations.

You need to assess the amount of interest in a story before you go to a news conference, because that determines how early you need to turn up to get a good place. You will need to know where the main speaker will be sitting so you can position your microphone for the best sound quality. If hundreds of press are likely to be there you may need to arrive several hours ahead of the start if possible. If the event is of only local interest, 20 minutes to half an hour will be enough time to set up.

Will there be an opportunity for one-to-one interviews before or after the main conference, or will you have to make do with the material recorded during the 'presser'?

It is important to establish the ground rules before a news conference. Will there be an opportunity for one-to-one interviews before or (more usually) after the main conference, or will you have to make do with the material recorded during the presser?

Press conferences are a good place to meet new contacts and establish relationships with press officers and others who can help you. If you are offered individual interviews with footballers and managers, for example, that is the time to try to earn their trust – and ask for their personal contact details.

Photocalls

Photocalls are stage-managed media events similar to news conferences with the emphasis on the picture opportunities they offer the media. They sometimes take place before or after a formal news conference.

The traditional accompaniment to the announcement of a new manager or player at a football club is the photo opportunity on the pitch, where the new signing is paraded with club scarf and a shirt with his name on it. It's a TV and newspaper cliché. Politicians' election visits are carefully planned so that the 'right' pictures appear on the evening news – the would-be prime minister with nurses/teachers/people from ethnic minorities, for example. Camera crews and reporters look for the slip-ups amidst the spin.

Sometimes what happens at a photocall becomes the story. When Prince Charles appeared with his sons William and Harry on the ski slopes prior to his 2005 wedding, the brief question and answer session began with an inquiry from BBC Royal Correspondent Nicholas Witchell about how the young princes were looking forward to their father's wedding. The microphones picked up the Prince of Wales muttering: 'Bloody people. I can't bear that man. He's so awful, he really is.'

Remember

- Always arrive in plenty of time for news conferences
- Establish the ground rules – will there be one-to-one interviews?
- Find a good position for recording
- Try to find the story behind the 'spin'
- Use media events as a chance to network and improve your contacts.

Protests and demonstrations

Some pressure groups and campaigners will tire of lobbying through press releases and letters to the local papers. They'll stage a protest or demonstration. Demos focus attention on issues, but they have to be considered in context. To what extent are the organisers setting the news agenda, and therefore manipulating us as journalists? There is a trade-off between the drama these events provide and the threat to the independence of the news organisation.

Demos focus attention on issues, but are the organisers setting the news agenda, and manipulating us as journalists?

The BBC used to have a rule about not previewing demonstrations. It was felt that publicising the event gave the organisers free advertising to attract bigger crowds than they would otherwise get. Current practice suggests the rules have changed. When musician and anti-poverty campaigner Bob Geldof announced the Live8 series of concerts in 2005, he attracted worldwide coverage (or at least coverage throughout the major part of the world where rock'n'roll is a cultural force). He used it to call on people to march on Edinburgh to protest at the G8 summit of world leaders. The demo at the summit was the biggest in Scottish history with more than 200,000 people taking part. Much of the publicity on the day attached to breakaway 'anarchist' elements who clashed with police, but Geldof and U2's Bono were welcomed by the G8 leaders and won what they claimed to be significant concessions over the cancelling of debt in Africa.

In another example, the pressure group Fathers 4 Justice, campaigning for the rights of absent fathers to have access to their children, achieved public notoriety and no little sympathy by dressing as superheroes and climbing public landmarks including Buckingham Palace, the Foreign Office and the Severn Bridge. Many of their protests caused widespread disruption to traffic, and could not have been ignored by local media. When Fathers 4 Justice threw flour-bombs at the prime minister, Tony Blair, from the public gallery of the House of Commons in May 2004, it was international news. And four months later, no editor could resist Batman scaling the Queen's balcony.

But there is a limit to such activity. When the *Sun* reported early in 2006 that Fathers 4 Justice were planning to kidnap the prime minister's son, the leader of the group said that would be going too far. Matt O'Connor said: 'If our position is constantly undermined by extremists, we will shut down the Fathers 4 Justice campaign.' He did, but others revived it a few months later.

Outrageous stunts attract coverage, and violent elements of an otherwise peaceful protest will become the focus of attention. Just as the clashes with the police at the G8 demo in Edinburgh were the lasting images of that event in 2005, so the reporting of a series of protests in 2010 against increased university tuition fees concentrated on the violent 'occupation' of Millbank, a building containing Conservative Party offices, and an attack on a car taking the Prince of Wales and Duchess of Cornwall to the theatre. Responsible reporting should explain the context of such obviously televisual moments – that they happened against a backdrop of thousands of people protesting peacefully – but it is an uncomfortable truth that whatever a reporter or presenter says, powerful news images linger in the memory of viewers.

Remember

- Don't be manipulated
- There is a need for impartial, balanced reporting
- Isolated violent episodes should be reported in the context of what else happened.

THINKPIECE NEWS PROCESSING

There is a problem for people working in modern broadcast newsrooms, particularly those in the larger organisations where journalists are working for numerous outlets, including online and interactive services. The problem is that many journalists (often very capable people who have either had or will have great careers as producers, reporters and presenters) find themselves in the role not of news gatherers but of news processors. They rewrite press releases or make new versions of stories that other people have gathered and written. The news processors could be forgiven for asking if what they are doing is proper journalism.

They are certainly one step removed from most of the sources outlined in this chapter. But successful broadcast journalists – those who hope to lift themselves above this bottom rung of the career ladder – will question the information they are processing, and check it out with primary sources wherever possible.

Paul Chantler and Sim Harris were prescient in their 1997 book *Local Radio Journalism* (Focal Press) when they warned that new technology was leading to one of the biggest dangers of all: 'There could be a tendency to think of news as that which simply appears on the screen or the printer. Never forget that real news is what you go out and find through your own efforts.'

The printer – in the sense of the machine in the corner of the newsroom that provided a landline feed of copy and 'rip and read' bulletins, rather than the printer linked to your computer – is now old technology. And it is simplistic to suggest that what you find out for yourself is the only 'real news'. But the warning is sound more than a decade on. It can be argued that 'proper journalism' is still the craft of finding new stories.

Nonetheless, journalists have always reworked material collected by others. The sub-editor on a newspaper and the producer in radio or television take others' work and where possible improve it.

In television, where teamwork is so important, several reporters can work on one package. The senior correspondent will usually write and present the item, but interviews and sequences of shots within the finished film may have been collected by others. A producer will have been assigned to coordinate the different ingredients and supervise the assembly of the final product. Any member of the team may need to check the facts, or other people's written copy, as they go along. It is a poor researcher who accepts others' data unquestioningly, and a poor reporter who sticks to the research brief when events in the field suggest the details he has been given are wrong.

Wherever possible go to primary sources. That became the mantra of the BBC's local online news services after a series of users complained about inaccuracies in stories based on local radio copy. Radio journalists in the pre-digital age did not have to worry about accurate spelling. Some spellings – of names, for example – might be deliberately spelled differently to aid pronunciation.

Now, online journalists are involved in re-sourcing – not just re-versioning – material, and in finding fresh stories. They are content providers in their own right. The decision in the BBC not to rely on unchecked local radio copy was controversial within the organisation at the time, but it vastly reduced the number of basic journalistic mistakes, such as names, places and facts that were wrong. Mostly mistakes happened because accurate spelling was not essential in radio and it is online. Other errors were easier for the audience to spot because web pages are permanent while the spoken word is transient.

Hugh Berlyn, then Editor of BBC News Interactive, English Regions, sums up the change in approach:

'It used to be the case that online journalists in the BBC were just processing other people's stories. The attitude was, "We don't need more journalists, we've got plenty in television and radio." But since we decided not to rely on local radio copy, that has changed. Our people have to be content providers. They know how to source a story and they know right from wrong. True, they don't get out of the office much, but that's true of regional newspapers these days.'

Wherever possible go to primary sources.

THINKPIECE   AN ETHICAL DILEMMA

Protests are good copy. They can turn ugly, leading to clashes with opponents or the police. The Poll Tax demonstrations in Margaret Thatcher's era turned into riots. The Countryside Alliance's march against the fox-hunting ban under Tony Blair's premiership led to confrontation with police in riot gear. The coalition government of 2010 faced mass protests early in its term, first over rising university tuition fees and then public spending cuts, with violence, vandalism and injuries to protesters and police.

Often broadcasters will be told about a demo in advance – even before the police or other authorities know about it. That is because the protesters want publicity for their actions. Public opinion is their principal weapon. It helps their case if they get coverage even before the police arrive. To what extent is it acceptable for broadcasters to collude in what might turn into criminal activity?

The Ofcom Code says 'material likely to encourage or incite the commission of crime or to lead to disorder must not be included in television or radio services'. But that does not prevent journalists attending illegal demonstrations.

The BBC *Editorial Guidelines* say 'comprehensive coverage of demonstrations, disturbances and riots is an important part of our news reporting', but:

- 'We assess the risk that by previewing likely prospects of disturbances we might encourage them.

- We withdraw immediately if we suspect we are inflaming the situation.'

> Ofcom: 'material likely to encourage or incite the commission of crime or to lead to disorder must not be included in television or radio services.'

There are also special rules for live reporting. There must be a delay in transmission, or the chance to cut away and record material for use in an edited report, if the level of violence or disorder becomes too graphic.

Estimates of the number of people involved should be treated with due scepticism. Report wide disparities and name the sources of the figures.

Courts and tribunals

Courts and the judicial process have been a mainstay of news reporting since the first modern newspapers were published. The reason for attending courts is not simply because the institutions themselves are important parts of our constitution – even though they are. Nor is it because 'justice has to be seen to be done' – even though that is a fundamental principle of British law. We cover courts because they provide great stories. Murder, rape, robbery and massive fraud all end up in the courts. That's why it's important that journalists understand the rules governing the various courts – juvenile, magistrates', crown, civil, courts of appeal, coroners' – and tribunals.

The law on contempt of court is designed to prevent evidence that could prejudice a fair trial appearing in the media before it has been presented in court. There's more on the law that applies to journalism and broadcasting later in this book.

Crown court and higher court listings are available online at **www.courtserve2.net**. Magistrates' court lists are available from the court clerks. You will need to make regular checks about forthcoming cases, because preliminary hearings are often postponed or adjourned, and there are many potential delays in the judicial system.

When a case comes to court, you need to make the same assessment as you would for any media event. Will there be so many media there that you will need to turn up especially early to get a place on the press bench? It's normally 'first-come-first-served', although access to some large trials is by ticket only, or a special pass arranged with newsrooms in advance. Sometimes an electronic feed of events in the court will be relayed to a separate press room.

Court reporting presents special problems for broadcasters because, while live text-based communications (such as Twitter) have been allowed in some courts, to date there is no acceptance that electronic recording media should be allowed inside court rooms. The Criminal Justice Act 1925 makes it an offence to take pictures in court and to publish those pictures. It means that broadcast journalists have to be imaginative in telling court stories, while sticking to the legal requirements to be fair, accurate and contemporaneous.

Court reporting presents special problems for broadcasters because . . . to date there is no acceptance that electronic recording media should be allowed.

Television has particular problems. How do you tell a story with no pictures? Courtroom artists are one solution. Pastel sketches show the accused or witnesses in the dock, usually being cross-examined. It may surprise viewers to know that artists are not permitted to sketch inside the court itself. Their remarkable work is done at speed and from memory. Computer graphics, placing figures in virtual court rooms, are a more recent and often more time-consuming alternative. Graphics artists will visit courts and make notes of the interior layout to create a virtual representation of the scene. The faces of defendants and witnesses, taken from stills or video taken outside court, will be added to the digital image to replicate the scene inside.

An option favoured by Sky News during the 2003 Hutton Inquiry into the circumstances surrounding the death of government scientist Dr David Kelly and the child abuse trial of pop star Michael Jackson in 2005 is the most elaborate, ambitious and expensive – a full re-enactment of the court proceedings using actors.

In all but two US states TV cameras are allowed in court. This version of justice being seen to be done does not yet extend to TV cameras in British court rooms. There is a fear that witnesses would play to the camera or would be afraid to appear if they could be widely recognised by TV viewers. The idea that people would play to the camera was also used as an argument against the televising of Parliament as recently as the 1980s.

Remember

- Learn where to find information about forthcoming court cases
- Check court listings regularly
- Prepare for a court visit as you would for any media event
- Know the law on court reporting and contempt
- Be aware of the problems broadcasters – and in particular TV – face when reporting court proceedings.

Government bodies

Every government department has its own teams of press officers, many of them regionally based. The Central Office of Information used to be an apolitical source of information working within civil service guidelines. After the 1997 election of New Labour there was growing concern among media commentators about the politicisation of the Civil Service – and, in particular, government press officers. When dealing with them, you need to be aware of the risks of 'spin' – the manipulation of journalists by the political parties' marketing specialists or 'spin doctors'.

There are also dozens of public bodies set up by government, sometimes known as quangos. They include everything from the Arts Council to the Health and Safety Executive. Most have press officers looking for publicity, and are able to help when stories about their area of expertise are in the news.

Politicians

Broadcast journalists spend an inordinate amount of time persuading newsworthy people with a story to tell, or a valued opinion to express, to talk into a microphone. We also talk to politicians. Elected representatives thrive on what one of their number famously called 'the oxygen of publicity'.

MPs and councillors will issue press releases and call newsrooms either in person or through their press representatives. Anyone with a political cause to promote will want to appear on the media. Some develop a reputation as 'dial-a-quote merchants'. Whether what they have to say is worth reporting depends on the story. If the purpose of their involvement appears to be self-publicity, you may prefer to ignore them.

Council leaders, their opposition counterparts, local cabinet members and (in some cities) elected mayors, who may have considerable power, are worth cultivating as contacts.

Whenever a journalist deals with a politician, the journalist must be aware of the political agenda and the need for impartial reporting. At election times this is especially important and there are specific, legally enforceable guidelines on the interviewing of candidates. These have been drawn up to ensure impartiality in the electoral process, and are available online, in section six of the Ofcom Broadcasting Code (**www.ofcom.org.uk**).

If you are looking for fringe or minority political opinion, just type the specific area of minority interest plus 'blog' into a search engine. The blogs will lead you to news sources and potential interviewees.

Councils

Local government is a prime source of controversy, a mainstay of local news reporting. Planning rows, controversial policy decisions and occasionally corruption all make headlines. These days, most broadcast organisations do not consider it worthwhile covering council meetings and they certainly don't bother with council committees. But professional relationships with councillors and council press officers are worth fostering. And it is worth remembering that debate in council chambers can often be filmed or recorded when newsworthy decisions are being made. This is the stuff of local democracy and can lead to lively actuality.

Trading standards departments offer a steady flow of consumer stories. Raising public awareness of citizens' rights is part of their brief. So, they often enlist the help of reporters to expose wrongdoing. Such stories can offer two bites at the same cherry: the exposé followed by the court case. The reporter earns the kudos of helping to uncover law breaking. And where suspected criminality has been exposed by investigative reporting, trading standards can be offered the evidence to support a prosecution – and a follow-up story.

Remember

- Don't be manipulated – beware of 'spin'
- Cultivate national and local politicians and government officials as contacts
- Remain politically impartial
- Remember the need for balanced reporting
- Know the guidelines on election coverage.

Communities

Schools, churches, voluntary and residents' associations, clubs, societies, special interest groups and online communities often welcome coverage of their affairs. Trade unions and business organisations can provide interesting copy. Consumer watchdog groups, both statutory and voluntary, also have stories to tell.

Beyond the reporting of organised groupings, many broadcasters are concerned that they do not fully reflect the communities they serve. The quest to represent those who are

Many broadcasters are concerned that they do not fully reflect the communities they serve.

traditionally underrepresented in the news continues, and it is at a local level that it can be most effective. Winning the confidence of potential news sources is a vital skill, whether they are cabinet ministers or costermongers, successful rappers or suspected rapists.

Local radio fosters a sense of local identity. Community radio stations, some of which are not on air permanently but granted short-term restricted service licences (RSLs) by Ofcom, are usually run by local people. They frequently encourage contributions from anyone in the community with a story to tell. Hyper-local news blogs perform the same function. Some feature video and audio content.

Remember

- Cultivate local contacts
- Try to find stories from groups who are not normally represented in the media.

Tip-offs

Tip-offs to journalists take many forms. A tip might be information from trusted freelances, for which they will expect to be paid an appropriate fee when the story has been investigated and (hopefully) confirmed. Or it might be a call from a member of the public. Radio stations and regional TV encourage listeners and viewers to call in with stories. It is a cheap way of finding exclusive material, and is always worth the effort involved in checking those stories that don't make it to air. It is also a way of engaging groups who otherwise feel excluded from the media. The BBC's local television pilot in the Midlands, between December 2005 and August 2006, focused on encouraging contributions from people and communities not given a voice by traditional media.

There are also anonymous tip-offs. Sometimes they offer an immediate lead to a story. Someone has noticed armed police surrounding a house. A siege is in progress. The caller doesn't want to get involved, but thinks the story should be on the news. At other times, anonymous tips need to be treated with a healthy scepticism. It could come from someone with a grievance, or be well intentioned but inaccurate. The message could be malicious – a hoax.

For example, a radio reporter was once hoodwinked into broadcasting that a gorilla had escaped from a local zoo, and was a danger to the public. The source was the zoo owner, who made several phone calls to the newsroom reporting on the primate's progress. The station duly reported that a gorilla was on the loose. It wasn't until the reporter rang the zoo back, to say he was on his way to the scene to report the growing crisis, that the owner admitted he'd made the story up. Was he trying to drum up trade on a slack Sunday afternoon? Or just playing a practical joke?

The only way to avoid being hoaxed is to find a second source for the story. If you receive an anonymous call, always ask for extra information that will help check it out. If someone says there's an MRSA outbreak at a hospital, ask for as many details as you can of who has been affected and on which wards. If you then approach the hospital with a series of facts, even unsourced ones, it is much harder for them to deny the story. It is more likely that they will correct any mistakes in your information, and you will end up with what you hoped for – an accurate story.

If you receive an anonymous call, always ask for extra information that will help check it out.

Off the record

When a tip-off is from a trusted source who doesn't want to be named, the question of *off-the-record* information arises. It's important both parties understand what this means. There are varying interpretations and the ground rules have to be made clear in each case. It might be that the informant did not mind the information being broadcast so long as they were not identified as the source. It might mean the story should only run if it can be confirmed by somebody else. Or it could mean that the information is simply guidance to the reporter in the pursuit of the story.

> **A source cannot turn round after revealing some juicy titbit of information and say: 'Oh, by the way, that last bit was off the record.'**

There is a useful guiding principle of the off-the-record briefing, used by the *Washington Post* reporters Bob Woodward and Carl Bernstein in *All the President's Men* (1974, Simon & Schuster), the story of the Watergate scandal that brought down US President Richard Nixon. They made it clear to sources that nothing could be placed off the record after it had been said. This means that a source cannot turn round after revealing some juicy titbit of information and say: 'Oh, by the way, that last bit was off the record.' The *Post*'s style guide says: 'We do not allow sources to change the ground rules governing specific quotations after the fact. Once a quote is on the record it remains there.'

In investigative stories, you may be dealing with *whistleblowers*, insiders prepared to give you information about an organisation for which they work. They may lose their job if they are identified. If you promise to protect a source, the responsibility for that decision is yours. It is a fundamental ethical principle of journalism that you should not reveal sources. Historically, UK law has not automatically protected journalists who want to keep information secret, and reporters have faced imprisonment. But the 1998 Human Rights Act incorporated the European Convention on Human Rights into English law. Article 10 upholds freedom of expression, which includes journalists' right to protect their sources, particularly when the story is in the public interest.

These niceties are important, but not much use to the reporter defending a libel action, when the story has to be justified by witnesses prepared to give evidence in court.

Remember

- Beware of anonymous sources
- Question the motives of people offering tip-offs
- Seek a second source where possible
- Understand what you and others mean by 'off the record'
- Protect your sources.

A CLOSER LOOK

PROTECTING SOURCES – THE LEGAL POSITION

The right of journalists to protect their sources was established in English law after a six-year legal battle. In the case of Mersey Care NHS Trust against Robin Ackroyd, the High Court decided – in accordance with Article 10 of the European Convention on Human Rights, which gives a right to freedom of expression – that a journalist could only be ordered to reveal a source if there was a 'pressing social need'.

Ackroyd, a freelance journalist, was ordered by the High Court to say who gave him medical information for a *Daily Mirror* story about the Moors murderer Ian Brady. The trust that ran Ashworth secure hospital took the paper to court to find out who had leaked confidential medical records. The *Mirror* had fought the case all the way to the House of Lords, but lost, and had to reveal that Ackroyd was their source.

The trust then pursued Ackroyd through the courts. Mr Justice Tugendhat delivered the ruling in Ackroyd's favour in the High Court in February 2006. The journalist had been supported by the National Union of Journalists (NUJ). The union's general secretary Jeremy Dear told the trade journal *Press Gazette* it was a fantastic verdict for all journalists: 'The fundamental point of principle – that there is a strong public interest in upholding journalists' right not to reveal their sources – has been maintained.'

Ackroyd told the BBC at the time:

Robin Ackroyd: 'Journalists protect their sources because they have a professional duty of confidence to them.

'Journalists protect their sources because they have a professional duty of confidence to them. It is not a standpoint we take because we are being difficult or precious. I do not reveal confidential sources of information as an overriding matter of conscience.'

When Ackroyd won his case on appeal Mr Justice Tugendhat said that there must be a 'pressing social need' before an intermediary [the journalist] will be required to disclose her or his source. The judge concluded that Ackroyd was 'a responsible journalist whose purpose was to act in the public interest'.

The ruling depended on a series of competing factors – the right to medical privacy against the right to protect sources. The judge said courts should apply a test of 'proportionality' to such conflicts. One fact that helped Ackroyd win was his proven track record as a responsible investigative journalist. But during the six-year battle, none of his contacts could be sure they would remain confidential as a source, and his career suffered.

The issue of journalists naming their sources was also highlighted when Dr David Kelly was identified by the government as the source of a BBC report that the government 'sexed up' a dossier about the reasons for going to war with Iraq (see Case study 3.3 later in this chapter for further details of the case and the subsequent Hutton Inquiry into Dr Kelly's death).

The Foreign Affairs Committee chairman, Donald Anderson MP, accused reporter Andrew Gilligan of changing his story when he gave evidence to them. The chairman said journalists should have to name their sources if they were making allegations under parliamentary privilege (the committee's hearings are covered by privilege, which means accusations made during their business cannot be subject to a libel action).

Jeremy Dear, of the NUJ, told BBC News Online that 'whistleblowers' must be protected as they 'will not come forward if they think they are going to be grassed up at a later stage'.

He said one of the roles of journalists was to expose wrongdoing and bad practice by public institutions and big corporations: 'For that reason it is the golden rule of journalism that we don't betray our sources and are prepared to go to prison to uphold that principle.'

Other news media

No matter how good your news organisation, you are not going to get every story first. There are other journalists in other organisations trying just as hard to find stories. So, it is vital to check other media organisations. That means reading newspapers, watching TV, listening to radio, checking news blogs and subscribing to podcasts.

In large cities there may be several local or regional radio stations, and they will all be listening to each other, hoping they haven't been beaten to an item of news. If they have, common sense dictates that the listener will not have been listening to both stations at once, so an item will be lifted, checked and run in the next bulletin by the station that missed it first time round. *Checking the information is vital. Just because somebody else reported it first does not give you legal immunity from libel or other legal actions.*

Spoilers

Rival regional TV stations monitor each other's output and are fiercely jealous of the other's exclusives. The 'exclusive' may not be a whole story – a key interview on a story everybody's covering will inspire just as much envy.

Tabloid newspapers are famous for running 'spoilers' – stories designed to spoil the impact of their rivals' scoops or cheque-book sign-ups. The spoilers will often take the form of a story written to suggest the beaten party has a story just as good as or better than their rivals'. This practice is not common in broadcasting, partly because cheque-book journalism (paying for stories) is not common in broadcast news.

A different agenda?

The newsroom of the independent local radio (ILR) station in Coventry, Mercia Sound, prided itself in the early 1980s on never being beaten to a major story by the local newspaper the *Coventry Evening Telegraph*. Few radio stations can make that claim today. Newspapers often have many more journalists than radio stations covering the same patch. So, radio stations end up following newspapers – not a proud boast for a medium that has immediate access to the means of broadcasting information.

But that should not stop the drive to be different. Sue Owen, the Managing Editor of BBC Radio Stoke, has the confidence to say: 'Newspapers simply do not set our agenda. We set our own. We should be doing something different.'

BBC2's *Newsnight* reports the front pages of the next day's papers, and most breakfast programmes feature a review of the morning's papers. A healthy respect for other journalists' output should not detract from the drive to be first with the news.

Remember

- Know what the competition is doing – check them out regularly
- Never use other media organisations' information without checking it
- Be confident – don't let other media set your agenda
- Always aim to be first – and accurate.

Freedom of Information Act (FOI)

Being first to report the news doesn't necessarily mean racing round chasing ambulances. Patience and a cool head are virtues, particularly if you are using the Freedom of Information Act 2000 as a research tool. Information released under the Act, often at the request of journalists, can take months to emerge because of the appeals procedure built into the Act. But when it finally comes into the open, that information may be dynamite.

You can make an application, in writing, for information to any public authority. They have 20 days to respond. They may charge a fee, according to a published scale of charges. They may be able to argue that collecting the information will be too costly. If they can't or won't respond, they may issue a Refusal Notice. Then the appeal process starts. Under the Act, authorities have a duty to provide advice and assistance to applicants.

The Act covers government departments, councils, NHS bodies, schools, colleges and universities, and the police. It also applies to the Houses of Commons and Lords, the Northern Ireland Assembly and the National Assembly for Wales. The Freedom of Information (Scotland) Act 2002 covers Scottish public authorities.

The *Daily Mail* requested details of an exchange of letters between the Metropolitan Police Commissioner Sir Ian Blair and a senior civil servant written in the immediate aftermath of the shooting by armed officers of Brazilian Jean Charles de Menezes at Stockwell tube station in 2005. The letters showed that the Commissioner had tried to block the Independent Police Complaints Commission's inquiry into the killing. He said he should be allowed to suspend the section of the Police Reform Act that requires information to be supplied to the IPCC. The *Mail*'s headline asked if the Met Chief had become a 'law unto himself'? The *Mail* heard about the letters during Sir Ian's evidence to a parliamentary committee, on 13 September 2005. The FOI request resulted in a story on 1 October. That was quick work. The Act is a valuable tool for investigative journalists, but don't expect a story on the same day.

Here's another interesting example, bearing in mind what we said earlier about police voice-banks. In August 2006 the *Press Gazette* reported that a reporter found out via an FOI request that more than 5,000 incidents (5,083 to be precise) took place over a weekend when a police voice-bank reported nothing had happened.

Anyone can request information under the Act. The Information Commissioner's Office will rule on requests that are refused. It is an independent public body set up to promote access to official information – though it is also charged with protecting personal information.

Details of how to make an application under the Act are explained on the Information Commissioner's website **www.ico.gov.uk**.

Often, a contact will make the initial inquiry and journalists can act on the results. When the government decided against a blanket ban on smoking in public, the charity Cancer Research UK made an application under the Act. They knew that research in Northern Ireland showed more than 90 per cent of the public supported a total ban, and they wanted the results of the consultation exercise in England. Three months later – in February 2006 – the government line changed and Parliament voted for a total ban.

Responses to the Act, by government departments for example, are officially 'made public'. That doesn't mean issuing a press release: it may just mean publishing the information on a website.

So, it is a question of knowing where to look, and then interpreting the information. Just because it is available to everyone doesn't mean everyone will be looking for it.

There is a very good guide to using the Act written by investigative journalist Heather Brooke (with a foreword by *Private Eye* editor Ian Hislop). *Your Right to Know: A Citizen's Guide to the Freedom of Information Act* (2006, Pluto Press) explains how the Act can be used by reporters. It includes advice on the law in practice (including in Scotland) and even a chapter on business reporting showing how to get hold of contracts, tenders and performance evaluations. Heather Brooke's website **www.heatherbrooke.org** has links to examples of FOI reporting and tips on how to prevent public authorities trying to block journalists' requests for information.

Interactive news as a source

Interactivity means more feedback from viewers – and more story ideas.

The mass of TV content on the Internet and mobiles means viewers can select which stories they want to watch, or tailor their viewing to news about subjects they have pre-selected. The RSS system (Really Simple Syndication) means web users choose topics and are alerted when stories on those topics are available. News and sports content was the 'driver', in the jargon, for this type of video on demand. Interactivity means more feed-back from viewers – and more story ideas.

Today's viewers have more control of the broadcast process than they could ever have imagined in the pre-digital age. Many broadcasters see the red button and apps such as the BBC's iPlayer as more than just another service. They believe they encourage viewers to be more involved in the news-making process. Viewers will get in touch by text and email with comments and opinions on stories and their treatment. They might also offer new stories. Still others will be bloggers – with their own sites offering information, opinion and occasionally new stories with video or audio treatment.

User-generated content (UGC)

The opportunity for viewers, listeners and Net users to share their experiences of breaking news stories means witnesses – to terrorist attacks, police operations and natural disasters – are easier to find than in the days when tracking down sources relied on journalistic legwork and phone bashing. These **citizen journalists** are a valuable news source, and may provide eye-witness accounts, via comment boxes on websites, and pictures, from mobile phones, digital video and stills cameras.

Gary Duffy, UK Editor of the BBC News website, says: 'If there's a sudden explosion, oil refinery fire or terrorist attack, or anything like that, within minutes now we expect to have user-generated content on BBC output.' A specialist hub, staffed by a team of journalists, is responsible for getting content to the websites and to television and for passing on contacts to radio stations.

Matthew Eltringham, Editor of the BBC College of Journalism website, worked in the unit. He says material from the public proves its value on all types of stories:

'There's obviously the breaking news, where you want immediate eye-witness accounts of what's happening around you, but we use user content in lots of different ways. We ask people to talk about their own experiences – whether it's pension funds, drugs or sexual harassment in the army. If it's a particularly strong case study, we'll use them in our coverage across television, radio and online. In a way it's a shortcut to finding the human aspects of the stories, but it's incredibly effective.'

The BBC said in April 2006, after a year-long review called Creative Future:

'Increasingly, audiences of all ages not only want the choice of what to watch and listen to when they want, they also expect to take part, debate, create and control. Interactivity and user-generated content are increasingly important stimuli for the creative process.'

Blogs

Blogs are a fantastic way to track down first-person testimony, witnesses to stories and events, and expert opinion. There are news-based blogging communities, many offering 'citizen journalists' the chance to report their own news. The business models for successful news blogging are in their infancy.

Shayne Bowman and Chris Willis, who run the **Hypergene.net weblog**, offered a definition of 'participatory journalism' as early as 2003. In *We Media: How Audiences are Shaping the Future of News and Information*, they defined citizen journalism as the act of citizens 'playing an active role in the process of collecting, reporting, analyzing and disseminating news and information'.

They described 'a bottom-up, emergent phenomenon in which there is little or no editorial oversight or formal journalistic workflow.

While the term 'citizen journalist' is no longer attracting the buzz it once did (with some pro-fessionals asking if there would be as much enthusiasm for 'citizen surgeons'), non-professional contributions have enriched the mainstream, broadened the range of news outlets, particularly at hyper-local level, and increased the diversity of views represented across the media.

On almost any running story, you can enter the story subject and the word 'blog' into a search engine and find someone commenting on the story or, better still, involved in it. On breaking news, subject-based blogs are more use for finding expert opinion than hard facts, because bloggers are usually amateurs, who can't keep updating their sites as news develops.

The ethical questions about the use of amateur reporters are still being debated. Editors agree they should never be in the position of asking a member of the public to endanger themselves to get original material for broadcasters. Health and safety considerations apply just as they would to your own staff. The National Union of Journalists produced a code of practice for what it called 'witness contributors'. The code – aimed mainly at protecting the livelihoods of the union's members and preventing the abuse of members of the public by cost-cutting editors – argued that 'the integrity and reliability of material and the safety of bona fide newsgatherers may be challenged and compromised by the use of "witness contributions"'.

They said that organisations using them should 'accept that appropriate and agreed payments will be made to witness contributors for all uses of their material and that the terms of licensing will be easily available and clear'.

Access to the means of distributing news material is no longer the exclusive preserve of professional journalists.

Contrast that with the disclaimer on an ITV news website in 2006: 'By sending us your video footage/photographs/audio you agree we can broadcast, publish and edit the material and pass it on to others for similar use in any media worldwide, without any payment being due to you.'

The reality is that access to the means of distributing news material is no longer the exclusive preserve of professional journalists. But there are potentially millions of people who are now able to contribute to news media with or without payment.

Former BBC Home Affairs Correspondent Andy Tighe offers a word of caution:

'It's fantastic in so far as it enables us to get information and perspectives from a much wider range of people, and they find it much easier to tell us what they're doing. So it's an important advance in news gathering. It does make our journalism more responsive and more democratic. The downside is if we open the gates completely, without any mechanism to check what we're being told.

'We have to be pretty careful we don't throw the baby out with the bathwater. It's great to involve more people and make them part of the story telling. On the other hand, there's a reason so many of us go to journalism college, spend a lot of time in local television and radio, or whatever it might be, getting trained so that we develop these skills, this ability to be a little bit careful, a little bit cautious and to really not always take things at face value. That's what journalism's all about, and we mustn't forget that.'

When an oil depot in Hemel Hempstead caught fire in December 2005, BBC News 24 was evangelical in its requests for viewers' contributions. A caption beneath the headline OIL DEPOT BLAST read: 'Send footage to **yourpics@bbc.co.uk**', a presenter repeated the request, and, to assist those who might be struggling with the technology, a message on the on-screen streamer, or tickertape, advised: 'For help in sending pictures 0208 576 8200.'

Greater rigour needs to be applied to checking pictures from your audience than to input from trusted professionals. Sky News fell for a hoax when it broadcast a picture sent in by a viewer in March 2006. The shot purported to show heathland fires raging in Dorset in the west of England. It wasn't until the picture was printed in the *Guardian* that a reader pointed out there were two North American elk in the middle of the shot.

But checking the authenticity of pictures – or any information – is part of basic journalism. The technology hasn't changed that.

Pictures are difficult to fake at short notice. Information is not, so there's a need for great caution. The BBC had to apologise – and took the unusual step of removing a story from its website – when it fell for an untrue tale from an Israeli tabloid newspaper in 2011 that a rabbinical court had sentenced a dog to death by stoning. By the time they took it down, the story had been shared by 50,000 Facebook users and appeared on 'most-read' and 'most-shared' lists. A less serious dog-related *faux pas* happened in 2005 when a tornado struck Birmingham, causing millions of pounds of damage. One eye-witness account posted on a BBC website was from Dorothy worried that her dog Toto had been swept away. Fans of *The Wizard of Oz* will recognise the reference.

Remember

- Extra caution is needed when using information from the public
- Check facts wherever possible
- Check the health and safety implications
- Beware of hoaxers.

Blogs by journalists

Many journalists produce their own blogs. It means they get feedback from readers, viewers and listeners. This is a way of gauging public opinion, and can provide story ideas. But there is a danger that responding to the blogging community can be time consuming, and a risk that the journalist loses sight of the wider audience of which the bloggers may be only a tiny part.

Some people inside the BBC, where blogging is successfully practised by senior editors and leading correspondents such as political editor Nick Robinson, think there is a danger of 'over-cooking' the idea. Not every story nor every reporter needs a blog. Used wisely though, blogs help you stay in touch with your audience and help the audience engage with your news medium.

THINKPIECE   USER-GENERATED CONTENT – THE CHALLENGE

Hugh Berlyn, of BBC News Interactive, says that when a big news event happens: 'Probably the first pictures we get are submitted by our readers and we use them. But what responsibility do we have for that person being near the bus bomber or whatever? I don't know. It's a big question.'

And who takes legal responsibility for the content of these contributions? Emily Bell, writing in the *Guardian* in December 2005, noted that 'the realities of mainstream media and citizen journalists living together have begun to bite'. She highlighted the *Daily Telegraph*'s 'snap and send' initiative, asking readers with a 'front row view of some major event' to send in a picture. The *Press Gazette* reported concerns by the Chartered Institute of Journalists that the terms and conditions applied to senders of photographs included an agreement 'to indemnify Telegraph Group Ltd against all legal fees, damages and other expenses that may be incurred . . . as a result of a breach of the above warranties'.

The copyright in such pictures usually remains with the contributor, while their agreement to terms and conditions licenses the newspaper [or broadcaster] to use them. This is the arrangement the BBC introduced for viewers' videos shown on local TV. Contributors signed a licence agreement, but received no payment.

In the *Telegraph* case Bell, the editor of *Guardian Unlimited*, points out that, if the newspaper were sued as a result of printing or uploading to its website a picture that breached copyright, privacy or libel laws, then one would expect the newspaper to fight the case and pay the costs. She wrote: 'Pursuing a reader would be a marketing disaster for the paper.'

There's also a concern, voiced among other places in *Journalist*, the magazine of the National Union of Journalists, that the contributions of unpaid members of the public might be used in preference to the work of professional journalists.

Photographer Pete Jenkins wrote that an NUJ member arriving at the scene of the tornado in Birmingham in 2005 was 'surrounded by locals waving their fashion accessories and demanding money in exchange for (very) dodgy smudges'.

Emily Bell, writing in March 2006, asked:

'Is there a difference then between the professional journalist and the citizen contributor? By the very definition there is – one is casually contributing their expertise, the other is paid for an ability to make judgements on how to convey stories or content in the most effective way. But the idea that what the professional journalist can provide will always in all circumstances be qualitatively better than a citizen journalist is not true any more – if it ever was.'

The ethical and legal issues have been around for nearly a decade but remain unresolved. What do you think?

- Why shouldn't a broadcaster use any material they can to tell a story?
- What checks should be applied to viewers' or listeners' material to ensure it is safe to broadcast?
- Should members of the public charge a professional rate for their contribution to news programmes?
- Are TV stations exploiting viewers' goodwill when they use their video or photographs? If so, how does this differ from newspapers filling column inches with readers' letters?
- Is the NUJ's Witness Contributors' Code of Practice a sensible response to the issues raised by the use of citizen journalists? Or is it a Luddite reaction to new technology?

Mark Byford, former BBC Deputy Director-General: 'News is about immediacy, but it's also about being accurate and being right.'

Whatever the source – if in doubt, check it out

Most news editors believe it's important to be first and it's important to be right, but it's more important to be right than first.

Mark Byford, the BBC Deputy Director-General, explained their approach in an interview in the *Guardian* in June 2005. He said: 'News is about immediacy, but it's also about being accurate and being right. It's better to be right and second than first and wrong. To be almost right or broadly right is not good enough for the BBC.'

Sky News has a reputation for being first with breaking news, but the man who presided over the growth of that reputation, Nick Pollard, has another passion: 'Accuracy, accuracy, accuracy. It certainly drives me mad and I hope that it drives younger people mad to see anything wrong.'

CASE STUDY 3.1	GETTING IT WRONG

The tragic consequences of getting it wrong were illustrated in January 2006 when the world's media reported that 12 miners had survived underground after a pit explosion in West Virginia. For nearly three hours waiting families celebrated before they were told that all but one of the men had, in fact, died.

The mistake was apparently due to a misheard radio message from rescuers to their command centre. As the euphoria at a 'miracle escape' spread, no journalist appears to have checked with authoritative sources, because there were no authoritative sources. The command centre had issued no official statement. Church bells pealed in celebration and the rolling news channels duly broadcast those celebrations. The reporters possibly got too close to the story and were caught up in the excitement of the miners' families. The result: misinformation was reported as fact.

Writing in the *Guardian* soon afterwards, media consultant and blogger Jeff Jarvis wrote: 'Hours after the terrible truth emerged, network executives and newspaper editors fell over themselves issuing justifications and excuses: they listed their sources and said they did the best they could with what they were given.'

Jarvis said the lesson of this was: 'You can't trust the news.' He argued that, in an age of instant communication and constant coverage, the public was left to judge the reliability of the news for themselves. 'The public is the editor.'

News, Jarvis said, is not a product, it's a process. 'It is time for journalists to tell the audience not just what they know, but also what they do not know. And it is time for journalists to admit that, in the end, they don't decide what is true. The public makes that judgement. So journalists must arm the public to do that job. We get to the truth together.'

The Internet as a research tool

The importance of checking sources is never more critical than when taking information from the Internet. The World Wide Web is a fabulous resource for journalists. Search engines offer immediate information at our fingertips. But there is no guarantee that any of the information is reliable.

Learn to focus your searches, and identify which sites can be trusted. If you are searching for an old news story about a topic, on Google for example, refine your search to 'news'. If you are looking for the website of a British organisation, select 'pages from the UK'. If you are looking for pictures, select 'images'.

Use quotation marks to refine your search. If you are looking for information about Roy Saatchi (a former BBC editor), you won't want information about Saatchi and Saatchi the advertising agency, Roy Keane, the former footballer, or the Scottish hero Rob Roy. So type 'Roy Saatchi' and only the exact phrase will be found.

Official sites of recognised organisations, such as universities and government bodies, can usually be relied on to give the official views of those bodies, and to store information. The name of a government website will have the suffix .gov; universities and other academic organisations have .ac.uk in the United Kingdom; non-profit organisations have .org, or .org.uk.

So much official information is now available online that 'computer-assisted reporting' is an important discipline within journalism. The phrase is a misnomer, because, as some practitioners have pointed out, nobody talks about 'telephone-assisted reporting'. The computer is just another tool for the journalist. You need to investigate what information it can give you access to, and analyse that information to see if it is worth presenting to the public.

CASE STUDY 3.2 THE INTERNET – A WARNING

Perhaps the most dramatic example so far of the unreliability of the Internet came in December 2004, on the twentieth anniversary of the Bhopal chemical disaster in India. A producer on BBC World was asked to find a spokesman from Dow Chemical, the company involved. An interview with Jude Finisterra followed. Mr Finisterra admitted the company's responsibility for the disaster and offered $12 billion compensation.

But Finisterra was not a Dow official. He was a hoaxer from a group calling themselves the Yes Men, online political activists, who had electronically hijacked part of the Dow website. His interview ran on BBC News 24 and Radios Two, Four and Five Live. The hoax was soon uncovered, but the BBC's only consolation was that its response and apology was 'speedy, frank and open'. Worldwide headlines suggested the corporation's reputation for accuracy was damaged.

> '[BBC online content] . . . has become an important place of record for news in the United Kingdom and beyond.'

The constant flow of information into newsrooms from viewers and listeners via text messaging and email, and journalists' access to blogs, micro-blogging, social networks and podcasts mean there has never been so much research material available to reporters. It is instant information, but little of it can be treated as instantly authoritative. Everyone and anyone has access to the Web and mobile phones. Not all websites can be treated as reliable sources of information; text messages even less so.

BBC online content is widely used as a journalistic resource. Gary Duffy, a BBC News web editor, sums up the organisation's influence and responsibilities:

'I don't think there's a news organisation in the United Kingdom whose journalists don't go out clutching print-outs from our website. One PR man from the nuclear industry was trying to get us to correct something he disputed. He said to me: "If we don't get it changed on your website, lazy bastards for years will be reprinting this as fact."

'It has become an important place of record for news in the United Kingdom and beyond.'

Is it new?

A serious problem with web pages is that there is often no way of telling if they are up to date. BBC web pages usually include a date when the material was posted. Most websites do not. Unless whoever posted the information keeps it updated or removes it when it is no longer current, the misleading page just hangs around in cyberspace waiting to undermine future researchers. It's as if you went into the newsagent and were sold last year's paper – with the date removed.

The BBC has provided an impressive volume of news background material online. Because it is produced within BBC guidelines of fairness and accuracy, this information is among the most reliable of any web resource.

But mistakes still occur. There are fewer checks before web content is aired than for most other broadcast outlets. BBC News online content is always checked by two journalists, but that is not true of all the corporation's websites. Web surfers may not recognise the distinction. On 22 November 2005, the front page of Radio Five Live's website (not a BBC News site) proclaimed 'George Best dies' and invited surfers to 'click here' for coverage of 'the death of the Manchester United legend'. Those surfers would have had some difficulty finding what they were looking for. George Best was still alive. Apparently someone preparing obituary material had pressed the wrong button. The mistake – a bit of 'finger trouble' by someone who was uploading other information from Five Live at the same time – was rectified within about 20 minutes. The legend died three days later.

Most reliable news sites (and the BBC is *usually* reliable) offer links to external sites, with warnings that the host of the main site can't be held responsible for other sites' content. Follow these links and you are in uncharted and dangerous waters. But you can use a selection of sites to cross-reference information and make a judgement about what is to be trusted.

CASE STUDY 3.3   GETTING IT RIGHT – THE IMPORTANCE OF NOTE TAKING

The importance of checking facts and the accuracy of sources was highlighted by the Hutton Inquiry into the death of civil servant Dr David Kelly in 2003. Dr Kelly killed himself after being named as the source of a BBC story about the reliability of the intelligence information on which Tony Blair took Britain to war in Iraq. Hutton cleared Tony Blair's government and damned the BBC.

The government had been accused of 'sexing up' the dossier claiming Iraq had weapons of mass destruction. Reporter Andrew Gilligan said in an early morning two-way on Radio 4's *Today* that the government probably knew the claim that weapons of mass destruction (WMDs) could be deployed in 45 minutes was wrong or questionable. He said the 45-minute claim had not appeared in the first draft of the document because intelligence agencies did not believe it was necessarily true. Hutton said: 'The allegations reported by Mr Gilligan . . . were unfounded.'

Hutton pointed out that Gilligan's notes of his conversation with Dr Kelly did not fully support the most serious of the allegations that he had reported.

It wasn't just the reporter who came under fire. The editorial controls of the BBC were criticised by Hutton: 'The editorial system which the BBC permitted was defective . . . in that Mr Gilligan was allowed to broadcast his report at 6.07 am without editors having seen a script of what he was going to say and having considered whether it should be approved.'

The BBC's Chairman Gavyn Davies, the Director-General Greg Dyke and Gilligan resigned. Dyke and the reporter still believe the essential truth of the story. No WMDs have been found in Iraq.

The corporation commissioned its own report into the consequences of Lord Hutton's criticisms. Ron Neil, a former Director of BBC News and Current Affairs, and his team, concluded that the BBC should improve the training of its journalists. Spending on training was doubled and a new 'virtual college' of journalism was set up.

The Neil Report stressed the importance of good note taking: 'Accurate and reliable note taking is an essential and prime journalistic craft.' Neil said that, where practicable, interviews with sources should be recorded on tape, and if that might inhibit the source, full shorthand or longhand notes were the best alternative.

One consequence of Neil is that it highlighted shorthand (always an essential skill for print journalists) as a valued skill for broadcasters. There are many places where electronic recording is not allowed (courts and tribunals, for instance). The journalist with the best shorthand note is always popular among colleagues and rivals. At the adjournment or conclusion of any high-profile court case, there is a huddle of reporters trying to agree the exact words used by a key witness or a judge summing up or sentencing.

Andrew Marr, the BBC's political editor at the time of Hutton, wrote in *My Trade* that shorthand is 'invaluable to anyone in journalism'.

The Neil Report: 'Accurate and reliable note taking is an essential and prime journalistic craft.'

The BBC did not go so far as to insist that it would only recruit journalists with a knowledge of shorthand. But senior managers confirmed at meetings of the Broadcast Journalism Training Council that shorthand was a desirable skill for job applicants. And Neil concluded that note taking should be part of all BBC journalists' training.

Details of the evidence to the Hutton Inquiry can be viewed at **www.the-hutton-inquiry.org.uk**.

CASE STUDY 3.4   GETTING IT RIGHT – REACTING TO INFORMATION

The speed with which breaking stories change offers massive challenges to 24-hour news operations. The desire to get it first has to be balanced by the need to get it right. The credibility of any news organisation depends on its accuracy. Cynics coined a slogan for CNN, the US station that was the first to offer 24-hour news: 'Never wrong for long.' Getting something wrong and then correcting it quickly just isn't good enough.

The rush to be first does not always lead to inaccuracy, but it can cause confusion. To the viewer that may be almost as bad. Research by the BBC shows, however, that viewers of rolling news are sophisticated consumers. They want to be told as much as the broadcaster knows. If it is properly sourced, they can then make up their own minds.

Here's an example of Sky News responding to new information as it became available.

Two weeks after the suicide bombings in London on 7 July 2005, there was a second series of attacks, this time unsuccessful. Three tube trains and a bus were again targeted, but the bombs did not go off. The day after the second attacks, the police released four CCTV pictures of the suspected bombers and a man was shot dead by armed police at Stockwell tube station.

At 4.55 p.m. Sky News carried the headline on its Sky News Flash lower third caption SUSPECTED SUICIDE BOMBER SHOT BY POLICE AT STOCKWELL.

The *Live at Five* sequence carried the headline: 'Marksmen shot dead a suspected suicide bomber as he boarded a train at Stockwell.' During the lead report a new caption appeared under the strap 'Breaking News': SOURCES: SHOT MAN NOT CONNECTED TO BOMBINGS.

At 5.05, at the end of the first package, newsreader Anna Botting linked live to crime correspondent Martin Brunt at Scotland Yard who reported: 'I can only tell you what I'm picking up from security sources. It's believed that the man who was shot this morning wasn't one of the four bombers that police are still hunting.'

By 5.07 the News Flash caption had changed to SOURCES: SHOT MAN NOT CONNECTED 4 ON CCTV (*sic*).

A minute later (5.08) reporter Nicola Hill, in a separate live two-way from Stockwell, said: 'Sir Ian Blair [the Metropolitan Police Commissioner] said he thought the gentleman shot here was directly connected with yesterday. Martin's just told us he wasn't.'

Martin Brunt explains what had been happening:

'The key to it was being stood outside Scotland Yard. I just saw an awful lot of people, some I knew and some I half knew – people of all ranks. Four chief constables stopped and said hello – not all of whom I knew – and between them all, right down to the lowliest PC, I got little bits of information, like bits of a jigsaw. That helped me put together what was going on so I could confirm it by putting it to somebody senior later on.'

At 5.10, presenter Anna Botting was talking about the 'shooting dead . . . of a suspected, or perhaps not, suicide bomber'. The caption had changed to SOURCES: SHOT MAN NOT ONE OF FOUR CCTV SUSPECTS.

At 5.12, Martin Brunt was live again, offering new information from his sources:

'Although they believe, and this isn't confirmed, they believe this man that was shot by police this morning wasn't one of the four bombers from yesterday, he was a terrorist suspect, and the police's interest in him did emerge after yesterday's bomb attack, and I think it's important, I'm told, to make that plain. Although he wasn't, they believe now, one of the four bombers from yesterday, he was somebody who emerged of interest to them yesterday and was considered a terrorist suspect.'

The BBC *Six O'Clock News* stuck to the suspected suicide bomber line. Security correspondent Gordon Corera said in a live two-way: 'The police are being very clear that the individual who was shot in Stockwell this morning was directly linked to the attacks yesterday.'

The dead man was Brazilian. He was unarmed. And innocent of any involvement in the bombings. The fact that he was not a terrorist was not confirmed by the police until the next day (Saturday). The weekend's news agenda was dominated by apologies and statements of regret from Sir Ian Blair and senior politicians, and by the political, diplomatic and legal repercussions. The story continued to run for years afterwards.

The early reporting of events had been subject to police 'spin' – an attempt to sanitise a very serious mistake. The best of the reporting emphasised the attribution of sources – where the information came from: 'what I'm picking up from security sources'; 'the police are being very clear'; 'they believe, and this isn't confirmed'.

Healthy scepticism – never cynicism – aids good reporting. In this case it also meant Sky News were first to suggest the enormity of the story – that the police had shot an innocent man – Jean Charles Menezes.

Remember

- Check every fact
- Use secondary sources where possible
- If in doubt, leave it out
- Use your contacts to challenge 'official' sources
- Maintain your objectivity – don't get caught up in rumour
- Learn which Internet sites you can trust
- Record conversations with sources if possible
- Always keep accurate notes, preferably using shorthand.

Forward planning

While news programmes give the impression of being responsive to events on the day, much of their content has been planned in advance. This can be anything from pre-recorded interviews to packages telling embargoed stories or illustrating stories that are in the news that day. There are also features on newsworthy issues that have no *peg* to a particular moment in time, and exclusive stories – the product of investigations for example – that can be aired whenever the broadcaster feels they will have most impact – usually as soon as possible, but on a 'slow news day'.

There can be no guarantee that enough news will 'break' on a given day to fill news programmes.

The importance of forward planning cannot be overemphasised. There can be no guarantee that enough news will 'break' on a given day to fill news programmes.

Most editors will tell you that usually about half of any day's output is pre-planned. This changes if big stories break. Coverage of those stories takes over, and the planned material is dropped. If it's a slow news day, the proportion of pre-prepared content increases. Items are taken off the *shelf* and used to fill programmes.

Larger newsrooms will have a *planning desk* with dedicated teams of journalists reporting to a planning editor. Planning departments within BBC Newsgathering prepare material that can be accessed by all the corporation's newsrooms. In any organisation, all reporters, researchers and producers are encouraged to contribute to the *diary*.

The newsroom diary

The most important tool for collating information from all the different news sources, and planning coverage of news, is the newsroom diary. It contains all the stories that news planners and field reporters know will be happening on each day. On a typical day almost half the stories covered will be from the diary.

Larger organisations will maintain their own diary of key national events. Smaller stations can subscribe to online diary services – listing everything from court cases to football fixtures. These will have contact names and numbers so the sources can be asked for details, localised information or interviews.

The diary is kept up to date by the forward planning teams. In a small local radio newsroom that may mean the editor keeps a watching brief, while anyone else can add to the diary if they have useful information.

Stories that break during the news day, or exclusives uncovered by correspondents, are known as **off-diary** stories.

Nowadays the diary will be in electronic form but years ago it would literally have been an A4 page-per-day diary with handwritten entries. Newsroom management software, such as ENPS (Electronic News Production System), allows the information to be presented to different people in the production process in the form that is most useful to them. A TV producer will want to know where his reporters and camera crews are being sent. A sports producer will want to know that day's fixtures. The camera desk will want to know the whereabouts of crews and an estimate of how long each job is likely to take. The programme editor will need to know what stories will be available in time for the bulletin. The online editor checks the deadlines throughout the day so he can refresh his content whenever new stories are available.

The diary file

Press passes. Without accreditation journalists and any technical crew are unlikely to be admitted to the event

It is also good practice to keep a hard copy file of all forthcoming events. This should include copies of **press releases**, whether they arrived in the post or had to be printed from email. Reporters need their own copies of releases to take on location and they need to know where to find them at short notice.

The same filing cabinet can contain **press passes**. An increasing number of events – including royal visits and sports fixtures – require special passes issued by the organisers. Sometimes these are issued to news organisations, but on other occasions the individuals attending need to be accredited personally.

Without accreditation journalists and any technical crew are unlikely to be admitted to the event. Sometimes accreditation is needed for legitimate security reasons, particularly at high-profile events where senior politicians are involved. Frequently, accreditation is arranged by PR companies so the organisers of an event know who has turned up, and can check on the coverage it received. It can be argued that an NUJ (National Union of Journalists) press card or Sky News security pass should be enough to prove the credentials of a bona fide representative of the news media. Operationally, having to apply for accreditation is a nuisance. Practically, if you can't get in, you can't do your job.

Remember

- Forward planning is essential to any news operation
- The diary is the central point of reference for the newsroom
- Keep the diary up-to-date
- Apply early for accreditation to events
- Know where to find your press passes.

CONCLUSION

So how does the information you've gathered from your sources become a news story? You need to assess it according to the criteria we discussed in Chapter 2. You need to talk to the people involved and work out how the raw facts can be turned into a story for your station and made relevant to your audience. And you need to do that in time to meet deadlines.

Editors and producers give a lot of thought to the best way to treat stories. In the news broadcasters' ideal world, cameras would record every newsworthy moment, there would be great pictures to show on TV and actuality sound for radio. Despite the spread of CCTV and the ease of video recording on phones and lightweight camcorders this rarely happens. Cameras, both professional and amateur, record many events, but news is much more than pictures of things happening.

Much of what we call news depends on the interpretation of journalists. How to tell a story, in words, sound and pictures, and present it on air is the subject of the rest of this book.

FURTHER READING

Brooke, Heather (2007) *Your Right to Know: A Citizen's Guide to the Freedom of Information Act*, London: Pluto Press. A handbook from a journalist who uses FOI every day in her work.

Harcup, Tony (2009) *Journalism: Principles and Practice*, London: Sage. Practical and ethical advice on finding stories and how to treat them.

WEB LINKS

www.courtserve2.net Details of forthcoming court cases.

www.google.com The world's favourite search engine.

www.the-hutton-inquiry.org.uk All the evidence presented to the inquiry.

www.ico.gov.uk The information commissioner's website.

www.nuj.org.uk The journalists' union site, including codes of practice.

www.ofcom.org.uk The site of the regulatory body Ofcom.

www.heatherbrooke.org Heather Brooke's site with details on using FOI and other investigative journalism.

CHAPTERFOUR
THE INTERVIEW

In this chapter, we'll look at:
- How to prepare for an interview.
- Interview techniques.
- The questions to ask.

JOURNALISM is about asking questions. Lots of them. And the right ones. Journalists need an inquiring mind. We want to know more about the world about us, even if it means uncovering awkward truths. From conversations with friends and relatives to confrontations with prime ministers, the interview is the most important means by which journalists gather information. In the world of broadcasting, the interview is also one of the most important ways of providing information to viewers and listeners.

We also look at the different types of interview you will use, and show you how to get the most out of every one you do.

A television interview on the street. BBC Midlands Political Editor Patrick Burns questions a political expert for *The Politics Show*

WHAT IS AN INTERVIEW?

An interview is a structured conversation. It's not a conventional conversation in which both people are interested in what the other has to say. It is a series of questions and answers, where only one party – the interviewer – is asking the questions. It follows that an interview is only as good as the questions that are asked. We'll explain how to ask the right questions in differing situations. And how, sometimes, interviewing is not about asking questions at all.

Some interviews are live on air; others recorded for future broadcast. But most are neither on air nor recorded electronically; they are part of your research before you interview anyone for broadcast. All these types of interview form part of the news-gathering process.

We will look in detail at the broadcast interview: those conducted to provide information and those designed to challenge authority figures. We'll pay particular attention to the need for preparation.

We look too at different types of broadcast interview – including the studio, down the line, the two-way (when one journalist questions another), and the doorstep. And we consider how to approach different types of interviewee, from senior politicians, rock stars and top sportsmen to the recently bereaved.

A CLOSER LOOK

A BRIEF HISTORY OF THE INTERVIEW

The interview is the most important news-gathering weapon in the broadcast journalist's armoury. It is also a way of challenging opinions and orthodoxies, and at its purest can become an entertaining or informative programme in its own right. Political discussion programmes have been a mainstay of the schedules since the early 1950s. Chat shows came along a little later.

It may come as a surprise to those of us who have enjoyed the verbal joustings of John Humphrys on BBC Radio Four and *Newsnight*'s Jeremy Paxman that it was not always so. The journalistic interview is a relatively modern invention – the broadcast interview even more so.

There's a famous bit of black-and-white footage from 1955, where the Labour Party leader Clement Attlee is approached by an eager but ever-so-polite chap with a microphone who asks if he'd like to say anything about the coming election. The great statesman's reply? 'No.' That was in an age before television became the most important medium of political information. Can you imagine a modern party leader refusing the same opportunity?

Attlee himself was described (by Labour cabinet minister Douglas Jay) as a man who never used one syllable where none would do. Indeed, he once answered all the questions prepared for a 15-minute broadcast in five minutes. Barely three years later, Robin Day on ITV conducted a confrontational interview with the prime minister Harold Macmillan.

A hundred years before Mr Attlee's famous reply, the idea of the interview as a journalistic tool had yet to be established. The first 'modern' interview with a public figure was apparently the *New York Tribune* editor Horace Greeley's verbatim account of a discussion with the Mormon Church leader Brigham Young in Salt Lake City in 1859.

Now interviews are the mainstay of story telling in broadcast journalism – first-hand eye-witness accounts from people at the heart of the story. Not everybody loves them though. The journalism trainer Michael Rosenblum says bluntly: 'Interviews are boring. They make better radio than television, but the really good radio, Radio Four documentaries, are full of natural sound and events and have an arc of story to them. Mediocre people rely on interviews to carry them. Obviously, Jeremy Paxman is an exception, but people look at him and rationalise their own crap interviews.'

> **Interviews are the mainstay of story telling in broadcast journalism – first-hand eye-witness accounts from people at the heart of the story.**

So, even if you have secured the key interview, you have to do it well and use it well.

PREPARING FOR AN INTERVIEW

Knowing what you want from an interview

Remember the five Ws? As we explain in Chapter 2: What's the story? and Chapter 5: News writing, the information presented in a news story can be summed up by answering the questions 'who, what, where, when, why (and how)'. It follows that your questions in any interview will almost certainly start with those words. But before you start asking questions there is only one of those words that matters. That word is 'why'. Why are you conducting the interview? Why do you want to talk to this person? Why will this interview help tell the story?

Often the reason why you're interviewing someone is to find a soundbite – a short clip that sums up somebody's opinion or reaction. You need to focus on the key question that will elicit that response. There's no point recording a five-minute interview when you only want a 20-second answer. Equally there's no point running through the five Ws. Those will have been answered earlier in the piece. Colour and drama will result from a more relaxed approach: 'Hey, did it hurt?'

When you know why you are conducting the interview you can decide what questions to ask.

Ask yourself: 'What do I want to know?' and structure the interview accordingly. If it is to learn the facts about a news event, then it is an interview to gain information. If it is to challenge an authority figure, then it is investigative or adversarial. If it is to elicit a personal response to events, it will be an emotional interview. Sometimes you will be talking to someone simply because of who they are – the celebrity interview. But you still need to be clear why.

> **There's no point recording a five-minute interview when you only want a 20-second answer.**

In any interview, be bold. And don't be afraid to be nosy. As long as you are polite, you should dare to ask the questions to which everybody wants the answers.

- What is the point of the story?
- Why am I asking these questions?
- What do I need to know?
- What can this person tell me that others cannot?
- How can I get the best from this interviewee?
- How can I make them trust me?
- Which part of their story needs challenging?
- What conclusions will the audience draw from this interview, or from the clip I choose?

Research and preparation for interviews

Research and preparation are central to all successful broadcasting. But never more so than when preparing to interview somebody. This is usually the first point at which your professional expertise comes into contact with the outside world. Suddenly there's someone in the story-telling process that isn't part of your team. And sometimes – in the case of politicians, captains of industry and other public figures who've been trained in media presentation – they're on the opposing team. They have skills to challenge your own. More about them later – but, remember, most of them have been on a course lasting a few days at most, whereas this is your lifetime career choice.

BBC Radio Two's Jeremy Vine says: 'The most important thing about an interview is to be briefed, and briefed, and briefed, because you don't want to be discovering key facts that everybody else knows during the interview.'

Research need not mean hours of back-breaking work. In a newsroom, you will be unconsciously researching breaking stories all the time simply by being aware of what's going on in the world and watching your own and others' news bulletins. But if you don't know enough about a story before you are sent to interview somebody, you must know where to find information fast. The Internet is the first port of call these days. It is almost entirely full of nonsense, so you need to know which websites can be relied upon.

For example, if the Chancellor of the Exchequer is coming to town and you have the opportunity to interview him, you may already know which aspects of government financial policy are proving the most controversial, whether economic growth forecasts are living up to Treasury predictions, what impact fuel prices or interest rates are having on local people and businesses, and which social groups in your patch are most affected by changes in the benefits system. But you will want to look up facts and figures. You need to know where to find them. Government websites are a good starting point. The whole process of 'researching' a brief news interview with one of the most powerful men in the country should take less than 20 minutes.

Research is also the key to longer interviews. A specialist correspondent will be expected to have detailed knowledge of their subject. The health correspondent, for example, must know government health policy, the administrative structure of the health service, the performances of local hospital trusts and the waiting lists for operations. They must also have a range of specialist contacts, providing access to the people – usually patients, doctors and nurses – who can be interviewed to provide the human stories that illustrate the issues of the day.

General reporters need to know how to access specialist information quickly. Contacts are vital. So too is knowing how to use search engines. When you make notes, jot down the source of the information in case you are challenged. The successful interviewer wins the respect of their subject by being well informed. The journalist who wins that respect gets better answers.

Remember

- Keeping abreast of the news is a short cut to informed interviewing
- Learn which websites can be relied upon
- Know how to use search engines effectively
- Note the sources of all information

CASE STUDY 4.1   CHALLENGING THE PRESIDENT

Irish journalist Carole Coleman told RTE radio she was nervous for days before a ten-minute TV interview with US President George W. Bush:

'Immediately I settled into this intense preparation period. I thought about nothing else for five or six days, even in my sleep.

'When you're given an opportunity like that you hope in your heart you're going to be the one that cuts through the fudge. Otherwise there's no point being there. You really have to challenge him. Otherwise the interview's a waste of time.'

Coleman revealed that before the interview the White House had requested a list of topics she would cover. On the day, officials mentioned some things they didn't want discussed – including Michael Moore's documentary *Fahrenheit 911*, which attacked Bush and the invasion of Iraq. Coleman had never intended mentioning the film. But she did say during the interview that people were angry about the invasion. It started a lively exchange, with the President repeating the phrase: 'Let me finish, please.' He gave what Coleman later described as 'a daggers look'. The confrontation made headlines in the US and back in Ireland.

President Bush was used to a more deferential approach from American reporters. Coleman, RTE's Washington Correspondent for two years, said: 'I had to challenge him. It wasn't that I didn't like him. I was just doing my job. My personal attitude to Bush was neither here nor there.'

Remember

- Coleman's experience illustrates the need for the journalist to maintain control of an interview
- Don't be overawed by people in positions of power. Most politicians expect tough questioning and have been schooled to deal with it. They are ordinary people in extraordinary positions who have been given power temporarily
- Ask the questions the audience expects to hear
- Don't allow your personal feelings to colour your professional judgement

See Workshops and Exercises

INTERVIEW TECHNIQUES

Putting people at their ease

1 People speak more fluently if they are relaxed. It is always in your interests to put your interviewee at ease. If that means spending time with them and making them feel special, then do it. If it means paying a compliment to someone you find obnoxious, so be it.

Making people feel comfortable starts even before the moment you enter their home, welcome them to the studio or meet them on location. You need to reassure people when you first contact them (if not in person then on the phone or by email) that they will be treated fairly and your intentions are sincere. Explain what programme the interview is for, if it's likely to be edited, and how much will probably be used. They need to have confidence that you are professional and know what you are doing.

2 They will also want to feel they have some control over what happens next. This may be difficult when you and your crews are rearranging the furniture in their living room. One BBC cameraman used to joke that he ought to work for Pickfords, the removal company. Be courteous throughout and remember that this is someone's home, their personal space. Don't comment adversely on the decor.

3 You need to remain calm and unruffled even if you are only five minutes from your deadline. Any signs of anxiety will be picked up by your interviewee, and result in a weak performance by both of you.

4 Take care how you address people. An elderly person might prefer to be called Mrs Jones rather than Hilda, which she might consider too familiar. A celebrity would be used to people calling them by their first name. Even before he was knighted, not many people would have called Sir Paul 'Mr McCartney'.

5 Lead people through the technicalities: 'Look at me, not the camera.' 'Don't worry about the microphone.' 'We'll be live when that red light goes on at the end of the adverts.' Explain that you need to take a sound level by asking them to tell you a little about themselves (see also Chapter 7: Location video and sound).

6 Before a TV interview, tell people how much of them the camera can see. Show them a monitor if possible. It stops them worrying about dirty shoes. If it's someone you're likely to want to interview again, it also assures them that they can look good on television. Demystifying the process usually helps people relax and give their best performance. The BBC's Jeremy Vine says of interviewing people who aren't experienced interviewees:

'I do think that as professional broadcasters we underestimate the extent to which coming into a studio and talking to somebody and having five minutes to say your bit – and you're never going to get that five minutes again, and it's live – we underestimate how frightening that is.

'It's easier to help them on radio because if they're sitting there in front of you, you can look really encouraging, nod and smile, and all of that. Television's slightly more difficult, because a person who wilts on television almost can't be reached. They're really on their own. It creates a great deal of loneliness when you're at the front end of a camera. They need to know we're not going to trap them – we just want to hear the story.'

7 Your conversation before recording starts can touch on the subjects you'll cover, but don't rehearse the interview in full. It kills the freshness you're looking for, and leads inexperienced guests to fill their conversation with lines like 'as I said earlier' and 'as I already mentioned'. John Sergeant, with more than 30 years' experience in TV and radio, much of it confronting senior politicians, says the easiest interviews are those with people used to being interviewed:

'What's the hardest interview? It's someone who has no experience being interviewed, who can't concentrate on the question and who rambles on, and you've got to bring them back to the main point – people who are inarticulate for all sorts of reasons and are not thinking in a sensible way and you're trying to grapple with their thought processes.'

8 Always respect your interviewees and don't judge them. Chris Tarrant says his early days in regional television were spent 'interviewing nutters', but he would not have succeeded

in the industry if he had gone round insulting members of the public. Don't bully or patronise people, just because their communication skills are not as accomplished as your own. Jeremy Vine says:

'I just don't think the interviewer needs to try to look clever-clever or superior or to blindside the interviewee or make them look silly. The purpose is just to get them to say as cleanly and as clearly as possible what they want to say.'

9   Sometimes you don't have time for introductory niceties. Someone may be brought into a radio studio while you are live on air. Give them an encouraging smile.

10 Your duty of care to your interviewees doesn't end when you turn off the mic. Thank them and compliment them on their performance. Reassure them that it sounded great. Take contact details if you haven't already done so. Don't switch off the charm until you've parted company. You might need them again.

Remember

- Relaxed people make better interviewees
- Explain technicalities
- Don't patronise people
- Take contact details of all interviewees

Victoria Derbyshire

Eye contact

Always try to maintain eye contact during an interview. It shows you are interested and encourages the speaker.

For television, you also want your interviewee to keep looking at you. If they are uncertain or embarrassed they may look away, perhaps to somebody else, or straight into the camera, which looks unnatural. You'll need to explain that to them.

For radio, conducting an interview face to face is much easier than down a line or over the phone because of the eye contact. Victoria Derbyshire of BBC Radio Five Live says:

'It makes a huge difference. The eye contact is really important. You can also pick up things by their facial expressions, which give you a clue as to something that perhaps they're not telling you. Or something that they want to share but don't have the confidence to share. You can see it in their eyes.

'You also can see if they're not happy with the question because of their body language, and you can share that then with the listeners.'

If it's appropriate, you will want to appear friendly and considerate. Eye contact and an open posture – that's keeping your arms and (if sitting) your legs uncrossed – will help somebody relax. But be sensible. Don't stare. People don't like it, and it's rude.

You're probably wondering how you can maintain eye contact if you're operating a recorder or writing notes. Technical operation shouldn't be a problem, because you will have set your recording levels before you start, and then you can concentrate on the content of the interview. Writing notes does not prevent you looking up frequently. Note taking is not a calligraphy class.

Remember

- Maintain eye contact whenever possible, but don't stare
- It helps to be friendly

Taking notes

Taking notes is just as important for broadcast journalists as it is for their newspaper counterparts. Not everything you witness will be recorded on tape, disc or SD (secure digital) card.
This is especially true of court reporting, inquests and other hearings where electronic recording
is not permitted. But it also applies as you go about the business of collecting facts about a story.
And a written note of what somebody said while you were recording will help you as you edit.

The traditional tool of the journalist is shorthand. It's an invaluable
skill. It is much quicker to read a shorthand note than to find a quote
from a recording, play it back and transcribe it.

Shorthand is an invaluable skill for broadcasters.

The importance of note taking was stressed in the Neil Report, the
BBC's internal response to the criticisms of the Hutton Inquiry into the
death of Dr David Kelly in 2003 (see Case study 3.3). Dr Kelly took his
own life after being named as the source of Andrew Gilligan's report that the dossier on Iraq's
weapons of mass destruction had been 'sexed up'. Gilligan, when pressed, could not produce
notes from his interview to substantiate his claims. The implication of the Neil Report was
that the BBC would have been in a stronger position to defend itself if the reporter had a full
note – preferably in shorthand – of the content of his private meeting with his source.

> ### TIP BOX
>
> **We must take accurate, reliable and, wherever possible, contemporaneous notes
> of all significant research conversations and all other relevant information.**
>
> **We must keep records of research including written and electronic correspondence,
> background notes and documents.** Research should be kept in a way that allows
> double checking, particularly at the scripting stage, and if necessary by another
> member of the team.
>
> **We must keep accurate notes of conversations with sources and contributors about
> anonymity. A recording is preferable where possible.**
>
> BBC Editorial Guidelines

Shorthand takes time to learn and longer to get up to speed, but many reporters swear they
could not do their jobs without it. Teeline is the preferred system of shorthand for most
journalism students. It's easier to learn than the older Pitman method, although harder to
achieve the really high speeds an old-fashioned secretary would have needed. You will only be
able to keep up your best speed if you use your shorthand every day.

The BBC recognises the value of electronic note taking, even recording people without their
consent, using small cameras, recording over the telephone or using discreet digital audio
recorders. But the intention of unauthorised recordings is to ensure accuracy and avoid legal
challenges rather than for broadcast. Permission to broadcast these recordings is only granted
in exceptional circumstances.

Remember

- Accurate note taking is a vital journalistic skill
- Learn shorthand and keep up to speed
- Use recording equipment when allowed, but make it clear to contributors if
  the recording is likely to be broadcast

ASKING THE RIGHT QUESTIONS

If you are a 'news junkie', as most journalists have to be, interviewing people in the news is relatively straightforward. You are asking the questions any reasonable member of the public wants answered. The skilled professional does so with courtesy and impartially. Playing devil's advocate is an acceptable ploy – challenging the interviewee with their opponents' views – but not at the expense of objectivity. Nobody should be interested in your opinions, and you should not express them.

An interview may appear to be a conversation, but it is not a discussion. One person is asking questions and the other answering them. You are the facilitator. *Your job is to elicit information and opinions, not offer your own.* Sometimes an interviewee will try to gain control by turning the question back on the interviewer. To avoid being intimidated, you need to have stock responses to hand. If you are asking an anti-drugs politician if he ever dabbled in soft drugs during his university days, he might respond: 'We all did things in our youth. Have *you* ever taken cannabis?' It would be reasonable to point out: 'I'm not standing for public office. Would you answer the question, please?'

> The journalist has to be a 'five-minute expert on everything, but a ten-minute expert on nothing'.

Nobody is an expert on everything in the news. It has been said that the journalist has to be a 'five-minute expert on everything, but a ten-minute expert on nothing'. From your professional experience and knowledge of news and current affairs, you will have gleaned enough to be able to discuss – or interview someone – on any topic for five minutes. But a longer conversation would require serious research.

Former political correspondent John Sergeant has good advice on preparing your questions:

John Sergeant, former political correspondent: 'The great interviewer is the person who could certainly answer the questions themselves.'

'You should have a pretty good idea how the person's likely to respond, because no one is so quick on their feet that they can get a reply from someone and then immediately think of the perfect follow-up question. What is the standard argument against this? What are they going to say? Why on earth wasn't this done? Or why was this prisoner released early?

'You've got to have, if you can, some idea how the official, the person in authority, is going to respond to that because it usually leaves open an enormous series of questions and you've got to get to that very quickly. If it's live, that's even more important.

'The great interviewer is the person who could certainly answer the questions themselves, and who certainly knows the subject very well. The idea that the great interviewer is some sort of ingénue, or some innocent who goes forward and says, "I don't know much about this, but tell me what's happened," that's ridiculous, and it just does not work.'

Don't think too hard

A successful interview – from the journalist's point of view – is one where you maintain control. That means asking the right questions. How do you think of the best questions? That's easy. Don't think too hard. What would any sensible person want to know: your friend in the pub, the shopper in the supermarket queue, or your next-door neighbour? What would they ask if they had the chance? That's the question you ask.

Remember the five *W*s: *Who, what, where, when, why?* And perhaps *how?*

When gathering eye-witness accounts at breaking news events, a simple 'What happened?' may be enough. Or even 'Please, just tell me about it.' Follow up with: 'What happened next?' or just 'And then . . . ?'

John Sergeant says if you know your questions won't be used on air, it doesn't matter how you put them: 'If it's recorded, you just want the quote. So it's a question of how you achieve that. You can say, "Oh come off it", "What do you mean?" or "Do you really mean that?" It doesn't matter how it's phrased.'

Occasionally a less obvious approach will be necessary. You may want to wrong-foot a politician to expose hypocrisy or inconsistency. That might involve setting up one predictable answer so that the follow-up has more bite.

Here's Peter Allen of Radio Five Live pressing home his advantage in an interview with Liberal Democrat MP Sarah Teather. The party leader Charles Kennedy had admitted he had a drinking problem – something he'd repeatedly denied in public. He was under pressure to resign.

Allen: Was it all about the drinking for you, or was it the way he was running the party?

Teather: For myself it was the former, erm . . .

Allen: The drinking?

Teather: Yes. It was.

Allen: But you knew all about that.

Teather: Yes, I did. We all encouraged him to . . .

Allen: So you don't mind him drinking [but] you don't want us to know about it.

Teather: Well, I think he had a right to try and deal with the matter privately. However, when we first, you know, we first raised this with him, after there was a number of major events about 18 months or so ago, not long actually after I was first elected, was when I first became aware of the problem. We sought reassurance that this was something he was going to take treatment [for], and he was going to take the matter seriously.

Allen: How long ago was that?

Teather: Oh, it's been in the public domain. This was around April of 2004.

The interview took place on 6 January 2006. Allen succeeded in establishing just how long Lib-Dem MPs had known of their leader's problem, and that they tried to keep it from the public. Teather's interview was among many by disaffected MPs. Charles Kennedy resigned as party leader the next day.

Remember

- Ask what the audience wants to know
- Be courteous and impartial
- An interview is not a discussion – your views are unimportant
- Maintain control of the interview

How to structure an interview

Every interview has a structure. Longer interviews have a more obvious beginning, middle and end, and take the audience on a journey of discovery.

You will want your questions to flow from the previous answer. It is often suggested that each question should contain a separate, distinct idea to avoid confusion. As a broad rule, this is good advice. But sometimes a double question will be more use if both parts are related. It does away with the need for the reporter's voice interrupting the interview clip.

'What's your favourite school dinner, and why?'

'What about Murray's performance? What does that say about his chances for Wimbledon?'

Don't be afraid to repeat the question, or ask it in a slightly different way, if the first response is disappointing or evasive. When you get a good answer, don't rest on your laurels; follow through with another strong question.

Most recorded news interviews operate on a different principle. You are after a soundbite for use in a package. It's like a football match that's decided by a Golden Goal. When you've got it, game over.

The opening question

It is good practice to inform interviewees of the topics on which they will be questioned and helpful to let them know how long the interview will last. We are not in the business of ambushing or trapping people. The exception is when we are exposing criminal wrong-doing.

It is never a good idea to provide a list of questions in advance. It restricts the opportunity to challenge what has been said. If you have agreed you will only ask pre-arranged questions, the interviewee is at liberty to offer an incomplete answer and refuse to expand on it in a supplementary enquiry: 'I've answered the question we agreed. I didn't agree to answer that. Please move on.'

The BBC's guidelines say we can only give a broad outline of question areas because the direction the interview takes will be dependent on what is said. But it sometimes helps to let your interviewee know what the opening question will be. It helps them relax, because it offers them the chance to mentally rehearse their first response. For this reason, professional media trainers suggest to their customers that they should always ask what the first question is going to be.

This tactic doesn't have to work. You may decide to stay in control. The late Tony Maycock, of Central TV News, was once interviewing a senior Staffordshire policeman, who asked what the first question was going to be. Maycock replied: 'You've been on one of those courses, haven't you? To tell the truth, sunshine, I haven't a clue what my question will be till that camera starts rolling.'

Given that the police officer knew why he was being questioned, this was perfectly acceptable practice, and would comply with today's Ofcom Code, which requires only that interviewees are informed of the area of questioning. Being too prepared can destroy spontaneity.

Don't read your questions

Make a list of questions before an interview, if you must, but don't feel you have to stick to it. Before a longer interview, it can help order your thoughts, which is useful if your newsdesk has asked you to cover a series of points. But if you write out a list, and read from it verbatim, it will probably sound as if you are reading, and the interview will be stilted and unnatural. Better to jot down a crib sheet of key words or bullet points.

Interviewees will notice if you are reading questions, and will not be flattered. In a Channel Four programme in 2006, *Ricky Gervais meets . . . Larry David*, the writer and performer of *The Office* and *Extras* and the man who created *Seinfeld* and *Curb Your Enthusiasm* were in fits of laughter recalling interviewers who had confronted them with a list of written questions. They mimicked the way the interviewers looked down at their notes, without making eye contact with their subject.

> **Make a list of questions before an interview, if you must, but don't feel you have to stick to it . . . a crib sheet of key words is more useful.**

Larry David: I say to them sometimes: 'Put that away. Talk to me.'

Ricky Gervais: You wanna hear [*laughs*], you wanna hear: 'That was an amazing answer.'

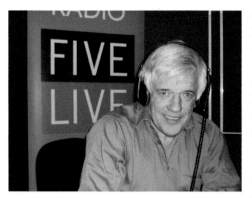

BBC Radio Five Live's Peter Allen: 'Listen to the answer.'

Others who see you reading questions may not see the funny side. Either way you lose. You need to maintain control of the interview and the respect of your interviewee.

As the interview draws to a close, you can refer to your crib sheet of key words to check that you've covered all the ground. Shelagh Fogarty of BBC Radio Five Live says: 'Sometimes if I really want to set out a couple of points before I ask the question, I'll formally write it out. But by and large I just add little notes that remind me of the point I aim to get at.'

You should be listening to the answers, and taking into account what has been said as you formulate your next question. This maintains the natural flow and stops you asking something that has already been answered. Asking something the audience already knows the answer to makes you look stupid.

Peter Allen of BBC Five Live says: 'Listen to the answer. Listen to what the guy or woman is saying, and then you probably won't have to write down a second question, because the second question will occur as you're really listening to what they're saying.'

He says he frequently hears interviewers failing to pick up on points because they've moved on to the next written question.

> **'Listening is as important as asking the question.'**

'The more important the person the greater the tendency to think "I must write down the six questions I've got to ask here" and not follow your head. A little bit of briefing obviously helps, but you should know enough to ask a few intelligent questions.'

Helen Boaden, Director of BBC News, says: 'Sometimes it drives me mad when I hear or see interviews where they've obviously got their ten questions and this person has just said something completely riveting or unexpected, and they just go on to question number eight. Listening is as important as asking the question.'

If you don't understand an answer, seek clarification. Don't be embarrassed. Ignorance is not the same as stupidity. If you don't know something, there's a good chance most of the audience won't. Have confidence in your judgement.

It's an old lawyer's trick, beloved of politicians, to try to gain control by quoting numbered paragraphs from obscure statutes. Don't be fooled, and don't fall into the trap of using the technique yourself.

Keep your questions simple, clear and concise. They are not an excuse to show off your knowledge of a subject, or to showcase the longest words in your vocabulary. Even if they are to be edited out of the final broadcast, long-winded questions can lose the interviewee's attention. In a confrontational interview, they will give the interviewee more thinking time than you would ideally want them to have.

Knowing when to shut up

The biggest mistake during a broadcast interview is to talk over the answer. In conversation it is natural to punctuate somebody's comments with encouraging verbal tics – 'Yes', 'That's right', 'OK', 'I see', 'How interesting', and, almost unconsciously, lots of 'Mmms'. It encourages the person you are talking to and is considered polite. But in a recorded interview, whenever you are not asking questions – shut up! That doesn't mean you can't encourage somebody to talk more. Nodding in agreement works well. So does the simple device of maintaining eye contact – a basic courtesy.

If someone is fluent and interesting, you won't want them to stop talking. A simple 'and?', 'so?' or 'why?', or a gesture of encouragement from the interviewer should work better than a lengthy follow-up question.

The silent question

Sometimes silence is better than asking a supplementary question. Most people take their cues to speak from pauses in conversation. Silences are awkward. People like to fill them. If you don't speak, they may feel obliged to. This is a useful technique with shy or inexperienced interviewees. They may feel they have done enough by providing the shortest possible answer, but what *you* want is for them to open up more.

Non-verbal communication is vital in all interviews. Nod encouragement. Smile when appropriate. Look quizzical if you need further explanation. But don't give away too much of your excitement if in the middle of a draining emotional interview your subject comes up with a killer soundbite. Read the interviewee's facial expressions and body language.

Repeating part of somebody's answer – reflecting the thought back to them – usually results in an expanded answer.

To take an example, the doyen of US reporters Ed Murrow, featured in the George Clooney film *Good Night, and Good Luck*, had a technique he shared with younger colleagues. According to his biographer Joseph E. Persico, Murrow told juniors that a direct question often results in the same answer the interviewee has given dozens of times before:

'Then begins the waiting game. He thinks he has given you the definitive answer. You manage a slightly uncomprehending, puzzled expression, and you can watch his mind work. "You stupid oaf, if you didn't comprehend that, I'll put it in language you can understand" and proceeds to do so. Then, in the course of editing, you throw out the first answer and use the second one.'

Remember

- Explain areas of questioning but don't give the questions in advance
- Listen to your interviewee's answers
- Don't rely on written lists of questions
- Know when to shut up
- Don't be afraid to repeat or reword questions to get a different answer

Time references

When you are recording an interview, bear in mind when it is going to be heard. If you interview a football manager on a Friday about Saturday's game, it doesn't matter if he refers to 'tomorrow's match' in a clip broadcast on the Friday. But if you want to take a grab for Saturday morning's bulletins, it's better if there is no reference to 'tomorrow'.

Often you will be required to record preview material for future bulletins and you will need to explain to the interviewee how it is going to be used. Most people won't mind talking about 'today's event' in a cut to be used on the day of an event, even if the interview is recorded several days in advance.

Similarly, it is worth asking interviewees not to use phrases like 'as I told you earlier' or 'as I told you before' because they will have to be edited out if only a short clip is to be used. Nervous interviewees may not be able to comply with that request – it's another detail to think about while concentrating on getting a message across. But it's worth asking, as it can save you time in the edit.

- When recording, think when the interview will be heard
- Avoid confusing time references
- Explain to interviewees when their contribution will be broadcast

TYPES OF INTERVIEW

It helps to differentiate between the types of interview broadcast journalists conduct and what they are for.

In an attack on the language of PR people, John Humphrys joked that Radio Four's flagship morning programme should bear the catchline 'Arguing and interrupting . . . for a better *Today*!' Humphrys could start an argument in an empty room. He says arguing is fun.

> **Interviewing is part of the process whereby political leaders argue things out in front of the rest of us.**

And important. He points out that interviewing is part of the process whereby political leaders argue things out in front of the rest of us. Then we decide who has the better case and deserves our vote. It's a vital part of democracy. So is a free flow of information. The kind of interviews conducted to gather information do not always have to be argumentative, aggressive or even – to use what Humphrys calls a 'limp-wristed' word – robust. They can be friendly, chatty even.

Recorded interviews

Recorded interviews follow clear patterns. Hard news interviews need to be short and to the point as a deadline approaches. Feature interviews can be longer and more relaxed, but are still restricted by the need to turn the material around in a limited time. Your ear will, with experience, become attuned to selecting sound clips as people talk, and remembering them ready for the edit. During a reply you will hear your 'in' – the first words of the clip you will use – buried within an answer, and then you will hear your 'out' – the last words of the clip – shortly afterwards. You get used to mentally calculating the gap between them – between ten and 20 seconds is usually about right. When you've heard the clip you can relax. Provided you've asked the right questions, you can draw the interview to a close.

Much of the time you will have to listen back to what you have recorded, making notes of in and out points, time codes and durations. All this takes time, and it takes a lot more time if you have recorded 20 minutes when five would have been enough.

It takes experience and confidence to know when to stop recording. Think back to your preparation. Is there anything else you would have expected them to say? Has the interview raised new questions you still want answered? If the answer is 'no' on both counts, stop recording. The chances are, of course, that this is when the interviewee comes out with a cracking soundbite. Don't worry. Just press record again and ask them to repeat it. It may not be as spontaneous, but at least you've got it, and even your editor won't know they said it better the first time.

> **It takes experience and confidence to know when to stop recording.**

Documentary makers have the luxury of taking more time over interviews. Longer programmes require more material, and editing schedules are less fraught than on news. But the discipline learned in news reporting is invaluable to journalists making longer-form programmes.

- Hard news interviews tend to be short and to the point
- Interviews for features can take longer
- Get used to listening for usable clips
- Learn when to stop recording

Informational interviews

In an informational interview an interviewer tries to find out what has happened in a breaking news story. It can be live or recorded, and offers a fresh voice – a source of information other than the journalist.

Subjects for news interviews have a natural pecking order. Eyewitnesses are vital in any hard news story: fires, bombings, shootings. They tell the personal experience of people caught up in a news event and its emotional impact. The interviewee may have only limited knowledge of the bigger picture, but first-hand accounts are gold dust; they're usually the first clips in packaged versions of the story.

The spontaneous live interview most often takes place as news breaks. An eyewitness may be the first person spoken to: the caller to the radio station; one of the first people approached by a reporter on the scene. The interview may start by seeking information – 'What happened?' – but it soon becomes an *emotional* interview – 'How has this affected you?' (hopefully, not the hackneyed 'How do you feel?', which usually sounds crass and begs the answer, 'How do you think, dimwit?').

Even as the quest for more eyewitnesses continues, there will be a need for an authoritative informed source, perhaps from the emergency services or the government. They may have information that gives the viewer or listener the bigger picture. If there is a matter of public policy involved – such as the government's spending on rail or road safety – this type of informational interview may develop into an *adversarial* interview.

In a developing story, the presenter or reporter apparently knows as little as the audience. Sometimes this is true, but often a producer or researcher will have spoken to the interviewee before they go on air. The presenter will be told through their headphones or earpiece what the interviewee should be able to say on air. Lines of questioning or even particular questions will be suggested.

TIP BOX

Eyewitnesses and informed sources – for example official spokespeople – add colour, immediacy and authority to reporting. They also save the reporter the need to summarise what is better told as first-hand evidence or expert opinion.

Interviewing experts

Experts will often be used to interpret information, particularly where the facts are sketchy or require specialist explanation. When interest rates are raised by the Bank of England, a financial expert can explain the likely impact on the economy. A mortgage expert may be asked to speculate on the likelihood of the interest change affecting house prices. A large proportion of the audience will be home owners, or live in mortgaged homes, and the expert can make the story relevant to them.

> **When talking to experts, ask them to avoid using jargon . . . otherwise you will have to explain it to your audience.**

Former senior police officers are often asked to comment on policing. What was the Metropolitan Police's 'shoot-to-kill' policy after the terrorist bombings of July 2005? It led to the death of Jean Charles de Menezes, an innocent man, at a London tube station. If ever there was a case where reporters should stick to the facts and leave opinions to others, this was it. Former policemen could attack or defend the policy without compromising the impartiality of the interviewer.

When talking to experts, ask them to avoid using jargon – the specialist language of their trade. Otherwise you will have to explain it to your audience.

The choice of experts and opinions that are given air-time leaves the broadcaster open to criticism. Impartiality and even-handedness should apply to the selection of expert interviewees as much as to the content of reporters' and presenters' scripts.

When choosing experts, try to avoid 'dial-a-quote merchants' – people who promote themselves relentlessly on radio and TV. Former radio news editor Mike Henfield says:

'Regional radio and TV is full of them. Many an expert wheeled in by TV newsrooms isn't able to say more than a well-informed viewer. We used to have "China watchers", but now that country is more accessible, we appear to have self-proclaimed terror experts in the studio instead.'

It may seem obvious, but make sure the expert is who you think they are. In May 2006, there was much hilarity in media circles when BBC News 24 interviewed the wrong man as an 'Internet expert'. The hapless victim had been rushed into the studio from the BBC's reception area by mistake. He obligingly bluffed his way through the interview, even though English was not his first language. It later transpired the interviewee was an applicant for a job at Television Centre. He *was* there for an interview – but not that kind.

Remember

- Eyewitnesses are essential in hard news stories
- The simplest questions are often the best
- Experts can add authority to your reporting, but choose them carefully

Emotional interviews

Often the emotional impact of an interview will be the most important element. The facts can be explained by the presenter or reporter. What the interviewee offers is the human impact or drama of the story.

This is true of eyewitness accounts of news events, or first-hand testimony in human interest stories, including the reporting of sporting triumphs and failures. Lengthy questions rarely get the best response from someone in a state of anxiety, shock or even elation.

The most successful approach to any emotional interview involves winning people's trust. Sometimes that is as simple as sharing their enthusiasm at a time of great elation – the successful sports team on its victory parade, for example. They want to talk, so interviewing them is easy. Sometimes the hardest part of the job is getting them to shut up.

> **For some victims the process of being interviewed can be cathartic – it helps them come to terms with what has happened.**

But dealing with people in distress requires great sensitivity. For some victims the process of being interviewed can be cathartic – it helps them come to terms with what has happened. It may be the first time they have been able to express their feelings. But for others, the idea of talking publicly about private matters is abhorrent.

The initial approach should involve some expression of sympathy and an acknowledgement that they might not want to talk. This might seem obvious, but it is amazing the number of people who go in feet first. The BBC advises that requests for interviews with people who are injured or grieving should normally be made through friends, relatives or advisers.

Longer reflective interviews – particularly with people who've undergone great physical or mental trauma – depend on building a rapport with the subject. This can take time, and can be emotionally draining for the reporter.

At a time of grief, great care needs to be taken. Media intrusion and insensitivity are not generally welcomed by audiences. But most people want to know how people respond to tragedy and misfortune. There may be hypocrisy in this, but it is not the journalist's job to second-guess the audience's response. Instead, it is advisable to be aware of these mixed emotions and take account of them.

Emotional interviews can illustrate political issues, or be at the heart of human interest stories. The following examples work because they bring the stories to life and create an emotional response in the audience.

1 BBC Midlands' health correspondent Michele Paduano reported on a 33-year-old cystic fibrosis patient's hopes of a transplant. Mark Allen, struggling for breath, offered his thoughts on what the operation would mean:

'It will change my life. It would mean I could be how I used to be. I could go out with friends. I could not be on oxygen. I could go more than 20 minutes away from the house. I could live independently again. I could go out to work again. I could just have a normal life that everyone else takes for granted.'

His mother Maureen:

'Nothing's worse than seeing your own child suffer, and that I find heartbreaking, when I can hear him coughing and being sick . . . I know that every morning he dreads actually getting out of bed, because that's such an awful time . . . you can't put things right, and, as a mother, obviously that's what you always want to do is put things right.'

2 An 85-year-old Burma Star veteran, Norman Auld, was interviewed on the 60th anniversary of the end of the Second World War on BBC News. He was visiting a primary school to share his experiences. One of the children asked how he'd felt about being at war. His understated reply was that it was 'disappointing – I'd been told to go so I had to go'. But during an interview by reporter Denise Mahoney, he was near to tears as he recalled his unit being shelled and the death of a friend: 'And we had to take him down the track and bury him, and that's the worst thing I've ever done [puts hand to face] . . . and it still gets me.'

3 And a stroke patient campaigning against hospital ward closures in Evesham, Worcestershire, emphasised the human impact: 'They gave my life back to me, and I feel very, very strongly about this. We've got to save our hospital.'

Remember

- Approach interviewees with sensitivity
- Use intermediaries (friends, relatives, advisers) if necessary
- Avoid the question, 'How do you feel?'
- For longer, reflective interviews, invest time in your subject

Adversarial interviews

Challenging, or adversarial, interviews can be among the most entertaining parts of any broadcast. The BBC's *Newsnight* has a fine band of reporters, many working on investigative or in-depth accounts of stories behind the news, but few viewers would deny that the programme's unique selling point is the lively confrontations between its presenters and senior politicians. The most successful presenters are well briefed and will have done enough research to counter any challenges from their interviewees. They will often appear to know more than the interviewee.

Closed questions are . . . useless for uncovering information about a news event or for providing soundbites.

In adversarial interviews, a broadcasting convention about always asking 'open' rather than 'closed' questions does not apply. The open question seeks to get the interviewee talking. 'What happened in the meeting?' 'Why does the government want to introduce this policy?' 'How can you justify your attack on the Prime Minister?' A closed question can be answered very briefly, often with the single word 'yes' or 'no'.

Closed questions are obviously useless for uncovering information about a news event or for providing soundbites. 'Were you on the tube?' 'Yes.' 'Did you see the explosion?' 'No.' 'Did you hear it?' 'Yes.' 'I suppose people panicked?' 'No, not really.' And so on.

But a closed question can have a dramatic effect in an adversarial interview. It was a closed question, 'Did you threaten to overrule him?', that Jeremy Paxman famously asked the home secretary, Michael Howard, 12 times. The topic was the political fallout over the dismissal of the head of the Prison Service, Derek Lewis, in 1997. After repeating the question eight times, Paxman even pointed out: 'It's a straight yes or no answer.' But the Home Secretary refused to offer anything so straightforward.

Paxman later said he kept repeating the question because the producer told him the next item wasn't ready. If he'd thought of an open question, there might have been no reason to repeat himself, and we would have been denied a memorable television moment. The Paxman interview and Ann Widdecombe's observation that the Home Secretary had 'something of the night' about him came to haunt Mr Howard, who went on to become Conservative Party leader but lost the 2005 general election.

Jeremy Vine, a former *Newsnight* presenter, says:

'Political interviewing is a particular art form and it may be that it's becoming more and more of a minority sport. I've learnt through bitter experience that embroidering questions to politicians is a bad idea. The thing to do is to really sharpen them, to have the facts right and the attitude right, and to chase them down when they don't respond.'

Vine says interviewing politicians should not be all about conflict:

'We've been through a period where political interviewing has become very gladiatorial, and it probably needs to get a bit shrewder. There probably need to be rather fewer fireworks in it, because we've ended up in a situation where they seem to have clammed up and they're not telling us anything.'

'You should only be combative when it becomes plain they're not prepared to answer the question.'

If you are recording what you expect to be an adversarial interview, it can be worth asking a soft question to start with, so that at least you have something to work with if your adversary walks out. Veteran BBC broadcaster Peter Allen says: 'I think you should only be combative when it becomes plain they're not prepared to answer the question. Give them a chance to say what they've got to say. Don't launch straight into the aggression.'

CASE STUDY 4.2   OLD ADVERSARIES

Here's Jeremy Paxman interviewing George Galloway, newly elected MP for Bethnal Green and Bow, on BBC1's election night programme, 6 May 2005. Standing for the Respect party Galloway, a former Labour MP, had defeated Labour's Oona King.

Paxman: Mr Galloway, are you proud of having got rid of one of the very few black women in Parliament?

Galloway: What a preposterous question! I know it's very late in the night but wouldn't you be better by starting by congratulating me for one of the most sensational election results in modern history?

Paxman: Are you proud of having got rid of one of the very few black women in Parliament?

Galloway: I'm not . . . Jeremy . . . move on to your next question.

Paxman: Are you proud . . .

Galloway: 'Cos I've got a list of people who want to speak to me.

Paxman: Ah, are you pr . . .

Galloway: If you ask that question again, I'm going. I warn you now.

Paxman: Don't you threaten me, Mr Galloway, please.

Galloway: You . . . you're the one who's trying to badger me.

Paxman: I'm not trying to badger you. I'm merely asking you whether you're proud of having . . . (*Galloway is talking, saying* 'I've actually got. I've actually got . . .') having driven out of Parliament one of the very few black women there.

Galloway: You are actually conducting one of the more, even by your own standards, one of the most absurd interviews I have ever (*cutaway of Paxman looking skyward*) participated in. I have just won an election. Can you find it within yourself to recognise that fact? Can't you find it within yourself even to congratulate me on this victory?

Paxman (*sarcastically*)**:** Congratulations, Mr Galloway.

Galloway: Thank you very much indeed.

Paxman: How do you propose to . . . ?

Galloway: Thank you very much (*waves and goes to remove mic*).

Paxman: Oh, I see. It's another occasion when you're not wanting to talk to someone who doesn't agree with you.

Galloway (*in background*)**:** No . . . no, no, no, no . . . no no no no. Actually, Jeremy . . .

Paxman: All right. (*turns to studio guest*) David Lammy, what do you make of Mr Galloway?

[David Lammy, the Labour MP for Tottenham, is black.]

See Workshops and Exercises

Jon Snow in his autobiography *Shooting History* describes his frequent encounters with the Iron Lady herself, Margaret Thatcher. He says it was 'sometimes akin to an execution'.

'Well, Jon, how are you?' she would ask, not apparently wanting an answer, but delighting you that she remembered your name. 'I do find these European sessions perfectly frightful,' she would go on, then there would be some small talk, and then we would start. The moment the camera rolled, the iron would return to her demeanour. Some harmless question would issue from my lips, and she'd sit bolt upright. 'How can you ask such a stupid question?' she'd bellow.

'Damn me,' I'd think, 'have I said something silly? What a fool I am . . . I'm so sorry.' Then I'd pull myself together and remember, for an inadequate moment, that it was *I* who was supposed to be shaping the questions, and *she* who was supposed to be answering them.'

Snow's example, written to amuse, nonetheless illustrates the key question – who is in control of the interview? Both parties can be fighting for that control. It usually leads to the kind of fireworks that make for entertaining broadcasting. Some attempts to control the agenda involve interviewees trying to take the heat out of the situation, by blocking or stonewalling. These interviews are invariably less entertaining.

Prepared statements

Some interviewees will want to read from prepared statements, usually agreed with their lawyers before they face the media. In extreme circumstances that may be inevitable – perhaps with the lawyer reading the statement on the courtroom steps. But whenever you have the chance to challenge somebody who wants to read from a script, point out how artificial and contrived it looks.

> **Whenever you have the chance to challenge somebody who wants to read from a script, point out how artificial and contrived it looks.**

Lawyers, their clients, and any other potential interviewees who think prepared statements are a good idea are rarely able to read from a script and make it sound sincere. You've seen it on TV. You know it always sounds as if they have something to hide. Tell them there is no reason why they shouldn't take legal advice first about how they should answer, but they would be better off answering questions spontaneously.

Consulting notes

Interviewees who want to consult notes during an interview should also be discouraged. If it is a TV interview, looking down at their papers will make them look shifty. If it is radio, they will sound hesitant as they scan the notes. It's best to advise interviewees to put their notes to one side. They will feel comfortable that they are there – as a safety net – and probably won't need to look at them. Don't simply take their notes away. It's rude, and will make your interviewee feel insecure.

'No comment'

Some people – usually celebrities – will say they are only prepared to answer questions on certain subjects. Explain that a polite, non-committal response to controversial questions serves them better than a blanket refusal. The formula phrase 'no comment' always sounds like a euphemism for 'I've got something to hide.'

Nobody has to take part in your programmes. Broadcasters faced with restrictions on interviews are within their rights to inform their audience, but only if it's relevant to the story. In the interests of accuracy, you should make the distinction between refusing to comment, refusing to answer questions, refusal to take part in a programme and not being available for interview.

Press officers

Some people will insist that a press officer or other associate is present during an interview. It happens frequently during political and showbusiness interviews. The advice from Jim Beaman, a university lecturer and former BBC trainer, in *Interviewing for Radio*, is: 'Agree, but on condition that they do not interrupt or interject during the interview.'

You then have to decide whether you will allow the interviewee to stop the recording to consult their adviser. Beaman says you should, within reason, allow this to happen. We suggest that you should never allow politicians such an opportunity. Other cases should be considered on merit.

The doorstep

The doorstep is an unannounced interview. The term can apply to any approach to someone without giving them prior notice, not just those that literally happen on their doorstep. Clearly this breaches the normal ethical convention of arranging interviews with consenting people and telling them what they are going to be asked about. It should only be used when other attempts to secure an interview have failed, only with prior approval from a senior editor, and only in accordance with the professional guidelines outlined in Chapter 6: Location reporting and production.

> **The doorstep . . . should only be used when other attempts to secure an interview have failed.**

The practicalities of the doorstep are that you will normally be recording as you approach the subject, and you will probably have only one chance to ask your question. So, you should have that question very clear in your mind. This is rarely the time for a subtle approach.

When you are reduced to knocking on a door in the hope of catching your interviewee unawares, expect the unexpected. Many people in the news will refuse to come to the door. But others have been known to answer the door with a paper bag or even a fruit basket over their head, or to cover their face with a newspaper or umbrella. In the multi-award-winning feature length documentary *Capturing the Friedmans*, a suspect in a child abuse case confronts a TV crew with a pair of underpants on his head – Fruit of the Loom, we're informed. More aggressive interviewees (particularly those being accused of criminal behaviour) may attack a reporter or camera crew, or pour water – or worse – on them from an upstairs window. Discretion is the better part of being attacked by a Rottweiler.

Remember

- Know your facts and be thoroughly briefed
- Anticipate the likely answers
- Closed questions can be useful in adversarial interviews
- Always stay in control
- Discourage interviewees from reading their answers or consulting notes
- Challenge restrictions on interviews
- Seek editorial permission before doorstepping
- Prepare for the unexpected

Vox pops

Vox pops – a series of comments from a variety of people – are a great way to include a sample of public opinion in your programmes and to add colour to reports that would otherwise suffer from a lack of lively soundbites.

> **Three or four pithy eight-second comments will have more impact than half a dozen longer ones.**

They should be approached in the same way as all other forms of interview – the difference is that, instead of asking one person several questions, you are usually asking several people one question.

The term *vox pop*, or these days even *voxes*, comes from the Latin *vox populi* or *voice of the people*. Americans used to call them *man-in-the-streets*, though *person-in-the-street* has taken over. Americans also call them *triple As* – which stands for 'Ask Any Asshole'. That's no way to talk about your audience!

Stand-alone vox pops are still popular on some stations, but most of the time you will use them as part of a wider feature. Then the key is to keep them snappy. Three or four pithy eight-second comments will have more impact than half a dozen longer ones.

Don't kid yourself that vox pops represent a true reflection of public opinion. Any sample taken in a shopping centre during the daytime, for example, cannot be representative of the population at large, because many people will be at work. Also, it is essentially self-selecting, consisting only of those people who choose to be interviewed by a stranger with a roving mic. So, be careful how you use them on sensitive issues and at sensitive times – such as during an election campaign.

None of this means, however, that you should not strive to show a diverse cross-section of people. If your selection includes young and old, an ethnic mix, disabled people, and even a sample of well-dressed and scruffy individuals (for TV), the audience will know you have tried to canvass a broad range of views.

Of course, not all vox pop sequences need to represent everybody's viewpoint. Sometimes the story dictates the type of person you want to speak to – an education story might lead you to conduct vox pops with parents outside a school; a story about Islamophobia might require a vox pop outside a mosque. If you are looking for memories of the 1950s, there's no point talking to teenagers.

Here are some tips for carrying out vox pops:

1   Make sure that, wherever you go, you have permission to be there. Public places – on the street and in parks – are fine. Many shopping centres are privately owned and you must seek the management's permission. Airports, bus and railway stations, schools and hospitals and their car parks are also no-go areas without official consent. If you are refused admission, wait outside on the public highway and approach people there. As long as you are not causing an obstruction, you are well within your rights.

2   Be polite – nobody is obliged to talk to you, even if you do represent the mighty BBC or Sky News. Explain that they will be doing you a big favour by helping with your report. One trick is to approach people who cannot escape – at a bus queue or taxi rank, for example. The potential 'victims' might be grateful for a way of passing the time. Remember, though, that everybody in a bus queue is a public transport user, so it might not be a great idea to ask their opinion of a rise in petrol prices. For that you might get a livelier response on a garage forecourt.

3   It can also help to approach groups of people who appear to know each other. One friend will egg on another. Sometimes a conversation or disagreement will emerge. These may be useful, but think how they will sound in the final edit. Will you be able to reflect the spontaneity of the moment in an eight-second extract? And if it's television, are all the speakers on camera at the same time? A good cameraman will try to show who's speaking, but won't jeopardise the shot to chase actuality from someone outside the viewfinder, because they may stop speaking at any moment. You must maintain as much control as possible of what you are filming. It may be better to pair people off before you turn the camera on them, but you might risk losing that special moment.

4 Usually there is little need to ask more than one question, so you need to have prepared that question well. How you phrase the question is crucial. It must be instantly
   and clearly understandable to everyone.

   If the same question is asked of each interviewee then the answers should cut
   together nicely. It is usually best to avoid the reporter's voice – so the question needs
   to elicit a self-contained response, preferably not one that requires an elaborate set-up
   in the preceding voice-over or studio link. Avoid closed questions (those that lead to
   a yes/no response), and don't be afraid to stay silent; if you keep looking at someone
   encouragingly, they'll probably keep talking.

5 Some questions can assume knowledge on the part of the interviewee, particularly
   if it's a subject 'everybody' is talking about. In February 2005, 'What do you think
   about the Queen missing Charles' and Camilla's wedding?' would guarantee a response
   on the streets. In May of that year, did the hordes of happy Scousers celebrating
   Liverpool's return from a historic comeback in the Champions League final even need
   to be asked a question before they volunteered their views?

6 But sometimes you need to inform people before you can ask their opinion. When
   the Food Standards Agency announced the withdrawal of hundreds of products
   containing the banned colouring Sudan 1, Radio Five Live had a reporter outside a
   supermarket within half an hour. He had to tell people about the scare – and then
   record their reaction. Most were shocked when they learned the reason for the ban
   – the risk of cancer. It made lively radio.

Vox pops have been a mainstay of TV coverage of controversial or amusing issues for
years. Esther Rantzen's *That's Life* programme always used to feature an extended vox
pop near the top of the show. Often the same crowd would gather at the same location
(usually a local market) and the same faces would feature in successive weeks. They
became micro-celebrities in their own right. But for news and current affairs coverage, it
looks lazy if the same person repeatedly appears – particularly in the same programme.
You are not on the lookout for television regulars – you need a variety of opinions. If
you come across a genuinely famous face, consider whether they are worth a separate
interview. A *Midlands Today* crew found the comedian Harry Enfield in a queue at Alton
Towers. And students from Staffordshire University spotted Nick Hancock, the presenter and comedian, buying a ticket at Stoke-on-Trent railway station.

Grabbing them at a bus stop
– radio reporter Charlotte
Foster conducts a vox pop

   Throughout the process of gathering vox pops – approaching people, persuading them
to talk on mic, suffering rejection, coaxing a response, monitoring your sound levels –
always remember to think how the clips will edit together. It's a tall order, and it's no
surprise that many seasoned reporters don't like doing vox pops at all.

   In a (mostly light-hearted) ITV show *It Shouldn't Happen to a TV Reporter*, the usually
fearless and intrepid BBC war correspondent and presenter Jeremy Bowen said: 'They're
totally humiliating and awful to do I think, because you have to go up to people –
complete strangers – and ask them a daft question.' Another of Britain's most respected
war reporters, Jon Snow, the presenter of Channel Four News, said: 'There is something
absolutely devastatingly grim about it.' And the distinguished Sir Trevor McDonald
called vox pops 'fairly useless'. But he didn't explain why he thought so, and it has never
stopped ITV News using them.

**Always remember to think
how the clips will edit together.**

   Vox pops are here to stay, and they offer an opportunity to aspiring
broadcasters. They are one of the tasks that local radio news editors
regularly entrust to students on work experience. And in bigger newsrooms they can provide a chance for newcomers not yet on the reporting roster to pace the streets with a microphone. The senior reporter is

putting a story together that the editor thinks will benefit from vox pops. The junior can offer to do the voxes, gaining experience and sparing the senior journalist the trouble.

If you're the lucky junior sent to do voxes, there are some technical matters you need to consider:

1 Location is important because background noise will set the scene on radio and the background is always an important part of telling the story on television.

   In radio, the greatest barrier to a good edit is background noise. If background sound levels jump too harshly, clips may sound ugly when joined together. Roadworks and traffic noise are intrusive. Music is particularly distracting as only a short snatch will be heard behind each interview and the snatches will not join together.

2 For television, watch the sound levels too, but also vary the background of the shot to avoid jump-cuts (the appearance of one person miraculously changing into another against the same background). Varying the background means moving the camera – tiresome but necessary. Keep the shot sizes the same (a medium close-up – MCU – works best), and try to alternate which side of the camera the reporter is standing, so that the eyelines of the interviewees vary from left to right. When you edit the pictures it is aesthetically more pleasing if a person looking camera right is followed by a person looking camera left and vice versa. Also it gives the impression of a conversation or debate (in the same way that alternate eyelines are used for cut-away questions in longer interviews).

3 When introducing vox pops in your script try to avoid the stale old formula of 'We went into the street to find out what people think', or 'So what do people on the streets of Paisley think?' Better would be 'It's divided public opinion . . .' or 'People are really angry/confused/happy about it . . .' and then cut straight to the vox pops. Sometimes no linking script is needed at all – the audience expects to hear a range of views on a controversial subject.

4 Always end a vox pop sequence on a particularly strong comment and, if appropriate to the tone of the story, a funny one. It is not always a good idea to start on your strongest clip, because it may make those that follow look weak by comparison.

5 The visual demands of television mean that more samples are needed for a TV vox pop than for radio. For example, you might talk to ten people and get four great answers. That might be enough for a radio vox pop. But if all four people are facing camera left, you have a problem. It's usual to alternate the direction in which interviewees are facing. As mentioned earlier, it is visually more satisfying to the viewer, because it conveys the impression of a conversation between your contributors. So, you need to do more interviews for a television piece – this time with everyone facing camera right – until there are enough to choose from.

6 Sometimes you can 'flip' a TV picture in the edit – reversing the image so that someone looking left is now looking to the right. But you can't always do that. Any writing on screen will appear back to front. So company logos, writing on T-shirts or shop signs in the background will immediately look wrong. To the perceptive viewer so will the buttons on a man's shirt. But don't worry too much about reversing somebody's hairstyle. If you flip a shot of a man with a side parting, the parting will be on the wrong side. But he probably won't notice. The television image will look the same as he sees himself every day in a mirror. His friends and relations might notice though.

Always end a vox pop sequence on a particularly strong comment.

Beware. Vox pops are not an easy option or a quick fix for a dull story. They have to be included on merit – often because of their entertainment value, but also because they shed new light on the topic.

Remember

- Relevant vox pops can liven up a story
- Ask people the same question
- Try to get a diverse mix of interviewees
- Approach people in queues – they can't escape!
- Be aware of background music and noise levels
- For TV, keep shot sizes the same, but alternate the direction interviewees are facing

Live interviews

Live interviews hold no fear for well-prepared interviewers. But they can be daunting for beginners. To stay within the 'comfort zone' you need to be disciplined and stick to the areas you have researched.

1 Stay in control of the interview. If you are live, you can't edit out your gaffes.
2 You need to concentrate and choose your words carefully. An RTE radio presenter, Ryan Tubridy, asking Carole Coleman about her controversial interview with George Bush, said: 'What was happening with all the people round George Bush – his courtesans?' We think he meant courtiers.
3 A strong beginning and end are important. Think hard about your first question. It must be one that will elicit a fluent response and preferably not cause the interviewee to clam up. If you appear too aggressive and put them on the defensive, you will struggle. Prepare plenty of follow-up questions.
4 An interview should end on a high. Save a good question till last, and rehearse your closing comments. If you are in a studio, you will know what comes next and be ready to link to it. If you are on location, think how you will hand back to the studio.
5 Timing is vital in all broadcasts. In a live interview, sticking to time requires collusion with the interviewee. Arrange hand signals so they know when to stop talking. If your subject is proving awkward and tries to keep talking, you need to take control by interrupting politely and firmly.

6 Occasionally you will run out of questions. The late Barney Bamford, a BBC reporter, had a solution to this: 'It's easy. I just lean forward, look intense and ask: "Just how serious *is* the situation?" Works about 90 per cent of the time!'
7 Talking over someone to end an interview can sound messy, but should never be rude. You, the broadcaster, are in charge, because you control the microphones and sound levels. A simple 'thank you' is usually enough. A phrase like 'that's all we have time for' is not a good idea. It begs the question, 'Who says?' You can't expect audiences to respect your running orders.

The pressure of live broadcasting adds an extra frisson to an interview. As you listen, assess the relevance of the answer and whether it is interesting or not. You may need to interrupt even if there is plenty of time left. Look out for people who start listing points, 'First, let me say . . .' Can you afford to let them go on to 'fourth' and 'fifth'? When you know there are 30 seconds left, that should be the time to ask a final question with an answer which is likely to be quite short. It's good practice when briefing the interviewee to warn them what the closing question is going to be, and ask them to answer it concisely. Experience will help you judge how much more needs to be said when timings are shouted in your earpiece.

Shelagh Fogarty: 'Edit with your ears, not with your eyes.'

Cutting an interviewee short can sound rude. Watching the clock is important, but not as important as the output. Provided you don't crash into what's coming up next, bring things to a natural close. BBC Radio Five Live's Shelagh Fogarty has good advice: 'Edit with your ears, not with your eyes.'

Remember

- Structure a live interview so you can begin and end powerfully
- Practise ways of interrupting without appearing rude
- Stay in control
- Practise timing your closing comments

Down-the-line and telephone interviews

Radio

Down-the-line interviews (or DTLs), where the interviewee is in a remote location, offer particular difficulties. The subject may be in another studio or on an outside broadcast (OB) unit. The connection with the studio may be via microwave or satellite link, ISDN (a broadcast quality phone line), Skype or landline.

Telephone interviews are a form of down-the-line interview. They are an almost instant way of covering breaking news. You are unlikely to have enough reporters to send out on every story. Even in a well-staffed newsroom, you almost certainly won't have the time to get out, record an interview, and play it back or return to the studio in time for the bulletin on the next hour. The *phoner* is the staple of local radio bulletins.

The sound quality of telephones, even 3G mobiles, is never as good as that of a broadcast line or face-to-face chat. But this is not a serious problem. Paul Chantler and Peter Stewart in *Basic Radio Journalism* say:

> **Research shows that the listener does not mind phone cuts at all. In fact, he or she thinks the story is actually more 'immediate' if it is done on the phone. It sounds to them as if you have reacted fast to a story . . . So phone audio not only makes use of radio's greatest strength – its immediacy – but also makes good economic sense for small stations with few staff and limited resources.**

> **Editorial guidelines insist you should tell someone in advance if they are being recorded.**

Editorial guidelines insist you should tell someone in advance if they are being recorded for broadcast. Even before they consent, though, it is good practice to make the call on the line you will be recording. Calling from the newsroom and transferring to a studio or, worse, having to call back later wastes your time and theirs. The longer you take, the greater the risk of someone saying no. 'I'd like to record your comments. Is it OK if I press the button now?' is rarely refused.

When you are recording, remember to 'ride' the sound levels – close your mic while they're speaking and drop the interviewee's level while you ask your questions. The audio will be clearer without interference from the other end of the line.

If you are after a simple soundbite (as is usually the case with interviews for radio news bulletins), listen for the 'in' and 'out' – the start and finish of the cut you will use. When you have what you want, politely end the interview.

Longer confrontational interviews require a slightly more aggressive tone on the telephone than if you are speaking to someone face to face. They can't see your body language.

Five Live presenter Shelagh Fogarty has a useful tip for signalling to an unseen interviewee (or a co-presenter) that she wants to ask a question:

'I just take a little breath in – not massive but audible – as though I'm about to ask them something. So what you haven't done is start your question and had that awful radio moment when you half-interrupt a guest and then they carry on speaking. Your breath indicates to them that you have something else to say.'

Fogarty reckons it works with most contributors unless they're nervous or so focused they carry on regardless. If they won't stop, she says, you just have to wade in. The audible breath trick works too on outside broadcasts when you don't have eye contact with your co-presenter.

TV

It's obvious that someone on the phone or in a remote radio studio cannot see the person asking them questions, but many viewers do not realise that the same applies to most remote television interviews. The vision link goes only one-way – from the remote location back to the studio. It would be too expensive (and too much trouble) to provide a television picture from the studio back to the remote location.

This means all the visual signals you give your subject in a face-to-face encounter are no longer available, which is disconcerting. If they are on an outside broadcast (OB), listening to you through an earpiece, there will be all the distractions of their own environment and an uncertainty about when to expect the next question.

The interviewee should be told clearly where to look, usually straight into the camera. In a live interview, when the interviewee is within the broadcast's transmission area, they may be provided with an off-air monitor, so they can see their interviewer. But it may be a distraction to viewers if the interviewee keeps looking at the monitor.

> **If you are being interviewed via satellite link . . . there will be a delay in the sound reaching you.**

If you are being interviewed down the line as a location reporter, you may want a monitor. If you are linking within the interview to a video clip or package you may want to introduce it by looking down at the monitor. Even if you don't have one, it is a convention to look down to where it would be. It's easier than looking blankly at the camera.

If you are being interviewed via satellite link, there will be a delay in the sound reaching you because of the time it takes the signal to reach the satellite and return to earth.

Remember

- Down-the-line interviews are like talking on the telephone
- For TV, advise your interviewee where to look
- Be aware of time delays caused by satellite links

The two-way

The two-way – a reporter questioned by a presenter – is a type of interview. But it follows different rules from the interview with a guest contributor. For a start the reporter should know all the questions in advance. As the reporter, you will have agreed them with the programme producer or the presenter. Usually you will have written or suggested them yourself. It follows that there is no excuse for not knowing the answers.

The two-way is an artificial device, scripted to create the impression of a conversation. It became increasingly common during the 1990s when live location broadcasting became cheaper and easier to do, and is now a staple of television and radio coverage of major stories.

BBC Radio Stoke's Stuart Fear awaits his cue on a two-way

You will hear questions, and instructions from the studio, via an earpiece or headphones. The producer's comments can be distracting. It's like trying to hold a conversation with someone on the telephone while somebody in the same room is speaking to you. Concentration and practice are the only ways to master this art.

BBC presenter Huw Edwards has this approach from the studio end:

'I will talk to every correspondent about the questions. We will agree questions quite often. One or two correspondents have been very happy not to agree a specific question. Andy Marr [former political editor], for example, because we were two fairly political animals, former lobby correspondents, he'd be happy to say, "I kind of want to talk about what Blair's up to on this." He didn't mind what the question was as long as I was driving towards that area, which actually made for a better exchange, because the form of words I used would trigger him off.'

Edwards explains, using a staccato voice

'Sometimes the danger is you-ask-a-question-and-they-answer. A bit unavoidable I'm afraid, especially if you've got an inexperienced correspondent (and I've been there myself) very worried about form of words, maybe on a difficult legal story where you have to get the form of words absolutely right, they don't want to be involved in some kind of cosy exchange. They want to just deliver what they've got. In which case, I've got to just say "Let's join her now." They don't want to be waylaid by any other considerations.'

Being interviewed on a two-way makes you realise what it is like to be on the receiving end. You might feel you are not in control, which is very disconcerting. You will have more control than most of your interviewees, however, because you know what questions are coming.

The experience is proof that both parties in an interview must feel comfortable. The best interviews are those where each feels they have some control.

Remember

- You can agree the questions for a two-way in advance
- Interviewer and interviewee should be on the same 'side'

TIP BOX

IN SEARCH OF THE SOUNDBITE

If you are recording an interview – whatever the style or subject – you will almost certainly want to edit it. That may mean cutting your own words out, or cutting the interviewee's words down. But most often it is to find a soundbite – a short clip expressing the key point made by the interviewee. The clip might be used in your own report, in another reporter's package, or on another platform: clips from TV interviews regularly appear on radio or on news websites; if someone is not available for TV but says something on radio, the clip will be used on TV bulletins with a graphic.

The key to securing a good soundbite is to frame your question so the answer will sum up the respondent's position – their view, reaction or account of what they have witnessed.

'What did you see?'

'What happened?'

'What's your opinion?'

'What do you think?'

'How did it affect you?'

But preferably not: 'How do you feel?' You should structure your questions to help the interviewee express their answer in the best way they can.

It's good practice to advise interviewees not to use your name in their answers. You may have to edit it out later, and that may not be possible if the vocal inflection (whether the voice goes up or down) makes the clip sound odd without the missing name. It's flattering to think you are on first name terms with celebrities, but not very helpful in the production process.

If you are preparing a packaged news report, you will know what you want from each of your interviewees. You are looking for the 10- or 20-second clip that sums up their contribution to the story. You learn to listen for 'in' and 'out' points, the beginning and end of the cut you will use.

If somebody is close to saying something clearly but messes up the answer, tell them not to worry and ask the question again. Sometimes you may wish to phrase the question differently to help them. If *you* make a mistake during a question, pause long enough to make an edit, and ask it again.

> **You are looking for the ten- or 20-second clip that sums up their contribution to the story.**

John Sergeant suggests you ask yourself a question after the soundbite interview:

'Have I actually got them to say on tape what I want them to say? Have I actually got on tape the quotes that I need, and the bits that I need to work into the programme, or the item, or whatever it is I'm interviewing the person for?'

Children

Children can be a fantastic source of lively comment. But Ofcom and BBC Guidelines say they should not normally be interviewed without the permission of a parent, guardian or other person of 18 or over *in loco parentis*.

The guidelines say that under-16s should not be asked for views on matters likely to be beyond their capacity to answer properly, without such consent.

The child's age, stage of development and degree of understanding should be taken into account when deciding whether consent is essential.

The BBC suggests an exception may be vox pops on non-sensitive subjects, where it is not controversial for children to hold and express their views. The Editorial Guidelines give no examples, but these might include discussing favourite sports or pop stars and reactions to school trips or holiday activities.

CASE STUDY 4.3　　INTERVIEWING CHILDREN

We've all heard the warnings about appearing with 'children and animals'. Steve May, a sports presenter on Radio Four's *Today* programme could see the funny side when he attempted a live interview with a seven-year-old football prodigy. It's also a priceless example of the dangers of asking closed questions.

May: Hallo, Jack.

Jack: Hallo.

May: Hi, Jack. How you doing?

Jack: Good.

May: Excellent. Now you want to sign for Manchester United, I know, don't you?

Jack: Yeah.

May: But you can't until April the fourth, because that's when you're eight years of age, because football regulations mean that you can't sign until eight. But that's what you really want to do, isn't it?

Jack: Yeah.

May: Yes. Are you a big Man U fan then, obviously?

Jack: Yes.

May: Right, and your speciality is scoring double hat-tricks, isn't it?

Jack: Yes.

May: Tell us about that.

Jack: Mmm, what did you say?

May: Your speciality . . . (*starts to laugh*)

John Humphrys (*interrupting*)**:** How many goals have you scored?

May (*still laughing*)**:** Something like that. You scored 37 goals last season, didn't you?

Jack: Yeah.

May: And what your speciality is is scoring six goals at a time, isn't it?

Jack: Yeah.

May: Right, and what's your ambition in football? (*laughter in studio*) What's your ambition in football? Why do you want to be a professional footballer?

Jack: Because I like football.

May: Yeah, yeah, absolutely. I suppose that's a good answer. Your favourite player?

Jack: What did you say?

May: Who is your favourite player?

Jack: Cristiano Ronaldo.

May: Absolutely. For Man U, and I've got a note here to say that your ambition is to buy a fast car and a big house for your parents. Is that your dad's ambition for you?

Jack: Yeah.

May: OK. Lovely. Jack, thank you very much indeed for joining us. Good luck with your career.

Jack: OK.

May: You take care.

Jack: Yeah.

May: Yeah. Absolutely. There you go.

Humphrys: Well done, Steve.

May: Never work with children and John Humphrys. That's the idea.

Humphrys: He got direct answers, didn't he? Which is more than we get most of the time. Give a lot for a one-word answer occasionally here we would.

The interview made it on to the *Today* website for the amusement of fans of the programme and students of how not to do it. Steve May proved himself a sporting presenter in more ways than one.

Vulnerable people

'Meaning of vulnerable people':

This varies, but may include those with learning difficulties, those with mental health problems, the bereaved, people with brain damage or forms of dementia, people who have been traumatised or who are sick or terminally ill.

Ofcom Broadcasting Code

Ofcom says persons under 16 and vulnerable people should not be questioned about private matters without the consent of a parent, guardian or other person of 18 or over *in loco parentis* (in the case of persons under 16) or a person with primary responsibility for their care (in the case of a vulnerable person), unless it is warranted to proceed without consent.

Remember

- Don't expect children to understand the interview process
- Be aware of the guidelines about interviewing children and vulnerable people

Celebrity interviews

Many young people entering journalism want to interview famous people. The reality of the celebrity interview is that it can be the toughest test of the integrity of the interviewer. Political spin is but a pale imitation of the control freakery beloved by most 'stars'.

Press agents will attempt to dictate the areas of questioning that are allowed: the plot of the movie, but not their private life. Film stars are stationed in hotel rooms, and interviewers are corralled into ante-rooms awaiting their five minutes (or less) 'exclusive' access to the star. You meet famous people, but what follows has precious little to do with journalism.

Two cameras are set up (by the film company) awaiting the conveyor belt of interviewers. One is on the star, and you can request the other is on a 'two-shot' (proving you were in the same room together). Alongside the star may be a personal assistant, furnishing them with a glass of water or applying make-up, and someone with a stopwatch. The star may be willing to talk for hours but the minder with the stopwatch does the dirty work, calling time on the interview. But they won't interrupt the star, so shrewd interviewers will save a question they know the star will want to answer at length until the end.

Nina Nannar, ITV News: 'If there's something personal you want to ask, you save it till about the third question.'

Nina Nannar has interviewed numerous 'A-list' Hollywood stars as Arts and Media Correspondent for ITV News. She's done 'junket' interviews with everyone from Brad Pitt and Angelina Jolie to Britney Spears. Miss Spears' publicist (at an interview before her marriage) insisted: 'Miss Spears will not answer questions about Justin Timberlake, virginity or September 11.'

Nannar says:

'If there's something personal you want to ask, you save it till about the third question. Two questions about the latest film, then in with the one you really want an answer to. Even if they say, "I don't really want to answer that question," you've got something.

'The really big stars like Tom Cruise and George Clooney can be absolutely charming, really gracious – and they remember you.'

When Tom Cruise agreed to a truly 'exclusive' interview – he'd requested that Nina was the only journalist he spoke to – Nannar says she was treated 'like a queen': 'They couldn't do enough for me because I was the one the star had asked for. It was just before I got married and he was great, hugging and congratulating me.'

David Braithwaite, a specialist in organising film star interviews for BBC Radio Five Live, says his job is about developing personal relationships with people from film studios and specialist PR companies:

'It's about being professional, not about meeting stars, but about knowing this is someone we can get on air, they'll say something good or controversial and they'll be a good interview.

'Most film companies prefer junkets, because they have control. You're split up in terms of regional and national press, radio and television. They also have another group for ethnic press, all treated differently. If you're national and you have a big audience you get treated better than if you're a regional journalist.

'When I go along to an interview and they tell me I've got ten minutes, I arrive and I say, "So how long have I really got?" And they say eight minutes, and then as the junket goes on it can go down to six minutes.'

At film company junkets, BBC Five Live likes to use ISDN lines or radio cars with wireless links, leaving the presenter in the studio. 'Every director and A-list film person who's been in London, we've done.'

When a guest comes into the studio, it's a bonus, a tribute to Braithwaite's persistence, and to the status of Simon Mayo and Mark Kermode's review show.

'Sometimes we get people on an ISDN line for great lengths of time and that's as good as coming in. [Film director and former Monty Python star] Terry Gilliam was the ultimate professional. He sat there, had his headphones on and held his own mic.'

Braithwaite says there's sometimes a trade-off with PR companies to secure big names:

'I'll put on a guest that I don't think is overly great for five minutes at the top of the film slot, so that I'm going to get somebody else later. We don't just do A-list stars. We will do a director of obscure documentaries. We can say we do everyone.

'It's about what gets on air. The people I meet – I've met Nicole Kidman, seven or eight minutes in a room, shake hands, do the interview and go – I meet them but I don't really meet them. They're like press conferences. You've got to treat them like a news item.'

CASE STUDY 4.4   THE CELEBRITY INTERVIEW – A LESSON FROM HISTORY

There is nothing guaranteed to make experienced journalists cringe more than hearing a fawning celebrity interview. You know the sort of thing: reporters who act like the longest-serving paid-up member of the artist's fan club, rather than an informed, reflective observer. Instead of asking the probing questions the wider public might want to hear, they give the star an easy ride. Soft questions include:

'Tell me about your latest album.'

'What attracted you to the part?'

'Have you a message for your British fans?'

This type of questioning of celebs is common in an age when politicians are shown little or no deference. As long ago as 1982, Mrs Thatcher's Defence Secretary John Nott walked out on interviewer Sir Robin Day when he was described as a 'here-today-gone-tomorrow' politician. John Nott is best remembered – by journalists at least – for that incident alone.

And yet pop and film stars, who more than any others in the media are part of a here-today-gone-tomorrow celebrity culture, are given undue respect by reporters. Sometimes the reporter acts like an adolescent fan, their critical faculties swept away in haze of stardust. The result is just embarrassing.

Bob Dylan, more than most pop performers, can be said to have stood the critical test of time. There are many examples of what can only be described as silly questions from Dylan's mid-sixties press conferences. And we all know what happens when you ask silly questions.

'Why do you sing?'

'Why? Just because I feel like singing.'

'How many people who labour in the same musical vineyard in which you toil, how many are protest singers, that is people who use their music, use the songs to protest the social state in which we live today; the matter of war, the matter of crime, or whatever it might be?'

'How many?'

'Yes.'

'I think there's about 136.'

'You say about 136 . . . or do you mean exactly 136?'

'Either 136 or 142.'

'Do you care about what you're singing?'

'How can I answer that if you've got the nerve to ask me? You've got a lot of nerve asking me a question like that. Do you ask the Beatles that?'

And Dylan had the perfect rejoinder to a journalist in Stockholm, who hid behind others' opinions and – an even greater sin – hadn't done his research:

'They've said that you must be the ultimate beatnik.'

'What do you think . . . I won't tell anybody what you say, what do you think?'

'Not your personal comment?'

'No. What do you think?'

'I have no opinion about that.'

'Well, why?'

'Because I haven't heard you sing . . .'

'You've never heard me sing, and yet here you are sitting here asking me all these questions!'

It's been said that there's no such thing in journalism as a stupid question, only stupid answers. No. There are stupid questions.

Sports interviews

> **Sports organisations are hugely conscious of their public image. They try to control the way their sport is reported.**

The approach to interviewing sporting personalities and administrators should be no different from any other interview. The same journalistic rigour and integrity should apply. But, as with the celebrity interview, modern professional sport can be controlled by agents and press officers, who want to insist on what their clients will be asked and what they will not answer. Nowhere is this more true than in the 'big business' that is football. The idea of football as 'big business' pervades modern journalism, largely because of the large sums involved in the sale of sports rights to broadcasters, and the transfer fees and wages for players. But football clubs are not truly 'big' businesses in a FTSE 100 sense.

Sports clubs earn their money from broadcasters, who collude in promoting their image, and from the fans, who pay at the ticket office, the club shop and in Sky Sports subscriptions. Therefore, sports organisations are hugely conscious of their public image. They try to control the way their sport is reported. The following advice is based on the way major sports clubs, and in particular Premier League football teams, control access to their personalities.

Previews

Sports personalities need the media – not least to add value to their lucrative sponsorship deals. Football managers' pre-match press conferences, usually on a Thursday or Friday before a weekend game, are part of the process of keeping the fans informed of and involved in events at the club. But modern football managers are trained in how to avoid answering questions. They are media-savvy and wary of the press. They know, for example, that unguarded comments in the heat of the moment can mean charges of bringing the game into disrepute, and disclosing which players they want to sign can lead to inflated prices on the transfer market.

You must aim for trust and honesty in your dealings with high-profile figures. But that trust can only be won over a period of time. And in an age when there are sackings within the first few weeks of a season, time is the one thing football managers don't have much of. Regional reporters often get to know managers at one club and develop the relationship at another.

From the club's viewpoint, the preview press conference is free publicity, a promotional device to provide upbeat messages ahead of the match. In practice, managers may be working to their own agenda. Apparently unguarded comments may have been carefully thought through, sometimes to put pressure on the club chairman or board, or to give messages to their own players or those they might want to sign from other clubs. It's up to you to interpret those messages. Don't be afraid to ask the question the supporters want asked.

Radio Five Live and BBC TV's Garry Richardson told a Good Practice training workshop for BBC local radio reporters that they should not be nervous about the big question: 'Never

The need for fairness and impartiality applies just as much to highly paid sportsmen as to . . . any other walks of life.

think you can't get the interview you actually want. Always ask – you never know – always aim high.'

There are rich pickings for reporters prepared to ask provocative questions. But the need for fairness and impartiality applies just as much to highly paid sportsmen as to people from any other walks of life. Knowledge of their sport and an understanding of the difficulties of their job are always appreciated. So too is good time keeping.

Think of your audience. If you are working for a local station that is part of a network, that means thinking of the network's needs too. Some of the personalities you meet will be big names whose opinions can make headlines.

Post-match

Barely a week goes by without a football manager being hauled before the FA for 'bringing the game into disrepute' in an after-match interview. Media trainers now tell soccer managers that the first interview after the game is not the place to vent your frustration at a referee's shortcomings. They are advised to take their time, calm down and if possible speak to a trusted assistant before going before the cameras. Nonetheless, getting it off your chest publicly can be more satisfying than getting it off your chest privately. Some managers may consider the FA fine a price worth paying.

Some football interviews have become the stuff of legend. Kevin Keegan's 'I'd love it if we beat them. Love it!' rant, against Manchester United, and his on-air resignation as England manager left interviewers almost speechless. Be ready for the unexpected when passions are running so high.

Veteran manager Ron Atkinson once told reporters he never commented on referees' performances, 'and I'm not going to break the habit of a lifetime for that prat'. Big Ron, of course, often found his tongue led him into trouble.

Mark Bosnich, the Chelsea goalkeeper, launched an astonishing attack on his club after a UEFA cup defeat to Hapoel Tel Aviv. The trip came barely a month after the 9/11 terrorist attacks. Players had been told it was up to them whether they made the journey, because they could be terrorist targets in Israel. A weakened Chelsea lost 2-0.

Bosnich complained – live on Channel Five TV – that whatever he did at the club he wasn't given a fair chance. He worked hard in training, he said, but when the team sheet was posted he wasn't on it. Interviewer Steve Lee remembers the studio director in London telling him, through his earpiece, to get Bosnich to say more of this. Bosnich obliged. He played barely half a dozen more games for Chelsea. Within a year he had tested positive for cocaine. Soon afterwards the club sacked him.

The most successful manager in English football Sir Alex Ferguson avoided some of the flak of confronting the after-match interviewer by refusing to talk to the BBC at all for years. But his comments were available online, on Sky Sports and on MUTV, the club's own TV channel. His words could be reported by the BBC, even if they could not always use the audio.

Remember

- Resist restrictions on the subject of your interviews
- Don't be afraid to ask the questions the public wants asked
- Always be fair to your interviewee – even the famous ones

CONCLUSION

How many interviews have you read with minor celebrities, or even the latest person to be evicted from a reality show, where they say their ambition is to have their own 'chat show'? The implication is that interviewing people on radio or television is easy. Anyone can do it. Well, they can't. High-profile TV personality Davina McCall and even the former Prime Minister Harold Wilson were critically condemned as talk show hosts. Interviewing is a specialist skill, and a very important one for broadcast journalists. You should prepare for every interview, and treat every interviewee with respect.

Few people master every kind of broadcast interview. With practice you will find your niche. With more practice you will develop your talent to become an all-rounder. But practice never makes perfect in this game. Experienced professionals can all point to recent failures. There is always more to learn.

FURTHER READING

Adams, Sally (2001) *Interviewing for Journalists*, London: Routledge. A useful introduction, though weak on broadcast techniques.

Beaman, Jim (2011) *Interviewing for Radio*, London: Routledge. The most detailed guide to the types of interview you'll conduct in radio.

Chantler, Paul and Stewart, Peter (2003) *Basic Radio Journalism*, Oxford: Focal Press. Sound advice on interviewing alongside other radio practice.

Harcup, Tony (2009) *Journalism: Principles and Practice*, London: Sage. Practical advice on finding stories and how to treat them.

Snow, Jon (2004) *Shooting History*, London: Harper Perennial. His career in journalism, including his account of interviewing Margaret Thatcher.

CHAPTERFIVE
NEWS WRITING

In this chapter, we'll look at:

- The skills involved in writing different types of story for different outlets.
- How to develop a script.
- How to begin and end your stories.
- The best kind of words and phrases to use . . .
- And those to avoid.

BROADCAST journalists write words that have to be read but also words that have to be spoken and sound natural. Broadcast scripts should not sound as if they are being read out loud. In that sense broadcasters have more in common with the dramatist than with newspaper reporters. Unlike the dramatist though, the journalist deals in fact rather than fiction. But in any form of oral story telling, it is essential to communicate instantly and to engage the listener in your narrative.

It's possible to re-read a newspaper story if the meaning is not clear, but nobody watches the TV news with their hand poised on the remote control ready to play back a recording of what they've just heard. The audience needs to understand the story on first hearing.

Similarly, when we write for online audiences and text services, the readers do not want to decipher complicated grammatical structures. They want information – and they want it fast. If they weren't looking for instant news, why would they subscribe to a feed to a mobile phone?

A CLOSER LOOK

ODD FACT

It seems odd today, but in the days of 'steam radio' BBC bulletins were read 'first at normal speed, then at dictation speed so that listeners can take notes'.

This idea developed a venerable history. In World War Two, American short-wave stations and the BBC World Service offered 'dictation speed news', so that servicemen in remote camps and even on ships could jot it down and report it to their comrades. The Shipping Forecast on Radio Four is still delivered at 'dictation speed'.

In this chapter, we'll explain that the most important thing to remember when writing news is to use good conversational English, whether you are writing for television, radio, online or text services. Clear spoken English is easy to understand. We are in the communications business; so anything that detracts from communicating gets in the way of the story.

Most news organisations have a *style guide* – summing up the in-house conventions for script writing. Many are available online. We'll explain the reasons for them and look at examples.

We'll round the chapter off by looking at sports writing; the differences between radio and TV scripting; and how the writing skills of the broadcast journalist have to be adapted for online work, where the words are, for a change, meant to be read rather than spoken.

Good journalism begins – and ends – with good standards of English. The BBC newsreader Huw Edwards says:

'Standards of writing are rather depressing – I could put it much more strongly. It is a growing problem.

'When I go to mark external papers [for university courses and others] I'm horrified by what people consider to be acceptable news writing. I'm not looking for great style. I'm really talking basics. I preach this when I go to schools and I see teachers vigorously nodding at the back of the hall.'

Edwards, who writes all his own scripts for the *Ten*, wonders why the education system isn't, in his view, working:

'I get the results of it in front of me every day. Why should I sit there using my time correcting basic grammar and basic punctuation mistakes which can really cause trouble for me on air? It really irritates the hell out of me.'

John Sergeant, now best known for his appearances on light entertainment and magazine shows, stresses the importance of consistent grammar. The former political correspondent with both BBC and ITV News says:

'You've got to decide, for example, whether collective nouns are going to be "is" or "are". So "the government is" or "the government are", but once you've decided that, you obviously must be consistent within your piece. You can't say, "The government is considering this. They want to do that," because that's a grammatical howler. You're moving away from the structure of the English language and that has an integrity of its own which you may not be able to get back to if you're sloppy about these things.'

BBC news correspondent and presenter George Alagiah says:

'You've got to write as if you're talking. I came into this business because I like to communicate; I like to write.

'When you're reaching between five and six million people, accessibility is absolutely key. The writing has to be engaging and it has to be rooted in experience. You need to know your audience. Succinctness and accessibility are quite hard things to do.'

Huw Edwards says good writing helps people get jobs:

'If people turn up here for jobs, submit an application form (which I will often see), and it's written nicely – good English, nothing fancy, nice clear concise English, grammatically watertight – it will stand out from the rest of the crowd and that person will be interviewed.'

ADVICE FOR EFFECTIVE NEWS WRITING

Good conversational English

If you invite someone into your home, you are almost certainly hoping they will be good company. You expect good conversation on subjects that interest you, presented in a way you understand, even if the topic is quite complicated. It wouldn't be a bad thing if your guest was witty and entertaining, but above all they must never be boring. It's a tall order for any visitor to meet all those requirements, and yet this is exactly the pact we make with broadcast journalists every time we switch on the news.

We expect the news to be interesting, understandable and sometimes entertaining. We expect the news readers and reporters to know what they are talking about. We don't expect them to sound as if they are reading something they don't quite understand.

A broadcast news script must sound like natural conversation. The advice from Peter Elliott, the author of the BBC Style Guide back in 1979, holds good today: *Write as you would talk. Better still, write as you would hear.*

> **People get up to all sorts of things while they listen to the radio: they drive, do the housework, fix the car, cook, have sex.**

You have to attract the listeners to what you are telling them. People get up to all sorts of things while they listen to the radio: they drive, do the housework, fix the car, cook, have sex. And surveys have shown, perhaps surprisingly, that they do many of those things while they're watching television too. Each of those potential listeners is alone in their thoughts, if not necessarily alone in physical space. You have to connect with those thoughts. You talk to the listener one to one.

When a broadcaster's words have been spoken they disappear into the ether. They are not available for clarification. They must make sense on first hearing. And the words must hold the listeners' interest, so they want to hear more. In the 1931 Hollywood classic *The Front Page*, a newspaperman says: 'Who the hell's gonna read the second paragraph?' The suggestion is that a headline and the first paragraph are all most readers bother with. In broadcasting, if the listener doesn't stay with you beyond the first paragraph, you haven't just lost them to another story on the same page; you've lost them to another station. Online, you've lost them to another website.

Remember

- Write as you would hear
- Speak to one person
- Make immediate sense

Tell it to your friends

The advice of editors to reporters offering a story in the newsroom applies to journalists writing copy: 'How would you tell it to your friends?'

The idea of telling a story to a group of friends works well because everyone can imagine themselves in a social situation: in a pub or café, at a party, round the dinner table. As others chip in to a conversation, you have to earn your right to be heard. In news, the competition is not other people's jokes and anecdotes, but other websites, other stations and the other things listeners could be doing.

Peter Allen of BBC Radio Five Live says most people can tell a story, without notes, but they complicate things by writing it down:

'It's a good exercise to be given a microphone and told to "Go". They'll be amazed at just how good they are at telling a story without any notes because most of us can.

'The other thing that people do without a script is they tell it simply. They say: "I've just seen a car crash. I think three people were killed. It was terrible. There was a bloke coming down the road and the other one went head on. One was a Jaguar, the other was a Mercedes, I think. They were obviously going too fast."

'And they think, "Oh I've just told a story," whereas if they tried to put that into a script it wouldn't have the immediacy or the power. When you just tell it as it comes into your head, it comes out in an immediate, easily communicated way.'

A CLOSER LOOK

THE ORAL TRADITION

Broadcast journalism is as much part of a long tradition of the spoken word as the medium of story telling. Ancient civilisations relied on word-of-mouth communication. The Greek poet Homer may have spoken his epics or sung them to a lyre – a primitive stringed instrument (think Bob Dylan without the harmonica). Scholars have worked out that the *Iliad* and *Odyssey* were probably not written by one man. It was most likely hundreds of years before they were written down. The rhythm of verse helped poets through the centuries remember the flow of the narrative. Songs served medieval balladeers in much the same way.

The stories in the Bible belong to an oral tradition. Most of the New Testament stories about Jesus were not written down until decades after his death. Shakespeare wrote his plays to be performed, to be spoken on the stage, long before scholars decided they were the finest examples of written English.

The essayist and critic William Hazlitt said in 1819: 'To write in a genuine, familiar, or truly English style is to write as anyone would speak in common conversation.' Hazlitt was encouraged to take up journalism by Samuel Taylor Coleridge, a poet.

The critic and author Cyril Connolly rather pompously observed that 'Literature is the art of writing something that will be read twice, journalism what will be read once'. Broadcast journalism isn't read at all; it is heard once. As BBC Radio News's style guide pointed out, who reads Cyril Connolly any more?

Broadcast speech belongs in the long oral tradition – a lineage with a proud history and important lessons for us:

● Write as anyone would speak
● Remember that it will only be heard once

Be concise

People who can communicate perfectly well in casual conversation and in some cases write perfectly good essays, or even newspaper copy, become afflicted by all manner of verbal tics when they write for broadcast. For young people entering the profession it is probably a hangover of school or university days when they were asked to write essays of a certain length. In an essay, every word is a step nearer the target; more words mean less work still to be done. In a news script, there is no place for padding or superfluous words.

> **In a news script, there is no place for padding or superfluous words.**

People speak an average of three words every second – that's 180 words a minute. In a half-hour news programme, if every second were taken up with speech (which it is not) that would be a total of 5400 words. A feature in a broadsheet newspaper may be 1000 words long. So you can see that words are at a premium in broadcasting. Each word in a news script not only has to be used precisely, it has to justify being there. Concise writing is essential.

BBC Five Live's Peter Allen says: 'Most writing is just too complex; too many sub-clauses; too much thought; too much trying to compress lots of facts into a single sentence. A sentence should have a thought in it, I think. Just one idea. Bump. Full stop.'

> **Read words out loud when you have written them . . . it is an invaluable discipline.**

A script has to sound right. Follow the rhythms of natural speech. Check this by reading words out loud when you have written them. You will have to overcome your self-consciousness, but speaking the words you write is an invaluable discipline.

Make sure you know the meaning of every word you use, and understand how it fits into the grammar of the sentence you are writing. If you don't understand it, what chance does the listener have?

Remember

- Use each word precisely
- Cut out superfluous words
- Read your scripts out loud

Keep it simple

Complicated sentence structures and long words are difficult to understand. We could warn here against dangling participles, passive verbs and stacked modifiers. But too much grammatical analysis goes against the best advice in this chapter: KISS – Keep it simple, stupid!

Simple sentences means active sentences. Subject, verb, object in that order. It is a direct and strong way to deliver information. The subject is usually a person or people doing something. It is better to say somebody did something than to say something was done *by* somebody. 'Rooney scored the first goal just before half-time' rather than 'The first goal was scored just before half-time by Rooney'. The audience wants to know who scored. So tell them. Beware of other structures that delay the important information: 'It was just before half-time that Rooney scored the first goal.'

Some passive sentences just sound wrong. 'Father Christmas was believed in by the children' or even 'Father Christmas was the object of the children's belief' are both ugly constructions. They sound awkward and unnatural. When you start a sentence with his name, you expect Father Christmas to be doing something.

Usually, it is best to have just one idea in each sentence. Consider this: 'After at least 78 people died in Chile's worst earthquake in 50 years, scientists are warning of a tsunami which could affect Easter Island and other parts of the Pacific Ocean.' It is clumsier and more difficult to read than using two sentences. 'At least 78 people have died in Chile's worst earthquake in 50 years. Scientists are now warning of a tsunami which could affect Easter Island and other parts of the Pacific Ocean.'

Sir David Nicholas, former editor of ITN, the provider of ITV News in Britain, said every sentence must stand on its own legs with no hanging thoughts or subordinate clauses.

> **Clarity is all. It may be necessary to lose some detail to clarify what is being said.**

Clarity is all. It may be necessary to lose some detail to clarify what is being said. As long as none of the accuracy of the statement is lost, that is usually worth doing. Here's a link to a radio report as it appeared on the BBC's national news service:

A spokesman for Tony Blair has indicated that the government's Health Improvement Bill – which restricts smoking in enclosed public spaces in England – will be published tomorrow as planned. The cabinet has so far failed to come to an agreement about the extent of a smoking ban – it's likely that there'll now be more discussion on the issue. From Westminster, here's Mike Sergeant.

And this is how BBC Radio Stoke rewrote the same link, losing none of the sense and only a little of the detail:

The government's plans to ban smoking in enclosed spaces will be published tomorrow as planned. The cabinet has so far failed to agree on the extent of the ban. From Westminster, here's Mike Sergeant.

We no longer have the source of the information (the rather vague 'spokesman for Tony Blair'), we've lost the name of the bill (who cares?) and we are no longer told the ban will apply specifically in England, but that would surely be understood by a listener to an English radio station. The shorter version has to be preferable for the purposes of broadcast journalism. It is certainly easier to understand.

Remember

- Use simple, active sentences
- Stick to one idea per sentence
- Clarity is all

TIP BOX

GREAT WRITING

Great writing is a matter of opinion. One man's idea of great journalistic writing is another person's idea of pretentious drivel. But few can fail to be impressed by the words that capture an idea or a moment so that others can only say: 'I wish I'd said that.'

Your favourite from the archive might be Brian Hanrahan during the Falklands War in 1982, ad libbing on BBC radio to fill a hole in the script because the government censors wouldn't allow him to report the numbers of aircraft on a mission: 'I counted them all out and I counted them all back.'

Or the simple use of the word 'biblical' in Michael Buerk's description of the Ethiopian famine in 1984, in a report that inspired Bob Geldof's Band Aid and Live Aid fund-raising campaigns: 'Dawn – and as the sun breaks through the piercing chill of night on the plain outside Korem, it lights up a biblical famine. Now. In the twentieth century.'

Or Martin Bell on Soviet troops leaving Czechoslovakia in 1990: 'They outstayed a welcome they never had . . .'

Good style comes in many spheres of writing. The great sports writer Hugh McIlvanney described the British boxer Joe Bugner as having 'the physique of a Greek statue but fewer moves'. Alan Bennett, who wrote the hugely acclaimed series of TV monologues *Talking Heads*, said of his own mother: 'A sausage had only to be hoisted on a stick to become . . . an emblem of impossible sophistication.'

Learn from the experts, and don't restrict your influences to other broadcast journalists.

Pithy, terse and brilliant. Witty too. Learn from the experts, and don't restrict your influences to other broadcast journalists.

How to tell your story

When you sit down to write your copy, ask yourself how you are going to tell the story to a friend. What do you want to tell them? What will they want to know? And what do they need to know? You want to grab their attention. But there is a world of difference between being the girl who makes everyone laugh in the pub and being a successful stand-up comedian. Similarly, to be a successful journalist, your story-telling skills need to be developed to professional standards. We'll now consider some of the guidelines and techniques that will help you write well.

Style guides

There is a big difference between the language suitable for a BBC Radio Four bulletin and that of the local commercial radio station. Within the BBC, Five Live is less formal than Radio Four. ITV News has adopted a more tabloid style than the BBC. But the BBC Radio News Style Guide, which is available online, warns writers that there is no such thing as 'trying to be a bit more Radio Four'. That is just an excuse for flabby prose. The difference between networks is one of tone, not the way stories are told: 'The same species of clear, straightforward English will stand you in equally good stead whichever outlet you are writing for.'

The spoken language evolves and what was common usage for one generation may not have the same meaning for the next.

Each organisation has its own style guide – a useful book or online resource to be consulted by news writers, setting out the preferred usage of the language.

Many style guides point out common mistakes. Most recognise that the spoken language evolves and a word with a clear meaning for one generation can have a different meaning for the next.

Here's an example of what's considered correct modern usage from the Sky Sports News Writing Style Guide:

Effectively/in effect

Effectively means *with (good) effect;*

Don't use it to mean *in effect,* for example:

. . . the game was effectively over by half time . . .

But the right-winger was used *effectively*.

And from the BBC News Style Guide:

Effectively is often confused with *in effect*. **If something is effective, it produces a satisfactory result, so** *effectively* **means with** *a satisfactory outcome. The outbreak of plague in Skegness has been effectively contained* **means the rest of us are safe.** *In effect* **means** *in practice,* **and often indicates an unplanned outcome, as in** *The new tax has in effect made it more sensible for Geoff to remain on benefits.*

Another adverb often used wrongly is *literally*. It is literally the opposite of 'metaphorically,' so it should never be used before a metaphor. Don't say: 'Cole literally flew down the wing.'

Be careful how you use everyday words. You often hear 'on either side of the road' or 'either side of half-time' when the speaker really means on 'each' or 'both' sides.

There are many more examples in style guides online.

See Workshops and Exercises

Accuracy

You will notice a theme running through a lot of this chapter – and a lot of this book – the need for accuracy, both in the reporting of facts and the use of language.

> **Keith Waterhouse: 'Words are facts. Check them (spelling and meaning) as you would any other.'**

The credo of Joseph Pulitzer, who gave his name to the renowned US journalism prize, was: 'Accuracy, accuracy, accuracy.' Keith Waterhouse, a great British journalist and author, advised journalists: 'Words are facts. Check them (spelling and meaning) as you would any other.'

Mistakes slip into copy under the pressure of deadlines. They occur too when you are writing about something unfamiliar. Many in your audience will not know the detail of what you're talking about, but some will care passionately about the subject. For example, the two-hundredth anniversary of the Battle of Trafalgar produced a series of inaccuracies and howlers.

A reporter on BBC *Breakfast News* commented (twice) on flags being 'risen'. Christ is risen – it's biblical language. Flags are raised.

A BBC Radio Four report spoke of HMS *Victory* being 'anchored' in Portsmouth Harbour. It is in dry dock.

The BBC's *Ten O'Clock News* referred to 'the HMS *Victory*'. HMS stands for Her Majesty's Ship. Would you refer to the Queen's shoes as 'the her shoes?'

And most confusing of all, a link from Independent Radio News for their network reported: 'Lord Nelson was fatally wounded and supposedly said to his right-hand man: "Kiss me, Hardy".'

Nelson did not have a right hand – he lost most of his right arm in Tenerife – so the phrase 'right-hand man' is confusing. Is it meant to imply that Hardy was some sort of gofer for the admiral? Hardy was the captain of HMS *Victory*. He was with the Admiral when he was shot. Hardy continued to command his ship and visited the wounded Nelson twice before he died. Nelson was attended below deck on the *Victory* by the ship's surgeon, a steward, a chaplain and a purser. He had a secretary, who was killed in the early stages of the battle. And then there was Admiral Collingwood, who commanded the right-hand column of British ships of the line at Trafalgar. To describe Hardy as Nelson's 'right-hand man' is sloppy, to say the least. It may work as a newspaper headline (where the 'joke' is implicit) but does not suit broadcast style.

If it's any consolation to modern reporters, the very first newspaper account of Nelson's death – in the *Gibraltar Chronicle* of 24 October 1805 – was also riddled with inaccuracies, claiming the Admiral was shot once, had his wound dressed and returned to the deck, was shot again and then survived till the evening. His last words, in this account, were: 'Thank God! I have outlived this day, and now I die content!' Slapdash journalism from two centuries ago!

UTV Radio's news mission statement said: 'We don't deal in half-truths or speculation . . . We check facts and source our stories.'

The Ofcom Broadcasting Code says: 'News, in whatever form, must be reported with due accuracy and presented with due impartiality.'

The BBC's policy is that it considers accuracy more important than speed. There is no justifiable argument for inaccuracy in journalism, but the BBC's position is not merely a statement of the obvious. According to its Editorial Guidelines, accuracy is often more than a question of getting the facts right. Facts and information should be weighed to get at the truth.

> **Accuracy is often more than a question of getting the facts right. Facts and information should be weighed to get at the truth.**

The presenter Evan Davis explained in an online article that it is not the case that 'comment is free and facts are sacred', as he had always supposed. 'Far from being precious nuggets of valuable information to be cherished, most facts are left discarded and unused.'

Davis argues that the audience wants the journalist to make judgements on their behalf, about the significance of the available facts and the pattern that fits them together.

So how do you avoid inaccuracy?

Remember

- Check every fact
- Only use words you understand
- Check the spelling and meaning of unfamiliar words
- Don't report rumour as fact
- Be bold – if you are sure of your facts, use them

See Workshops and Exercises

Keep it up to date

Precision also applies to any references to time in your script. Broadcasting and the Internet replaced newspapers as the main source of news because they are immediate, and not subject to printing and distribution deadlines. People expect to hear about what is happening now, not what happened yesterday.

We know from Chapter 2: What's the story? that immediacy is one of the factors that makes a story newsworthy. News has to be new. We've also mentioned that when you record interviews you should be aware of when the recording is likely to be broadcast, so that there are no misleading references to time and dates. It is equally important to write stories in a way that keeps them bang up to the minute. That means using the present tense where possible.

> **People expect to hear about what is happening now, not what happened yesterday.**

In the aftermath of Hurricane Katrina in August 2005 there was widespread looting in New Orleans. It would have been accurate to lead a news bulletin with the phrase: 'lawlessness continued this morning', or 'lawlessness has continued'. But it had much more impact to say: 'lawlessness is continuing'. This underlines the fact that the law breaking was not under control. It keeps the audience wanting to know more.

Even after an event, it is important to keep the information as immediate as possible. 'Two people have been killed and seven injured in a road accident', rather than 'two people were killed . . .'. And if the information is being reported the morning after the event, consider updating it by saying: 'The police are investigating a road accident that killed two and left seven people injured.'

You might even want to project forward to future events: 'The police will begin interviewing witnesses today . . .'

Writing for online audiences, it's usually best to avoid time and date references altogether, because the story can be accessed long after you have written it. References to yesterday, today and tomorrow or even 'next Tuesday' are confusing.

Remember

- Report what's happening now, not what happened yesterday
- Use the present tense where possible
- Think of ways to keep stories fresh
- Avoid time and date references in online stories

Use short words not long ones

Never use a long word where a short one will do.

Never use a long word where a short one will do. That advice was one of the rules from English novelist George Orwell in *Politics and the English Language*, written in 1946. The man who gave us 'Big Brother' and 'Room 101' (both from his novel *1984* and both the titles of twenty-first-century TV series) is still relevant today.

So use:

- start *not* instigate
- dead *not* deceased
- cut *not* eliminate
- fire *not* conflagration
- truth *not* veracity
- end *not* terminate

Another word that creeps into scripts all the time is *however*. The BBC presenter John Humphrys got it right in his *Lost for Words*, aptly subtitled *The Mangling and Manipulating of the English Language*. He wrote: ' "However" instead of "but" is clumsy. Any word that requires a pair of commas to surround it before it is allowed out in public should stay at home.'

And don't feel the need to replace the perfectly serviceable 'said' with its many alternatives: affirmed, announced, asserted, claimed, commented, observed, stated, and so on. Phrases such as 'expressed the view that' are ugly and unnecessary. 'Had this to say' is a broadcasting cliché.

Use short phrases rather than long ones

Many of the phrases in everyday speech are fillers used to buy the speaker thinking time. Just as you wouldn't expect to hear 'you know' or 'if you see what I mean' in a broadcast script, you shouldn't use 'at this moment in time' or 'at present' when the perfectly serviceable 'now' will do. Similarly, 'more than' is more concise than the rather pompous 'in excess of'. Some common phrases can be replaced by a single word.

So use:

- although *not* in spite of the fact that
- to *not* in order to
- during *not* in the course of
- scarce *not* in short supply
- thought *not* was of the opinion that
- because *not* owing to the fact that
- if *not* in the event of

You will find your own examples as you think harder about the language you use.

Remember

- Use short words instead of longer ones
- Use short phrases or single words where they can replace longer phrases

Use short forms

In everyday speech we shorten common phrases. 'I will' becomes 'I'll', 'we will' becomes 'we'll', 'you are' is 'you're', 'they are' is 'they're'. These short forms, or contractions, are the best form to use for broadcast scripts. They are conversational and concise. If you speak it that way, then write it that way. You'll find we do it in this book all the time. It may not be the best written English style, but, hey, we're broadcasters!

Many natural contractions are pronoun–verb combinations, such as the examples above. There's never any harm in using the short form. Others have to be used more judiciously, particularly when they involve a negative. It's usually acceptable to say 'isn't, aren't, hasn't, haven't, don't' and 'won't'. But if you want to emphasise the negative, avoid the contraction. 'The prime minister said he will not resign' is stronger than 'The prime minister said he won't resign.' That is because you can put emphasis on the word *not* when you read it.

Contracting 'has' or 'is' into ''s' at the end of a noun also usually works. So 'The president's appointed a new secretary of state' or 'The president's on his way to Camp David' are fine and work well.

Contraction doesn't work though when it becomes an excuse for sloppy speech. Don't use 'wanna' instead of 'want to'. And if you use 'could've', be aware it's short for 'could have' and not 'could of'. Most broadcasters avoid the use of slang expressions, but some commercial radio stations aimed at younger audiences encourage the kind of street language an older generation would frown upon. Offensive language remains taboo.

If it sounds right, contract and use the shortened version, because it's how we all speak.

The general rule is: if it sounds right, contract and use the shortened version, because it's how we all speak and what the listener's ear is attuned to.

Remember

- Contract words and phrases where it sounds natural to do so
- Avoid slang – unless it's part of your house style
- Leave out the contraction if you want to emphasise something – particularly a negative
- Make your scripts sound like everyday speech

Who said what – attributing stories

Good journalistic practice requires information to be properly sourced. The listener needs to know who is responsible for what they are hearing. In newspapers the attribution often comes at the end of the paragraph, after the reader has read the main point of the story. Here's an example from a newspaper:

British forces could be pulled out of Afghanistan within five years, the head of the army has disclosed.

The *Daily Telegraph*, front page, 27 February 2010

The story would not work well as a broadcast script in this form. For a start it is not a natural way to speak. The man at the bar wouldn't say: 'My dinner will be in the dog if I don't return soon from the pub, a mobile phone call from my wife has revealed.' He might say: 'My wife's phoned to tell me . . .' etc.

A broadcast version of the *Telegraph* story might read:

The head of the army says British forces could be pulled out of Afghanistan within five years.

There is another problem with giving information before it is attributed. Contentious statements can be given authority because they are heard first from the mouth of a trusted newsreader.

Consider this sentence: 'The prime minister took the country to war on the basis of a lie and must pay the price by losing his job.'

It sounds like the opinion of the newsreader until we get to the next sentence: 'That's the view of the mother of a soldier who died . . .'

If listeners know who's saying something, they can judge the authority of the information. So it's easier for the audience to give them the source of the information first. Occasionally a controversial quote may be strong enough to start a story – but make sure the attribution is clear.

Remember

- Make the source of your information clear
- The source of a contentious statement usually needs to come first

Avoid direct quotes

Direct quotes appear all the time in newspapers. What somebody says appears between sets of inverted commas. It's the nearest readers of newspapers can get to hearing somebody say something. Radio has the advantage of being able to use the actual sound of somebody saying something, and on television we can see them saying it. These interviews can run at greater length online.

There are still times when we want to quote what somebody has said – in the intro to a story for example – and that's when dangers arise. On radio in particular it is difficult to tell whether you are reading your own words or somebody else's. Direct quotations should be used sparingly.

Bob Geldof said the Live 8 concerts had been 'full of hope and possibility and life'.

BBC News, 3 July 2005

This works because the quotation is short and easy to follow. Any longer though and it might be difficult for the listener.

Look at this example from the BBC TV interactive service just before a G8 summit in Scotland, where the cancellation of debt in Africa was to be announced:

Gordon Brown told the BBC: 'It is a lifetime's work where we empower the people of Africa and the developing countries to make decisions for themselves.'

If this sentence were to be broadcast on radio it would be difficult to work out to whom 'we' refers. Is it the British government, all the governments of the G8, citizens of developed countries, the BBC? Using *indirect* speech would make it clearer. 'The chancellor said it was a lifetime's work where the G8 countries empower the people of Africa and the developing countries to make decisions for themselves.'

So, *it's usually better to use indirect or reported speech.* The tense as well as the person linked to the verb changes in reported speech: 'I am' becomes 'he was'.

Direct speech: Jaldeep said: 'I'm going to the concert in Hyde Park.'

Reported speech: Jaldeep said he was going to the concert in Hyde Park.

The word 'that' could be included in the second example: 'Jaldeep said that he was going to the concert in Hyde Park.' But what's the point? It is a superfluous word. Strike it out. The word 'that' is almost always unnecessary in this type of sentence and can usually be omitted.

Punctuation

Punctuation in a broadcast script should be kept to a minimum, to make it easy to read. Full stops are essential, but inverted commas are almost always unnecessary: colons and semi-colons are impossible to express in speech. We speak in phrases rather than perfectly formed sentences. So there is no harm in writing that way.

Remember

- Use short words instead of long ones
- Use short forms (contractions) of phrases such as can't, don't, won't
- Attribute your stories – make the source clear
- Avoid direct speech

If you follow these simple rules you will develop a clear, concise way of expressing yourself. Many people master these techniques, and then allow sloppy expressions to cloud the clarity of their writing. When you know how to spot these intrusive phrases they are easy to avoid.

Clichés

A cliché is a hackneyed and over-used expression, and, boy, are they over used in journalism! Julia Cresswell, the editor of the *The Penguin Dictionary of Clichés* defines a cliché as:

'an expression that does your thinking for you: an expression so well established in the language that you know exactly how it is going to end once someone has started saying it, and which conveys instant meaning without your having to work out anything for yourself.'

Aha, you're thinking. That's handy. Phrases I can use so that everybody knows what I mean. They'll be really useful if I'm up against a deadline. And that's fine. If you want to produce turgid and predictable copy.

Andrew Boyd, in *Broadcast Journalism: Techniques of Radio and Television News* (Boyd, A., Stewart, P. and Alexander, R. 2008, Focal Press), summed it up:

'Clichés and journalese are devils disguised as angels. They lie in wait for the moment Inspiration turns her back, before overpowering her, stealing her clothes and sneaking up on the reporter as a deadline approaches.

'Hapless hacks are usually so intent on beating the clock that they fail to see through their disguise and welcome these saboteurs as saviours.'

Let's have a look at some examples of cliché (and journalese) from just one *hour* of twenty-first century broadcasting:

. . . a huge security operation – BBC News

. . . a huge boost to the economy – BBC News

. . . in a comfortable condition – BBC News

. . . scientific studies – BBC News

. . . will add some time to your journey – BBC London News

. . . on your supermarket shelves – BBC News Channel

. . . quiet confidence – ITV News

. . . flying the flag for Britain – ITV News

. . . singing London's praises . . . hot contenders . . . top of an exclusive pile . . . so good they named it twice – Sky News

. . . face a major hurdle – Sky News

. . . a battle of wills – Sky News

. . . fears are growing – Sky News

. . . all-time highs – Sky News

. . . the best sporting action from all around the globe – Sky Sports News

. . . Jack Nicklaus rolled back the years – Sky Sports News

. . . trained negotiators – BBC Radio One

. . . enjoyed a huge boost – BBC Radio Two

. . . keeping a very close eye on – BBC Radio Four

. . . ring of steel – BBC Radio Four

. . . cut up rough – BBC Radio Four

. . . walking tall – BBC Radio Five Live

. . . sales have rocketed – BBC Radio Five Live

All those phrases were used by news readers and reporters. People turn on the news to hear fresh information – not stale and predictable phrases. A fun test that can help you avoid some of these pitfalls is to apply the opposite word to a phrase. You'd never say '*un*trained negotiators' or 'walking small'.

It has become a cliché of books on news writing that they all seem to offer the old joke: avoid clichés – yes – like the plague. Better to avoid them like any nasty disease.

Be realistic though. Mike Henfield, a seasoned radio news writer, says: 'When the chips are down (there's a cliché for you), there's often very little alternative when you need a shorthand way of telling a story. By all means avoid really obvious ones – but sometimes they're a necessary evil (another one!).'

Remember

- Avoid clichés where you possibly can

Jargon

Journalism is all about interpreting events and information in everyday language – language people understand. Every business has its jargon, a language specific to the job in hand. For those in the know it can be, though isn't always, the best way of communicating. There's a lot of jargon from the world of broadcast journalism in this book. But you wouldn't expect your mother, your sister or the bloke in the pub to understand 'voicers', 'two-ways' and 'pressers'.

Don't expect your viewers and listeners to understand jargon.

So, don't expect your viewers and listeners to understand the jargon of the legal or medical professions, or that of the emergency services.

If someone is pronounced *dead on arrival* at hospital or *DOA* that means death was certified at that point because someone was available to do so officially. It doesn't always mean they died on the way to hospital. If they died in a road accident, say so.

If a policeman tells you an HGV and a private motor vehicle were involved in a fatal RTC it means someone died in a crash involving a lorry and a car. We don't all watch police dramas, so we don't all know that.

Presenter Jeremy Paxman on *Newsnight* debunked the jargon, and indeed the mixed metaphors, of international diplomacy by quoting BBC Radio News coverage of the Middle East peace process. The radio reported: 'The road map was derailed before it got off the ground.' Paxman's sardonic tone said it all. Incidentally, 'road map' is defined in Nick Webb's *The Dictionary of Bullshit* (2005, Robson Books) as a noun meaning 'a plan, but a little more vague'.

Remember

- Learn to recognise jargon – the specialist words and phrases used by specific professional groups
- Even if you understand a phrase, don't assume your audience will
- Try to dissuade interviewees from using jargon – you will end up interrupting them to explain their meaning

Journalese

Journalism has its own ugly jargon – a form of the English language beloved of many newspaper journalists and abhorred in almost equal measure by most broadcasters. Former BBC news editor Rick Thompson says in *Writing for Broadcast Journalists*: '. . . the language of broadcast news is infected by the virus of so-called journalese. It is rampant. And there seems to be no known cure.'

Journalese is the jargon of bad journalism. Dozens of journalese words infect the pages of newspapers, many of them chosen because they are short and fit neatly into headlines.

Journalese is the jargon of bad journalism . . . the problem with journalese is that people don't speak like that.

Shock. Bid. Probe. Clash. Plea. Blast. Slam. Row. Short words are always preferable to longer alternatives, but only where their meaning is precise and not sensational. The weakness of these headline words has been exposed by the growth of online news. Search engines will not recognise the clichés and puns of tabloid sub-editors; they will recognise words in everyday use. The need for search engine optimisation (SEO) dictates that we should write headlines in plain English.

Another type of journalese is the use of the stacked phrase, cramming adjectives and nouns into unwieldy phrases that are difficult to say on air and often look ridiculous, even in print: five times Olympic gold medal-winning oarsman Sir Steve Redgrave; *X Factor* and *Britain's Got Talent* judge Simon Cowell; double-Oscar-winning actor Tom Hanks. 'London Mayor Boris Johnson' is more clearly expressed as 'the Mayor of London, Boris Johnson' or 'Boris Johnson, the London Mayor'.

Newspapers also seem to have an obsession with age: the 30-year-old mother-of-two; the 61-year-old rocker; the 36-year-old midfield maestro. Better to say 'Angela Johnson, who's 30 and has two children; Bruce Springsteen, who's 61; David Beckham, who's 36. That's if you consider age an important part of the story. It probably isn't. In January 2006 the *Daily Mirror* described the Education Secretary Ruth Kelly, who was under pressure to resign, as a '37-year-old mum-of-four'. You would not want that phrase in a broadcast, especially not in a political story.

The problem with journalese is that people don't speak like that. Nobody says: 'Drinks probe cheat makes shock eleventh-hour bid to end row.' They say: 'OK, I'll get my round in!'

Remember

- Learn to recognise journalese
- Treat it as any other jargon – leave it out
- Don't be obsessed by people's age unless it's relevant to the story
- Journalese might work in a newspaper headline, but not in an online headline or the spoken word

Officialese

Politicians and businessmen have their own languages – often employed to disguise the real meaning of what they are saying. *Downsizing* means people lose their job. *Human Resources* or *HR* means people. And the word *issue* has become a euphemism for *problem*. But the two words do not mean the same thing. If there's a problem, that's part of the story.

You should avoid euphemisms in all your writing. For clarity, always say 'died' rather than 'lost their life' or 'passed away'. When you are trying to get to the meaning of officialese, cutting out euphemisms is equally important.

Here's an intriguing one from John Clare, the chief executive of DSG International (that's the electrical shops Dixons and Currys to you and me). He told an interviewer on Radio Five Live's business news: 'We're putting some exciting new executions into the marketplace.'

The idea of exciting new executions surely whetted the appetites of any horror fans in the breakfast audience. What did he have in mind? Celebrity disembowelling? What do you think he really meant?

Also on Five Live, when commuters were trapped in London after the terrorist bombs of 7 July 2005, many complained of being charged up to three times the normal rate for hotel rooms. A spokesman for the hotel trade was asked to explain this apparent exploitation. He said it was an example of 'yield management'. Now, yield management is a perfectly respectable term for dealing with supply and demand, notably in the airline and hotel businesses. In this context, though, the jargon seemed callous.

And in another business bulletin, Sir Nigel Rudd, the chairman of Boots, commenting on a proposed merger with the pharmacy chain, Alliance Unichem, said there was 'complementarity' between the two companies. Faced with a light-hearted challenge about whether there really was such a word, Sir Nigel laughed and confessed: 'I don't honestly know. I probably just invented it!'

Remember

- Officialese should always be challenged
- Avoid euphemisms
- Where possible, convert official language into plain English

Hype

There's a temptation to make stories sound more important than they are by using exaggerated language. Resist that temptation.

Professional rivalry and personal pride mean most journalists want to impress their editors and colleagues, and excite audiences. So, there's a temptation to make stories sound more important than they are by using exaggerated language. Resist that temptation.

According to BBC Radio Four, the French President Jacques Chirac committed a 'monumental' blunder with a comment in July 2005 that the only thing the British have ever given European farming was mad cow disease. Napoleon won monumental victories – the French built the Arc De Triomphe because of them. Nelson won a monumental victory at Trafalgar – otherwise there would be no column in Trafalgar Square. Nobody is planning a monument to M. Chirac's bad-taste jokes.

The spread of early man into the Americas was described on BBC Radio Five Live as 'a hugely controversial area'. But it isn't. Are they talking about it in your supermarket? We doubt it.

A BBC TV regional breakfast bulletin reported: 'Crucial talks between West Midlands fire service and union leaders take place this week in a last-ditch attempt to avoid strike action.' The sentence has all the hallmarks of a hastily written Sunday overnight filler. The clichés 'crucial' and 'last-ditch' add little to the sense.

The UTV Radio mission statement – for radio stations with a style they themselves describe as 'tabloid, punchy and to the point' – makes it clear they avoid 'tabloid excesses'.

Remember

- If a story is worth reporting, there is no need to use hype
- Exaggerated language runs the risk of appearing ridiculous

Numbers

Numbers present real problems for broadcasters, particularly on radio. Television can explain with a graphic; charts or simple figures on screen let the eye take in what the ear is hearing. It is important the words match the picture – don't say *one in five* if the graphic says *20 per cent*.

Radio is a poor medium for dealing with numbers.

But radio listeners will struggle to take in big or complicated figures. The BBC News Style Guide says bluntly that radio is a poor medium for dealing with numbers. A story with too many figures numbs the listener.

Psychologists have proven there's a limit to how many numbers people can retain. The art is to simplify. Round up or down where appropriate. And always start a story by identifying a trend or somebody's reaction, rather than getting bogged down in the numbers. So:

There's been a big increase in the number of people unemployed and claiming benefit.

Or:

The Prime Minister says he's disappointed by the rise in unemployment.

Rather than:

The unemployment figures have risen by 37,000.

Be particularly wary of percentages. A rise in interest rates from 4 per cent to 5 per cent is not a 1 per cent increase. It's a 25 per cent increase, although to say so in those terms would be confusing.

Doubling a figure is an increase of 100 per cent, not 200 per cent. If something goes up 200 per cent, it triples in cost.

Try not to mix decimals, fractions and percentages in the same story. Listeners do not have the opportunity to sit back and ponder the figures. A bulletin is not a mental arithmetic test. A bemused audience will certainly switch off mentally, and may switch off physically.

When writing about figures, be careful about the use of words such as 'number' and 'amount' and their close relatives 'fewer' and 'less'. It's 'the number of people on hospital waiting lists' not 'the amount of people'. Fewer means smaller in number (fewer coins, for example); less means smaller in quantity or a smaller amount (less money).

Even if you get the numbers right, watch how they fit into the sense of what you are saying. Avoid nonsense like this from BBC *Midlands Today*, reporting on improvements at a secondary school: 'Exam results have rocketed from 11 to 34 per cent.' No, they haven't. It's likely that there were results for 100 per cent of the exams taken, both this year and last. The meaning was probably that the pass rate improved.

There is a masterclass on the use of numbers on the BBC College of Journalism website. It is one of the most valuable resources on the site for established journalists. Newcomers to news writing would be well advised to visit it before they go anywhere near a bulletin. The link is at the end of the chapter.

Remember

- Simplify numbers where possible
- Round up or down if appropriate
- Don't mix decimals, fractions and percentages
- On television and online use graphics to explain numbers

Using good English in your copy

If you take the advice above, you will already be able to construct clear, understandable broadcast sentences. Think what you want to say. Work out how you want to say it. Then consider how each strand of information, clearly expressed, should come together in the finished copy.

A good story is more than a collection of facts. It has a narrative structure. That structure should attract and keep the attention of the audience. You need to understand the story before you begin to tell it. Marshal all the information into a structure that tells people what they need to know in a sequence they can easily follow and comprehend. What you tell them should make immediate sense in its own right. People might want to find out more about the story – that's a good sign, because it shows you have interested them in the subject – but they should not be left asking questions you should have answered. Weblinks should be included in the online version of your story, so

> **A good story is more than a collection of facts. It has a narrative structure.**

that related stories and background information are easy to find, but the reader should not have to click away from your story to know what it is about.

Putting the story together – the five *W*s

The key ingredients of most news stories can be summed up in the five *W*s – who, what, where, when, why.

- Who was involved?
- What happened?
- Where did it happen?
- When did it happen?
- Why did it happen?

Some textbooks on journalism suggest 'how' is important too. It depends on the story. How something happened is often complicated. In the case of a train or air crash, it's best left to the accident inquiry. In any case, 'how' or 'why' will rarely be the main point of the story.

It is not necessary to have all the *W*s near the top of the story. But who was involved and what happened are almost always in the introduction.

'Who' is particularly important because most news is about people. Sometimes it's one person: 'A three-year-old local boy has become one of the youngest members of Mensa, the society for people with high IQs.' Or 'who' could refer to a lot of people: 'Householders across Scotland are welcoming the news that their council tax won't be going up after local authorities agreed a freeze in payments.'

If the 'who' is well known you may name the person or give them their title, or both, straight away.

'The former Prime Minister Ted Heath has died.'

In this example, to say 'a former Prime Minister has died' would be unduly vague. To say 'Ted Heath has died' would not deliver enough information to younger people who might not have heard of him. He died 31 years after leaving power, so we can't assume everybody knew who he was.

If someone is not well known, there's no point identifying them straight away, as their identity is not among the main points of the story. The name can come later, perhaps in the second paragraph.

Headline writing

Opening with impact

They're the first thing the audience sees or hears, but often the last thing to be written. The headline has to capture the attention, sum up the key point of the story, and tell people why they should want to know more. Teasers midway through a programme serve the same purpose. They trumpet why this story is news.

Online headlines need to make sense in their own right as summaries of the story. Several versions of the headline may be needed for the same story depending on the number of characters (letters and spaces) permitted by the web-page template: 'Warning as floods hit parts of UK' for the sidebar listing top stories; 'Warnings as heavy rainfall causes flooding in UK' at the top of the story. The words in online headlines are picked up by search engines and given greater prominence when rating the story than words lower down the item. So, to attract the most readers, writers need to apply the basics of SEO and make sure the key words in the story are in the headline. Tabloid puns don't help.

> **Headlines . . . need a sense of urgency. They need to be brief and punchy.**

Broadcast headlines need to make sense too. They also need a sense of urgency. They need to be brief and punchy. So they are often written in the present tense.

The government is urging GPs to improve their service to patients by keeping their surgeries open for longer.

A teenage girl is in hospital after being repeatedly stabbed at school.

Shorter bulletins may not have headlines at all. Longer programmes will have headline sequences that are as long as some radio stations' news summaries. They serve as a hard sell for what's to follow. Here are the headlines from a ten-minute Radio Four weekend summary:

A powerful earthquake has struck off the coast of Chile. More than 70 people have been killed. A tsunami warning has been issued across the Pacific.

The Conservatives have set out the themes on which they'll fight the general election. But activists meeting in Brighton will be told the path ahead won't be easy.

In sport, the Premier League leaders Chelsea are in action against Manchester City but the match began with a public snub for their captain John Terry.

Here's Sky News from later the same day:

A massive earthquake in Chile has left at least 122 people dead, destroying buildings and roads and cutting off power. Several other South American countries are now on tsunami watch.

George Osborne's blamed Gordon Brown for Britain's economic woes. He told the Conservatives' spring conference that the country cannot afford another five years of Labour.

Fabio Capello's told Sky News today that Wayne Bridge could still play for England in the World Cup. Bridge made it clear he's not ready to forgive John Terry in a deliberate snub ahead of Manchester City's match against Chelsea today.

And here's an example of a headline sequence from BBC TV News in 2005, suggesting that sports news can and should be given – on merit – the same treatment as hard news:

After the best series ever, England's cricketers regain the Ashes – for the first time in eighteen years.

A superb century from Kevin Pietersen wrecks Australia's chances on the final day of the fifth test.

We'll have the full story of the day's play and the celebrations at the Oval.

Also tonight, after the violence in Belfast local leaders are told to back the security forces.

In Niger, food is still not getting through to many of those who need it.

Motorists are told not to panic buy at the petrol pumps.

And President Bush in the centre of New Orleans, on the day one of his top officials resigns.

> **Powerful actuality and punchy interview clips should be included in headline sequences to add impact.**

Powerful actuality and punchy interview clips should be included in headline sequences to add impact. An up-sound of a key interview or announcement creates drama and can improve the rhythm of a sequence. Many headline sequences are backed by music and punctuated with sound effects, notably the signature 'bongs' of Big Ben on ITV News and David Lowe's distinctive, pulsating BBC News theme (based on the Radio Four pips). But the music always comes second to the words.

Remember

- Headlines need a sense of urgency
- Online headlines need to tell the story
- Search engine optimisation should be applied to any web headline
- Be brief and punchy
- Use actuality to add impact

Closing heads

Many programmes close with headlines. They are a summary of the day's top stories, and may be written in a different style from the opening heads. The purpose is to summarise the news, not to tease. Similar sequences occur in the middle of longer programmes, perhaps after an ad break. Here's BBC Radio Four news from the day of that Chilean earthquake in 2010.

One of the strongest earthquakes ever recorded has struck Chile, killing more than a hundred people. The quake has set off tsunamis which pose a threat to communities across a vast expanse of the Pacific Ocean.

The Conservative Party has set out the themes on which it will fight the general election. David Cameron says the party offers real change for Britain.

Remember

- Closing heads inform rather than tease
- They should summarise the whole of the story

The menu

A headline sequence is known as a menu – it tells what is on offer and whets the appetite. The example above from the day England regained the Ashes was followed by two regional headlines. Viewers would be in little doubt they were to get comprehensive coverage of the cricket story – but not at the expense of the international or local news agenda. That didn't stop some viewers complaining to the BBC's *NewsWatch* programme that the cricket was given too much prominence. And you may agree, given that England did it again in 2009, and 2011. But the 2005 win *was* the first in 18 years.

A CLOSER LOOK

SEARCH ENGINE OPTIMISATION – WHY HEADLINES ARE EVEN MORE IMPORTANT IN THE DIGITAL AGE

Video on demand means viewers can choose their own news agenda to suit their interests. You might assume headlines are no longer important, and that they are a hangover from newspapers and traditional media. Perhaps you consider they are only important to broadcasters working on traditional 'appointment to view' bulletins, and on rolling news. Think again.

Headlines have never been more important. Vin Ray, founding head of the BBC's College of Journalism, says headline writing skills are at a greater premium than ever before. That's because it is the headline – summarising the story – that determines what people will watch. The headline is the only thing many viewers of interactive digital TV or news websites will see. They need to appeal to 'scanners' – people scanning the web in search of interesting content. Just as key words determine the web content that appears on an Internet search, the words in headlines determine which stories are sent to viewers using automated news feeds on phones and computers. When we're using mobile media, the displays are so small that lists of headlines determine what we watch and read.

So news writers need to remember the principles of search engine optimisation (SEO). It's a cumbersome phrase for making the most of search engines – ensuring Google and the like deliver eyeballs to your site rather than others. SEO is a useful revenue stream for Internet marketing companies: journalists need to know how to do it for themselves. In headlines, that means using the key words that will be picked up by people searching for your story. Don't let the Web template tempt you into using abbreviations, nicknames and short forms that might not be entered into a search by a potential reader. If it's a story about Manchester United then 'Manchester United', 'Man Utd' or 'Man U' will yield the right result; 'Reds' or 'Red Devils' might not.

Nobody will access the finest content in the world if the headlines that lead to it are not compelling.

The buzz phrase for successful interactive operations used to be that 'content is king'. But there's plenty of good content around and what news organisations are fighting over are audiences. Nobody will access the finest content in the world if the headlines that lead to it are not compelling – and picked up by the search engines.

Intros and outros

Hooking the listener

The introduction to a story is known as an *intro*. That's an abbreviation well known in print newsrooms and to reporters writing online copy. It may be called an *intro* or a *link* in UK TV newsrooms. Americans prefer to call it the *lead*. In radio, the words that introduce an item may be known as a *cue*.

Whatever you call it, the idea of an intro is to hook the viewer or listener. And as any angler will tell you, that's the hardest part of the game. The best way to tell a story is almost always to give the main facts first. But how you do it can vary. The intro might be a dramatic or exciting sentence in its own right. It could include a telling quote, an amazing statistic or a witty turn of phrase.

Here's the lead to ITV News' 10.30 pm programme in February 2006:

Forget the Great Train Robbery. Forget the Northern Bank in Belfast. Britain's biggest ever robbery took place in the early hours of this morning in Kent. Sources have told ITV News tonight that as much as 40 million pounds in bank notes was taken. A security manager and his family were abducted by men pretending to be police officers. They told them unless they co-operated their lives would be in danger. Tonight the man's employer Securitas said it was a brutal crime. Our reporter Harry Smith is live in Tonbridge tonight. Harry . . .

The first sentence can be as short as those above, but should not be more than 20 or at the outside 30 words long. People speak at an average of three words per second (a useful guide when calculating the length of your script). So 20–30 words is roughly between seven and ten seconds – a comfortable time span for the listener to take in your meaning.

Here's an example from BBC Radio Four:

The American Secretary of State Hillary Clinton has arrived in Afghanistan on a surprise visit. (15 words)

This addresses the questions *who, what* and *where* and the use of the word 'surprise' tells you it was unexpected, and therefore newsworthy. Here's another intro from an earlier edition of the *Today* programme. It's longer because the story is more complicated:

The Health Secretary, Patricia Hewitt, is calling for GPs to do more to meet local demands – if necessary by extending surgery hours into the evenings and weekends. (27 words)

Again the *who* and *what* questions have been answered. We also know *how* GPs are expected to meet local demands.

Sometimes the content of two stories is connected. The lead will draw them together. This is known as an *umbrella* lead because it covers more than one story.

Michael Brown, the official in charge of organising the response to Hurricane Katrina, has resigned tonight. Mr Brown has come under severe criticism for his performance, and President Bush has now acknowledged that mistakes were made.

As the recovery work goes on in New Orleans, 45 bodies have been found in a hospital there. Reports suggest that the bodies were those of some of the hospital's patients.

(BBC TV News)

The stories about an official's resignation and the discovery of bodies in a hospital are both aspects of the aftermath of the hurricane. You might want to consider whether the political angle is more important than the hospital deaths. How might the story have been written if you judged the deaths more significant?

When a cue or link introduces a package, the cue should be written first. The information in the package then flows from what the presenter has said. *Never* repeat the information from a link in the opening line of a package. It sounds clumsy, wastes time and makes the audience think the reporter hasn't been listening to what has just been said. The reality is, of course, that the package was most likely pre-recorded, and the reporter probably wrote the link for the presenter to read. The reporter has made himself sound foolish. In larger newsrooms, the correspondent in the field will have suggested material for the cue and left it to a producer back at base to write. It's important they liaise to avoid repetition.

> *Never* **repeat the information from a link in the opening line of a package.**

When writing your story, never raise questions that can't be answered. If in doubt, check it out. If still in doubt, leave it out.

Remember

- Hook the listener
- Write the intro first
- Include only the vital facts – cut out the merely interesting
- Never repeat information from the link at the top of a package

The pay-off

The last words of a package or programme are important. They're your final chance to make an impact – the last impression. It is weak to close a report without a pay-off. Tagging a standard out cue (SOC, e.g. 'Gary Hudson, BBC News, Birmingham') on to the last interview clip or piece of actuality is lazy. Ending on an interview – unless it is a particularly dramatic and punchy clip – rarely works, and it may leave the final say to one party in an otherwise balanced story.

How a story ends is as important as how it begins.

Most newspaper reports are not read in full. In the traditional inverted pyramid, less important information comes lower down the story and is often ignored. But the broadcaster wants the listener to keep listening. So, how a story ends is as important as how it begins.

The well-crafted pay-off is an opportunity to tie up loose ends, to summarise, or to predict future developments. Try to look forward without speculating or being bland. Variations of 'What happens next remains to be seen' or 'This story will run and run' aren't good enough.

Possibly the laziest example of any of this occurred in a BBC *Midlands Today* report about a metal sculptor, Len Clatworthy. Len was asked, towards the end of a lengthy feature, about his future plans. His reply was a non-committal 'Who knows'. The reporter provided a pay-off (mainly because the editor had recently issued an edict insisting that reports should not end on interviews). The reporter's words: 'Len Clatworthy, a man with an uncertain future. Who knows what the future holds? Certainly not Len himself.'

Remember

- A pay-off can summarise the story
- It can tie up loose ends
- It can project forward
- Avoid obvious or bland statements
- It's the last thing the listener hears, so make sure it has impact

---

TIP BOX

THE INVERTED PYRAMID AND THE CHRISTMAS TREE

Boris Johnson, then a Conservative MP and later Mayor of London, was accused in 2004 by a posse of tabloid reporters of having an affair. He told them their stories were an 'inverted pyramid of piffle'. He'd borrowed a phrase from the teaching of journalism. Johnson is a journalist; he was the editor of the *Spectator* at the time. But most readers who saw the comment in the next day's papers would have been mystified by the phrase.

In conventional newspaper writing, the facts are organised in order of importance. Less vital information comes last so the sub-editor can cut the story from the bottom to fit the page. This construction is known as an inverted triangle or pyramid. It works for newspapers because, as we've heard, people often don't reach the end of a story before moving on to something else in the paper. It doesn't matter if the sub cuts out the summarising paragraph at the bottom of the story. But broadcasters have to begin *and* end well to hold the audience's attention throughout a programme.

So let's suggest another model. What about a Christmas tree? Not a luxuriant Norwegian spruce but the type a child would draw – a simple diagrammatic representation.

Think of the intro as the top of the tree. If it's bright enough you can put a star on it! Below the intro the branches flare out and then there's another narrow bit. This is the second place you have to put emphasis, the second opportunity to grab the audience. It's the start of the package or edited report.

In radio, a package needs to start with powerful actuality, an audio clip or a telling introductory phrase in the voice-over. In television, it would be a strong opening picture, perhaps with dramatic actuality sound.

Here the Christmas tree broadens to a wider base. This is where your story fills out.

And the Christmas tree needs a solid base. That's your pay-off or outro – the final summarising thought or phrase that rounds up the item or projects the story forward.

Remember, it's one Christmas tree. The link and the report, the top and the branches, are part of the same story. Nothing grates on the listener quite as much as hearing the same information repeated. We've all heard this sort of thing:

intro or cue

start of package

Newsreader: Three people have been injured in a fire at a house in the Llandaff area of Cardiff. It broke out in the early hours of this morning. Jeffrey Walsh has the details.

Reporter: The fire broke out in the early hours at a house in the Llandaff area. Three people were injured . . .

sound bite

The Sky Sports News writing style guide sums it up well, taking into account that the intro may be written by newsroom subs while the reporter is preparing their script on location:

link

Don't give the whole story away in the intro – save something for the reporter. Ensure that the last line of the link is different to the opening line of the package. Reporters should think what the top line of the intro is likely to be and avoid that as their top line.

soundbite

pay-off

When you are writing your own intro, write it first. The rest of the report follows from it. If it's a feature item, you may even be able to write your cue before you leave the newsroom. It saves time when you file your report or edit your package later.

The Christmas tree structure of broadcast stories

Almost all of what we've learned so far applies across the whole range of broadcast output. Wherever the spoken word is the means of communicating – that's all TV and radio, and much online content – the rules of good conversational English apply. Both written and spoken content demand well-structured story-telling. And it's essential to be concise, with no wasted words. Let's look now at how this advice can be applied to specific contexts.

APPLYING THE ADVICE

Sports reporting

If ever there was an area where the conventions of good news writing seem to be in danger of falling into misuse it is sports reporting. Sport is hugely important to audiences. Watching and playing sport are major sectors of the leisure industry. Sport is entertainment as well as information. Sports reporters tell people what they *want* to know rather than what they *need* to know. So it's up to us to tell them to the best of our journalistic ability. That means avoiding jargon and cliché just as we would in a well-crafted news report.

Some sports reporters believe there is a language specific to their trade, and which sports fans expect. The argument goes that we are giving the fans what they want. The fact that half the audience switches off mentally as soon as they hear that 'Rooney made no mistake from the spot' doesn't occur to them. They're proud to be hacks, and it's probably a long time since they consulted a dictionary, which would point out that a hack is 'a literary or journalistic drudge'.

There could be an argument made, though it would be a pretty poor one, that the only people who read the sports pages of newspapers are sports fans, so it is perfectly acceptable to

The sports reporter has to speak to some people who switched on to learn about world events and others waiting for the weather report.

use sporting clichés in newspaper copy. But news broadcasting must be different. Mainly because it is *broad*casting not *narrow*casting. We are not talking to narrow interest groups. We are addressing a wide audience. Just as the political correspondent has to make politics relevant to people who say they are not interested in politics, the sports reporter has to speak to some people who switched on to learn about the latest world events and others who are waiting for the weather report.

Even though its audience is probably made up exclusively of sports fans, Sky Sports News, the most watched all-sports channel in the UK, has no time for peddlers of cliché. Its style guide is quite specific. It has a list of phrases it doesn't want to hear. Among the banned expressions:

- denied by the woodwork
- writing on the wall
- history was made
- gifted them a goal
- marching orders
- outfit – as in Hungarian outfit/Spanish outfit etc.
- just what the doctor ordered
- on the stroke of
- nothing more than a consolation
- international duty
- winning ways
- have it all to do
- top flight
- but they hadn't read the script – and other variations on the theme
- unveil – statues and plaques are unveiled – managers are appointed
- headed home
- long-range effort.

And of course:

- no mistake from the spot.

Audiences want lively content, not dull and predictable phrases.

Sky Sports News bans these phrases because scripts without clichés are more likely to engage audiences: they want lively content, not dull and predictable phrases.

Football Lexicon by John Leigh and David Woodhouse (2004, Abbey Books) is a hugely entertaining warning against resorting to phrases so hackneyed that these academics put them in their book. It's the first alphabetical glossary of the language of football. The authors pass no judgement but their analysis pokes gentle fun. Here's their entry for the simple word *effort*:

Effort: Perhaps surprisingly, an *effort* can also be a goal: 'Notts County have pulled one back, another *effort* from McSwegan.' But more typically, when a goal fails to materialise, an *effort* will be described as long range or speculative.

In a recommendation of the book in his column in the West Bromwich Albion matchday programme, TV football presenter Adrian Chiles asked:

'Why is a successful penalty taker always said to have "made no mistake"? Nowhere else in sport, or indeed life, are you said to have "made no mistake" when you accomplish something relatively straightforward: "Well done for paying the gas bill, darling, you made no mistake there."'

The authors of *Football Lexicon* sum up the attitude of fans to the way players speak:

'The clichés and set phrases – sick as a parrot, over the moon, game of two halves – to which players and managers seem to turn at every juncture have indeed been echoed so gleefully and frequently by the public that the mockery of these commonplaces has itself become commonplace.'

'Sick as a parrot' and 'over the moon' have been parodied to extinction. But 'game of two halves' enjoyed a form of post-modern revival in 2005, when Liverpool came from three down at half-time to win the Champions League Final.

Remember

- Address the whole audience
- Try to broaden your audience
- Avoid clichés

Writing for radio

It's a cliché beloved of people who've worked all their lives in radio that it's a superior medium to television because the pictures are better. Think about it. Every picture conjured up by a radio script exists in the mind of the listener. It's their personal version of events. The film version of a beloved novel fills fans of the novel with dread. Will the hero be as attractive as I've imagined him? Will the heroine be as feisty and gorgeous? Will the locations match those in my imagination? The 2005 film remake of *Pride and Prejudice* drew comparisons not only with the novel but with the earlier TV version. When J.K. Rowling told Harry Potter fans 'That's my Hogwarts' they were reassured that the school they saw in the films was what the author had in mind.

So, description is the key to evocative radio scripts.

Introducing audio

Voice reports and interview clips brighten radio bulletins. They deserve better than predictable introductions. The tried and tested 'Laurence Lee reports' should not be overused. 'From Moscow, here's our correspondent Laurence Lee' is similarly unimaginative. Try to vary it.

'Laurence Lee explains.'

'Laurence Lee has been following the story.'

'Laurence Lee has the background.'

'. . . as Laurence Lee, who's been following the story, now explains.'

Similarly, you can vary the way you introduce audio clips in bulletins or within reports. In radio, the listener needs to know **who's** speaking. Sometimes announcing the name will be enough. 'Here's the rail workers' union leader, Bob Crow' or simply 'RMT union boss, Bob Crow'.

> **It is almost always essential on radio to introduce someone by name before we hear them speak.**

There's never a need to include your recorded question at the start of an interview clip. Cut out the question, and write into the clip. 'Mr Crow was angry at the suggestion that his members are unwilling to support him . . .' 'Why was Mr Crow unhappy?' 'So what made the union leader so upset?' 'Mr Crow rounded on his critics . . .' With so many options, 'I spoke to Bob Crow and asked him . . .' is unimaginative and unacceptable. Avoid 'I spoke to' unless you want to sound amateurish.

Pick up on a previous clip to introduce the next one. 'While the union leader was in a combative mood, his counterpart at the train company was more reserved . . .'

While it is usually best in a radio bulletin to introduce a speaker before we hear them, it's possible in a longer feature to use a short clip before the speaker's identity is revealed. The clip can then continue.

'I absolutely refute that view.' **Conservative spokesman Andrew Mitchell.** *'We believe the government has . . .'*

Remember

- Introduce a speaker before you hear them
- Cut out your question before an interview clip
- Write into the clip
- Don't say 'I spoke to . . .'

Writing for television

Writing for television follows the same broad guidelines as writing for radio – good conversational English is paramount. But the added dimension of pictures requires changes to vocabulary and syntax – the grammatical structure of your sentences.

Write captions rather than narrative sentences – but captions that move the story along.

The biggest difference between TV and radio is that there is much less need in television to be descriptive. Viewers don't need a description of what they can see on screen. The worst television scripts fail because the words don't fit the pictures, but it is almost as great a mistake to describe what viewers can see for themselves.

Sometimes 'writing' for television means not writing at all. Pictures with natural sound – the sound recorded at the scene – may be more effective in helping tell a story than the same pictures with a voice-over. Actuality gives viewers a sense of authenticity, of 'being there'.

Television interviewees do not have to be named in a script before they speak. That is a radio technique. An on-screen caption can supply the name and a brief description of the speaker.

> Actuality gives viewers a sense of authenticity, of 'being there'. Television interviewees do not have to be named in a script before they speak. That is a radio technique.

Here are some guidelines:

- Let the pictures tell the story
- Use as few words as possible to deliver the information
- Think of the script as a series of captions
- Make the words fit the pictures, but . . .
- Don't describe what people can see for themselves
- Allow the pictures to 'breathe' using natural sound
- Don't name interviewees to introduce them – use captions
- Never use 'wallpaper', i.e. pictures that are simply there to cover the narrator's words. This isn't proper television; it's radio with pictures.

Read your script – out loud – for accuracy and ease of delivery. Do so without looking at the pictures. Errors can creep into scripts simply because the writer is concentrating on making the words fit the pictures.

Remember

- If in doubt, check it out
- If still in doubt, leave it out

TIP BOX

NEWSWRITING FOR BROADCAST – SOME DOS AND DON'TS

What do I want to say?
How can I say it naturally?

DOs
- Remember the rules of story telling: 'who, what, where, when, why and how'
- Write clear, concise sentences
- Use short rather than long words
- Start with the most important/most recent fact(s) of the story
- Make sure all the vital points are included
- Follow a narrative thread (*beginning, middle, end*)
- Stick to the facts
- Avoid unnecessary adjectives
- Avoid clichés
- Avoid repetition
- Avoid confusion
- Keep sentence structure simple
- Use active – not passive – sentences whenever possible
- Cut out any words that can be cut out
- Check the meaning of words
- Check facts
- While doing all this, avoid complicated, compound sentences with too many subordinate clauses, dangling participles, conjunctions and other bits added to them, just to make them sound more important, while still trying to keep to the sense of what you are trying to write, notwithstanding the difficulty of maintaining the audience's interest despite your periphrasis and obfuscation!
- Learn to *edit yourself* – read out loud what you have written to ensure it makes sense
- Count the words (three to a second) to check how long your piece is.

DON'Ts
- Use jargon or journalese
- Use clichés
- Use foreign words or phrases when there is an everyday English equivalent
- Use words you don't understand
- Write sentences that are too long or too complicated to understand on first hearing
- Invent or assume anything
- Use lengthy direct quotes (reported speech, e.g. *He said: 'I am not happy being here because I don't like being told what to do by that rascal Hudson.'*)
- Offer opinions by inserting unnecessary adverbs (e.g. *Luckily, they escaped from the fire . . . Fortunately, a local postman spotted smoke . . .*)
- Use unnecessary adjectives
- Use words such as 'stated' or 'commented' or phrases like 'expressed the opinion that' when the simple word 'said' will do instead
- Hype up the story – just stick to the facts
- Write a story you don't understand. If you don't understand it, how can you expect the audience to?

A CLOSER LOOK

THE ART OF WRITING 'SLIGHTLY OFF THE PICTURES'

The following passage is not from a textbook. It is from a blockbuster novel, but is the best description we have read of the art of writing a television news script.

It was a specialist art form, difficult to learn, and some in television news never quite succeeded. Even among professional writers the talent did not receive the recognition it deserved, because the words were written to accompany pictures and seldom read well alone.

The trick . . . was not to describe the pictures. A television viewer would be seeing . . . what was happening on the screen and did not need verbal description. Yet the spoken words must not be so far removed from the pictures as to split the viewer's consciousness. It was a literary balancing act, much of it instinctive.

Something else TV news people recognised: the best news writing was not in real sentences and paragraphs. Fragments of sentences worked better.

Extract from *The Evening News* by Arthur Hailey (1990)

Writing for online

Online writing is the only time broadcast journalists write to be read rather than heard. But writing news online can follow the same guidelines as writing a broadcast script. Online journalism definitely does not have to be written in newspaper style.

But it is not good enough to simply upload your broadcast scripts onto the Web. Otherwise you get this, from Staffordshire-based Signal Radio's website:

> The search is on for a mum after a baby boy was dumped on a Staffordshire doorstep.

It is not good enough to simply upload your broadcast scripts onto the web.

> The little boy, thought to be three weeks old was left at a house in Post Office Lane in Rugeley (pronounced Rouge . . . lee).

Apart from anything else, it begs the question: why don't Signal Radio's journalists know how to pronounce the name of Rugeley, a town in Staffordshire?

Despite the practice of some commercial local radio stations, uploading scripts at the touch of a computer key, the full range of online skills for writers includes preparing headlines, single paragraph summaries, longer stories, and cross-heads. There are also picture captions to write and interactive boxes and hyperlinks to insert.

Online journalists learn the technical skills to import still pictures, graphics, audio and video, and the art of writing summaries to differing lengths to fit the templates on content management systems.

The BBC pioneered online news in the UK. Its sites are the most visited news websites in the world, and it is the UK's biggest employer of online journalistic talent. A clear house style has developed, which would-be online journalists need to learn.

But the rules about grabbing an audience are the same as for all forms of broadcasting. Hugh Berlyn, Editor of BBC News Interactive, English Regions, sums it up: 'Content is king. If you haven't got a fresh, interactive, easy-to-use site, the punters will just go away.'

Headlines

Online headlines differ from newspaper headlines, because big, bold typefaces won't attract attention to a web page; clever use of search engine optimisation will. Instead the number of characters (or letters and spaces) is limited by the font size within the content management template rather than the need for a huge font to grab attention.

The number of letters available is not as restrictive as in newspaper layout. You don't need to use journalese words such as *probe*, *clash* and *row* to fit the length of the line. Online writing does not have to follow a tabloid style.

But there are limits imposed by the page template. In the BBC system, a grey box appears on screen and writers have to tell the story in four paragraphs within this box. This is the version sent to mobile phones. Extra information can be added outside the box for the online version. Headlines used to have to be written to a length of 31 to 33 characters, to fit the Ceefax text pages on television. That limit still applies to online headlines.

Summaries

It is common to have a brief summary of the story on the front page of a website. The BBC has title pages – or index pages – for each of its local news sites. A one-paragraph (or par) summary of the story appears underneath the headline. The BBC style is to write the summary in the present tense. This version also appears on digital radio scrolling text and on BBC 'big screens' around the country.

The four-par generation

Most stories on BBC sites are written in just four paragraphs. All but the biggest stories will have a maximum of 250 words. Those four pars also appear on digital text and mobile phones.

Hugh Berlyn says:

> **Hugh Berlyn: 'We are breeding a four-par generation. Stories need to be told in a maximum of four pars. We as journalists have to live with that or die.'**

'Young people today don't watch traditional news bulletins or sit and read long newspaper articles as their parents did. They are reluctant even to scroll down text on a web page. All our indications suggest our users read the top four paragraphs. Only if they are thoroughly engaged will they read much more. We are breeding a *four-par generation*. Stories need to be told in a maximum of four pars. We as journalists have to live with that or die.'

Longer stories can be used, but they will be subdivided by newspaper-style *cross-heads*, one or two words in bold splitting up the text.

Maurice Blisson, a veteran freelance journalist who's written for network and regional news as well as BBC online, says:

'You put in cross-heads just like a newspaper after every four pars or so. You rarely write more than eight pars, though you might for a lengthy court case. The cross-head is a visual thing. You can also liven it up by putting a *quotebox* in. There's a place on the template to put the quote and another place for the name and it does it automatically.'

He sums up the tone of his online work:

'I write in a fairly light newspaper style. I think of it as traditional *Daily Express* or *Daily Mirror* style without the clichés and the journalese. There are specific things you have to do. You have to tell the story in the first four paragraphs for the text services. You must fit your facts and your location into those four pars. There's a template that tells you if you're going to bust.'

Maurice concedes that a lot of online work is re-versioning other people's original material: 'It's 95 per cent re-hashing what others have written.'

When those others are broadcast journalists more used to writing for radio, there can be a lot of work to do. Hugh Berlyn explains:

'We're definitely looking for writing skills. Newspaper journalists have those skills. People from local radio take longer to retrain. Spelling is obviously important, but a lot of people trained in radio don't think it matters, for obvious reasons.'

Sky News Interactive uses stories of between eight and 12 paragraphs, usually with three headlines (for different pages on the site) and two pictures. Their red-button Sky News Active service (on satellite TV) was launched with ten text sections and eight mini video screens. Now Sky News online offers a short summary bulletin alongside dozens of video stories and the opportunity to watch the rolling TV news channel.

Writing online copy means ignoring those guidelines about broadcast writing that relate to the spoken word, but not the principles of concise and accurate use of English.

Remember

- Online writing has to be read not spoken
- Check spellings
- Don't use contractions such as *isn't, aren't, hasn't, don't*
- Direct quotes *can* be used online – perhaps in a separate box
- Use graphics to explain numbers

Writing for social networks and SMS

Text (SMS) news flashes to mobile phones have become one of the most popular ways for people to keep up with the latest news. They are a quick way to find out what's happening so you can watch fuller coverage later, without breaking into what you are doing.

Writing text flashes is a tight journalistic discipline, because you don't want to bombard subscribers with more information than they want. Adam Harding, Deputy Editor of Sky News Interactive, summed up the writing style in 2005: 'One story. One sentence. One chance to get it right. 140 characters maximum.' Since those comments, that character limit has become even more significant – thanks to Twitter.

Most major news organisations promote their core services through social networking sites. A TV programme or radio show might have its own pages on sites such as Facebook, and there are hundreds of broadcast outlets on Twitter, sending news flashes in fewer than 140 characters and TinyURL links to millions of potential viewers and listeners.

Look at today's top stories online. Decide which, if any, would be worth a news flash to mobile phones. Now try writing those stories in fewer than 140 characters. It's not easy.

WRITING FOR CHILDREN

Writing for children is a particular skill. The BBC's *Newsround* is targeted at nine-year-olds. Lizo Mzimba is second only to John Craven as the programme's longest-serving presenter. He says they cover two types of story – things that children are interested in, and things they might not be interested in at first glance, but really ought to know about.

'It's all about language and presentation. We'd use simple, straightforward language and put everything into context. We'd never talk about the Middle East Peace Process, but we would explain what's happening now and what has been happening for more than 50 years, and what's likely to happen in the future.'

The rule about knowing your audience is rarely more important than when addressing this group of viewers. 'Kids are interested in entertainment (Harry Potter and that sort of thing), sport, mostly, and they're interested in the environment. They're worried about the planet and what we're doing to it.'

Mzimba says nine-year-olds will never say they're interested in politics:

'But if you say to a nine-year-old: "How big is your class in school? Is it too big?" or "Are you interested in the threat to the planet from what people call global-warming?" a lot of that's related to politics.

'We'd never start a story: "The government has issued a White Paper on education," but we would say: "Schools are being offered millions of pounds to improve the standard of education."'

He says you have to be reassuring and honest with children:

'Children get worried after a terrorist attack. You can't say: "No, don't worry. There won't be any more." But you can say: "The police and security services are working very hard to make sure things like this don't happen again." You have to be honest with children.'

Explaining 'adult' news to children is a challenge. Done well, it is one of the most satisfying jobs in journalism. Mzimba told the authors, shortly before leaving *Newsround* to become the BBC's Entertainment Correspondent: 'We get a lot of mail from adults saying *Newsround* is the only news programme they really understand.'

CONCLUSION

Once you've read this chapter, you should have an understanding of the guiding principles of good broadcast writing. You will be aware of the range of writing skills you may need in your career to produce everything from snappy radio headlines to online copy.

The only way to become fast and fluent as a writer is to practise. If you're not working in a newsroom yet (or on a course that involves a lot of writing every day), do it in your spare time. Take a newspaper and re-write the stories in it for broadcast. That is an easy way to start because the key news points should already have been picked out for you. Then go online, or better still out into the community where you live, and try to find original stories to write.

Much of broadcast journalism involves teamwork. Most writing does not. Writing well is one of the most satisfying aspects of the job because what you create is all your own work. Learn to enjoy it.

FURTHER READING

Boyd, Andrew, Stewart, Peter and Alexander, Ray (2008) *Broadcast Journalism: Techniques of Radio and Television News*, Oxford: Focal Press.

Ford, Simon (2006) *Writing News for Local Radio*, Nottingham: Booklaw. A comprehensive look at the art from an experienced BBC practitioner.

Hicks, Wynford (1998) *English for Journalists*, Oxford: Routledge. A clear and accessible guide to grammar and usage in all types of journalism.

Hicks, Wynford, with Sally Adams and Harriett Gilbert (1999) *Writing for Journalists*, Oxford: Routledge. One of the definitive works on writing for all journalists, although aimed at print specialists.

Humphrys, John (2005) *Lost for Words: The Mangling and Manipulating of the English Language*, London: Hodder & Stoughton.

Thompson, Rick (2011) *Writing for Broadcast Journalists*, second edition, Oxford: Routledge. Lively, often witty and always definitive – an invaluable guide.

Webb, Nicholas (2005) *The Dictionary of Bullshit*, London: Robson Books.

WEB LINKS

www.bbc.co.uk/journalism/skills/writing A wealth of BBC training resources, including advice from BBC journalists, workshops and online exercises.

CHAPTER SIX
LOCATION REPORTING AND PRODUCTION

In this chapter, we'll look at:

- The best working practices for different stories and situations.
- Health and safety.
- Preparation *before* you leave the newsroom.
- Radio, TV and online reporting.
- Dealing with user-generated content (witnesses' pictures and video).
- The legal and ethical guidelines for journalists on location.

GETTING out and about and meeting people are among the greatest joys of being a reporter. Foreign correspondents speak of the thrill of being eyewitnesses to history. But even a murky morning outside Middlesbrough magistrates' court beats being stuck at a desk in front of a computer screen. The best reporters prefer being out on a story to the glamour and big salaries of presenting in the studio, or climbing the greasy pole of management.

Military strategists will tell you that no plan survives contact with the enemy. The same is true of journalism. So, who are our enemies? We're not talking about those (often-powerful) people who may have good reason – in their own terms – for not wanting your story broadcast. Very few of them will take to the streets to prevent you doing your job; they're more likely to try taking out an injunction. We're talking about, to quote Harold Macmillan: 'Events, dear boy, events.' Those events – beyond your control – include hanging around in the cold and wet for hours on end, the mic going dead, or the satellite link going down; and when it comes to children and animals, the old actors' adage applies – you might as well raise the white flag.

This chapter examines the practical considerations of news gathering in the field.

THE BEST WORKING PRACTICES

Be prepared

When Robert Baden Powell wrote *Scouting for Boys* in 1908, there was no such thing as broadcast journalism. But the motto 'Be Prepared' could have been written for us. There's no substitute for preparation. That means research and forward planning. A *recce* (short for reconnaissance) or site visit lets you work out where you should position your microphones and cameras. It helps you find locations for the *pieces-to-camera* or *stand-ups* by a reporter. Sometimes there will be a *pre-shoot*, a chance to shoot material that helps tell the story before the day on which it is broadcast. If you are covering an awards ceremony, for example, you might want to film the nominees at home or at work. You would not be able to do that on the day of the ceremony itself, because they will be busy getting ready for and travelling to the event.

You will almost certainly want to talk to potential interviewees on the phone before visiting them. You can check their availability, and what they are likely to say, and explain what the story involves. Seeking written permissions, printing off location maps and drawing up realistic shooting schedules are all part of good newsroom practice on diary stories. For breaking news, you might have to forget all of these and rely on one thing – *experience*. And not just your own.

News gathering is a team effort. The experience of the whole team is brought to bear on big stories – editors, producers and reporters will discuss the way to cover a breaking event, and each will try to achieve the best results possible within the organisation's capabilities and budget. A small radio station with limited resources has to make compromises on big stories; staff find themselves working hard for long hours.

You can tap into expertise on any story. Never be afraid to ask older colleagues how they have covered similar stories in the past. It may seem a surprising admission by people dealing with what is new and often surprising (otherwise it wouldn't be news), but most journalists will agree there's no such thing as a new story.

> **Never be afraid to ask older colleagues how they have covered similar stories in the past.**

There have been natural disasters, terrorist attacks, political scandals and almost every imaginable form of criminal activity before – and people who have covered those stories. This is not a recipe for formulaic or predictable reporting. But it is a reminder that there is no point in reinventing the wheel, if you'll excuse the cliché.

Newsroom meetings

Most newsrooms will have at least one meeting a day – usually at the earliest opportunity in the morning after most staff have come on duty. The morning meeting sets the agenda for the day. The stories that are likely to be covered are known as the *prospects*. This will include diary items and breaking stories to which reporters and producers have yet to be assigned. In a well-staffed newsroom, some reporters will be assigned researching duties, on the understanding that, if new stories break during the day, they are available to go on the road. They are in 'coiled spring' mode – waiting to be unleashed on 'the big one'.

There will also be *forward planning* meetings in which story ideas for the future will be discussed. These might include diary stories, new developments in *running stories*, embargoed material and ongoing investigations. Planning desks are at the heart of all successful newsrooms. On a 'quiet' or 'slow' news day, almost all the bulletin content will be a result of their efforts. Planners fix technical facilities and feed points, transport and accommodation, and arrange any special passes that are needed to cover events.

See Workshops and Exercises

The main bulletins on terrestrial TV and longer, speech-based radio programmes will also have *production meetings* in which editorial and technical staff discuss the logistics of getting the programme on air. These meetings are important in providing an operational framework, but, inevitably, on most days the running order will change several times as new stories break and some of those that looked likely to make it to the bulletin fall by the wayside. Often the running order changes while the programme is on air. Stories break, items overrun, edited packages miss their feed time, live links go down. Anything can happen in the next half hour – and probably will.

In the midst of all this you, the reporter or producer, are planning to go out and cover your story. And you know that there's a more than even chance that something will go wrong. So, how do you play the percentage game, and reduce the chances of letting down your editor, your station, your audience and yourself?

Below are some tips. Every one is based on the bitter experience of not one, but hundreds of broadcasters. Show us a broadcast journalist who denies falling prey to any of these pitfalls, and we'll show you a liar.

Everyone has a story of when they messed up. Helen Boaden is the Director of BBC News, a former controller of Radio Four, producer, presenter, reporter and executive producer in television:

'The worst thing I ever did, I was so excited about a story I drove off in my car and only halfway to the story did I realise I'd left the tape recorder behind, which, given the fact that it was radio, was a bit of a problem.'

Before you leave the newsroom

Do your research

The best way to cover any story is with more background knowledge than you are ever likely to need. Then, when you write the story, the hardest decision becomes what to leave out. Check the Internet and your cuttings library for information. Read all the newspapers. Research the station's archive. In television, find out what pictures are available on related stories. Larger broadcasters will have dedicated library services with a willing librarian to help.

> **TIP BOX**
>
> ### A NOTE ON ARCHIVING
>
> Libraries have a computerised search facility. The old principle of 'rubbish in: rubbish out' applies. When you are archiving your own material, remember that the information you provide will probably be retrieved by somebody else who doesn't know the story as intimately as you do. Label your images clearly. Cross-referencing helps.
>
> The first TV report of a murder might include pictures of the victim, the murder scene and a police press conference, with interviews. The pictures of the scene will be valuable in future reports about the case but might also be used in stories about government policing policy, crime statistics or police resources. Do the shots include the activities of scene of crime officers, police photographers, door-to-door enquiries, patrol cars, fingertip searches, plain clothes officers or incident control rooms? All could be useful. Armed police are increasingly common on Britain's streets. But it is still worth noting shots of police officers with pistols drawn or using Heckler and Koch machine guns. Be specific.

When you are archiving your own material, remember that the information you provide will probably be retrieved by somebody else who doesn't know the story as intimately as you do.

Permissions

Before you record or film at any location you need to make sure you have permission. As soon as you have a microphone or camera in your hand you are not treated as a member of the public, even though you are one. It's a shock to newcomers to the business, but you cannot always expect special treatment because you are part of the media. And you are often prevented from going to places everybody else can wander through with impunity.

Never assume – just because somebody tells you it will be OK – that you have the authority to enter private property. Private, in this case, includes public buildings such as schools and hospitals and their car parks, and places that encourage most other people to enter, such as shopping centres. You will need permission from the head teacher, the hospital's chief executive (or communications department) or the shopping centre manager respectively. It's not enough that a doctor or shopworker says you're welcome to record what's happening. It is your responsibility, not theirs, to get the proper permissions. That usually means a verbal agreement from the right person, but, if they are not likely to be around, a written note or email will help satisfy overzealous security staff.

> Never assume – just because somebody tells you it will be OK – that you have the authority to enter private property.

Here's an example of how inexperience led to two student journalists losing their exclusive video. A young mother in Stoke-on-Trent, who did not know she was pregnant, went to bed one night unaware that next morning she would have two extra children. She gave birth to twins in the family bathroom in the middle of the night. A few days later, she agreed to an exclusive interview with the two students.

The twins had been taken to a hospital's baby care unit and the mother asked a nurse if the students could film them there. The nurse agreed, so the students thought they had permission. It wasn't until they had all the footage they wanted of mother, father and the surprise arrivals that a hospital official arrived and confiscated their tape. The students lost all their footage of the babies.

Nobody has a right to take away your pictures. But if you don't have the proper permissions it's much more difficult to argue your case. On a practical note, if you are in danger of somebody wanting to take your material, have a blank tape or memory card in your pocket and practise a little sleight of hand. Camera crews in politically sensitive parts of the world do this all the time.

> There is usually no problem with recording or filming from the public highway.

There is usually no problem with recording or filming from the public highway, but you may be accused of causing an obstruction. If the police ask you to move on, there is usually no alternative but to comply. There's more on police guidelines about dealing with the media later in this chapter.

Health and safety

Health and safety considerations come into play every time you leave the newsroom. Health and safety training for reporting in the field is essential for all journalists. As a reporter or producer it is your responsibility to assess the safety of a location before you leave the newsroom, and to update that assessment as circumstances change.

Generic health and safety assessments will apply to day-to-day news assignments. Workplaces will insist on the completion of hazard assessment forms for particular high-risk situations. Some stories present obvious dangers. Journalists and technical crews will be given hostile environment training before they are sent to war zones, for example, and similar training is available for those covering demonstrations where violent disorder is likely. There are also rules to be observed every time you record or film in public locations. Cables laid in public places can be a hazard. If a passer-by trips over an unattended cable, the broadcaster is liable. If a radio reporter or camera person walking backwards to grab an interview bumps into somebody, the broadcaster is liable. If a lighting rig or a radio car gets in the way of people going about their everyday business, the broadcaster may be liable.

You have a duty of care to your station's staff too. A radio engineer in the West Country was killed when the telescopic mast of a radio car hit overhead power lines.

Nobody can predict everything that might go wrong on a location recording or shoot, but the *risk assessment forms* available in all well-ordered newsrooms cover most eventualities and repay the time spent filling them in. Completing one before you go out shows you considered the possible risks. If anything goes wrong, and you can't prove you made reasonable efforts to prevent it, you would be liable and your insurance would be invalid.

Foreign assignments often include exposure to hostile environments. So hazard assessment is vital. These can include operating in countries at war or prone to civil unrest and terrorism. Many regions have extreme levels of crime and lawlessness. This can include banditry and the kidnapping of foreign nationals, particularly those from Western nations. A responsible news organisation will also require the completion of risk assessment from its workers in places with extremes of climate or terrain. Mountains and deserts are as great a danger to the inexperienced as war zones. So is the reporting of severe floods, hurricanes, earthquakes and volcanic eruptions.

High-risk events at home, where completing a hazard assessment is essential, include riots and civil disturbance, serious public disorder, firearms incidents such as hijackings and sieges, and terrorist attacks – suspected or real. Where there's a bomb threat, or the suspicion of chemical, biological or radiological substances, exercise extreme caution.

> **One of the guiding principles of covering riots and disorder in the streets is to find a safe vantage point.**

One of the guiding principles of covering riots and disorder in the streets is to find a safe vantage point, usually above the action. For radio reporters this provides a commentary position. For TV, it is a secure camera platform. Reporters and producers may have to negotiate with householders, shopkeepers or landlords for access to an upstairs window or balcony. The reward for these delicate conversations, occasionally involving payment of a facility fee, is risk-free, quality coverage.

Remember

- News does not just happen on the day
- Forward planning is essential to broadcast journalism
- Research and set up as much of the story as you can before you go out
- Make sure you have permission to record or film
- It is almost always OK to film in the street
- Consider health and safety, and complete a risk assessment if appropriate

You are what you wear

We'll leave fashion tips to the experts (though, trust us, there will be plenty of comments about appropriate dress in Chapter 14: *Presentation*). Dressing to do the job well is about more than looking good. Sports producer Mitch Pryce, a veteran of World Cups and Champions and Premier League football for ITV and BBC, says his first piece of advice to young journalists is: 'Get a decent pair of shoes.' You'll spend a lot of time walking, and a lot of time hanging around outdoors. High heels are rarely a good idea – even for women! Comfort is all-important.

Decent waterproof clothing is a must. A warm, weatherproof jacket can be kept in the car. Make sure it's one that won't look out of place in front of a court or in the middle of a field. And when you're choosing your life-saving, and perhaps expensive, winter warmer, don't just admire yourself in the mirror. Listen too. If the fabric rustles, the sound may be picked up on a mic, and the coat will be useless for broadcasting.

Select a jacket with lots of pockets – for pens, notebooks, briefing sheets and your mobile. Female reporters may find handbags a hindrance on location.

Keep a hat handy – not necessarily to be worn on camera, but to avoid that drowned-rat look. Wellingtons are a must for muddy country lanes and fields. Fishing waders are handy if you have to cover floods. Keep them in the boot of the car along with an umbrella. If you're a TV reporter, make sure the design of your brolly is not a distraction. Company logos should be avoided (there are rules against product placement and advertising within programmes). Some programmes will provide you with an umbrella decorated with the show's own graphics. During a downpour, though, heavy raindrops may be heard on mic, sometimes even drowning out an interview or live report. You may have to put the brolly down just before you go on air.

When possible, a reporter's clothing should suit the location and the story. In the city, reporters should look businesslike. On a farm, casual country clothing is in keeping with the environment. In a war zone, helmet and flak jacket are not a question of style; they are essential for health and safety.

> **When possible, a reporter's clothing should suit the location and the story.**

Reporters are better off avoiding blatant fashion statements. It is a distraction from the news. BBC presenter Michael Buerk's comment that Oscars correspondent Rosie Millard was due an award for 'best-supporting dress' drew attention to Ms Millard's low-cut outfit rather than her news report.

If the idea of 'appropriate' dress is a little vague, then think about the clothing that will help you do the job more easily. That would obviously mean wellies or waders for floods, and a weatherproof coat for anything outdoors in winter. But it is not just a question of comfort. The way you dress can also make the job easier, because your clothes give strangers messages about you. If you want to be treated as an equal when you go to interview a business executive, wear a suit. If you are visiting an eco-warriors' protest camp, dress casually and practically, and avoid designer labels. It sometimes helps not to be seen as an 'establishment' figure; on other occasions you will want to present yourself as the very model of conventional respectability.

Know where you're going

Obvious. Yes, but if you're in the West Midlands and somebody tells you there's a fire in a street in Willenhall, where do you go? Well, Willenhall's between Walsall and Wolverhampton, isn't it? Maybe. Unless they're talking about the Willenhall in Coventry, 20 miles away.

There were riots in the streets of Wood End in the 1990s. BBC Breakfast News duly showed a map of the village of Wood End in North Warwickshire. Unfortunately, the riot was on the Wood End council estate in Coventry. It's easy to pick on Coventry (check out the pronunciation of Styvechalle and Cheylesmore if you want to know the dangers *that* city presents to broadcast journalists), but these quirks occur throughout the British Isles.

Street names will often get confused in transmission from newsdesk to reporter. Hagley Road and Hagley Street may be miles apart. One may be a main thoroughfare, the other a sidestreet. Check it out online or in an A–Z street map. Use websites such as Google maps, theaa.com for routefinder facilities. They will not only find the street, but tell you how to get there.

Satellite navigation is a great tool if you can afford it. But so is common sense. On entering a strange town, stop at a service station to buy a local street map. Keep maps of places you

> **Satellite navigation is a great tool if you can afford it. But so is common sense.**

regularly visit in the car. And if you are travelling on a strange road in what might be the wrong direction, remember that the sun rises in the east and sets in the west. At night you can find north by locating the Pole Star from the Plough constellation. If it's cloudy, stop and ask for directions. If it's raining and nobody's on the streets, try petrol stations, pubs or shops.

Be punctual

'Be punctual, be polite and ask questions' – that's the advice newspaper feature writer and interviewer Lynn Barber offers beginner journalists in Tony Harcup's *Journalism: Principles and Practice*. She's quite correct that reporters need good manners and the ability to interview. But it is equally obvious that punctuality has to come first. If you're not there on time – or better still before time – you can't cover the story.

The importance of punctuality is not unique to journalism of course. In the movie *The Fabulous Baker Boys*, a down-at-heel piano player says to a singer who turns up late for an audition: 'Punctuality – the first rule of showbusiness.' Michelle Pfeiffer's character replies sarcastically: 'This is showbusiness?' You may feel the same about broadcast journalism on a wet, winter weekend shift at Radio Rubbish. But you still have to be there on time.

Sports reporters will have their own personal horror stories of when they missed the kick-off. It might have been because their car broke down, because of traffic congestion or because their train or flight was delayed. Whatever the excuse, there's no justification for not building a reasonable margin for error into your travel plans. Britain's roads are congested. Trains get delayed. Flights are subject to weather and air traffic controllers. A lie-in or a little more time at home reading the newspaper may be tempting, but you're better off getting to the location, and then relaxing. Take a newspaper or book, or listen to the radio.

Remember

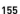

- Dress appropriately for the weather conditions and for the job
- Keep waterproofs and an umbrella in your car
- Plan your journey
- Be on time, or better still early

RADIO ON LOCATION

The best radio reporting has strong *actuality* – sound recorded on location. First of all, a radio reporter looks for strong interviews: first-hand eyewitness accounts in the case of a breaking event; the words of the key news makers in other stories. Next there are the background noises that draw the listener into the scene. These are the sounds that separate the event being covered from our normal world.

Most of us operate in a sound landscape so bland we don't think about it.

It's worth taking the time to shut your eyes and listen – to recognise the ordinary so you become attuned to the extraordinary and the newsworthy.

Our workaday world takes place against a backdrop of traffic noise, birdsong, perhaps aircraft passing overhead or music blaring from somebody's home or car. In a city or large town these elements are rarely far from our ears. A dog might bark or children shout. We take little notice. But there are other sounds that clearly place us in a location, and which can transport our listeners there too. The echoes and splashes of the swimming pool. The excited chatter of schoolchildren at playtime. Some sounds relay their own drama: police sirens during a terrorist alert; the roar of the crowd at a football match; loudspeaker announcements from a water company's vans during a hosepipe ban; leather, willow, chants from the Hill.

> **There really is no substitute for actuality sound in news reporting. You can't fake it back in the studio.**

There really is no substitute for actuality sound in news reporting. You can't fake it back in the studio. And if you try to – by spending considerable time and effort mixing in sound effects – you are cheating your audience. That would be dishonest and would not be journalism. It would be fiction.

Description

Painting pictures with your words is one of the delights of radio journalism. Some of your description may be scripted. You can also try ad-lib commentary 'on the hoof'. This works in both recorded and live situations.

Peter Allen of BBC Five Live says:

'Some of the best radio is when you go to the scene of a train crash or an earthquake, and just paint pictures, just tell people what you can see. In a way you can do it more powerfully than a television camera ever can. It's a fantastic medium, radio. I really do believe in its power.

'It's the time I really feel a buzz, when I get out of the studio. You haven't got a computer screen, you haven't got anything written down, and you simply have to make it up.'

Remember

- Listen for background sound that helps set the scene
- Record and use actuality sound
- Describe what you can see

Personal space and mic technique

Seated interview position for radio

Recording a radio interview is an intimate experience. You will need to be close to your interviewee, and you need to explain why. Most mics work best about 25 cm from the sound source – roughly a hand's span from the mouth of the subject. Stand at right-angles to your subject to avoid staring them in the face. Face-to-face confrontation usually makes people back away, and you will find yourself chasing them across a room.

If you are sitting, you may need to position yourself alongside the interviewee on a sofa, or on chairs angled so your knees are almost touching. This might not be how you would normally sit, but the important thing is to get good quality sound. Television interviewers too suffer unnatural postures to get the shot right. If you are not relaxed though, how can you expect your interviewee to be at ease? They are probably not as used to radio interviews as you are. You are the expert; you need to take the lead. Charm and confidence come into play here, making your subject comfortable while invading what they are unconsciously aware of as their personal space. Just remember to use a decent deodorant, brush your teeth and don't have a Balti the night before.

Use your charm too to entice executives away from their desks. People like to be on familiar territory. Sitting behind a desk is a way to feel secure or assert power. It can also produce stilted, pompous, predictable dialogue. Besides, it is very difficult to operate a microphone across an expanse of wood and piles of paper. Use that as an excuse to invite your interviewee to another location – perhaps the factory floor (which has background sounds to help tell the story).

Interviews can take time, so it's vital you are comfortable. It's no use fidgeting once the interview is under way. You will lose concentration and start thinking about your aching arm or sore bottom instead of the next question. Make sure your interviewee is comfortable too.

Being close to the interviewee means you have to move the mic less, so there's less danger of handling noise. Grip the mic firmly but not too tight, taking up any slack in the cable with your fingers. Don't tug at or stretch mic cables, as strain on the connections can cause clicks on the recording.

Beware of jewellery and coins rattling. A ring may click against the mic as you hold it. A bracelet may jangle. And interviewees, particularly if they are standing up, may jingle coins in their pocket. It's a common nervous reaction. Be aware of it and politely ask them to take their hand from their pocket. Even clothing can rustle or brush against a mic causing distracting noises. And trailing leads can bump against furniture.

- Make sure you are relaxed
- Put your interviewees at ease
- Position yourself to get good sound
- Avoid handling noise on the mic
- Be aware of distracting sound

Grip the mic firmly but not too tight, taking up any slack in the cable with your fingers

Sending material back to base

Radio reporting used to involve some live work – probably via a radio car or phone line – and a lot of driving back to base to edit tapes. But not any more.

Broadcasters use portable links, technically called wireless audio codecs, but known in the newsroom by trade names. The full name of the 'Comrex box' is Comrex Matrix Portable – a device for doing cheap outside broadcasts over phone lines. Programme and off-air cues (a conversation between the studio and reporter) can be sent over the same phone line.

Now there are apps for the iPhone, iPad and similar devices that enable broadcast quality OBs from anywhere with a 3G phone service. The quality of 3G signals can vary but they are usually reliable; Wi-Fi hotspots are much more dependable.

A pocket computer phone revolutionised radio news gathering in BBC local radio in 2007. It became possible to record quality audio, edit a simple package in the field and send it back to base without going anywhere near a radio car or an ISDN line.

Unusually the system was developed not by BBC engineers in London, but by journalists at BBC Lincolnshire. Senior broadcast journalist Andy Roche, who had a background in

The Comrex box – a portable reporting device in action

A PC phone, running Windows mobile, complete with windsock. It can be used to record, edit and transmit audio

BBC Radio Lincolnshire's William Wright interviews celebrity chef Jamie Oliver on a PC phone

computers before joining the BBC, recognised the potential of the software in a new PDA phone from O2, the XDA. He contacted the company behind the recording software – a small specialist operation in Maastricht. The Dutch team was in almost daily contact with the Lincolnshire journalists as the pilot scheme developed.

They discovered that the input sockets on the phones were not robust enough to use external mics, but the internal mic was more than good enough for most everyday journalistic applications. The phones had manual level control and simple single-track editing, with a familiar wave form display. The audio could be sent back to the radio station over the mobile network or on broadband from Wi-Fi hotspots.

Files could be transferred in MP2 format to play on the Radioman playout system (a higher quality audio format than MP3). Or they could be sent as .wav files.

Like other smartphones, they could also take pictures for use on websites and video to share with television on breaking news stories.

The pilot scheme started with the XDA phone and other models were tested. The XDA proved the most reliable and some were still in use nearly five years later. Project director Roche says: 'These phones became standard issue for all our journalists. Even when the phone companies were thinking of them as an old model, we carried on using them.'

In the meantime, the personal phones carried by most reporters were becoming increasingly sophisticated and journalists started using their own phones for broadcast purposes. The internal mic on most iPhones delivers decent audio in most environments, and unlike the old XDA, the iPhone will take an external mic for high-end professional use.

The quality of the audio can be adjusted to reduce the transfer time. When BBC Lincolnshire gave phones to its freelance non-league football reporters they reduced the transfer rate to half that used by news reporters. Even with reduced audio quality, Roche says it made a huge difference to the station's reports: 'Previously you got them on crackly mobile phones, and sometimes you could hardly hear them, with all the crowd noise at the grounds. Suddenly you could actually hear what they were saying.'

The value for breaking news is immense: 'Most people always have their phone with them, and now they can produce quality audio for a radio report. You can send a minute of audio in 30 seconds on a wireless broadband link, and quality live stuff through the 3G network.'

The station gave the phones to Red Arrows pilots, based at nearby RAF Scampton, when they went on their annual training trip to Cyprus. The pilots produced audio diaries of their training schedule.

And the phones can also be given to other contributors with a story to tell. For ME Awareness Week, a sufferer produced a compelling audio diary, explaining how she became tired after performing simple household tasks: 'I've been gardening for five minutes, and I've got to sit down now because I'm totally exhausted.'

She admitted she would not have been able to explain the effect of ME so well in a conventional interview. Roche explains the advantage of this type of user-generated content:

'The simple reason this works better than giving somebody professional recording equipment is feedback. We've all given people recorders for a week, and then had hours of material to listen to, and not had the time. But this way, they can record a short piece and send it to you, and you can give them instant advice and encouragement. They send you one or two minutes and you ring them immediately. You can tell them if the background noise was too loud, for example, and ask them to do it again.'

The iPad – with Luci Live software developed over several years by the Dutch company – proved itself as a professional tool when BBC Lincolnshire were able to broadcast live from an offshore wind farm. The kit enabled the reporter five miles out into the North Sea to broadcast live and play back pre-recorded clips in studio quality over the 3G mobile phone network.

TELEVISION ON LOCATION

Using the language of film making

A TV reporter is like a film director. You use the camera to tell a story. The difference is that the movie director has control over almost every part of the action. He might have planned a location shoot where the only variable is the weather. Rain or cloud might determine whether the scene can be filmed or not. That's why the movie industry flourished in Hollywood, California, where it's usually sunny. For the film director, sets have been built, lighting planned, focal lengths measured, microphones positioned and actors rehearsed. In the modern blockbuster, he might be filming actors against a green screen, with the wizards of computer-generated imagery waiting to insert the action. The TV reporter has hardly any of that control. The trick is to take as much control as you can, but to be flexible and to respond to the events around you.

Whether you are working with a crew or shooting material yourself, it is essential to understand the language of filming. That includes its grammar. It helps you choose your shots and to appreciate what is and is not possible (see Chapter 7: Location video and sound).

The grammar of film making is the same for film and television, and for online video. The vocabulary is the same too. You need to know how to describe what you want to the subject and to the camera person. We're in the communication business, after all. 'Can you get a shot of that over there?' usually isn't good enough.

The late BBC Foreign Correspondent Brian Barron said filming a report is like doing a jigsaw. You compose the story in your head as the day unfolds, mentally moving the pieces of the jigsaw around until you're settled on your final structure.

Pieces-to-camera

On location you will almost certainly want to do a piece-to-camera (PTC) or *stand-up*. If there's time. And if it's essential to tell the story. They're not compulsory.

Of course, it's good to see your face on the telly – that's probably one of the reasons you became a TV journalist. And it's true that audiences like to see who's talking to them. But the stand-up must serve a purpose within the piece. Think hard about how you are going to use it.

Placing the reporter at the heart of the action is a legitimate reason for a stand-up. It lets the audience know you were there, which gives you authority. Make sure there is plenty of action in the background as you film. There is no excuse for a PTC against a blank wall. It looks as if you are about to be shot by a firing squad rather than a camera.

Experienced, and bold, reporters may want to place themselves in the action at the key moment in the narrative – the finish of a race, the arrival of the prime minister, or as the winning captain lifts the cup, for example. But remember, if you fluff your lines at that point, you won't be able to use the shot. And unless you have another camera angle available, you will have no pictures of that moment for use in headlines or as archive.

Another good reason for the stand-up is to explain part of the story for which there are no pictures. For example, if a public body issues a statement, but will not offer anybody for interview, a PTC outside their headquarters may be a quicker way of summarising their statement than a graphic.

Make sure you're not trying to say too much. If you are having trouble remembering your words, the piece-to-camera is probably too long. As a guide, 15 to 20 seconds is usually about right.

Among the clichés of TV reporting are stand-ups at the start and end of reports. The opening stand-up can set the scene, but may not be the best visual image to open your piece.

The closing stand-up allows you to sum up the story and sign off – useful in some stories but not all. And they definitely won't work if you're linking live on location to your own package as part of a two-way.

On a complicated legally sensitive story, you will need to be word perfect. Write the words down first and learn your script like an actor. At other times you can ad lib around key words and phrases.

Whenever possible, try to introduce movement – of yourself, the camera or both – into your PTCs. Even the shortest stand-up is likely to be the longest shot in your piece, so it's worth taking time to get it right.

> **Even the shortest stand-up is likely to be the longest shot in your piece, so it's worth taking time to get it right.**

Locations for TV interviews

Television interviews can be spoilt by a poor choice of location or background. The best talker in the world shot against a distracting or irrelevant backdrop will appear less interesting.

Try to talk to people in their natural environment – a bus driver in her cab, a builder laying bricks, a businessman in his factory (usually better than an office).

You should avoid excessively noisy scenes, but if the audience can see the cause of the noise, background sound is much less of a problem on TV than on radio. A lawnmower off camera could be an annoying distraction, but if you are interviewing a cricket groundsman and the mower can be seen on the other side of the pitch, the shot may work.

Choosing a background for interviews is particularly difficult when you are indoors and space is limited. Don't shoot against blank walls or windows if you can help it. If the room, or what's going on in it, is relevant to the story, take people to one end of the room or even into a doorway if it is the only way of getting the room in shot.

In documentaries you may see people interviewed with an attractive fireplace (and perhaps even a vase of flowers) behind them. When you do, ask yourself how many rooms are arranged so that you sit with your back to the fireplace.

Remember

- Pieces to camera should help tell the story
- Introduce movement into your stand-ups
- Choose your backgrounds carefully
- Make sure there is space between the subject and the background

Recording voice-over on location

You may have to record voice-over (V-O) for a package on location. This is known as *track and rushes*. The pictures (rushes) and V-O (track) will be sent back to your edit, where they'll be assembled. You need to be aware of what shots you have and how the story fits together when you write your script.

You also need to find somewhere with as little background noise as possible to record your V-O. A quiet room, without echoing walls, is ideal. Inside a car works too. Use the mic close to your lips with the gain (level control) turned down, to reduce the background sound. Use headphones to monitor the sound quality and make sure there is no 'popping' on the mic.

If you are using tape and have to send it back for someone else to edit, record the V-O over colour bars (*on the stripe*, as it's known), so that it can be found easily when the editor is spooling through.

- Choose a quiet spot to record location V-O
- Use the mic close to your lips with low gain

Using viewers' videos

It has become so easy to take still pictures and video on mobile phones that 'user-generated content' (UGC) is as much a part of broadcast journalism as the eyewitness account. There are also so-called 'citizen journalists' reporting events online. The simplest way to find contributors and use their material is through the social networks where it is posted. To gather unshown material for your own coverage, on-air pleas and captions requesting phone pictures and video are common on breaking news stories. The user-generated material often becomes the topic for separate reports. Reporters in the field also join the quest for the material usually captioned on screen as 'viewer's video'. The radio equivalent might be an audio recording of a dramatic event. Radio reporters should remember that video cameras record sound too.

It's not too many years since domestic camcorders were a luxury. Nowadays every home seems to have one. But cries of 'get the video, Mavis' are less common than you might think when disaster strikes on the doorstep. If a terrorist bomb explodes, an aircraft crashes or armed police break into the house next door, self-preservation is the first instinct, rather than 'I wonder if the TV would like shots of this?'

There was extensive home video footage of the 2004 tsunami, because it affected coastal areas packed with holidaymakers. Taking holiday pictures is one of the main reasons people buy video cameras, so hundreds of people caught up in the tragedy were able to take pictures later seen on news bulletins around the world.

Almost all mobile phones and many digital stills cameras can take video.

Almost all mobile phones and many digital stills cameras can take video. While moving pictures are highly prized, camera-phone stills can also help tell a story. The quality of moving pictures from mobiles is usually poor by normal broadcast standards, but the newsworthiness of an event will determine whether it is acceptable.

CASE STUDY 6.1   WITNESS VIDEO

The first major use of mobile-phone video in mainstream broadcasts in the UK came during the July terrorist bombings in London in 2005. There was enough material from commuters caught up in events to fill a separate package within the BBC's coverage. Sky News too made extensive use of shots taken on the tube within seconds of the bombs going off. Both organisations were well equipped to handle these pictures prior to transmission, as they had been experimenting for several years with ways of using camera-phone technology to enhance their own reporting. The idea that a TV journalist can be live on air at the scene of a breaking news story, even before the camera crew arrives, is hugely attractive to editors. Broadcasters are prepared to accept poorer picture quality in the short term in the race to tell the story first.

Just as television reporters will seek out domestic video of news events, radio can accept poorer quality recordings where the content is newsworthy. BBC Five Live ran a recording from a listener's Dictaphone when police raided terrorist suspects in the aftermath of the July 2005 London transport bombings. The man, whose home overlooked the flat on the Peabody Estate in West London where two of the men were arrested, had recorded loud bangs and armed police officers shouting to the men inside the flat. The recording was crackly and distorted but dramatic – and made compulsive listening.

The same episode led to one of the scoops of the year for ITV News. When pictures of the arrest of the two suspects appeared on their 6.30 and 10.30 bulletins, they were captioned 'EXCLUSIVE: ITV News/Daily Mail'. ITV News secured the pictures from a man who'd taken them, according to first reports, with his girlfriend's DV camera. A bidding war had already started when ITN decided they needed to increase their financial clout. News Editor Deborah Turness called the *Daily Mail* newspaper, because she had shared stories with them before. The joint bid helped stave off a late attempt by Sky News to win the rights. Turness brokered the deal with the amateur cameraman and the *Mail* without even seeing the moving pictures. The man was trapped within a police cordon, but a grabbed frame sent by email convinced her she must have the footage.

Turness told the *Independent* newspaper shortly afterwards that the deal broke new ground in the kind of deals television can do with newspapers. The *Mail* had exclusive stills of the arrests. ITV News had exclusive TV pictures without having to pay the full asking price. Crediting the newspaper on screen – as part of the large 'EXCLUSIVE' caption on the top left of the picture – helped prevent other newspapers from lifting the pictures for their own editions. Otherwise there would be little incentive for a newspaper to work with a TV programme that could show the pictures the evening before the paper came out. The graphics department of ITV News sent the paper 25 high-quality stills from the ten minutes of rushes on the DV tape. Despite legal warnings, other TV channels lifted the pictures complete with the 'exclusive' logo. The BBC report acknowledged that the scenes had been 'sold to a commercial broadcaster'.

Broadcasters like to think of themselves as being at the cutting edge of audio and video production, but the newest technology can catch us out. Highly dramatic pictures of cars being swept down a flooded main street in Boscastle in Cornwall in 2004 were taken on a new hard-disk domestic camcorder. The first TV crews on the scene did not have the software to download the shots on to their edit systems. The first use of those pictures on air came after a cameraman pointed his own lens at a playback monitor. Later BBC engineers worked out how to retrieve the pictures in all their glory, rather than off a flickering screen.

The debate about what constitutes 'broadcast quality' is an argument engineers have had with journalists since broadcast news began. It continues, but the engineers have lost! There was a time when pictures taken by professional cameraman would be rejected if they didn't show the correct wave pattern on an oscilloscope – even if they showed a perfectly comprehensible picture on a television screen. The quality argument has been reduced to this: do the pictures or sounds tell a really important story? If the answer is 'yes', then they will be used, no matter how shaky, grainy, fuzzy or distorted. This is not an excuse for subjecting viewers to second-rate images. Too many wobbly or badly focused shots will quickly make the audience queasy. These shots have to be used sparingly. The duration on screen is directly proportional to the news value of the pictures. If the pictures are exclusive, that adds a little extra to what will be tolerated.

Release forms

You may have charmed the video tape from the hapless home video enthusiast. You may have transmitted the video clip from the mobile phone back to your newsroom. You may have the camcorder in your hand ready to wire it up to your mobile edit. But that doesn't mean you can use the pictures. Copyright normally rests with the person who took the pictures, so it is best – to be legally covered – to get their written permission to use the material. Most

> **Copyright normally rests with the person who took the pictures, so it is best – to be legally covered – to get their written permission.**

organisations have a standard release form to be filled in by those contributing material. It's a good idea for reporters and producers to keep a handful in the car. This document will also act as a receipt and a legal contract if money changes hands.

It is usual to arrange for all rights in material gathered in this way to be transferred to the broadcaster. This allows unlimited future transmissions, and for the news organisation to sell on the pictures to other broadcasters. The Boscastle flood pictures mentioned above were sold worldwide. The BBC made so much from them they felt obliged to go back to the original cameraman and offer him more money. He declined, asking instead that a contribution be made to the town's relief fund.

Exceptionally, other arrangements will be made. The nationally known motorcycle stunt rider Eddie Kidd was seriously injured in an accident at the Bulldog Bash, a huge gathering of bike enthusiasts in Warwickshire, organised by Hells Angels. One of the crowd caught on video the moment Kidd's bike leapt the track at Long Marston airfield. It appeared to be slowing down after landing, but toppled over the edge of a steep embankment. Eddie Kidd's back was broken; he was lucky to be alive, and his stunt career was over. As a fellow biker, the amateur cameraman did not want to profit from the stunt man's injuries, but he allowed the BBC to use the pictures on condition that a donation to a bikers' charity was made every time they were shown.

Every time you use somebody else's pictures, remember the law of copyright. Copyright belongs to the person who takes the pictures (or if they are a professional the person who employs them). You can't use anyone else's pictures without their permission.

Giving people cameras

'User-generated content' is not just about waiting for people to send in material or seeking it out after an event. Ever since lightweight DV cameras came on to the market, journalists have been lending them to people to make their own video diaries and to report stories from their own viewpoints. This can make compelling television.

The authored report (a first person narrative from a contributor) has an important place in the modern news balance. It enfranchises groups who might otherwise not have a chance to air their views on mainstream media.

Cameras producing pictures of broadcast quality are so cheap that within the budgets of big news organisations they are almost disposable. But that doesn't mean you should give them to everybody.

Ask whether what anybody can produce (with a little basic camera training) will provide exclusive or otherwise unavailable footage that enhances the story telling. The key question is one of access – the secret of much good documentary making. A homeless person with a camera may give a better account of their plight than a homeless person being followed by a video crew, where the presence of the team prejudices the authenticity of the material. There's an example of the results of giving a contributor a camera in Chapter 11: The package.

Remember

- More people than ever are carrying video and stills cameras, often on their phones
- Video cameras also record sound that might be useful for radio
- Check copyright and ask for a written release
- Make use of authored reports
- Consider lending lightweight cameras to contributors

Pressers and press packs – regular scenarios

No two stories are the same but the situations you find yourself in can be. You will often find yourself at a news conference – or 'presser' – or in a pack of other reporters chasing the same tale. These situations are daunting the first time, but you soon get used to them and learn how to prepare.

At times you may need to co-operate with other journalists from rival organisations. In practice, reporters are not lone wolves – they often hunt in packs. Many on-the-road reporters spend more of their working day with their rivals than with colleagues from their own newsroom. They trade favours, information and occasionally audio and video material. Sometimes their editors never get to know about these arrangements, which can make life easier working in the field.

The news conference

Always arrive in good time for press conferences, so you can set up your equipment and find a seat where you will have good eye contact with the people at the top table when you ask your questions. The pressures of a small radio newsroom mean you will not have the luxury of being first to arrive and claiming the best position. You will be covering many stories in the day. So time management is the key. Can you bag your seat at the presser and then continue writing the earlier story you were working on? Can you make those vital calls on the mobile while you are waiting? Can you set up at the presser and *then* file the earlier story in time for the bulletin?

It's helpful to establish the ground rules with the press or media liaison officer at the conference. Can you plead early deadlines so you are in and out swiftly without missing anything? Do the speakers have to leave at a certain time? Is there a photo call and if so what form will it take? Most importantly, is there an opportunity for separate one-to-one interviews? If there is, that's good news, but you should record the presser anyway, in case the plan changes. If the conference overruns, the one to ones may be cancelled.

If you arrived early, there is a better chance of being first in the queue for the one to one, but bear in mind that, deadlines permitting, it can be better to go second. The interviewee will have been warmed up and had a chance to order their thoughts. But you never want to be late in the pecking order. Interviewees will have become bored, and may rush their answers to get away.

In large set-piece news conferences, such as the monthly gatherings with the Prime Minister at 10 Downing Street, there are standard procedures and favoured reporters will get priority.

High-profile news conferences raise a contentious point, on which editors will differ. Does it matter who asks the questions as long as you get the answers? Everybody ends up with the same material from the conference itself. If you have an exclusive point to pursue, a one-to-one interview after the main event is the best time to reveal your hand. And yet interviewers' questions are often included in reports of news conferences.

The next time you see that happening, ask yourself whether the reporter's question was really necessary to tell the story. Or was it a case of the reporter and the news organisation giving themselves a pat on the back for getting their question in?

The press conference: arrive in good time to set up your gear

Remember

- Arrive early at press conferences
- Ask if there will be one-to-one interviews
- Everybody gets the same material from a 'presser'

Media scrums

You may find yourself involved in a media scrum. We've all seen them on television. The bigger the story, the bigger the scrum: hordes of TV and stills cameras; radio reporters shoving microphones into people's faces; newspaper reporters brandishing mini-recorders and notebooks. They're not an easy place to record sound and video. Often they follow a *stake-out* of somebody or somewhere in the news. They can be great fun, or they can degenerate into fights.

They can also be intimidating and intrusive. That depends on who is at the centre of the mêlée. Is it a public figure who can expect this level of attention? Is it a criminal who cannot reasonably expect privacy? Or is it an otherwise innocent member of the public who does not deserve to have their privacy invaded and might even be frightened?

The BBC guidelines suggest it will sometimes be appropriate to make pooling arrangements with other media organisations, and at other times it is proper to withdraw.

So, there are times when it is right to pull out, but when should we get stuck in? A Sky News crew edged their way into one scrum live on air. Gerard Conlon, one of the Guildford Four who were wrongly jailed for IRA pub bombings in the 1970s, emerged from the House of Commons after an historic meeting with the Prime Minister. The Sky News reporter was live on air at a different entrance to the House. The camera was transmitting to the satellite truck via microwave link. So, the team had the freedom to march down the street, still broadcasting, and edge their way into the pack. It was exciting and innovative television.

And there's another incentive for getting stuck into the scrum. Many local radio stations will consider it a job well done if you manage to shove your microphone so close to the interviewee that it can't help but appear on the TV news. Indeed, in the early days of commercial radio, reporters were paid a bonus if their mic, with its prominent station logo, made a TV appearance. Station managers still consider it part of the reporter's job to get this free publicity. It helps the station's profile.

Remember

- Media scrums can be exciting, but don't expect top quality recorded material
- They may be intrusive

Doorstepping

In an age where cold callers invade our homes via phone and email with sales patter for everything from double glazing to Viagra, it may surprise you that broadcasters are sensitive about the rights and wrongs of doorstepping.

Doorstepping should not take place unless a request for an interview has been refused or it has not been possible to request an interview.

Doorstepping is not just any interview on a doorstep, and the term doesn't apply to journalists knocking on doors in the normal course of enquiries. The term is defined in the Ofcom Broadcasting Code as:

The filming or recording of an interview or attempted interview with someone, or announcing that a call is being filmed or recorded for broadcast purposes, without any prior warning.

It doesn't include people in the news being recorded in public places, or vox pops, where opinions are sought from random members of the public.

The Ofcom code says:

Doorstepping for factual programmes should not take place unless a request for an interview has been refused or it has not been possible to request an interview, or there is good reason to believe that an investigation will be frustrated if the subject is approached openly, and it is warranted to doorstep.

The BBC guidelines say that all proposals to doorstep people, whether or not they have been approached for an interview beforehand, have to be 'referred up'. If there has been a prior approach, a senior editorial figure, or for independent programme makers the commissioning editor, must give approval for the doorstep. Where there has been no prior approach, Controller Editorial Policy must give approval (there is an exception for daily news gathering). The Controller will normally only give permission for a doorstep if there is clear evidence of crime or significant wrongdoing, or good reason to believe an investigation will be frustrated or allegations avoided if the individual is approached openly.

Notwithstanding these rules, doorstepping has become a staple of consumer reporting. The reporter or camera being attacked became a cliché of this type of television. Central Television's *Cook Report* set the standard in the 1990s, with programmes structured to lead to a confrontation with an alleged wrongdoer. The BBC's *Watchdog* and *Rogue Traders* were among those who followed the trend. But what works for cowboy builders doesn't necessarily yield dividends from more astute 'victims'. In 2009, Ryanair chief executive Michael O'Leary turned a doorstep by the BBC's *Panorama* into an opportunity to promote his airline and to condemn the programme makers' 'biased agenda'. He chatted for nine minutes stressing he'd give an interview of whatever length the reporter wanted as long as it was unedited. The BBC put the uncut version of the doorstep on their website.

Approaching the bereaved

Most reporters dread the *death knock*. It is an insensitive but commonly used term for calling on the recently bereaved to request interviews, or to ask for home video or photos of someone who has just died. It is an uncomfortable experience, and difficult to avoid guilt at intruding on grief. But people react differently in times of distress. Some may want to talk – to unburden their own emotions or to pay tribute to a lost loved one. Others may react angrily. The sensible rule of thumb for reporters and producers is to learn when to take no for an answer – which should, in these circumstances, be the first time it is said to you. An approach through an online tribute – a Facebook site, for example – is less intrusive than a knock on the door. Tribute sites will usually yield information useful to the reporter, without upsetting people in distress, but securing an interview, through whatever medium, requires old-style diplomacy and sensitivity.

Most BBC journalists will defend the corporation's approach as the most sensitive and appropriate way to treat people. Its Editorial Guidelines are clear:

We should normally request interviews with people who are injured or grieving following an accident or disaster by approaching them through friends, relatives or advisers. We should not:

- **put them under pressure to provide interviews**
- **harass them with repeated phone calls, e-mails, text messages or knocks at the door**
- **stay on their property if asked to leave**
- **normally follow them if they move on.**

The Ofcom Broadcasting Code is more succinct: 'People in a state of distress should not be put under pressure to take part in a programme or provide interviews, unless it is warranted.' The definition of 'warranted' has yet to be defined in law.

More on editorial guidelines

Whenever legal and ethical judgements have to be made, editorial guidelines can be consulted. The BBC's Editorial Guidelines – more than 350 pages in the 2010 edition with more detail online – are the best-known example. They used to be called Producers Guidelines, but now include the relevant sections of the Ofcom Broadcasting Code. They are available online at: **www.bbc.co.uk/guidelines/editorialguidelines**.

Whenever legal and ethical judgements have to be made, editorial guidelines can be consulted.

The Ofcom Code, which is also available on the Internet at **www.ofcom.org.uk**, replaced the regulatory codes of the Independent Television Commission (which governed independent television), the Radio Authority (commercial radio's regulator) and the Broadcasting Standards Commission, which controlled taste, decency, fairness and privacy.

These guidelines are the result of years of experience and case studies, drawn up by senior editorial figures, many of whom have had to make critical and controversial decisions in their own careers. The BBC guidelines are approved by the BBC Trust, a body appointed by the government to regulate the corporation. The guidelines are constantly reviewed by the corporation's Editorial Policy team of senior managers. Ofcom maintains a similarly rigorous regime of review and control.

The guidelines are not just a sop to viewers' and listeners' pressure groups. They are a working tool, consulted by broadcasters every day.

Just as there is no such thing as a truly new story, there should be no contentious issue that isn't covered by the guidelines. If one arises, be assured there will soon be a policy about it. In short, there is no greater reservoir of experience to draw upon.

The guidelines, either those of the Ofcom Code or the BBC, are more than just a legal framework. They are a one-stop shop for any reporter worried about the appropriate way to approach a delicate story. They cover accuracy, fact checking, impartiality, fairness, consent, privacy, crime and anti-social behaviour, the use and treatment of children in broadcasts, politics and public policy, war, terror and emergencies, religion and the editorial integrity and independence of the broadcaster. They also tackle the conflicts of interest brought about by the modern broadcast environment, in which co-production and content bought in from independent producers are an important part of the mix.

A CLOSER LOOK

THE REPORTER'S ROLE – A POLICE VIEW

Ofcom sets out a legal and ethical code for the work of broadcasters, including reporters in the field. But journalists are not above the other laws of the land, and will often find themselves dealing with those who have to uphold those laws – the police.

The interests of the police and reporters are not mutually exclusive. Often the police will want help from the media. The most obvious examples of this are appeals for witnesses to crime or accidents. Reporters cultivate police contacts and they are a valued source of information. But there may be conflict too.

Police constables maintain traffic flow and crowd control at major incidents. They are on duty at crime scenes to prevent anyone interfering with evidence. But they are not allowed to give *ad hoc* media interviews.

The police have their own guidelines for police–press relations. The Metropolitan Police drew up ground rules after consultation with media representatives including the National Union of Journalists.

The Met's guidelines said:

1 Members of the media have a duty to report from the scene of many of the incidents we have to deal with. We should actively help them carry out their responsibilities provided they do not interfere with ours.
2 Where it is necessary to put cordons in place, it is much better to provide the media with a good vantage point from which they can operate rather than to exclude them, otherwise they may try to get around the cordons and interfere with police operations. Providing an area for members of the media does not exclude them from operating from other areas to which the general public have access.
3 Members of the media have a duty to take photographs and film incidents and we have no legal power or moral responsibility to prevent or restrict what they record . . . Once images are recorded, we have no power to delete or confiscate them without a court order, even if we think they contain damaging or useful evidence.

The Met's guidelines go on to cover issues including dealing with bereaved and distressed people who are subject to media attention, and advice that the media must obtain recorded permission to enter private property while accompanying police officers. The BBC's advice on 'tag-along raids' echoes this.

West Midlands Police produced an A4 folder with no fewer than 12 inserts covering everything from media training courses to an A–Z guide on subjects from 'accidents' to 'young offenders' (an A–Y guide).

Staffordshire Police's media unit produced a pocket guide for their officers. It also included advice which is helpful for reporters to know:

● The presence of a photographer or a reporter at an accident, crime or disaster scene does not of itself constitute an unlawful obstruction or interference.
● The taking of pictures or the asking of questions should not be restricted, even if the police officer disagrees with the nature of the pictures or questions.

- If a distressed or bereaved person requests an officer to ask the media to leave them in peace, the officer can pass that request on to journalists, in the spirit of 'victim support'. This is advice on which journalists and editors can base their own decisions, unless there is an identifiable Breach of the Peace, when journalists, like any citizens, have a duty to disperse.
- Journalists should carry press credentials and produce them if requested by an officer.
- Journalists have a right to photograph and report events that take place on public property.
- The police can invite journalists on to private property where an event of public interest has occurred, but the journalists have to respect the rights of the owner of the property and may have to leave.
- Access to crime scenes can be denied for evidence gathering and forensic examination, but the reasons for denying access should be explained.
- As long as a journalist does not break the law or interfere with an investigation, a police officer should not impede the journalist.
- It is reasonable for a police officer to ask a journalist to move his or her vehicle – even if it is legally parked – if it could obstruct the movement or parking of emergency vehicles.

Metropolitan police guidelines: 'Once images are recorded, we have no power to delete or confiscate them without a court order, even if we think they contain damaging or useful evidence.'

'Journalists have a right to photograph and report events that take place on public property.'

While the guidelines of the police forces offer a more liberal approach to journalists, the anti-terror laws of the Labour governments of Tony Blair and Gordon Brown suggested a harsher regime. The stop and search powers of Section 44 of the Terrorism Act 2000 were used to prevent photography in designated areas, but the Association of Chief Police Officers warned in 2009 against the Act being used against photographers, and the European Court of Human Rights ruled the Section 44 powers illegal in January 2010. The Counter-Terrorism Act 2008 banned the filming of police officers, but a Home Office circular in 2009 said legitimate journalistic activity would be a reasonable excuse and therefore a defence under the Act.

Awareness of this range of advice leaves you better equipped to cover big stories with a heavy police presence – and to deal with individual officers as you go about your day-to-day business. Remember that courtesy is more productive than confrontation.

CONCLUSION

Reporters and producers on location are under a lot of pressure. In radio, you will almost certainly be alone. That is why it helps to prepare as well as you can before you leave the studio, where others, like the planning desk or your editor, will have been able to help you.

It is almost always a good idea to arrive early for a story, but that advice may not always be possible to follow. We're well aware of the pressures of busy newsrooms. So, perhaps it's better to offer another platitude. Don't panic. Think on your feet and respond to changing circumstances. Remember, no plan survives first contact with the enemy.

FURTHER READING

Beaman, Jim (2000) *Interviewing for Radio*, Oxford: Routledge. Practical advice on dealing with interviewees and how to structure interviews in different locations.

Chantler, Paul and Stewart, Peter (2003) *Basic Radio Journalism*, Oxford: Focal Press. The role of the reporter on location.

Frost, Chris (2001) *Reporting for Journalists*, Oxford: Routledge. Useful on the preparations you need for working in the field – not broadcast based though.

Ray, Vin (2003) *The Television News Handbook*, London: Macmillan. Strong advice based on the experience of television practitioners.

WEB LINKS

www.bbc.co.uk/guidelines/editorialguidelines The code by which BBC journalists operate.

http://stakeholders.ofcom.org.uk/broadcasting/broadcast-codes/broadcast-code/ The site of the regulatory body Ofcom's Broadcast Code.

CHAPTERSEVEN
LOCATION VIDEO
AND SOUND

In this chapter we'll look at:

- News gathering and reporting in the field.
- Recording audio for radio and the Web.
- Radio tips and techniques.
- Working with a TV crew.
- Working as a video journalist.
- Filming techniques.
- Getting the story back – the ways your stories reach the airwaves, including live transmission from radio cars, microwave and satellite links, 3G phones, and the use of fixed and wireless broadband connections.

GETTING out of the office to cover a story – any story – is one of the joys of broadcast journalism. There's an excitement and an expectation – the thrill of not knowing exactly what might happen or how people will react to you. And you have to capture the essence of it all in sound or on video. Unless you are very familiar with the recording kit you're using, the job becomes extremely difficult.

AS ALWAYS – BE PREPARED

Health and safety

The risk assessment of any location must include a consideration of how safe it will be to operate your equipment. Clearly, in a war zone or a riot a video journalist is at greater risk than a three-person TV crew. A reporter and a sound recordist can keep watch for danger while the camera operator concentrates on filming. But even routine domestic stories present dangers – not just for yourself, but more importantly for members of the public. Trailing cables can trip people up. Is there somewhere to park your radio car or satellite truck, legally, without it causing an obstruction?

As we explained in Chapter 6: Location reporting and production, newsrooms have risk assessment forms for you to fill in whenever you identify hazards beyond the routine of daily news gathering. When you are taught how to use a new piece of kit, the health and safety aspects of using it should be explained to you.

Before you leave the newsroom

Newsroom planning involves working out what equipment you need to cover a story and the logistics of how the story will be transmitted. What distances have to be travelled? Will a reporter be able to return to base to edit, or will they be on location feeding output for several hours or even days? Do you need live links, location editing, and feed points for audio and video? Or can you rely on Wi-Fi hotspots? Do you need to book overnight accommodation?

Local radio newsrooms cover a small patch. Reporters spend much of their time travelling to and from base. They edit and voice most of the material collected in the field back at the studio. National news gathering relies on reporters based around the country in regional centres. Travel times are an important factor in how long it takes to cover a story.

Foreign news operations have correspondents based around the world, but covering stories can still mean lengthy flights or overland journeys to locations that are not served by regular transport links. The technical resources available vary hugely, particularly in developing countries, and news crews have to take all the equipment they need with them.

Whoever you work for, making sure the equipment is up to the job is the first step before you go out on the road. If you are using unfamiliar equipment, try it out before you leave the newsroom. Always ask how new kit works, and have a look at the instruction manual if you get the chance. Being caught out in front of an interviewee or when you arrive in a foreign hotel room is embarrassing and unprofessional.

Check your batteries

Most electronic recording devices use batteries. Do you have batteries ready to use? Are they fully charged? It's almost incredible how many interviews have been lost because the reporter left the newsroom with dead batteries or, worse, no batteries at all. Bear in mind that pieces of kit you may use only occasionally – radio mics, for example – need their own batteries. It's always handy to carry spares.

The biggest problems occur with shared equipment. In any newsroom, make sure you know whose job it is to make sure batteries are charged, and, if they're not around, do the job yourself. On foreign assignments make sure you have an international adapter so you can plug in the battery charger – and your mobile phone.

> In any newsroom, make sure you know whose job it is to make sure batteries are charged, and, if they're not around, do the job yourself.

Check your tapes

You might be using audio or video tapes, hard-disk recorders or memory cards. Whatever the medium, do you have enough recording capacity for the job in hand? Always carry spares in case the unexpected happens. There's not much worse, professionally speaking, than watching exciting events that you can't record because of your own failure to prepare.

If you are on a big story, don't think simply in terms of how much recording time you have available. You may need to send a tape or memory card back to base or to a satellite truck with only a few shots, or a single key interview on it.

A classic how-not-to-do-it documentary, *Stalking Pete Doherty*, broadcast on Channel 4 in 2005, recorded the moment when the interviewer, who had been trying to document the life of the rock star *du jour*, Pete Doherty of the Libertines and Babyshambles, found himself alone with his subject at last. Doherty suggested this was the time to do the interview. The tape ran out.

Remember

- Prepare the logistics of your shoot
- Check batteries (make sure they're charged) and carry spares
- Make sure you have enough recording capacity (take spare tapes or memory cards)

RADIO ON LOCATION

Radio reporting on location – the history

The technical challenge of radio reporting has always been how to capture location audio – interviews, actuality, the reporter's voice – in the highest sound quality with the least physical effort.

Technological advances have transformed radio reporting within the lifetimes of many working in the industry today. The legendary Richard Dimbleby, the father of David and Jonathan the television presenters, was the first BBC war correspondent and, according to the US Museum of Broadcast Communications, the virtual founder of broadcast journalism. During the Second World War, he reported from Allied bombing raids; from the Normandy beaches; was the first radio reporter to reach the concentration camp at Belsen, and the first to enter Berlin.

The BBC developed portable 'midget' disk recorders to be operated by reporters in the field without an engineer. The terms *portable* and *midget* were misnomers by modern standards. The machines weighed 40 pounds – about the same as a soldier's rucksack – and the reporter had to carry his personal kit as well. The Riverside Portable recorded on to double-sided ten-inch disks. It got its name from the gramophones taken on picnics in the 1930s. Under fire, it was no picnic to operate one.

Magnetic tape was a German invention, copied by the Allies after the war. For radio programmes, it was a revelation and dominated the medium for half a century. Programmes could be recorded and edited very simply. A classical music performance that lasted an hour and ten minutes could be condensed into an hour's transmission slot. Or a long-winded interview with a politician could be cut down.

For several decades the most reliable portable recorder for news reporters was the Uher – pronounced 'ewer'. Many people working in news today recall the Uher fondly – it was the size of a large handbag and heavy, but trusty and rarely broke down. If your batteries lost their charge you could buy replacements at any corner shop. And you could see, through the Perspex lid, that your tape was in place and turning at the right speed.

The Uher also had record level meters the same size as the ones back in the studio, so it was clear to see whether the sound you were recording was too quiet or, worse, too loud and therefore likely to distort on playback.

Elderly relatives may have told you about the first video recorders. They were four times the size of today's DVD players and could only record up to one hour's programming. The picture was comparatively fuzzy, whereas a modern domestic recording is an exact digital copy of whatever was broadcast. Similar advances have been made in audio recording and for a while it looked as if domestic and professional news recording equipment would converge.

The digital revolution

As early as the 1980s radio reporters were using cassette recorders, the 'professional' equivalent of the Sony Walkman – the personal stereo that was everywhere before iPods and MP3 players.

Then the digital system MiniDisc was developed, and it looked like the answer to a station manager's prayers: a professional piece of kit at a high-street price. Reporters went out with domestic recorders and a high-quality professional microphone that probably cost twice as much as the tiny recording deck. The controls are fiddly, and the record level meter a little awkward to see, but used properly MiniDisc gives results of the highest quality.

Digital recording means you only record the electrical signal from your microphone or line sound source. That signal is converted into a binary code, and once encoded it will not change. You are not recording the tape hiss or distortion typical of analogue copies. And each copy will be as good as the original, not subject to increasing amounts of tape noise. MiniDisc players never matched the robustness and longevity of the Uher, but, at a fraction of the cost, they were virtually disposable. An advantage of MiniDisc was that it was possible to perform simple edits on location. A reporter could select in and out points on an interview clip by adding inaudible markers to the recording. The resulting soundbites could be played back instantly. The separated tracks could be shuffled, and played back in any order, which meant that a simple package could be produced in the field. Solid-state recording on to removable media, such as SDHC cards of the type found in cameras, offered similar flexibility. But for most purposes – and certainly for journalists in the field – the technology was becoming almost too complicated. Which is why the next technical breakthrough was, if anything, a simplification of what had gone before – not to sell in a domestic market, but to serve the practical needs of professional journalists. It's a mic that records, without any messy cables.

For straightforward news reporting the self-contained microphone with built-in recorder has become an industry standard. The FlashMic combined a high-quality Sennheiser mic with one-button recording on to internal flash memory with a capacity of several hours. Internal markers can be added to recordings, if needed, and the recorded sound files can be quickly transferred for editing or played back live using a USB connection. The FlashMic was advertised as ideal for press and broadcast journalism, radio interviewing and podcasting. So, unlike the cassette and MiniDisc recorders, it was developed with professionals in mind. Radio news reporters need no longer take to the streets carrying the equivalent of an upmarket personal hi-fi.

FlashMic

Modern machines will have *automatic level control (ALC)*. What ALC does is to flatten out the incoming signal to a consistent level that is neither too low nor too high. It should guarantee no distortion on playback. It would appear to be a useful tool, but the problem for professionals is that because *all* the recorded sound is at the same level, as soon as there is a pause in what you mean to record, any background noise may be boosted to fill the gap. You might be on a pavement, interviewing a fire officer at the scene of a fire. When he pauses at the end of a sentence, or to collect his thoughts, traffic noise swoops in to fill the gap. You might think his next comments would be drowned out by the cars and lorries. But no, as soon as he starts speaking again the din subsides. It is an odd effect and disconcerting for the listener. Radio professionals call it *surge* or *pumping*, and they hate it, because it is an unnatural distortion. Domestic recording decks have had ALC for years. But there are few circumstances in which it should be used by broadcast professionals. Most people use the FlashMic's automatic level control; it almost always gives broadcast standard results, but the manual advises that, as with all automatic gain systems, a degree of pumping may be audible.

You might get away with using automatic level control in perfectly quiet conditions, but it is better to set the levels manually and alter or *ride* them as you monitor what you are recording. Cheaper equipment has pre-set ALC, but on more sophisticated kit it is possible to adjust threshold settings and attack and release times. Trust us, it is simpler to use manual level controls.

Remember

- Digital recording means you can make multiple copies without reducing the sound quality
- Avoid automatic level settings
- Be prepared to ride the levels

The **omnidirectional** takes in sound from all around.

Gun mic

Omni mic

Microphones

Whatever you are recording onto, the sound will only be as good as the microphone you are using. And the mic will only be as good as the person using it. If you move the mic around too much, there will probably be handling noise: the cable may rattle, causing scratching effects on your recording. If you use the wrong type of mic, you may record sound from the wrong direction or sound that is horribly distorted by wind noise or electrical interference.

If you work in a radio newsroom, the chances are the options will have been taken away from you. There will be a standard piece of kit taken out by every reporter on news jobs. The mic will have been chosen according to its fitness for the job, its reliability based on the chief engineer's past experience, and almost certainly its cost. But you still need to know what type of mic it is to get the best results from it. And if you fancy producing outside broadcasts or covering sports events, it's worth knowing a little about the other microphone types.

Microphones are described according to the way they pick up the sound and according to the direction from which the sound is received. All pick up sound waves, vibrations in the air, in a similar way to your eardrum.

The standard news-gathering mic for radio can be an *omni*, short for omni-directional. It picks up sound from any direction, and is useful for interviews and close-up sound recording.

The gun mic used by TV reporters can be held further away from the interviewee and kept out of camera shot because it is directional; in other words it only picks up sound

Ribbon mic

Lip mic

The **cardioid** has a heart-shaped area of pick-up.

The **hypercardioid** is more directional than the cardioid.

Dead   Dead

from the direction in which it is pointed. It will be a *capacitor* or *moving coil* type. The capacitor or *condenser* type has an electrically charged capacitor plate, and needs an electric current to work. The electricity can be supplied by a battery in the mic itself, or from the recorder. You need to know if you are using this type of microphone because you will have to make sure the battery is charged for it to work. If it is operating from the power in the recorder, known as *phantom power*, then it will be a small extra drain on the recorder's battery.

The moving coil, or *dynamic*, mic has a wire coil attached to a diaphragm vibrating in a magnetic field.

There are also *ribbon* mics, where the vibrations are picked up by a diaphragm of foil, usually a thin strip of aluminium, vibrating in a magnetic field. These are expensive and most often found in studios, where they are used for high-end music recording. They are hardly ever used in the open air because they pick up wind noise, which distorts and crackles. An exception is the *lip mic*, a type of ribbon mic which, as the name suggests, is held close to the lips. These are the microphones favoured by many sports commentators, and are also used in TV edit suites for recording voice-over. They only pick up sound at very close range. So, they cut out crowd noise while relaying the commentator's voice. Effects mics will be placed around the ground to pick up sound from the crowd and the pitch to be mixed in on transmission. Nowadays many commentators use mics attached to headsets. These are likely to be dynamic or condenser types.

We mentioned that the standard TV news-gathering mic is likely to be directional. Technically its *polar pattern* (or polar diagram) – the direction from which it picks up sound – is known as hypercardioid. The *gun* or *rifle mics* used by TV news crews are covered in fluffy wind covers, which trap a layer of air through which the sound travels, preventing wind noise and '*popping*' on the recording. They are often referred to as a dog. Prince Charles used to ask sound recordists: 'Does it bite?' Longer guns are even more directional – you'll have seen them in documentaries about the making of wildlife films, and in spy movies.

Hypercardioid is a more extreme version of the polar pattern known as cardioid, or heart-shaped. Sound is collected from a heart-shaped area around the front of the mic.

Some mics record in a figure-of-eight, receiving sound from the front and rear but not the sides. They're sometimes called bi-directional. These are handy in studios for recording an interview where interviewer and subject are sitting either side of the mic.

Apart from strongly directional mics, the type of most use to broadcast journalists is the omni-directional, which as the name suggests collects sound from all directions. It's not much use if you want to eliminate heavy background noise, but can be effective if used close to the subject. They're commonly used by radio reporters. The tiny personal mics used by TV crews are usually omni-directional. They can be attached to the recorder or camera by cables or by radio link.

The FlashMic is a condenser type available in omni-directional and cardioid versions.

For lengthy radio interviews on location, personal mics attached to yourself and your interviewee do away with the need to stretch across chair arms and coffee tables. If you are using two mics, be aware of how you are going to mix the sound into the recorder. A small mixer might be the answer, or else you could record on to separate stereo tracks and adjust the balance and levels in the edit.

A useful tip when recording in a noisy area is to hold the mic very close to the speaker's mouth and turn down the record level accordingly. The mic will pick up the voice and cut the background noise to acceptable levels.

Protecting your mic outdoors

Just as the fluffy 'dog' protects TV gun mics from wind noise, a foam windshield is usually provided for reporters' stick mics. It fits on top of the mic and keeps some wind noise at bay, though not as much as the dog. What it won't protect the equipment against is pouring rain. The BBC advises its radio reporters to carry a condom . . . to slip over the end of the mic in a downpour. The windshield can be placed over the top of the protected mic, so that the makeshift waterproofing doesn't alarm interviewees.

- Different mics record sound in different ways
- Try to choose the best mic for the job
- Protect your mic from wind and rain

Recording indoors

Personal mic (a.k.a. clip-on mic or tie mic)

Wherever you record sound it is important to take control of the environment. Normally that is easier indoors than outside. You might not be able to halt the traffic on the M6 or divert the 1030 flight from Manchester to Malaga, but you can, politely, ask for a quiet room in which to conduct an interview.

Listen to the acoustics of the room. Clap your hands if necessary to hear any echoes. Bare walls, tiles and wooden floors will echo. Soft furnishings (curtains, carpets and upholstery) help dampen reflected sound. Avoid bathrooms and kitchens. Standing or sitting next to curtains can help.

The trend for laminate flooring played havoc with sound recording. One radio producer, confronted with an interviewee's newly modernised home – all wooden floors and no curtains – had to hire a room in a local B & B to ensure sound without echo. She said hiring a room at an hourly rate during the daytime did nothing for her reputation.

Often, you will want background sound to add colour to your interview: to prove you are on location, and haven't just invited everyone into the studio. Then you might be faced with the opposite problem to those above. For example, you might have to persuade the managing director who has set aside a nice quiet room for the interview that it will be better conducted on a noisy shop floor.

'Turn it off' – the problems of distracting sounds

Indoors it's easy to unplug telephones so they don't interfere with your recording. It's also important to remember to switch off mobile phones – your own and your interviewee's – while you are recording. If other people are in the room, ask them to switch theirs off too.

Clocks, fridges, freezers, air-conditioning units and other electrical equipment can also be picked up on your recording. You should ask if they can be turned off. And remind people to turn them back on again; you won't be popular if you've left a freezer full of food to defrost.

Fluffy dog wind shield

Setting a level

Normally, you should set your sound level before you start recording. Exceptionally, if you're at risk of missing something, you can start recording first and then adjust the levels immediately. If your settings are as they were the last time you recorded in that location, there is a fighting chance you will have usable sound. Recording on-the-fly like this happens more frequently than you might expect. The demands on the radio reporter are such that you may have just completed a live two-way or returned from feeding material via the radio car to find that a press conference has already started. Or you may be outside a court as the key witness emerges and starts talking to a television camera ten yards away.

Usually you have control over the situation and can take time to do things properly. The recorder has a pause mode and, while it is in pause, you set the record levels by directing your microphone at the sound source and monitoring it. If the sound source is a human voice, make sure the speaker is talking at the same level when you come to record. A shy interviewee may be reluctant to speak up before the interview proper. It used to be thought good practice to ask an innocuous question such as: 'What did you have for breakfast?' These days many people say: 'I didn't have any breakfast', which adds up to less than two seconds – barely time to look at the audio meters, never mind adjust them. A more imaginative approach may be needed: 'Tell me about your holidays.' 'Tell me what your job involves.' Sometimes it's best to ask people to identify themselves with their name and title, spelling out any difficult words. You may wish to record this as an audio note.

Some reporters have problems monitoring their own levels. They sound-check at one level – usually *sotto voce* because they don't want to be overheard. Then, as they launch into the report proper their voice booms out much louder. Avoid this temptation. If you're happy for thousands of people to hear your words over the radio, it shouldn't matter that a few people within 20 yards or so can overhear you. Counting into the microphone – 'one, two, three, four, five' or even, like a rock show roadie, 'one-two, one-two' – is a poor way to take your own level. You will probably count in a monotone, all at the same level, whereas your voice report will contain many ups and downs, just like a normal conversation. So it's better to sound check with the words you will be using.

Use headphones

It is surprising how many radio reporters conduct interviews without wearing headphones. The headphones or *cans* are your quality control. Your ears are the best judge.

Monitor the sound going into your recorder and you can ensure that the levels will be correct when it is played back. In news gathering with tight deadlines it is not good enough to assume you can boost the level on playback if it's a bit quiet. There may not be time to play with the levels before your recording is on air.

Worse still, if sound has been recorded too high it will distort, or on some digital systems disappear altogether. This is irretrievable. Distorted sound cannot be restored. Recording it is wasted effort. If it was a key interview with a witness who has left the scene, you will never be able to recapture the moment. You have failed to do your job.

You wouldn't take a photograph without looking in the viewfinder. Don't record sound without monitoring it. Some radio reporters prefer a small earpiece – it's less intrusive, but not as reliable as cans, which should encase your ears and eliminate the sounds you are not recording.

Monitor the sound through your ears

Useful extras

There are a few accessories worth taking out with any microphone kit. These are a small desktop mic stand, lengths of extra cable and gaffer tape. Leave them in the car until you need to use them. They come in handy for formal news conferences. The mic can be mounted on a desk and the cable laid to where the reporter is sitting. The tape helps keep it out of the way of fumbling hands and feet. The reporter can then operate the controls on the recorder in comfort, and concentrate on what is being said. If you don't have a mic stand or there's no room for it on the table, tape your mic to someone else's, but make sure you ask first!

You may have seen, on television coverage of major news stories, radio reporters crouching under a desk with their microphone hand held aloft to record press conferences. This is a bad idea for a number of reasons. First, it makes your arm ache and after ten minutes or so it is unbearable. You can't concentrate on your recording if you are engaged in an endurance test. Second, it is hard to earn the respect of your interviewee if you are crawling around on the floor at their feet. Third, even if you don't ask questions, it is decidedly undignified and does your reputation and that of your radio station no good at all.

Remember

- Control the recording environment
- Remove the source of distracting sounds if you can
- Set your levels before you start recording
- Always monitor your recording – preferably with headphones
- Don't forget the extras (cable and mic stands)

TELEVISION ON LOCATION

On the road with a camera crew

> **If it is potentially unsafe for one person to be responsible for technical operation, a second person is vital.**

Most television news reporting is carried out by a reporter with a camera crew. In domestic reporting the crew is usually one person, who's responsible for operating the camera and recording sound. In more dangerous locations, and that includes many foreign assignments, there will be a sound person too. If it is potentially unsafe for one person to be responsible for technical operation and watching their own back, a second person is vital.

It wasn't always so. Early BBC news reporting, on film, used two-person crews: one for the camera, the other for sound. In ITV there was a third person, a lighting electrician. Greg Dyke tells a story of when he was a young researcher on an ITV programme. A car pulled up on location with no one in the back. The future Director-General of the BBC asked why.

'He's the electrician's driver.'

'So where's the electrician?'

'He prefers to use his own car so he can claim the mileage.'

That was an example of the infamous 'Spanish practices' when trade union rules dictated ITV crewing policy. But Margaret Thatcher's government of the 1980s, with its determination to limit trade union power, and the advent of ENG – electronic news gathering – changed that.

ENG – or PSC (portable single camera), as it was known in the BBC – was the first major technical advance. Video took over from film as the medium for recording news events.

Then the Betacam system replaced U-Matic. In the U-Matic tape system, the camera was attached by an umbilical cable to the recorder, carried by the sound person. It would have been impossible for a camera operator to carry the heavy recorder. To this day, sound recordists who carried those recorders slung over one shoulder complain of back problems.

Betacam introduced the camcorder to television news. It also brought us the *one-man-band* – the camera person who did sound. The economic advantages are obvious. The practical problems of one person carrying camera, tripod, and often lights are harder to justify. Carrying the 'sticks' or tripod certainly endears a reporter to the crew. But always ask first. Don't just pick up a camera person's kit. These are the tools of their trade.

The introduction of single-person crews had another benefit – cameramen or women became used to working in tight two-person teams, not with a sound recordist, but with a reporter. People who had previously seen their responsibilities as purely technical became part of the journalistic process. They helped to tell the story, contributing filming ideas and adding an extra pair of critical eyes to the news-gathering process.

The value of a good camera person can never be overestimated. They will suggest shots that help tell the story, and will often pick up pictures or storylines you miss. There may be times though when you are expected to operate the camera yourself. Increasingly, the video journalist is a key player in television news gathering.

Operating the camera yourself – the video journalist

Video journalism is not just a way for news operations to save money. Journalists can bring greater intimacy and authenticity to their reports by operating their own cameras. Because the technology and the manpower (one person instead of two or three) are cheaper than traditional crews, the reporter can spend longer on the story, get closer to the people involved and uncover much more detail.

Lightweight, low-cost digital cameras producing pictures almost up to the quality then considered acceptable for broadcast came on the scene in the 1990s. Debates followed about the technical quality of the pictures and about who could and should use them. Today, the only practical restrictions on journalists 'one-man-banding' seem to be health and safety and human imagination. The video journalist or VJ is here to stay.

BBC Security Correspondent Frank Gardner, an Arabic speaker and Middle East expert, emerged as a leading video journalist after he was based in the Gulf in 1997:

'By then I'd picked up a lot of tips by watching how cameramen work. I did all my own films after that, and just shot everything for the BBC, because it was the right thing to do, rather than hiring a crew who didn't really understand what a sequence is (which you need to be able to do to make a film really watchable). So I've been pretty much a one-man-band most of the time.'

There are obviously situations where it would be folly for one person to act as reporter and camera operator. In riots, war zones and natural disasters, it is dangerous not to have someone watching your back while your eye is to the viewfinder. It's physically impossible to report from inside a courtroom, film witnesses going in and out, and have the camera ready for a stand-up outside at the end of the session. Frank Gardner, incidentally, was not alone when he was shot in Riyadh in 2004. The attack left him disabled. His cameraman Simon Cumbers died.

But there are stories where the portability of lightweight cameras and the flexibility and personal involvement of the VJ can be advantages. The BBC's PDP (Portable Digital Production) programme produced many mini observational documentaries, which benefited from intimate access to their subjects. Hundreds of journalists – and technical staff – were trained to operate DV cameras and to use laptop editing systems. The confusing 'PDP' label was dropped from BBC training in 2006 in favour of the clearer description 'video journalism'.

Remember

- It has never been easier to take your own broadcast-quality pictures
- Lightweight cameras give access to situations where a crew might be intrusive
- Video journalism enables you to control a story from beginning to end
- There are some situations where, for health and safety reasons, it is impossible to work alone

The rule of thirds: in a landscape, and a shot of a vehicle

Look at the lines; the lines in the picture draw attention to the subject

The language of film making

When you shoot pictures, you need to understand the language of film making. It helps you to think in pictures – to work out what you want to say televisually – and to use the pictures to tell the story.

Composition

You want every shot in your piece to look beautiful, but in news coverage events do not unfold to suit the camera. You have to do your best with what happens in front of you. Fortunately, there are rules to help you.

The rule of thirds has been used by artists and photographers for centuries to produce pleasing compositions. Mentally divide your viewfinder into thirds vertically and horizontally, like a noughts-and-crosses grid. The horizon or a distinct horizontal line in the landscape (a river or road, perhaps) should be a third of the way up or a third of the way down the screen.

People should be a third of the way across frame – looking into or walking into the two-thirds space, rather than walking out of frame. If you are walking alongside somebody, allow space in front of them for them to walk into. Stop and allow them to clear the frame at the end of the shot. It makes a good edit point.

Another technique is to have a point of interest in the foreground and strong action in the background – for example, the flashing lights of a police car in the foreground with police in riot gear behind. Strong foreground action against an imposing backdrop also works – think of the television coverage of the London Marathon, where runners are frequently shown against a background of familiar landmarks. Shots with both foreground and background interest give depth to the image.

Some people have a natural eye for a good shot. They're usually the people who were good at art in school. But you can learn composition. Whatever the subject, try to look at the lines in the frame. Are there lines, perhaps created by a row of trees or buildings or a stack of shelves, that draw your eye to one part of the picture? If there are, can you place your subject in that part of the picture? The effect is visually satisfying.

Remember

- Use the rule of thirds
- Strong foreground and background give depth
- Look at the lines

Sequences

Each shot in a news report should be there for only one reason – to help tell the story. But isolated shots will not tell the story very well. The pictures need to flow from one to the next. The best way of making your story flow is to film sequences – collections of shots that fit together. A sequence is usually an event filmed with different shot sizes and from different angles. You will often need to film the same action repeatedly to get enough shots for an edited sequence.

With a single camera you can create the illusion of a multi-camera shoot by shooting the same event several times from different angles. Make sure though that you maintain *continuity* – the appearance of continuous action – between shots. There's more on continuity later in the chapter.

Shooting sequences also helps you edit your pictures, because you can shorten or lengthen the action to fit your story. If you take a single shot of a top athlete running 100 metres, it will take just over ten seconds. If you shoot the same thing three times (each time on a different shot size or angle), you have 30 seconds of rushes to play with. So you could create a sequence much longer than ten seconds. Or, by cutting from the athlete starting the run to a close-up, and then back to the finish of the run, you could condense all of the action into six or seven seconds.

You may find it helpful to sketch out your ideas on a *storyboard*. The storyboard is a standard tool for feature film makers and for many documentary directors. Divide a piece of paper into squares. Sketch roughly what you want to see in each shot in a separate square. Add notes about camera moves.

In news, you will rarely have time for a storyboard. But it is useful for longer features and for designing graphics sequences.

Remember

- Shoot sequences, not single shots
- Think of the edit
- Use a storyboard if it helps and you have time

Shot sizes

Different sizes of shot perform different functions in our story telling. The diagram below shows a summary of them.

These are filming conventions that you will recognise from TV, movies and news coverage. Shots of people are graded from the long shot to the big close-up. A long shot shows the whole body; the big close-up shows detail of the face.

Lights on   CU

Band on Stage   WIDE

L. hand   CU

R. hand   CU

Singer   CU

Drummer   MCU

Band   WIDE

Crowd   WIDE

Example of a storyboard

GV
General view

WIDE
Wide of the action

LS
Long shot

MLS
Medium long shot

MS
Mid-shot

MCU
Medium close-up (the interview shot)

CU
Close-up

BCU
Big close-up

Illustrating shot sizes

MCU – the interview shot

MCU

The most important shot in your arsenal is the medium close-up – the standard shot for television interviews. It enables the viewer to see the subject's face clearly, their clothing, body language and the setting in which they are being filmed. It also allows enough space at the bottom of the screen to superimpose a caption giving their name and title without obscuring their features.

A reporter asking questions will stand directly alongside the camera, as close as possible. This has the effect of drawing the subject's eyeline round just away from the camera without their looking directly into it.

Always advise interviewees to look at you and not at the camera.

The effect of the standard interview shot is that we see three-quarters of the face. It is important the viewers can see both eyes. It keeps them interested in the face.

The interviewee needs to look at the reporter and not at the camera

A face in profile is a face partly turned away from you – and therefore a face that is talking to somebody else. You, the viewer, do not feel part of the conversation.

So, why does the interviewee address the reporter rather than talking directly to the camera? It's a convention from documentary film making that helps assert the authority of the narrator's voice. The reporter is the mediator of the story. When the reporter talks on camera, he looks straight into the lens. His eye contact is with the viewer, not a third party.

When you accept material from contributors or lend a video camera to someone to make their own film, you will probably want them to address the camera like a reporter. They are telling their own story.

Experienced interviewees, particularly politicians who may have done down-the-line interviews from remote studios, will ask: 'Where do you want me to look?' It's probably one of the things they were told to ask on a media training course. Ask them to look at you and ignore the camera.

The interviewee should be framed so that their eyes are looking into free space at the side of the shot. If the centre line of the head were to be exactly in the middle of frame it would look as if the subject were looking away from the interviewer. This gives the impression that they are trying to avoid the questions, and also that they don't really want to be there. It's unfair on a willing interviewee if poor framing gives a misleading impression of their motives.

The shot should also give the interviewee a little, but not too much, headroom – space above the head. Too little headroom and they may look unnaturally tall; too much and they appear too short. Camera operators will spend time adjusting the height of the tripod so that the eyeline of the interviewee is level, irrespective of their height relative to the interviewer. Their eyes will then be more than halfway up the screen. If someone's nose is almost at the exact centre of the screen, and they are looking neither up nor down, they're in the right position.

You may have heard stories of Hollywood leading ladies having to stand in a trench so they

would be level with a particularly short leading man. Or of a leading man standing on a box for the *two-shot*. On a news shoot, you don't have time to dig trenches, but a little manipulation of the topography may be permitted (stand the shorter person on a box or a step, for example). The idea is not to mislead the audience – you should never do that – but to present people as naturally as possible. The heights of your contributors are rarely part of the story (unless you're covering basketball), so there is no point confusing the viewer by filming somebody looking up or down. They'll be wondering what or who they're looking at, and miss what they're saying and the point of the story.

It's worth remembering that, when you are facing the camera, your left and right will be the opposite of the camera operator's. So give instructions to move out or in as 'camera left' or 'camera right', the way events are seen in the viewfinder. It is usually considered good practice to alternate the direction in which interviewees are looking during a piece. So, you need to remind the cameraman: 'We're probably using this after the first one we did, who was looking right, so can we do this one looking camera left, please?'

You will always want the background to an interview to help tell the story (see Chapter 6: Location reporting and production). It's a useful shorthand for the viewer, adding extra information while the interviewee is talking. The leader of an industrial dispute may be interviewed in front of a picket line. The spokesperson for a protest

The interviewee should be framed so that their eyes are looking into free space at the side of the shot

movement stands in front of banner-waving demonstrators. A winning golfer chats in front of the packed gallery around the eighteenth hole.

Beware, though, of being manipulated by those with a political or commercial agenda. Is it appropriate to film a protest leader in front of the half-dozen people who bothered to turn up when he is claiming massive support for his cause? Would it not be more accurate to show the wider picture – with most of the street empty? And just because somebody represents a particular commercial concern, you don't have to film them in front of their advertising hoarding. Product placement is not allowed in British-made news programmes, and there is a ban on 'undue prominence' for commercial services.

Anyone who has ever seen after-match interviews with football managers and players will know that every professional football ground has an interview room with a board behind the interviewee filled with sponsors' logos. There may be separate boards for different broadcasters: one with a Sky Sports logo plus the sponsors; the other with BBC Sport, perhaps, and the same sponsors' logos.

This is part of a commercial arrangement involving the clubs, the competition's organisers (UEFA, the FA or the Premier League, for example) and the broadcasters who have paid for the rights to the event. There is no obligation on news crews to use these interview rooms, although in the real world you have to go where your interviewees are.

Close-up (CU) and big close-up (BCU)

The close-up (CU), in which the picture cuts off just below the subject's neck, offers a more intimate look at the subject and is appropriate when the speaker is intense, emotional or under pressure.

The big close-up, or BCU, cutting off the top of the head and chin and concentrating on eyes and mouth, is rarely used in news except for the most emotive content. It used to be standard practice for the camera to zoom in if someone started crying. But audiences are more aware of the techniques of film making these days. Caution should be exercised. Does the camera appear to have been too intrusive?

The two-shot

When two people are featured in a shot, it's known as a two-shot. It has a variety of uses.

It can be a shot of two interviewees.

Or it can be a shot of the interviewer and the interviewee. A static two-shot taken from behind the interviewer used to be a common way of introducing the interviewee. These days you are more likely to see a walking two-shot, sometimes with the interview starting on the move, using radio mics.

(a) Close-up (CU)
(b) Big close-up (BCU)

It is rarely a good idea to conduct a lengthy interview on a two-shot. If two people are in frame all the time, the shot will be so wide that there will not be enough detail in the face of the speaker to keep the interest of the viewer. Another problem with the static two-shot is that the interviewer and interviewee are likely to be facing each other and will therefore be in profile. There is no eye contact with the viewer and, again, not enough of the speaker's facial expression can be seen. Interviews conducted on a two-shot are also difficult to edit.

If you must start an interview on a two-shot – in a live or 'as live' situation perhaps – try this common technique. After your introductory comments and first question, the camera zooms in to a single shot of the interviewee – a conventional MCU. At the same time the reporter steps round alongside the camera, into the same position as for a regular interview. This draws the eyeline round so the speaker is no longer in profile and the viewer can see both the speaker's eyes. As the interview closes – and on a pre-arranged signal or instruction from the gallery – the reporter steps back round in front of camera as the operator zooms out, widening the shot. The reporter thanks the interviewee and delivers his or her closing lines to camera.

The over-the-shoulder two-shot

Over-the-shoulder two-shot

The over-the-shoulder two-shot is useful for editing. It enables you to jump from one point in an interview to another. The back of the reporter's head is towards the camera, so the movement of their mouth is not visible. This means the shot can be dropped over any question. When filming these shots it is vital to be aware of how they might be used in the edit. It is tempting to relax at the end of the interview and, while the cameraman concentrates on the shot, interviewer and interviewee share a joke. This will not work if the subject of the interview has been a serious one. You will need to advise the interviewee what's going on so they adopt a suitable expression.

The reverse two-shot

By moving the camera you can take a *reverse* two-shot, over the shoulder of the interviewee favouring the interviewer. You may wish to record *cutaway questions*, or *reverses* as they are also known, repeating questions you have already asked. Or you can do listening shots. They're sometimes known as *noddies*, but the temptation to nod during them should be resisted as it gives the impression you agree with everything being said. These shots can be edited in later if needed.

Most news reports rely on short soundbites and there is no need for reverse questions or even two-shots. Up against tight deadlines, it's easy to ignore them. But the day will come when you are in an edit truck and you wish you'd taken the extra moments to do the two-shot. It's worth developing the discipline of doing them every time you film, or at least every time you have time to.

Cutaways

Over the shoulder and reverse two-shots are known as cutaways because you cut away to them during the edit. Close-ups – of hands for example – serve the same purpose. These shots are not dependent on *sync* sound, the term for any shot where the picture has to match the sound, usually because we can see someone's lips moving. A cutaway is a picture that can be used over the sound from another picture.

Cutaways can disguise an edit point in an interview. The sound may flow seamlessly but the picture will not. Without a cutaway, the viewer would see a *jump-cut*. The jump-cut is where the action jumps from one part of a scene to another. It happens all the time in really old newsreel where film stock has degenerated and frames are missing. It also happens if you

The reverse: a useful editing device and an opportunity to ask cutaway questions

cut a section out of someone's answer. Suddenly their head jumps from one position on the screen to another. There are ethical considerations in all this, because the cutaway disguises the edit. You should not set out to deliberately mislead the audience. Alternatives are discussed in Chapter 12: Editing.

When shooting sequences, you will need details of the action. For example, when showing someone painting a picture, you'll want to cut to the close-up of brush on canvas. Be conscious though of *continuity*, the need to make the action appear continuous when you edit. If you cut back to a wide shot, the brush must appear to be in the same position and not to have jumped across the canvas. And the close-up should not show an almost-finished work of art when the wide shows it's barely been started – or vice versa.

Annette Martin, a director on factual programmes from *Top Gear* to *Countryfile*, says: 'You can never have enough cutaways. Do your shoot. Get your cutaways. And then get more.'

A set-up shot – let the interviewee clear shot to assist the edit

Set-ups

Every time you interview someone think how you will introduce them into your film. The best way is with set-ups – a shot or preferably a sequence of shots of them doing something, and preferably something exciting or at least with bold movement. The advantage of a sequence is that the length can be adjusted in the edit depending on how much you need to say to introduce the interviewee. You will not normally need to say somebody's full name and title – that can be done with a caption – but you may need to lead in to what they are about to say.

Some set-up shots are so tired from overuse that they have become visual clichés. Regular viewers of television news will recognise these examples. The academic takes a book from a shelf and thumbs through it. The MP walks across College Green (outside the Houses of Parliament) or down the stairs in Millbank. The elderly woman makes a cup of tea. The chief constable/government minister/football manager is seen in a wide shot at the head of a table during a press conference.

Like all clichés, these shots save time because they save the need to think. That doesn't mean you have to do the same.

Paul Myles, a senior trainer at the BBC's Centre for Video Journalism, says:

'The politician on College Green and the man taking a book off the shelf are exactly the kind of set-up, staged television the BBC is so keen to get away from. But sometimes there's no time for anything else. The politician comes out of his office and will only give you two minutes.'

Myles and his colleagues encourage video journalists to spend time with their subjects, filming people as they go about their daily business, rather than directing them for the camera. Snatches of comment or interview from the subject can be grabbed as you go along, rather than inserted from a set-piece interview. This technique leads to very naturalistic, highly watchable films.

Remember

- Learn the names of different shots and their uses
- Get cutaways
- Try to film imaginative set-ups
- Spend time with your subjects

Crossing the line

You will hear camera crews and directors talk about the *line* and warn about not crossing it. At first it sounds like warning children about stepping on cracks in the pavement. Watch out for the bears! In practice it is a very useful way of making sure that what you film does not confuse the viewer.

The line is best explained by looking at the way a football match is televised. The main cameras are on one side of the pitch. As the director cuts between them, perhaps to go from a wide shot to a close-up of the player on the ball, play continues in the same direction. Chelsea are kicking left to right; Arsenal right to left. If the second camera were on the opposite side of the pitch, the teams would appear to be kicking the other way when the director cut to the close-up. If he then went back to the wide shot, the teams would appear

To avoid crossing the line, the subject in the close-up should be facing the same direction as in the wide shot

to be attacking the opposite goals again. Very confusing. This is because the action has *crossed the line.*

In all film making, directors do not want to confuse the viewer so they try not to cross the line. If you have only one camera you need to be especially aware of this. Make sure any action continues in the same direction. If someone clears shot left of frame they should enter the next shot right of frame. If a golf ball is played from right to left of screen we need to see it arriving on the green from the same direction.

The only time crossing the line does not seem to jar in the mind of the viewer is when pictures are set to music. This means pop videos can cross the line several times a second. You may use music in features, but you will rarely be able to in hard news.

The imaginary line in an interview runs between interviewer and interviewee. The camera stays on one side of it, so that a reverse angle or cutaway question will show the interviewer facing the opposite direction on screen to the interviewee. This gives the impression of two people talking to each other. It is this final impression that is the most important thing. If it looks right, it is right. The *line* is a useful tool, but like all tools it can be discarded if it is not helping you to do the job. And you *can* cross the line if you take the viewer with you. You can move the camera across the line as you shoot, or track around the subject, and use the shot in your piece.

If the close-up is from the opposite side to the wide shot, viewers are left wondering in which direction the cyclists are travelling

Remember

- Keep the camera on one side of the action
- Film interviewer and interviewee facing in opposite directions
- Crossing the line doesn't matter in music sequences
- You can cross the line if you track round the action, 'taking the viewer with you'

Continuity

You should aim for continuity whatever you shoot. For example, if you cut from a wide shot of a chef chopping vegetables with the knife in his right hand, to a close-up of the knife in the left hand, it will look odd. If the first shot showed carrots but the second shot has leeks, that too will jar with viewers. A wide shot of the chef wearing his hat followed by a close-up without it will not work either.

The reverse angle in an interview shows the interviewee facing the interviewer

You need to be aware of the possible breaks in continuity as you film. If you are alone, this is difficult. Feature film crews have a member of the team whose only job is to ensure continuity between takes. And still there are continuity mistakes in the biggest-budget Hollywood blockbusters, with websites, chatrooms and TV programmes delighting in exposing them.

The easiest way to ensure continuity in news features is to enlist the aid of your subjects. Tell the chef, 'Make sure you keep your hat on.' And explain why.

One of the biggest mistakes is to take a break in mid-sequence and return to filming later. 'Now where were we? Did you have your hat on?' Finish the sequence, and *then* have your cup of coffee.

Whenever you shoot a set-up sequence, think what will come next in the finished piece. What exactly are you 'setting-up'? If you are cutting to an interview, then do the set-ups of that person in the same location. In particular, make sure that you don't jump from indoors to outdoors or vice versa. Watch enough TV news, and it won't be long before you see a shot of someone walking into a building followed immediately by an interview with them outdoors. We know why it was done: the lighting was easier outdoors for the interview (no need to use fiddly artificial lights); the easiest shot was the subject going into the building (no need to ask them to go in, come out again, and walk past the camera without looking at it). The result is lazy television and it looks odd.

Remember

- Concentrate between shots to ensure continuity
- Enlist the help of your subjects
- Don't break from shooting mid-sequence
- Do set-ups and interviews in the same location

If you get it wrong, both parties will be looking the same way, and the illusion of a conversation is lost

Tracking

When the camera moves over the ground it is known as tracking. In news coverage, tracking usually means the cameraman is walking. When the budget allows, it will be mounted on a *dolly*, which runs along a track, like a narrow-gauge railway line. Again, bigger-budget productions might allow for a stabilising device such as Steadicam, a harness with a counterweight. You see them all the time on the touchlines at televised football matches. In news, you will probably be relying on your own (or the camera person's) expertise to achieve a wobble-free shot.

Where action is unfolding in front of the camera there is rarely a need for tracking. 'Point and shoot' is the best approach to news events. Keep the camera absolutely still and let the action take place in front of it. But tracking shots – and other camera moves – help when there is a shortage of action to film. Crime and court reporting are good examples. If it is known that an attacker fled down an alleyway, a tracking shot down the alley will illustrate this.

Tracking shots can also be *POV* shots. POV stands for *point of view* – what somebody sees as they are walking along. It's another useful technique in crime scene reconstructions.

Tracking with a subject can also add movement to a story that would otherwise be a series of static scenes. If you want to demonstrate how busy someone is, it is better to film them racing between meetings than sitting in a series of meeting rooms.

Pans and tilts

The pan (short for panoramic shot) is a camera move on a horizontal plane – left to right or right to left (but never both in the same shot). The tilt is a vertical move – up or down. Both pans and tilts can be achieved using the pan handle on the tripod. The pan handle is not so called because it looks like the handle of a frying pan (although it might). It is the handle that helps you pan.

The most important things to remember about pans and tilts are that these shots must have a purpose and they must have a beginning, middle and end. One of the most common and annoying faults of people using a home video camera for the first time is that they pan and tilt (often at the same time) aimlessly and endlessly. This is known as 'hosepiping' because the camera is being waved around at random like an uncontrollable garden hose. It might be fun for the kids, but most adult gardeners will tell you it's not the best way to water the lawn.

If you must pan, decide what you are panning from and to. If it's a view across typical English countryside, start with a landmark like a church tower left of frame then pan right to reach another landmark or natural feature, such as a copse. Make sure the pan lasts no more than the three or four seconds you would reasonably expect to use. Cutting in or out of a moving shot looks ugly so any longer is pointless. Record enough at the beginning and end of the pan – say four or five seconds – to use as separate static shots if needed.

Pans and tilts may last longer in features and documentaries, where the pace of story telling will be affected by the director's choice of shots. In news, stick to the guidelines above and you won't go far wrong.

The zoom

(a) The wide shot (b) Zoomed in

The zoom lens – a lens that can make far-away objects appear closer to the camera – is one of the most useful and also the most abused controls on any video camera. The best thing the zoom does is enable you to change the shot size without moving the camera. The worst thing it does is to encourage inexperienced operators to zoom in and out to the annoyance of the viewer. Excessive use of the zoom is particularly irritating when the camera is handheld, as witnessed on all the worst holiday videos. Whenever the camera is handheld, the zoom should be as wide as possible. As soon as you zoom in, you magnify the effect of any camera shake. Even experienced professionals using tripods will be unable to prevent some camera shake if they are working 'at the end of the zoom'.

Only ever use optical zoom. Modern cameras have a digital zoom facility, beyond the range of the optical zoom. It is an electronic enhancement of the picture – blowing up the available pixels to fill the screen. It results in a loss of picture quality and is not suitable for most professional purposes.

The shot we call a zoom – the act of zooming in or out of the action – also has to be approached with caution. You see zooms all the time in news coverage – usually on regional programmes when not much is happening in front of the lens. Exterior *GVs* (general views) of buildings will often include a pull-out from a window to see the whole of a house or office block. Occasionally a zoom-in will highlight an interesting feature.

Mostly though, zooms are a boon to lazy reporters because they fill time and can cover sloppy scripting. Great film makers rarely use zoom shots, however, unless it is for dramatic effect. Watch any feature film and it will be rare to see a zoom at all. John McLeod, a senior news correspondent who worked for both ITV and the BBC, refused to use them in his reports. His argument was that they were 'unnatural'. They were the only movement the camera made that did not replicate the way our eyes see the world. We can look up and down (the tilt), turn our heads from side to side (the pan), look at things in detail (the close-up), or take a broader view (the wide), but nobody (unless they are a T-1000 Terminator sent back from the future to kill a boy who will grow up to be a resistance leader) has eyes that zoom in and out.

Remember

- Camera moves can make shots more interesting
- There has to be a start and an end point for any camera move
- Moves should rarely last more than three or four seconds
- Use zooms rarely, if at all
- If you are handheld, keep the zoom as wide as possible

A CLOSER LOOK

PRESSERS AND PRESS PACKS – REGULAR SCENARIOS

Many news-gathering situations occur frequently and it's possible to prepare for them. Not every news conference or press briefing is the same – but there are similarities.

The news conference

When you are sent to cover a news or press conference, plan what equipment you will need. If it is indoors, as most are, TV crews may need lights. Some press conference rooms, at police headquarters buildings for example, are in regular use for the purpose and have their own TV lighting built in. Ask your producer or researcher, or better still the organisers of the conference, before you leave the newsroom.

You will need enough mic cable to run from the top table to the camera or to where you are sitting as a radio reporter. Alternatively, use radio mics. They are a better option on health and safety grounds too. No one will trip over your cable.

In large set-piece news conferences, the bigger radio stations will have more than one microphone and TV will have more than one camera. If you have the option of more than one audio channel, one will be a mic on the main speaker (or a feed from an audio desk of a mic on the lectern), the other a mic you can use for your questions. Similarly, one camera will be on the main speaker; the other will take wide shots, cutaways and a shot of you as you ask your question. Make sure you sit where the second camera can see you clearly.

Media scrums

It is easy for reporters to operate effectively in media scrums. Just shove your microphone to the front and start recording. For a lone person with a handheld camera, the scrum is the worst of working environments. You will have no

For a lone person with a handheld camera, the scrum is the worst of working environments.

protection against being jostled as you try to maintain focus and framing. The chances of securing steady usable shots are not high. The chance of recording quality sound (without an undue emphasis on the grumbles and complaints of those around you) is minimal. Ask yourself if you need to be in the thick of it. Might you be better off dropping back and getting a steady, wide shot that tells the story just as well? Here are some tips:

- Don't zoom in – as we've said, the zoom magnifies camera-shake and makes steady shots almost impossible.

- Use your ears – listen, preferably through your headphones, for the actuality sound you want to hear. When the subject at the centre of a scrum has said something relevant and usable, consider whether you can then drop back and get the wide shot of the scene.

- Stand your ground. Don't be intimidated, but resist the temptation to fight for position. When you are operating equipment you are more vulnerable than a reporter with a notebook who may be trying to elbow their way past you.

The camera

The growth of video journalism has been made possible by the reduced costs of cameras that can produce a broadcast quality picture. The gulf between home video equipment and professional cameras has all but disappeared in the last decade.

The cameras used most often by video journalists are at the top end of the domestic camcorder market. They will be similar to the ones used by students on broadcast journalism courses, which means today's graduates have an advantage over the journalists of earlier generations. They are more likely to be multi-skilled when they start the job.

Cameras using SDHC (Secure Digital High Capacity) cards are capable of producing high-definition widescreen pictures – as good as anything on most TV news stations worldwide and of a higher specification than you'll need for broadband content. The Sony Z1 became the instrument of choice for the BBC's regional video journalists in 2005. Then Panasonic introduced their P2 system – solid state with high-powered memory cards. The cards could be 'hot-swapped', allowing continuous recording, with no gaps while tapes are replaced. Video files transferred to the edit system at up to 640 megabits per second (Mbps), much faster than the time it takes to *digitise* tapes, which have to be played back in real time. The Sony NX5 is effectively the flash card version of the Z1. It records on to SDHC cards. These are classified according to data transfer speed and performance. Class 10 is the most efficient.

The professional operator should always use the manual settings.

These cameras have automatic functions aimed at the domestic user. Mum or dad won't want to bother with lots of tricky buttons to press at family parties: they want to just point and shoot. But the professional operator should always use the manual settings. They ensure you have control over the picture quality at all times.

White balance

Cameras are electronic instruments. They're clever, but not as clever as the combination of the human eye and the human brain. A white shirt looks white to you and me whether we are indoors or outdoors. The camera will see it differently because different types of light favour different parts of the colour spectrum. Daylight is mostly blue. Artificial light is more yellow.

Always do a white balance

These differences can be shown on a scale as *colour temperature*, measured in degrees Kelvin (or K). Daylight in the UK measures around 5000 K. Sunrise and sunset are much lower. Ordinary household bulbs are nearer 3000 K – more yellow on the scale.

Before you take a shot, the camera needs to be told the colour temperature. This is known as a *white balance*. If we tell the camera an object is white, it will make it look white and adjust all the colours in the picture accordingly, so that they look natural too.

You need to do a fresh white balance every time you move between different types of light, outdoors to indoors, or from fluorescent to tungsten lighting.

The process of white balancing is usually straightforward. Zoom in on a white object – a white wall, a white shirt or a sheet of white paper. If you are using a piece of paper, hold it directly in front of what you are filming, rather than immediately in front of the camera lens (because it is the light on the subject that you need to measure – not the light a few centimeters from the lens). Then press the camera's white-balance button. The image in the viewfinder will flash and then set itself to the appropriate colour temperature. What you see in the viewfinder when you zoom out to the wide shot will look the same colour as what you are seeing around you with your own eyes. Pre-set white balances (for outdoor and indoor shooting, for example) allow you to move rapidly from one lighting environment to another. But professionals will point out that even outdoor light changes – particularly as the sun moves across the sky – so you should white balance outdoors every hour or so.

You can create a warmer, or more orange, picture by white balancing on a light blue object. Or make things look blue by white balancing on something yellow. Such techniques can replace the use of colour filters. They can be practised through trial and error, but have little use in news reporting and are best left to experienced operators.

Electronic editing systems can compensate for mistakes with your white balance. But that takes time. It's better to get the white balance right from the start and apply any artistic adjustments in the edit.

Exposure

Your picture should not look unnaturally dark or light so you need to control the exposure – the amount of light let into your camera. You do this by changing the *aperture* and occasionally the *shutter speed*. The aperture setting acts like the iris of your eye, controlling the amount of light let in. Smaller aperture settings allow less light in – you can see this on your viewfinder.

A CLOSER LOOK

F-STOPS – MEASURING THE APERTURE

Aperture is measured in f-numbers, and they can be confusing to non-photographers. Because f-numbers are the ratio of the focal length (the distance from the lens to its focal point) to the aperture diameter, smaller numbers mean a larger aperture. As the numbers on the scale increase, the amount of light is halved at each stop. The f-numbers don't double though, because of that ratio formula. Don't worry about this. In practical terms you will see the result of changing the f-stops in your viewfinder.

These are the numbers you'll see on your camera and how they relate to the amount of light being let in.

f-stop	1.4	2	2.8	4	5.6	8	11	16
light entering lens	1	1/2	1/4	1/8	1/16	1/32	1/64	1/128

The shutter speed also affects the amount of light let into the camera. A fast shutter speed allows less light in than a slow one. You will need a larger aperture if you decide to use a faster shutter speed.

So why change the shutter speed? It depends what you are filming. A fast shutter enables you to capture fast action without blurring. A very slow speed creates an interesting deliberate blurring effect, which can look good behind graphics sequences or in stylised reports. Adjusting the shutter speed can also get rid of the annoying stripes that appear on video and computer monitors when they are shot by video cameras.

In very bright lighting conditions – outdoors on a sunny day – you may want to use a *neutral density* filter. It is a feature built into many cameras – the equivalent of giving your camera an electronic pair of sunglasses. The neutral density filter is usually applied using a separate control marked *ND*.

Your eyepiece viewfinder should show when pictures are correctly exposed. Flip-out LCD (liquid crystal display) screens are useful, but outdoors in sunlight you won't be able to see the picture clearly enough to check the exposure. The best tool on a professional camera for checking exposure is the *zebra* feature. Zebra stripes are diagonal black and white stripes that appear on the picture in the viewfinder – but *not* on your recording. If you set the zebras to 100 per cent, they will show on areas that are too bright or over-exposed. The most useful setting, particularly when setting up interviews, is 80 per cent. The zebras should appear on the nose, forehead and cheekbones of your subject. The patterns on darker skins will appear smaller than on Caucasian subjects. Adjust the exposure accordingly.

Focus

Only after you have set your white balance and exposure should you worry about the focus. But focus is the most important of your camera settings. Small errors in white balance and exposure can be corrected in the edit – but *when something is recorded out of focus you can never make it sharp again.*

Never leave auto focus switched on. The camera will *hunt* for focus as objects move in and out of the centre of the frame. The result looks decidedly amateurish.

You should usually control focus using the focus ring on the lens. This is the best way to change focus when an object is moving towards or away from you. Some cameras have a focus button which switches to auto focus for as long as it takes to sharpen up your picture; this can be useful.

Rotating the focus ring to pull focus

To set focus, zoom into your subject. Choose a part of the subject that has clearly outlined features. If it's a person, zoom in on the eyes: that's where you'll find the most detail on anybody's face. Then turn the focus ring until the picture is sharp. When you zoom out to reframe your shot, the subject and everything immediately in front of and behind it will be sharp in the frame.

After you have focused, everything within the lens's *depth of field* will be sharp on screen. The depth of field is the distance from the nearest to the furthest points at which objects appear to be in focus. Manipulating depth of field is a useful device. It enables you to *pull focus* – to change the part of the picture that's sharp, and so switch the viewer's attention from one thing to another. You'll have seen this in drama when two people are talking, or in news and documentaries when an object in the foreground gives way to what's happening behind it, or vice versa.

The pull focus: the foreground and background are in different planes of focus. Rotate the focus ring to go from one to the other

Reducing the aperture size increases the depth of field. A narrow depth of field, created with a wider aperture, will mean your subject is in sharp focus, but objects in front of and behind it appear blurred or *soft*. If your subject strays closer to or further from the camera, it will go out of focus.

To set up a pull-focus shot, frame your shot so that the two subjects, at different distances from the camera, are in view. Use a wide aperture setting, so that only one of the subjects is in focus at a time. Practise rotating the focus ring so that the plane of focus moves from one to the other, before you start recording. When you're sure just how far to rotate the ring, press the record button. Hold the shot for a few seconds before you pull focus.

In bright sunlight the field of focus will be so deep you might not be able to pull focus. Try using the neutral density filter to reduce the light coming into the camera, or move further away from the subjects and zoom in. Operating on the end of the zoom is another way of reducing the depth of field, but you can only do so if you are using a tripod. Otherwise there will be too much camera shake. It's a matter of trial and error. Full-time camera operators take a long time setting up their artier shots, but the results are rewarding. They add a professional gloss to your filming.

Often the problem you face filming in available light (that is, without professional lighting) is that there is not enough light. Indoors in gloomy buildings, or at dawn and dusk, you might need to use another electronic trick – the camera's *gain*. Gain boosts the exposure of the picture. It might be added using the flywheel or ring that changes the f-stop settings or with a separate switch on the side of the camera. Gain has a disadvantage. It makes the picture grainier and less sharp. The graininess is known as 'noise' and is measured in decibels (or dB). Video cameras usually offer 9 dB or 18 dB of gain. 18 dB is always noticeable, and you may prefer, if possible, to use artificial light.

Remember

Every time you take a shot you need to check:
- White balance
- Exposure
- Focus

And
- Don't use autofocus
- Practise pulling focus

Only when white balance, exposure and focus are set (and sound levels have been checked) should you press the record button. Make sure the record symbol (usually a red dot in the corner) is showing in the viewfinder. If you are taking lots of shots, it's very easy to get 'out of sync' and think you are recording when you're not. Most professional camera people have fallen into this trap at one time or another.

Follow the red dot.

A portable camera light with barn doors

Three-point lighting for an interview

The lighting kit

Lighting

As soon as you start using professional lighting, the quality of your pictures, particularly in indoor locations, steps up a gear.

As well as showing what might otherwise be in the dark, lights can create mood and a sense of depth in your pictures. They can also highlight a particular part of the shot. But for the single-person operator, new considerations come into play – mostly about health and safety.

A small light can be fitted to the top of your camera. It will use a lot of battery power, but the improved picture quality should repay reduced battery life. Switch it off as soon as you have finished a shot. Be careful. If you get too near your subject with a camera light, you may bleach out their features in the recorded shot. A single light source also flattens the image. A camera light will not give any impression of depth.

To create depth, you need more than one light. You will need to plug your lights into a separate power source, usually the mains, and that means trailing leads. There's always a risk of someone tripping over loose cables, so you can't use mains lights unless you have complete control over your working space. You should also use a circuit breaker to avoid fusing electrical systems. Television lights can take a lot of power. A redhead, so-called because the 'head' of the lamp (not the bulb) is by convention coloured red, offers 1 kilowatt of light. A blond (yellowish in colour) offers 2 kilowatts.

Lights are mounted on their own stands. There are movable flaps, called barn doors, on the front of the lamps to help you direct the light.

Three-point lighting

The traditional TV rig for lighting an interview or talking head is known as three-point lighting. Three lights are used, each with a different function.

- The **key** light, with hard-edged shadows, brings out the main features of the face. It will be placed in front of the interviewee, on the same side as the interviewer.
- The **filler** light, with a softer edge, lightens or 'fills in' the shadows cast by the key on the other side of the face.
- The **back** light is placed behind the interviewee to one side. It gives depth to the picture – a 3D effect – making the subject stand out from the background. It can be very flattering, adding sparkle to a subject's hair.

When you use artificial lighting indoors, be aware of the obvious light sources in the room. Your lighting scheme should echo what looks natural to the viewer. If there is a window or a lamp in the picture, the viewer expects that to be a source of light. When blue natural light from a window is competing with the yellowish light from your lamps, a transparent blue film or gel can be placed over your lights. Your lights are then complementing the daylight with more blue light, rather than competing with it. This helps achieve an accurate white balance. The gel can be attached to the barn doors with bulldog clips or clothes pegs.

But remember, if you are on your own, lights are heavy to carry around and take time to set up. Keep a lighting kit in the car, if you can, but expect to use it only on pre-planned shoots or when you have plenty of time.

The tripod

Whenever possible use a tripod to make your shots steady and free from wobble. There's a vogue in reality TV shows and some news coverage for verité-style handheld camera shots. These can add excitement and a sense of 'being there' to your coverage. But too much camera movement is disconcerting for the viewer. The best handheld camera shots are those that use the advantages of not being mounted on a tripod to get into situations where a tripod would get in the way. But the operators still keep the camera steady.

The Steadicam – a counterbalance system worn by the operator to keep shots stable – offers steady shots on the move. But Steadicam is a specialist area of camera operation and too cumbersome to use for news coverage.

A stable platform for your camera is essential if you're shooting something that isn't moving – scenery or buildings, for example – or filming yourself. The tripod's height can be adjusted, which helps you set up an interview or piece-to-camera with the camera at the subject's eye level. The tripod should have a spirit level to ensure vertical and horizontal lines do not appear at odd angles in your pictures. There are few sights more upsetting than a shot of a lake that appears to be sloping from one end to the other. It brings new meaning to the old joke about wanting to take up waterskiing, but not being able to find a lake with a steep enough slope.

The Rosenblum effect

The American TV producer Michael Rosenblum has been a key figure in the BBC's video journalism training. He says the idea of a TV news operation being planned around the availability of five or six cameras is like a newspaper's reporters sharing only five or six pencils. He persuaded the BBC that, if they didn't embrace the new technology of cheap, lightweight cameras and editing, they had no future as a producer of broadcast programmes.

Rosenblum says traditional broadcasters are reluctant to embrace change:

'**Institutionally they're not really prepared to cope with the ramifications of what all this means. They pay lip service to it, and they try, but they're not really psychologically or emotionally prepared to embrace the reality of what has to come.**'

He says TV stations don't need studios: 'People are going to work at home, and feed their stuff online with fibre-optic and Wi-Fi. This is all here. The way they work now is extremely cost and journalistically ineffective. Either they get it or they'll be fundamentally out of business.'

His advice to trainees who don't want to become multi-skilled: 'Either understand how to do this and skill yourself, or learn how to sell life insurance.'

The five-shot method

Any event can be filmed as a series of sequences, and the easiest way to shoot a sequence is to use the five-shot method, based on Michael Rosenblum's teaching.

This is taught on BBC video journalism courses. Rosenblum insists on people-led television. Stories are always about people, and there's no place in his world for exterior shots of buildings. So, this method applies to filming people – but it can be adapted for any shoot. If you are with someone, and they're doing something, these are the shots you need:

The five-shot technique:
(a) hands; (b) face; (c) wide;
(d) over-the-shoulder;
(e) shot-of-choice

1 The **hands**. What is this person doing? Look at their hands. Get a close-up of the hands. Focus. Press record. Hold it for ten seconds.
2 The **face**. Who is this person? What is their expression? Are they concentrating on what they're doing? Are they enjoying themselves? Are they unhappy? Get a close-up of the face. Focus. Record. Hold for ten seconds.

3 The **wide** shot. Where is this person? What is their environment? Are they at home, at work or at leisure? Step back for the wide. Focus. Record. Hold for ten seconds.

4 The **over-the-shoulder**. What or who are they looking at? This may be a high-angle shot looking down at what the hands are doing, or a shot from behind. Move yourself and the camera. Focus. Record. Hold for ten seconds.

5 The **shot-of-choice**. This can be an alternative wide, or an unusual angle suggested by the setting or the activity, a high-(top-shot) or low-level view of the scene, perhaps. Move yourself and the camera. Focus. Record. Hold for ten seconds.

These shots are interchangeable in the edit. When the action is continuous or repeated (working at a desk or bench, for example), they can be taken in any order. Each shot will act as a cutaway between any two others. You will choose the best two or three seconds of each shot to match the others.

The technique is flexible. If you're filming someone kicking a ball, the shot of the hands will be replaced by a shot of the feet.

You need to monitor the sound as you record, to make sure it is usable throughout. Don't talk over the shot while you are recording. You may decide that to maintain the continuity of sound in the edit, you are better off not switching the camera off between shots.

When you edit, you don't have to use all five shots every time. That will depend on the length of the edited sequences. If you use the shots over someone speaking (voice-over or interview), the duration may be determined by the audio.

The five-shot method has at least three steps in common with the five Ws approach to writing news stories (see Chapter 5: News writing). The face shot tells us *who* is doing something, the hands show us *what* they're doing and the wide shows us *where*.

Don't move the camera

When you have framed your shot, don't move the camera. Keep it steady. Steady shots are so much easier to edit. Cutting in and out of moving shots invariably jars – the viewer feels cheated because they expect to see how the move finishes. Wobbly shots, or shots where the framing changes midway through, are a distraction.

Move the shot to follow the action only if you are sure how the action is developing. It may be better to re-frame and shoot the new action separately, keeping the camera running to capture continuous sound (which helps in the edit). You can link from one shot to the other with a cutaway if there is a continuity break.

If you must move the camera, make sure there's a good reason: to follow the action or to move smoothly from one point of interest to another.

Sound on video – a reminder

Great sound helps pictures to tell stories. Good actuality sound is better than voice-over at letting the viewer know what's happening on screen. You need to monitor sound whenever you shoot. Wear headphones or an earpiece whenever the camera is running, and watch the levels. You will have two channels of sound on the camera. If you are working with a sound recordist (a rarity in news or video journalism), they can monitor and mix the sound from different sources as it is recorded.

In the absence of a sound recordist (i.e. almost always), use your second audio track as a back-up for the main sound source. For example, you may be filming someone wearing a radio mic. Set their audio level manually and keep an eye on the meter in the viewfinder as you film. Use the on-camera mic on channel two as a back-up, in case the signal from the transmitter fails. Set the level on channel two slightly lower, so if there is a sudden loud noise it won't distort on the recording.

Monitoring your audio through headphones allows you to check not only the volume but also the quality of the sound you are recording. You should be able to hear if your subject is clearly on mic, or if you have accidently flicked the wrong input switch. Some cameras (the Sony NX5 for example) record from an internal mic as a default setting. So if an external mic is plugged in but the input on the camera is not switched to the mic setting, the recording may sound tinny or hollow. The level meter will show that you are recording sound at the right volume, but won't tell you that it's unusable. With headphones on, you'll pick that up straight away and be able to change your input settings to record perfect sound.

Remember

- The five-shot method helps you shoot sequences
- Steady shots are easier to edit
- Maintain continuity of sound

Transmission – getting the story back

Technology has revolutionised the way stories can be transmitted from the field. Satellite transmission is now commonplace, and broadband and wireless networks, particularly in built-up areas, are making long-distance reporting ever cheaper. As bandwidth increases, live links from anywhere on earth look increasingly possible. We are not yet in a Wi-Fi world. Developing countries and remote regions are not wired up for unlimited broadcasting. But the domestic (UK) landscape has been transformed.

Outside broadcasts (OBs) historically relied on microwave links to fixed receivers. The radio car or TV links vehicle needed to be within a 'line of sight' of the receiving station. Line of sight did not literally mean you had to be able to see the receiver – it could be many miles away, and a tall mast would mean the reach would be much further than the eye could see from ground level.

Engineers kept maps of the regions their vehicles covered, showing sites from which a strong signal could be transmitted, and also the blind-spots, areas where hills and valleys, or even tall buildings, prevented a signal getting through. Sometimes a chain of vehicles would be needed to deliver a signal. This had obvious costs in equipment, manpower, time and effort. There were problems too with permissions for parking vehicles on site (you needed the consent of the landowner). Many stories could not be covered live. Despatch riders – freelance or staff motorcyclists – ferried tapes back to the studio or to the nearest available feed points.

Satellite communications changed news gathering forever in the late twentieth century and continue to do so. The advantage of satellite transmission is that all you need is to point a satellite dish at the right point in the sky and you can transmit from anywhere in the world.

Early satellite transmission was costly, and the equipment cumbersome. Sandy Gall of ITN became a broadcasting hero, taking a small, diamond-shaped satellite dish by mule into Russian-occupied Afghanistan in 1985.

Now, satellite links vehicles are used every day by regional news operations. They are expensive and have to be used sparingly even in the best-funded organisations, but they mean a 'live' is possible from almost any location.

As the costs of satellite time came down, more satellite transmissions were possible, and satellite phones became a viable alternative for lower-resolution broadcasting from remote locations. Inmarsat's M4 system, the first of which weighed about seven kilograms, has been used for 'videophone' reports from around the world.

During the invasion of Iraq in 2003, 'vehicular videophone' was used by reporters 'embedded' with US troops. Portable M4 sat-phones and tracking-antenna systems offered live video reports from reporters with troops on the road to Baghdad and on warships in the Gulf. The hardware involved a dish about a metre across and a heavy dome that could be fitted to 4×4s or flatbed trucks.

Inmarsat's BGAN (Broadband-Global-Area-Network) offered another breakthrough less than two years later – better picture quality and a fully mobile base station. The highest bandwidth terminal weighed just over two kilos, was fully portable in a back-pack, and could be operated, the manufacturers said, by 'non-technical staff', anywhere on the planet.

In the developed world, wireless broadband connections (Wi-Fi) are being used to send location reports back to base. The picture quality is improving all the time.

Paul Clifton, the transport correspondent for BBC South, pioneered Wi-Fi transmission of packages edited on a laptop:

'The most spectacular use of this was in New York (2005). I flew with Sir Richard Branson on a Virgin twenty-first anniversary flight, just me and my little hand-held camera and a laptop. My ITV opponent brought a cameraman, and also his news editor, who had a small camera to look helpful.

'I shot most of the piece on the plane, edited on the plane, and just picked up a handful of shots and a piece-to-camera on the tarmac at JFK. I then simply squatted down on the tarmac beside the plane, edited in the final shots and hit the "send" button. With a strong wireless broadband signal, the story was on air 20 minutes later in the UK. That was 24 hours quicker than the team from Meridian. It was even quicker than any of the six local New York crews (who'd come to film Branson with Pamela Anderson), because they could not get back through customs quickly.'

Clifton, working with a camera person, also filmed, edited and broadcast from a moving train – believed to be the first time this had been achieved anywhere in the world. He explains:

'Southern Railway had fitted wireless broadband to the London Victoria to Brighton line. After talking at length to T-Mobile, who fitted it, we reckoned it was just about possible to send a compressed-quality (not as good as normal but much better than videophone) file whilst the train was running at 90 miles an hour. The transmission would be picked up by a succession of base stations mounted along the track, and in theory would automatically be reassembled into a single file. It was, though we only just made it in time. The file was still trickling through as the train pulled into Brighton station, and as passengers started getting off.'

Clifton says that, with Wi-Fi broadband hotspots now pretty much everywhere, we no longer need despatch riders or satellite trucks to send edited packages: 'Any McDonald's, airport lounges, many railway stations, all Caffé Nero shops etc. etc. are now TV edit suites! I often cut and file from the back of my car sitting in a car park.'

Clifton uses Final Cut Pro on a Mac, and converts the sequence into an H.264 file, a form of QuickTime Movie: 'This is the current "best available" format, essentially a form of MPEG-4 [the broadcast video standard]. That's about as far as my technical knowledge goes. I then send that over a Wi-Fi broadband link to a computer in Southampton.'

Technology is making this sort of transmission simpler all the time. A programme called Snapfeed works out how much material you have to send and how long it will take to send it at varying degrees of picture quality. Senior Broadcast Journalist Phil Simpson, a BBC trainer, explains: 'It assesses the amount of time available, and gives you as much bandwidth as it can. If you have a two-minute story and 30 minutes to send it, it'll assess what bandwidth is needed to get the highest-quality resolution.'

Remember

- It is possible to broadcast by satellite from anywhere in the world
- Satellite is no longer the only option for sending material from remote locations
- Packages can be transmitted by wireless broadband

CONCLUSION

An increasing number of technical skills are needed by modern broadcast journalists. Many of the new technologies improve our news gathering and make it easier to send stories back from the field.

There is an increasing demand for all journalists to be multi-skilled. That means many radio broadcasters, particularly in larger organisations such as the BBC, have learned video production skills. But you should never let the technology get in the way of the journalism. You should embrace new technologies when they enhance our ability to tell stories to an audience. Video journalism allows a more intimate relationship with your witnesses and contributors. Often, you will not be the storyteller; you will be the facilitator who allows contributors to tell their own story through your technical expertise. It's still broadcast journalism.

FURTHER READING

Chantler, Paul and Stewart, Peter (2003) *Basic Radio Journalism*, Oxford: Focal Press. How radio professionals go about the job.

Ray, Vin (2003) *The Television News Handbook*, London: Macmillan. Experts, many of them household names, on how it's done.

Watts, Harris (1997) *On Camera: Essential Know-how for Programme Makers*, London: AAVO. The first and still among the best – a guide to TV production.

WEB LINK

www.bbc.co.uk/journalism Includes guides to using equipment in the field.

CHAPTER EIGHT
SPORTS REPORTING AND COMMENTARY

In this chapter we'll look at:

- The impact of sports rights.
- Sports news coverage.
- Diary events in sport.
- Commentary skills.

IT has to be the best job in the world – watching sports from the best seats in the house and getting paid for it. If you're a sports fan, that is. If you're not, then you'll never make it as a sports journalist, and you won't want to. But many reporters find themselves covering sport as part of their everyday routine. Not every news provider has a separate sports department, even though sport is an important part of the modern news agenda. Sports stories make it on to the front as well as the back pages of newspapers. All broadcast journalists have to be aware of sports stories.

There's no place in the broadcast newsroom for anybody who says: 'I'm not interested in sport.' You may find yourself on shift alone late in the evening, and needing to put together a summary of cricket or football results for a late bulletin or the breakfast news. You need to be familiar with the terminology and even the jargon of sport and write it in a way audiences will understand.

In this chapter, we'll look at the skills and experiences applicable to sports reporting – and the specialist skills of the sports commentator. An understanding of these will also help the general reporter called in to cover sports events. Some people make a distinction between sports journalism (covering sports stories) and sports broadcasting (coverage of live sports events). But journalism skills are essential for both. In 2006, the BBC management brought sport within the remit of its journalism board – a recognition that sports are part of the mainstream news agenda.

There is a strong emphasis in this chapter on football reporting. That is because football dominates sports coverage. Look at any newspaper, or listen to BBC Radio Five Live or Talksport. And the Sky Sports News channel on TV is usually Sky Football News. That doesn't mean broadcasters are not interested in other sports; a specialism in a minority sport can be an invaluable career asset. But the reality of the modern world is that football is a dominant cultural force – and not just on sports programmes.

SPORTS RIGHTS

The broadcast journalist working on sports programmes is covered by different rules from news broadcasters – mainly because of sports rights contracts.

Most top sports events are covered by contracts with strict rules about how the event is covered, and what can and cannot be broadcast. Huge sums change hands, and the contract will be enforced in the courts by the parties to it – usually the event's organiser and the broadcaster that made the highest bid for the rights to cover it. Separate rights may be sold for radio, TV, Internet and mobile phone updates. Live and recorded coverage will be negotiated separately.

For example, from 1992 to 2006 Sky Sports had the exclusive rights to live Premiership football on TV. BBC Sport had the TV highlights (*Match of the Day*) from 2003 and BBC Radio Five Live had the network radio commentary rights. Sky's live TV monopoly was broken (at the insistence of European competition commissioners) when the Irish pay-TV company Setanta bid successfully for two of the packages of live Premier League matches for 2007 onwards. TV rights to the Barclays Premier League sold for £1.7 billion in 2006 – a 65 per cent increase on the previous three-year deal. As if to prove football's dominance of broadcast sport, that's more than ten times what Sky paid for all the cricket controlled by the England and Wales Cricket Board, including Test matches. Setanta's failure to attract enough subscribers led to the company going into administration and the closure of its live action and sports news channels in June 2009. But the Premier League's revenues did not suffer. US-controlled broadcaster ESPN took over the Setanta packages, and launched its own live sports channel six weeks after Setanta folded. The Premier League TV deal for 2010 to 2013 was worth £1.782 billion.

Rights issues can be confusing in a converged world where traditional broadcast services are available online. Many BBC local radio stations with commentary rights for their local football clubs cannot run those commentaries on their streamed radio services because they do not have the Internet rights.

Journalists working for organisations with broadcast rights to a tournament get better access than the rest of the sporting press.

Journalists working for organisations with broadcast rights to a tournament get better access than the rest of the sporting press. There are usually obligations for players (and managers) to be interviewed after the event as part of the broadcast deal. While the reporter working for the rights holder is guaranteed an interview, others wait their turn and may be disappointed.

The deal will prohibit commentary on the event or the use of extensive pictures of the action by all but the rights holders.

Usually news coverage is allowed outside the terms of the contract. News organisations are covered by the copyright law of 'fair dealing', and by news access agreements, allowing them limited access to show up to a minute's highlights of a football match, for example, within 24 hours of the match taking place. Oddly the news access agreement does not extend to Sky Sports News, because it is not considered a news channel by the regulators, or to sports programmes.

For weekday regional TV news programmes, news access is extended to include the first full-length programme after a weekend's sporting action. Hence the popularity of goals round-ups on Monday evening programmes.

Reporting Saturday afternoon's events on a Monday evening would appear to break most conventions of broadcast journalism. It undermines the immediacy of television as a medium. Defenders of the practice will point out that Monday is the best day to evaluate the full weekend's football programme, now that games are played with various kick-off times between Saturday lunchtime and Sunday evening. The truth is that regional TV has been doing this since all the games kicked off at 3pm on a Saturday.

The goals round-up has become a routine for TV producers and – to some extent – the audience, although there can be few real fans who have not seen their team's goals on TV before 6.45 on a Monday evening. Many will have subscribed to see them on the Internet or their mobile phone. The days of the Monday round-up are surely numbered.

To students of media law it is a mystery why news access agreements exist at all. In 1991, the BBC tried to claim that British Satellite Broadcasting was in breach of copyright for showing the goals from World Cup matches to which the BBC had exclusive rights. But Mr Justice Scott ruled that the goals could be shown under the law of 'fair dealing' for reporting current events. It is a condition of 'fair dealing' that the copyright owner is acknowledged, and that the use does not compete commercially with the copyright owner. Fair dealing for the purpose of reporting current events does not apply to photographs, however, and in 2005 the BBC stopped showing the front pages of the day's newspapers on its online news review, because lawyers advised there was a 'considerable risk of litigation' from copyright owners including paparazzi photographers. The advice has not been tested in court.

Remember

- Sports rights contracts can determine what you show
- News access agreements allow news reports of sporting events

Rules and regulations

A fundamental of reporting any sport is knowledge of the rules of the game(s). Just as court reporters need an in-depth understanding of the risks of contempt of court, sports reporters need to know not just the laws by which a game is played but the rules of the competition and the administrative structure of the sport. Sports institutions and regulations are taught on specialist sports journalism degree courses. But you can do much to find out these rules yourself.

Sports governing bodies have their own websites. Many give valuable background information that you can use when you are covering an event. They also explain the rules of the competitions they organise. These can change frequently, and can sometimes be confusing. For example, Twenty20 cricket, the limited-overs county competition drew big crowds from the start, but in its first few seasons the structure of the competition was modified to improve its appeal. When the number of games in the three regional groups was increased to eight, each county played three teams twice and the two other teams once each – an unprecedented arrangement. It's a journalist's job to understand these complicated rules and explain them to the audience.

Sky Sports and BBC Five Live's commentators had to explain cricket's rules (in the complete absence of any official comment) when England's Third Test against Pakistan came to an unprecedented end in August 2006. England were awarded five penalty runs when Pakistan were accused of ball tampering. The Pakistani players protested by refusing to leave the dressing room after tea. The umpires and batsmen took to the field and then left. Pakistan tried to return, but the umpires said they were too late, and play could not continue. With no play, the crowds at the Oval sat in ignorance of what was happening for over an hour and a half, until they were told play had been abandoned for the day. Eventually – after calls to the International Cricket Council headquarters in Dubai – England were awarded the match. In the meantime, the commentators (and other broadcasters) were left to speculate. Only by researching – live on air – the game's extensive (and sometimes obscure) rule book were they able to keep the audience accurately informed. People at home knew more than the 23,000 paying customers at the ground.

There was less confusion among spectators at Aintree when the 1993 Grand National became 'the race that never was', but the estimated 300 million television viewers worldwide relied on a series of swift decisions by the BBC production team and presenter Des Lynam to interpret events. After a second false start, 30 of the 39 runners in 'the world's greatest steeple-chase' carried on running. The race was declared void. Esha Ness came in first, but goes down in history as the answer to a trivia question rather than a Grand National winner. Thanks to information from the broadcasters, punters at home knew they'd be enjoying a refund from the bookies long before the 'winning' jockey. (Lynam also famously ad libbed through high drama at the Grand National four years later when the race was postponed because of a bomb scare and the evacuation of the course.)

The regulatory framework of sport provides stories in its own right. For example, the World Anti-Doping Agency had to test its strict liability rule (whereby an athlete is automatically disqualified for a positive drugs test) against international law and human rights legislation. That was a complicated story to tell, requiring research into international law.

A BBC *Panorama* investigation, 'FIFA's Dirty Secrets', was shown late in 2010, just before FIFA's announcement of the venue for the 2018 World Cup. The allegations about corruption in the hierarchy of international football's governing body would have been a meaty story at any time. But the timing of the broadcast, and the suggestion that it destroyed England's chances of hosting the world's biggest football tournament, became a major political story. An easier sports administration story to tell was the reinvention of rugby league in Britain as a summer attraction with the establishment of the Super League. The idea was to improve attendances. It worked.

Sports journalism *v.* sports broadcasting

The relationship between sports broadcasting and journalism has always been an uneasy one. Punditry and opinion (often from ex-players) is mixed in with reporting.

There is also an element of commercial cross-promotion as channels that have rights to an event report on the build-up to that event. The free-to-air Sky Sports News channel helps promote the subscription-only Sky Sports channels.

The level of opinion allowed in sports coverage differs from that in news reporting. Outspoken comment *is* allowed.

The level of opinion allowed in sports coverage differs from that in news reporting. Outspoken comment *is* allowed. BBC Radio Five Live's commentator Alan Green has made it a trademark – to the annoyance of some Premier League managers (and many sports fans). But the sports broadcaster is still governed by the same laws of libel as news reporters. 'Fair comment' is no defence unless you are commenting on provable fact.

THINKPIECE	JOURNALISM OR BROADCASTING

Raymond Boyle of the University of Stirling, in *Sports Journalism: Context and Issues*, says there's an institutional and cultural distinction to be drawn between sports broadcasting and sports journalism. He says some sports broadcasters (notably Henry Blofeld of Test Match Special) don't really see themselves as reporters or journalists, while others (Des Lynam) have insisted that what they do is very journalistic.

Boyle says sport on television is dominated by entertainment rather than journalism values, and points out that, while there are big audiences for sports events, broadcasters perceive there to be less demand for investigative documentaries about sport.

In support of his argument Boyle quotes the former Liverpool striker Michael Robinson, now a popular sports presenter in Spain. Robinson told the *Observer* in 2005 he now sees himself as a journalist who wants to 'invade living rooms'. He despises the way sports broadcasting, and that of football in particular, has been 'hijacked by ex-pros' in England.

Robinson said:

'There is a screaming necessity for a journalist, because they all speak now in a certain argot, they all sit down comfy, comfy – and there's no journalist saying, "Why?" They need to be challenged. It's all happy families. I consider the BBC to be the mother and father of all television but they've become totally prostituted.'

The journalist and author Eamon Dunphy is also a former professional player. He often causes controversy in Ireland with his outspoken views on football and politics. He told Boyle:

'You are very inhibited if you are in a contractual arrangement with an organisation. You do not hear the idiosyncratic voice on television as much as you ought to. It's not cultivated. The media should be working for its readers and viewers. If that leads you into direct conflict with managers and players, then you have got to do that. But of course rights to events are important as well. So there is a fine line to walk on this.'

Sports news is big business, and BBC Sport has the most visited sports web pages in Europe. Sky Sports' web presence is popular too. Club websites are often the first to carry breaking stories of injury and transfer news. Other journalists rely on them increasingly.

The BBC remains committed to a strong 'journalistic spine' in its sports coverage and says the news agenda should never be determined by the sports rights it holds. The organisation's commitment to strong sports journalism was underlined by the appointment of Roger Mosey as BBC Director of Sport in 2005. He is a former Head of TV News, Controller of Radio Five Live and editor of the flagship Radio Four *Today* programme. Mosey's next job was to take charge of the 2012 London Olympics for the BBC. His successor as Director of Sport, Barbara Slater, was a former Olympic gymnast and vastly experienced sports producer, but she too had started at the BBC in news.

Sports news coverage

Larger broadcast organisations will have 'sports news correspondents'. It's an acknowledgement that sports coverage goes beyond reporting events. Sports news correspondents cover more than just sports stars and sports events. Sports stories may find their way into news programmes because of the celebrity of those involved or the controversy an issue generates. There can be political and social implications of sport too – as in these examples:

1 Governments talk of the importance of widening participation in sport to improve the health of the population.
2 Major sporting events are used to regenerate inner city areas. The Manchester Commonwealth Games of 2002 meant world-class sporting venues were built, to be inherited by local athletes, and in the case of the City of Manchester Stadium, Manchester City FC.
3 The continuing delays and rising costs of the new Wembley stadium were a major news story, particularly when the developers ran hugely over budget and failed to open in time for the 2006 FA Cup Final.

4 The business opportunities offered by the successful London 2012 Olympic bid – and the reluctance of some in the local community to relinquish their homes and businesses for redevelopment projects – were stories in the build-up to the games. In contrast to the Wembley saga, the Olympic stadium was completed a year ahead of the games.

5 And then there are sporting drug scandals. The reporter who is well briefed on the characteristics of performance-enhancing drugs will be in heavy demand for two-ways.

Even within the tightly media-controlled world of professional sports, good contacts, sheer tenacity or good luck can produce exclusive stories. BBC Radio Five Live's Juliette Ferrington was the first reporter at the England training camp one morning during the 2006 World Cup. She saw something that was to make headlines throughout the country. The big story in the build-up to the tournament had been Wayne Rooney's metatarsal injury. The broken bone in the foot of England's most talented player had dominated the back – and some of the front – pages for the month before the tournament.

Ferrington says:

'It was the first time we'd seen him kick a ball, run with a ball, turn with a ball, since he was injured. I broke the story and I was everyone's best friend that day – even the dailies [newspapers], a lot of people who missed it, the daily journalists, the Sunday journalists, everyone asked: "What did you see?"'

Rooney went on to play in the tournament, didn't score, and was sent off in England's quarter-final defeat, on penalties, against Portugal. Ultimately a disappointment then – but not as much as Rooney and the team's performance four years later in South Africa. It takes an imaginative reporter to find a new twist on the misery of being an England football fan.

Remember

- Sports news is about more than reporting events
- Sporting issues make strong running stories
- Traditional reporting skills – tenacity and hard work – can still break sports stories

REPORTING EVENTS

Specialist equipment for sports reporters

Radio and TV reporters providing voice-only reports at live sports events normally do so via ISDN – a broadcast-quality phone line. To connect to the line in the press box, you will carry your own outside broadcast unit, packed in a small flight case or shoulder bag. This will be mains powered, preferably with battery back-up. You may also need to record interviews. It is vital to check equipment before leaving the studio or your home on match day:

- Are all the parts there?
- Are you sure they're working?
- Have you tried a test recording?
- Have batteries been charged?
- Will you need an electrical extension lead? If you're not sure, take one just in case.

At the end of the match there is usually a need to pack equipment away quickly – probably because you need to get to the tunnel area to record interviews with managers and players.

Bizarrely, given how much sports clubs are paid by broadcast companies, the operational needs of the media are often overlooked when stadia are designed. Coventry's Ricoh stadium opened at the start of the 2005–6 football season. The TV gantry is on the opposite side of the pitch to the TV interview room.

It's during the rush to pack equipment away that it is most likely to get broken or lost. The connecting jacks on mic and headphone cables can become detached when they are stuffed hastily into bags.

They may not belong to you, but these are the tools of your trade. Take care of them. And don't blame the station engineers if they go wrong. It is usually not the engineers who abuse equipment.

Previews

Clubs arrange pre-match press conferences at which journalists have the chance to question managers about forthcoming fixtures.

At some clubs broadcasters may be excluded from the conference itself. TV crews may be allowed to film the opening moments to use as set-up shots. The exclusion of broadcast reporters is at the request of print journalists, who want a chance to pursue their own stories without microphones recording everything. It is an understandable plea because the presence of a mic destroys any chance of exclusivity for the newspapers.

Radio and TV may have the opportunity to conduct one-to-one interviews either before or after the main press conference. This is the chance to ask your own questions and to try to secure exclusive comments. Players too will be offered for interview. Any one to one is an opportunity to get a story that others have missed, or to develop an angle that will provide headlines beyond your own output.

A CLOSER LOOK

KNOW YOUR SPORTING AUDIENCE

The demands of different audiences are rarely better illustrated than at a football club's press conference. The national media want different stories from the local media.

In October 2005 Aston Villa's Premiership derby with Birmingham City took on added significance because the teams were on equal points just above the relegation zone. Local reporters were keen for team and injury news. But the national story was Villa manager David O'Leary ruling himself out of the job of Irish international coach.

Later that season, when it was known that England coach Sven-Goran Eriksson was to step down after the World Cup in the summer, media questions to English managers of Premiership clubs focused on whether they wanted to be considered for the national job. But local reporters still needed to know what was going on at the club itself, and they were often anxious not to antagonise the 'boss' by pressing him about his international ambitions.

When Steve McClaren of Middlesbrough got the job, journalists on Teesside breathed a sigh of relief – they didn't have to ask him about it any more. McClaren went on to earn the nickname the 'Wally with the Brolly' when England lost at Wembley to Croatia and failed to qualify for Euro 2008. He began to rebuild his reputation with success in Dutch football, away from the merciless attentions of English reporters.

Match day

Reporters attending matches need to prepare with background information and statistics just as if they were a news reporter covering a diary story. Most are fans of the sports they cover, so a lot of the background will already be known to them. But a specialist football reporter can find himself covering a minority sport of which he has little knowledge. When Great Britain's women won gold in curling at the Winter Olympics in Salt Lake City in 2002, there was frantic research into a sport many reporters had previously dismissed as 'housework on ice'.

Freelance sports reporter Steve Lee has built a reputation for reliability and always doing his homework. That's why he's used by the BBC, ITV and Sky Sports programmes. He says: 'There's no excuse for not being statted up these days. If it's football you're covering, there's soccerbase.com, which is fantastic, and the various football yearbooks. It's at your fingertips, even in the press box if you want it.'

It's increasingly common for broadcast reporters to use their mobile to check the stats or to have a laptop linked to the Internet sitting alongside their outside broadcast equipment. If something happens, they tap the player's details into a website such as soccerbase (run by the *Racing Post*) and can announce with confidence it's the player's first goal in 18 months or their second booking in ten games. The Internet means that a much bigger range of statistics is available to you during the match than you had time to research before kick-off.

Sports reporters usually need specialist *press passes* to attend an event. These often have to be applied for in advance. Accreditation may be needed for the competition (for example, the Premier League) *and* for a particular game. You may need a pass specific to the event with a laminated photo ID issued by the organiser. Tickets for regular fixtures such as football matches will normally be left at a special press window at the ground, at the club's reception or at the entrance to the press room. Arrangements differ according to the venue. Before your first visit to a ground, it's worth speaking to someone who's been there before or telephoning the club to ask how to find the press entrance. Match-day stewards and police officers do not always know. Much time and legwork can be wasted getting into a football or cricket match. Walking the entire circumference of a stadium lugging a heavy outside broadcast kit is not the best preparation for great broadcasting.

There can be administrative errors, even at the best-run events. Hundreds of media representatives might be expected, so losing one ticket – yours – is not necessarily a sign of the club's gross incompetence. Stay cool and try to resolve the problem. Make sure you carry your press card or workplace security pass as proof of identity. If the doorman can't help, ask him to find a club official who can.

Contrary to popular myth, a press card or BBC pass is not a golden ticket to any event. They certainly don't impress the 'Jobsworth' at the gate. But they can help sort out misunderstandings.

Sports reporters also need to pay special attention to travel and parking arrangements, particularly if large crowds are expected. It is usually better to arrive well before the paying public. You will avoid most of the traffic and the crowds on the way in. Arriving early will allow you time in the press room to check out any late team or transfer news. Time spent at a sports ground on match days is usually of more value professionally than time spent in the newsroom or at home.

Post-match

Most football clubs have press rooms where the managers will hold post-match press conferences. But first the managers will visit the flash interview room, where a single TV camera provides a feed to broadcasters who have bought the rights to live coverage or recorded highlights of the game. The advertising boards on the wall have the names of the TV company and the competition sponsors on them. There's a separate board for each TV station.

You will probably need a separate *tunnel pass* for the post-match interview area. This will be given to you when you arrive at the ground or in the press room. Pitch-side access will be covered by yet another ticket. Sports clubs are fond of controlling access to their stars. As we've explained, it can be in their commercial interests.

Interviewers await the managers, and also try to grab interviews with players. At most clubs, the interview room is near the players' tunnel and the dressing room, so it may be possible to approach players in person. Usually, though, the request for an interview with a player is made through club press officers. Any time you can spend getting to know sports personalities when the cameras are not rolling is time well spent. These are the moments to establish a rapport, and to ask for mobile numbers.

Radio stations with live broadcasting rights will usually have an ISDN feed point in the tunnel area. In the English Premiership, BBC Five Live has points for live inserts near the players' area at all clubs. Other radio reporters will record interviews to be played down the line from the press box, or persuade interviewees to come to the press box so they can chat to the presenter back in the studio.

The mixed zone

At bigger sporting events, the mixed zone is an area where sports journalists from organisations that have not bought broadcast rights will wait to get interviews with sportsmen and women and team managers. It's a free-for-all, and those with the best contacts – those who know the players already – will be the most successful.

For the 1999 Rugby World Cup in Wales, ITV Sport contracted former Welsh Rugby Union international Nigel Walker, who'd been freelancing for Eurosport, to cover the Wales team. His personal knowledge of players and coaching staff was invaluable, and a major stepping stone in his career. He later became Head of Sport for BBC Wales.

The mixed zone is usually an area that all the players and coaches have to pass through on their way out of the dressing room. But that doesn't mean they will want to stop and chat, particularly if they've just lost a cup semi-final. The famously enigmatic soccer manager Gordon Strachan wouldn't talk to TV reporters in the mixed zone even when his team had *won* an FA Cup semi-final.

Be bold – and ask the questions the fans want answered.

Mixed zone interview arrangements are not exclusive to match days. They are also arranged at training sessions for major events.

The language barrier

Reporters have to be bold, not only in what they ask and how they ask it, but in tackling the language difficulties at international events.

Steve Lee, who was working for the BBC at the 1998 World Cup, recalls an ITV reporter making the first approach to Romania's star Gheorghe Hagi. The ITV man had insisted: 'I know Spanish. He'll know Spanish because he played for Real Madrid.'

The player obliged and an interview in faltering Spanish followed. Lee's response was to ask:

'Gheorghe, a few words in English please?'

'Why yes, of course, what would you like to know?'

The interview that followed with the multilingual Mr Hagi was not only more fluent than the Spanish version, it was of considerably more use to a British broadcaster. The lesson from this is obvious. If you are working for an English language broadcaster, try to gather your material in English.

BBC Radio Five Live's Juliette Ferrington recalls a similarly helpful Luis Figo of Portugal answering in English at a team press conference at the 2006 World Cup in Germany. But his coach Luiz Felipe Scolari's only English words in response to her question were: 'I don't answer questions in English.' Ferrington concedes: 'He was quite cool, because he would not answer any questions in English, even though you knew he spoke English.'

She'd asked him about taking over the England manager's job. His answer ran – in translation – on Five Live, BBC World Service, in newspapers and on television.

Remember

- Get to the venue early
- Most sports interviews take place under controlled conditions
- Make sure you have the correct passes
- Be bold – ask the right questions

Commentary skills

Sports coverage relies on one specific form of journalistic expertise – live commentary. The great commentators grace their sport and become synonymous with it: Richie Benaud on cricket; Henry Longhurst and later Peter Allis on golf; football's John Motson.

Encyclopaedic knowledge and diligent research mark out the best commentators. But they have another thing in common – a passion for their sport, a passion they can transmit to audiences.

An over-opinionated commentator, or one who is too partisan, can be seriously annoying.

Good commentary appears fluent and seamless. But, like all broadcast speech, it consists of different elements combined for effect. An overload of factual information serves the listener as poorly as too little description of what's happening. An over-opinionated commentator, or one who is too partisan, can be seriously annoying.

Description

Americans call it play-by-play or calling the action. Describing what is happening requires knowledge of the rules of the game, its terminology and jargon, and above all the players. In team sports, recognition – preferably instant – is vital. More words are of course required on radio or a webcast than on television, where the words have to complement the pictures.

'Gerrard . . . Rooney . . . one-nil.' (TV version)

'Gerrard, right-footed through the middle for Rooney to chase. Rooney – good first touch – on to his right – beats the keeper. One-nil to England.' (Radio version)

On TV, a caption at the top of the screen will tell viewers the score in a live match. On radio, the question of how often to repeat it is a matter of judgement. It usually depends on the station. It is normal before and after ad breaks on commercial radio, or when returning to coverage from other reports on a BBC station.

Background

The commentator includes what he already knows from his experience of covering the sport. This can include contextual, factual or anecdotal content. In practice it's usually indistinguishable from researched material.

'Ernie Els with a hole-in-one at the Postage Stamp . . . that's the hole where Gene Sarazen hit an ace at the age of 71 in the 1973 Open.'

Research

However good your background knowledge, you need to research and prepare for specific events. This information includes players' names, individual and team statistics, statistical analysis, biographical detail, historical context, and anecdotes gleaned during the research process. To the casual listener these facts appear to be your own background knowledge and add greatly to your credibility.

Research helps fill a lull in the action, or the wait between events. Athletics coverage relies almost exclusively on research and background knowledge. A commentator may describe what the athletes are doing as they warm up, and speculate about their mood, but that is something the audience can usually see for themselves. The expert should add to the audience's knowledge, not simply repeat what they can see.

> The expert should add to the audience's knowledge, not simply repeat what they can see.

In a fast-moving event such as a horse race, you are lost without research. You will need to know horses, jockeys, trainers and owners, and the betting odds. You then have to recognise the runners, often as they're bunched together. The colours of the horses and the jockeys' caps and silks need to be memorised. Commentators will note which horses are wearing nosebands, visors, cheek pieces and blinkers. It's a complicated specialism. Few people who are not racing fans can cover a horse race.

Football is a fast-moving sport too, but there are long periods when the ball is out of play, at throw-ins or during injuries, for example. Then you draw on your reserves of research. Typically, a commentator on a live match will have 150 snippets of information – factoids, if you like – at their fingertips. If you have a summariser alongside you – an ex-player, perhaps – there's time to draw breath, consult your notes, or even access the Internet to find new facts.

'That's his seventh goal in as many games . . . and his first for England.'

Opinion and bias

Richie Benaud, the great Australian cricketer and broadcaster, has sound advice for sports commentators:

'First of all get your brain into gear, and when you've got your brain into gear, only add to the picture. What you have to do is not describe to people what has happened, but to explain to them why it has happened.'

In a radio interview about his craft, Benaud singled out as the greatest commentators Henry Longhurst and Dan Maskell, the voices of golf and tennis respectively in their time, because they only ever added to the television picture. And for devotion to research and preparation, Benaud praised racing's Peter O'Sullevan. In his early days at the BBC, Benaud spent a day following O'Sullevan, who advised him to stay quiet, take notes, and ask questions at the end of the day over a beer.

If outright partisanship is usually taboo, expressions of opinion are almost inevitable given the enthusiasm shown by most commentators. Outright bias is best left to summarisers.

If an ex-pro from one of the clubs in the game is sitting next to you, you will want him to reflect his passion for the club and provide professional tactical analysis. If he does that, there's no need for you to do the same.

> An English audience for an England football match will want England to win. A UK audience for the same event will be divided.

Sometimes, sharing a point of view with the audience – being a fan – is accepted: on a club website or local radio station, for example. But many local radio stations cover more than one club. Aston Villa fans don't want to hear a Birmingham City supporter on BRMB or Radio WM. But they still want to know how their closest rivals are getting on.

An English audience for an England football match will want England to win. A UK audience for the same event will be divided. Experience tells us that most Scottish international fans support two teams: Scotland and anyone who's playing against England. It's good advice to take the example of the former Australian cricket captain. In his 40-year broadcasting career, Richie Benaud never referred to the Australians as 'we' or 'us'.

Statements of the obvious don't help the listener either: 'I don't believe he wanted to do that!'

Reaction

There's no harm in a natural response to events. Exclamations and expressions of surprise, wonder and amazement are all part of the mix. The late Dan Maskell, the 'voice of Wimbledon' for 40 years, peppered his tennis commentaries with an expression that became his catch-phrase: 'Oh, I say.'

Remember

- Sports commentary relies on extensive research and background knowledge
- Radio commentary requires more description of the action
- Expressions of your own excitement are acceptable
- Consider the audience before expressing any bias

The lone voice

Sports commentary is available across all media, and the economics of media businesses mean that, for smaller audiences, commentators work alone. A lone voice covers the event, often in a cramped seat in the press box, alongside others doing the same thing for club websites, Internet and mobile phone services and local radio. The lucky ones are operating with headphones and a mic on an ISDN line; others use a telephone.

It's possible to earn a respectable living working for the Internet and premium-rate telephone services set up to satisfy the demands of the growing betting industry. Gary Capewell began commentating on horse racing while still a broadcast journalism student. He covers hundreds of miles a week visiting race courses for phone and Internet services (including William Hill radio and RaceCall). And he also works from home. Using a Skype link on a PC in the corner of the family dining room in Uttoxeter, he can watch race meetings on TV and broadcast internationally.

Capewell's preparation for a phone commentary is as meticulous as when he's at the racetrack:

'I always have lots of extra snippets of information – bits and bobs I can throw in if there are quiet moments, either before the race or if there aren't many runners and one horse is way out in front. If I'm watching a race from Ireland, say, where they're often covered by just one camera, I need all that extra information to fill if I can't make out exactly what's going on.'

The commentary team

Maintaining fluent commentary for 45 minutes or longer at a football match is hard work. That's why bigger stations share the load. BBC Radio Five Live will have two commentators at a football match, each doing half of each half's play. There will be a match analyst with them – usually a player, ex-player or manager. When the analyst is summarising the action, there's a chance for the commentator to make a brief scribble on their notes, keeping tag of scorers, bookings and sendings-off.

Five Live have also experimented with two commentators together in rugby league: one describes the play when the home side is in possession; the other picks up when the other side has the ball. It's a different and entertaining approach, but would be unlikely to work in sports such as association football (soccer) where possession changes more frequently.

At big tournaments, broadcasters will team their commentators with a regular summariser and a producer. These three-man units will work, travel, and usually eat and socialise together. At the Germany 2006 football World Cup, BBC TV had five of these teams; ITV Sport had three. Producer Mitch Pryce, who worked with commentator Jon Champion and the ex-Liverpool and Republic of Ireland international, Jim Beglin, for ITV, said it was an exciting time but very hard work:

'We covered 17 games in 25 days, taking in 11 of the 12 venues, and 21 of the 32 teams in the tournament. We took 11 internal flights and drove thousands of miles. On our day off we drove three hours to Dortmund to see Brazil v. Ghana.

'Normally commentators spend the best part of a week preparing for a game, but in a big tournament you're doing it day by day, telescoping your normal work schedules to fit everything in. You just don't stop. The most important thing is that you all get on and get on with the job.'

Pryce repeated the frenetic schedule for ITV at the 2010 World Cup in South Africa. In between, most of his work, as a freelance, was for BBC *Match of the Day*.

Working with a co-commentator

The BBC's Guy Mowbray: 'If I'm still talking during the second replay, I'm doing a bad job.'

Compared with the frenzy of working alone, life is a little more relaxed for the commentator working with an experienced summariser. The expert, usually an ex-player or manager, offers informed opinion, a change of voice for the listener, and a breathing space for the commentator to catch up on their notes. Conversation replaces the need to carry on regardless.

The BBC *Match of the Day* commentator Guy Mowbray says:

'It's much easier with a co-commentator. He's the expert. He's the one who's played the game, so let him give the opinions. You just call the action. You can argue with them at times, but don't get ideas above your station.'

Mowbray also has advice on when to introduce the summariser after a goal: 'The first replay you can still be talking about what has just happened, but the second replay belongs to my colleague to analyse. If I'm still talking during the second replay, I'm doing a bad job.'

The role of the producer

At big events, the location sports producer makes life easier for a commentator and his summariser. He'll locate the stadium media centre and pick up match tickets from the host broadcast service. For ITV's Mitch Pryce, at World Cup games this meant not only collecting three commentary position seats for his team but also 'observer' seats for reporters from ITV News and the UK breakfast TV service.

Pryce observes: 'Contrary to popular opinion, you don't then sit back with your feet up and watch the match.'

Mitch Pryce at the World Cup 2006: 'You don't just sit back with your feet up and watch the match.'

The producer in the press box is an integral part of the commentary team, although you won't hear his voice on air. He's watching the action and has his own input. Pryce says:

'I can talk to the commentator through his headset, but I prefer not to interrupt their flow. I'll usually write something and put a piece of paper in front of him. Sometimes the commentator will slip his headphones off and ask something off mic.'

When Radhi Jaida scored for Tunisia against Saudi Arabia in 2006, Pryce was able to tell Jon Champion that Jaida was the first Bolton Wanderers player to score in the World Cup finals since Nat Lofthouse in 1954. Champion used the statistic – as did the next day's *Daily Telegraph*.

As Champion and Jim Beglin were concentrating on the replays of Wayne Rooney's sending-off for England against Portugal in the quarter-final, Pryce was watching the action on the field and saw Rooney's altercation with Manchester United teammate Cristiano Ronaldo. That part of the story became a huge talking point in the British media but might have been missed by the ITV commentary team at the time without the producer's involvement.

Pryce says:

'As field producer, I am the link between the studio gallery and the action. It's down to me to pass on to the commentators how long they have to talk about the team line-ups, links to studio and to commercial breaks; also to ensure the right on-air promotions are delivered without interfering with the action. In return I can pass on any editorial issues back to base that might affect the studio discussions. For instance, to confirm that Graham Poll really *did* issue three yellow cards to the same player as happened in the Australia v. Croatia World Cup match in Stuttgart.'

Sports producing at the highest level is a rewarding and exciting job. And occasionally producers get to broadcast too. Pryce interviewed Henrik Larsson live to an audience of eight and a half million people after Sweden's Euro 2004 game with Italy. Pryce says: 'It helped that we were staying in the same hotel as the Swedish team, and I'd said hello to him in the lift!'

Remember

- Sports commentators are part of a team
- Summarisers are the experts
- The producer is a fixer and extra pair of eyes

CONCLUSION

Sports reporting can mean free tickets for the best events in town – but you have to work long and hard to win the right to be there. Even if Chelsea are playing in the Champions League, someone has to cover the league match on a rainy night in Grimsby. Only the elite of sports broadcasters have any guarantee of being at the biggest events, and there's no guarantee at all if your employer doesn't have the broadcast rights.

But if you love sport – all sport at whatever competitive level – a great life awaits in sports broadcast journalism. Like foreign correspondents you will see the world at somebody else's expense. And there's less chance of being shot.

FURTHER READING

Andrews, Phil (2005) *Sports Journalism: A Practical Introduction*, London: Sage. Covers many practical problems – but is light on broadcast skills.

Boyle, Raymond (2006) *Sports Journalism: Context and Issues*, London: Sage. A look at theoretical issues in sports journalism and broadcasting.

USEFUL REFERENCE BOOKS

Most sports journalists will need at least some of these to hand for background and research:

- *IRB International Rugby Yearbook*
- *Rugby League Yearbook*
- *Rules of Golf*
- *Sky Sports Football Yearbook*
- *The Directory of the Turf*
- *Wisden Cricketers' Almanak*.

WEB LINKS

The sites of sports clubs and governing bodies and the sports news sites should be bookmarked on your computer:

news.bbc.co.uk/sport
www.iaaf.org
www.cricinfo.com
www.formula1.com
www.golfonline.com
www.racingpost.com
www.rfl.uk.com
www.rfu.com
www.skysports.com
www.soccerbase.com
www.thedirectoryoftheturf.com
www.tennis.com
www.wada-ama.org

CHAPTER NINE
FOREIGN REPORTING

In this chapter, we'll look at:

- Operational – preparation and travel.
- Language and cultural problems.
- The dangers – particularly in hostile environments.
- The role of local fixers and minders.
- The importance of specialist training.

FOREIGN correspondents are the journalistic elite. Theirs is a world of travel, adventure, excitement and, yes, glamour. It can also be a world of danger – of greater risk than any other job in the modern media.

The risks can be appealing to some people, but for most the attraction of foreign reporting is the chance to witness world events and interpret those events for an audience at home. More than any other group of reporters they are providing 'the first draft of history'. And, of course, they get to travel the world at someone else's expense.

We'll also reflect on the differences between being based overseas and 'parachuting' in to cover stories. Most news organisations have fewer permanent overseas bureaux these days. It is easier than ever to travel around the globe and reach the world's troublespots. But does that mean the reporter is less aware of local culture, and therefore less able to report with authority on the impact of events on local people?

We'll also consider the role of 'embedded' journalists based with military units in times of war. Does embedding compromise their independence? And how much safer is it than acting as a 'unilateral' – operating without military assistance?

A JOURNALISTIC ARISTOCRACY

The broadcaster and writer Andrew Marr describes foreign correspondents as an 'aristocracy'. In *My Trade* he says of foreign reporters:

Though the trade is old, the real glamour of the job reaches back only about 70 years, from roughly the time imperial soldiering and missionary exploration began to decline. Unlike missionaries, foreign correspondents had a moral message not for the natives out there, but for the folks back home. Ever since the first wars involving fascism, in Abyssinia and Spain, the foreign correspondents of the democracies have been bringers of warnings. They have been adventurers who returned not with loot but with information.

BBC TV News' Europe Editor Gavin Hewitt agrees with his colleague about the prestige attached to foreign reporting, although he stresses it's just as important to report well on domestic issues. He says some of the blame lies with the television industry's obsession with awards:

'It is true that time and time again people get recognised on the whole for the work they do abroad. There seems to be greater interest when you're reporting from Afghanistan, Iraq or America or whatever.

'Obviously our principal duty is to reflect what's happening in our own society. It's been a criticism in the past that we reflect what happens around the world with fantastic reports and brilliant cameramen. Why don't we do the same in the UK? I think there's a little bit more of an emphasis on trying to do that.'

In response to Andrew Marr's 'aristocracy' comment, Sky News' Ian Woods, who was based in Washington DC for four years, says he never felt like an aristocrat, but he knows plenty of foreign correspondents who lived like a lord on expenses.

Another inference of Marr's comment is that foreign correspondents are like old-fashioned imperial adventurers, who have little regard or respect for the people whose countries they visit. This was true of newspaper correspondents of the type parodied by Evelyn Waugh in the comic novel *Scoop*, written before the Second World War. Modern broadcasters have to apply journalistic principles of objectivity and cultural neutrality, and will find empathy with the people they report on. Finding the human interest angle in a story is even more important in cultures that differ from what the audience knows. Humanity is the shared bond with the viewer or listener.

Big stories require management and organisation, so producers and fixers will be sent too. There are journalism jobs in foreign news other than those for on-screen talent.

The larger news organisations maintain foreign bureaux – permanently staffed offices around the world. They're usually in capital cities – Washington, Paris, Moscow, Beijing – where major political stories will happen and a country's media are based. When big stories break, they serve as regional bases. The North America correspondent will set out from Washington or New York to cover election campaigns in the Mid-West or hurricanes in Florida. When there are not enough staff in that part of the world to cover a major disaster – the tsunami of Boxing Day 2004, for example – extra reporters and crews will fly in from the UK. These big stories require management and organisation, so producers and fixers will be sent too. There are journalism jobs in foreign news other than those for on-screen talent.

Foreign travel

Travelling abroad is part of the appeal of being a foreign correspondent or producer. Being ready to travel at a moment's notice is part of the job. Keep up to date with the jabs you would otherwise need for only the most exotic holiday destinations.

Keep your passport handy at all times, and up to date. Many countries will not let you in unless your passport has at least six months left to run.

Many reporters keep a bag permanently packed ready for short-notice assignments. It should include the documentation, currency and medical supplies you will need for the first few days in a strange environment. You need to plan for the worst case – an earthquake perhaps with no fresh water and little shelter. Unless your operational area is restricted to, say, northern Europe, it's difficult to plan what clothing to take, because you won't know what weather or temperatures to expect.

Passports

Keep your passport handy at all times, and up to date. Many countries will not let you in unless your passport has at least six months left to run. Newsrooms are full of stories of reporters who were sent to breaking foreign news stories simply because they were the only one in the office who had their passport with them.

Many experienced foreign reporters keep two passports. This makes it easier to travel between countries at war or with strained diplomatic relations, particularly in the Middle East. For example, many Arab countries will not let you in if you have an Israeli stamp in your passport. In Syria you will be denied entry if you have a stamp from another country's border crossing point with Israel. There are similar restrictions about travelling between Turkey and Cyprus. The Foreign Office does not keep a list of these 'incompatible countries' but you can check by phoning their individual embassies.

To apply for a second passport you will need a letter of support from your employers explaining that your work will take you to incompatible countries.

Even if you have only one passport, keep a photocopy of the main pages separate from the passport, in case it gets lost or stolen. It's also worth keeping a couple of passport-sized photographs with you. They're sometimes needed for local accreditation.

Visas

Working abroad differs from travelling abroad. Countries you can enter freely as a tourist may require a work permit or visa.

The US is a case in point. Most visitors from the UK no longer need a visa to enter the States, as long as they plan to stay no more than 90 days. But working journalists require a special 'I' classification visa. It's granted to people working on news or information programmes, whose work involves the normal news-gathering processes, such as interviewing people or covering events. British journalists working for US media, on reality TV programmes or dramatic reconstructions for documentaries, will find they need a different category of visa. The details can be checked on the US embassy website (**www.usembassy.org.uk**).

Visas for India can be obtained in person on the same day from India House in London or the Consulates General in Birmingham or Edinburgh, but you'll need a special permit if you are filming a documentary.

When you apply for a visa, try to get one that will be valid for as long as possible and for multiple entry to the country. You may want to return.

When you apply for a visa, try to get one that will be valid for as long as possible and for multiple entry to the country. You may want to return.

Whichever country you are visiting or planning to work in, the Foreign Office website (**www.fco.gov.uk**) is a useful first port of call. It has details of entry requirements, and web links and contact details for all countries with embassies or high commissions in the UK. There is also good advice on currencies, customs, medical precautions and the British government's assessment of the current security risks.

Driving licence

Don't forget your driving licence. Keep it with your passport. In many parts of the world you will want to hire a car, or to be able to drive a crew car. There's road safety advice and information about local traffic laws on the Foreign and Commonwealth Office website (**www.fco.gov.uk**).

If you are hiring a car abroad, make sure you are fully covered when you sign the contract and that there are no exemptions or hidden costs.

Insurance

If you travel abroad regularly, you will want insurance cover against the usual hazards of travel such as lost luggage and unexpected medical bills, but the travel insurance you bought for your holiday will not cover visits to war zones or natural disasters. Larger organisations will have their own cover. Check what's available to you under your conditions of employment. If you are freelance, consider taking out specialist insurance. The National Union of Journalists can advise.

What to pack

Packing for foreign work need not mean taking enough clothes for an indefinite stay. Use hotel or local laundries. Buy cheap clothes on location and discard them at the end of the trip if they won't fit into your travel bag.

Women should be aware of the sensitivities of locals in Muslim countries and wear clothes that cover their arms, legs and chest.

You will need waterproofs and sensible footwear. And emergency medical supplies.

A basic medical travel pack is available from Boots and other high street chemists. You can add your own extras. Your pack should include sterile hypodermic needles – there's a high risk of infected needles in parts of Africa and the Far East. Water purification tablets are essential in developing countries and in areas affected by disasters such as famine, earthquakes and flooding.

You will want good maps of the area where you are operating, and satellite phones for communications.

In war zones, your organisation will provide you with helmets and flak jackets. You should expect to travel in vehicles with some level of armour plating, and to carry a personal GPS (global positioning system), so your employer always knows where you are.

> **Water purification tablets are essential in developing countries and areas affected by disasters.**

CASE STUDY 9.1 TSUNAMI 2004 – TRAVELLING LIGHT

ITV *News at Ten* presenter Julie Etchingham was working for Sky News when she received the call on Boxing Day 2004 to cover the Asian tsunami. She took a sleeping bag, mosquito net, water purification tablets, medication and the kit she always had on standby as a reporter. Despite the devastation across many thousands of miles, the damage was restricted to coastal areas. Many reporters found themselves in comfortable hotels just a few miles from scenes of almost unimaginable destruction. She says: 'There were still holidaymakers by the swimming pool. It was bizarre. You'd got this extraordinary disaster unfolding and people still sitting reading Jackie Collins by the pool.'

But the relative comfort didn't make the job easy, as she explains:

'It was 12 hours in the air, an hour on the ground to put your bags down and get your bearings, and then straight down to the feed point and the live point. Then I was live for about 12 hours and I did that for two weeks day in and day out.

'The other anchor who was there was Jeremy Thompson. We literally worked in a shift pattern. He would do ten hours on: I'd do 12 hours off. Then we'd just swap round, and we were also doing it for Five News, because it was just when Sky News took over the Five News contract [from ITN], and I was working as a presenter for them. We had one ridiculous afternoon when Jeremy and I were both on, on different paths to the truck on two cameras. Then I would leap over and do Sky News for the rest of the evening, so it was pretty demanding.'

Just over six years later, Etchingham was anchoring coverage of another devastating earthquake and tsunami – this time in Japan for ITV News. The role – on conventional appointment-to-view programmes – was much less demanding; the result was arguably more polished and attracted bigger audiences. But it couldn't match the energy and excitement that went into covering the 2004 event.

Currency

Travelling abroad on holiday, you probably take foreign currency or travellers cheques, or rely on the convenience of 'hole-in-the-wall' banking. Some of the places you visit as a journalist may not offer such ready access to your money.

For longer overseas trips, you will usually want a cash advance or 'float' from your employer. Taking large cash sums in US dollars is helpful. The dollar is negotiable almost everywhere (although it's still not welcome in Cuba).

> **Remember to keep every receipt. You will need to account for the money later . . . Don't be tempted to exaggerate your expenses.**

Remember to keep every receipt. You will need to account for the money later. We've already heard that foreign correspondents can 'live like a lord' on their allowances, but don't be tempted to exaggerate your expenses. One correspondent was found out after he claimed for a lawn-mower – he lived in a flat.

The advice to travellers on the Foreign and Commonwealth Office website includes information about foreign currency.

Remember

- Keep your passport(s) and jabs up to date
- Check visa requirements
- Take your driving licence
- Make sure you are insured
- Keep a bag packed
- Research your destination before you leave
- Take a cash advance
- Make sure you have good communications – satellite phones and GPS

Language

It goes without saying that a knowledge of foreign languages is useful for anyone working abroad. You are unlikely to get a posting to Paris without workaday French. And French is spoken in many former French colonies. Spanish is useful in much of Central and Southern America (although in Brazil they speak Portuguese). In all parts of China the language is written the same, but words are pronounced completely differently in Mandarin and Cantonese speaking areas.

If you are to be based for any length of time in a non-English speaking country, you will want to learn some of the language. But the modern foreign correspondent visits so many countries that only a fanatical linguist could keep up with the demands.

The BBC's Security Correspondent Frank Gardner speaks fluent Arabic that has served him in two careers, banking and journalism:

'Almost the only sensible decision I took as a teenager was to embark on a difficult language that would then be useful. I thought, well, I could go and learn Mongolian, but it's not going to be much use outside Mongolia, whereas Arabic is a lingua franca in about 20 countries and a lot of those countries have got oil. So therefore, there should always be a job.

'I could not have done the reporting I did in Yemen or Saudi Arabia without Arabic. I've been detained in both countries several times. I was arrested by the Saudi authorities once, and without Arabic I would not have got out.'

Gardner was able to interview a kidnapper in Yemen. The man spoke no English, and Gardner had nobody with him who spoke English: 'If I hadn't had Arabic, I wouldn't have got the interview.'

Gardner uses a wheelchair after being shot by Al Qaeda in the street in Riyadh in June 2004. His cameraman Simon Cumbers died.

'I honestly thought that having Arabic was like a sort of armour, but the people who shot us were not interested in negotiation or discussion. I did plead for my life in Arabic and they didn't accept it. They decided to just put me away. But these were hardcore psychopaths. There have been many times since, for example covering the intifada in the West Bank in Gaza, where Arabic has been really, really useful.

'And also I don't like having to do journalism with a government minder beside me – a government minder/interpreter – because then you just hear the government version of events, and I prefer to be able to do it myself.

'Arabic has allowed me to do proper journalism, to go on my own to countries with a pack-up camera, that goes in the back of my rucksack, and go and do the interviews myself without having a whole big team of producers, lights and cameramen and interpreters. It's allowed me to do it on my own, which to my mind is the purest journalism.'

Remember

- Language skills are useful – but not all languages are equally useful

Local guides

News organisations rely on local guides and fixers to organise their itinerary, set up interviews and smooth the way for reporters and crews. Some do little more than translate; the best are freelance journalists based in the country, with inside knowledge and contacts to help you look good. Some fixers fall into the role by chance: it can be a good source of income in an economy disrupted by war or natural disaster.

The fixers are the unsung heroes of foreign reporting – the ones left behind when the journalists have gone. Larger broadcast organisations will have a global network of them.

The most important quality in a fixer is trust. You must be able to trust them and they should trust you. Your lives may depend on it. You can expect to rely on people your organisation has used before, or trust can be built on a personal relationship. If you are charged with finding a fixer to help cover a foreign event, it is probably the most important part of the job.

Frank Gardner says he learned never to trust Saudi government minders after he and cameraman Simon Cumbers were shot. The minders had told them the location was safe:

'They weren't dishonest. They were just incompetent, and I've always distrusted going with minders. I've avoided them whenever I can.

'The mistake we made was believing that the Ministry of Information minders knew what they were doing and were an accurate judge of the security situation in Riyadh. They weren't. They misjudged it horribly. My cameraman's dead and numerous lives were ruined because of it.'

Trusted local guides should be your surest guide to any local customs that might affect your news gathering. For example, you should not try to arrange an interview in a Muslim country at a time that clashes with the call to prayer. And if you are in Japan, there is strong business etiquette associated with the exchange of business cards. If you have time, get some cards printed with your details on one side in English and on the other side in Japanese.

Remember

- Only use guides you can trust
- Be wary of government minders
- Be aware of local customs

Logistics

Getting pictures and sound back from remote locations is a big headache for broadcast organisations. We've seen in Chapter 7: Location video and sound how wireless broadband and satellite connections have made that easier in recent years. But getting people to and from places where things are happening can still be a nightmare.

The first reports of many major foreign news stories in recent years have been through social networks. The uprisings across the Arab world in 2011 generated huge amounts of video from mobile phones and amateur cameras. Those involved in anti-government protests sought to boost their cause internationally and at home by posting dramatic pictures online. Social networks buzzed with messages encouraging locals in Tunisia, Egypt, Libya and other countries to rise up. But the broader picture – which of the protests were proving successful – was rarely clear to audiences in Europe and the USA until foreign correspondents arrived to try to make sense of difficult local politics. Getting news teams to the scene of international stories is often just as difficult and dangerous as being there.

George Alagiah, of the BBC, says the importance of logistics was brought home to him as a correspondent in southern Africa:

'I would say television journalism is 75 per cent logistics. How do you get in, and more importantly how do you get out? More than once, in the beginning, I managed to get into places – I was one of the first people to get into Somalia, before 1992, before the invasion – and I hadn't really sorted my way out, and I was beaten on one occasion by the competition, rather annoyingly.'

Alagiah says you can do now, with two or three people, things that ten years ago might have taken five people. But you still have to get them in and out on time, and you have to think of sources of power for your technology: 'There are still large chunks of the world where you do need to take that with you, or organise it.'

Alagiah was presenting the *Six O'Clock News* in July 2006 when the BBC mounted one of its more spectacular logistics exercises. Correspondent David Shukman was live from a tiny boat on the Amazon river with a second camera mounted on a balloon, offering dramatic wide shots over the rainforest.

Remember

- Plan the logistics of your trip
- Make sure you have a way of getting your story, and yourself, out of the country
- Consider power sources for your equipment

The dangers

Harassment, physical violence, kidnapping and even murder are occupational hazards for reporters covering domestic news in many countries.

Journalism is a dangerous trade in many parts of the world – and not just for foreigners going into war zones. Harassment, physical violence, kidnapping and even murder are occupational hazards for reporters covering domestic news in many countries.

The West Bank, where Israeli troops have targeted news gatherers, topped one recent list of the worst places for journalists to operate. The massacre of at least 32 media workers in the Philippines in November 2009 – the worst atrocity of its type in recent memory – distorted the number of journalists killed that year. Cardiff University's Centre for Journalism produces a list for the International News Safety Institute. In 2009, Mexico with 11 dead, Russia, 9, Somalia, 9, Pakistan, 8, Iraq, 5, Colombia, 4, India, 4, Georgia, 4 and Afghanistan, 3 completed the bloody Top Ten. Mexico was the most dangerous country for journalists three years in a row according to the International Federation of Journalists (IFJ).

In the first decade of the twenty-first century, according to the IFJ, the number of journalists and media staff killed because of their work averaged 120 a year. Most of these were operating in their own countries in peacetime – many of them murdered by people who knew they would probably get away with it (66 per cent of the murders of journalists worldwide in 2009 were reported to be unsolved).

For those on foreign assignment, there have been few more dangerous places than Iraq during the conflict that followed the US-led invasion. Western journalists have been killed by roadside bombs set by insurgents and by the so-called 'friendly fire' of US troops.

And sometimes there is danger despite your own precautions. Frank Gardner says, of being shot in Saudi Arabia:

'We were very unlucky. We had government minders with us. We weren't going off on our own. We asked to film the edge of an area where there'd been trouble in the past, only if it was safe. Our minders from the Saudi government said: "It's safe. You can come with us. No problem."

'They took us there, and quite clearly it wasn't safe and an Al Qaeda team drove past and happened to see us at that time. If we had finished filming five minutes earlier, we would have gone back to the hotel and nothing would have happened.

'They happened to see us. The cell leader said: "They're infidels. You must kill them." In a way it was a racist killing. If we'd have been brown skinned they wouldn't have stopped. They shot us because we were white Western Europeans, not because we were journalists, but just because we were infidels, non-believers, in their minds.'

Hostile environment training

Responsible news organisations will not send reporters or crews to war zones without hostile environment and first aid training (HEFAT). It is part of the employer's duty of care to its employees.

A HEFAT course will typically last a week, and parts of it will be conducted by former military personnel, usually SAS or Royal Marines. It will include:

- first aid, including battlefield dressings
- the use of protective equipment, including body armour
- what to do if you come under fire
- what to do in a minefield
- dealing with roadblocks and checkpoints
- vehicle hijacks
- using body language to escape an angry crowd
- how to avoid being kidnapped
- what to do if you *are* kidnapped
- how to behave as a hostage.

Much of the course will be about improving your awareness of risk, avoiding confrontation and defusing potentially volatile situations. The experience can be frightening. There will usually be a journalist or two 'shot' during role-play simulations, and people are often reduced to tears.

Details of the organisations running courses can be found on the website of the Dart Center for Journalism and Trauma, a body of journalists, journalism educators and medical experts (see Web links at the end of this chapter). The Dart Center tries to improve the coverage of conflict and tragedy by giving journalists a better understanding of trauma and emotional distress. They're also concerned about the emotional well-being of journalists themselves.

War reporting

Edwin Starr sang: 'War! What is it good for?' Few would disagree that the late Motown legend's answer, 'Absolutely nothing', is true. But truth is the first casualty of war, and it is an uncomfortable truth that war has been very good for the careers of many broadcast reporters.

Rodney Pinder, director of the International News Safety Institute, and a former international correspondent, writes on the organisation's website (www.newssafety.com):

'Successful war reporting can enhance a career like little else. But more journalists and bosses are coming around to the view that no story is worth a life. They are reining in some of the wilder impulses that can prompt home desks to drive field journalists deeper into danger to match or outstrip a competitor. Dead journalists, after all, don't tell tales.'

The Channel 4 News presenter and veteran foreign correspondent Jon Snow says in his autobiography *Shooting History*:

'War brings you extraordinarily close to the people you work with. Your team become brothers and sisters, in an intense, almost familial conspiracy both to stay alive and to tell the story of what you have seen more graphically, more coherently, more speedily than anyone else.'

No story is worth a life . . . dead journalists don't tell tales.

Two British television journalists were killed by a roadside bomb in Iraq in May 2006. They were with American troops and were working for the US network CBS. It brought the total of media staff killed in the conflict to 127, since the invasion of 2003, according to the International Federation of Journalists.

The IFJ General Secretary Aidan White said: 'This was a tragic example of how journalists embedded with occupation forces face the same perilous conditions that have affected many local reporters.'

In 2010 in Afghanistan another British journalist, Rupert Hamer, and two soldiers died when their armoured military vehicle struck a roadside bomb in Helmand province. He was embedded with the US Marines. It happened just over a week after Michelle Lang, a Canadian reporter, died with four soldiers in a similar incident in Kandahar.

Embedding

The idea of 'embedding' reporters with troops was not new to the invasion of Iraq. Richard Dimbleby famously flew with the RAF on raids over Germany in World War Two. He and others reported from numerous allied operations.

But the move by the Pentagon in 2003 to welcome embedded reporters, even laying on 'media boot-camps' (hostile environment training courses) was seen by many media commentators as an attempt by the military to control media coverage.

The BBC's Gavin Hewitt, who was embedded with the US 3rd Infantry during the invasion of Iraq, says he had no problem with the practice:

Gavin Hewitt, BBC News' Europe Editor

'It did give us a front row seat at the war. The advantage of embedding on this occasion was that you were right at the heart of the action, but it was always very important to be honest: when people came across to you and said "Well, how is the war going?", not to extrapolate from what you were witnessing that you knew how the war was going. You knew how your unit was going, or you might pick up a little bit from divisional level.

'I think, alongside all the other material that was coming in, embedding provided some very useful material. I would always run an embed in a conflict, but I'd also run everything else that I could as well from all the other sources, and I wouldn't, just because you've got good access, elevate that necessarily.

'I think embedding works absolutely fine. Where it becomes slightly problematical is that, of course, you are dependent on this unit for your safety, and in certain circumstances that does create a bond. But I think you have to be honest with your audience and honest with yourself.

'Nobody censored me either on radio or television. Nobody looked at my reports. So I think it was invaluable in some of the things we were able to point up, and in retrospect turned out to be very important.

'We saw a lot of civilian casualties, and I realised that the way the Americans were fighting the war, which was if they were attacked, they replied with very considerable force, that, and I said this, if the war went on too long, you would alienate the population. And of course as time has gone on, we've seen some of those problems.

'The looting was clearly an issue in the battle for hearts and minds, which I think it's just possible we might have won. The fact they took a decision to stand by as neighbourhoods were ransacked was a huge blunder.'

A US press analyst Mark Jurkowitz, of *The Boston Globe*, described the coverage provided by 'embeds' as like looking through a drinking straw: 'There is plenty of information, but it only allows us to see a narrow slice of the war.'

The ITN reporter Terry Lloyd died with two other members of his team when they were caught in cross-fire near Basra, during the invasion of Iraq in 2003. He was not embedded. Subsequent reports suggested he was killed by a US helicopter gunship.

Lloyd's TV exclusives had included the gassing by Saddam Hussein of 5000 Kurds in Halabja in 1988, and the discovery of mass graves in Vukovar, in the former Yugoslavia in 1994. In an obituary in the *Guardian*, the former ITN editor Sir David Nicholas wrote: 'One can be certain that he would not have entered into a foolhardy enterprise.' Terry Lloyd's fate highlights the risks of operating in a war zone outside military control.

It may be that staff news reporters working for Britain's news media will never be allowed to operate as 'unilaterals' in war zones again. There was certainly a greater dependence during the Afghanistan conflict on third-party footage – the pictures shot by army cameramen and supplied to the media by the Ministry of Defence. These pictures help tell the story. A news cameraman probably could not have taken them without unnecessary risk, and as long as the source and context are made clear to the viewer the loss of editorial independence is a price worth paying.

A CLOSER LOOK

WORKING SAFELY ABROAD – A CODE OF PRACTICE

The International News Safety Institute (INSI) – a coalition of media organisations, press freedom groups, unions and humanitarian campaigners – has developed a Code of Practice for journalists working in dangerous parts of the world.

The INSI recognises that the work of journalists and media staff can never be completely safe, but says it will strive for the elimination of unnecessary risk, in peace and in war. This is their code.

1 The preservation of life and safety is paramount. Staff and freelances equally should be made aware that unwarranted risks in pursuit of a story are unacceptable and strongly discouraged. News organisations are urged to consider safety first, before competitive advantage.

2 Assignments to war and other danger zones must be voluntary and only involve experienced news gatherers and those under their direct supervision. No career should suffer as a result of refusing a dangerous assignment. Editors at base or journalists in the field may decide to terminate a dangerous assignment after proper consultation with one another.

3 All journalists and media staff must receive appropriate hostile environment and risk awareness training before being assigned to a danger zone. Employers are urged to make this mandatory.

4 Employers should ensure before assignment that journalists are fully up to date on the political, physical and social conditions prevailing where they are due to work and are aware of international rules of armed conflict as set out in the Geneva Convention and other key documents of humanitarian law.

5 Employers must provide efficient safety equipment and medical and health safeguards appropriate to the threat to all staff and freelances assigned to hazardous locations.

6 All journalists should be afforded personal insurance while working in hostile areas, including cover against personal injury and death. There should be no discrimination between staff and freelances.

7 Employers should provide free access to confidential counselling for journalists involved in coverage of distressing events. They should train managers in recognition of post-traumatic stress, and provide families of journalists in danger areas with timely advice on the safety of their loved ones.

8 Journalists are neutral observers. No member of the media should carry a firearm in the course of their work.

9 Governments and all military and security forces are urged to respect the safety of journalists in their areas of operation, whether or not accompanying their own forces. They must not restrict unnecessarily freedom of movement or compromise the right of the news media to gather and disseminate information.

10 Security forces must never harass, intimidate or physically attack journalists going about their lawful business.

Remember

- Foreign reporting can be dangerous – and not only in war zones
- Never visit a risky country without proper hostile environment training
- Embedding produces valuable front-line reporting, but you will be unaware of the bigger picture in the conflict

Working in a foreign bureau

Maintaining foreign bureaux is expensive. At the height of the insurgency against the foreign occupation of Iraq, BBC World Affairs Editor John Simpson said (during a debate in London on Reporting the Middle East) that a quarter of the corporation's foreign news budget went on maintaining its bureau in Baghdad.

Nowadays, correspondents do not merely report from world capitals. They use the bureau as a base for covering a region of the world. Usually the office will be shared with a national broadcaster from the host country, so that technical costs, such as lines and satellite feeds, can be shared. There will usually be an arrangement about using the host's audio or pictures.

For example, in Moscow, Sky News used to use the AP (Associated Press) studio. Feeds to the UK from there cost $500 a time. But then they struck a deal with NTV, a Russian commercial station. NTV was given an office at Sky News HQ in Osterley, west London. Sky News built their own small studio in Moscow, and linked it via fibre-optic cable to NTV, so there were no more lines/satellite costs.

Sometimes a bureau will be established in a country that ceases to be as significant politically as when the bureau was set up. One option is to close it down. Another is to use it as a base for covering a region of the world. That was what happened in South Africa in 1994, when the BBC's George Alagiah was there:

'The South Africa story itself had ceased to be a television story. Up to 1994 you had the Mandela factor. Then peace broke out and the story moved into parliament. My job was to turn this into an Africa bureau. It was just another place to be based, and we flew in from there to Kinshasa or Nairobi or Sudan.'

Using his specialist knowledge of African affairs (he'd been Africa Editor of a magazine), Alagiah was able to interpret events across the continent. He says old-fashioned journalistic skills were vital: 'Make the calls and make contacts.'

Informal sources such as aid agencies and business people could be contacted on mobile and satellite phones, often with invaluable results:

'I spent the best part of three months [in 1997] watching the Mobutu regime in Kinshasa collapse [in the Democratic Republic of the Congo], and my best source was a businessman. I didn't name him because he didn't want to be known, but he was a trader, and so he had trucks moving up and down the country, he had little shops, offices all over the place, and he was getting information. There were times when CNN was running stuff saying such-and-such a place is surrounded by rebel troops and I'd phone him and say: "Have you got anything?" And three hours later he'd come back and say: "There's nothing. Absolutely nothing."

'So those informal things are really crucial – the information sources – and they're rarely the official ones. Almost by definition the official sources in some of these places are bankrupt. They're just not working. They're institutionally defunct.'

Covering foreign politics

Covering the politics of a foreign country presents two major problems. First, most of your audience will only be interested if they believe the story is relevant to them. Second, the political elite in most countries will have no interest in engaging with the foreign press unless it suits their international policy aims.

We are conditioned in the UK into believing that US politics matters to us. The US is seen as the world's only global superpower. Its economics and politics impact on the world stage. So a lot of US politics is reported in Britain. But, for all the talk, mostly by British politicians, of a 'special relationship' between the two countries, public opinion in the UK is of little interest to American politicians. There is no electoral advantage in talking to the British media.

Ian Woods spent four years as Sky News' Washington correspondent, living on Capitol Hill, about a mile from the office. He says: 'We were painting in broad brush strokes – the big picture – most Sky News viewers wouldn't be interested in the minutiae of American politics.'

But there was a big problem:

'The attitude of the White House to foreign media was summed up during a presidential election campaign, when one of the people closest to [President George W.] Bush was asked about the demands of the foreign media, and he said: "They're like vermin." That was their attitude. You were treated with complete disdain and you just had to smile through it.

'None of the American government departments will give foreign broadcasters the time of day. They don't see the point. (The exception is the State Department, whose job is to deal with foreign affairs.) They won't answer your questions, do interviews or even return your calls. They've got enough on their plate with their own media.'

Sky News has the problem of not being shown in the US, so there is little awareness of what it does. Occasionally, Woods said he would introduce himself as being from 'the sister station of Fox News'. Fox News is the notoriously right-wing channel owned by Rupert Murdoch's News Corporation. Sky News is, of course, bound by the British regulatory framework of remaining politically neutral. Nonetheless, Woods says the link with Fox News played well in the 'Bible belt' of middle America. But, on the east and west coasts, where political opinion is more liberal, he would introduce himself as being from 'British TV' – although most people assumed that meant the BBC.

The BBC does have a worldwide reputation, which makes the job of BBC correspondents a little easier than their independent counterparts. Gavin Hewitt, who has also spent time in Washington, says: 'We are lucky in so far as when the White House does think about foreign broadcasters we usually are at the top of the heap.'

But Hewitt, too, acknowledges that getting to the heart of the administration was notoriously difficult: 'It is very important to work hard, and to turn up at press conferences, and to try and see people, and to, as far as you can, get within the bubble.'

Woods says:

'Washington's full of commentators, analysts and pundits so you mostly interview them. You get to know second- and third-tier people in the hope they'll become first-tier people. You find out who talks to the Defense Secretary every day, and you talk to them rather than talking directly to him. It can be a bit frustrating because it's always second- and third-hand reporting.'

Hewitt says there's so much source material in English in the US that there's a danger for foreign correspondents of living off the wires and the all-news channels:

'You need to go out and realise that, outside of the coasts, middle America is a very different place, and you need to go there frequently.

'It's a challenge. We all know this country's swamped with Americana, offbeat stories about wacky America and those crazies over there and all the rest of it. It's both interesting and a kind of disservice because America's not full of crazies or full of religious fanatics or the stereotype that's developed. There's a lot of impassioned argument over there between pretty sensible people and I sometimes think our reporting is drawn to either the strident or somebody you can say is a nut with a gun. But we do ourselves a great disservice if we go for the caricatures.

'So it's actually a slightly more difficult job than people often think. People think it is more easy than elsewhere because of the language, and the culture seems so accessible. That's one of the challenges in our broadcasting – not just to reinforce the stereotypes.'

Woods agrees that getting out of the office is essential to doing the job properly:

'In four years, the United Nations was the only political story where I could truly report first hand. You were able to grab an ambassador and talk to them, which you can't do in American politics. You had the same access to the key players as the US media. In fact, I felt I was able to be more accurate than the US media, who were so caught up in the White House spin that they were blind to what opponents of the war [in Iraq] were saying.

'I was there for two months in the build-up to the invasion of Iraq [in 2003] and then I was at the Pentagon, in the bunker, covering the briefings and we had a permanent line in there.

'The best stories I did were outside Washington – hurricanes (even before Katrina), and wild fires in California. We were competing on equal terms with American journalists – in Washington you aren't on the same playing field.

'Outside Washington, I found people genuinely helpful and genuinely interested that a British broadcaster wanted to talk to them. I spoke to Arnold Schwarzenegger in California, Jeb Bush in Florida – state governors were happy to see us – and Ray Nagin, the Mayor of New Orleans after Hurricane Katrina. And we did a 15-minute sit-down with Presidents Bush senior and Clinton when they were raising money after the tsunami, because they wanted international help.'

Finding the stories that matter to your audience

Finding stories is never a problem in the US. The challenge, as Gavin Hewitt says, is to avoid stereotypes. In other parts of the world the correspondent will have to persuade the foreign desk to take an interest in stories from places the audience may not have heard of.

Laurence Lee, who was based in Moscow for Sky News, and later worked for Al Jazeera's English language channel, says:

'You look for hard stories that really press the buttons at home. Stuff that people can relate to even if they're in a country nobody's ever heard of – heroin smuggling into Tajikistan, people trafficking, the big geopolitical stuff about the oil in Central Asia, the use of gas supplies as a political tool – stories that travel well.

'First you've got to persuade the foreign desk in London, and then make them relevant to people at home.'

CASE STUDY 9.2   WHEN THE LEVEE – AND THE STORY – BREAKS

Ian Woods and his crew with the Sky News Winnebago – $10,000 a week well spent

Ian Woods at the wheel

Sky News' Ian Woods explains how, when a big story breaks, the correspondent drops everything – including his holiday plans. This is how he covered the aftermath of Hurricane Katrina, which devastated New Orleans and other Gulf Coast communities in August 2005.

'I was on holiday in New York to watch the US Open tennis at Flushing Meadows. I went to the theatre to see the Monty Python musical *Spamalot* and [US Secretary of State] Condoleezza Rice was there. She came in for a lot of flak because she was at the theatre while this natural disaster was taking place – and I was at the same show! I'd already realised what a big story it was. We had somebody there and Sky were sending out presenters from London, so I just rang the office and said: "This is stupid me being on holiday while we've got the biggest natural disaster in this country in years."

So I left my wife in New York (she had to drive back to Washington), and caught a flight to Houston, which was hundreds of miles away but the nearest I could get. Then I hired a big eight-sleeper Winnebago for $10,000 a week (they were at a premium!) and drove all day to get to New Orleans. It was 300 miles or something like that. Some of the Sky crew that came out ended up sleeping in the Winnebago. All the hotel rooms for miles around were full of refugees. I was on somebody's floor in a sleeping bag in Baton Rouge 80 miles away. So every morning we had to get up at five in the morning, drive 80 miles, work for 15 hours and then drive back to Baton Rouge.'

Lee says there were not a lot of big stories in Moscow itself, so, again, the trick was to get out of the office – and all over his part of the world:

'I visited 13 countries. We'd work to a cycle, planning two trips every month. While the producer was planning and finding a fixer in the country where the next story was, we'd knock off a couple of stories in Moscow. I'd tell the desk: "Next week we're going to Kazakhstan, but in the meantime there's this story about a paedophile ring that's been broken up in Moscow."'

Lee says the stories for Sky News always had to be relevant to their audience:

'We covered the heroin smuggling out of Afghanistan into Tajikistan and there were all these people swimming across the river that makes up the border – it's 800 km long – carrying this heroin. Then they were stuffing it in their shoes and the chassis of cars and into railway carriages. We saw somebody whose slipper was cut open by security and it was full of heroin. There's evidence that all this stuff that Westerners are shooting into their veins is being sold to drug dealers and the money is going to fund the resurgence of the Taliban in Afghanistan, which I think is pretty interesting to anybody.'

Sometimes the British angle is clear, as when British technology saved the lives of a group of Russian submariners in August 2005. A Priz submersible, with seven crew on board, was trapped by cables on the floor of the Pacific Ocean. A remote-controlled British submarine was sent in an RAF aircraft to help. Lee says: 'Obviously there was lots of interest. I did 28 lives [news reports] in a weekend. Our little studio virtually paid for itself.'

On other occasions the impact of the story took longer to sink in:

'Covering the Orange revolution in Ukraine [in 2004–5] was probably the most satisfying thing I did. It was a piece of history and I was there. But more than that it was the moment I felt I persuaded London that there were things worth reporting in this part of the world.

'It started badly. I could hear the studio in London saying: "Why should we care about Ukraine?" and a presenter says: "Well it's the biggest country in Europe and the inventor of the helicopter was Ukrainian." I'm thinking is that the best they can do – the inventor of the helicopter! And then it's: "Laurence Lee is in Kiev . . ." They've completely undersold the story, and then I've got to build it up again. There were a hundred thousand people on the streets!'

When Lee got hold of video from election monitors, showing the way the election had been rigged, the story took another turn:

'People were going round beating the opposition up, and they destroyed loads of votes and you could see it all happening. That was an exclusive, which we later let the BBC and others have.

'Within two or three days the story had developed such a head of steam that you didn't need to explain it, and it was leading the bulletins for a week.'

Stories that can be linked to events at home also have a good chance of making it. Here's another example from Laurence Lee:

'When there was a cold snap in Britain we decided to do a piece on a place that's statistically the world's coldest town. You know the sort of thing: "If you think it's cold here, have a look at this place."

'It's in Yakutia, which is a region of Siberia and it's bigger than India. So we fly six hours from Moscow to Yakutsk, the capital of Yakutia. Then we drive in a clapped-out minibus for two days to the mountains in the north of Yakutia. This town, Oymyakon, has recorded temperatures down to minus 71. It was minus 41 and people were just going about their daily business. They didn't even think it was particularly cold.

'The schools were still open. There were kids going to school. A bit of frost on the ground in Britain, and schools are closing all over the place, but here it has to be minus 45 before they think about closing them.

'We'd travelled two days to get there, spent three days living with a family, they were reindeer herders, and two days getting back, but you know it's the sort of story that people are just going to go "wow". That's really interesting the way these people live. It's part news, part *National Geographic*.'

Remember

- Foreign bureaux are bases for covering large regions of the globe
- Don't rely on agency pictures and wire feeds
- Build your own contacts
- Tell the stories that matter to your audience at home
- Get out of the office as much as possible

CASE STUDY 9.3   EXPLAINING THE WORLD – A FOREIGN REPORTER AT WORK

This is an example of how foreign reporting provides a window on the world. It's one of an award-winning series of five pieces Laurence Lee did for Sky News prior to the Russian presidential elections of 2004. He travelled across the country from Moscow to Vladivostok, explaining how people live and offering amazing facts – 'part news, part *National Geographic*'.

Pictures	Sound – VO and sync
 A series of shots of Lake Baikal, beginning with a wide pan	How big is Siberia? Well, consider for instance Lake Baikal. It's one of those few places to offer statistics so stupendous as to be almost meaningless. The oldest and deepest lake in the world, it's a mile down before you reach some of the hundreds of species unique to its waters. It's bigger than all the American Great Lakes put together. Only in Siberia could its size feel appropriate.
The shots include close-ups of ice . . . and a handheld zoom looking through the ice	
Piece to camera, pointing down	Do you know, there's 20 per cent of all the world's fresh water right under there.

Pictures	Sound – VO and sync
Reporter's feet	It's just the weirdest place.
Van driving across lake	During the winter the great lake becomes a road, even if the fact of that makes the mundane appear ridiculous.
Tracking shot – driver's POV	Every spring when the ice starts to crack they lose about half a dozen cars to the depths.
Driver Sergei	Sergei remained impossibly calm. Up sound of Sergei speaking (calmly).
Motorcycle and sidecar	So, if a ten-ton truck is OK, then these fellows have nothing to worry about. They live on an island, right in the middle of the lake. [Up sound 'Good morning,' as they drive past the reporter].
Wides of town in lake	It's almost as if they were faced with a life of exile in Siberia and decided they might as well go the whole hog.

Pictures	Sound – VO and sync
Yelena greets her long-lost uncle	Yelena, our guide from the mainland, came in search of an uncle who hadn't surfaced for 30 years. She found him too.
Interview with Yelena's uncle	(voice fades). Translator: The one problem we have on the island is with the electricity supply. Other than that it's fine.
A street scene with electricity poles	They find a way to get supplies through when they can.
Clothes shopping	There's more stuff in the shops. It just depends how much money you have.
Daytime fireworks	(Sound of fireworks.) The closest town to Baikal is Irkutsk where two-thirds of a million live in slightly decadent remoteness.
Ice sculpture	

	Pictures	Sound – VO and sync
	Shots of skiers	They're holding a winter games. Hardly an outsider here. Just a chance to celebrate each other.
	Vox pop	Translator: 'There's nowhere else like Siberia. It's got everything.'
	Vox pop	Translator: 'Siberia may be cold, but it's very beautiful.'
	Wide shot of Irkutsk	(Local music in background.) Some of the earliest inhabitants here were former slaves, escaping the Tsarist autocracy of Western Russia.
	People shots	These then are the descendants of Siberia's pioneers, whose exploration of the east mirrored the conquest of the American West.
	Railway tracking shot	The Trans-Siberian railway was built at the turn of the last century to make travel easier for explorers and peasants alike,

Pictures	Sound – VO and sync
Wide shot of train on mountain pass	
Interiors of train	. . . and today our carriage is still awash with long-distance human traffic.
Family in carriage	A family dividing its time between Russia and China – three days from Beijing to Irkutsk.
Businesswomen on train	In the next compartment some local businesswomen who've been buying Chinese clothes to sell to the Siberians.
Getting off the train	(Up sound of footsteps.) We got off the train at the southern tip of Lake Baikal. They were already waiting for us.
Trackside fish salesman	This is smoked omul, a relative of the salmon, and it's the staple food and the staple income source for many. (Upsound trading.) It's only five minutes till the train moves on. They need this trade to survive. Omul's dirt cheap. They have to sell fast.

Pictures	Sound – VO and sync
Train departs	Siberia has always been synonymous with suffering.
Close-up of local woman	But these people have no one to complain to.
Wide of woman on fish stall	They seem to feel no self-pity.
Pull focus from woman in foreground to reporter eating omul	And they refuse to submit to the harshness of the place. But they have each other and of course they have the great lake.
Reverse of Lee looking out over the lake	Laurence Lee, Sky News, Lake Baikal in Eastern Siberia.

CONCLUSION

Foreign reporting can occasionally be glamorous. It is often dangerous. It requires a level of professional commitment beyond the routine of turning up at the office every day and being sent out on a story.

Even foreign stories need to justify their place in the bulletin. If you are based in a foreign bureau, you are the eyes and ears of your organisation in that region of the world – not just the city where you are based. You need to identify and report stories from many countries, and work out the logistics of how to cover them. Or you might be 'parachuted' into a big global story, where you will be pitted against not just your own country's but the world's media.

Foreign correspondents are part of a journalistic elite – even an aristocracy. To maintain their position most of them work long hours in difficult and occasionally dangerous conditions. If you aspire to join them, weigh up the impact on your lifestyle. Don't expect a settled home life, or to see much of your children.

FURTHER READING

Many foreign correspondents have written their memoirs. The following are all entertaining and informative.

Adie, Kate (2002) *The Kindness of Strangers*, London: Hodder.

Alagiah, George (2001) *A Passage to Africa*, London: Little, Brown.

Alagiah, George (2006) *A Home from Home: From Immigrant Boy to English Man*, London: Little, Brown.

Gardner, Frank (2006) *Blood and Sand*, London: Bantam.

Gardner, Frank (2009) *Far Horizon*, London: Bantam.

Hewitt, Gavin (2005) *A Soul on Ice*, London: Macmillan.

Marr, Andrew (2005) *My Trade*, London: Macmillan.

Simpson, John (1998) *Strange Places, Questionable People*, London: Pan.

Simpson, John (2001) *A Mad World, My Masters*, London: Pan.

Simpson, John (2002) *News from No-Man's Land: Reporting the World*, London: Pan.

Simpson, John (2003) *The War Against Saddam: Taking the Hard Road to Baghdad*, London: Pan.

Snow, Jon (2005) *Shooting History*, London: Harper.

Tumber, Howard and Webster, Frank (2006) *Journalists Under Fire: Information War and Journalistic Practices*, London: Sage. An examination through first-hand testimony of the way journalists operate in war zones.

WEB LINKS

www.dartcenter.org A global resource for journalists covering violent and traumatic events.

www.fco.gov.uk The Foreign and Commonwealth Office site, detailing the precautions to be taken when visiting foreign countries.

www.ifj.org The site of the International Federation of Journalists, with updates on the number of journalists and media workers killed worldwide.

www.newssafety.com The site of the International News Safety Institute.

www. usembassy.org.uk For details of US visa classifications.

CHAPTER TEN
GOING LIVE

WHEN Mark Austin took over as the presenter of ITV News' main 10.30 programme at the start of 2006, he said: 'I want to take the programme to the story.' It was a strong assertion of the importance of being live at the scene of events.

As early as the 1980s there was a saying in the US: 'If it ain't live it don't jive.' In television where the US leads Britain often follows. That has never been truer than in the growth of live coverage of news events. It predates the advent of multiple 24-hour news channels, and was made possible by new technology enabling live links to be set up quickly and relatively cheaply from remote locations. Satellite time used to be expensive and only available to national networks. Now satellite links are so common that most people working in regional TV news in the UK can't remember when they were not in daily use on their programmes.

When the Americans were setting the trend for going live, their news values were distinctly tabloid. Even at network level US stations have never majored in foreign news – unless it's news from a country where US troops are fighting a war. So, Rick Sanchez earned a reputation on Channel Seven in Miami for chasing ambulances, reporting via live links from south Florida's crime scenes. He said: 'I just go where the bodies are warmest.' It led to an undiluted agenda of often sensational crime coverage where the significance or importance of the story itself was valued less than the live drama it produced. Ambulances were highly prized. Bodies even more so. As a reporter with so much live broadcasting experience, Sanchez suffered a surprising fall from grace: he was sacked from CNN in 2010 for alleged anti-Semitic remarks during a live radio interview.

An obsession with live two-ways has definitely crossed the Atlantic, even if UK TV news is rarely so tabloid. We don't chase ambulances, but editors do appear to value live coverage simply because it is live.

Mark Austin, presenter of ITV News

The art of the two-way

The ability to talk live on air and unscripted has never been more highly prized. It is no longer the preserve of presenters, but has to be practised by all reporters in radio and TV, usually in the form of live two-ways – question and answer sessions with the studio – or the 'throw', where the studio 'throws' to the reporter who picks up the story and runs with it.

It was a live unscripted two-way that landed Andrew Gilligan and the BBC in such trouble with Tony Blair's Labour government, and led to the resignation of the BBC's Chairman and Director-General (see Case study 3.3). Among the BBC guidelines arising from the case was this: 'We should not normally use live unscripted two-ways to report allegations.' But that didn't stop the widespread use of two-ways on the BBC and elsewhere for all other types of reporting.

Great presenters have the ability to ad lib and to cope with changing events – and studio mishaps. Reading an autocue convincingly was never enough, and now reporters too need the same live skills as studio presenters.

You will have an earpiece through which you can hear studio output. You should hear all the studio sound, including instructions from the gallery, but without your own contribution. This is known as *clean feed*. The clean feed lets you speak naturally in response to questions or instructions from the studio without hearing yourself back.

Without clean feed, a reporter on a satellite link hears their own voice a second or two after they have spoken. The delay is caused by the time it takes for the signal to reach the satellite and return to earth. Hearing your own words coming back at you is disorienting. No one can broadcast well under these conditions.

Reporter Steve Lee of Sky Sports has suffered this problem several times: 'It's one of the worst things that can happen on a two-way. You almost inevitably stumble over your words because it's impossible to think.'

If an engineer has accidentally flicked the wrong switch and you hear a delayed feed of your own voice, there are no easy ways to cope. You can remove your earpiece or turn it down (assuming you can find the volume control under pressure), but if you need to listen for the next question there is no choice but to soldier on. The safest option is to apologise and explain the problem on air. Audiences are more forgiving than you might think; they quite enjoy a glimpse of 'behind the scenes' difficulties.

So, technical hitches can spoil the flow of your report, as can the difficulty of remembering what you need to say. How then do you gain the fluency and confidence to go live? How do you work without a script but still get it right?

On-air miles

Kirsty Young, the presenter of *Desert Island Discs* on BBC Radio 4 and former presenter of Five News on terrestrial television, has watched the trend for live reporting grow: 'The great thing about 24-hour news and radio stations like Five Live is that there are now some crackingly fluid individuals who can stand and just tell you a story.'

Young advises broadcasters to start in radio where you can learn a lot quickly: 'Don't be seduced by the glamour and apparent big bucks of television. In radio nobody is worried about making hugely expensive mistakes, so you're more likely to be given your head.'

She says the experience she gained at BBC Radio Scotland helped her get used to being live on air, and today's best reporters have done the same:

'They've earned what I call their "on-air miles" because they have been on air, and there's nothing really to substitute for that. I think that one of the great things the 24-hour era is throwing up is people who are very fluent. For me, being on radio for a few years really

helped me overcome the idea of simply talking. That's what we do for a living – quite an intimidating thought, when you think about it – communicating. Being on air really helps.'

Hospital radio and community stations are good places to start, because keen volunteers are always welcome. Your ambition may lie in being a news reporter, but don't restrict yourself to just doing the news. Offer to present music or sports shows, anything where you're just talking, mostly without a script. Clock up your own 'on-air miles'.

Enjoy yourself

Simon Cole, Deputy Head of Sky News, says on-air reporting is about confidence, and he encourages their reporters to enjoy what they do.

He's suspicious of training reporters to perform, and critical of the BBC:

'Sometimes they go through the BBC machine and they come out without a lot of character. They have these trained movements, like the "behind me" wooden move. They have to do things that way – you have to check this, you have to do that – and you actually inhibit sometimes the reporter's natural effervescence or exuberance.

'What I've always said to my lot is, forget all about the BBC. I don't want you to do BBC. Do Sky, which is go out there and have fun, because if you're enjoying the story, if you're really into it, the viewer will pick up on it.

'Our people are told to just be natural and give it some. I think that's important. The whole image of Sky is of a vibrant throbbing station.'

Remember

- Talking live and unscripted is an important skill for a broadcaster
- You can only get better with experience – your on-air miles
- Act naturally and enjoy it – don't appear wooden

CASE STUDY 10.1   THE IMPORTANCE OF GREAT PICTURES

When a series of explosions devastated an oil depot in Hemel Hempstead in December 2005, it was described as the biggest fire ever seen in Europe in peacetime. 24-hour news wasn't around during the Great Fire of London, so that claim may never be proved, but it was certainly the biggest fire ever seen on television. Buncefield was also the biggest news story to break on a Sunday morning since the death of Diana, Princess of Wales.

Sky News' Geoff Meade was at home in bed and awoken by the explosion: 'I thought it was a plane crash. You are at home with your loved ones, and you convince yourself we've just escaped another Lockerbie.'

Professionalism – the urge to find out what was happening and report it – kicked in within seconds: 'When I looked out of my bathroom window it seemed like the whole horizon was on fire.'

He immediately called the newsdesk and was on air in minutes: 'It was a different experience because the story had come to me. It crossed the line between the professional and the personal.'

Meade's telephone reports included vox pops with guests evacuated from a hotel: 'I just thrust my mobile phone out and said: "Would you speak to Sky News please?" What I'd have done if they'd told me to bugger off I daren't think.'

Duty editor Roger Protheroe recalls:

'Within 45 minutes we had viewers' video off phones. We had so many images we did a whole package on them later in the day. Some of the stills were sensational. It was the biggest response we'd ever had on any domestic story.'

BBC TV received their first picture, a still, at 6.16 a.m. – about 13 minutes after the explosion – and the first moving image seven minutes later. There had been no on-air request for pictures at that stage. They received 15,000 images throughout the day.

Once satellite trucks were in place, broadcasters soon had live feeds showing pictures of the blazing depot and the plume of smoke spreading across the Home Counties. Those pictures dominated the next several hours of live coverage to such an extent that viewers rarely saw the people in the studio anchoring the programme. On Sky News, it was over an hour after the live pictures began rolling that the first studio face appeared. It was Political Editor Adam Boulton explaining why his Sunday morning programme would not take place as normal. His studio guest, the cabinet minister John Reid, commented on the incident and said: 'I understand fully why you might leave to nip over for a press conference or whatever.'

Sky News presented viewers with information as they received it, running the latest video in a split screen alongside the live shot. They ran uncut rushes of vox pops with witnesses, including the reporter asking an interviewee to move so 'we'll just get the flames over your shoulder', and thanking a contributor: 'Cheers, mate, lovely talking to you.' The reporter Enda Brady had been with Sky just three months and did not realise the vox pops were going to be 'hot rolled':

'It was an eye opener for me. When you're doing voxes you think you're just after three lovely clips and nobody will hear the other stuff. I was still learning the Sky way of doing things. But it worked. It added immediacy to the story.'

Although the studio presenters were not seen as the story developed, reporters *were* shown, even when what they were reporting was their own predicament. Geoff Meade told the studio – and viewers:

'The police are quite adamant our satellite truck has to relocate, so we might not be able to bring you these pictures for much longer. The police are saying it is hazardous to us to be in this area, so they are evacuating the area around Leverstock Green.'

His words added to the drama, and gave viewers a powerful impression of how events develop during a large-scale emergency.

Meade sums it up: 'On a story like that the normal rules of neat and tidiness go out the window.' His own bathroom window perhaps.

The Deputy Head of Sky News Simon Cole was delighted: 'Yes, we were lucky, but, you know, old hack gets out of bed in his pyjamas and does the business. It was fantastic and led the way.'

Pushing the limits

Technology is making it easier to report and present from live locations. Mark Austin made good on his promise to take the ITV News programme to the story during Israel's attacks on Hezbollah fighters in Lebanon in summer 2006:

'Part of the job that I took was whenever possible to present the programme from locations. We did it for two weeks in first Beirut and then Tyre. I just think it adds something to the viewer. I am then able to report as well, so I can double up. That would not have happened five–ten years ago. Now we try and do it more often than not, if there's a big breaking story.'

On 24-hour news channels, 'lives' fill time as well as being a quick and easy way to update a story. And if your reporter and satellite truck are already in position, they are cheap too. Sky News has set daring precedents in the use of two-ways. Reporters are often required to speak to camera when important events are imminent, rather than just after they have happened, keeping the audience in a state of heightened expectation even before a crucial court verdict is announced or a key politician walks out of an international conference. Keeping talking like this requires great fluency and huge amounts of confidence.

Jeremy Thompson, a 30-year veteran as a foreign correspondent with ITN and Sky News, is one of the 24-hour channel's most senior presenters. He's not afraid to take risks – to busk it. When US and British troops invaded Iraq in 2003, Thompson showed daring in his approach both to covering the war – and to what he could get away with on air.

'I just went in with a truck, crossed the border illegally into Kuwait and just busked it. We weren't embedded. We just busked it, with me and the engineers on the truck, a cameraman and a producer, and we just rock'n'rolled. When we were on the road to Baghdad, as soon as we got across, we started interviewing Iraqis as the British troops were coming in. I heard in my talkback that in London they had Geoff Hoon on, and they were talking to him, and I just shouted down the line: "Give him to me, give me the Defence Secretary."

So they said: "Oh, Defence Secretary, Jeremy Thompson is in Iraq," and he obviously went: "Oh dear."

'I said: "I'm surrounded by Iraqis. You've just sent your troops in to liberate and save them, and they don't seem that pleased . . . so what have you got to say to them?"'

Art or artifice?

As well as their obvious value in filling time on rolling news, two-ways are a way for correspondents to expand coverage of important stories on terrestrial television's main bulletins. This means facts and analysis should be saved for the two-way, not repeated from the package.

Some viewers think the reporters on two-ways are so fluent that they must have Autocue. They almost never do. Others wonder whether the questions and answers are rehearsed. The truth is there is rarely time for a full run-through, although the reporter will have suggested the questions to the producer or presenter before they go on air. A two-way is not the same as an interview – even though it copies the question-and-answer format. The appearance of spontaneous questioning is a pretence. The reporter knows what questions to expect and can jot down bullet points or even write out whole answers before going live. It is not uncommon to see reporters pacing alongside satellite trucks trying to remember their lines. But usually there is no time for that.

So reporters are valued today as much for their competence in live, unscripted broadcasts as for their ability to tell a story in a well-crafted package. But this doesn't mean writing skills are any less valuable. The best exponents of the two-way speak as they would write for broadcast. They construct sentences that sound right on air whether they've been written down first or not. Most of the best do it well because they have had years of practice. Although the growing demand for live contributions is a relatively modern phenomenon, many experienced older hands in TV newsrooms found it a straightforward skill to accomplish. It was almost as if it saved them the trouble of having to bother writing things down.

The BBC's Martin Bell was a master of this art, which is probably why he became effective as a straight-talking Independent MP and then a UNICEF ambassador later in his career. In fact, his preferred method of working on location – even on news packages – did not involve committing the words to paper. He would pace up and down collecting his thoughts as the picture editor compiled a sequence. Then on cue he would deliver flowing prose. His words never appeared on a screen nor even the back of a fag packet. The value of Bell's approach was that, if the words were easy to remember and deliver without writing them down, they would be easy for the audience to understand. For a professional with many years in the field this process worked superbly, and the words rarely failed to enliven and enhance the pictures. Bell spoke of his words 'caressing' the pictures. For newcomers, doing a voice-over without a script is a difficult skill to master. But worth trying – if only as an exercise in plain speaking.

The growing importance of being available to 'go live' has thrown up another dilemma that Martin Bell summarised, eloquently as ever, in the BBC publication *50 years of BBC Television News*. Despite his 'lucky' white suit, Bell was injured by shrapnel in Sarajevo in 1992. But he looks back fondly on that period in his career as a 'golden age':

'I see the war in Bosnia as belonging to a golden age of journalism. It was the last one we could report in the time-honoured way, by going into the field and finding things out, making sense of them and reporting them in a considered but rapid manner. This is hard to do in the age of rolling news, which requires its practitioners to be tethered for long periods to the satellite dish, to answer questions from distant anchors.'

Bell admits his comments may be 'an old soldier's prejudice'. But his concerns are supported by another term, probably too inelegant for Martin Bell, used by a lot of industry insiders to describe today's satellite reporters. They are known as 'dish monkeys'. The expression does little credit to the performing skills of modern TV correspondents, but it underlines how they operate. 'Tethered to the satellite dish', they are fed titbits of information by producers and researchers. Sometimes those other journalists are in the field working alongside them, but often the material is being gathered from wires and other sources thousands of miles away back in the studio. The reporters then repeat what they've just been told by somebody else. Perhaps 'dish parrot' would be a better description than 'dish monkey'.

Sky News Crime Correspondent Martin Brunt echoes Bell's fears:

'I spend a lot of time standing outside somewhere reporting the elements of a story that isn't moving at all and sometimes the reason it's not moving is because I'm not able to get away from being on air. I remember [when failed London transport bombers were arrested in July 2005] monitoring the siege in west London, and they kept me talking, speculating about what was going on. I'd been talking for about 20 minutes and Scotland Yard had sent somebody down to see me. I could tell that they had something to tell me and they were hovering at my shoulder and I just said [to the studio]: "If you can go away for two minutes and talk to somebody else I might have something to tell you."

It was a very senior guy [press officer] from Scotland Yard and he had a piece of paper in his hand. He did enough for me to get a sense he was there. He moved slightly into my eyeline, and I had to engineer myself away from being on air.'

The idea of speaking on air unscripted is of course nothing new to those who make a living from sports commentary. The late John Arlott was revered among cricket fans. His informed description, flawless analysis and much-mimicked Hampshire burr helped make radio's *Test Match Special* a broadcasting institution around the world. When he was asked for the secret of his art, he said that even though he was speaking live he always worked out exactly how his sentence would end before he started it. Sound advice to anyone in live broadcasting.

Arlott was of course a fine writer. Imagine the pictures to accompany this description of the day Geoffrey Boycott scored his hundredth first-class century. Boycott was the first to achieve that feat in a Test match, and he did so at Headingley in his native Yorkshire in August 1977: 'All Yorkshire knew he would do it, so they came in their thousands, and long before play began the dense, patient crowds in their long crocodiles to the turnstiles ensured that the gates would be closed.'

It could be a good descriptive piece of radio, or the opening of a TV news package. In fact, it is from Arlott's report in the *Guardian*. As we say, he was a good writer.

Remember

- Be bold – don't be afraid to push the limits
- Use clear, concise language at all times
- Beware of being tied to the dish

A CLOSER LOOK

THE TWO-WAY – A MASTERCLASS

John Sergeant has been a fixture of British broadcasting for more than four decades. He was a foreign correspondent on BBC radio, the BBC's Chief Political Correspondent, Independent Television News' Political Editor and later a reporter and presenter on programmes such as *The One Show*. He was live on air outside the British Embassy in the final days of Margaret Thatcher's premiership, when he was famously pushed aside by her press secretary Sir Bernard Ingham as she emerged from the building. The British Press Guild voted it the most memorable broadcast of 1990, ahead of footballer Paul Gascoigne's tears at the Italia 90 World Cup.

Sergeant won a permanent place in the nation's affection on *Strictly Come Dancing* with viewers repeatedly voting for his return to the celebrity ballroom contest despite his incompetence on the dance floor. Since *Strictly* he has presented documentaries on subjects as diverse as India's railways and the origins of Father Christmas.

He called his autobiography *Give Me Ten Seconds* (2001, Macmillan) – a reference to the precise time keeping needed by broadcasters on two-ways. Here he gives us some tips gleaned from those hundreds of hours waiting outside No. 10 Downing Street and in the corridors of power.

If you tell a professional broadcaster they have ten seconds to go, it isn't a vague discussion. That's it. It's got to be ten seconds. I used to find, if I was doing a two-way for ITN, that I might be given one minute 50 seconds in all. I might be given two minutes, or I might be given one minute ten seconds for the whole thing, and I found it extremely difficult to be counted through all that. Sometimes they give you, 'you've done a minute', and then 'ten . . . nine . . . eight', as if you're some sort of machine. You're not a machine, but it's useful to know when you're

John Sergeant, former Senior Political Correspondent at the BBC and ITN

about to get to the end, and I used to find it was good if someone just said in my ear, 'ten'. Sometimes they'd say, 'ten, John' or 'John, it's ten', and it was enough for me to realise that I've got to wrap up.

I would try and work out a final sentence, so if you were discussing some particular problem facing the prime minister, or some decision that had to be taken, you might then say: 'But whatever happens he must decide by the weekend', or: 'This is the sort of subject that has got to be resolved quickly'. You'd know that was going to be your final thought. What you can't do is end your interview, your two-way, on some kind of vague or pathetic note. It's got to have something quite firm or definite. It's useful, when you're trying to work these things out in your mind, to have a very solid and strong thought to end on.

You'd usually have the sentences you would need at the beginning of the answer: 'The key thing to remember about this is . . .'

You'd then decide how much history you'd give: 'This is a problem they had to cope with two or three years ago . . .' or whatever it was.

You'd then know as you were moving towards the end of your reply that you had to reach firm ground. So you can go off into the sea, you can do all sorts of strange things, you can have all sorts of diversions, but you then come back to the main point. And that usually is an answer to the question.

So, that's how you work it out. But if you work out every sentence and try and memorise it, then you can't succeed.

So, you've got to allow yourself that quite a lot of that answer is going to be extempore. And why do you do that? Is it out of bravado? No, it's because you want to do really well, and to do really well in a two-way, you can't prepare it. You've got to wing it, because then you might be just surprisingly articulate, and the only way you can do that is to be under a great deal of pressure.

You don't quite know what you're going to say, and the audience sense that you're thinking about what you're going to say, and that you're reaching the main point, like in an ordinary conversation. If you do that, the listeners are following you very closely.

> 'You've got to wing it, because you might be surprisingly articulate, and the only way to do that is to be under great to pressure.'

It's a curiosity about my trade, but in newsrooms they tend to be just looking at you on the screen and seeing Big Ben behind you or something, but real listeners are actually listening to your words.

So it's very important that you shouldn't look nervous; you shouldn't look as if you're under terrific pressure; but the words that you're using and the thoughts that you've got are absolutely vital, because, amazingly and wonderfully, the audience stretched across the British Isles are listening very carefully to what you're saying. And that's the fun of it.

The lessons from John Sergeant's masterclass include:

1 Don't look nervous

2 You can't memorise every sentence in advance

3 'Winging it' makes you perform at your best

4 Know how you are going to end

5 Always end on a firm and definite note

The throw

When the studio 'throws' to a reporter on location, the idea is that the reporter will pick up the story and run with it. Usually that involves a live piece to camera, but there can be other elements – the illustrated two-way.

From a radio car, you will be able to report live and play in your own audio clips – an interview perhaps or some actuality at a scene.

Live location mixing of television pictures is available on some satellite trucks and in self-contained, fully portable systems. Usually, though, reporters will link to video played in through the gallery back at the studio. This may be rushes, an interview clip or a cut package sent back moments earlier. The reporter needs to give the gallery a cue for them to play in the clip. This will be a form of pre-arranged words ('as he told me a few moments ago . . .' or 'says he's not happy about it . . .', for example).

Sometimes the director will 'float in' pictures of whatever the reporter is talking about. If the reporter has a monitor he will see the shots and be able to talk over them, matching words to the changing shots. If there's no monitor, there'll be an instruction from the gallery ('on pictures' or 'on video') and the reporter will hear that via the earpiece, and ad lib over the pictures. This requires good communication between gallery and location, and an understanding from both ends of exactly how long the pictures are and what they show.

Remember

- The key to a successful throw is good communication between the studio and the location
- Know your in and out cues

Editorial justification for the 'live'

While live reporting has added immediacy and freshness to television news coverage, there has to be an editorial justification for it. Let's inject a note of caution from BBC broadcaster John Humphrys, presenter of BBC Radio Four's *Today* and BBC TV's *Mastermind*. He summed up the dangers of being too obsessed with 'going live' in his 1999 book *Devil's Advocate* (Hutchinson).

Television news does too many things because they are possible rather than because they are necessary. I have never understood why we must 'go live' to a reporter on the scene two seconds after we have seen the report. You know the sort of thing.

'Over now to Kate for the very latest. Kate, what's happening?'

'I've just told you what's happening in my report, cloth ears, and if you weren't listening properly I'm buggered if I'm going to tell you again.'

Sadly they never do say that, but I live in hope.

Although Humphrys didn't know it, a version of his imagined scenario had indeed happened a couple of years earlier. A reporter standing in front of a camera after nightfall in a snow storm at a crime scene was asked the ubiquitous: 'What's happening now?' on a live outside broadcast for BBC *Midlands Today*. His reply: 'Not a fat lot!' earned a serious rebuke from the editor.

THINKPIECE   WHEN LIVE COVERAGE DISTORTS THE STORY – AN ETHICAL QUESTION

The role of the journalist as an interpreter of information is thrown into sharp focus in war. Pictures – and opportunities for 'lives' – may be available from one side of the conflict and not the other. This dilemma arose during the first Gulf War, and again during the invasion of Iraq 12 years later.

In 1991, for the first time in an international conflict, press conferences – by Allied commanders – were broadcast live. Viewers saw live reports from correspondents in war zones, including those in Baghdad, though never from the Iraqi front line. The absence of an accurate Iraqi perspective and the inaccuracy of some of the reporting meant the picture was never complete.

A reporter for CNN in Tel Aviv appeared live, wearing a gas mask, saying there had been a Scud missile gas attack. In fact, there had been no gas in the missile, which carried a conventional explosive warhead. This was misleading and dangerous reporting. The Israeli government had suggested it would respond with nuclear weapons if there were chemical or biological attacks on its citizens. US President George Bush had already said he was getting some of his information about the war from CNN before it was confirmed by the Pentagon. If the Israeli prime minister had been watching CNN, might he have pressed the nuclear button? We know of course he did not, but the thought that he might have done surely brings into the sharpest focus the need to check facts – even in the heat of a major incident.

During that war, a newspaper reporter, appearing on CNN's *Larry King Live*, remarked that it was all very well showing live press conferences, but exposing the mechanics of journalism did the viewers no favours. He said it would be like giving his notebook to his paper's readers and telling them to make sense of it for themselves.

There was precious little interpretation as American generals proudly showed video of laser-guided bombs destroying military targets – and scrupulously avoided any pictures that suggested real people were being killed. The role of the journalist – either during or after those news conferences – should have been to put the 'smart-bomb' pictures in context, pointing out that most of the Allied ordnance was not 'smart' at all. Conventional weapons were being used to carpet-bomb Iraqi troops on the ground. But there were no pictures of that. So, the military successfully commandeered the airwaves – with the compliance of the broadcasters.

During the Invasion of Iraq in 2003, embedded journalists moving with US and British forces were able to report live from the battlefront. But again there were few pictures from the Iraqi side. (BBC correspondent Gavin Hewitt discusses his role as an 'embed' in Chapter 9: Foreign reporting.)

It is an abiding criticism of war coverage that journalists show the 'bang-bang' – the guns and missiles being fired, but not the consequences of the weapons on human beings. There are two reasons for this. One is practical – if the camera crew is with an army firing weapons, they are unlikely to be able to cross the lines to gather pictures from the other side. There have been few recent conflicts where the media on both sides have had equal access to the military. The second reason for not showing the carnage of war is an unwillingness to offend viewers. Judgements of taste and decency are made all the time by editors and producers, and they don't always get it right. Strong writing can allude to what the viewers are not seeing without showing the most gruesome images.

Broadcast journalists have an ethical responsibility to report impartially, independent of external pressures, and a legal responsibility to be politically neutral. That is difficult to do and harder to maintain. Facts, we are told, are sacred. 'Opinions,' Clint Eastwood says as the San Francisco cop Dirty Harry, 'are like assholes. Everybody has one.' But, inevitably, opinions come into play when journalists select which facts to report and which sources to quote.

Presenters of rolling news programmes, particularly on radio, often find themselves commenting on the news, but they have to be careful not to be involved in political controversy. Shelagh Fogarty, BBC Radio Five Live presenter says: 'We make our feelings known on subjects, but not political subjects, not subjects that are sensitive. We make our feelings known about lifestyle things, because that's what people want to hear.'

There have been few recent conflicts where the media on both sides have had equal access to the military.

Challenging facts, and their sources, and separating them from propaganda and spin are among the first duties of any journalist. Establishing the 'truth' of any situation is a near-impossible goal. Truth is almost always subjective. But striving for an accurate and balanced account is fundamental to the job.

Presenting live

Just as reporters have had to learn the traditional presenter's skills of talking live and unscripted, so today's presenters have to be accomplished live reporters. Interviewing contributors and linking to reporters and packages are only the beginning of it.

Jeremy Thompson has reported live from wars in Kosovo and Iraq, from the devastation of the 2004 tsunami, and from the middle of the Mall during the Queen's Golden Jubilee parade in 2003. Sky News uses a digilink – a radio link to the camera, freeing it from the need for an umbilical cord to the satellite dish. It also frees the presenter to be much more ambitious, as Thompson explains:

Jeremy Thompson of Sky News: 'Look, there's some people over there. Let's go talk to them.'

If you get it right and you get the kit in place and you've got the right people out there telling the story and you've got a good story to tell, it works. As long as you tell people what you're doing. As long as the audience know – don't worry about the cameraman, he's got to come with me – talk to the audience. The key thing about the presentation business is as long as you're not fazed by it, as long as you're not bothered, they won't be. The one thing you don't want to do is to embarrass the people who're watching or make them feel uncomfortable. My view is if you cock it up, just say: 'Sorry, bit of a mistake.' Just get them along with you. I'll say: 'Look, there's some people over there, let's go talk to them,' and go. That might not always work, but take people with you, take people on the ride. As long as they're on a voyage of discovery with you, as long as you know what you're doing and you're confident about it and you're not fazed, they won't be. And I think people like the idea of 'bloody hell we're there, wow', and peering round corners, picking our noses and finding out what's going on. When there's a big story it clearly is hugely compelling. The number of tales I've had back, we all have, of people who said they had no intention [of watching], but suddenly a big story comes up and they're sat there rooted, and it's actually better drama than fictional drama on telly.

Julie Etchingham: 'The language evolves, because you're finding out the facts the whole time.'

Julie Etchingham, later of ITV News, presented with Thompson from the disaster relief centre in Phuket after the 2004 tsunami:

Most of the presenters [at Sky News] have had experience as reporters. If you are in the field as a presenter, you naturally use a more fluid language. If you are describing a scene and you're doing much more stuff live, then the language used is inevitably different. If you look at the way a link into a carefully crafted package is written for the *10 O'Clock News* on the BBC, it is in very different terms to the way I would read a link or say a link into a package if I was in the field. It's much more driven by the spoken word.

That has big upsides and big downsides, because it can get much more woolly and can get very sloppy. But at the same time if it's done well, and you're in the field where the story's happening, it can be far more compelling. So actually you think much more about the spoken word and the way it's expressed, rather than crafting beautiful sentences if you've got all day with just one link to write for a package. So it's a different approach totally.

The 2004 tsunami presented particular problems of tone and content. Etchingham was on air 'living the story', gathering information as teams of reporters in the field uncovered the enormity of the event:

The language evolves, because you're finding out the facts the whole time, and actually finding the right language to describe it, particularly something like that where it is so harrowing. It's very easy to suddenly start talking about a disaster in glib terms, frankly, because you're saying it hour in, hour out, and you're talking about the endless figures of the death toll rising. It's very easy just to get glib about it, and you have to make sure that you're always conveying the scale of the story, without slipping into anything that becomes a cliché.

3G phones

Mobile phones can be used for the first live television reports from a breaking news story. Although the technology has revolutionised the ease with which a reporter can go on air, using it is a comparatively primitive experience. There will be no talk back or clean feed. Instead the telephone screen shows a tiny thumbnail picture of whatever you are pointing the phone at (yourself, if it's a piece to camera) and the wider screen shows programme output. As soon as you see yourself on the bigger screen, start talking. The system is rough round the edges, but it works.

Remember

- New technology allows you to be more ambitious
- Don't make the audience feel uncomfortable
- Apologise if there's a mistake – then move on
- Take the audience with you
- Find the right language for the story
- Don't use clichés

CASE STUDY 10.2   EVENT TELEVISION – WHEN ONLY LIVE COVERAGE WILL DO

Some news events so grip the public imagination that live coverage is the only way to watch them. They become a shared audience experience. Mobile phone updates or downloading video-on-demand cannot compete with live viewing.

These events are rare. A survey by Cardiff University researchers of the three British rolling news channels that were on air in 2005 said that the phrase 'breaking news' is often little more than a device for maintaining a sense of drama. They showed that, even if we accept the channels' definition of breaking news, it forms only a small part of their content (3.6 per cent during their two-week survey).

But when there is massive public interest, the battle between Sky News and the BBC News Channel is fiercely competitive. After the ITV News Channel closed at the end of 2005, the two big fish were left in the sea. And, appropriately, it was a huge sea creature that provided their first head-to-head encounter. The appearance of a northern bottlenose whale in the heart of London was a once-in-a-lifetime story.

The whale, normally a deep sea creature, found itself off course and stranded in the River Thames. On Friday, 20 January 2006, the story was presented as a great novelty. But it soon became clear that the mammal was in distress and in danger of running aground. Readers of the next morning's newspapers, and people who'd heard about the whale on radio or seen it on TV the night before, tuned into rolling news channels on the Saturday morning to see what was happening – and they witnessed an extraordinary day-long rescue attempt.

Events unfolded within a timescale that almost perfectly fitted a leisurely Saturday afternoon's viewing. By lunchtime the volunteers from British Divers Marine Life Rescue had succeeded in approaching the whale in shallow water, calming it and surrounding it with inflatable pontoons – all viewed live from helicopters and cameras on the bank of the river.

Teams of BBC and Sky News presenters and reporters offered running commentary and interviewed experts and people involved in the rescue. Sky News talked to people watching from the river bank, while the Skycopter provided live pictures. The flexibility of the aerial coverage – from a thousand feet up, but with a long lens gyroscopically stabilised to provide remarkably close pictures – proved the winning element in their programming.

The BBC had a helicopter too, but it was refuelling when the most dramatic moments of the afternoon took place. News 24 (as the News Channel was then known) was showing a loop of rushes from earlier in the day, as the Skycopter, broadcasting live pictures, tracked two inflatable boats, with the whale sandwiched between them, gingerly heading a few hundred yards downstream to a waiting barge. They were live on air, shortly after 2.30 pm, as rescuers strapped the whale into a giant cradle and lifted it onto the barge. And the live shots continued as the whale on the barge was taken out to sea, past the Houses of Parliament, the London Eye and other landmarks.

It was almost an hour after it happened that the BBC showed – at 3.32 pm – recorded rushes of the whale being lifted from the water. It was bad luck that their helicopter was grounded during the key moments (the Skycopter was refuelling later in the afternoon as the barge made its 40-mile journey to the sea), but a graphic on that evening's BBC1 news was bad journalism. It said the whale was lifted on to the barge at 3.30. That was when the BBC had first shown the pictures – an hour after the event.

The value of the live element of a fast-moving story was underlined late in the afternoon. Sky News packaged the events of the day in a recorded report at the top of the hour at 5 pm. Even as the report concluded, on an optimistic note about the whale being ready for transfer to a deep sea vessel, the breaking news strap across the lower third of the screen announced that the whale had taken a turn for the worse and was unfit for the transfer. It had developed breathing difficulties. The whale suffered convulsions, and died just off Gravesend in Kent at 7 pm.

The animal's plight was reported worldwide. It was a story of little political significance – although it helped reopen a debate about conservation of marine mammals. But it captured the public imagination in a way few 'hard' news stories do. It was not a story that merited interruptions to mainstream programmes – although presenter Clare Balding on the BBC's *Grandstand* advised viewers that live coverage was available on News 24. Many viewers took that cue to switch over.

The whale story happened less than a week after a feature on the front page of the media section of the *Guardian* headlined 'Rolling news RIP'. Paul Mason, BBC *Newsnight*'s business correspondent, argued that downloaded video-on-demand exposed the inadequacies of rolling news channels. Mason's arguments were well reasoned, suggesting 'that the concept of "story" – an editorial process whose outcome is a narrative with a beginning, middle and end and hopefully a meaning' had been lost. The 'day the world prayed for a whale', as the *Mail on Sunday* put it, showed that reports of the death of rolling news were greatly exaggerated.

Live radio reports

Radio reporters are often required to report live. It might be from your mobile phone, from a remote studio, from a radio car, a portable OB unit or even a microwave link on a back-pack. The advantage of a radio two-way over its television equivalent is that nobody can see you reading your notes. So make plenty. As ever, preparation is all.

Some reporters, confident of their conversational writing style, will write out their whole answer, knowing they can deliver it in a way that sounds natural. This may be essential if the material is legally contentious. Others will jot down key words and phrases, with particular attention to names they need to include. Names are easily forgotten when the adrenalin starts

> **Names are easily forgotten when the adrenalin starts to flow.**

to flow. Presidents and prime ministers can become anonymous when the excitement of going live addles the reporter's brain. Remember, although the two-way sounds like an interview, it is not. The questions you are asked will have been agreed beforehand, with the producer and the studio presenter. So, that gives you time to concentrate on the technical side. That means making sure you are in a comfortable position where you can see your notebook.

If you are in a crowded street, take a look around and make sure nobody is hanging about waiting to spoil your moment. A shouted 'hello mum' will disrupt your flow and sounds insensitive and inane in the middle of a serious report.

Remember that the most annoying, inarticulate youth has as much right to be in a public place shouting inanities (though obviously not swear words) as you do to be broadcasting. Never lose your cool. Just as you need a certain charm to encourage people to be interviewed, you may need to charm any potential live 'audience' to behave while you are on air. Most passers-by are intrigued by live radio. Those who are determined to get in on the act can often be 'bought off' with the offer of a quick recorded interview, after you've done your report. Explain that you need to talk to people with strong opinions on the story. If they agree, their contribution could even work as part of a vox pop. Or it might just buy you time to get the job done. Either way, you don't have to use it.

The satellite phone is a vital
tool for reporters

Satellite phones

The satellite phone is an invaluable tool for international reporting. The first casualty of war is no longer truth. It's communications. An aggressor has to destroy an enemy's communications. And a frequent consequence of natural disasters such as earthquakes and hurricanes is also the destruction of communications infrastructure.

So, reporters in war zones and places blighted by nature's excesses cannot rely on getting a decent mobile phone signal. That is where satellite phones come into play. Sat-phones are a vital tool for international reporters. They communicate directly with satellites rather than mobile phone masts. They are a must-have accessory for international reporters.

Remember

- Try speaking from key words and phrases rather than writing everything down
- Two-ways are not like other interviews – you can prepare your answers
- Use tact and charm to prevent interruptions in public places
- Satellite phones are essential tools for foreign reporting

The 'as-live' report

Such is the modern obsession with live reporting that, when resources are not available to go live, news editors may want 'as-live' reports instead – recorded inserts that look or sound live. On TV, this is often achieved by a reporter on a single camera walking through a location, conducting interviews on the move. It is an opportunity to be more ambitious than you might be in a live situation where your mistake or a slip by a guest could ruin the piece. You can choreograph the camera to give a series of different shots, moving gracefully from one to the next by tracking or panning.

Sometimes overlay or cutaway shots will be added later – perhaps to give the impression of a two-camera shoot. The editing of an 'as-live' report will be minimal – often no more than 'top and tailing' – and the time saved in the edit can be put to good use on location, making sure you achieve the best possible take.

'As-lives' can be effective, and are sometimes the best way to tell the story. Often, though, the 'as-live' is a cosmetic device to make the story appear more immediate and interesting.

Under no circumstances should you claim that a recorded report or interview is live. It is dishonest and your sins will find you out. It's not just that play-out systems can fail you – tape grinding to a halt or computers going down – events can overtake you too.

Under no circumstances should you claim that a recorded report or interview is live.

For example, a report on Central News in the West Midlands about a fatal stabbing in Rugby was introduced: 'For the very latest we cross to Rajiv Popat in our newsroom.' When the reporter had finished, presenter Michelle Robinson continued: 'Rajiv, thank you for the update from the newsroom, and in the last few minutes Warwickshire police have named the man they believe was killed . . .' Who had the very latest? Clearly not the reporter in the newsroom.

Remember

- Never pretend that an 'as-live' report is live

A CLOSER LOOK

MR COOL – THE LYNAM TOUCH

Calm under pressure is the trademark of the finest live presenters. Des Lynam made his name as the coolest of sports presenters. In a world noted for frenzied over-the-top reportage, where the excitement of sporting action was almost always delivered in swathes of hyperbole, Des was Mr Cool.

Never was this better shown than in his announcement of the most sensational story of the 1988 Seoul Olympics. During a live broadcast on the BBC's *The Olympics Today* he announced:

'I've just been handed a piece of paper here that, if it's right, it'll be the most dramatic story out of these Olympics or perhaps any others. It says Ben Johnson of Canada has been caught taking drugs and is expected to be stripped of his hundred metres gold medal, according to International Olympic Committee sources.'

Lynam's expertise enabled him not only to present the information in a calm and authoritative way, but to interpret the significance of the event live on air. The 'world's fastest man' was stripped of Olympic gold for being a drugs cheat. It remains one of the greatest scandals in modern sport.

CONCLUSION

Live reporting and presenting are core broadcast journalism skills. Nobody can work on air for a network outlet without a fluent live presence. It has never been so easy to broadcast live from anywhere in the world, and the technology is getting cheaper. So, the demand for live broadcasters will only increase.

It is a skill worth practising constantly, at home, in the car or whenever you are alone. Try ad libbing from research notes, and then from memory. Only with practice will your confidence improve, and with confidence comes fluency.

FURTHER READING

Ray, Vin (2003) *The Television News Handbook*, London: Macmillan. Advice from top professionals on the pitfalls of live reporting and presentation.

Trewin, Janet (2003) *Presenting on TV and Radio*, Oxford: Focal Press. Excellent advice on the best preparations for live broadcasting.

CHAPTERELEVEN
THE PACKAGE

IN this chapter, we'll look at the art of structuring and writing the recorded report – the package. The reporter pulls together interviews, actuality and their own narrative to tell the story.

The well-honed package is still the best way of telling a story concisely and directly. The skills of packaging news have enjoyed a renaissance because more and more packaged news is available on a variety of media. Video-on-demand is available online and on phones and other hand-held devices. Interactive news services offer stories as easily digestible packages.

On rolling news channels, the skills of live reporting are particularly prized, and for a while in the 1990s it looked as if fluency in a two-way would become the defining characteristic of successful broadcast journalists. But reports of the death of the package were exaggerated. Packaging skills are essential both for on-air reporters and for the far greater number of news journalists working as behind-the-scenes producers and on broadband and interactive services.

Multimedia packages, using software such as Macromedia's Flash, extend the boundaries of the traditional package. Journalists can combine text, audio, video and graphics in revolutionary treatments of stories. The traditional time restrictions no longer apply. Interviews can be viewed at length, as well as used in edited form. Linear story telling can be augmented by non-linear techniques, allowing users to explore parts of the story that interest them.

We'll show how to enhance the package when appropriate with music or graphics. The abilities to 'think in sound' and 'think in pictures' – where the musical phrase or graphic image becomes an integral part of the story telling – are the hallmark of the best reporters. These skills are especially valuable whenever journalists stray from hard news into feature and human interest territory.

It has been said that hard news writes itself. This is true when broadcast journalists reach a certain level of competence. Creative use of graphics and music requires another level again of production expertise.

THE RISE OF THE PACKAGE

In July 1954 BBC TV presenter Richard Baker announced: 'Here is an illustrated summary of the news. It will be followed by the latest film of events and happenings at home and abroad.' British television news was born.

On that first evening, there was an illustrated news summary, read by radio announcer John Snagge, with still photographs and maps. That was very much 'radio with pictures' – a phrase still used as a criticism of weak television reporting. The spoken summary was followed by the newsreel – moving pictures of events in the news. The use of filmed footage set the tone for the next half-century. Film, and later videotape, of events became the staple of any TV bulletin.

The first BBC bulletins suggested the corporation didn't trust television as a news medium. Moving pictures were considered far too exciting for the viewers. The early Television Service ended its evening transmissions with a recording of Home Service radio's nine o'clock news, over a caption. Richard Baker remembers it being described as 'news for the blind'.

The revolutionary *News and Newsreel* was a response to the threat from independent television, which was due to start in 1955. Sure enough, ITN burst onto the scene, with newscasters promoted as personalities and a new breed of thrusting reporters. Its most enduring legacy was a less deferential approach to interviewing politicians.

Melvyn Bragg in his series *The People's Channel* celebrating the fiftieth anniversary of ITV said: 'ITN blew away deference and insisted that the newsmakers explained themselves . . . but more than anything, at home and abroad, ITN put people and their stories at the heart of the news.'

Bragg's programme showed a clip of the foreign correspondent Michael Nicholson reporting from camps in East Pakistan in 1971. Children were dying of malnutrition. The veteran reporter explained his technique:

'You don't look at hundreds of thousands. Numbers are meaningless to the viewer. But you hold a dying child in your arms and say: "By the time I've finished my commentary this child is dead." And that has impact . . . Call it melodrama. Criticise it if you like, but it gets to the heart of the viewer and that's what you're after.'

If you watch old TV packages (old reports from the BBC and Independent Television News are viewable online), you will see that they appear slow by comparison with today. Shots are held for longer and lengthier interview clips are used. Documentary story-telling techniques influenced early TV news reports. The rise of music video in the 1980s means modern audiences are more comfortable with rapid cutting, but in a factual report too much editing can be a distraction.

The package and its simplified sibling, the wrap, are important parts of radio news too. Although radio might think of itself as the Senior Service – it was around years before television – sound editing was the younger relation of picture editing. Editing sound recordings on the old wire recorders had not been possible, but film had been cut into story sequences since before the earliest days of Hollywood. In Britain and the US, magnetic recording tape was a post-war phenomenon. Indeed the first tape recorders used in the English-speaking world were seized by allied troops from defeated Germans in World War Two.

So, the package became not only the preferred way of telling a story in pictures and sound throughout the latter half of the twentieth century; it has survived into the modern era as both the most useful way of delivering news in downloaded formats and as a staple of rolling news.

Nick Pollard, the Head of Sky News until 2006, explains:

'We generate an awful lot of non-live picture content, far more, I suspect, than any one person would ever be interested in seeing in the day. The other fascinating thing with online and video-on-demand offering is that it does to a large extent potentially cut out the editorial management as a filter. It does allow a customer – a viewer – to say: "I want a lot of that and none of that. I want lots of stuff about Victoria Beckham and football and *The X Factor*. I don't want any of that rubbish about foreign news and Europe and finance and politics. It doesn't interest me at all." Or the reverse.'

Statistics from BBC News suggest users of online news *are* more likely to go for the 'dumbed-down' option – sport and celebrity rather than politics and international affairs. The early users of new technologies are usually younger people, and more of them are men. As the technology spreads, the interests of the wider population will be represented – though don't bet against sport and celebrity leading the news download charts for many years to come. Any editor will tell you they are modern obsessions.

Don't forget the intro

Although this chapter focuses on the package, remember that it will almost always be introduced by a link or cue – whether the words are read by a newsreader or appear as a few lines on a website. As we said in Chapter 5: News writing, you need to avoid repeating what the audience already knows.

Vin Ray, who has run TV masterclasses using the BBC's top correspondents, says in *The Television News Handbook*:

> **Vin Ray: 'The cue, or intro, should "sell" your story rather than "tell" it.'**

As far as it's possible – and it isn't always – the cue, or intro, should 'sell' your story rather than 'tell' it. Nothing will kill your piece quite like a cue that says it all and leaves you to repeat what's already been said. A good cue will leave the viewer ready and anxious to hear more.'

Ray points out that many correspondents don't write their own intros – an editor, producer or presenter does. But the correspondent needs to know what's being said and how it sets up the piece so the two flow seamlessly together. Among the most annoying things you can hear on radio or television is repetition of an exact phrase, or worse a whole sentence, in a package, after you've already heard it in a cue.

Remember

- Don't repeat in the package what the audience has already been told

RADIO

The feature

A packaged radio feature may contain several voices – reportage, interviews, commentary – actuality sound recorded on location, and music, sometimes for background or impact, sometimes featuring the words of a song. Shorter wraps – voicers with interview *clips* or *cuts* – are mini-features.

Making an impact

The opening words or sounds in any report have to grab the audience's attention. Should it be a snappy soundbite or an imaginative use of actuality sound? Should it be voiced on location or in the studio? Whatever you choose it has to make an immediate impact.

If you have recorded gun shots, explosions or screams at the scene of an incident, these would almost certainly be the most dramatic actuality in the report. But to use those sounds at the top of the piece, without clear explanation in the presenter's cue, would almost certainly be to waste them. The sound of sirens works as a dramatic scene setter, but other noises need to be put in context. Establishing the context need not take too long, though:

'This was the moment police negotiators knew they had failed.' [sound of gunshots]

'Three anxious hours came to an end with a controlled explosion.' [loud bang]

Having grabbed your audience's attention, it's then possible to backtrack and tell the story chronologically.

Listening for an 'in' and an 'out'

The best soundbites are self-contained and self-explanatory.

In Chapter 4: The interview, we highlighted the importance of listening to your subject's answers. Remember: *two ears, one mouth; listen twice as much as you speak*. You are not listening for content alone. You are listening for the grammatical sense of what is said, and for speech patterns and rhythms. These will help you identify the 'in' and 'out' points of any clip – the points at which the selection will start and end.

The clip must make complete sense in the context of the piece. A scripted introduction can set up an idea to clarify what is said, but the best soundbites are self-contained and self-explanatory.

You are looking for comments that are lucid and jargon free. If someone uses a jargon term, you have to waste valuable seconds explaining it.

As a general principle, you should be looking for emotion and opinion in interview clips. Facts can be explained by the reporter. Sometimes an expert will be offering factual information, but you still want it explained in an engaging way.

Soundbites

During an interview, and later while listening back or reviewing rushes, you will be trying to hear a usable clip. Sometimes the soundbite will jump out at you – and at everybody else.

When the US-manned space programme was relaunched two years after the loss of the orbiter Columbia, Wayne Hale was deputy programme manager of the Discovery mission. As astronauts prepared to inspect the heat shield on the shuttle, to see if it had been damaged by foam breaking off the fuel tank during the launch, Mr Hale answered questions from journalists about the risks involved. He said: 'The Columbia accident made us realise that we'd been playing Russian roulette with the shuttle crews – that we had been very, very fortunate in the past that the foam did not cause critical damage.' The 'Russian roulette' comment made it on to every bulletin, and was being quoted in discussion of the mission for days afterwards. Those two words summed up the dilemma that NASA had faced for years.

The Prime Minister Tony Blair announced new anti-terrorist measures after the London bombings of July 2005. He said: 'Let no one be in any doubt. The rules of the game are changing.' That quote was used as a headline on most of the coverage of the story. It was used, as audio only, behind pictures of police on the street, as the opening of a BBC TV News report – an unusual and effective story-telling technique. The quote was repeated days later in follow-up stories. We know that politicians and their advisers think long and hard about the language they use. Journalists will be given advance copies of their speeches with key phrases – the day's 'soundbites' – highlighted. Not since his (or Alastair Campbell's) 'the People's Princess', on the day of the death of Diana, Princess of Wales, had a Blair comment received such wide currency.

Linking to audio

Questions should be edited out of interviews unless they are short and challenging.

When you are linking to interview clips (soundbites or 'grabs'), your script should introduce the interviewee and set up what they are about to say. Normally that means naming them before they are heard. A simple descriptive statement works well: for example, 'The company's finance director is Lorraine Butler' or just 'Company Finance Director Lorraine Butler' followed by the clip. Never use phrases such as 'I spoke to . . .' or 'I went to see the company's finance director Lorraine Butler and asked her . . .' And always cut out your opening question. These tips will prevent you wasting words, save you time scripting and make your pieces snappier. For a TV report, of course, even the simple description is unnecessary – you can put the name and job description on a caption.

To vary the way you introduce an interview, or to aid the story telling, you might want to write into the clip; for example, 'The company's finance director Lorraine Butler says the job cuts are inevitable' followed by her comment. Often it is easy to do this by simply paraphrasing the sentence before the one you've chosen. In the example above, Ms Butler may have said: 'The job cuts are inevitable. These are difficult times and sadly we've had no option but to look at a programme of redundancies.' So you turn the first part of what she said into indirect speech and that becomes the link to a clip starting with: 'These are difficult times . . .'

Bridging between clips of sound also requires special thought. The idea is to carry the narrative forward. Setting up a new clip with a question is usually a lazy, and therefore unacceptable, way of doing it. Questions should be edited out of interviews unless they are short and challenging. Otherwise, introduce what is about to be said with a statement.

Here's an example of introducing an interview from a BBC report into the takeover by HMV of the bookshop chain Ottakar's:

'The author, Antony Beevor, was one of the leading critics of the takeover.' [clip of Beevor]: 'I think the outcome is entirely expected . . .'

This is from a BBC Radio Sheffield report of a gas explosion in Chesterfield:

'Pat Kerry, who lives next-door-but-one, says there was an almighty explosion.' [clip of Kerry]: 'It was completely out of the blue. Blew out the boiler. Blew out the pilot light.'

Who's interested?

Choosing what to put into a story – the interview clips, the actuality and the facts for your script – means choosing what to leave out. Harsh decisions have to be made.

The rule of thumb should be: if it's interesting to you, then it's interesting to the audience. If in doubt, leave it out. You need to be honest. And brutal.

Just because you enjoyed the company of a particular interviewee does not mean that they help tell the story. It's easy to be won over by the charm of someone who turns out to be incapable of speaking in coherent sentences in front of a microphone. You probably told them they'd be on the six o'clock bulletin, so you have to include them, don't you? Well, no.

> It's a big mistake to promise, or even suggest, to anybody that they will be appearing at a certain time, or at all.

It's a big mistake to promise, or even suggest, to anybody that they will be appearing at a certain time, or at all. The news agenda changes. Stories move on or get overtaken by events. Most of what you do in your career will be at risk of being dropped by an editor and may never be transmitted. In a small local radio station, where it's all hands to the wheel, almost everything does get used. Otherwise you'd never fill the bulletins. But the larger the organisation for which you are working, the greater the chances of your story being dropped. A handful of reporters will be repeatedly entrusted with the lead package on the biggest stories. Only technical failure will prevent those getting to air. But most of the time, you will be putting your best efforts into something that may be dismissed at a programme editor's whim. This is not because you have done a bad job. It may be that the story simply does not fit the day's mix – 'There are already two crime stories; we don't want a third,' or 'We've had too much sport this week.'

Living with rejection is one of the hardest lessons for trainee reporters. It's not usually personal but it always feels like it. You should aim to be so good the editor doesn't want to miss out on your work. Producers want your piece because they know it will make the programme better. That's why you have to be brutal – your report has to be of the highest standard because it has your name on it, and you want your name to be a benchmark of quality.

Treat the contributions of interviewees as you would your own script. Are there unnecessary words? Can they be edited out? Does the clip summarise the speaker's position accurately? Are they speaking with passion? What is the most interesting or enthusiastic part of their contribution?

Keep it clean

The value of clear, clean sound cannot be stressed enough. Noisy backgrounds and interruptions make editing a nightmare. It is best not to link from pristine studio-quality voice to an interview with heavy background noise. It jars on the listener's ears. It can take a second or two to adjust to what is being said and in that time the sense may be lost. Nonetheless, *some* background sound is essential when you are on location. Otherwise, what is the point of being there rather than in the studio? The background helps paint the audio picture for the listener. Remember, the pictures are better on the radio. It's been said so often that it's a cliché, but it's only true so long as there is an artist with a microphone to paint those pictures.

> Background sound is essential when you are on location. Otherwise, what is the point of being there rather than in the studio?

On location, unplanned interruptions may occur: someone comes into the room; a car drives past; an aircraft passes overhead. Sometimes, background sounds will add to the sense of being there: an ice-cream van at the seaside; a helicopter at an army base; a school bell in a playground. At other times, disruptive sound will put your interviewee off their stride and you may need to break off the interview. There may be occasions when you accidentally speak over your interviewee. You think they have finished making their point, and start your next question; you find yourself speaking over the most exciting thing they've said. The solution should be to pause and record that part of the interview again. It's no use thinking you can make up for poor recording in the edit. You can't.

Running wild

An important aid to editing, which is often overlooked in the haste to get a story on air, is the recording of **wildtrack**. Taping 30 seconds of 'atmos' (short for atmosphere) on location can save precious minutes back in the newsroom, and may even salvage otherwise unusable audio. The wildtrack, which has no speech on it, bridges gaps in edited sound. It is particularly useful when there are jumps in background level between one clip and the next. You might even want to record enough wildtrack to lay behind the whole of your voice report.

Using music

A musical performance recorded on location is always a sure-fire way of transporting the audience to the scene of the story.

Remember that recorded music is not free. Your station will have to pay a royalty.

Music can liven up a radio feature, either to create an atmosphere or to make an editorial point. A few seconds of music can set the tone of a piece. You need to use enough of it for the audience to recognise the tune, and then you can fade it beneath interview or voice-over. It is never a good idea to use music as a bed beneath the whole of a package.

A musical performance recorded on location is always a sure-fire way of transporting the audience to the scene of the story. Make sure you have permission from the performers to use it. There is a news access agreement drawn up by the Musicians' Union that means MU members have to give permission for unpaid use of their work in news programmes.

Recorded music can add flavour to features. You can use music to punctuate or underline the content of a story. Popular songs do this particularly well. If you want to highlight the words of a song, fade into and out of those words rather than playing the whole of a verse or chorus. Even if you are featuring the very first words of a song you will probably want to edit out the musical intro.

Try to be original in your choice of music. For decades, Rod Stewart's *Sailing* was overused on features about boats. Pink Floyd's *Money* and Abba's *Money, Money, Money* were similar clichés on financial reports.

And remember that recorded music is not free. Your station will have to pay a royalty to the performer and composer of the piece, just as if it were played in a music programme. The use of music has to be logged so that payment can be made.

Remember

- Make an impact at the top of your package
- Make sure you have clean sound
- Be imaginative when you introduce soundbites
- Be brutal in your edit – if in doubt leave it out
- Use lots of actuality sound
- Use music imaginatively

CASE STUDY 11.1   PULLING IT TOGETHER – USING ACTUALITY

Here's an example of a radio package from the reporting of an earthquake in May 2006. Rachel Harvey's piece for BBC Radio 4 News uses actuality sound and an interview to paint an audio picture of the relief operation. Note how the two separate pieces of actuality are explained in the script.

CUE: The United Nations has said that 'enormous progress' is being made in getting aid to those affected by the earthquake on the Indonesian island of Java. However, congestion on the roads is still said to be hampering efforts to get supplies to more remote areas. Up to two-hundred-thousand people have been made homeless by the disaster, in which more than five-thousand-eight-hundred people are now thought to have died. Thousands more were injured. The epicentre of Saturday's earthquake was near the city of Yogyakarta, from where our correspondent, Rachel Harvey, reports:

SOUND: CHILDREN SHOUTING; HELICOPTER NOISE

HARVEY: Helicopters are a welcome distraction for traumatised children. They're also the quickest way to deliver aid across the stricken region. Heavy traffic is clogging the roads, so taking to the air is often a better option. Emergency supplies are reaching main distribution points, but the rural villages which were hardest hit by Saturday's earthquake are only getting a trickle. So, as Kendar Subroto, of the United Nations Children's Fund, explains, some survivors have decided to take the initiative:

SUBROTO: Instead of waiting for aid workers to go to these villages, they came to us. And this morning, for example, we have stands of people, representing various villages, saying how bad the situation is there, and we provide support to them.

HARVEY: Accurate information is crucial to ensure that the right help reaches the right places. Shelter remains a priority. Thousands of people are still without tents and must now face a fifth night in the open. It'll be easier to create temporary camps once the rubble is cleared. The Indonesian military is making a start on that.

SOUND: SHOUTING; COLLAPSING NOISE

HARVEY: A damaged house pulled down with a few ropes and a lot of brute force. Things are moving forward here – but there's a long way to go.

BBC Radio 4 1800 bulletin, 31 May 2006

TELEVISION

Picture power

While devotees of radio will tell you it is a more powerful medium than television because the pictures are better, that old chestnut is a tribute to the power of the human imagination rather than Marconi's technology. But it can't be denied that radio is usually more immediate – all you need is the human voice to tell the story. You don't have to wait for camera crews, satellite trucks or even for someone at the scene to post pictures online. New technology is making it easier to report live on TV – reporters can be on screen using mobile phones – but it is still the case that television works best when the pictures tell the story.

The power of pictures can never be underestimated. If a picture paints a thousand words then 25 frames a second – 25 different pictures to make up a moving image – equals 25,000 words a second. One second's video is obviously not worth *that* much, but it's pretty powerful nonetheless.

The art of television reporting is to make sure that it never becomes simply radio with pictures. Strong images lead the story telling. And pictures should never be used as 'wallpaper' just to cover the cracks in poor scripting.

Kevin Bakhurst, Controller of the BBC News Channel and a former editor of the *Ten O'Clock News* on BBC1, explains the value of picture-led stories:

'This is TV news not radio news. The two years I was on the *Ten*, it was really important to the programme – picture power and the story telling with packages – as well as lives – it's good to mix them. Some bulletins can stray too far away from that. You think at the end: "I didn't really see a good picture story in that programme."

'Look at any of the most memorable TV news stories of the last couple of years, and you'll remember them because they were picture stories, not because they were live correspondents.'

Every package should start with a strong image, but not necessarily the strongest image. Often the narrative flow is more important than putting the strongest or the latest pictures first. The defining moment of a story – the picture that sums it all up – will probably already have been used as a headline. But your audience wants to know how that moment has been reached.

Consider a football match. You might show a spectacular winning goal or a controversial sending-off as a headline, but in the package you almost always tell the story of the match in chronological order. Chronology is the most straightforward way of telling a news story too.

Sometimes the most dramatic pictures *are* the story. The coverage of a triple suicide bombing in Baghdad in October 2005 inevitably started with the most dramatic pictures, because the explosions happened within sight of the hotel used by the foreign media. They had been caught on video. Caroline Hawley's report on the BBC began with shots of the explosion followed by the commentary: 'A strike in the heart of the city. A massive bomb captured on camera.' Pictures of the inside of the journalists' hotel followed. Hawley concluded with a piece-to-camera cradling a 'razor-sharp piece of shrapnel', which had landed near the BBC offices.

Remember

- Television is not radio with pictures
- Start with a strong image
- Tell stories chronologically whenever possible
- Never use pictures as 'wallpaper'

Making it relevant – the visual metaphor

Sometimes, the story is seen by broadcasters as important but potentially boring. They don't want it to be 'worthy but dull' so they use gimmicks to engage the audience. This kind of treatment is at the heart of the debate over 'dumbing down'. Does popularising important issues devalue them? Or is it the best way of involving more people in complicated debate?

Does popularising important issues devalue them? Or is it the best way of involving more people in complicated debate?

ITV News used a metaphor from reality television to report the 2005 Conservative Party leadership contest, borrowing the music from *Big Brother*, and describing the elimination process, as MPs voted to reduce the number of candidates, as 'evictions from the *Big Brother* house'. When the field was reduced to two, David Cameron and David Davies, Tom Bradley reported: '*Big Brother* now becomes *Love Island* as Tory members decide who is their ideal partner.' Daisy McAndrew's report, on the night of the final vote by MPs, used a graphic, blending the face of David Cameron, the favourite in the race, with that of the Prime Minister Tony Blair, pointing out the similar backgrounds of the two opponents. Deborah Turness, the editor of ITV News, has strong views on making stories relevant:

'You see on other news channels and programmes what I call process journalism. It's lazy. It's a story because it's around and everyone else is doing it. "How shall we do it? Well, a few GVs, a bit of a graphic, piece-to-camera, sign-off, Bob's your uncle!" No!

'I always say to people, when they say it'll be fine: "Fine isn't good enough to make it into an ITV News programme."

'We've got half an hour to distil the entire world, surely we can make it exciting, gripping and dramatic. I think news is the best drama on TV, because it's real, it's completely unpredictable and when you turn on your TV, you do not know what you are going to get.'

But Turness is clear that some reporting – notably from foreign correspondents – does not need elaborate treatments: 'Our films from people at the sharp end are never going to have graphics in them. Those are eye witness reports and those are always going to be the most important things we do, but elsewhere we need to be creative.'

Patrick Burns, BBC Midlands Political Editor, is proud of the way *The Politics Show* on BBC1 sets out to popularise issues of the day:

'Any old fool can take a complicated story and render it complicated. It takes someone who's really on top of the issue to simplify it so an audience can understand it and still keep to the truth of the story and what's really going on.

'It's quite Reithian [a reference to the BBC's first Director-General Lord Reith, who is identified with the public service aims to inform, educate and entertain]. We're bringing complicated stories to the greatest number of people.

'Our political coverage changed with *The Politics Show*. It used to be enough to take the pictures of a debate in Westminster, show a few pictures of industrial decline in West Bromwich or wherever, and get a couple of MPs into the studio for a debate. That's easy to do. But what could be caricatured as "dumbing down" takes a hell of a lot more intellectual rigour, doing it so you don't insult the intelligence of the committed viewer and so that you engage the interest of the less committed viewer.

'I call it "cool television". You try to find something that isn't obvious but becomes a visual metaphor for the story. Looking at Wyre Forest before the local elections a few years ago, most people knew that they had this independent MP Richard Taylor who won two general elections campaigning on the health service, but hardly anybody knew where this place was. It's a shame that it's named after a forest because the defining feature is the River Severn. It would have been easy to dig out the library pictures of the hospital protests and Dr Taylor's election win, but we thought it was important to let people know about the area. So we started the piece at Bewdley, which is an attractive riverside town. They were pretty pictures. If you're going to use a river as your theme, pick part of it that's attractive. And it let me say things like for Labour to recover from their collapse it was like pushing water uphill.

'Another piece asked whether the West Midlands had lost its political clout at Westminster because we didn't have local MPs at the cabinet table and in positions of power. We went to a boxing gym and did lots of close-ups of punch bags and used that as a metaphor for political clout.

'My colleague Sarah Thackray did a piece about whether new drugs should be prescribed for Alzheimer's sufferers. She used a recurring image of a cinema projector showing an Alzheimer's patient's old cine footage of his family holidays. She said his memories were as transient as each frame of this home movie footage. Once they were gone they were forgotten and looking at them was the only way he could rekindle these memories. The piece kept returning to these cine shots – an ingenious recurring image.'

Remember

- Think imaginatively
- Think pictures

Sometimes a visual metaphor is inappropriate to the story, but you still have a lack of pictures. Here's an example of making the most of what you have from BBC Midlands video journalist Robin Punt, reporting in June 2006 on the story of a paralysed man determined to visit Switzerland for an assisted suicide. All that was available was a single interview with a subject who couldn't move.

The interview with Noel Martin was shot entirely in his own home. Mr Martin was unable to walk or feed himself after a racist attack ten years before.

Pictures	Sound	Robin Punt's comments
	Actuality sound of electric wheelchair Mr Martin: 'You're not living, you're existing . . .	This shot [of Mr Martin being helped through a door by a carer] was just a grabbed shot. It was what he was doing at the time. He'd agreed to do the interview, and I wanted to make the whole experience as easy for him as possible. So there weren't a lot of set-up shots.
	because in order to live you have to be able to feel.'	After a shot showing how difficult his life is, underlined by his own words, you've got to see him. So this is the main interview shot.
	Voice-over: And he can't feel . . . he can't move . . . he can't drink – or do anything unassisted.	This is a cutaway, a pan up [tilt] as he sits gazing into the garden.

Pictures	Sound	Robin Punt's comments
	Paralysed from the neck down after a racist attack in Germany, Noel Martin from Edgbaston in Birmingham wants to die.	Somebody lighting a cigarette for him just shows his dependence on others.
	'It's my decision. God gave me a free choice,	This is a really tight close-up. It serves as a cutaway too but the intimacy is everything. If you go for lots of medium shots there's no involvement.
	. . . made me in his own image and he gave me a free choice to what I want. And I'm making that decision. I'm not saying it's best for other people, but for me that's the decision.'	Cutback to the interview. You want to see him saying this.
	Question: 'What do your family feel about this decision?' 'I don't know, I've never asked them. It's up to them what they feel.' Question: 'They haven't tried to stop you?' 'They can't stop me. Each person is supposed to . . .	A wider shot from a different part of the interview. I was able to zoom in and out as we did the interview. Most of us are just used to turning up and asking questions, but when you've only got one interview it helps to vary the shot size. The wide shows him in his home, a very nice home, with ornaments on the mantelpiece, and you can see he's quadraplegic. I was able to butt the two clips together, because he doesn't move and so there's no jump. I trailed the question in over the outgoing shot (the original question is on the wider shot). If you can do that even by 12 frames, or half a second, it's so much smoother.
	If you're a man or a woman, you're in charge of your own destiny.'	This shot is really close. Any closer and the camera would have been in his ear.

Pictures	Sound	Robin Punt's comments
	V-O: Noel Martin planted this garden,	This shows the controls of the chair, obviously, and two close-ups together work well. It's better than a close-up then a wide, which just looks like an obvious cutaway.
	restored his beautiful home, with his own hands years ago.	The silhouette from the rear shows his isolation, and the natural light lets you look at his garden. I like doing silhouette shots because they put people in the context of their surroundings.
	From his chair, he can see the memorial built in honour of his wife Jacqueline – she died from cancer six years ago.	This is the POV [point of view] shot. We get to see what he sees, and it gives us a sense of then and now: the man who built the garden, but who can't work on it any more. This is the killer fact, and the shot underlines it. You don't know until this point that his wife died. He has no close family. It's terribly sad.
	Question: 'So you know what you want now?'	I pulled focus from the memorial back to the leaves, which brings us back to him in his chair.
	'I know what I want, simple as that.'	It was easy to use his sound out of vision because he was such a clear talker. Sometimes you need lip sync to tell what people are saying.

Pictures	Sound	Robin Punt's comments
	Question: 'Even when you're sitting there and they're going to administer a fatal injection, you really want to go through with it? You're not going to stop anyone at the last minute?' 'I'm not afraid of dying. Dying isn't a problem. Living is a problem. Dying is no problem. I'm just moving on.'	The light has changed on this shot, so it's not quite so moody somehow. When you're relying on natural light you have to live with that. The reverse two-shot. I'm not a particular fan of putting myself into stories like this, but I'm sitting there able-bodied and I think it makes a point.
	V-O: On the 23rd of July next year, his 48th birthday, Noel says he'll end his life with the help of two doctors at a clinic in Switzerland.	In a way this shot doesn't work at all technically, because his position in the room has changed. But it's a different angle and I think it does the job. He reverses out of frame to end the piece. Simplicity was the key throughout.

Library pictures

Sometimes there are no new pictures to tell a story. The story could be the latest development in a long-running saga or a follow-up to an earlier report. It is then that you rely on the archive or library. A well-kept library, with a searchable database, is a great asset to any news organisation. Huge resources were spent converting tape libraries to digital storage.

Whenever you use library footage, or file tape as the Americans call it, it is important the viewers are aware they are not looking at new pictures. You can do this by using an on-screen caption or in voice-over.

Sometimes pictures are used as a generic example of something you can't film on the day: a particular model of car or aircraft; the production line of a factory threatened by industrial action or closure; shots of a celebrity who's in the news but not making public appearances. In these cases a simple 'library pictures' caption will do.

Other pictures from the library are shots of well-known events: the 11 September attacks; the 2004 tsunami; the London bombs of July 2005; the invasion of Iraq; the coalition press conference in the garden of 10 Downing Street after the 2010 general election. In these cases it is obvious to viewers what they are seeing and the script will explain why they are looking at familiar images.

Other specific events are not as well defined in the public consciousness, and it is important to explain the context. Shots of the tornado that hit Birmingham in 2005 might be used in a feature about extreme weather conditions. A date caption would help, although plastering dates all over the screen is no substitute for proper scripting. You should write to library pictures as precisely as to any others.

Many agencies keep libraries of pictures that broadcasters can buy. The broadcaster pays a licence fee to use the shots. The Imperial War Museum has an extensive resource of images from the First and Second World Wars and other conflicts, which regularly appear in news reports and documentaries. A word of warning – they can be expensive.

Wherever you get your pictures from, you should take the same care in editing them as pictures that have been shot for your piece. You obviously have no control over the way library pictures are shot, but you have total control over the way they are used.

Remember

- Script library pictures with as much care as any others
- Label library shots clearly – do not deceive your audience
- Beware the costs of agency pictures

Mike Ward: 'We are in a user-driven environment rather than a producer-driven environment.'

User-generated content

Contemporary broadcasting makes increasing use of content from users of the media. Americans talk of the new journalism being 'a conversation not a lecture'. Most British journalists would like to think they have never lectured their audience, but you get the point.

Mike Ward, who taught online journalism at the University of Central Lancashire, says we are in a 'user-driven environment rather than a producer-driven environment'. Users – the audience – can scrutinise and challenge traditional news providers. Major news organisations become facilitators, or even partners, for content providers, the so-called citizen journalists.

Pictures from contributors are likely to be the first to tell a story. In January 2009, when an Airbus passenger plane successfully ditched in the Hudson River after hitting a flock of geese on take-off from New York's LaGuardia Airport, it was reported first on Twitter. A still photograph on twitpic showed the floating plane with passengers scrambling to safety – the defining image of the 'Miracle on the Hudson'.

CASE STUDY 11.2   THE TWITTER REVOLUTION

Numerous political protest movements have grown through online networks and the pictures produced by activists become a key part of the story telling. Reporters integrate user-provided content into their coverage. In Iran in June 2009, when demonstrators took to the streets after contested presidential elections, their stills and video were the primary source of the reporting. Copyright considerations became secondary, with one user of the Flickr website collecting Twitter images from the protesters and begging news organisations to use them, writing: 'The individuals that took these photos, risked their lives to do so and it is incongruous that having done so they would not wish these photographs to be used by the world media.' He argued that constant press coverage was the only thing preventing a massacre [of the demonstrators]. Footage of the death of 26-year-old Neda Agha Soltan captured on amateur video became a rallying point for the opposition. She had been shot in the chest by a pro-government militiaman, leading to what was described as 'probably the most widely witnessed death in human history'.

While the BBC used still pictures and amateur footage from Tehran extensively, they were cautious; typically, dramatic video of a bus on fire and an apparent stand-off between protesters and security forces was accompanied by the warning: 'The BBC cannot verify the authenticity of this video.' Meanwhile the Iranian authorities tried to block BBC websites being accessed in their country, attacked social networks such as Facebook and Twitter and media-sharing sites including YouTube, and restricted mobile phone services and Internet bandwidth. Thousands of arrests and a number of executions of protesters followed. The 'Twitter Revolution' did not bring down the government of President Mahmoud Ahmadinejad.

People caught in extraordinary events may take pictures on their phones. Mobile phone pictures from a tube train bombed in the terror attacks on London transport in July 2005 provided an early UK example. Another was a year later, when BBC special correspondent Richard Bilton interviewed a Briton, Tony Lteif, at his home in Surrey after he fled Israeli attacks on Lebanon. The report included video from Mr Lteif's mobile phone of his taxi ride from Beirut into Syria, and of the chaotic scenes he saw at the border crossing.

The war artist story on the next few pages is an example of user-generated content (UGC) contributing to a well-crafted video package. The story ran as part of the ninetieth anniversary commemorations of the Battle of the Somme on BBC local and regional TV.

The story is that of an artist, Rob Perry, who specialises in painting and drawing the landscapes left by First World War battlefields. Regional BBC had featured his exhibitions before, but had never followed him to France to see him working from his mobile studio. In 2006, though, the BBC lent Rob Perry a camera to take with him. They also interviewed him at home in Stourbridge in the West Midlands. The interview and the artist's shots from France were combined to produce two feature-length pieces.

For the first item, the trained artist's eye produced some captivating images. A chance meeting with a former professional cameraman (visiting the battlefield with a group of military history enthusiasts) meant he also had someone to help with some of the shots.

The journalist who edited the piece left in a sequence where Rob jokes about the problems of talking to camera. Paul Myles, a trainer with the BBC, advises video journalists to use humour in their work whenever possible. It can show another side to the subject, even on the most serious stories.

War artist

Tracking shot

Music: Bach Suite for Cello No. 1 in G.

Music fades under Rob Perry's voice: 'As you drive through the battlefield area you just can't help but notice how many cemeteries there are dotted about.

Interview

War and its effects are something we should just never forget.'

War artist

 Cutaway tracking shot

Voice-over: 'For 15 years artist

 Rob driving

Rob Perry has toured and painted the battlefield of the Somme in northern France.

 Rob in trench

He's made over 40 trips from his home in Stourbridge to these fields, the farmland where ninety years ago this weekend

 Tilt up to show landscape

20,000 soldiers died in a single day of fighting.

 Slow zoom on still

Inspired by his cousin, a private in the Royal Warwickshire Regiment who was killed here, this is Rob Perry's video diary.'

Music fades

War artist

Walking piece to camera

'Actually I hate doing this, don't you, do you hate talking on the television?

Voice off mic: 'Well, I'm behind the camera mostly.'

Rob: . . . 'especially when you don't know what to say and you find yourself going, well, er, arr, um, err . . .'

Wide in woodland, Rob walking. He clears frame

'It's not a very easy subject to tackle, this, because the ground cover is so even.'

Tilt down to Rob working

Pause.

'So I now start working back into it with pen, making all these very fine hatching lines to try to bring a bit of character into this rather bland surface cover of grass.'

Close-up of hatching

Upsound of pen scratching paper.

Low angle of artist

'The grass of course follows the profiles of the remains of the shell holes and the ridges.'

Music fades up: Mozart Piano Concerto No. 23 in A Major.

War artist

Close-up of sketch

'So there is interest there, but it is quite difficult to find.

Albert street – tracking shot

Birmingham's very closely tied to the town of Albert. Albert was

Albert street scene

the epicentre of the Battle of the Somme.

Tower

But after the war the city of Birmingham

Albert street

adopted the town of Albert and helped with the

War artist

	Rue de Birmingham sign	reconstruction, raised funds
	Interview	and helped the rehabilitation of the population.'
	Rob in cemetery, walking to camera	Music rises.
	Close-up of headstone	'Now here's a headstone to an unknown soldier of the Royal Warwickshire Regiment. My grandmother had three cousins who were all killed on the Somme,
	Wide of cemetery	two of them with known graves, but one Bob Dean, with no known grave,

War artist

	Rob kneeling pats the headstone	so who's to know if this isn't Bob here?'
	Rob rises and clears shot	Music
	Start of tilt	Voice over: 'Tomorrow, Rob meets the historians attempting to find
	End of tilt – Rob with historian	the site of one of the biggest tunnel networks on the Somme.
	Rob working on large canvas by night	And in the dark and the pouring rain trying to capture a unique image of this massive World War One battlefield 90 years on.' Music fades.

Remember

- Integrate user-provided content into your coverage

Voice-over

We've already described how to write for broadcast in Chapter 5: News writing, but great scripts only work if they complement the rest of the package – the pictures, natural sound and interview clips.

Writing into interview clips is an art in itself. On TV – unlike radio – there is usually no need to introduce the speaker by name. A caption will do that. As in radio, there is almost always no need to use the question. Some clips need no introduction at all. One speaker may follow naturally from the one before, either because they are continuing the narrative (in a hard news story, perhaps) or because they are offering an opposite point of view (a political item).

Remember to avoid repetition. The reporter's first words should not repeat the words in the link. The first words of an interview should not repeat the reporter's introduction to the speaker.

Here's an example of how not to do it:

Reporter's voice: Examinations of the house have revealed what investigating officers are describing as a significant degree of violence.

Clip of Detective Superintendent: Something has occurred in there with some significant degree of violence . . .

Central ITV

And here are some better examples:

Reporter's voice: Two men are dead. It could so easily have been many more.

Clip of surgeon: We had people brought in with stab wounds to the chest . . .

BBC Midlands

Reporter's voice: Well-off schools will be obliged to help others.

Clip of education specialist: A third of the extra money of a specialist school has to be spent helping neighbourhood schools, and that's the whole point of the initiative . . .

ITV News

Reporter's voice: Two weeks ago his parents were called to collect the 14-year-old from school because his hair was the wrong length.

Clip of boy's mother: Too short, and it wasn't in the school prospectus.

BBC Midlands

Linking to soundbites

When you link to soundbites, let your words carry the story forward. Remember, a caption will probably be the best way of naming the speaker.

The opposition health spokesman says the government's policy will lead to longer waiting lists for patients . . .

One expert, who's studied the background of successful asylum seekers, says the approach is misguided . . .

This man has lost his home and all his belongings in the flood. He's still searching for his missing wife and child. He's desperate . . .

Natural sound

A great weakness of novice TV reporters is using too many words of voice-over and not enough actuality sound from the pictures. Whenever possible, use the actuality to set the scene. Let the pictures breathe, and give the viewer time to take in what you are saying.

Vin Ray, the first director of the BBC College of Journalism, says in *The Television News Handbook*:

'We don't live in a silent world, yet you wouldn't know it to see some television packages. Use as much natural sound as you can. Natural sound really helps the pace of a television package and helps viewers assimilate the pictures and the words they are looking at and listening to.'

> **Vin Ray: 'We don't live in a silent world, yet you wouldn't know it to see some television packages. Use as much natural sound as you can.'**

How to judge the pace of the package is summed up by Ray in the old saying from broadcast newsrooms: 'It can be as long as you like as long as it's quick.'

A well-paced piece will appear to fly by, whatever its duration. It leaves the audience keen for more. Plenty of natural sound draws the viewer into the piece. It reinforces the sense of 'being there' – the old, but still relevant, idea of television as 'a window on the world'.

The piece-to-camera

Many packages will include a piece-to-camera, or stand-up (when to use them is covered in Chapter 6: Location reporting and production). It's worth remembering that these should be treated like any other shot in the package. If it doesn't fit, drop it or change it.

When you record your PTC (or stand-up) on location, you should have a clear idea of how it will fit into your piece. But you may need to drop it if the story has changed by the time you edit the package. Apply the same ruthless quality control to the PTC as you would to all your shots.

Longer pieces-to-camera may benefit from shortening. Some will work better if they are partly covered with pictures or cutaways.

Remember

- A package can be 'as long as you like as long as it's quick'
- Words should complement the pictures
- Avoid repetition
- You don't need to name interviewees in voice-over
- Use actuality sound – let the pictures breathe
- Treat stand-ups critically, as you would any other shot

THE ONLINE PACKAGE

The non-linear online package is the closest thing to a new form of journalism since the advent of broadcasting. Traditional broadcast journalism is a linear form. Stories have a beginning, middle and end. You want the audience to stay with your story, so you give it a narrative arc, based on old-fashioned story-telling skills. Viewers and listeners should want to know what happens next. If they stay till the end, you've done your job. When your story has finished, the audience is presented with a new one.

But graphics-based online story telling can be different. Online, using a programme such as Flash, different story-telling elements can be linked. Video, still photographs, sound, text and graphics can all be used to tell the story. Soundslides, combining audio, still pictures and minimal text, can be particularly effective. Because of the way the different elements are linked, users can decide how much or how little they want to see or hear. There's a linear thread, but the user controls the length of the experience. It's similar to skipping from one story to the next in a newspaper – except it's much more exciting.

Some of the best online treatments of stories are on US websites. Many UK newspapers have seen broadband as an opportunity to train their reporters as video journalists. Most of their early efforts looked amateurish (although they will obviously get better), and UK newspaper companies have largely overlooked the potential of a medium that marries broadcast and newspaper skills.

A Long Island-based newspaper, *Newsday*, achieved 12 million hits in a day and won a Batten Award for Innovations in Journalism with a report, the 'Cost of War'. The in-depth account of the impact of the war in Iraq had audio commentary, video footage, top-quality news stills, interviews with Iraqis and Americans, personal testimony, blogs, cutaway graphics of weapons systems, diaries, traditional reportage and much more. It demonstrated how a non-linear package can appeal to different audiences. Its content could just as easily satisfy a liberal opponent of the US-led invasion of Iraq in 2003 as a paid-up member of the National Rifle Assocation.

Video-journalist and educator David Dunkley Gyimah, who blogs at **www.viewmagazine.tv** (and won first prize in the same US awards as *Newsday*), says the use of Flash for online journalism is a revelation: 'Broadcasters have finally awoken to a piece of kit only recently the preserve of animators and designers.'

Interactivity

> **[Users] can skip what they're not interested in, or delve deeper into what fascinates them, perhaps accessing archive or external links.**

The most successful online packages have a high level of *interactivity*. It's a broad concept. A conversation is interactive. So is playing a game. Reading a novel is not.

Interactivity in online journalism takes several forms. If a story is constructed in a modular form, with a lot of different elements, users can choose their own path through it. They can skip what they're not interested in, or delve deeper into what fascinates them, perhaps accessing archive or external links.

Users may be able to interact with the technology – bookmarking points they can return to later, or changing the screen layout, to make text easier to read or images easier to view. They may be able to enter their own preferences so that the presentation is tailored to their interests. The package 'learns' things about the user, and offers, for example, the option of restarting a piece of video from the point at which the viewer left off.

Interactivity might also mean the user interacting with other users and the journalist. Pop-up email boxes and the 'have-your-say' features on BBC web content were early simple forms of this. Now the journalist need not be the only creator. More complex versions of the production model include the opportunity for live blogging or for media content from the user (user-generated content) to be added to the treatment. Online communities can be created around the story.

When you are planning an online package you will probably be unclear what features might be added as the story develops. Some will be suggested by feedback from users. Then your content will be truly interactive.

Remember

- Online story telling can be non-linear – the user chooses a way through the content
- Combine text, stills, graphics, video, audio and user content
- Online packages can appeal to different target audiences at the same time
- Use graphics programmes such as Flash
- Make your package interactive for users

CONCLUSION

The traditional TV or radio package is probably as good a way of telling a linear story as has ever been devised. All the elements can be edited and crafted into an easily digested form that's convenient for viewers and listeners to understand.

But there are new horizons and new challenges. The limits of non-linear story telling have yet to be explored. There is clearly an appetite for the new form. Many young people prefer playing video games to watching TV. They still use TV, but fewer are engaged by scheduled news programmes. Interactive journalism offers a way to attract that audience, and the opportunity to expand the limitations of traditional broadcast journalism.

FURTHER READING

Chantler, Paul and Stewart, Peter (2003) *Basic Radio Journalism*, Oxford: Focal Press. Expertise on producing wraps and features for radio.

Ray, Vin (2003) *The Television News Handbook*, London: Macmillan. TV reporting explained with many examples from senior practitioners.

WEB LINKS

www.viewmagazine.tv David Dunkley Gyimah's web-based magazine *The View* with examples of 'post-video journalism' and integrated multi-platform video journalism.

Beckett, Charlie (2010) *The Value of Networked Journalism*, downloadable at **www2.lse.ac.uk/media@lse/POLIS/documents/Polis%20papers/ValueofnetworkedJournalism.pdf**.

A report from the director of Polis, the journalism think tank at the London School of Economics and Political Science, looking at networked journalism – public participation in the news production process.

CHAPTER TWELVE
EDITING

STORY telling is at the heart of journalism. Shakespeare used a quill pen. George Orwell used a typewriter. J. K. Rowling uses a word processor. Broadcast journalists use computers to manipulate words, pictures and sound.

The hands-on craft skills of putting together news packages have been practised for years by radio reporters. Now, increasingly, television reporters have to perform the same techniques in their medium. Online journalists need to know how to assemble a web page and input media – text, graphics, stills and edited audio and video.

Editing is the process of selecting information for broadcast. It means leaving out what is unwanted, and choosing the material that best helps tell the story. It is an electronic process that replicates the role of the sub-editor in newspapers. The 'sub' cuts unwanted copy, checks the grammar and content of what has been written and orders what remains into the final story. In modern broadcast journalism, reporters are required not only to write, but to select pictures and audio clips and present them in a narrative structure that will tell the story.

What software?

There are dozens of digital editing software programs for both radio and television. Trade names include Avid, Quantel, Adobe Premiere, Final Cut Pro (in television) and SADiE, Adobe Audition, RadioMan, Audacity, Burli, Pro Tools (in radio).

Whatever the name, the programs have much in common. Most involve assembling the picture or sound information on a computer screen in a sequence from left to right – the *timeline*. Raw media clips may be collected in folders known as clip boxes or bins – a term from film editing. (Each shot, on a strip of film, was hung from a rack, with the trailing end dropping into a large bin, like a dustbin. Waste material ended up literally on the cutting-room floor. On a computer, deleted material is more likely to end in a wastebasket, which isn't a basket at all. Emptying the computer's wastebasket means deleting files.)

Most edit programs can be run on laptops – giving you the flexibility to take them into the field. Extra disk space on removable hard drives may be needed to cope with large amounts of video. Typically an hour's video of broadcast quality will take 14 gigabytes (GB) of disk space.

Which are the most user-friendly editing programs? That depends on the user. Picture editors trained on Avid systems may swear by them. Journalists usually prefer systems designed to make the edit process as simple as possible.

A typical state-of-the-art set-up controls ingest (the input of video material from every source), output (the playout of video into programmes) and editing. Edit systems will be linked to news production systems. MOS (media object server) protocol allows video, audio and graphics to be played according to the running orders prepared on newsroom computers.

Non-linear editing

Digital editing systems are non-linear. This means that sound and pictures do not have to be laid down in a strict chronological sequence. In modern non-linear systems, the raw audio or video has to be transferred to the edit program. This takes time if the source is tape rather than a computer file. But once it is ingested, manipulating the pictures or sound is comparatively simple.

Some journalists see editing as a chore, but it should not be. It is a creative challenge and a chance to enhance your story telling.

A CLOSER LOOK

LINEAR EDITING – THE WAY WE WERE

Analogue video editing – the technique used for nearly two decades after electronic news gathering took over from film – involved pictures being dubbed across from one tape to another. A news report had to be assembled from the start to the finish in strict linear order. Each shot was dubbed across in the order and at the exact length it was to be used in the final report. Changing shots was tricky because a new shot or shots had to be chosen to fit exactly the same space as what was replaced. If major structural changes were needed, the edited sequences had to be dubbed onto yet another tape, with a consequent loss of picture and sound quality. The audio and video on each copy, or generation, of analogue tape was of poorer quality than the last. Too many dubs made the material unbroadcastable.

Dubbing digitally holds no such danger, as each copy is technically identical to its source.

Editing analogue audio tape was also complicated. Each length of quarter-inch tape had to be stored on separate reels before they were joined together. Sound was usually recorded at a tape speed of seven-and-a-half inches per second (ips) for speech, or 15 ips for music. A ten-second clip of interview would therefore cover 75 inches of tape. That's nearly two metres. So, editing long features required great discipline and organisation, managing huge lengths of tape and switching reels frequently. And that was just for a single track. For a multi-track edit, you needed the equivalent of a small recording studio.

RADIO EDITING

Sound editing systems present sound as waveforms. You need to get used to the idea of 'seeing' your sound. The peaks and troughs in the wave make it really easy to see where words start and finish. Editing is much more straightforward than in the days when you had to spin the spools of an analogue machine by hand, running quarter-inch tape across the playback head and listening for the beginnings and ends of words.

Layering sound and multi-tracking have also become easier in recent years. You can put commentary, interview clips, wild-track sound and music on separate tracks and then adjust the level of each in turn. Or you can play back material through a mixer and adjust the levels as you go along.

With a system like Adobe Audition, you save your audio files into a clip-box that appears on the desktop, and then move them on to the timeline. Then the fun begins as you cut and shape your package.

Multi-tracking

Multi-tracking – laying down several tracks on top of each other and then adjusting the sound of each track to the right levels for the finished project – is comparatively simple with software such as Audacity, which is free to download.

The limitation on its practical use is how many tracks you can comfortably view on screen. Most professional broadcasters suggest that three or four tracks are the most you can use

RadioMan editing – multiple tracks show on the timeline

quickly in a news production environment. Anisha Shah, a broadcast journalist with less than a year's professional experience at BBC Radio Stoke, told us: 'I've used up to five tracks. That's about the maximum. Any more and I can't see what I'm doing.'

SADiE, which is used for longer-form radio programmes such as documentaries, is a little more sophisticated. It takes longer to master, but more tracks can be viewed comfortably on screen.

If you want to record music, use a program such as Pro Tools, which can be found in many professional recording studios. Editing music is straightforward in most programs – the rhythms of the music can be seen on screen.

The principles of most systems are broadly the same and, if you have learned on one, you should be able to pick up others fairly quickly.

- Editing software is non-linear – you can move audio to anywhere on the timeline
- Multi-tracking – layering your sound – is limited only by what you can see on screen

Making an edit

You should edit first with your brain, then with your ears, then your eyes. The sound is the most important thing. On playback make sure you can hear everything clearly. The timeline helps you to 'see the sound'.

Each track can be edited separately. You can isolate the playback sound on the track you are editing, so it is all you hear on the speakers or in your headphones while you're working on it. You can see the peaks and troughs in the waveform and zoom in for more detail. A continuous series of peaks represents a word. The low points, or troughs, are the gaps between words. You move the cursor to one of these points to make an edit.

Make sure, when you remove words or phrases, that you maintain the sense of what is being said. Allow pauses between the words you join together to maintain the natural breaths or gaps in everyday speech.

Levels

Sound levels have to be balanced before your edit is complete. You need to ensure that all speech is distinct and understandable, and not obscured by the background sound on other tracks.

You also need to make sure that the level of your finished edit is not too low or too high for station output. You should not rely on engineers, or the newsreader in a self-op studio (who has enough to think about), to 'ride' the levels because you haven't done your job properly.

Overall sound levels should peak between 5 and 6 on a PPM (peak programme meter) for speech output. On a digital LED (light emitting diode) meter, you don't want to see too many red lights flashing.

In a busy newsroom, you will almost certainly be using headphones. They make it easy to hear every nuance of the sound, which is great for editing accurately, but does not bear much resemblance to how most people use radio. Most people listen while they are doing something else and your broadcast is competing with background noise, which can be anything from traffic noise to screaming children. If your station broadcasts on an AM frequency, the sound will be even more indistinct.

If you get the chance, play your finished piece back through domestic speakers. Can you hear everything that is supposed to be there? This is how most people will hear your work at home or in the car.

Using music

As we explained in Chapter 11: The package, it is never a good idea to lay a bed of music beneath the whole of a package. Instead, you should feature it where appropriate. You can lay a long piece of music down as a single track and then lift it to audible levels in the mix, but this is not usually the best way. It's usually better to edit out the musical phrases or the parts of a song you want, and drag them to the appropriate place on the timeline.

Unless there is a hard 'in' or 'out' to the music you are using, always lay down a few seconds before and after the phrase you want so you can fade in and out. How long the fade should last depends on the pace of the music and the impact you want it to have in the piece. A rapid fade-in will be punchier; a slow fade-in can build expectation.

Remember

- Edit first with your brain, then your ears, then your eyes
- Get used to 'seeing' your sound
- Check your levels (sound should peak slightly into the red)
- Monitor the edit on headphones
- Play back through small speakers

TV EDITING

Editing pictures on Final Cut Pro, one of the edit systems used by video journalists

TV editing on modern software is extremely versatile, and elaborate effects can be achieved relatively quickly.

Pictures can be frozen, slowed down or speeded up; they can be reversed or re-sized (to allow 'zooming-in' on a point of interest); the shot can be 'flipped' so that left becomes right; colours can be 'corrected' (if the camera's white balance was wrong) or changed for dramatic effect (sepia tones or black and white, for example). You can add all manner of fancy wipes, fades and mixes and even do your own graphics.

Split-screen editing – showing more than one moving image on the television screen – is a simple task. All you do is make your picture smaller to fill the part of the screen you want it to occupy. Then do the same with the shots you want to appear in another part of the screen.

Ingesting or digitising

The process of transferring video to the computer on which it will be edited is known as digitising or ingesting. The most important discipline in this process is to label the media as you ingest it so you can find your shots quickly.

Cameras recording to SDHC (secure digital high capacity) cards will create separate media files for each shot and give each file an identification number. But a string of consecutive numbers is difficult to keep track of without copious notes. It is better to retitle the files when you transfer them. Abbreviated descriptions of the shots will help: for example, 'ext GV' for an exterior GV (general view); 'int' (interview); PTC (piece-to-camera); 'CU' (close-up), and so on.

When video clips from tape are ingested on to a computer they can be selected one at a time, and then digitised, or you can view the material in lengthy sequences, marking *ins* and *outs*, and *batch digitise*. Batch digitising means you can choose your material and then leave the computer to wind the tape and transfer the shots to the hard drive. Just make sure there are no breaks in the time code to confuse the machine while you're away.

Whatever the source of your clips, labelling them accurately as you go is the only way to guarantee finding them again quickly. Make sure the title of a clip gives enough information so that someone other than you can work out what it is. Producers and editors may need to access the material for a headline shot. Other reporters or sub-editors might take over the story later in the day. Longer versions of interviews may appear online. So 'man walking' is not as helpful as naming the man walking. Words such as 'cutaway' and 'interview' may help *you* put a package together, but they're not much use to anybody who is coming to the material fresh and doesn't know what pictures are available. The single word 'interview' could apply to anybody. If it's an interview with the football manager Arsène Wenger, then 'wenger interview' or just 'wengerint' would be better. Similarly, shots of Wenger in the dugout might be labelled 'wenger dugout' to distinguish them from 'wenger presser' or 'wenger training'. You should then add 'CU' for close-ups, 'MS' for mid-shots and so on.

TIP BOX

KEY LEARNING POINT – LABEL YOUR STORIES

It is always worth taking time to label clips and stories properly even in the excitement of late breaking news. The bigger the story, the more important the labelling. Huge amounts of video are shot on big stories. Retrieving the right shots from the archive when there is a new development in the story, days, or even years, later, becomes almost impossible without proper labelling. Correct spelling is more important in the computer age than ever before, because a search of an archive will not show a misspelt name or catchline.

Time code

Alongside the picture and sound, professional video carries digital information that helps us edit. This is time code. It is presented in hours, minutes, seconds and frames usually across the bottom of the picture on a playback machine (UK TV pictures have 25 frames per second). It restarts every time the camera records. So, when you're using tape, a shot that starts three minutes, ten seconds and four frames into the tape will appear as 00.03.10.04 on the time code. If several tapes are to be used on the shoot, the camera can be set so that the 'hours' reading on the time code begins with a different number for each tape. Tape one will be set to 01.00.00.00; tape two to 02.00.00.00. And so on. Recordings on non-tape systems are numbered in the same way; you can reset the code if you change media cards.

Time code is essential for editing. When you mark the in and out points of a clip into the edit program, it is the time code that gives the computer information about where the shot begins and ends. The computer doesn't make rational decisions such as ending a shot when the subject has left the frame, or stopping an interview at the end of a sentence. The computer just reads the numbers.

A warning. As well as continuous time code, cameras can record 'time of day' code, so that the information on the timecode is the time of day at which the shot was recorded. This presents problems for edit systems, because they don't like a 'break' in the time code. When they are trying to ingest material from tape, any break in the code (i.e. if the numbers are not continuous) will stop the digitising process. That includes breaks in the code just before the shot you want to use, because tape requires a brief pre-roll time to get up to speed. If the

Pictures on a timeline on Avid Express Pro, as used by BBC video journalists

numbers on the time code during this pre-roll are not continuous, the edit system will not be able to ingest the material. For news reports, make sure you are recording continuous time code.

Timelines – a reminder

The programme information on digital editing systems is presented on a timeline. Pictures and sound can be added at any point on the line. The media – the clips of raw footage or audio – are stored on a hard drive, within the edit computer itself, on a separate drive linked to the terminal, or on a server linked to the whole newsroom.

The medium is not stored on the timeline, which means cuts made on the timeline do not affect the raw data, which is stored elsewhere.

Cutting the end off a shot on the timeline does not mean you have lost the end of the shot. It does not show in the edited piece, but it has not been deleted.

This means there is an almost infinite opportunity to change the edit. Resisting the temptation to tinker endlessly is one of the disciplines experienced broadcasters learn quickly.

Remember

- Label your shots clearly
- Make sure you have continuous time code
- Material cut from the timeline is still stored in the system

Picture assembly

Fancy wipes and dissolves are almost always a distraction. A straight cut from one shot to another maintains the narrative flow.

Edit systems will give you dozens of options of how to switch from one shot to the next. By all means experiment with them, but, as a rule of thumb, *don't use them*. Fancy wipes and dissolves are almost always a distraction from the story. A straight cut from one shot to another maintains the narrative flow. You need a strong editorial justification to depart from this.

Cut or mix?

In news reporting, as in feature films, the rule has always been that video mixes, or dissolves, should be used only sparingly. The dissolve – fading in one image as another fades out, rather than cutting from one to another – usually denotes a passage of time. So, it is a useful story-telling device. It is also a way of editing within an interview to show the audience that something has been cut out. It is an alternative to cutting within an interview and then using a separate shot – a cutaway – to disguise the join. Used this way, the mix is an ethical device. It lets the viewer know what is going on: the televisual equivalent of [. . .] in the middle of a print interview, which tells readers that some words have been omitted from the published quote.

The increased use of the mix on television is a product of technology rather than a development in the grammar of film making. Editing can be much more creative thanks to digital non-linear editing. In the days before videotape, pictures were literally cut from a length of film and taped together. Then video arrived and pictures were assembled by recording them, one after another, from a rushes tape on to a second tape. Both film and video required extra equipment to do anything other than a simple cut between shots. To mix between shots on film, two separate reels had to be prepared, known as A and B rolls. They were played back simultaneously through a vision mixer and the resulting image was recorded. In videotape editing, a third recording machine was needed at a cost of thousands of pounds in each edit suite.

Computer edit programs can add dissolves automatically and almost instantly. It takes only a few seconds to drag and drop the dissolve on to the timeline, and perhaps another few seconds to render the image. So, it is much easier to apply a dissolve or a more complicated video transition between images. A single operator can do the work of a TV gallery.

So, has the grammar of TV reporting changed? Not really. Even though it is easy – and cheap – to apply a dissolve or a wipe to a sequence of pictures, it does not mean that is the best way to tell a story. Technical effects can distract from the narrative. You *can* do it, but that doesn't mean you *must* do it. Watch feature films, or documentaries, and you will see very few vision mixes. They are used only for dramatic effect. There is usually very little reason to apply them to news reporting.

Fading to black

Some picture editors will include a brief fade to black within a piece as a pause for thought or to denote a change in mood. This device should be used with caution, if at all. It invariably slows the pace of the piece, and can suggest the item has come to an end. It can upset output engineers too. They watch the programme as it is broadcast to check the technical quality of the signal. They are not necessarily concentrating on the detail of the story. So, if the screen goes black they think the signal has been lost. A 'do not adjust your set' graphic might be flashed on to the TV screen before you have time to explain the black was meant to be there. Many producers ban the use of black within reports for the above reasons. You should warn the gallery in advance about any black moments in your piece, but it's easier not to have to bother. Ask yourself if the black is really necessary.

For most TV output it is unnecessary to fade to black at the end of an item. Just make sure there is enough video at the end of the piece to allow the gallery to mix back to the studio. Extending the last shot by one or two seconds is enough. And don't have an edit point less than three seconds from the end of an item. If the vision mixer cuts out sharply, there will not be enough time for the viewer to take in the final shot.

When you are cutting video for the Web, you may want to fade to black at the end. There is no vision mixer mixing to the next item. From the user's viewpoint the piece is self-contained, so a fadeout, rather than an abrupt end to the pictures, is more pleasing.

Video tricks

Most edit systems have a range of effects and tricks that would have had a 1960s TV director drooling over his vision-mixing desk. If they are overused you are in danger of producing something that looks like the product of a 1960s LSD trip.

There is very little need for elaborate effects in hard news reporting. In features they may be used sparingly, but only if they assist the story telling. Page wipes run the risk of turning your journalism into a parody of a cheesy 1980s promotional film.

Split-screen is becoming more common in news packages. But remember that, if there are two images running simultaneously, there is twice as much editing to do. Can you still meet the deadline? And will there be too much visual information for the viewer to take it all in? The story telling has to come first.

When to cut

The pace of any piece of edited video – the speed at which events appear to unfold in front of the viewer, regardless of the length of the piece – is determined by the edit. Some one-and-a-half-minute items appear to drag, while a five-minute feature can leave the viewer wanting more. 'Any length you like as long as it's quick' is a useful mantra. You should always leave the viewer wanting more, because it shows you have maintained their interest right till the end.

One of the hardest skills to master, even when you are familiar with editing technology, is how long each shot should be. The simple answer is that a shot should run to its natural length. And the natural length depends on the shot. A static shot with not much happening in frame will look tired after three seconds. A shot full of action will sustain interest for ten seconds or longer.

Camera moves complicate the decision, which is why not moving the camera is the easiest option for beginners.

You should not cut on a camera move.

BBC video journalism trainer Paul Myles explains: 'Avoid cutting on a move – a zoom, pan or tilt. It's weird for the viewer. You leave people asking: "Where was that shot going to end?"'

Cutting from a wide to a close-up, or vice versa, almost always works well. This simple principle lets you build up sequences of shots of the same subject or action. A change of viewpoint – picking shots from different camera angles – helps keep the edit interesting too.

But there are some combinations of shots that should be avoided. A cut from a wide to another wide of the same subject rarely looks good. Editing between moving shots usually looks ugly even if the camera move has been allowed to end. So avoid cutting from pan to pan or zoom to zoom – or joining together combinations of pans, tilts and zooms. A left-to-right pan followed by another left-to-right pan is just as upsetting visually as a left-to-right followed by a right-to-left. Zooms in and out, in any variation, never work next to each other.

Jump cuts and cutaways

If the transition from one shot to the next jars, or simply looks wrong, it can mean you have made a **jump cut**. A jump cut can be a cut between two parts of the same shot – such as sections of an interview – or a problem with the continuity of the action on screen. For example, one shot shows a woman reaching for a pen; in the next shot she is already writing.

The way to avoid jump cuts is to use a cutaway – a separate shot showing something different – over the join. In an interview this may be a close-up, such as detail of the hands or face (though not the mouth); a reverse shot of the interviewer (the 'noddy'); a reverse two-shot (in which you can't see the lips of the person speaking); or shots of what the person is talking about.

Televisually, cutting to shots of what's being described by the speaker is usually the most satisfying option for you and the viewer. You are using sound and pictures to complement each other. Instead of just hearing someone talking about something, you are seeing it as well. Your interview becomes more than just 'radio with pictures'.

Changing shot sizes during an interview helps avoid jump cuts too. As long as the speaker's head is in the same position, a switch from a wide shot to a close-up will not jar.

Remember

- Use mixes and wipes sparingly in news
- Be wary of fading to black
- Don't cut on a camera move
- Avoid jump cuts

Audio mixing

The sound on documentary and feature films is 'dubbed' after the initial edit. In feature films, that may literally mean actors voicing their words all over again. In current affairs, 'dubbing' does not mean re-voicing the spoken word. But it may mean balancing the sound of interviews, natural sound on film or tape, music, audio effects and voice-over.

In news, a rough sound balance should be carried out as you go along. Dip the background noise so it is still audible but isn't drowning out the voice-over. Mix or cross-fade the sound from one shot to the next if there would otherwise be a clash in the levels.

Trailing audio

You will often want to 'trail' the audio, fading it out after a shot change, or lead into a shot by fading up the sound before you see its source.

The narrative will flow more easily if you occasionally introduce a new sound before you see its source.

One of the big mistakes beginners make is to assume that, whenever you cut a shot, you cut the audio to exactly the same length as the video. This is not a good idea. It can lead to a staccato 'stop–start' effect. The change in sound, every time the picture changes, emphasises that you are watching a succession of separate shots.

Instead, you will often trail sound in or out of shots, cross-fading using the mixing tools on your edit package. The narrative will flow more easily if you occasionally introduce a new sound before you see its source. This is particularly useful for introducing interviews. You hear a new voice and, a couple of seconds later, see who's speaking. The technique works nicely over a set-up of somebody doing something. You hear the voice, so you expect to see the speaker talking. Unless the framing of the set-up is very similar to the interview, you probably won't need to cut away to anything else before the speaker appears in vision.

Sometimes you may want to use wildtrack or continuous sound off one shot over a sequence of shots. This works over street scenes and wide landscapes. If there is an identifiable source of sound in the picture, though, you will want to hear it. For example, if there's a powerful motorcycle passing down the street, you should be able to hear its engine over the rest of the traffic.

Music will usually be faded in and out too, unless there's a strong start or end to the music itself that you want to feature.

Watch your 'sync'

Interview clips and featured sound are sometimes known as 'sync', or even SOT (sound on tape) or SOF (sound on film). The importance of sync (and where the term comes from) is that the picture is 'synchronised' to the sound. If the sound track is displaced by just a few frames from the picture it goes with, the effect is most disturbing. If you are 'out of sync', people's mouths do not move in time with what they are saying. You must avoid this. It looks unnatural – because it is.

You will usually move the sound and picture from a shot together as linked clips. If you move a track, either audio or video, separately, the displacement will be shown on the timeline as a plus or minus figure (e.g., '+ 00.03' or '– 00.03' if you are three frames out one way or the other). Move the offending clip by the appropriate number of frames and link the pair together again.

The importance of natural sound

Every shot from a location shoot will have its own natural sound. Natural sound gives the viewer a sense of being a witness to events, of 'being there', without distraction from a voice-over or staged interviews. It can be raised in the mix to highlight what's in the picture and to punctuate the voice-over.

The natural sound from dramatic news pictures should always be highlighted: the explosion; the collapsing building; people cheering or screaming. Don't talk over it. And sound with less obvious narrative impact is important in setting the scene and helping tell a story: the traffic on a motorway; children shouting in a playground; the roar of a sports crowd.

Background sound is important in every shot. No jet aircraft ever took off without making an almighty roar. If you can see people playing music in a shot, let's hear the music.

Every pause for natural sound allows the report to 'breathe'.

Every pause for natural sound allows the report to 'breathe'. It lets the viewer take in what the reporter or interviewee has just said. End-to-end words make a report more difficult to understand and less interesting for the viewer.

The most important thing to remember when editing pictures with natural sound is that we do not live in a silent world. Viewers expect to hear the sound appropriate to the picture, even when there is a reporter's voice on top.

Imagine shots of the outside of two buildings – a Victorian town hall and a stately home. Architecturally they may look similar. But the sound on the town hall shot would probably be traffic noise and the bustle of a town centre; the sound at the stately home might be occasional birdsong or the bleating of sheep. Think how odd the two pictures would seem with the sound transposed.

Background sound is so important that it was once someone's job in the newsroom just to make sure it was right. Before videotape, 'mute' film – that's film without recorded sound – was often used for shooting news. It was cheaper to send a single cameraman with a wind-up film camera than a two-person sound crew. Station assistants had to find sound effects from discs to go with the mute pictures. On transmission, the sound effects were often played out live from a gramophone deck. 'Prov town plus tweet' was a particular favourite – a recording of the traffic noise in a provincial town with a single bird tweeting. Viewers never knew that the same bird was heard in shots of towns and cities up and down the UK.

Remember

- Cross fade sound between shots if necessary
- Try using audio to introduce speakers before you see them
- Watch the sync on clips when people are speaking
- Feature natural sound
- Always use background sound – we don't live in a silent world

Voice-over

The reporter's carefully crafted voice-over (V-O) has to be added to the timeline at some stage in the edit. But when? And how?

We've already read in Chapter 5: News writing that the words should complement the pictures, not fight or contradict them. If you do not have location editing, you will send pictures back to the studio, either with a motorcycle dispatch rider (a DR), or via a satellite or broadband link. What you send is known as 'track and rushes'. The track is the voice-over recorded on location; the rushes are the uncut pictures. As the reporter, you need a clear knowledge of the pictures, even though you may not have seen them before writing the script. It's unlikely you will be able to change the script once it has been sent. You also need to give cutting instructions to the editor or producer, highlighting what shots are available and how they should be used. This can be done on the script itself (tucked into the tape box, perhaps) or by phone or email.

Editing on location or back at base, either by yourself or with a craft editor, is a much more flexible operation. You can choose whether to lay the words down first or later.

Back at the studio, some news organisations have soundproof booths for recording voice-over. Others rely on microphones in edit suites. Lip mics, of the type used by sports commentators, are often used. They have the advantage of picking up clear sound close to the mouth without 'popping' – the distortion caused by the breath at the end of some consonants. They cut out much of the background noise from sports crowds, so they're ideal for reducing background chatter in a busy newsroom, or traffic noise if you're in the back of a van on a location edit.

Words before pictures – or vice versa?

Should you lay down your voice-track before the pictures, or should you cut a sequence of pictures and then add the words?

A good writer will be able to tweak their script to fit the shots.

There is no right or wrong answer to this question, and the approach you use may be determined by your deadlines. If the reporter is ready to record voice-over and the pictures are still not available (perhaps they are still being ingested or haven't even been shot yet), then laying the track down and cutting to it is a quick way to get a news item on air.

But, if you put the track down first, even if you have a good knowledge of the shots you are going to use, the pictures become constrained by the words. The edit is less flexible and will probably be less well crafted. You will have to use your shots in a set order – and more particularly for a set duration. A shot that is probably worth only three seconds will be stretched to four or more to fit the script. An arty camera move will have to be ditched because it takes too long. There's less chance too to use the natural sound on each shot, which as we've heard in Chapter 11: The package can help the piece to breathe.

So, as a rule of thumb, cut your pictures before committing the words to the edit. A good writer will be able to tweak their script to fit the shots, trimming or embellishing a word or phrase here and there to match the pictures. If you feel you don't have enough to say to cover every last second of the shots, all the better. Natural sound should fill the gaps.

Remember

- Laying down pictures before V-O usually produces better films
- Sometimes you will need to record your V-O before you see the pictures
- You need to know the pictures before scripting

Layering video

Just as digital editing allows multi-tracking of audio, you can also work with any number of video tracks. This means you have options for a series of sophisticated effects. The edit tools enable you to achieve:

- multi-screen or split screen
- re-sizing pictures within other pictures
- moving pictures around the screen
- text and graphics effects

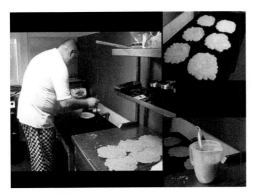

A split-screen effect on Final Cut Pro

To achieve a multi-screen effect you will need to reduce the size of a shot so that it fills a smaller space on the screen. It's surprisingly easy to do (in Final Cut Pro, for example, this is done by applying a 'wire-frame' and dragging the shot down to its new size – a process that takes ten seconds or under). Or you can feature just a part of the shot, by dragging the edges in to change the framing. For example, if you drag the right-hand margin of one shot to the centre of the screen and the left-hand margin of another into the centre, and put the two shots on top of each other on the timeline, you will see one half of one shot and the other half of another. This is a *split-screen*.

It looks sophisticated, but consider when you use it whether the viewer can take in all that is happening on screen. It works best when at least one of the shots is a continuation of what has gone before and is already familiar to the viewer.

Talking to yourself – a device to be used rarely, but it shows what the technology can do

Split-screens can produce some quirky visual effects. If you film on a locked-off shot, with a camera on a tripod so that it cannot move, you can film one half of the shot separately from the other and match them later. You would be able to appear twice in the same shot and have a conversation with yourself. You are unlikely to want to do this in a news story, but in lighter features the possibilities are endless.

Overleaf is a more mundane effect that enhanced the story telling of a video journalist on BBC Local TV in 2006. Laura McMullan was operating out of BBC Radio Stoke, so she did not have access to BBC television's graphics department. She created her own graphics sequence in the edit on Avid Express Pro, by layering video on the timeline.

The background shot of the man in the garden is the bottom layer of the sequence (a). Others are introduced on top, one by one, to build the graphic effect. The second layer from the bottom is the letter from the council (b). The last three layers are the words that have appeared on top of the picture (c) to (e).

(a) A man on a riverbank. He has cleared the site next to his garden to give him access to go fishing with his grandson

(b) But he has received a letter from the council warning that clearing the brambles was illegal

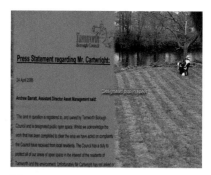

(c) It tells him the riverbank is 'designated public space'. The graphic is animated – the words appear to move out of the letter and on to the right of the screen

(d) More words from the letter – he's been told he 'didn't have permission' to landscape the riverbank

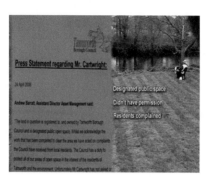

(e) A final comment from the letter – 'residents complained'

(f) Timeline – showing the layers of the edit

Remember

- Split-screen effects are easy to create
- They may be difficult for viewers to follow
- Layered video can produce backgrounds for graphics

THINKPIECE   ETHICAL EDITING

We've suggested ways of using edit systems to enhance your story telling. You will discover as you practise that the possibilities of applying an increasing range of sophisticated and dramatic effects are limited only by your imagination. It follows that you can make things appear to happen that have never happened. Or change the sense of what someone is saying.

As soon as you misrepresent the truth or distort the facts as you understand them, what you are engaged in is not journalism. It is trickery or fraud, and completely unethical.

Sound engineers will claim that, with a long enough audio recording of somebody's voice, they can make them say anything. It's probably true, although it would take considerable skill to make it sound natural. It's not an exercise you would ever want to try in a newsroom.

Some politicians prefer to do live interviews, because there is more chance of getting their views across than relying on the edited version put together by a reporter. But that does not mean the reporter has deceived the audience by leaving out the politician's preferred quote. It means the reporter has chosen the words from the interview that he considers most significant or newsworthy. In a democracy, most voters would think that is more important than allowing an unchallenged platform for politicians.

Few people complain that they have been misrepresented by clips of them broadcast on news bulletins. That's because journalists strive to make sure a clip they choose represents an interviewee's view accurately. The charge that someone has been 'quoted out of context' is much more likely to be levelled at newspaper reporters, who can take phrases from separate sentences and write them up as if they were a coherent self-contained quote.

It's harder to distort the sense of someone speaking in a television interview, because chopping the words about would make the picture jump. A clip could be used out of context, but journalists are looking for a clip that sums up the interviewee's viewpoint accurately and concisely; otherwise, why would they have interviewed that person?

There are other ways television can mislead an audience. If clips and shots are chosen carelessly, the story can be distorted. Using cutaways to disguise jump cuts in an interview could be regarded as dishonest, although there are probably very few members of the audience who are not aware that television packages are edited rather than live. Because audiences understand the process, it can be better to leave the edit in, mixing between soundbites so the jump cut doesn't jar.

If you must use reverse questions, recorded after an interview, you should ensure the wording is exactly the same as it was the first time you asked them. Some American producers have been known to insist that reverses can only be used if the interviewee was present when they were recorded.

Another ethical consideration relates to the use of cutaways. When people's reactions are involved, they should be as near to contemporaneous as possible. For example, it would be unfair to show a cutaway of the audience at a press conference sitting stony faced after the Prime Minister has cracked a joke, if in reality they laughed uproariously. Or the other way round.

Whenever you use footage from the library rather than new material, it should be clearly labelled as such, either in the script or on a caption, perhaps using the date, the title of the event (e.g. 'First Gulf War', 'Ryder Cup 2006') or a phrase such as 'library pictures' (the Americans prefer 'file tape'). Sometimes generic footage will be used (perhaps of crowd scenes or particular locations), and there is no risk of deception. It matters if you show old war footage to describe new fighting without making it clear these are not the latest pictures. Does it matter if you show old shots of oil wells in a story about rising fuel prices? Most viewers would think not.

Whenever you use footage from the library rather than new material, it should be clearly labelled.

As for fancy video effects, as long as the viewer can tell they are fancy video effects (layered shots, graphics or electronic wipes, for example) rather than a use of the technology to fool the viewer, that's acceptable. Re-enactments of events by actors should be clearly labelled as such, and you should only show details of which you are absolutely certain. There is no place in journalism for making pictures up, any more than you can make up the facts of a story.

See Workshops and Exercises

CONCLUSION

Edited audio and video is an important part of radio, TV and online news. The more editing you do, the more familiar you will become with the software and the more tricks of the trade you will learn. The short cuts to working more quickly are vital for journalists. Deadlines are constant these days. You need to work swiftly and accurately. But you will also want to learn how to be creative with your editing.

Editing is one of your key story-telling skills. Remember the advice about being a 'jack of all trades and master of some' (Chapter 1: Introduction). Reporters who've mastered editing are in big demand in modern broadcast newsrooms. It is in your interests to become a skilled editor. And it can be hugely fulfilling and a lot of fun.

FURTHER READING

Bordwell, David and Thompson, Kristin (2007) *Film Art: An Introduction*, Maidenhead: McGraw Hill. A well-established film studies guide with chapters on editing.

Kauffmann, Sam (2006) *Avid Editing: A Guide for Beginning and Intermediate Users*, Oxford: Focal Press. Practical advice for Avid users.

Murch, Walter (2001) *In the Blink of an Eye*, Los Angeles: Silman-James Press. A top Hollywood editor's guide to his art.

Weynand, Diana (2009) *Final Cut Pro 7*, London: Peachpit Press. Practical guidance for Final Cut Pro.

Wohl, Michael (2009) *Final Cut Pro 7 Advanced Editing*, London: Peachpit Press. Advanced practical guidance for Final Cut Pro.

CHAPTER THIRTEEN
GRAPHICS

THERE'S been an exponential growth in the complexity of electronic graphics in the past few years. Words and images created in computers have transformed the way television and online journalists can tell stories.

Modern graphics present a whole new range of technical, presentation and writing considerations for broadcast journalists. In television they have led to exciting new ways of explaining complicated stories. Online they have changed the nature of story telling. Online journalism no longer needs to have a narrative arc created by the journalist. Interactive applications mean you can offer alternative ways for the user to investigate the story, and find out as much or as little as they want. This non-linear story telling involves providing not just one story line but layers of story lines, all accessible through graphics.

We'll look at the guidelines for using graphics and explain how they can enhance television packages and online content. This chapter is about using graphics in journalism. It is not a software tuition manual. There are other books that will help you learn specific programs, such as Macromedia's Flash (one of the best tools for creating multi-media packages). A program like Flash will take at least 15 hours of concentrated study to learn. But don't worry if you haven't mastered it at this stage in your career. At most places you work you will be part of a team, and there will be experts on hand to offer advice.

But remember the guiding principle of successful broadcast journalism – if you are multi-skilled, you will be more employable. It's worth learning still picture editing with Adobe Photoshop, a graphics program such as Flash and basic web-authoring software. Then you can concentrate on the journalism.

Time is money

The real cost of graphics is time, not software. What was once available to Hollywood block-busters can now be seen every night in news bulletins. One reason for this is the increased memory power of computers. Far less kit is now needed to render complicated images within a timescale for broadcast. But the biggest factor determining the use of graphics in journalism is still how long they take to prepare.

Letters and numbers on screen can be animated (made to move) almost instantly; the time taken to render three-dimensional movement is less than it ever was; but it still takes as long for a graphics designer or online journalist to find, draw or import graphical images, to lay out pages, add script and build sequences.

A graphics sequence lasting 15 seconds on screen may take several hours to prepare. Compare that with how long it takes to shoot 15 seconds of video, and you'll see that graphics have to be used sparingly.

Newsrooms have dedicated graphics designers. They will always be busy and demands for complicated sequences should be made as far in advance as the story allows. You might be fighting for their time with a colleague. Documentary programmes have to book and pay for graphics as part of their budget.

What can we do?

When is it appropriate to use graphics? How complicated should they be? The BBC spent a reported million pounds revamping their weather graphics in 2005. The result was hugely unpopular with audiences, and they had to change them. The Holy Grail of any graphical representation on TV used to be the ability to present information in three dimensions. TV graphics started with 2-D cardboard cut-outs, maps on boards with a graphics operator sliding another piece of cardboard out of the way to reveal place names. In those days – within memory of some senior television correspondents – 3-D would not have been complicated and expensive; it would have been impossible.

By the middle of the first decade of the twenty-first century, 3-D was both possible and affordable. So, the BBC weather map became three dimensional. The map of Great Britain was tilted to allow the virtual camera to sweep across the country and below the cloud line. But tilting the country 'backwards' made Scotland tiny and the Home Counties huge in the foreground. There was an outcry from viewers outside the south of England. The Scottish National Party said the map gave a 'distorted' view of Scotland. BBC managers, hugely conscious of accusations of metropolitan or London bias, had to respond. The map was tilted back to a more traditional upright form. All that was left for the viewers to complain about was the dreary brown colour of the 'green and pleasant land'. Viewers notice graphics. Get them wrong and there will be a reaction.

> **Viewers notice graphics. Get them wrong and there will be a reaction.**

Remember

- Book graphics as early as you can
- Graphics take time to prepare
- Spoken words should normally match those on screen

BREAKING THE RULES – AND MAKING NEW ONES

It was always a golden rule of television news that words being spoken have to match any words written on screen. Nowadays some news and sports news channels look like particularly confusing web pages, with more words than anyone could take in at one time. But regular viewers soon become familiar with the format. They realise that these stations are telling several stories at once, and you don't have to follow all of them.

For example, most of the screen on Sky Sports News operates as does a conventional television programme. There's also a headline strap at the bottom of the screen, and down the right-hand side there are statistics (league tables and results), unrelated to the main story.

For most TV output, though, the graphic is there to help viewers understand the story being told. Expecting somebody to take in one set of words through their ears and another through their eyes is expecting too much. It's not that such a feat is mentally impossible. It's just that it requires an unreasonable level of concentration. Try listening to a radio drama while you are watching a football match on television. The attention wanders.

An exception to this rule has always been the *name super* (see Captions below) – people can read captions identifying somebody speaking on screen while they are listening to what that person is saying. In a round-up of locations, a one-word place name is acceptable too – although it is normal to allow a breath for the audience to take in the information. A caption informing viewers that what they are watching is *library pictures*, or in the American idiom *file tape*, doesn't intrude on the viewers' understanding either. Many people will not notice it, but ethically it is important we identify when people are seeing something that is not newly filmed.

Similarly, if events have been recreated and filmed to help tell a story, the word *reconstruction* is used on screen. This is an important ethical consideration too. Viewers should never be confused about whether what they are seeing is actual footage of a scene or a re-enactment of it.

Some channels will identify themselves with a 'dog' – short for digital on-screen graphic. It stays in the corner of the screen throughout their output. Because it is always there, it doesn't interfere with the viewers' understanding of what they are watching.

The big change that occurred in the era of 24-hour news was the recognition that viewers of rolling news channels want more than the story being told at that moment. They switch on these channels for news of what is happening now *and* for a round-up of the day's key events. They don't want to wait for an 'appointment to view' the bulletins on other channels.

Split-screens, breaking news graphics across the lower third of the screen and moving tickertape strap-lines, usually along the bottom of the picture, are techniques pioneered by Sky News and borrowed by other rolling news stations. It is still important to recognise what information is essential to the viewer, and what might be considered add-ons or 'bells and whistles'. But there is definitely an audience for information beyond the main story being told.

There were good examples of the different ways journalists can use on-screen information when the former Conservative Prime Minister Sir Edward Heath died in July 2005.

Sky News ran library pictures of Sir Edward and had a 'Sky News Flash' strap across the bottom of the screen with the caption 'Former PM Sir Edward Heath has died aged 89'. The first moments after such a story breaks are frantic. News crews and satellite trucks are mobilised, but it is too early to expect to see pictures from them. The station relies on telephone interviews. When Sir Edward died, people who knew him were interviewed. A caption identifying the telephone interviewee briefly replaced the headline. The phrase 'Former cabinet minister voice Lord Brittan' appeared on Sky News for just over five seconds – about the same duration as a caption on an in-vision interview.

The ITV News channel (which has since closed) had different library shots, but an almost identical caption to the one on Sky: 'Breaking News: Former Prime Minister Sir Edward Heath has died at 89.' Their telephone interviewees were not so easily identified by viewers. A caption saying 'Lord Tebbit, former Conservative cabinet minister' appeared for less than two seconds. ITV News had a rolling ticker-tape of the rest of the day's headlines – everything from Tiger Woods' win in the Open golf to the movie premiere of *Willy Wonka and the Chocolate Factory*. But for people switching on – perhaps in response to a news flash that appeared on ITV1 moments earlier – there was little to identify the voices they were hearing.

BBC News 24 (now the BBC News Channel) also ran library shots. Their caption 'Ted Heath dies' assumed a greater level of knowledge on the part of viewers. In a headline, it was reasonable to expect a UK audience to recognise the name of a former prime minister. Throughout the BBC's telephone interviews the name of the interviewee, 'Tony Benn, former Labour MP', for example, remained on screen. The ticker-tape offered a potted biography of Sir Edward – bullet points about key moments in his career.

> **Viewers of rolling news channels want more than the story being told at that moment. They switch on these channels for . . . a round-up of the day's key events.**

Each channel used their graphics in a different way to support the story. The BBC had the clearest coverage – there was never any doubt who was speaking, and there was instant background detail. Sky News, with a more expansive headline, probably offered younger viewers a better explanation of who Ted Heath was. The ITV channel used the graphics to keep viewers abreast of the rest of the day's news.

Captions

Name captions, identifying a speaker in an interview, are among the simplest type of television graphic. They are also known as 'supers' (short for superimpositions) or 'Astons' (after the machine that generates them). They can be added live on transmission using a caption generator, usually the Aston machine. This used to be done manually by an Aston operator, but now newsroom production systems automatically insert and remove captions, according to instructions typed in by journalists. Captions can also be introduced during an edit.

It is important to know your organisation's house style so that captions produced by different journalists are consistent on screen. Do you use capital letters for people's names, or upper and lower case? How are initials and titles used?

Is it   David Cameron M.P.
        (Con) Witney
Or   DAVID CAMERON MP
        (CON) Witney

Or   DAVID CAMERON M.P.
      (Conservative) Witney

Or any of the variations in between? We prefer the second of these examples. Your style book will determine which you use. Other examples that need clear guidance include the ranks of police and military personnel, and the titles of religious leaders of all faiths.

Graphics in links

Graphics can be used to point to the content of a story during a studio link. The presenter may have an *inset* box over their shoulder with a picture appropriate to the story – guns for a story about armed crime, a picture of the Chancellor of the Exchequer (or the historic red briefcase) for a budget report, or a wicket for the cricket scores.

Full-screen CSO (colour separation overlay) is also common. The whole screen is a graphic representation of the story, either a still or moving image. The presenter is superimposed on top of the image electronically. It looks as if they are standing or sitting in front of it.

Or the presenter could be standing in front of a giant screen, like Sky News's newswall.

The images behind the presenter have to be simple to understand and should not detract from the words being spoken. Any written words should match those of the presenter. You also need to round figures up or down in your script.

The opening sequence of the BBC's evening news became a graphics-rich environment when the programme relaunched on a new studio set in spring 2006. The technology had an effect on how the programme was written, with multiple screens available to show different images. ITV's *News at Ten* also became more complicated: from 2009 the traditional image of Big Ben was all but replaced in a re-branding exercise that involved a graphics makeover but retained the familiar 'bongs' in the headline sequence.

BBC presenter George Alagiah says in the early days of the relaunched *Six* there was sometimes too much information on screen:

'There was one thing where they scrolled up a list of all this criminal legislation. The idea was: "Look how much the Home Office has done." But it went up so fast and so small that nobody ever could read it, and that annoys somebody, because if they think they're meant to be reading it, and they're trying to keep up with it, and they can't, they get frustrated, and they don't hear the corresponding script being read. If they're not meant to be reading it, they're thinking why is that there? All it needed in the script writing was a sentence to say: "Just to mention all the acts the Labour Party's passed would take half this programme." And that relates it to the screen to say: "Don't worry. We're just trying to show you how much there is. Forget about reading it. That's why it's going so fast."

'That was a classic example of how having the ability to put more stuff on screen means you've got to think more carefully about how you write it.'

The 'breaking news' bar

A bar across the lower third of the screen is often used for simple headlines and to explain the story on screen. On 24-hour news stations, it's also used to announce breaking news. The term 'breaking news' is somewhat undervalued by its overuse on these channels. The term 'latest' is often preferred nowadays.

The information on the bar can be changed during an item, summarising the key points of the story. Here's an example from BBC News 24 in a studio two-way about the regulator

Ofwat's recommendations on the water supplier Thames Water. There was a hosepipe ban in force in the company's area, and the company had failed to meet its targets on repairing leaks from the Victorian pipe network.

During a studio two-way with a business correspondent, the top line heading said 'WATER WASTE'. The second line changed from 'No fine for Thames Water over leaks'

to 'Firm must spend extra £150m fixing leaks'
then 'Company failed to meet targets on leaks'
then 'Firm loses 894m litres of water per day'
then 'Profits up nearly a third to £346 million'.

The five sub-headings rotated throughout the two-way.

Ticker-tape headlines

Scrolling news across the bottom of the screen, or 'ticker-tape', has a variety of uses. CNN International has an on-air label for its ticker-tape strap. It's called the 'newsbar' when it is presenting news headlines. For sports news it becomes the 'sportbar', and for business news the 'bizbar'. This is probably a little over the top for British taste, but the labels sum up the way ticker-tape can be used.

Sky News found a way of providing a public service through their ticker-tape during the aftermath of the 2004 tsunami, offering holidaymakers in south-east Asia the chance to deliver a message to loved ones at home that they were safe and well. Similar messages appeared in the wake of the London bombings of 7 July 2005.

At other times the ticker-tape, or crawler, is most often used for a summary of the main three or four news stories of the day. Each story will be limited to two sentences, concisely written. Sky News and the BBC punctuate their ticker-tape headlines with invitations to viewers to text and email their comments and news stories.

Ticker-tape headlines perform one of the main functions of 24-hour news. Whenever you switch on, you will get a summary of the day's main news within a couple of minutes.

Full-screen graphics sequences

Graphics are used to help tell stories, and they can determine the way a story is told. It may be clearer to go for a studio-based graphics extravaganza than a conventional video package.

When graphics cover the full screen the script must match the images. The words need to be paced so that the images can be taken in comfortably. Sequences are usually built up as a series of pages. On-screen words are added page by page, and each page is revealed in turn.

A graphics sequence might have a headline ('Prime Minister's statement', 'Troop withdrawals', 'Water shortage' or 'Injury news', for example) but, apart from the headline, any words on screen should be matched exactly by what is said in the voice-over. It's unnecessarily confusing to paraphrase the words in the graphic. If the graphic says: '27% vote for Liberal Democrats', you should not say: 'Just over a quarter of people supported the third party in the poll.' You might say '27% voted Liberal Democrat' or 'there was a 27% vote for the Lib-Dems'.

If the words are a statement from a person or organisation in the news (usually somebody who has not been available for interview), they can be animated, so that they appear on screen as they are spoken in the voice-over. Too many words on screen at one time are a distraction. Three sentences or three bullet points are usually enough.

A simple chart in BBC graphics style

In television, design is usually left to specialist graphics designers, but journalists should have a creative input too. What background do you want? Should it be a still image or moving pictures? Should the background be 'washed out' or 'knocked back' so any words can be read more clearly?

As the journalist, it's your job to check that any pictures in a graphic are not potentially libellous. For example, if you were doing a story about a possible link between pesticides and cancer, and showed a range of products, you would have to make sure the link had been proven for each and every one shown. You might be using pictures of a tractor for this story: if it was from a library report of an organic farm, the farmer might sue.

Make sure too that you have copyright clearance for any images used. Material that wasn't shot by you is probably not your copyright and you can't use it without paying the copyright owner.

Charts

Graphics are the best way of explaining numbers on television and online. If you are using a chart – a bar graph or pie chart, say – you need to make it clear what the viewers are looking at, to explain the scale, and to make sure the numbers are simple to read (not too many noughts and not too many decimal points) and acknowledge the source of the information.

Once you are satisfied the figures are going to be easy to understand, you can think about embellishing the picture with other elements – stills or video. The numbers will probably be the last thing the graphic designer adds to the image, but the journalist has to think first about how the numbers will look and sound in the context of the story.

Acknowledging the source of the information is good journalistic practice and can be done with a simple caption in the corner of the screen; for example, a graphic about hospital waiting lists might have the caption 'Source: Department of Health'.

Maps

Maps have always been important in TV graphics. Even before graphics were used within stories, a map would be shown to tell viewers where in the world a particular foreign story was happening.

Maps can explain the location of a remote foreign province or the distance between the scene of a crime and the street where a getaway car was abandoned. They can show a parliamentary constituency or a crack house. A map helps explain the 'where' part of a story.

Major broadcasters use software such as Curious World Maps, which can zoom in to anywhere on the globe, or any UK street. The Curious program, which runs on a separate computer in graphics departments, revolutionised the speed with which maps can be produced. They look dramatic too with animated moves between world maps and countries, or between city maps and close-ups of streets.

Curious World Maps – created almost instantly by software which can find a street name or a postcode. They animate spectacularly too

Maps used to take hours and often involved thinly disguised breaches of copyright, using Atlases, the Ordnance Survey and the *A–Z* as sources. Now they are almost instant, and legally sound.

- Get involved in the creative process
- Be aware of potential libel
- Check copyright

Graphics in the studio

Television studios have become graphic statements in their own right. The back projections on the BBC1 news programmes and Sky News' video wall both show commitments to strong use of graphics in the channels' story telling.

Regional programmes do not usually have as much going on as the national outlets where graphics teams are bigger, but they too will have large screens for reporters to stand in front of. And occasionally the temptation to do 'virtual reality' is too much to resist.

3-D graphics from senior graphics designer Sue Keeling at the BBC's Mailbox studio. A look at the height of the Midlands' tallest building (it's not that big after all!), and the moment viewers were led up the garden path

Sometimes stories will be told in the studio using graphics, including 3-D virtual reality. Sky News presenter Martin Stanford enjoys 'walk and talk, show and tell stuff', and has been doing it for more than ten years: 'There are some subjects which lend themselves to "human interactive explainers". When they're great, they're really great.'

But there has to be a reason for explaining something this way. Stanford says:

'If you're going to put a human being in there, there has to be a strong motivation for doing it.

'The best example perhaps was our budget explainer, when we had a supermarket checkout, and a little car came over on the checkout, and it went through the infra-red reader, and "ker-ching" – petrol up 3p. And cigarettes came up. "Ker-ching." People still cite that to me. It was the stuff on budget day – which let's face it is quite dry – that people wanted to know, presented in a slightly more interesting fashion than just a load of charts.

'Economics and things can be really dull and dry, but if you get in there and you actually draw the graph in front of your chest and, as you can now, walk along behind it, and say: "This was the down-point when the budget hit the crisis. Then we had the growth period and look how it goes up," and you make sure it goes right through your face and over your head and then down. Suddenly, I think that's 15 seconds of watchable television.'

Rob Kirk, former Sky News Editorial Development Manager, says: 'Martin's very tactile with the graphics, which I think works very well. I like graphics that have a human dimension, because as a viewer I like to be led through the story.'

BBC correspondent Nick Higham has used extended graphics packages to tell complicated stories. He says the important thing to remember is not to get carried away with what the graphic *can* do, instead of what it *should* be doing:

'Sometimes we err too much on the side of entertainment instead of content, but the trick is to help the content. Graphics are a very good story-telling tool.

'Good television is mostly about showing real things and real people, but these things are very whizzy and get good feedback, both internally [within BBC News] and from outside.'

He says audiences love 3-D graphics when virtual objects appear around the studio reporter: 'There's an "ooh" factor when people see these things appearing in front of you.'

Martin Stanford agrees: 'It's the sort of "wow" factor, or "cor" factor!'

Both Stanford and Higham work closely with graphics designers. Stanford says: 'British television design is mostly staid and broadly quite flat. We've gone quite big – the design team here will use big fonts, but we haven't gone the American route. I can accept they might be over the top for a British eye, but they've got so much richness, texture and depth. Simple typological things. They think nothing of throwing three different fonts on screen, nice bold letters with lots of drop shadow and edge.'

Remember

- You need a good reason for putting a presenter into a graphic
- Don't get carried away by the technology
- Working with blue screen is a difficult performing art

CASE STUDY 13.1   WORKING WITH BLUE SCREEN – THE VIRTUAL REALITY GRAPHIC

Jeremy Vine became the new king of the BBC's swingometer at the local elections on 4 May 2006. He explained the difficulties of working with 3-D graphics in a virtual studio to DJ Chris Evans on Radio Two. He spoke of the problems of working in a space with nothing there, of working off a monitor (which, unlike a mirror, does not reverse your actions), and the amount of practice needed to get it right. Midway through the conversation, Peter Snow, an old hand at election graphics, joined in.

Evans began by introducing Vine and describing the virtual studio as 'the giant of all visual aids'.

Vine: You are in this space with nothing really. It's just a big blue curtain. I'm the only person who can't see anything at all, and these things appear around me, but they're not actually there. If I point my left hand it points on the monitor to the right, so I've now learnt how to do that, but I can't walk down the street.

I mustn't go anywhere near a mirror at the moment, because, you know, right-hand left-hand reverses it, and this works the other way round, but I have been practising and I've been practising the numbers . . . and I've suddenly realised that numbers are terribly important. We see politics as being gigantic human drama and all that, but in the end it comes down to how many councillors you've got and how many MPs and how many voters.

Evans: The great thing about the swingometer is that it shows us in the simplest way what is happening in the country. Yet, in order for that to happen, you have to deal with all these massive statistics. Now it used to be a physical thing. Now, you've just described, it doesn't exist, it's a virtual thing. You're just dealing with an invisible piece of technology. So how many hours have you clocked up on this?

Vine: Well, probably 24 so far in front of all these cameras and this blue curtain, because, as I say, I can't actually see anything. The peculiar thing is the really big jump forward. I mean, if you go back 25 years to the first time we saw Peter Snow and a computer, it was the 1979 election, and when Labour won whatever it was in 1979, I think it was 269 seats, the camera came behind Peter, focused on this computer screen, rather like the one you've probably got on your desk, and you saw he typed in 269 and you saw a little blue line. That was it. That was the graphic.

25 years later, the big change is the graphics don't just happen behind you, they happen in front of you as well. So you need to be aware, like I'm doing at the moment. I'm stepping backwards and forwards on this blue floor. If I walk forward too far, like I've just done, I actually go through a graphic and destroy my own legs, so the virtual and the real must never come into contact with each other.

We've had a problem with one particular graphic which is Ming Campbell. We've got this thing – Ming Campbell, the new Lib-Dem leader, will he drop the baton? Because he used to be a relay racer, he used to run around a track . . . we need the baton to drop. The first stage has to be a virtual baton, but then a real baton has to drop at my feet. And the only way to do that has been to get somebody into this set area standing near me with a blue sheet draped over them so they're invisible, and then they suddenly throw a baton at my legs. You just look around and you take it all in and you think this is absolute madness. I'm sort of jumping around in an ocean of blue.

When Peter Snow was introduced, he shared Vine's bemusement – and enjoyment.

Snow: I'm thrilled to hear Jeremy's finding the whole virtual reality scene somewhat bemusing. It is a madhouse . . . It's the best job in television. It's absolutely wonderful . . . You're in that studio and the graphics are telling you for the first time what's actually happening. Up pops a council in blue in Birmingham or something and you have to react to that live. It's terribly exciting.

Evans: What was the most your swingometer swung?

Snow: In the Dudley West by-election a swing of 29 per cent to Labour away from John Major's government, the whole thing blew up, the screen went blank, the House of Commons wouldn't forecast. It was total chaos. Old David Dimbleby, sorry, young David Dimbleby, immediately said: 'Peter, I think we'd better come back to me there. We'll come back to you later when you've sorted out your contraption.'If something goes haywire in the studio, sit back and enjoy it. Have fun. It is just a bit of fun, after all.

Vine: How on earth did you get used to the situation in the monitor where, when you extend your left hand it goes to the left, so it goes in reverse on the monitor? So everything goes the opposite direction to what you're expecting.

Snow: You've said it. It's an absolutely maddening problem. You'll get used to it, Jeremy, in about 30 years' time.

Evans: When I worked with the puppets Zig and Zag, the puppeteers had the same problem. There's a switch on the back of the monitor. You can reverse the monitor picture.

Vine: Yes, but Peter will tell you the problem with that, because then the percentages are all reversed. You can't read the numbers.

You can see why 'just a bit of fun' became Peter Snow's catchphrase. It *is* fun, but it is also one of the hardest jobs in television. And the efforts of TV producers and graphics designers to spice up 'dull' subjects such as politics open them up to criticism. The use of cartoon characters and Wild West scenarios led to accusations of 'dumbing down' after the 2008 local election coverage. What cannot be denied, though, is that computer simulations – variations of the 3-D swingometer – are a fairer representation of modern multi-party politics than the old two-way swingometer – a simple pendulum shifting between Tory and Labour.

For aspiring broadcasters there remains another problem with the trend for ever-more complicated graphics: it is very difficult to practise presenting against a blue or green screen without a virtual reality graphics studio. While the rest of television technology – cameras, editing, even transmission (via broadband) is within reach of most people's pockets – 3-D graphics studios are not. Yet.

See Workshops and Exercises

ONLINE GRAPHICS

Although TV journalists are unlikely to be asked to operate graphics equipment in TV studios, increasingly sophisticated graphics packages are available to online journalists. Adobe Photoshop has become the industry standard tool for digital image manipulation. Macromedia's Flash allows you to introduce animated graphics into the presentation and content of your online material. Maps and diagrams can be used to help tell the story. An animated map can show the progress of an event: flooding, military advance or the spread of disease, for example. Video and audio can be inserted.

If you are working online for the BBC, Sky News or most newspapers' websites, inserting still images or simple graphics such as quoteboxes is just a question of typing the words or cutting and pasting file names into the appropriate window in the software program. You will do very little that could be called graphic design. But if you are given control of web content at a small organisation where there is no house style, or if you have set up your own web space, then you can and should be as imaginative as you like.

Using multimedia graphics

As we explained in Chapter 11: The package, online story telling can be very different from that on traditional broadcast media. Radio and TV are linear story-telling media. You listen to or watch a story being told from beginning to end in an order determined by the journalist.

Online news can be linear – you can read a story from beginning to end, or play audio and video reports. But there is also the opportunity for non-linear story telling – for interactivity and for much more user choice in how information is accessed and produced. News reporting ceases to be a lecture and becomes a conversation. User participation can become the defining characteristic of the content, and there's as much opportunity for comment as for reportage.

Non-linear story telling opens up a whole new world of the imagination. You need to appreciate the strengths of each medium – text, still photographs, video, audio and graphics – and use each to best advantage. Educators talk about developing a 'multi-media mindset'.

The interface – the connection between your different media elements – will almost certainly be graphics pages. Built into the graphics will be links to launch other elements (animations, audio or video, for example) alongside space for comment and links to other related pages, including forums and blogs, encouraging more interactivity.

Each graphics page will offer a choice of routes for the user. The user chooses their route through the story. For this to happen your project needs to be constructed in modular pieces, all of which can have their own internal links and be networked with user-generated content.

Remember

- Graphics lead users through online stories
- Construct stories in modular units
- Use graphics to encourage interactivity

Graphics templates in web journalism

Many web journalists working for established media organisations find themselves using prepared templates to put content online. For example, all BBC News web pages look similar. There's a main story with a big picture and other stories beneath, each accompanied by a smaller picture. Sky News' interactive content has a different but still distinctive house style.

Journalists fill in templates rather than creating their own graphic design. There's a discipline to working on these sites that is very different from the freedom and flexibility of authoring your own multi-media stories. Headlines have to be a certain number of characters long; teases and stories have to be written to prescribed length. Quotes have to be put in 'quote-boxes', opportunities for user feedback in 'have-your-say' or comment boxes.

Writing to length is a core journalistic skill. Working on these sites will help you hone your craft. You will learn to upload video and audio and how to link between text and other media. And you will develop an instinct for knowing which stories will attract the greatest user response. These are fundamentals of multi-media journalism.

Remember

- Practise writing to exact lengths
- Learn to link between different media

CONCLUSION

Graphics are a vital part of television and online story telling. From the humble name caption to the virtual studio they provide information to viewers and users. They can make a dull story exciting, and a difficult concept easy to understand. They are particularly valuable in explaining statistics.

So, what are the limits of graphics reporting? It's no use creating *Jurassic Toy Story Lord of the Sith: Part Three: Reloaded* if it won't meet the six o'clock deadline. Three-dimensional graphics are a great tool in modern news programmes. But the time they take to produce means they have to be used sparingly, and only when they improve the story telling. Sometimes the viewer might wonder if the tail is wagging the dog.

Multi-media graphics packages take time too. They are better used as a growing resource on developing stories, rather than as a treatment for breaking news. Done well, they could be the future of modern journalism.

FURTHER READING

George-Palilonis, Jennifer (2005) *A Practical Guide to Graphics Reporting*, Oxford: Focal Press. Modern and well-informed introduction to the use of graphics in all media.

Quinn, Stephen and Filak, Vincent F. (2005) *Convergent Journalism: An Introduction*, Oxford: Focal Press. Drawing together the disciplines of multi-media journalism, including the use of graphics and graphical interfaces.

CHAPTERFOURTEEN
PRESENTATION

SHOWBUSINESS for ugly people. That's a phrase that was once used to describe politics but could easily have been applied to broadcast journalism. Not any more. Appearance is important, and those who take care over the way they look will get on. But there's much more to news presenting than simply looking good.

This chapter will explain the skills needed for reporters, newsreaders and studio presenters on radio and TV. It covers both studio and location, live and pre-record techniques.

We'll consider what not to wear and even what not to eat the night before a broadcast.

Electronic prompting, or Autocue, in the studio and on location should help make the job simple, but there are pitfalls for those who fail to master it.

Many news magazine and rolling news programmes are presented by two people. Dual presentation offers new opportunities and new challenges. Just what is on-screen chemistry? Who's in charge? And is there such a thing as an ad lib?

We explore the art of talking to time. It's no wonder Political Correspondent John Sergeant's autobiography was called *Give Me Ten Seconds*.

We also cover performing in a virtual studio.

CHAPTER FOURTEEN PRESENTATION

The vessel of information

News presenting shouldn't be about looking glamorous. It's about communicating information. Natasha Kaplinsky, one of the highest profile (and reportedly highest-paid) news presenters of recent years, is clear about the role:

'You're there as a vessel of information. You're not there to imprint your personality on the bulletin at all. People have turned on to see what the news might be.

'You really are there to be as neat and as smart as possible without even a piece of hair or jewellery being a distraction from the information. It shouldn't matter what you're wearing; you should blend into the background. Of course, there's room occasionally for a smile or some warmth. People like faces they're familiar with and faces they've come to know and trust, but you're not there to have your say, you're there to give them what they want to know.'

Not everyone involved in news presentation is a star. Most, even those on TV, will be pleasantly surprised if people ask: 'Don't I know you from somewhere?' But for the star names the rewards are great.

Many presenters prefer the flexibility of radio. Julian Worricker, who appears on the BBC News channel and BBC Radio 4, says:

'In TV there are a lot more rules to abide by; you're not as free to explore as on radio. You have to look in the right direction, nod at the right moment, make sure you follow the instructions. Otherwise, at least ten people are depending on you doing it, and if you don't, it all goes pear shaped. Radio is a little bit more relaxed.'

A CLOSER LOOK

THE NEWSREADER AS STAR

Two episodes in the career of newsreader Kirsty Young show how important the presentation of news has become. When Channel Five News started there were hundreds of column inches devoted not to the content of the new channel's bulletins, but to the fact that the newsreader was *standing up*. Later, after a spell sitting behind a desk (most of the time) at ITV News, she returned to Five. The channel's advertising campaign showed her (standing up, naturally) with the caption 'Kirsty' and in smaller letters '5.30 p.m. & 7.30 p.m'. A single name was enough to identify her. She was being given mega-celebrity treatment like Madonna, Kylie or Pele – people who are identified by one name – and the word 'news' was much smaller than the word 'Kirsty'.

Kirsty says:

'You'll never be more important than the story – neither should you be – but if people trust you, that's what counts. Look at Sir Trevor McDonald, who recently retired from the news. People find him a very trustworthy figure. They loved him. If he said it, they believed him.

'As important as beautiful graphics and beautiful studios are, I like to watch people tell me things, if they're people I trust.

'I think when people are younger they can be a little too serious, a little too earnest, because they're trying to have a gravitas they don't have. But we all get older. We get our wrinkles and we get more comfortable in our skin, and we hopefully get better at it, in any job, and reporting and presenting are just the same. So try not to be too po-faced in the beginning.'

Nowadays a news presenter standing rather than sitting will not attract headlines (although there was some controversy when the BBC's venerable *Ten O'Clock News* became the last of the major programmes to move their presenter from behind the desk).

Kirsty comments:

'In a way we could reasonably be accused of having started the whole bloody thing, by taking me out from behind the desk. We were trying to have a point of difference, because we were trying to shake the whole thing up a bit, and news, for so many years, was a very, very conservative medium: everybody sat behind a desk; everything was blue; they were usually all men, apart from the odd fragrant lady who was allowed to decorate the set.

'Essentially that's the way it was, and when we went on air, we were trying to say, a little bit naughtily but also with good intent, we wanted to approach it differently. A good way to do that was to take me out from behind the desk.

'When you innovate, sometimes you come a cropper, but you only have to look how much some of the things we did first are now used as a language everywhere to see we didn't get it completely wrong.'

The performance

All TV and radio presenting is a performance. It requires a lively mind and a cool head. In terms of approach and attitude there is no advantage in distinguishing between live and recorded performance. Experienced live presenters will talk of the buzz of doing a show live and how the butterflies beforehand help them perform. Those remarks disguise the preparation needed to do the job well.

Recording a radio voicer or TV voice-over, doing a piece-to-camera or filming an 'as live' report should be approached with the same sense of urgency as going live. The chance to retake or to have another go should not detract from your purpose, which is to produce an authoritative and polished performance. Knowing there will be another chance if you make a mistake might encourage you to try something more ambitious than when you are on air. Once the mic is live, though, your effort has to be spot-on.

The reporter who wins a reputation as a 'one-take wonder' will earn the respect of colleagues. But dependability is not just about impressing your peers. Getting it right first time buys you valuable minutes as deadlines approach.

Posture and preparation

Speaking is a physical activity. So you have to be physically prepared to speak properly on air. The air from your lungs passes through your vocal cords and sounds are then shaped in your mouth. So you need to have as much control as possible over your breathing.

Nick Pollard, the head of Sky News for ten years, was one of many local radio newsreaders who learnt the hard way about reading when you're out of breath:

'The best lesson I ever learnt was in local radio. Never, under any circumstances, run if you're late to read a bulletin. I did. I was working at Radio Merseyside. I was sitting there waiting for the clock to tick round to the top of the hour to read the bulletin, and then looked down and realised I'd forgotten to bring the bulletin in with me. There was about 15 seconds still to go, and I legged down the corridor, snatched up the bulletin, ran back to the studio and of course the microphone was already live. You cannot read after you've been running. I sounded like I was having a heart attack. I was gasping for air, unable to get my breath. People were phoning up saying: "Excuse me, I think your newsreader's having a heart attack on air."

'That's definitely my number one lesson. Never, ever run, if you're about to broadcast. Even if you're going to miss it, just miss it.'

Correct posture is the key to good breathing. You must prevent your ribcage from constricting your lungs. So, sit or stand upright and relax. Upright doesn't mean thrusting your shoulders back – your neck and shoulder muscles should not be tense. And relaxing does not mean slumping. If you are seated, place your feet firmly on the ground so they stabilise and balance your body, and don't rely on the chair back for support.

If you are about to read a radio bulletin, don't lean forward to the mic. Take a second to pull the mic towards you. Leaning forwards constricts your abdomen and the diaphragm – the muscles that help you breathe. Tight trousers, a belt or waistband, and even underwear can do the same – dress comfortably.

Fizzy drinks or strong curries are never a good idea before a broadcast. The effects on vocal delivery and other bodily functions are well documented.

Whenever you have the chance, and this should mean *always* unless there's a late story breaking, read through your scripts before you enter the studio. Check any difficult pronunciations, and change any tricky phrases. Know your material before you deliver it.

The easiest scripts to read are those you have written yourself. As you develop as a presenter, you'll write in a style that suits your delivery. If there's time, newsreaders should try to rewrite any awkward words or phrases in a bulletin so they can read them confidently. Producers and reporters are usually happy to let them do so, just as long as they don't change the sense of what is being said. Or the facts. That is why good newsreaders have to be good journalists.

Huw Edwards of BBC TV News, who writes all his own scripts, says, of being the sole presenter of a programme: 'You can set your own pace. You can put your own stamp on scripts, and deliver in the way you want to deliver.'

In the modern fast-changing news environment the idea of specialist news readers who have a background as actors rather than journalists is anathema to editors. It used to happen, but simply doesn't any more.

Anyone wanting a job in broadcast journalism because they fancy reading the news – and that includes many potential students applying for college courses – needs to know that the journalism comes before the broadcasting. And it has to be done well. If you need to check facts with a producer or reporter, do so. But be aware that they may not take too kindly to you asking questions as a deadline approaches. Particularly if all you are doing is changing a script they considered perfectly good when they handed it to you.

The best way to check a script for fluency and ease of understanding is to read it out loud. The weaknesses of words that appear fine on paper or on the computer screen are exposed by the simple test of rehearsing aloud.

> **The best way to check a script for fluency and ease of understanding is to read it out loud.**

Reading aloud also increases your familiarity with the material. If you know what's coming next in most of the bulletin, including the in and out cues of inserts, you are less likely to be fazed by late changes or breaking stories.

In a rolling news environment, there is less chance to check scripts before you deliver them. That's when you come to rely on the professionalism of your colleagues and their ability to write links that are easy to read. It is unlikely that anyone will be so adept that they will write in *your* style, but good writers will produce material that anyone can read fluently. You should aim to be one of those writers.

Remember

- You are a 'vessel of information'
- Don't run before you read a bulletin
- Stand or sit upright, but relax
- Don't lean into the mic
- Dress comfortably
- Check your scripts

Delivery

Confident delivery is essential to successful broadcasting. Nothing sounds worse than hesitant phrasing and awkward pronunciation. Whether you are reading from a script or ad libbing from background knowledge, you must have confidence in your material.

Chapter 5: News writing explained how good conversational English is the basis of effective communication. If you have checked your scripts and have faith in colleagues who might be writing late stories, you will have fewer nerves in front of the mic.

Much of a presenter's confidence comes from experience. Remember presenter Kirsty Young's advice in Chapter 10: Going live: there is no substitute for building up your 'on-air miles'. Get as much on-air experience as you can, whether it's in student radio, hospital radio or local radio. One national radio presenter joked of her co-host: 'You suspect he was making tapes in his bedroom when he was seven years old!' It was a tribute to his fluency on air.

Timing

The best presenters develop the art of talking to time, condensing what has to be said or filling to meet the time available. No programme format is open ended. Even rolling news has junctions to meet – headlines on the hour or half-hour, or links to live events, for example.

Continuity announcers have to fill gaps between programmes to the exact second. News presenters have to ensure their bulletin starts and ends on time. Reporters may be given ten seconds to 'wind up'. Play-out systems automatically record the duration of programme inserts and offer back timings – the amount of time left before the end of an item or bulletin. The computer has replaced the stopwatch in most galleries, but the human element, the presenter, is still the most important part of getting in and out of a show on time.

Any programme that is part of a network will depend on exact timing as you opt in or out. The local headline sequence on BBC TV bulletins, the tease half-way through the national programme telling viewers what's coming up locally, and the opt-out bulletin itself all have

> **Any programme that is part of a network will depend on exact timing as you opt in or out.**

to be an exact length so that viewers will not see the join as different parts of the UK leave the network for their own news and join it again later. The same is true of the regional slots in breakfast TV programmes. Many commercial radio stations take a bulletin, starting exactly on the hour, from Independent Radio News or Sky News Radio. Inserts on some digital services have to be an exact length to fit between recorded programmes – perhaps a two-minute bulletin or a 40-second summary.

So, how do you develop the art of talking to the exact second? It helps that most presenters deliver at three words a second – slightly faster on BBC Radio One and many commercial stations. But not everything can be precisely scripted – live inserts will overrun or fall short, and technical problems will occur ('I'm sorry, we don't seem to be able to bring you that report . . .'). So you need a range of strategies to fill out or cut short your programme.

- In a short radio bulletin the easiest way to fill to time is to take extra, short, copy stories into the studio with you. Repeating the main headlines also helps.
- If the bulletin ends with the weather report make sure you have three or four paragraphs of weather news, and that the first one or two lines will make sense on their own. *The rest of today will be mostly sunny with temperatures reaching 18 degrees Celsius . . .*
- Keep an eye on the clock from the start, and pace your content accordingly. It's no good linking to a 40-second voice report when there are only 30 seconds of the bulletin left. Don't be afraid to drop material while you are on air.
- Have a variety of sign-offs, or closing comments, ready. Experienced presenters will not need these to be scripted, but until you have grown in confidence write your closing words on a script and know how long it takes to say them (*That's all for now. We're back with more news in an hour . . .* Four seconds). Some stations will have a standard sign-off (*You've been listening to Smart Radio news – more in half an hour*), so you need to practise that and work out short phrases that will sound right immediately before it (perhaps trailing a news item you know is coming up later in the day).
- On TV, there will be a countdown in your ear from the gallery telling you how much of the programme is left. Get used to talking while listening without being put off.

There's no substitute for practice, of course. So, how can you practise on your own without a studio? To practise talking to time all you need is a watch with a second hand. Or even the counter on a digital music player. Look at your clock and tell yourself you're going to fill for ten seconds. Think about what you're going to say, then as the hand is ten seconds away from the next minute, just do it. Then try 15 seconds or 20. To replicate studio talkback try doing the same thing while you are listening to speech radio. Then try to remember what was said on the radio!

Pitch and intonation

The most important tool of any presenter – and the only tool in radio – is the voice. Emphasis and interest are conveyed by inflection and tone. It may be worth underlining key words in a script so that you can stress them as you reach them.

You have to sound interested in what you are saying. Otherwise why should the listener be? You also have to understand what you are saying. Otherwise what chance does the listener have?

One of the greatest sins of radio presentation is to emphasise the wrong words. We've all heard a strange stress on prepositions in phrases such as 'over to our reporter *in* Edinburgh' or 'they've been top *of* the Premier League *since* Christmas'. People don't speak like this, so it is a mystery why some broadcasters feel the need to do it when a microphone is live.

> **You may hate the sound of your own voice when it is recorded and played back.**

You may hate the sound of your own voice when it is recorded and played back. That's because you are hearing yourself as others hear you rather than how you hear yourself. When you speak, the sound of your voice enters your ears by a different route from the way others hear it. Your ears are on the side of your head (hopefully) and you are hearing yourself through your own head – what Andrew Marr has called 'the familiar baffling of bone and flesh'. The recording will be an accurate representation of the way you might sound on air, so live with it. But that doesn't mean you can't improve your broadcasting voice.

Regional accents

Gone are the days when the news was read in the clipped tones of received pronunciation (RP). 'BBC English' no longer means 'posh English'. Listeners are used to hearing a range of accents on air.

Local radio stations usually have several presenters with strong local accents, although the use of dialect (words and phrases specific to the area) would still be frowned on in a news bulletin.

> **Frank Gardner: 'If you've got a good story, and you report it well, and people can understand what you're saying, it doesn't matter what your accent is at all.'**

TV presenter Adrian Chiles jokes that his West Midlands accent has helped him in broadcasting. He says: 'They assume Brummies are thick, so when you can string two sentences together and ask a sensible question, they think you're a genius.'

The encouragement of regional voices has not hampered people with neutral or even 'posh' accents. BBC Security Correspondent Frank Gardner says:

'I got told once by somebody, a colleague who'd been to the same school as me: "Your voice is too posh to ever be on national television." That is just not true. If you've got a good story, and you report it well, and people can understand what you're saying, it doesn't matter what your accent is at all.'

Microphone technique

To get the best out of them, you need to know the technical capability and polar pattern of the mics you're working with (see Chapter 7: Location video and sound). Put more simply, you need to know how near you need to be to the mic to sound your best.

- In a radio studio, don't be afraid to be almost kissing the microphone (but beware of 'popping').
- On location for radio, with an omni-directional mic, keep it close to cut out ambient sound, or hold it a little further away to add background atmosphere to your piece.
- A gun mic on TV will be more directional – ensure it's pointing directly at your mouth.
- In a TV studio, the clip mic will be omni-directional, and needs to be secured within six inches (15 cm) or so of your mouth.
- Podcasters should recognise that more expensive mics will produce better results. But BBC tests have found that cheap headset mics, with 'noise cancelling', can produce results comparable to professional equipment.

Remember
- Be confident on mic
- Learn to talk to time
- Accents don't matter
- Know your equipment

Expect the unexpected

'We're going to end this programme and we're going to hand over to London where Five Live is going to continue because the BBC's facility which is in the centre of the city centre in Birmingham is being evacuated.'

Jonathan Aspinall, 10.15 pm, Saturday 9 July 2005

Whenever you are on mic, be aware of what might go wrong. It's not so much that what *can* go wrong *will* go wrong. It's more the case that what can go wrong won't be a disaster if you are prepared for it.

Concentrate to block out distractions. To remain focused when the unexpected happens is easier said than done. There is a famous clip of BBC newsreader Jan Leeming being startled by a studio light bulb that burst above her head and showered her with glass. Who wouldn't be surprised by that? More common are technical glitches within a bulletin – the wrong audio played in, the wrong video, or graphics that suddenly bear no relation to what is being said on screen.

CASE STUDY 14.1   COPING IN ADVERSITY

Perhaps the most famous example of news readers responding coolly when the unpredictable happened came at the top of the BBC's *Six O'Clock News* in May 1988. The top story was a breakthrough in East–West relations as the Cold War drew to a close. But that wasn't what made front page headlines in the *Daily Mirror* the next day. Their headline 'BEEB MAN SITS ON LESBIAN' and the sub-head '. . . while Sue reads on with woman chained to her desk' summed up one of the most bizarre episodes in broadcast journalism.

Two women in combat fatigues had broken into the studio and handcuffed themselves to the equipment: one to the desk, the other to a camera. They were protesting about Clause 28 of the Conservative government's Local Government Act, outlawing the promotion of homosexuality in schools. A live broadcast to the nation might seem a predictable target for demonstrators. What made it so unlikely was that the news studio was on the *sixth floor* of Television Centre.

Presenter Nicholas Witchell managed to sit on one demonstrator and hold his hand over her mouth, while Sue Lawley read the headlines and said: 'I am afraid we've rather been invaded by some people, whom we hope to be removing very shortly. In the meantime, if you can avoid the background noise, we will bring the news to you if we can.' Ms Lawley said years later this was 'pompous stuff – but what else was a girl to do?'

Anyone who has visited BBC Television Centre recently will know how hard it is to get past the security at the front desk, never mind into the studios. That did not stop campaigners for fathers' rights bursting into the National Lottery studios in May 2006 and interrupting a live broadcast.

Pronunciation

There's rarely an excuse for pronouncing words wrongly. Check pronunciation as you would facts. The BBC has a Pronunciation Unit, which checks how words are spoken for all outlets from quiz shows to news bulletins. They issue daily checklists of phonetic spellings of names in the news. If you don't have access to pronunciation experts, you can check a word you don't know by asking colleagues, or phoning libraries, language teachers or embassies. Local post offices can be helpful. Add pronunciation experts to your contacts list.

Network news readers often say their biggest challenge is unfamiliar foreign names. When famine struck Niger in Africa, the BBC's pronunciation of the country's name changed. It used to be pronounced like a shortened form of another African country, Nigeria (the accepted pronunciation, incidentally, of the river Niger). The new pronunciation sounded like a shortening of 'knee-jerk'. The modern version (nee-jer) avoids confusion with the river and with Nigeria, and recognises the French-speaking history of the country.

BBC football commentator Guy Mowbray has to identify familiar foreign players on *Match of the Day* most weeks and unfamiliar ones at international tournaments. He says there is nothing wrong with anglicising names: 'Some commentators try to be too clever. We can't know all about every different language. What matters is that the viewers know who you are talking about.'

> If an unfamiliar name crops up, most professionals' advice is to 'just go for it' . . . but in local or regional broadcasting, you can't bluff.

If an unfamiliar name crops up, most professionals' advice is to 'just go for it'. If you sound confident, listeners won't think you've made a mistake. But in local or regional broadcasting, you can't bluff. Many listeners will know you've got it wrong, probably because they live in or near to the village you've just mispronounced. Newsrooms need to have pronunciation lists available to all on-air staff.

We've all seen reporters repeatedly fluffing their lines in out-takes programmes such as *It'll be All Right on the Night* or *Auntie's Bloomers*, but the novelty has long since worn off. Most are not funny any more, especially when the light is fading and you are on take 47.

Many of the oft-repeated bloopers have one thing in common – the inability to pronounce a particular word or phrase. Everybody has words they stumble over. The trick is to avoid your particular *bête noire*. Use a different word. The thesaurus has plenty of synonyms for 'phenomenon'. Find another way to say it, or, if the problem word is a proper noun, the name of a person or place essential to the story, break it down into easy phonetic syllables. Visualise it that way rather than the way it is spelt. In a radio script or voice-over write it out phonetically.

Mahmoud Ahmadinejad, the President of Iran, might become *Mar-mood Armour-dinner-jad*.

Paris Saint-Germain, the football club, is usually pronounced *Paris San Jer-man* with the name of the city said the English way, and the rest with the French pronunciation.

Menachem Begin, the late Israeli prime minister, whose name still turns up in reports of the conflict in the Middle East, can become *Men-nak-im Bay-gin* – the underlining reminding you the name has a hard 'g'.

Remember

- Expect the unexpected
- Check pronunciations
- If you're uncertain – just go for it!

RADIO

A good conversation

Think of live radio as a good conversation, and you won't go far wrong. Some presenters have a mental picture of their listener. It may be a real person (a favourite aunt or grandfather, say) or imaginary (independent local radio's Debbie – see Chapter 2: What's the story? p. 21). But almost every radio presenter prefers to think they are talking to one person rather than the actual audience, who are probably too numerous to visualise.

> Concentrate on someone you know will be interested in what you're saying – a critical friend.

The idea of talking to millions, or even hundreds, of people at a time is daunting for most of us. You can't please them all. So, concentrate on someone you know will be interested in what you're saying – a critical friend.

Peter Allen is a Sony-award winning BBC Five Live presenter and a journalist with experience on newspapers and as a foreign correspondent for ITN. He says:

'Radio is just conversation. What makes a good conversation is someone who's got something to tell you. He tells you in an amusing, sharp, concise way: sometimes provocative; sometimes a little bit combative; never boring.

'I worked with Jane Garvey for years, and we got a Sony once where the judge said: "Peter and Jane are in conversation, but it's a conversation that includes the listener." That's the essence of the business – does this help me in a conversation with the listener? Are they understanding what I'm talking about? Am I talking their kind of language? Am I communicating with this person?'

Making mistakes

Peter Allen says you shouldn't be worried about making mistakes on air. Just apologise:

'If you have done something wrong and you stand up and say, "I think I got that wrong." Anger dissipated. Honour satisfied. People don't even bother to write the letter of complaint.

> 'If you've really got something badly wrong and you laugh at yourself, you will find that you are enormously popular.'

'Some journalists think if you make a mistake, ignore it, cover it up. No, don't. People love mistakes. If you've really got something badly wrong and you laugh at yourself, you will find that you are enormously popular. If you make a mistake and you sound embarrassed, then they're embarrassed and you've lost. But the bits which people remember are when something goes wrong and you simply laugh and say: "Oh, what a clown, look what I've done." People laugh at you. You laugh at yourself, and on you go. Absolutely no damage done.'

Remember

- Radio is conversation
- Admit your mistakes, and move on

Driving the desk

Most radio bulletins are *self-op*. The reader operates or *drives* the mixer on the desk through which microphone, audio inserts and any jingles or theme tunes are channelled. Nowadays the recorded inserts are likely to be stored digitally, ready for instant playback. There might also be live feeds from outside broadcasts or reporters on the telephone, on ISDN or web links. There might be up to a dozen channels to control. And sound levels have to be checked on each of them before transmission.

Modern digital desks allow the inputs to be changed to suit the operator. For example, if somebody prefers to have the mic fader on the extreme left of the desk, they can do so by pre-programming the desk. This is helpful for left-handed people. But there is a danger that, unless settings are agreed among station staff, someone called on to read a bulletin at the last minute might find themselves trying to operate a strange desk with all the controls in the 'wrong' place.

The versatility of modern equipment can mean a greater margin for error. Strong studio discipline is required and the station's operating guidelines have to be observed by all staff.

Older studio desks are likely to be hard-wired. The reader's microphone, for example, is always operated by the same fader – usually at the end of a row. It is likely to be alongside the controls for the second mic, which can be used by a separate contributor, perhaps providing a live voice report or presenting a sports bulletin.

Remember

- Check the levels on all inputs before transmission
- Know the controls on your desk

News programming

Longer-form news programmes, such as BBC Radio 4's *Today* and *The World at One*, the output of BBC Five Live and many speech-based programmes on local radio, have a control room similar to a television gallery. The producer and technical crew are in the control room (sometimes it's known as the *booth* or *cubicle*) and can see the soundproof studio through glass. It may be someone's job to answer the phones and put callers on air; someone else will play in audio and dial up contributors and OBs. The number of backroom staff will depend on the size of the station.

The producer can talk directly into a presenter's headphones or *cans*.

Headphones

Headphones are your link with the world outside the studio. You need to wear them to monitor output – to hear exactly what you and your programme sound like to the audience – and to listen to voices from the control room (your producer or technical operator). You won't be able to hear phone-in callers and other live contributors without your cans, because the studio speakers will be muted whenever your mic is open.

> **Headphones are your link with the world outside the studio. You need to wear them to monitor output.**

Muting the speakers is necessary to prevent feedback, or 'howl-round', the high-pitched screech produced by sound being picked up from a speaker and re-transmitted through the mic. For the same reason, phone-in callers are asked to turn their radios off. Otherwise,

> **Many professional broadcasters slip their headphones off one ear; it means they can talk to people in the studio . . . without shouting.**

the broadcast suffers from background whistling. Contributors in the studio need to wear cans to hear people on the phone.

Headphone levels are adjustable. Protect your ears by making sure they are not too loud. It might not be your mistake that damages your hearing – it could be a control room error. But it's your ears that will suffer – and they are two of the tools of your trade.

Many professional broadcasters slip their headphones off one ear; it means they can talk to people in the studio – colleagues or guests – without shouting.

Many presenters develop the art of working on *split-cans*, having one audio source (programme output) in one ear and another in the other ear. The second source may be another station's output or an audio feed from an outside broadcast. A presenter will then be able to link to the second source or relay information from it. You can only do this if you trust the second source. If the second source is something for which your station doesn't have the broadcast rights, but is live on another station (the FA Cup draw is a classic example from British broadcasting), an accomplished broadcaster will be able to repeat the information almost immediately.

A variation on this is monitoring TV output while you are broadcasting on radio. On BBC Radio Five Live, for example, a presenter may be watching a TV picture of a press conference (either on the BBC News channel or the live feed into the BBC newsroom). They will be able to take their cue from the TV monitor and link to the presser at the appropriate moment. This technique also works if you are linking live to events in Parliament – you can watch it live on the BBC Parliament channel – or to a televised sporting event.

Remember

- The presenter's headphones are the link with the production team
- Practise the art of working on split-cans

Checking for accuracy

The presenter is at the sharp end of any broadcaster's output – which is why some are so well paid. Contact with the audience brings a responsibility to make sure you get things right.

BBC Five Live's Rachel Burden says presenters need to be constantly aware of the need for accuracy:

'As a presenter you are quite vulnerable to what is being set up for you, and what is being written for you. In the back of my head is the thought: "Does this all make sense to me?" Is there anything glaring that needs to be checked? The next step is: "What's the story?" I look at each story and ask: "What is the key element here? What is the one question people at home will be asking?" And I try and build what we do around that.'

See Workshops and Exercises

Dual presenting

Successful presenters have significant control over a programme. The producer is in charge, but relies on the on-air skills of the presenter.

The presenter will have a close working relationship with their production team, and the presenter who has a strong journalistic input can be 'first among equals'. Working with a co-presenter creates a new set of challenges.

Shelagh Fogarty, who co-presented BBC Radio Five Live's *Breakfast* programme for seven years, says mutual respect and a flexible approach to who does what within the programme are keys to a successful on-air pairing: 'You hear all the time about presenters scrapping over stuff, and to me that's like a marriage where you argue about who took the bins out last.'

She explained her Sony Award-winning relationship with Nicky Campbell at the time:

'There's no trick of the trade. We get along. We're both pretty clear on areas of interest and they don't particularly clash that much. If we do bargain it's friendly bargaining, and the editor has a clear idea of how to play to our strengths.'

Presenters need to get on with each other, but it doesn't always have to appear that way to listeners. Peter Allen jokes that his on-air partnership with Jane Garvey, which also won a Sony, began as 'the grumpy old git and the sex-starved spinster'.

Garvey, who now presents Radio 4's *Woman's Hour*, explained how the radio relationship with Allen developed when we spoke to them during their time together at Five Live. She said:

'When we first started we didn't have the contact with listeners we do now. We've got the texts coming up in front of us on our screens. It's not scientific, but it gives you a fair idea of what gets people going. So, increasingly, I can be doing an interview with somebody and someone will text in a question which I will use. That's how fast the interaction is. We're closer to the listenership than has ever been possible before.'

The pair made a point of reading out listeners' comments, particularly the critical ones. Garvey said:

'It's reverse psychology and it actually stops them coming in! But we like it. Any reaction is better than no reaction at all. If it's a boring afternoon, Peter will do a deliberately ridiculous interview just to stir it up a bit. It doesn't do any harm. I don't mean something offensive. He'll just take a slightly ludicrous position.'

Allen said: 'We'll normally argue with each other. There's very little point in us agreeing. It sometime sounds like an old married couple – underlying affection, but quite cross with each other a lot of the time.'

Members of the audience responded according to which side of the argument they were on:

'You get letters which indicate that people look at you as a real friend. They say things like: "I'm very disappointed that you didn't pick up that point, Peter. I really thought you would, because I've always trusted you and you're a mate." It's a very immediate medium, radio. Better than telly. Telly's a bit plastic.'

Remember

- Working with a co-presenter involves 'give and take'
- Dual presentation on radio can include the listeners in the conversation

TV PRESENTING

Presenting the news on TV is a specialist form of communication but it has a lot in common with everyday conversation. When you tell somebody something, all kinds of natural tools help the process: eye contact, body language, hand gestures. You can use these in TV reporting and presenting, although there would appear to be limits about what viewers will tolerate.

Viewers are critical of how their news is presented. The letters columns of serious newspapers often feature comment about newsreaders. It happened when Channel Five's Kirsty

Young first stood to read the news; when Sky News and ITV News introduced their 'video walls'; when BBC newsreaders stood up at the start of bulletins.

And then there's the argument about whether one or two people should present the bulletin. BBC presenter George Alagiah is an experienced foreign correspondent with a sense of perspective about these things. He presented the early evening programme with Natasha Kaplinsky and then alone, when she left for Five News. He says:

'Remember, this is fashion. I won't be very popular for saying this, because every manager comes along and reinvents the wheel. I can remember when they were double-headed, and somebody comes along and says: "We really need the authority that comes with the single voice speaking for the BBC." Then somebody else comes along and says: "Actually we need a bit of warmth, so let's have a double-header." I don't want to sound too cynical, but let's not dress it up too much. Whether it's single-header or double-header, these are as much a function of fashion as they are of journalism.'

The presenter as team player

One of the biggest differences between TV and radio presenting is that television relies on a team of people to get on air. You can be alone in a radio studio and produce a memorable broadcast. In TV, there are studio and gallery crews (a producer, director and vision mixer, camera, sound and graphics operators, Autocue). Everyone in the team needs to know what's going on. If the presenter departs from the script for any length of time, or moves out of shot, everything starts to go wrong.

Producers like to think of their presenters as swans gliding effortlessly across the surface of a pond, with the unseen production team paddling furiously beneath the water.

Star presenters can be a reason for viewers to switch on. They trust them and welcome them into their homes. But the best presenters are more than just the mouthpieces of the news operation. They contribute to the journalism too. That is why almost all the top news presenters are trained journalists. Many of them have been correspondents in the field. Mark Austin, George Alagiah and Jeremy Thompson were foreign correspondents. Huw Edwards was a political correspondent. Julie Etchingham was a reporter.

The BBC News Channel's Matthew Amroliwala explains how the presenter on a rolling news channel is involved in the journalistic decision making:

'It is a team thing. You're keeping your eye glued to that top line for updates. As well as the information your own team is sending in your ear, there is a relentless stream of factual information from other news agencies and people on the ground, and it's a case of trying to weave all that in.'

'It's often the case that you spot something. You whisper it down the microphone to the gallery and suggest we should do this or that, and they make a judgement call on what's around.'

Matthew Amroliwala: 'As well as the information your own team is sending in your ear, there is a relentless stream of factual information from other news agencies and people on the ground.'

The presenter may be given the go-ahead to deliver information before it has been typed into a formal script. Then the presenter ad libs, perhaps reading from the newsflash on screen or from a print-out. They'll be making sense of the facts as they deliver them.

Amroliwala says:

'Quite often you are aware of the sort of things that might be happening during the course of the day, and in that sense you are able to prepare a bit of the background knowledge and that can sustain you in terms of explaining. You usually only get one line of, say, a Press Association snap on something, and the way you fill in the gaps is through, hopefully, having read into some of the background earlier in the day or knowing some of the background off the top of your head.'

This kind of presenting requires a keen journalistic brain – you are writing the story in your head as you go along.

Ad libbing

Ad libbing, speaking without a script, on hard news stories is notoriously difficult. There may be legal problems, if you are reporting the outcome of a court case, for example, or considerations of political impartiality. There will always be questions of tone – the right way to deliver information when you are not sure of its importance. Is this significant? How does it fit the bigger picture? You will become more confident about these decisions as you gain experience. The safest way to introduce new information is to attribute it (*according to the Press Association . . . our reporters on the ground say . . . there's a Twitter message claiming . . .*). Sometimes broadcasters get it wrong, but audiences are forgiving as long as they feel they are not being misled. They like to feel they are privy to new and exciting information.

> **Sometimes broadcasters get it wrong, but audiences are forgiving as long as they feel they are not being misled.**

On structured bulletins, there is less need to ad lib. Whenever possible you will want to stick to the script. It's safer to do so. But occasionally an ad lib comment will help fill time. It works well if there's more than one presenter. A cheery exchange brightens up the programme. But the best of these exchanges are thought about beforehand and often rehearsed. The exact words need not be scripted, but you should discuss what you want to say (and the response) with your co-presenter. Jokes rarely work unless they have been well thought out. Remember the old one about the secret of good comedy – timing.

Autocue

Most scripts for news programmes, even rolling news, are read from the prompting screen. Autocue is a trade name often used as a generic term for electronic prompting – the scrolling words that appear on a screen in front of the camera lens. The camera looks right through the screen, and the presenter reading the words is looking straight into the lens. This helps maintain eye contact with the viewer, the surest way of communicating effectively. A reader who keeps looking down at a script is unconvincing – they look as if they are not sure what they are talking about. Similarly, looking off camera – even for a split-second – makes you look shifty and undermines your authority.

Jane Hill, presenter BBC News

Jane Hill of BBC News says: 'I always say a trained monkey could read Autocue.' For presenters like her, who're used to ad libbing as stories break on rolling news channels, reading from the prompt is clearly the easiest part of the job. But how much training does the monkey need? There are several things worth knowing about prompting systems before you use them.

Most importantly, the prompter follows the presenter, not the other way round. It scrolls at your speed. An experienced operator will ensure that the words you are reading are always towards the top of the screen, so you can see and understand what's coming next. This helps your delivery. Sometimes on shorter bulletins you will need to operate the prompt yourself, either with a handheld control or a foot pedal. This is another discipline to master – but at least you are in control of the pace of the bulletin.

If you are having trouble reading from the screen, the font size can be changed. It's usually best to use the smallest font you can read comfortably, because then more words are on screen and it's easier to make sense of what's written. Technical instructions (e.g. 'Jane on Cam 1', 'VT' or 'OOV') can be included on the Autocue. It's up to you as presenter to ask for the information on the screen that helps you do a better job. You might want a note about turning to another camera, or for a tricky word to be spelt out phonetically.

It is important that you do not become a slave to the Autocue. Some presenters are like rabbits caught in headlights. When they have to leave the safety of the electronic prompt, they're lost. You need to keep your wits about you and your brain in gear. If you have a paper script in front of you, remember to turn the pages even as you are reading from the prompt.

When stories break or late stories come in, the *running order* (the order in which stories run) will change. Autocue will be updated, and it may not be available while that is happening. You need to develop the art of reading from a script, so that you can keep looking at the camera for as long as possible between glances down. This involves reading ahead and memorising the next few words before you deliver them.

See Workshops and Exercises

THINKPIECE   OVERPAID AUTOCUE READERS

Newspaper journalists appear to like nothing more than writing about their counterparts on television. So, when two of Britain's most respected and experienced broadcasters suggested that television newsreaders were overpaid for doing a very easy job, the columnists reached for their laptops.

Andrew Marr (BBC Political Editor and later presenter of *The Andrew Marr Show* and Radio 4's *Start the Week*) and *Today* and *Mastermind* presenter (and former TV newsreader) John Humphrys made their remarks at the Hay-on-Wye Literary Festival in 2005. The festival was sponsored by the *Guardian* at that time, so it was no accident that their comments were well reported and sparked a lively debate.

Marr said: 'Newsreaders, they really do come and go. I must say I have never quite understood why they are paid so much, why reading an Autocue, however adeptly, earns you quite as much money.'

Humphrys spoke from the experience of having read the *Nine O'Clock News*: 'Reading the news isn't work, whatever anybody says. You get paid a lot of money and it requires no brain.'

And then, as if to twist the knife in the injured pride of former colleagues, he continued: 'I have a four-year-old and I think he'll be ready in a couple of months.'

Strong stuff. But were they right? The *Daily Telegraph*'s distinguished radio critic Gillian Reynolds described it as a 'shoot out at the Autocue corral,' reporting that another distinguished name, Michael Buerk, had joined the attack. Reynolds wrote: 'If Fiona Bruce really is on £400,000 a year no wonder he's hopping mad. Buerk was a great television reporter, covering Africa's famines, wars, victims. Which battle has Bruce ever seen, beside the struggle to seem serious?'

Across seven columns of the same page there was an interview with 'a newsreader', who, with the benefit of anonymity, offered an insight into the economics of hiring and firing newsreaders, liberally spiced with industry back biting.

The *Telegraph*'s Ben Fenton reported: 'There are some presenters whose qualities are not universally respected by colleagues in the television news business, including

Natasha Kaplinsky on the BBC and ITN's Andrea Catherwood.' He then quoted the anonymous newsreader as saying: 'And I'm not sure how far Bruce can go, to be honest.'

The story suggested that the advent of Sky News and the value of 'credibility' had driven up the earning power of 'the men and women we invite into our living rooms every evening'.

It included a comment from the 'newsreader' justifying his colleagues' high salaries:

'When you are sitting in the studio and everything's going well then yes, all you are doing is reading from the Autocue.

'It's when the whole thing falls apart behind the scenes and you have to hold it together for half an hour of very complicated live television and not let the viewers know what's happened – that's when you earn the money. And when the BBC says there aren't many people around who can do that, they are right.'

Is it surprising that a broadsheet newspaper should quote an anonymous source so extensively on such an apparently trivial story? Not if you judge the *Telegraph* by the standards of *The Times*, whose treatment of the story was even more tabloid, not to say childish. It read like the script of a 1970s edition of *Blue Peter*. They published a double-page feature almost a month after the original 'story' broke with the headline *Here is the news: it's not as easy as it looks*. They sent no less than three reporters to the ITV news studios to 'try the job for themselves', with ITV news presenter Nicholas Owen judging them. The feature offered such glittering insights as:

'Oh well, I thought, I'll just keep pace with the Autocue. I later discovered that the Autocue keeps pace with the newsreader.'

'I'm supposed to ask him questions, only I can't hear a word he's saying. I assume that this is a technical hitch that will sort itself out, and for which I can hardly be blamed. Then I realise my earpiece has plopped out.'

'Now the voices are telling me that we've lost the VT and that I should apologise to the nation. Like it was my fault!'

Charlie Lee-Potter chipped in to the debate, with her column in the *Mail on Sunday*'s magazine. She was the voice of experience, having appeared on BBC *Breakfast News* and other programmes. Under the cross-head *Never mind the money – reading the news is the silliest job I've had*, she described it as 'a beauty contest for megalomaniacs with more money than brains'.

A month later one of the first callers to BBC Chairman Michael Grade, on a Five Live phone-in, asked him if the corporation was 'taking the mickey' with such inflated salaries for newsreaders. Grade said the figures in the newspapers (£400,000–500,000) were greatly exaggerated, but repeated the line that there was a free market for talent. He said: 'We pay them what *we* think they're worth, not what *they* think they're worth.'

The clearest insight into why some newsreaders earn so much came from Chris Shaw, Senior Programme Controller at Five, writing in the media section of the *Guardian*. He pointed out that he has negotiated dozens of presenters' salaries, and some of them earn less than £30,000 a year.

He recognised the unkind view that a presenter is 'basically a gob on a stick and should be paid in lollipops', but said 'authority, fluency and composure in a live studio plus grooming and good looks' are extremely valuable to employers.

Andrew Marr: 'I have never quite understood why . . . reading an autocue, however adeptly, earns you quite as much money.'

Shaw then argued that the main factor explaining why top news presenters can earn up to five times as much as the best-paid correspondents is that they are icons as well as newsreaders. 'They have been picked to represent the value system, the authority and the public service face of the channel on which they work. They are, if you like, the personification of our brands – our own walking talking poster people.'

Five's own Kirsty posters proved his point. Shaw said Trevor McDonald on ITV, Jon Snow on Channel Four and Kirsty Young on Five would almost certainly figure in the top three answers if you were asked who were the faces you most associated with those channels.

Michael Grade: 'We pay them what we think they're worth, not what they think they're worth.'

So, senior newsreaders have become marketing figures. It might not do much for their journalistic credibility. But it underlines the importance of news to a channel's identity, suggesting there is a bright – and for some highly profitable – future in the television news business.

Remember

- Presentation style – dual-headed or single-headed – is a product of fashion, not journalism
- Presenters contribute to journalistic decision making
- Practise ad libbing
- Don't be a slave to Autocue

Scripts

The script, whether it's on paper or in electronic form, is the foundation of any programme. It tells presenters and studio crew where they are and – if they stray from it – where they should be. It's usual to have a separate page for each story, so a story can be dropped easily when the running order changes.

If Autocue fails, you will want to read directly from the script. So you should remember to turn the pages as you go, even when you are using the prompt. Then, when you look down, you will be in the right place. You can leave the script on the desk unless you are reading directly from it. If you are standing, holding pages of a paper script can look messy. A clipboard used to be the solution. Now, in a move pioneered in the UK by Sky News, presenters will often be seen with tablet computers in their hand. These can be updated electronically, which means changes in the running order do not have to mean awkward shuffling of papers and the risk of losing your place.

If Autocue fails, you will want to read directly from the script. So you should remember to turn the pages as you go.

Talkback

Television presenters are given instructions and can hear what's happening in the gallery through an earpiece connected to the studio's *talkback* system. Comments from the director or producer go directly into your ear without being picked up on your mic.

> **Most modern presenters prefer open talkback, where they can hear everything from the gallery.**

There are two types of talkback – *switch* and *open*. Switch talkback means someone in the gallery has to press a switch to talk to the studio presenter. As presenter, you only have to listen to instructions specifically for you, rather than any background chatter, which can be a distraction. This means you can concentrate on your performance. But most modern presenters prefer open talkback, where they can hear everything from the gallery. This is particularly useful when news is breaking or running orders are being changed. You will be aware of why changes are being made and can prepare yourself for them. Working on open talkback requires discipline – one of the arts of presenting is to make the on-air communication as smooth as possible, even when there is frantic activity behind the scenes.

Julian Worricker of BBC News explains how open talkback helps a presenter respond to breaking news pictures:

'You can hear everything that's going on – what pictures are coming in – and you're trying to find the right bit of info to come out with. That's when it's at its most satisfying for a presenter. Most times you'll get the warning that you're going to have to do it, and if they get the chance they'll run them by you in the plasma opposite. Sometimes they haven't got the chance and you just pick your way through it as best you can.'

Worricker was on air in the week after the Boxing Day tsunami of 2004, responding to pictures as they came in:

'Even though you were conscious of the death toll at the time and realised that it was huge, you hadn't necessarily at that point seen pictures that quite tallied with those figures. You knew it was bad but you couldn't quite see why it was so bad. And then one or two pictures began to come in that you were talking over without any advance warning, and as you talked, and you looked, you thought, bloody hell, now I realise why so many people died.'

His BBC colleague Jane Hill says she can't imagine operating without open talkback:

'You've got to know if there's a problem coming up. If you're thinking you're about to talk into such-and-such a press conference and actually they're all screaming: "We've got the pictures, but we've got no sound. We can't hear them, we can't hear them," you've got to know about that, because your brain is filtering that, thinking, right, I'll explain that we've got no sound yet and keep talking over the pictures. If you're on switch, you can't hear that and you're on a hiding to nothing.'

She says working with open talkback is a skill some people have difficulty mastering:

'You can either divorce your brain, keep going on Autocue, keep listening to the director or the editor in the gallery, or you can't. You will get better at it with practice and you

> **Jane Hill: 'You can either divorce your brain, keep going on Autocue, keep listening to the director or the editor in the gallery, or you can't.'**

learn to filter out the things that aren't meant for you the more you do, but the bottom line is you're either born like it or you're not. It's very odd.'

A constant flow of information to the ear of an experienced presenter can be the making of many programmes, especially in sports coverage. For example, Jeff Stelling, the presenter of Sky's *Soccer Saturday*, handles an almost incessant stream of goals, scorers and statistics as he holds together one of the busiest shows in television.

The earpiece

The television presenter's earpiece is their lifeline – their connection to what's being said in the gallery and to the outside world. In a studio, it is usually a wireless receiver, though

Sky News presenter Martin Stanford with a tablet computer – the paperless script. He can scribble his own 'sticky-notes' while he is on air

hard-wired earpieces are still common. Regular presenters will want their own earpiece, moulded to the shape of their ear. They are available from hearing aid specialists and, curiously, high street opticians. Check which ear you prefer before buying – many people have better hearing in one ear than the other. If you have to share an earpiece, make sure there are antiseptic wipes available to clean it before you put it in.

An alternative to paper

As we've heard the script is the template for the shape of the programme. Printed versions of the script are normally considered essential for presenters to fall back on if Autocue goes down. But paper scripts can be awkward for presenters standing to read the news. A sheaf of papers is unwieldy, and it is difficult to change pages on a clipboard while you are talking.

Sky News introduced an alternative, years before the iPad. The idea of presenter Martin Stanford was to use tablet computers, with a wireless connection to the newsroom systems. Not only could scripts appear on the tablet, but he could scribble his own notes, access the Internet or send messages to colleagues.

He said:

'You can be in any one of several locations [in the studio] and yet still have the full functionality which we so live on here, of being able to read an emergency wire or research a quick breaking story straight away. You're not any more disadvantaged than anybody that's sitting in front of a PC.

'Even if I'm in mid-interview, and I can't speak, I can top line ("top line" is the instant messaging system in our software) a colleague or a producer or a director.'

Remember

- The script is the template for your programme
- Open talkback lets you know what's going on
- Presenters need to be able to access breaking news information

What (not) to wear

A TV reporter or newsreader's appearance should not distract from the news. But a large proportion of viewers will take notice of what people are wearing. Channel Four News' website had a section devoted to Jon Snow's ties. Peter Sissons was criticised for not wearing a black tie on the BBC when he announced the Queen Mother's death in 2002. There were comments from viewers when Jeremy Vine did not wear a tie for the first time on Sunday lunchtime's *The Politics Show*. The BBC's view was that most people do not dress formally on a Sunday.

Radio newsreaders used to wear a dinner jacket in the early days of the BBC. The idea is now comical. Today's rule is that news presenters should dress 'appropriately'. For studio presentation that means modern, stylish clothes that fit well. It helps presenters appear warm and engaging to the audience. The BBC stipulates that the announcement of the death of the monarch should be made in a black tie (for a man) or a black jacket or top (for a woman). Otherwise bold colours work well on television for women and formal jackets with collar and tie are best for men. But think how the colour scheme will look against the studio set.

It is always a good idea to look smart on television. You are appearing in strangers' homes, so it's only courteous to look your best. You will have your own idea of what looks best on you, but remember that the newsreader is not there to stamp their personality on the programme.

Patterns that don't work

Some clothing patterns simply do not work on TV for electronic reasons. Herringbone and houndstooth checks and narrow stripes will 'strobe' – wavy patterns appear on the picture. White shirts with no jacket will reflect too much light and cause contrast problems. Too much black will also absorb light and lose definition.

Colours that disappear

If you are working in a studio that uses electronic technology to superimpose images on the set, you will need to be especially careful what clothes you wear. Colour separation overlay (CSO), also known as blue- or green-screen, is used to produce weather maps, insets (a picture within the main picture) over presenters' shoulders, and backgrounds. Some studios are completely 'virtual' – they don't exist in real space and are electronically created, usually against a blue background.

If any part of your clothing is the same colour as the screen onto which the electronic image is projected (usually bright blue or bright green, as the name suggests) the image will appear on your clothes and that part of you will disappear.

Make-up

Presenters may need make-up to help them look natural under TV lights. For women, that may mean wearing more than normal. Powder reduces sweating and glare, noticeably on the forehead or cheeks, and can add definition to your features. Politicians use it. Don't be embarrassed by it.

Remember

- Dress appropriately – usually smartly if you are in a studio
- Avoid herringbone and houndstooth patterns
- In front of a blue or green screen, don't wear blue or green, as appropriate
- Make-up helps you look natural on screen

Co-presenting on television

Working alongside a second presenter requires new skills. Most presenters we've spoken to suggest that, far from halving the workload, co-presenting is harder work than being alone.

Mark Austin, ITV News

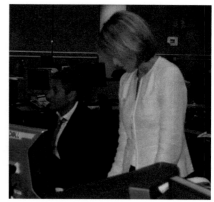

Mark Austin and Mary Nightingale: ITV News' success story

Jane Hill and Matthew Amroliwala: a successful on-air partnership

Nick Owen and Suzanne Virdee on *Midlands Today*: 'The key is friendship.'

Programmes have to be structured so that presenters can share the links. Whenever possible, producers will want interaction between the presenters. ITV News' Mark Austin who often co-presents says:

'Be absolutely clear about who's doing what when. There's nothing worse than both of you starting to speak at the same time, or not knowing where you're going to go next. Real clarity is needed. In a double-header, the most common problem is if there's confusion between the two of you about what you're doing, when you're doing it, who's doing it, and that can lead to total disaster. Happily, we know that's important, and we don't let it happen.'

In rolling news, it helps producers to be able to give instructions to one presenter while the other is conducting an interview, but the best moments for the viewer can be when both presenters are working together. That might mean 'flip-flopping' (alternately reading parts of the same link) or combining to offer different parts of the story and build the bigger picture.

The BBC news presenter Jane Hill says: 'When there are two of you, there's got to be give and take. When there's breaking news and it's busy and it's really fluid, you've got to understand when the other person's going to speak.'

She's developed an understanding with her regular co-presenter Matthew Amroliwala: 'We just look at each other and do a little hand gesture and we know what that means. It's so instinctive with us.'

On-air chemistry

Watching television news you will often see a male and a female presenter together. In America, the cliché is an older man (often likened to a favourite uncle) alongside a glamorous woman. Commentators talk about 'sexual chemistry' – the suggestion that the presenters look as if they fancy each other! Is this important? It's certainly a factor when producers put presenters together.

Nick Owen had an on-screen relationship for nearly 15 years with Anne Diamond, spanning the ITV breakfast channel TV-AM, and *Good Morning with Anne and Nick* on BBC1:

Anne and I always used to agree who would start an interview and the other would bide his or her time before nudging the other in the thigh. If Anne was doing the chatting, for instance, she would lean back to let me know I could take over. Or she would keep her position to tell me she was still following a particular line of questioning, so she didn't want me to change direction yet. Or, if one of us was finding it hard going, he or she would lean back without prompting, as if to say: 'Take over, baby, I need help!' A major element of our partnership was based on instinct, which sprang from our close friendship. We instinctively knew, when ad libbing, for instance, the right moment to come in. This applies to our times together at the start of breakfast television with TV-AM, and during *Good Morning with Anne and Nick* a decade later.

More recently, Owen has worked alongside Suzanne Virdee on BBC *Midlands Today*. He says friendship is again the key to success:

'It makes the whole experience really enjoyable if you're working with someone you've become close to, and that's been the case with Anne and Suzanne.

'Working on your own, you're terribly exposed if anything goes wrong. If there's somebody else – and I've been lucky to work for so long with good friends – between us we just get out of it.'

The *Midlands Today* studio is about to go live

Ad libbing becomes much easier alongside someone you get on with. Suzanne Virdee, who has also worked on BBC *Breakfast News*, says there's an excitement about presenting world events, with colleagues who are 'big players, big names'. But working with Nick has been her favourite job: 'We just do it as it comes. I'm the world's worst actress, so when we fill, it's never scripted. If I've got time, I might say to Nick: "I'll say something coming out of this." Then we just busk it.'

Regional programmes, with less hard news, offer more opportunities for humorous asides than national news. But friendship helps on the bigger stage too. Jane Hill says of her relationship with Matthew Amroliwala:

'We genuinely get on famously, and we're just very lucky. We did nearly five years together on the four till seven [pm] slot, which is pretty frantic, and the five o'clock hour is one of the biggest hours for audience, so it's an important hour. It was brilliant. We just worked really well.

'It is vital. People call us an old married couple, because we both hate it if the other one's off. The point of the job is, of course, that you have to learn to get on with anyone. But it does make a big difference, your co-presenter.'

Remember

- It's vital to have a good working relationship with your co-presenter
- Professional respect is the key to the relationship

Working in a virtual studio

Virtual studios can produce spectacular effects. The space you appear to occupy is created by computer graphics. You are usually working against either a blue or green screen. You may have a video wall behind you on which moving pictures and graphics are projected.

You need to be familiar with the script even if you are reading from Autocue. You will want to turn to the screen, or to your virtual surroundings, and then face the viewers again, picking up seamlessly without interrupting your natural flow. You don't want to sound scripted.

You can read in Chapter 13: Graphics Jeremy Vine's account of working with the complicated effects for the BBC's election coverage – complete with an 'invisible' colleague draped in a blue curtain. There is a whole new discipline for news broadcasters working with virtual effects, and wearing the right colour is the least of their worries.

You will have a monitor so you can see what the finished output looks like, but you have to resist the temptation to treat the monitor as a mirror. In a mirror all your actions are reversed (raise your right arm and the mirror image appears to raise their left arm). On a monitor, actions happen as the camera sees them. So, if you raise your right arm, the image in the monitor raises the right arm. Psychologically, it is tricky to overcome years of conditioning caused by looking at yourself in a mirror. You need to practise, particularly if you need to point to things on the screen or react to objects in the virtual environment around you.

Linking to interviews on a video wall

A common technique, used instead of a conventional filmed package, is to stand in front of a video wall, linking to clips of interviews, which will then be mixed to fill the whole screen. At the point at which the interviewee appears in the video wall, they should be looking towards you, the presenter. If they're facing away from you, it looks odd. So a lot of thought needs to go into filming this type of package.

It's no good coming back from location, deciding you haven't got enough shots to make a package and opting to do the report in front of a video wall instead. Your interviews will probably have been shot with people looking in different directions, so the eyelines will be wrong. Also, video wall sequences take time to set up and involve the whole gallery crew. They need to be planned in advance and shot accordingly.

Remember

- Virtual presentations have to be meticulously pre-planned
- In a monitor, your actions will be the reverse of looking in a mirror
- Interviewees on video walls should face the presenter

CONCLUSION

Throughout this book, we've emphasised the need for the modern broadcast journalist to be multi-skilled. We've spoken about the range of writing, production and technical skills you'll need. We also recognise that most (though not all) would-be broadcast journalists want to be on air.

The key to success as a presenter or reporter, particularly in the modern world where many people are on freelance or short-term contracts, is versatility. Within the broad term 'presenter' there is a range of skills to master. Some people will be good at a desk reading a bulletin; others will be happy to ad lib and hold together a breaking news programme; still others will use graphics imaginatively and be at home in a virtual studio or in front of a video wall. If you can become proficient at all these skills and more, you will be much more employable and much more successful in the long term.

FURTHER READING

Chantler, Paul and Stewart, Peter (2003) *Basic Radio Journalism*, Oxford: Focal Press. Solid basic advice for those looking to improve their newsreading and reporting techniques.

Mills, Jenni (2004) *The Broadcast Voice*, Oxford: Focal Press. Even seasoned broadcasters will find something new in this comprehensive book (and CD).

Trewin, Janet (2003) *Presenting on TV and Radio*, Oxford: Focal Press. An all-round guide to performing in news and current affairs from a practitioner.

CHAPTER FIFTEEN
THE PROGRAMME

THE range of broadcast news output now runs from brief headline reads on radio to 24-hour news channels on TV, with downloaded news content, podcasts and mobile phone services in between. Rolling news changed the agenda of all broadcasters. Video-on-demand through broadband meant another major rethink.

Broadcasters now have to consider not only what to put into a programme, but what *is* a programme. Are we happy to deliver our half-hour of news and current affairs, or must it be part of a bigger package, with opportunities for the audience to contribute and comment and web links to outside sources and even other news providers?

Comedy shows such as *The Day Today* and Charlie Brooker's *Newswipe* have given the conventions of news programmes a thoroughly deserved kicking. Never before has there been so much pressure to offer not only a professional service, but one that avoids self-parody.

We give examples of how programmes deal with breaking news, and give guidance on the production techniques you need to put a programme together:

- running orders
- timings
- bulletin content
- creating a balanced bulletin.

We canvass opinion on the way news programmes and interactivity will develop in the future, as the public are increasingly able to determine their own news agenda, whenever they want it, through mobile phones and wireless broadband.

The news agenda

Most news programmes are not full of exclusives. Indeed, much of the news agenda is predictable. That is why headlines, teases and striking audio or images are presented in a way that will keep viewers and listeners tuned in.

Online news and RSS services mean audiences can determine their own news agenda. They become their own editor. But viewing figures suggest traditional news programming is far from dead. Red-button technology was only the first of the interactive options open to news providers.

Nick Pollard, who ran Sky News for ten years, said in 2005:

'We will move towards a genuine on-demand service via the set-top box, because the next generation of set-top boxes will effectively have the hard drive divided in two, one under control of the customer, the other under the control of the company so we can drop things down there. If you had an hour or less available for news, you could drop on to that 12 stories of a couple of minutes long (or longer or shorter or a combination) and a little home-made EPG [electronic programme guide] that allows people just to view things in the way they want. That is then genuinely news-on-demand whereas the red-button offering that we have at the moment, the interactive news, isn't. It's semi-news on demand. It's streamed news.'

His successor John Ryley, writing in the *Independent* in September 2006, explained why traditional news channels, with so much content sitting on servers, were ideally placed to deliver news to mobile phones and other portable devices:

If you want a service of 20 video clips either sent by broadband to your PC or fired to your mobile, then it's likely to come from the 24-hour news channels . . . in news, anything can be made into anything else and reused on new platforms.

By 2011, when Sky News launched its iPad app, Ryley said it was one of the biggest developments in the 20 years since the launch of Sky News itself. He said tablets were the future of news consumption because they offer choice to 'find out instantly what's happening or go back in time and see how it happened'.

The BBC Technology Correspondent Rory Cellan-Jones wrote in his blog that Sky News on the iPad went further than anything he'd seen in delivering a television news service crafted for a tablet computer. Apart from watching, or pausing and spooling, live TV, the user could choose on-demand content with interactive graphics, background text features and photos. But Cellan-Jones said it didn't do breadth of coverage. The launch in March 2011 coincided with the calamitous earthquake, tsunami and nuclear alert in Japan – there was plenty on those events, but he'd looked for coverage of business and technology stories and found it wanting. In short, the Sky News app followed the pattern Pollard and Ryley had forecast several years before.

In the early years of the new online technologies, news services, from Sky and the BBC, on-demand via broadband or streamed to mobiles, proved to be more popular than longer-form entertainment programmes.

The appointment-to-view programme

Switching the radio or television on at a certain time of day to receive the news is quaintly old-fashioned. News is available at all times of the day, whenever people want it. So what is the role of the traditional appointment-to-view programme?

Chas Watkin, a BBC editor in the Midlands, says:

Chas Watkin: 'The programme is no longer the deadline. The story is the deadline.'

'Journalists are used to working to deadlines, but the deadlines have changed. The programme is no longer the deadline. The story is the deadline. When a story breaks people want to see video as quickly as possible. You do it as fast as you can. We've got to work fast without giving up our commitment to quality and accuracy.'

In a world of instant access to news, the traditional news programme might seem like a curiously twentieth-century phenomenon. But the truth is that most people are not news junkies – they have less interest in the full range of world events than most journalists. People may want to access selected news stories the way they download favourite music tracks, but that doesn't mean they don't want professionally produced digests of all the day's news.

The audience for the main channels' flagship news programmes is still many times greater than that of rolling new channels. The bulk of the UK population still trusts news organisations to present a summary of the day's events in an easily digestible form. Not everybody wants to wait around for stories to develop. Some people make sure they always catch the headlines, but don't bother with much else unless there's something that really grabs their attention. Others will watch the lead story and then switch off. So, there is still an important role for well-presented news programmes that grab an audience.

The Editor of ITV News, Deborah Turness, says:

'The demise of the appointment-to-view bespoke half-hour television news programme is overstated. For quite a long time to come, people are going to want to sit down, not have to click, not have to make a choice, just be delivered a news programme that will tell them what happened today in the world.'

She says their approach is different from the rolling news channels:

'Our strategy is blockbuster coverage of big stories. Send dishes, helicopters, anchors, everything. Just monster them. The second thing is exclusives from everybody, particularly our specialist units and our foreign bureaux. And the third thing is distinctive ideas like special series that we run, campaigns, features, and if every show has got some of those bits in it, then it's got the stardust that'll make people think: "Whoa, I'm going to watch this every night."'

BBC *News at Ten* presenter Huw Edwards says:

Huw Edwards

'I've no doubt there's a long-term future for it. At this stage, I can't foresee a time when BBC1 won't have big structured bulletins on, because they're still drawing five million viewers regularly. We know that people are accessing news on their mobile phones and in different ways, but you've still got five million people tuning in at night and that should tell you something. There's still a market for it. Looking towards the medium term – the next decade – I think it's inconceivable that these bulletins will disappear from the main channels.'

His opposite number at ITV News, Mark Austin, says:

'We're trying to make quite crafted half-hour news programmes and in many senses it's a dying art now, because all the emphasis is on breaking news and getting it on air as quickly as possible. Of course that has a role, and people want to dip in and out of that, but the real viewing figures show that people still want, and millions of people still watch, so-called appointment-to-view programmes, and only a hundred thousand or so watch each news channel.'

Helen Boaden, the BBC's Director of News, points out that news can increase the audience for the main channels:

'In a digital world where people have far more choice about what they want, the *News at Ten* actually attracts audiences back to BBC1, and that's because for lots of people it is their opportunity to sit down and say: "These are the most important things that have happened today. I trust the BBC to tell me what they are and tell them in a fair, impartial way," and I don't think that need in people is going to disappear.'

So, you no longer need an 'appointment-to-view' to keep abreast of the news, but news broadcasters want you to make that appointment.

Remember

- Audiences for bulletins are still many times greater than the audience for rolling news
- News-on-demand has not replaced the demand for news summaries
- Most viewers and listeners want journalists to be the 'trusted guides' to the news

---

CASE STUDY 15.1   THE MICHAEL JACKSON TRIAL

The influence of Sky News on the rest of the UK's news broadcasters could not have been illustrated more dramatically than at the end of the trial of the pop star Michael Jackson for alleged sex offences in 2005.

Jackson had been the biggest star on the planet and a mainstay of the red-top tabloids throughout the later part of the twentieth century. The former child star was the self-styled King of Pop. Increasingly bizarre stories appeared about his eccentric behaviour. Tales of plastic surgery, a strange friendship with Bubbles the chimp and an unlikely marriage to Lisa Marie Presley, daughter of Elvis, the King of Rock'n'Roll, only increased the public fascination in him and did little to harm his record sales. But the 'Wacko Jacko' stories took a sinister turn in the early part of the twenty-first century when he was charged with sexually molesting a 13-year-old boy. The suggestion was that Jackson's Neverland ranch with its funfair, zoo and a bedroom shared with young boys was the ultimate paedophile lair. It was by any standards a sensational tabloid story.

More than 2000 journalists from more than 30 countries gathered at the court in Santa Maria, for the verdict on 13 June 2005 at the end of a 66-day trial. It was the heat of the California afternoon. But, crucially for British broadcasters and for the BBC in particular, in Britain it was approaching ten o'clock in the evening – the time of the flagship BBC TV news bulletin. ITV News flashed – between programmes on ITV1 – that the verdict was imminent. ITV's main bulletin wasn't on air until 10.30 pm. So, they handed an audience to the BBC and Sky News.

The BBC's editor made a decision to stay with the story live until the jury delivered its verdict. It's a tactic Sky News had used frequently on all sorts of stories. Cynics might argue it helps fill time on a 24-hour channel. But it also guarantees you get the story first – or at worst equal first if some other channel dares to go live at the same time. It seemed that the BBC was buying into Sky News' philosophy and tactics on an essentially tabloid story. And not just on the BBC News channel, but in prime time on the most popular channel in Britain.

The BBC bulletin started conventionally, with titles, headlines and an introduction to the top story, but it soon developed into a waiting game as presenter Huw Edwards and reporter Matt Frei 'filled' until the jury's verdict.

When the BBC decided to devote the first half of the *Ten O'Clock News* to filling air-time waiting for something to happen – not daring to cut to pre-recorded packages for fear of missing something – they were playing Sky's game. Instead of offering an 'appointment-to-view', a digest of the day's news, they were behaving exactly the same as Sky News, the ITV News channel (which later closed) and their own BBC News 24.

It begged the question: 'If this is what BBC1 does, what exactly is the point of BBC News 24?' The truth is it didn't matter to the editor of the *Ten O'Clock News* that the BBC had a perfectly serviceable news channel that could have played the waiting game. The editor – and the channel controller – did not want to lose audience. The decision was taken to give the audience what they wanted, because if BBC1 did not do so, there were at least three other channels – including the BBC's own News 24 – that would. It is a rare news story where such a judgement call is so easy to make.

BBC correspondent Matt Frei spoke – very fluidly and very convincingly – in an extended two-way with presenter Huw Edwards for most of the first 15 minutes of the programme. When viewers were not looking at Frei outside the court, they were seeing a live camera shot of the crowd of fans nearby. The shot was not steady; it panned and zoomed as if the cameraman was not aware he was live on air. We learned later that inside the courtroom (where there were no cameras) the judge spent ten minutes opening envelopes containing the verdicts before the court clerk read them out.

Then the voice of the clerk Lorna Frey delivering the ten verdicts was heard over an exterior shot of the crowd, including a woman releasing a dove for every 'not guilty' verdict. Often the crowd's cheers threatened to drown out the clerk. A caption informed viewers that they were hearing the voice of the clerk and, apart from brief comments from newsreader Edwards, the viewer was mostly left to interpret the live event for him or herself.

When the verdicts had been delivered, it became clear that Matt Frei hadn't been idly waiting for the court clerk to finish. He'd been making notes of information fed to him from inside the court. He informed us that, as the second 'not guilty' pronouncement was made, Michael Jackson snapped his fingers and was handed a tissue with which he wiped a tear from his eye. Frei observed: 'He has been the ultimate choreographer of his own bizarre lifestyle.'

It was 10.21 pm, more than two-thirds of the way through the scheduled bulletin, before the BBC ran the first of its pre-recorded packages that evening. It was the 'backgrounder' prepared by reporter David Willis, who'd been following the trial from day one. This was the 'not guilty' version. Other versions, covering various other possible outcomes, including guilty on all charges, would never see the light of day. There followed a biographical piece looking back at Michael Jackson's career and controversial life. The BBC's *Ten O'Clock News* had returned to a more familiar format.

Over on Sky News, where until that point the coverage had been very similar to that of BBC1, a camera focused on the courtroom door. Graphics filled the bottom and left-hand side of the screen: on the left, a fast-changing list of the charges with the words 'not guilty' in bold; underneath, the words 'Sky News Flash: Michael Jackson cleared of all ten charges.' And so it was that Sky News, playing the long game, had the first shots of Michael Jackson leaving the court. That was at 10.28 pm.

The shots of Jackson leaving court were disappointing. He walked straight to a blacked-out SUV and helicopters tracked him back home to Neverland. The moment was, however, high in expectation. Even the BBC's correspondent had said there was the chance of a news conference on the courtroom steps. But BBC1 was by this time catching up with the rest of the day's news. Before the bulletin ended, a round-up of the Jackson trial by reporter Duncan Kennedy included the shots of Jackson leaving.

The ITV main news started at 10.30 pm on terrestrial channel three. They'd missed the main action. Later, ITV News missed the live shot of Jackson arriving back at Neverland.

The rest of the evening on all the news channels was taken up by reaction – including an extended press conference from the eight women and four men of the jury. They seemed to be enjoying what amounted to almost literally 15 minutes of fame; Andy

Warhol's words – if put to a stopwatch test – had never been truer. It went on so long that Sky News eventually put it on their interactive service, while the main programme returned to the studio for other reaction.

Michael Jackson's press conference never took place. On his website the singer compared the end of his trial to the birth of Martin Luther King, the fall of the Berlin Wall and the freeing of Nelson Mandela. Reporter Ben Ando summed up the hype on BBC Breakfast News next day: most people probably think the acquittal of a pop star is not so important.

Two days after the trial closed, a letter appeared in the *Daily Telegraph* asking how much the BBC had spent on its coverage. Why was it necessary to have separate, simultaneous coverage of the trial on BBC1 and BBC News 24, and eventually on *Newsnight*?

The BBC decision was justified (in their own terms) by a paragraph on another page of the same newspaper. It reported that the acquittal was watched by 7.9 million viewers on the *Ten O'Clock News*, two million more than usual.

The BBC itself said the figure was nearly three million more than usual and that they had a 36 per cent audience share – almost unprecedented in the modern multi-channel age. But they received more than 400 complaints. Bulletin editor Kevin Bakhurst appeared on the review programme *NewsWatch*, defending the decision to devote so much time to the story. He wrote on BBC Online: 'We knew the verdict was imminent, but that was the full extent of our knowledge.'

As if anticipating the inevitable comparison with Sky News, he continued: 'Obviously we set the threshold for covering breaking news much higher than the 24-hour news channels.'

So, who was the real winner? Arguably Sky News, which not only achieved its fourth highest ratings to that date, peaking at 1,069,000, but seemed to have changed forever the way its rivals covered breaking news.

Bakhurst, who later became Controller of the BBC News Channel, says the Jackson trial was not a watershed moment. He says the *Ten O'Clock* team were confident about holding for the verdict. Many of them had worked on BBC News 24 and their treatment was a natural response: 'That is the audience expectation now. If there's a story about to happen or happening, they don't expect you to opt out of it and go to something else. People will leave in droves.'

But it was a close-run thing: 'I think it was only two or three minutes away from us saying: "Enough. We can't go on doing this." It was unlucky it went on so long, but it was quite lucky it came when it did.'

See Workshops and Exercises

Rolling news – a different discipline

Rolling news has changed the way journalists work. The deadline is always with us. The impact of that on reporters in the field is clear, but it also changes the way producers and editors operate.

Kevin Bakhurst edited the BBC's *Ten O'Clock News* (the Ten) and then became Controller of the BBC News Channel (when it was still called News 24). He says there are clear differences in the approach to news programmes and to rolling news:

'A lot of the fundamentals are the same – the basic journalism and so on – but in terms of the skills of the producers and the output editors, it's quite a different set of demands.

'My view was that for too long News 24 was run on exactly the same basis as the bulletins, and actually 24-hour news and the expectation of the audience is different. People rightly expect a bulletin like the Ten to be a kind of bulletin of record, and that, unless there's a big breaking story, what you are told on the Ten is the definitive take on the story.

'On 24-hour news channels, we need to give the audience the latest information that we have, and tell them our assessment of it. Be open with them. You can take the audience along with you and you've got the time to say: "Look, this is the information. This is what we've got at the moment. We're checking it out." And then say if it's right or wrong.'

BBC Radio Five Live is Britain's only true national rolling radio news network. It has a less formal approach than Radio 4 – more of a conversation than a lecture, with phone-ins, email, text messages and Twitter feeds read on air.

Speaking shortly after audience research from the BBC's Creative Future project was published in 2006, Five Live Editor Matt Morris suggested how all BBC radio news might sound in future:

'The audience said they regarded us as authoritative, accurate, formal, trustworthy, but they wanted us to be modern, accessible, friendly. Their view was it was a kind of monologue. They wanted a dialogue. Ticking all those boxes, Five Live's there. That's why Five Live's successful. The question is: do we shift as other bits of the BBC shift towards us, and if we do shift, where do we shift to?

'Five Live has to maintain its conversational tone, but I don't want to drive it downmarket. Our interviews are the kind of interviews you might want to conduct yourself. I'm keen that Five Live is polite, friendly and treats everybody as if they've got something to say, and we're not going to get aggressive with people. On Five Live, you can listen to a conversation, not a row.'

He believes Five Live has an important public service role:

Five Live's Victoria Derbyshire: her phone-in is 'just a normal conversation'.

'We have to do our journalism in a way that's going to inform people and help them to live their lives, help them to make sense of the world. There's a whole range of things affecting people's lives that are getting much more complicated, and if we have got a role as public service broadcasters, it's got to be helping people to make sense of all that difficult stuff in a way that is not patronising, not paternalistic, but genuinely on a kind of peer basis.'

Morris says Five Live's approach is summed up by presenters saying things like: 'I don't get this. You'll have to explain this to me.' Morris says:

'It's always OK to say as a presenter: "I don't understand." It's absolutely fine, because, probably, then loads of other people aren't understanding it as well.'

'The audience understands that. "Whoah, hang on, let me hear that again." And that's what Five Live should be like. It's not saying people are thick and they don't get stuff. It's about how difficult some stuff is, and on the radio you've only got one bite at it. We shouldn't be afraid of having a second bite at things.

'What we've got to do is concentrate on the audience here. And not on making some kind of perfect product. I don't want perfection. I quite like warts and flaws – not lines going down – but I quite like the sense of "Stop a sec, I haven't got that".'

Presenter Victoria Derbyshire says: 'It's always OK to say as a presenter: "I don't understand." It's absolutely fine, because, probably, if you're not understanding it, then loads of other people aren't as well.'

Breaking news

Breaking news provides the greatest challenge for any broadcast organisation. Just as paramedics talk of the Golden Hour – the time in which casualties have the best chance of being treated successfully – there is a Golden Hour in news coverage. A swift response establishes a lead in covering events that can never be retrieved by reporters late on the scene.

Before 24-hour news channels on TV and radio, news editors and programme controllers would decide whether to break into programmes to provide a news flash or special programmes. That still happens for major incidents. The BBC interrupted Six Nations rugby coverage (though not during play) when the first UN-backed aircraft enforced a no-fly zone over Libya in March 2011. BBC1 and ITV1 broke into programmes when terrorists bombed London transport targets in July 2005. They shared coverage with their 24-hour services. And, for the first time, content provided by the audience became a major part of the output. Thousands of texts, mobile phone stills and clips of audience video informed the coverage. Viewers' pictures were used extensively on air and were to become some of the defining images of what became known as the 7/7 attacks.

Remember

- Rolling news programmes can lead the audience through a story
- Don't wait for the 'definitive' version of events
- Attribute your sources
- Use interactive services to encourage user content

CASE STUDY 15.2   LIVE TELEVISION *V.* THE INTERNET

The London bombings of 7 July 2005 showed that live television can still be a more immediate news source than the Internet. Terrorists go for high-profile targets. Cities like London, or New York on 11 September, are the hubs of major news-gathering organisations. The logistical problems of scrambling news crews to remote locations do not arise. Live links can be established quickly.

In London on the morning of the bombings, news on TV proved infinitely superior to online coverage, despite claims for the Internet that it is the most immediate and flexible of news media. It's a question of resources. When an organisation such as the BBC or Sky News throws resources at a story, the range of information being gathered is awesome. Online newsrooms, with a fixed number of staff and no ready pool of extra personnel to call on, cannot match them. Although user-generated content proved vital to the coverage, before Twitter there was no ready flow of eyewitness accounts in the early stages of the event.

On that summer morning, the BBC news website was reporting at least one person dead and several people injured at a time when the ITV News channel had a Reuters report of 90 casualties. The Reuters report proved inaccurate, but by naming the source the broadcaster was keeping its audience informed of the way the story was developing without verifying the information and presenting it as incontrovertible fact. The idea of telling the audience what we *don't* know alongside what we know for sure is one of the innovations of rolling news, and particularly of Sky News' approach.

Witnesses on BBC News 24, Sky News and ITV had already spoken of seeing several bodies in the wreckage of the underground trains and a double-decker bus. The online headline 'Multiple blasts paralyse London' was unchanged and there were few pictures, as eyewitness accounts, political reaction and expert analysis filled television screens. The information deficit for anyone relying on the Web must have been frustrating. BBC insiders say the lack of new information on their online news service was a result of unnecessary caution by duty editors. They clearly did not want to broadcast the untrue Reuters report, but they left out much that *was* confirmed.

The BBC Interactive Newsroom received 8000 emails and 1500 text messages before eight o'clock that evening. It proved its worth as a means of connecting with its audience, but as a primary news medium it struggled to match the effectiveness of television and radio.

7 July 2005 was the day citizen journalism became a force in British media. Stills and video from mobile phones were shown extensively. TV used material from viewers in reporter packages and in separate items explaining how people caught up in events had been able to record what went on because of the new technology. On the Web, the mobile phone pictures were mostly an available extra, rather than part of the main reports.

And TV also won on traditional news criteria. It carried the Metropolitan Police Commissioner and the Prime Minister live well before the Web reported their comments.

Sky News' head at the time Nick Pollard says their plan for big stories is well honed even though it's not written down:

'You bash the phones, start putting up maps of where these incidents are reported and, most crucially, try to get on the phone somebody who's seen what was going on, whether it's the managing director of London Underground or someone on a mobile phone standing outside a tube station.

'It's an awareness of the importance of chucking all your resources at the stories that really matter and being content to ignore the others.'

Sky News launched their Skycopter, with a reporter on board, offering live aerial commentary and scenes of the capital in chaos. They were lucky the helicopter was available. It had been recalled from Gleneagles that day because London had just been awarded the 2012 Olympic Games. Reaction to the winning bid would have been a big story, before events took over. The helicopter was going to be used for aerial shots of the sites in East London due to be redeveloped as Olympic venues. It was soon in the air over Aldgate tube station, showing live scenes.

Sky News also used their rolling ticker-tape graphic for messages from people reassuring loved ones they were safe. Sky News' impromptu service was in place several hours before the police set up an emergency information line for people worried about their friends and family.

The coverage included mobile phone video footage from inside one of the damaged underground carriages. It was one of the first times this technology had been seen in a major breaking story. It showed how members of the public have become news gatherers in their own right. Viewers' video of near 'broadcast quality' occasionally turns up on the news, but video on mobile phones added a new dimension. People carry their phones everywhere, whereas they are unlikely to have the family camcorder with them all the time. It's always a good idea these days to ask witnesses if they have pictures of an incident. Video from mobiles is usually of poor quality, but for the biggest stories it is used widely.

Among all the innovations, the London attacks also highlighted one of the weaknesses of 24-hour coverage – the desire to publish any information, however suspect or unhelpful.

Sky News' boss Nick Pollard told the *Independent* a few weeks later:

'Our philosophy is that we will tell viewers what we believe is going on. We will attribute every source, claim and figure that we quote. We will also tell viewers what we don't know. I have a feeling that viewers, who are now quite attuned to 24-hour news, understand the rhythm and dynamics of an evolving story and would rather be told what we believe is the detail of an unfolding story, rather than waiting until the whole story is known.'

It was probably this philosophy that prompted both the ITV News Channel and Sky News to run captions almost two hours after the first bombs, quoting a police source saying it was too early to say if the blasts were linked to terrorism. To any reasonably experienced journalist – indeed to any informed viewer – this was clearly not true. Reporting the comments of a cautious policeman or police press officer served no purpose. Within less than half an hour the Metropolitan Police Commissioner said the bombings were probably a major terrorist attack. Within an hour the Prime Minister said it was pretty clear there had been a series of terrorist attacks.

Sky News claimed credit for being the first to report a terrorist attack when other stations were still talking about a power surge on the tube system. A Westminster-based producer, Bob Mills, saw the bus that exploded in Tavistock Square and told the newsdesk there was absolutely no question it was a bomb. Sky News trusted his judgement and ran with the story. But the early statement from the police seemed to contradict what the station was reporting. The source was, as Nick Pollard says, 'attributed'. But the word 'police' carries an authority that could have misled viewers.

Sky News' Crime Correspondent Martin Brunt recalls his approach to covering the story:

'If you've been around a few years, you trust your instincts. You go with your urges. When the London bombs went off, I was put on air and all I knew was there'd been six incidents and people were talking about power surges. Inevitably, I started talking about the possibility of bombings and I knew from one phone call there was pandemonium at Scotland Yard. This sort of thing was what they'd been warning about and planning for. You could argue that, if we'd been talking about bombs and it turned out to be power surges after all, we'd be doing the terrorists' job. But we weren't wrong. It's sometimes worth taking a risk. I think if we are a little ragged round the edges it gives us some immediacy. It appears honest. We admit it if we don't know things and I think that's important.

'I think that's what 24-hour news has added – much more speculation in the early stages of a story.'

See Workshops and Exercises

Sports programmes

Sports programmes have much the same elements as news bulletins, even when the show is devoted to live coverage of an event.

There will almost always be a headline sequence, telling the viewer what to expect, a presenter who anchors the show, usually with the help of studio guests, live reporting and commentary and packaged reports. The packages might be player profiles or reports of other matches in the same competition.

There will be extensive use of graphics, particularly for league tables, performance statistics and for live analysis. Whether it's a former player talking soccer tactics on Sky Sports or an explanation of reverse swing during a cricket Test, technology is essential to the reporting. The programme close might be a musical montage of highlights of the day.

The network Big Brother

The relationship between network TV and the regions, and between national and local radio, is based on co-operation, but fraught with potential conflict. It differs in BBC TV and radio, in the ITV network and in ILR. But the relationship usually comes down to the hunger for exclusives: the desire of individual journalists and editors as well as reporters and producers, to beat others with the stories they cover.

The producer of a regional programme with a national story in his running order has to think of ways to make his treatment different from the network version. This is of particular concern on the BBC where regional news traditionally follows the network bulletin. The instinct is to shut up shop and prevent the network having access to your material, keeping anything exclusive to yourself.

Arguments that 'we're all on the same side', or even as Director-General Greg Dyke tried to insist 'one BBC', cut no ice.

But the relationship to the parent organisation means the regional television and local radio newsrooms have the benefit of the BBC's news feeds and access to the network's audio and pictures.

Here's an example of treating a national story differently for a region. A man wanted in connection with failed suicide bombings in London was arrested in Birmingham on 27 July 2005. It was the lead story on the BBC's national news. So, how would the regional TV programme deal with such a big story in their area without repeating what viewers had already seen? *Midlands Today* focused on the impact on the community in Hay Mills. A suspected bomb was left at the scene. Bomb disposal experts were called in, and part of the street was evacuated. Hundreds of people didn't know how long they would be away from their homes. Correspondent Peter Wilson's report covered these aspects of the story and included shots from an exclusive piece he'd done two weeks earlier on call with the Royal Logistics Corps bomb disposal team – the men brought in to deal with the threat. And there was a telling interview clip that summed up the local angle to the national story. John Bedder, the owner of a fish and chip shop just yards from the scene of the arrest, said: 'It's real now. It's not something you've read in the newspapers or seen on television, serious though that is. It's something on our doorsteps.'

ITV's regional structure has historically been one of its strengths. Regional newsrooms compete with their BBC counterparts and with other ITV companies in areas where the broadcast signal overlaps with their neighbours in the network. They'll also want to provide better coverage of local stories than their network 'big brothers' from ITV News. The ITV companies owned Independent Television News (ITN) but that didn't stop the rivalry at newsroom level. The merging of ITV's major companies into one main player was followed by cutbacks in regional newsrooms. They are no longer as well staffed (or as well paid) as their BBC counterparts.

ILR stations subscribe to an audio and copy feed from Independent Radio News or Sky News Radio. The benefit of being part of a network is clear. Local radio stations cannot afford to have their own staff covering national and international stories. So, they buy into a networked service. The network stories appear alongside staff reporters' coverage of local events.

Local TV

Once upon a time in the UK, there was national television and there was regional television. Regional TV was based on the reach of the transmitters set up to deliver analogue television signals across the country. The government offered licences to ITV regional companies to use these transmitters, and the BBC offered regional services based on these transmitters. So, all that followed is a product of the 1950s' TV transmission system. We had programmes like *Midlands Today*, *Central News*, *Calendar*, *Look North* and *South Today*. Now there is a new perspective with the government supporting local TV in selected cities. The culture secretary's initial target was a dozen or so services.

A CLOSER LOOK

REGIONAL TV – WHO'D BUY IT?

Tim Burke, Community Content Editor of the BBC's local television pilot in 2006, had an amusing, deliberately overstated but compelling argument why regional television is an outmoded idea in the broadband age. The local TV project was abandoned when the BBC Trust (the corporation's controlling body) ruled that they couldn't justify the cost from the licence fee or the 'negative impact on commercial media'. There had been substantial lobbying from regional newspapers that their web interests would be damaged by a local BBC service – although neither the quantity nor quality of video on newspaper websites improved in the years immediately after the Trust's decision.

Even so, Burke's case against *regional* TV remains strong. Addressing public meetings to promote the proposed service, he would begin: 'Let's assume the BBC doesn't exist. Let me float you an idea.'

Turning to someone in the front row, he would ask: 'Where do you live?'

As they began to answer, he would interrupt:

'I don't care. Because I'm going to base this service on transmitters. If you live in Cheltenham, you might not be interested in events in Birmingham, but I'm going to give you a service from Birmingham. You might be more interested in events in Bristol. Well, tough. And because of hills, and houses and offices blocking the signal, you might be lumped in with places you're not interested in. I don't care where you live.'

Turning to another audience member, he would ask: 'What time do you get home from work?'

Again, before there was time for a reply, he would continue: 'I don't care, because I'm going to put this service on from 6.30 for half an hour, with a little bit more after the *Ten O'Clock News*. I don't care if you miss it.'

'What are you interested in? . . . I don't care, because I'm going to appoint somebody, probably a middle-aged, middle-class bloke like me, to decide what the most important stories of the day are, and what order they should be shown in. And you won't have any input into that. We'd like you to have a say, so we'll put our phone numbers and email address on screen, but don't try ringing during the programme because we're busy.

'So I don't care where you live, what time you get in or what you're interested in. But I'm going to charge you a proportion of £130 [the TV licence fee] every year for this, and if you don't pay, I'll prosecute you. Now are you going to buy that?'

Put like that, regional television sounds like a very bad deal. Burke says:

'It's like giving somebody an iPod and saying you can only use it between 6.30 pm and 7.00. I'll download the tracks for you and decide what order they're in. Now pay me something every year, or I'll prosecute. Who would buy that? Nobody.'

The argument for continuing transmitter-based regional TV looks very thin in an age when satellite, cable and broadband can be used to deliver television services.

Anita Bhalla, the first woman to be elected President of Circom Regional, the European association of regional television stations, says people are interested in global events and local events. She expects regional television of the kind seen in Britain for 50 years to be squeezed out in time in favour of increasingly local content.

She says:

'People want to know about the places they live, to hear their own stories. For example, people in Shropshire want stories about Shropshire; they are curious about their locality. People want news on demand, when they want it and where they want it. They don't want to wait till 6.30.'

Apart from the coalition government's city TV plans, the strongest alternative to regional TV appears to be broadband local services with much of the content generated by the users. It means much more localisation of content – almost everything you see is likely to be within a 20-mile radius of your home. This was the model piloted by the BBC in 2006. It was also available on satellite, with six local services on a loop repeating every hour. The local ten-minute bulletins could also be sent to video iPods and mobile phones. BBC producers offered guidance to local people and community groups to help them tell their own stories, sometimes lending cameras and giving basic training to enable them to do it.

The opposition to the pilot from local newspaper groups, who saw it as the BBC encroaching on their territory – the provision of local news – was a factor in the BBC Trust's refusal to back the project. Without their role as the main providers of local news, the papers feared sales and advertising revenue would fall. Many local papers provide video content on their websites, but others have scrapped investment in video journalism because they can't make it pay at a time of falling circulations. Nonetheless, there are some job opportunities for broadcast journalists within the traditional newspaper industry.

Most business models for local television have struggled to produce quality news content. The BBC model, backed by the licence fee, the corporation's news gathering (including extensive grass-roots contacts through local radio), and access to BBC national and international coverage (and archive) looked, in early 2007, like the surest prospect of a quality local service for viewers across the UK. Now local TV looks like being available only in select major cities and not at all in the countryside.

Ian Johnson is a Midlands-based BBC cameraman, who has covered major UK stories, including the 1984 Libyan Embassy siege, which followed the shooting of WPC Yvonne Fletcher, and stories across Europe and the US for the BBC in the Midlands. He is now a video journalist and a strong advocate of local television.

He says:

'It's the way ahead. It's definitely what people want. People want big news – world and national news – and ultra-local news. They want to find out what's happening on their estate, in their village, in their town, but they don't care what's going on 20 miles away. Today we can deliver the TV equivalent of a local newspaper, whereas in the past you couldn't.'

Chas Watkin, the BBC Midlands News Editor, who supervised the local TV pilot, says the scheduled bulletins on satellite were successful, but broadband is the way ahead: 'It has to be a totally on-demand service to work.' Watkin says the broadband service came into its own on local election day in May 2006, when they were able to offer coverage of every local count: 'That was our best day. It's news that drives the hits. The audience want local news. They may also want something quirky – but they want good quirky.'

- Regional TV is based on signals from transmitters
- TV regions are not homogeneous communities
- Local TV can provide news from closer to home
- Broadband offers news-on-demand

Podcasts

> **A radio programme may be live, and a podcast cannot be live, but apart from that there is no difference.**

What is the difference between a podcast and a radio programme? A radio programme may be live, and a podcast cannot be live, but apart from that there is no difference.

There are good podcasts that sound just like radio programmes or features for radio, and bad podcasts that don't. For example, some newspapers tried podcasts with their reporters reading out features they had written for the paper. Adam Harding, a Sky News online journalist, asks: 'Why would you want to listen for five minutes to a person, who is not a broadcaster, reading something written for print, that it takes you a minute and a half to read for yourself in a paper?' These podcasts certainly bore no relation to Radio 4's *From Our Own Correspondent*.

Podcasts can be important tools for broadcast journalists. RSS feeds that tell users when a new episode has been updated mean you can develop subscriber networks. 'One-hit sub-scription' is what makes podcasts different from other sound files on the Internet.

BBC Radio Five Live developed some of the most downloaded podcasts in the UK with Mark Kermode's film reviews on Simon Mayo's programme. The station's editor Matt Morris said time shifting and portability were the attractions of podcasting:

'Time shifting was already there (you can go on to your computer and listen to output that was on last night streamed on the Internet – we do it all the time) but with portability, if you're a businessman, and you don't want to get up at 5.30, you can get up at 6.30, download *Wake Up To Money*, and listen to it on the way in to work.'

Professional broadcasters can make use of amateur content too. Chris Vallance, producer of a Pods and Blogs spot on Five Live, said:

'One of the things the new digital technologies enable is that, if you buy a computer now, you probably get nearly all the stuff you need to start recording audio, and if you don't have it, you can get it for free.

'In terms of mic technology, if you think about the quality of just those headset mics you can buy now, we did some tests and you can get results that are very similar to very expensive broadcast mics.

'There are no barriers to entry in most industrialised countries, and increasingly in the non-industrialised world. Given that that's the case, and given that there are people who are enthusiasts for playing around with sound, be they musicians, be they podcasters, be they bloggers who also do audio blogs, and you've suddenly got a vast pool of people who can send you sound from where they live. They can send you voice pieces, they can send you voxes, they can send you personal viewpoint pieces.'

One early project involved collecting material from survivors of Hurricane Katrina, which hit New Orleans in 2005. Six months on the BBC broadcast almost 50 minutes of material. Vallance recalls:

'The sound quality of all of them was good, and some pieces were exceptional. There was one beautiful mixed package. He said: "My name is Chris Decker. I'm a trainee Catholic priest," and then he faded up the road noise. Then he said: "When I first moved back to New Orleans, the noise outside my window was absolute silence, and now you can hear traffic." And he used that as a way into riffing about the reconstruction of the city. It was a beautiful piece of radio – very NPR sounding, not BBC at all [National Public Radio is the US public broadcasting service]. Obviously it's coming from his radio culture not ours, and was a very different sound for us.'

Podcasters will occasionally send Vallance unmixed tracks, and he'll do the production work. Most show high production values:

'Some of them don't, frankly. There are breath noises all over the mic, pops everywhere and strange wheezes, pops and crackles – but I've heard one or two of those go out on regular radio.

'There's definitely, among the good people, a high degree of craft skills. They probably wouldn't see themselves as journalists. They see themselves as podcasters.'

Vallance is not sure, though, how long the term 'podcast' will last. 'It just will become radio, if you talk about radio as a device you switch on and talk comes out of it.'

So, podcasting looks as if it's here to stay. It's radio, after all.

Remember

- Podcasting is the same as recorded radio programming
- RSS feeds mean subscribers can be told instantly when a podcast is updated
- Podcasters can provide source material for your own radio programmes

Phone-ins

Phone-ins are a staple of speech-based radio. They were interactive before interactivity became a buzz-word.

Text and email messages are part of the mix – but remember, if you are presenting or producing a phone-in, written messages have to be read out by a presenter. According to Jon Gaunt, who has been one of the closest things to a 'shock-jock' on UK radio, both at the BBC and commercial stations, reading messages aloud is less likely to attract further callers than a good argument on air.

BBC Five Live strives for conversation rather than argument. Victoria Derbyshire explains her approach to callers on a phone-in: 'You've got no idea what they're going to say, it's completely unpredictable, so you just have a normal conversation with somebody you've never met before – courteous, polite, curious, all the sort of basics, what, why, where, when.'

Five Live's editor Matt Morris said:

'For a long time there's been a relationship between a radio station and its audience through the phone-in. We've developed that through emails, and then almost unexpectedly into text messaging, which taps you into a much wider constituency.

'A typical programme may get 150 calls on a hot topic, of which you try and get maybe 30 on air. You can get thousands of text messages. You've got to beware of the tyranny of instant public opinion – but there's still something in tapping into public opinion in that way.

'Also text messaging gives you a lot of information about weather, road conditions and all that stuff. Peter Allen, the drivetime presenter, has referred to text messagers as our army of reporters. We've had that kind of interactivity, that relationship with the audience, for some time.'

The sports phone-in

A lively sub-genre of the phone-in programme is the sports phone-in. '606' is one of the best known programme strands on BBC Radio Five Live, and Talksport has a similar format on independent national radio.

Although all sports can be discussed, the obsession of callers and presenters since the earliest days has been football.

The sports phone-in began in Britain on local commercial radio. Veteran Midlands broadcaster Tony Butler invented the football phone-in as we know it, when he was sports editor of BRMB in Birmingham in 1974. It started on the new commercial station on a Sunday lunchtime. Butler had four live guests in the studio, in case he didn't get any callers. He needn't have worried. He says: 'I shall never forget it. We had 28 callers in an hour and a half. The most any of the other talk shows had at that time was ten.'

After a 'fact-finding' visit to the US and Canada, where he heard outspoken sports presenters arguing with phone-in callers, he developed his own strident style, delivered in a broad West Midlands accent.

Butler's show moved to a Friday evening, where it became a Midlands institution. He was parodied by the Brummie comedian Jasper Carrott, bringing his show to national attention. When he left BRMB he continued the phone-in on BBC Radio WM, and even for a time on TV, on the cable service Birmingham Live.

He says: 'It hasn't changed over the years. I suppose I've mellowed as the years have gone by, but it's the same show. You don't have to be balanced or anything like that, but you've got to be responsible.'

Butler worked for newspapers including the *Daily Telegraph* and was a regional journalist writing copy for the BBC's regional radio and TV bulletins before he became a local personality. His ethical position on phone-ins is clear: 'I've never set up calls. I won't do that. If they're not calling in, I'm not doing my job.'

Butler says there is a danger on a long-running show that the same listeners call repeatedly, and it can begin to sound too much like a private club:

'We do have regular callers, and I have to be diplomatic, shall we say. I have someone answering the phones, and she'll say: "We've got so-and-so on, and he's already been on this week. Shall I put him off?" The answer is, of course, yes.'

Butler's abrasive style frequently fell foul of the old radio regulating body, the Independent Broadcasting Authority. His catchphrase was 'On yer bike' to get rid of callers. That was deemed acceptable, even in the 1980s, but the IBA complained when he started exhorting listeners to 'get your prayer mats out', whenever Aston Villa were playing in Europe in the run-up to their 1982 European Cup victory. The IBA said it was offensive to Muslims. Butler pointed out that he had received ten prayer mats from Muslim football fans. He says: 'I wouldn't do it today because these are very different times, politically, but in those days the IBA were the bane of my life. They used to drive me spare.'

Butler continued his cult status on local radio and regional TV for 30 years. BBC Radio WM sent him to Germany for the 2006 World Cup with sports editor Mark Regan.

'We'd do inserts into programmes throughout the day, starting with breakfast, do the phone-in for an hour in the evening and finish at about ten o'clock. It started as 12 days in Germany. Then they extended it to 24 days. We were running out of clean clothes and booking hotels became a problem. Twenty-four days and I never saw a match except on the telly!'

When he went to Germany, Butler was 71 years old. He said then: 'As long as they keep paying me and as long as I've got an audience, I'll keep doing it.'

PHONE-INS – THE RISKS

Any form of live radio involving members of the public carries a degree of risk. Will they use it as a platform for offensive language or views? Will they inadvertently, or even deliberately, libel someone?

Here are the BBC's guidelines on phone-ins.

Because phone-ins are live, we should be ready to deal with contributions that may cause widespread offence, or break the law. We should also be careful not to allow phone-ins to become a vehicle for the opinions of the presenter.

The following practices may help to minimise the risks:

- Contributors to phone-ins should normally be called back and if necessary briefed before they go on air. Care should be taken to establish whether they are appropriate to put to air, and appropriate referral made in cases of doubt.

- A breadth and diversity of views should be sought and the requirements of due impartiality should be met.

- If a programme has attracted no callers then it should seek alternative content. Under no circumstance should programmes make up callers, or other interactions such as emails and texts. We must be honest with our audiences at all times.

- Presenters must be adequately briefed on the Editorial Guidelines and the law and should be able to extricate the programme from tricky situations with alacrity and courtesy. Emails and texts should be read before they are broadcast.

- When producing a phone-in on a difficult or sensitive subject, the production team should be briefed on how to deal carefully with contributors and, if appropriate, support systems should be in place. Particular care should be taken when children and young people interact with phone-in programmes.

- When a programme is contacted unexpectedly by someone wishing to share their difficult story, we should consider the implications and refer if necessary.

Remember

- Phone-ins are the principal form of audience interaction in radio
- They can entertain and inform, and be a platform for public debate
- Presenters and producers need to be legally aware and alert to the risk of contributors causing offence

'It just felt like the whole of London was under attack.'

Jon Gaunt, BBC London

Jon Gaunt: 'I thought it was going to be an easy day.'

The morning of 7 July 2005 produced some of the most remarkable local radio ever heard in Britain.

What made the suicide bomb attacks on public transport in London an exceptional breaking news story was that it came on a day when everyone was expecting to be covering a huge 'good news' story – London winning the 2012 Olympics.

BBC London, a local station for the capital, had the first eyewitness accounts as the drama unfolded, and in a model of restrained, factual broadcasting, Sony award-winning presenter Jon Gaunt reported only confirmed information, and insisted on air that the station was not interested in speculation or opinion.

Elsewhere in this book you will read the opinions of experienced rolling news journalists who believe modern audiences have a sophisticated grasp of the news-gathering process. They say you can tell people all the information to hand as long as it is attributed. The audience can make their own minds up what to believe. BBC London's approach on 7 July was arguably a more old-fashioned one. The decisions of Jon Gaunt, an often controversial presenter, and editor David Robey to stick to the facts as they knew them were informed by the need not to spread panic across the capital.

Here are some of the key moments of the BBC London coverage of the first hours of the story – and an insight into the behind-the-scenes tensions, with Jon Gaunt's comments on what he felt as the story unfolded and what he really suspected was going on.

Gaunt had spoken to his producer as he was on his way in to work on the train from his Northamptonshire home. It was his habit to talk through the content of the morning programme, billed as 'London's liveliest phone-in'.

I just said don't set anything up. Let's just do Olympics, Olympics, Olympics. I thought it was going to be an easy day.

Predictably, the phones 'went crazy' with people wanting to talk about the Olympic victory. After the nine o'clock news, Gaunt went on air with an opening link that summed up the euphoria in the capital.

'There isn't really much to talk about today except one major story. Is this just not the best news ever? When you saw the jubilation . . . it has put a spring in the step. It does make us proud to be British . . .'

At 9.15, travel editor Jules Wilson reported: 'We've got some major travel disruption . . . please stay clear of the whole tube network . . . they've got some incidents taking place.'

Gaunt reacted: 'We've sent reporters to Liverpool Street. If you're in the Liverpool Street tube station area, we need to hear from you now.'

The programme continued with a two-way with a reporter in Singapore, where the International Olympic Committee made its historic decision. There were calls too from ecstatic Londoners.

Then at 9.25, reporter Pete Wilson joined Gaunt in the studio with more on the incident at Liverpool Street.

By then I knew. Pete said they thought a bomb had gone off, but don't say anything on air.

Wilson: 'We've heard a report about a bang.'

Gaunt: 'An explosion?'

Wilson: 'No, a bang. It could have been a collision involving two trains which could have caused a power surge . . . there are reports of walking wounded. The advice is to stay off the tube.'

A trail followed for a phone-in the following Tuesday with the Metropolitan Police Commissioner, Sir Ian Blair. It included a clip of the Commissioner saying: 'My job is to make London safe.'

The 9.30 news headlines led with: 'Emergency services have been called to Liverpool Street station after reports of an explosion. It's thought the incident was caused by a major power failure. The station's currently cordoned off. TfL [Transport for London] are telling people to avoid the entire tube network. British Transport Police have confirmed there are walking wounded, and said paramedics have responded to one report of a person classed as life at risk. More on that as soon as we get it.'

I was of the opinion, surely we've got to say this is a bomb. I was very much in favour of 'Let's go.' I was thinking Ferrari [Nick Ferrari on rival, commercial station LBC] will be doing it. There was a lot of debate with the [control room] cubicle. What I do on air is I produce as I go along. I'd been on air on 9/11 and learnt a lot from that, but a lot of the backroom team didn't have much experience of rolling interactive news. Management weren't in at this stage and we ended up being cautious. You don't want to spread panic.

The travel report repeated the advice to avoid the tube network. Tickets were being honoured by buses.

At 9.32, the first witness was on air. The caller, Tyrone, said there were hundreds of police on the streets. There were loud sirens in the background of the call.

Tyrone: 'Can you hear me?'

Gaunt: 'Yes, carry on.'

Tyrone: 'It seems to be some sort of security alert that has affected the whole of the East London area . . .'

The first witness from one of the bombed trains followed immediately. One of the radio station's staff was on the tube with his wife.

Ian Wade, who was an accountant with BBC London, was on the train, and that's why we had the first witness on air.

Gaunt: 'BBC London's Ian Wade was actually on the underground.'

Wade: 'I was on the train it actually happened to, Jon. We were about 200 yards outside King's Cross and an almighty bang. Lights went out. Soot filled the carriage we was in and then the emergency electricity come on. We was in the actual carriage about 15 minutes. They started filing us out, they shut the line down for the electricity, and officials was walking us down. Now as I was walking out, I asked one of the officials what happened and he said one of the electric overhead lights fell down, he thinks, and hit the front of the train. There's people here crying. We was actually on the train it happened, I've never seen anything like it.'

Gaunt: 'Was there panic on the train when those lights went out? There must have been panic.'

Wade: 'To be honest with you, people were silent for about 15 to 20 seconds. You couldn't believe it. It was . . . some people were saying: "Oh, my God, help me, help me," and all sorts, banging on the doors and others were saying: "No, no, no. Don't open anything. If there's a fire outside we're going to be dead in minutes, if there's smoke coming in." But people were generally very, very good, you know. There's people keeping people calm, and saying: "Look, we're all right. There's no fire, you know, hang on."'

Gaunt: 'How long were you in the dark for?'

Wade: 'I would say 15 minutes but the train was absolutely, which is normal, absolutely packed, so there's . . . it was the busiest train I've ever been on anyway 'cos it was running slow, so it couldn't have happened at a worse time. It was almost like a bomb going off. There was just a boom.'

Gaunt: 'Any injuries?'

Wade: 'I'm just looking over. There's a guy with a short-sleeved shirt on. He's got cuts on his arm, but otherwise that's the first and only one I've seen actually injured, but other than that people are sobbing and covered in soot and all sorts.'

Wade said it had taken 15 minutes to walk along the track to King's Cross.

Gaunt: 'We want you to stay there for the moment until we can get a reporter down. If anything else happens, I want you to ring us back, Ian.'

What I do is produce on air, thinking where the next twist might be or where the next actuality is coming from. Ian Wade wasn't a reporter, but he was great that morning. We needed to have him available to go on air.

Gaunt summarised what they knew so far; the train was on the Piccadilly Line from Cockfosters; people were in the dark for 15 minutes; somebody said it was an overhead light that came down; keep off the tube for now. The next caller was equally dramatic.

Alexa: 'There was a really loud bang and the lights went out and everybody ducked and screamed. We were told to evacuate and we were asked not to run, but everybody ran.'

Gaunt: 'Alexa, you're obviously shook up. Take it easy now . . . We'll talk to the emergency services once they've got the time.'

Pete Wilson returned to the studio and reported the police and fire brigade had been called to Aldgate. It had been declared a major incident, and, yes, there were some casualties.

At 9.43, Gaunt issued a more detailed plea for witnesses: 'It's not helpful to speculate. We don't really know . . . In situations like this, I'll be absolutely straight with you, we rely on you as well. That's why we're an interactive radio station. If you were there, please give me a call now. 020 722 42000. You can also text 07786 200949 or email me gaunty@bbc.co.uk. We are going to do travel bulletins now every 15 minutes.'

The decision to increase the number of travel bulletins was taken by the travel unit, but the rest was all me. There were some people who thought we shouldn't be asking for calls, but I didn't want to just sit there and be a public information centre. We've got this great resource – the listeners – let's use it.

Gaunt: 'Don't bother ringing people back – put them straight through. We need to know what's happening now. As soon as we can talk to the emergency services we will.'

That's me getting annoyed with the cubicle. The normal practice is to ring people back, but there was a chance they'd ring off and be taking a call from a loved one asking if they were safe, and they'd be engaged when they tried to get them. And anyway, the phone lines were getting clogged up. You couldn't get through.

Gaunt: 'We were celebrating a great Olympic victory, but now for obvious reasons we are concentrating on that incident on the tube.'

We were still getting calls about the Olympics. Whether people hadn't heard what was going on, I don't know. We had to clear the lines.

The 9.45 travel bulletin reported King's Cross mainline station was closed, as were several roads. The police were asking drivers to avoid the City of London.

Gaunt: 'Jackie at Kilburn wants to tell me what's happened at Edgware. Jackie, what can you tell me?'

Jackie said she was driving down Park Lane and heard sirens coming from all directions. 'Police bikes, police cars, an ambulance went by, and I thought: "What the hell's going on down here now?"'

She gave more details, and Gaunt thanked her: 'If you find out any more, see any more, give us a call back. We need to go back to Ian Wade in a couple of moments. Can you get him back on the line, Abi, to find out what's going on at Liverpool Street now?'

This is me producing on air, and bossing it. Abi Lewis, my producer, had been with me for years. This is the way we work together. I'm not just a gob on a stick. I couldn't do that sort of radio, being told what to say next. You've got to be involved in your product.

Phil, a cabbie, called from near Russell Square station: 'It's unbelievable. It seems there's a major disaster.'

Gaunt: 'Let's not speculate. We know it's a major incident . . . come on London cabbies, come on white van men, come on white van women, just tell us what you can see. This is why we have interactive radio like this. Pick up the phone please, and please tell us. Obviously a lot of people will be concerned about relatives and friends who might have been travelling this morning. We will keep you informed and, as soon as we know something, we will tell you. What we will not do on this radio station, let me tell you, is speculate.'

I knew speculation wouldn't help. But I also knew this was a massive opportunity to build an audience. And I was right. The figures went up after this. During a period of terror, people want to know what's going on.

By now, just after 9.50, reporters were reporting from the scenes of the events.

Gaunt: '94.9's Anna O'Neill is at King's Cross. Good morning, Anna.'

O'Neill: 'Extraordinary scenes . . . police telling people to move away from the station and they're starting to cordon off the area. Fire engines, ambulances, police cars and vans. Hundreds of police men and women. Everybody confused. We're not being told very much indeed. We were told there was some kind of a power surge and that we needed to evacuate the station. People are crying, 'cos they don't know what's been happening and they've heard there've been casualties at Liverpool Street. People are shouting: "Get out of the station, get out of the station."'

Gaunt: 'Stay safe, Anna, we'll speak to you later. Ian Wade is back.'

Wade: (alarms sounding in the background) 'I'm in the station, King's Cross station, and I have to retract what I said earlier, Jon. Those who are injured are badly injured, there's a lot of blood in here.'

Gaunt: 'And how many people would you say are injured at the moment, my friend?'

Wade: 'In this room I would say there's probably about 30 or 40 people, but, as I say, it's very bad news. There's a lot of blood.'

Gaunt: 'If you don't mind me asking you, what kind of injuries are you seeing?'

Wade: 'A lot of head injuries. Because it's quite warm this time of year, a lot of people are wearing short-sleeved shirts so you can see a lot of arms cut up and faces cut up . . . this is definitely glass cuts. People are bleeding heavily. People like myself that are covered in soot. I can't fault the police or the ambulance or even London Transport. They're walking round tending everybody that's badly injured, I mean, I'm just slightly shaken.'

By then we knew it was a terrorist attack. Ian wasn't a reporter, but I was just treating him as an eyewitness. I knew he was an intelligent bloke, who wouldn't say anything he shouldn't have. But if he had described really terrible injuries, I didn't care. He was just telling us what he could see.

Gaunt introduced Kevin, another cabbie, at Aldgate.

Kevin: 'I saw a man covered in blood being led by the police. The emergency people are putting on orange chemical emergency suits at Aldgate East.'

Gaunt: 'I'm being told by my research team that's standard practice.'

Pete [Wilson] came on and said that. He was a good member of the team with that sort of knowledge. I could cut the mic and talk to the people in the cubicle and of course they're telling me lots of stuff. The last thing you want to do is spread panic. But you do want to make it sound exciting, because it is exciting.

Gaunt made another appeal to cabbies, white van men and women.

Gaunt: 'Please don't ring up with comments on the Olympics, please don't ring up to speculate. We want to know what's happening out there in London.'

The 9.58 travel update reported that the whole of town was taking the brunt of road closures. 'Avoid all the roads around the city.'

At 10.01, news reader Max Rushton said a 'power surge incident' had caused a number of bangs. People had been injured, one of them seriously. Clips in the bulletin included Ian Wade and Tyrone talking to Gaunt. It featured the Mayor, Ken Livingstone, on the use of compulsory purchase orders to clear the Olympic site and Sir Ian Blair on Olympic security. There was also US President George Bush, speaking on climate change at the G8 summit at Gleneagles.

By 10.05, the radio station was reporting the tube network was suspended. British Transport Police had informed them that two trains remained stuck at Edgware Road, but it was not yet known if they had collided. The official police line was that it was 'difficult to know exactly what's happened at the moment'.

Gaunt read out a text message from a listener who said the sound was deafening, there was a lot of smoke and absolute chaos at Aldgate.

Gaunt: 'We are getting a lot of calls about an incident on a bus. If you know anything about that, please get in touch.'

Text messages can be useful in an incident like this. But I don't ask for emails. There's no place for emails in a phone-in show. They allow people to go on at length and not to join in the debate. If you're an abrasive presenter like me, it lets people avoid being questioned. An email won't get another caller, but an argument will.

On this occasion, Gaunt was not inviting argument. He was after information. Another caller heard a blast from a station platform at Liverpool Street; the travel editor said traffic cameras were showing 'people everywhere' on the streets; the National Grid said they had no reported problems that would have caused power surges; the Royal London Hospital was preparing to take casualties.

There was a kind of other-worldly quality to it all. It just felt like the whole of London was under attack.

Gaunt summed up what was known so far and explained that they had not been able to interview anyone from the emergency services: 'They have many more important things to do than talk to a radio station. We're getting a lot of calls with speculation. I'm sure you'll agree that speculation is not useful at the moment.

I was a little embarrassed they [the emergency services] hadn't spoken to us. I fully understood their problems, but as a programme we needed to have spokesmen on. You're trying to make it sound authoritative and professional.

Amy, a first-time caller who'd been on the Piccadilly Line train, said she heard a 'very big bang': 'I've heard it might have been a light falling on the train, but it was too big an explosion to have been that.'

It's all about the trust you build with an audience. They might not even like you but they trust you. It's like Pavlov's dog. The reaction is automatic. Something's happened, so ring Gaunty.

At 10.19, reporter Anna O'Neill was on again: 'I've got some rather grim news. One man has actually shown me some footage that he recorded on his mobile phone of a bus exploding a few streets away just near to Euston station . . . some very devastating scenes there. It looks like some people lying on the floor. I couldn't tell you exactly what kind of injuries they've got, people lying motionless on the floor.

'The man who'd been at King's Cross was talking about people covered in soot and blood. We're not sure whether it is this power surge we've been hearing about this morning, or something more sinister is going on.'

> **Gaunt:** 'Of course, but let's not speculate on that. Just tell me about the bus. The bus was in Russell Square, I believe.'

O'Neill reports the man wasn't sure, because he was shocked. He saw the back of the bus explode. He filmed footage of it on his mobile phone. 'He hadn't actually captured the moment the bus exploded. What he captured was the seconds after that bus exploded, and as he gets nearer you can see people lying on the floor, and the bus basically in tatters.'

That footage was all over the *Six O'Clock News* on TV.

Gaunt reported complete and utter gridlock and advised people not to travel, before taking a call from Steve in Marylebone: 'I was in Tavistock Square, and about six vehicles in front of me, there was a line of buses and then . . . bang! You see the explosion. I don't know what caused it. You see either the side of a building fly across the road, or, as people have been saying, the side of a bus.'

> **Gaunt:** 'How far were you from the incident would you say?'
>
> **Steve:** 'Probably about no more than 50 metres.'

Gaunt: 'And you're a cabby, obviously, I can hear the meter in the background. What else did you see after that?'

Steve: 'Just chaos. People running across the square, kids on the floor crying, people cowering in the corner and just, basically, havoc really.'

Gaunt thanks the caller and repeats the plea for information: 'All we want you to do is say, "Jon, I saw this or I saw that."'

By this time we were getting calls with anti-Muslim messages. Why can't people express that view? Management were in the cubicle by then. There was a kind of censorship going on, I suppose. But I have to say the editor Dave Robey was spot-on with his news judgement that day.

At 10.18, Pete Wilson was back in the studio with reports from Scotland Yard of multiple explosions: 'It's the first time they've called them that so far this morning – multiple explosions across London. We're told that in the next ten to 15 minutes we'll get a full release . . . it now looks as if there is some kind of pattern, some kind of link as to what has happened across London this morning and that's what we're trying to establish as well.'

I knew then what was happening. The editor was saying we can't say it's Muslims or we can't say it's Al Qaeda, but it sure as hell wasn't the IRA.

Gaunt: 'On a day when we started off so jovial, having a laugh about the Olympics . . . it's turned into something else . . . It's an horrific day for London. There's no two ways about it. It's an horrific day for London, but we will not speculate. We will bring you the facts as we establish those facts.'

Latoya in Liverpool Street told of a big explosion, grey dust falling everywhere, an orange light which they thought was flames and a lot of people who were badly wounded. They were in the front carriages. 'As we walked down the track we saw the full extent of the damage, and it looked like the whole carriage had blown open and they were still rescuing people. There were bodies and er . . . that's it, I guess.'

Gaunt: 'Stay safe. Calm down, won't you?'

At 10.22 Pete Wilson had a full report that had come through from the Metropolitan Police in the last two minutes: 'At approximately ten to nine this morning, police were called to Aldgate station to assist the City of London Police and British Transport Police regarding an incident on the underground system.'

Wilson reported a major incident, and that it was too early to say what had happened. Across London there were further reports of multiple explosions. Police were responding to reports from Edgware Road, King's Cross, Liverpool Street, Russell Square, Aldgate East and Moorgate underground stations. Added to this there were confirmed explosions on a bus at Tavistock Place: 'There have been reports of numerous casualties, but again it is too early to say the numbers at this stage.'

Everybody knows these places. Even if you're not a Londoner, the story's made for radio because you don't necessarily need the pictures, because everybody's got a Monopoly board.

Gaunt: 'And every word you've said there was official from the Metropolitan Police?'

Wilson confirmed it was and said it was worth calling loved ones to say you're safe.

Gaunt: 'I've just tried to phone my wife but a lot of the mobile systems are down . . . please keep the phone lines free, please only ring us if you've got something you can tell us. Let's go straight now to Martin Edwards, who's at Royal London Hospital in Whitechapel. Good morning, Martin, what can you tell us?'

Reporter Edwards said the A and E entrance was closed to the public, there were walking wounded, people on stretchers, and an air ambulance on the scene.

The 10.30 headlines reported explosions in multiple locations: five tube stations and a bus in Tavistock Square.

The travel report said the tube network was closed, trains to King's Cross and Paddington were diverted, and there were road closures, including the Aldgate one-way system.

Off the back of the travel report, Robyn, a witness in Belsize Park, said she saw the bus in Tavistock Square and heard the explosion. There were people running, a number of wounded people. She'd heard on the radio they thought there had been a bomb at Euston station: 'It was a fairly large shock then, to see the bus explode right in front of me.'

Gaunt: 'Hold on. You actually saw the bus explode?'

Robyn: 'That's right.'

Gaunt: 'This is awful to ask you this. Tell me what you saw.'

You have to ask these questions. They'll speak to me because they trust me. People will say things on the phone that they won't say by the time you've got your microphone or your television cameras there.

Robyn: 'Sitting in the car and, of course, the debris of the bus raining down on to the car I was sitting in. I had my 15-month-old daughter sitting with me so of course my first response is to try to . . . cover her and of course praying that nothing's going to seriously damage the car that we're in. Then of course seeing the people in the road and . . . quite a bit of carnage, I suppose, and blood.'

Gaunt: 'How far away were you from it, Robyn?'

Robyn: 'Perhaps a block, if that. There were three or four cars between us and the bus . . .'

Gaunt: 'How's the child?'

Robyn: 'She was, of course, extremely frightened by the explosion, but of course didn't understand anything else that was happening, so . . . she's fine and I'm fine, and we're just, I suppose, in a state of shock.'

Gaunt: 'Of course, Robyn, to be straight, we all are this morning.'

She was great. She ended up on every news broadcast. It's an iconic image. I think in pictures so I could see it all. The explosion on the bus, the mother protecting her baby, and I thought of my kids. I suppose, to be cynical, I was playing the family man card, but somebody who doesn't have kids might not have asked that question.

The broadcast continued with Shep, another cabbie ('It's absolute mayhem here, mate . . . we've just been told there's another two buses blown up'); more eyewitnesses ('they said it was a power surge but a power surge can't do that to a train' . . . 'there were dead bodies on the track'); mobile phone networks jammed; and police and government statements.

Gaunt appealed for video phone footage for 'our TV station', but asked people to avoid the jammed mobile networks and use a landline if possible.

One text message read: 'I've got no words, I'm just crying.'

At 11.39, Gaunt read out internal wire copy: the BBC Security Correspondent Frank Gardner was reporting the explosions had 'all the hallmarks of a planned Al Qaeda attack'.

To be honest, you're thinking, This Is It. A bomb has gone off on my watch. It's the doctor whacking the electrodes on the chest in casualty. This is it. I said let's not speculate, and I knew what LBC would be doing, and I wanted to make our coverage distinctive. A lot of the people on our programme were young kids, and they'd never done a proper story. And a lot of them grew up that day.

As the enormity of the events became clearer, Gaunt's programme was carried across much of the BBC local radio network on 7 July 2005. Gaunt left the BBC soon afterwards to become a columnist for the *Sun* newspaper. The corporation decided his column, with its outspoken and controversial opinions, was inconsistent with working as a BBC broadcaster. He remained in demand as a TV and radio pundit (including contributions to BBC stations), and returned as a radio presenter on the independent station Talksport.

TIP BOX

Jon Gaunt's experience on 7 July highlighted a number of important working practices for broadcasters on live radio.

- You don't have to speculate. Powerful news radio can work without broadcasters or 'experts' speculating.

- Work as a team and put your trust in your team, but when you are on air, yours is the final voice, the final responsibility for the output.

- Somebody has to take control. It can be the producer in the cubicle or it can be the presenter. But you need to know who's in charge. You can't have too many chiefs.

- Be natural and be yourself. Gaunt has a reputation as an acerbic, opinionated phone-in host and commentator, but his professional range included the ability to respond on a human level to events, and to take responsibility for not spreading panic.

- Keep calm and keep a clear head. Think how the story could develop and prepare for those developments.

PROGRAMME PRODUCTION IN TV AND RADIO

Scripts and running orders

Every live programme has a script and a *running order*, sometimes known as a *run-down*. The programme goes on air with the production team knowing what to expect. But the thrill of working on news programmes, and the reason most broadcast journalists prefer it to any other form of programme making, is that running orders and scripts will change while you are preparing them, and also while you are on air.

Late news stories appear on the wire services, reporters in the field relay new developments, live interviews overrun, satellite links go down, juries return verdicts, Parliament votes on important legislation, sports results come through. Suddenly the running order you started with is redundant. Then the fun begins.

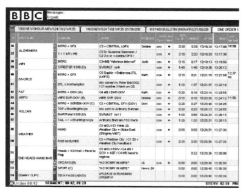

A running order in ENPS, the news production system

But programme staff need to go on air with an expectation of what the programme will contain. A producer needs to organise the range of technical resources and the teams of technical and journalistic staff that contribute to modern news output. The running order is the way to do that, even though it may end up as little more than a rough template for what follows.

Radio bulletins

Every station will have its own style guide for bulletins. Many local stations will insist on at least two local stories in the top three. The preferred style may be for a headline sequence followed by a sequence of stories. Or it may be a straight read without headlines.

The content should be flexible. At a time of international crisis, it's not appropriate to stick to 'two local stories out of three'. Normally, the newsreader is the final arbiter of content. The reader drops or adds stories on air to fill to time. On bigger stations or for longer bulletins, the producer will make decisions about content.

A CLOSER LOOK

ELEMENTS OF A RADIO BULLETIN

A radio bulletin will consist of a combination of the following elements.

Headlines	A series of phrases or sentences summarising the main stories of the bulletin. They may include audio clips.
Copy stories	Stories read by the presenter without audio. Usually no more than 20 seconds long.
Voicers	A reporter's voice report, introduced by a cue from the presenter. Voicers can be live or recorded and may be from a location or the studio.
Wraps	A voice report with one or more short clips of audio, usually from interviews. Introduced by the presenter's cue.
Packages	More complex features, with several clips of audio, possibly including interviews, actuality and/or location commentary, and music. Also introduced by the presenter's cue.
Clips	Audio introduced by the presenter. Usually soundbites from longer interviews. Sometimes called 'grabs'.
Vox pops	A series of tightly edited comments from members of the public. Introduced by the presenter as a stand-alone feature, or used as part of a package.
Two-ways	Question-and-answer sessions, live or recorded, with a reporter or correspondent who's covering a story, either in the studio or down-the-line from a location.

Interviews	Rare in short bulletins, but occasionally a presenter will interview someone in the news.
Weather	Usually in copy form, for use at the end of the bulletin. Weather reports can be flexible in length, so that you can finish the bulletin exactly on time. Write the weather so the first few seconds make perfect sense on their own (*and the weather, it'll be mostly cloudy with sunny spells*). You can then add subsequent sentences to fill to the end of the bulletin.

The content of every bulletin should be varied. The treatment of the lead story, unless it is very recent breaking news, will always include audio, whether it is a voicer, wrap or clip. There should be a variety of treatments available for bigger stories, so that, even if there is no new development, the lead can sound different in successive bulletins. The first version might be a voicer; the second could include an interview clip; the third might be a wrap incorporating elements of both.

Each story should be clearly marked with a catchline (a title for the story, also known as a *slug*), the duration of the cue, the duration of any audio and the out words (the last words) of any audio. On news production systems, such as ENPS or Burli, the length of the cues will be calculated automatically, and the information about the audio can be added by the journalist responsible.

Some news editors will prefer that a voicer is not followed by another voicer, and that one cue and clip is not followed by another cue and clip. A well-crafted bulletin may follow these guidelines, but it is more important to present the stories in the right order according to your news judgement. Listeners are more interested in the stories than the treatment.

Wherever you work, stick to the rules. But the newsreader who uses their experience to improve the bulletin, by making editorial decisions on air, will rarely be criticised.

Levels

The PPM – always check your levels

All items in the bulletin should be at the same level. The newsreader should be as loud as the voice reports and interview clips.

Output is usually shown on PPMs (peak programme meters), a semi-circular dial registering the peak volumes of the output. You should aim for speech to register between 5 and 6 on the scale. Music, which has a wider dynamic range, and so is easier to hear, should register between 4 and 5. Avoid dropping below 4, because that will be too quiet for many people listening at home. Any speech or music much above 6 will be too loud for the listener and may even distort (this is known as over-modulating or 'over-modding'). The exception is telephone quality voice – which you'll use a lot of on local radio bulletins.

Boost the volume on telephone speech (to over 6 on the scale) to compensate for the poor dynamic range of the audio.

Some digital desks have a series of LEDs (light emitting diodes) that flash green for acceptable levels and red for over-modding.

Equalisation

Equalisation (or EQ) controls on a radio desk change the frequency range of the output, just like a graphic equaliser on a home stereo. You only need to alter the EQ response of a channel if the audio you are playing out is too tinny or sounds muffled. Increase the bass response for something that sounds tinny or too bright; increase the treble for muffled or 'boomy' sound.

Remember

- Vary the content of bulletins
- On a local station, ensure local stories are near the top
- Mark your stories clearly with a catchline and timings
- Monitor the sound quality (levels and EQ)

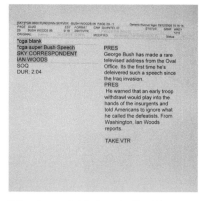

TV scripts – divided vertically with technical information to the left and script to the right

TV PROGRAMMES

Scripts

The key to a smooth-running TV programme is teamwork. Working as a team means communication between team members, so that everyone knows what is going on and what part they play in the programme. The information on the programme script is part of that communication.

TV scripts will be divided vertically, so that technical information is available alongside the newsreader or reporter's words. At a glance everyone in the production team can see who is on screen and on which camera or outside broadcast, when VT or graphics should be played in, and the duration and out words of each item.

TIP BOX

TEN-MINUTE TV NEWS BULLETIN – PROGRAMME TEMPLATE

Here's a suggested running order for a TV bulletin in a simple three-camera studio, with two presenters, one for news and another for sport.

Picture and sound sources are listed alongside the content, and the duration, of each section of the programme. Once you've decided on your content, the full script will have a separate page for each story, clearly numbered with a catchline at the top. Camera one is pointing at the main presenter; camera two is a two-shot; and camera three is a shot of the separate sports presenter.

This template has been used by student broadcast journalists as a starting point for bulletins on 'newsdays' when they replicate newsroom practice. By the end of the day, it will almost certainly have changed considerably.

	Technical Information – Camera/VT/sound	Content	Dur:
1	VT	Titles	15
2	Camera 1 + studio sound	Hello	5
3	VT + studio sound	Headlines	15
4	Cam 1 + studio sound	Lead intro	20
5	VT	Lead package	1 min
6	Cam 1 + studio sound	News Copy	15
7	Cam 1 + studio sound VT	News Copy + OOV	20
8	Cam 1 + studio sound	News Copy	15
9	Cam 1 + studio sound	Package One intro	15
10	VT	Package One	1 min
11	Cam 1 + studio sound VT	Short story + OOV	20
12	Cam 1 + studio sound VT	Wipe story + OOV	20
13	Cam 1 + studio sound VT	Wipe story + OOV	20
14	Cam 1 + studio sound	Package Two intro	15
15	VT	Package Two	1 min
16	Cam 2 + studio sound	Link to Sport	10
17	Cam 3 + studio sound VT	Sport One + OOV	30
18	Cam 3 + studio sound VT	Sport Two + OOV	20
19	Cam 3 + studio sound	Sport Three copy	15
20	Cam 3 + studio sound VT	Sport Four + OOV	20
21	Cam 2 + studio sound	Handback	10
22	Cam 1 + studio sound	Weather link	10
23	GFX + studio sound	Weather	40
24	Cam 1 + studio sound	Finally link	10
25	VT	Finally	1 min
26	Cam 2 + studio sound	Goodbye	10

Durations and out-words

Every link or cue must contain information about the audio or video that follows. The most important technical details for the gallery or control room are the length of the piece – its duration – and the final words of audio – the out-words. These are the cue for the next item in the running order. Directors, vision mixers, sound mixers and presenters await those cues. The information must be accurate if the programme is to run smoothly.

Durations – to the exact second – are easily noted. Stopwatches used to be a common tool in newsrooms. Today's digital editing systems tell you the length of a piece without having to time it for yourself. But it will be the reporter's job to tell the rest of the production team. If scripts have already been prepared as a deadline approaches, typing the duration into the newsroom computer system may not be enough. There may not be time to distribute revised scripts to the gallery and studio. Someone has to make sure people are told.

The out-words are usually the last three words of a script or interview. If a news organisation has a style which involves reporters signing off with a standard out cue (SOC) – for example: 'John Simpson, BBC News, Kabul' – then the letters SOC may appear on the script. Sometimes the 'out' is a repeat of words that have been heard only a few seconds earlier, so it is a good idea to make that clear. For example, if there is an interview clip in which someone repeats the phrase 'in my opinion', and those are also the out-words, then the script should read OUT: 'in my opinion' (second time). If the final audio in a piece is not words at all, but actuality or music, then that should be noted on the script, e.g. OUT: music fades.

Remember

- Communication and teamwork are the key to smooth-running programmes
- A running order is your programme template
- The running order should change in response to events
- Mark your scripts clearly with technical information (the source of the VT or graphic, duration and out-words)

CONCLUSION – THE FUTURE OF NEWS PROGRAMMING

So what is the future of news programming as we have come to know it? Industry professionals we have spoken to agree there is a need to embrace change and new ways of delivering news. But the consensus appears to be that we are in a period of evolution, not revolution. The Internet has changed global communications, but core journalistic skills remain.

Kevin Bakhurst, Controller of the BBC News Channel, predicted, shortly after taking the job in 2005, that the traditional bulletins had a healthy mid-term future (he'd been editor of the *Ten O'Clock News*) but change was likely to be significant over the next five years: 'The audience is already shifting to some extent. As audiences become more sophisticated, as the rollout of digital and Freeview continues, the News 24 [BBC News] channel is going to be a more and more important proposition for the BBC.'

He was right about the trend if not the timescale. The BBC iPlayer – allowing people to view programmes at any time – appears to have prolonged the life of the conventional bulletin.

Nick Higham, a long-serving Media Correspondent at the BBC, says we have to accept continuing change. We are not moving from a stable past to a stable future. 'Transition is the stable state.' Here's his assessment of the state we have reached.

'The audience or a section of it is getting its news from a much wider range of sources – especially electronic. We know that newspapers are in long-term decline. We know that people increasingly want and can get news updates on the move from mobile phones, and we know that the audience for conventional news programmes on television is declining, along with the audience for the channels on which those programmes appear, BBC1 and ITV, and we know that, although these things have made something of an impact, the combined audience for [news channels] is still not that great, so there is, you could argue, a kind of looming crisis for television news as a whole.

'I don't see any other way of dealing with that than confronting it and continuously trying to reinvent ourselves. The BBC has always been, institutionally, very good at reinventing itself. It sometimes takes an outside stimulus. If you go back to the 1950s, the BBC was dreadfully set in its ways and was given a huge kick up the arse by ITV, and responded in a dramatic and remarkable way. More recently the BBC has been very good at responding to changing audience behaviours and changing technologies. Our position online is extremely strong as a result of being early movers and doing it well. So, news has got to find ways of re-presenting itself, reconfiguring itself, redefining itself in ways that are going to be meaningful to people who have new and different technologies.

'There are two reservations. The audience itself does not move into the new technologies consistently. There are still very large numbers of people, particularly older people, who don't want and are not interested in all these new technologies. And the other problem you have is that the pressure of doing news in new ways on new technologies – the competition that is implied in all that, because lots of other people are doing this – all of that means a danger that you do things differently not merely in a cosmetic way, but in a fundamental way. And if you're the BBC that's a problem, because you undermine the brand and the promise and the service that we traditionally deliver.

'If you're not careful, you forget that our position in the marketplace is that we're trustworthy, in broad terms, and we mustn't forget that because we're trying to provide a new service for mobile phones.'

Nick Higham's view is that the democratisation of the media – the fact that anyone can get access to the Internet – strengthens the position of journalists, particularly with organisations – such as the BBC – that have a reputation for trustworthiness.

'Our stuff's reliable, so if you want to know, reliably, what is going on, if you want an authoritative statement, then the BBC is the place to go – and news organisations like that – because, although there is all this stuff around, and a lot of it may be very current and very new, judging its accuracy is a problem. The Internet is a huge great rumour factory, and it produces all kinds of fascinating stuff, but can you believe it? You've no way of knowing what you can believe and what you can't believe. Our job is to say: "This much we know and you can believe this much." If you then want to go off and swap gossip with someone online or blog or whatever, that's fine, but bear in mind that what you're seeing there may not be reliable. It may be hearsay. It may be half-truth. So there's a very important role for us, for the BBC and for other news organisations which have built their promise to the audience and promise to the readership on trustworthiness and reliability.'

He says there is a potential mismatch when news providers offer a forum for hosting blogs. There needs to be a clear separation between an authoritative news station and something that provides a forum for comment and exchange of views – just as there is on radio between a news bulletin and a phone-in.

This debate is at the heart of the future of broadcast journalism. Journalists are certainly all content providers in a converged multimedia age. It doesn't follow that all content providers are journalists. They never have been, and it is unlikely they ever will be.

There is a clear technological argument that anyone with access to the means of distributing media is in the same position as a traditional broadcaster. That is not the same as being able to command an audience and earning the trust of viewers and listeners.

Journalists have become used to dealing with new technologies, and learning new software. Nick Higham's argument that 'the stable state is change' is a compelling one for anyone operating in a modern newsroom. But the key skills of authoritative story telling within a legal and ethical framework are a constant.

Remember

- Journalists have to be jacks-of-all-trades, and masters of *some*
- Content is king

PARTTWO THE ESSENTIAL GUIDE

GETTING A JOB

THE JOB APPLICATION

Typically there are two ways of applying for jobs in broadcast journalism – a letter or email accompanied by a CV (curriculum vitae) and possibly a showreel, or an online application form.

You can prepare a letter, CV and showreel that would fit any job. But that is not the best way. Your application should be tailored to the job you are applying for. The biggest sin in any application is to show no knowledge of the organisation to which you are applying and its output. You are unlikely to be invited to an interview.

Online applications are tougher, because you have to fill in all your details, including all the tiresome stuff you repeat every time about your education, qualifications and experience. This is a chore, but it helps you focus. Include only the details that are relevant to the job and will make a positive impression. Most online forms (such as the ones used by the BBC) allow you to store the information and go back to it later. Don't rush. Fill in the basics, then return to the form when you have given serious consideration to the parts where you write creatively about yourself and the job.

If you are applying for a job in journalism, there is no excuse for an application with spelling or grammatical mistakes.

Use of language is a core journalistic skill, so many employers will use any spelling mistake or grammatical error as a reason for rejecting an application. It's an easy and sensible way to reduce the number of applications.

BBC presenter Huw Edwards, who looks at a lot of job application forms, says:

'I really am quite hardline about it. If somebody can't be bothered to get their stuff up to scratch if they're applying for a job, you just think, well, do I really want to take this on? You may be dealing with somebody who's got a really good aptitude, a really good journalistic approach, but the fact is they will be really badly let down by how they present themselves on paper. It's what the job's about.

'If you can produce good writing, you will stand out from the crowd and you are going to advance more quickly than other people.'

THE COVERING LETTER

Your covering letter, which may be an email, should also be concise – rarely more than a page, grammatically accurate and with correct spellings. One journalism student had an offer of a work placement withdrawn because she made a spelling mistake in her email accepting the offer. Imagine how much more important it is to be accurate in a job application.

It is fundamental that you spell the names and titles of people in the organisation you are applying to correctly.

Your letter should focus on why you are suitable for the job in question. Try to avoid clichés such as 'I am an enthusiastic, hard-working team player'. It's better to give brief examples of why you are a special candidate.

- Ask other people to describe your best qualities – it's better than trying to describe yourself.
- Have you achieved something of which you are particularly proud?
- Did you lead a team to success?
- Have you produced an original piece of journalism?
- Can you find a story?
- Do you write a blog with journalistic content?
- Have you been involved in a successful broadcast or website?

THE CV

When you apply for a job, you will include your CV, whether it's a printed document or something you do online. So how do you prepare a CV for maximum impact?

You need to keep it brief and to the point. Few editors will want to look at more than one or two pages. You will find CV templates in most word-processing packages. There is nothing wrong with these. It's how you fill them in that matters. Don't use fancy fonts. They are distracting and difficult to read.

A CV for a job in journalism should:

- be concise – most jobs in journalism are hugely oversubscribed, so editors faced with hundreds of applications will not be impressed by anything over two pages;
- emphasise your *relevant* experience – three weeks in a local radio station, even if it was unpaid, will carry more weight than two years' part-time work on a supermarket checkout;
- stress your key skills – any technical skills (camerawork, editing, software skills, shorthand) and legal training (the NCTJ law exam, for example) should be listed;
- include contributions to any broadcast or journalistic output – including hospital radio, student radio, websites and local newspapers – must be included.

Never lie on a CV. You will be found out. Maybe not the first time, but eventually. It may be on an application for your dream job that your lies are discovered.

Simon Cole, Deputy Head of Sky News, is looking for that extra something – but admits it boils down to a subjective decision:

'These days media courses, I think, are totally oversubscribed and what you get is a whole raft of really bright youngsters – they've all done a gap year, they've all done good works abroad, they've all done something interesting. They've done a postgrad, or a journalism degree, they've had work experience at CNN or the Beeb, or whatever – they've done a movie which is on DVD and all nicely set out for you, and they are all absolutely bloody fantastic – and so you think: how do I choose?

'And what it boils down to, to me, is – if you're sitting there – whether I like you or not. Whether I think you've got some character; whether you're going to have development potential to be whatever; whether you're a news editor or a reporter – because everyone wants to be a reporter, don't they? We all did – but these days the competition is so fierce, they've got to have something a bit different on the CV to get into my door and then they've got to sit on the couch and I've got to like them.

'For example, one person was very clever and they'd done some homework, and they'd heard that I'd got fridge magnets and so they brought in a fridge magnet that plays a tune.

That person didn't get a job, but they got a second interview. You've almost got to use a gimmick – you've got to be a salesman or a saleswoman because what you are selling is yourself. It's not a car; it's not a Ducati motorbike; it's not a Fender Stratocaster – it's yourself. This is your big chance because if you get a job at Sky, you've made it. Whether you stay with the company, or whether you move, you're going to have that on your CV and you are in the business.'

Remember

- Correct spelling and grammar are essential in a job application
- Keep your CV concise, with relevant experience near the top
- Know the output of the organisation
- Never lie

SHOWREELS

A good showreel – an edit of highlights of your best work – can be the difference between getting an interview and not. It can also be the difference between getting the job and not, even if you do not perform your best at interview.

It's best to make a showreel that's geared to the job for which you are applying.

Here's an unfortunate fact – most showreels are not viewed beyond the first minute. So, give the first minute the most attention. A montage of pieces-to-camera (stand-ups) or studio presentation is a good idea. Try to make it entertaining and varied, with a mix of hard and light stories. It lets the prospective employer know how you perform on screen. They can judge your voice, presence and whether the camera likes you. TV professionals talk about the 'magic box'. Some people who are attractive in real life do not necessarily look good in two dimensions. Others, who are not conventionally good looking, come across as strong and engaging personalities on screen.

After the montage, you should include a full-length package or two, so the employer can consider your writing skills, and use of pictures and sound. They will be asking if you can write to pictures, and tell a story.

You may want to include a hard news story, and a lighter piece. Don't make it longer than ten minutes and five will usually be enough.

A DVD presentation with a title page giving choices of shorter or longer content can help. Or you can do it online. Put a hyperlink or web address in your covering letter. You could host the showreel on your own website or post it on YouTube or a similar site. Having your own site is a good idea and shows professional commitment – as long as it showcases your journalism and isn't an extension of your social life. You won't want a prospective employer viewing your holiday photos or worse. Be wary too of what you put on social networks if it can be viewed by anyone, including a future boss.

A showreel tailored to a particular job description may take time, but it's worth the effort. Even if it doesn't get you this job it can be adapted for similar openings in future. Freelances looking to increase their portfolio of employers apply the same principle.

- If it's a reporter job, show your best reporting and any exclusive stories
- If the job is for a presenter, show your best studio work
- If you are applying to be a producer, include stories that show imaginative production techniques – graphics, perhaps, or visual metaphors.

Don't worry if all you have is student work. Professionals looking for someone suitable for a first job will recognise talent, even if the production values are not quite up to broadcast standard.

For a radio job, an MP3 or wav file attached to your email, a web link or a good old-fashioned CD does the same job as a showreel, and the same rules apply. Start with impact, then give examples of bulletin reading and crafted packages. Many broadcast journalism students will return from work placements in local radio with examples of their broadcasting skills, either off air or recorded as a demo in the studio.

Remember

- Keep a showreel brief
- Make it entertaining and varied
- Most editors only view or listen to the first minute
- Tailor your showreel to the job description

THE INTERVIEW

There are books and websites devoted to job interview techniques. They'll tell you about dressing well, making a good first impression and showing confidence.

But what are the questions interviewers ask when they are appointing people to jobs in broadcast journalism? They can be divided into four broad categories:

1 awareness of our output
2 story ideas
3 treatment
4 knowledge of broadcast law and ethics.

Awareness of output

Interviewers will want to know you have listened to or watched enough of their output to judge the content, treatment of stories and how it compares with the opposition. It is never good enough to claim a vague knowledge of what the broadcaster does. There is no excuse for not having heard or seen the latest bulletin. Listen in the car or on the train on the way to a radio interview. Watch on satellite or online if you don't live in the region where the TV station broadcasts.

If you're asked your opinion about the output, you should err on the side of enthusiasm. Otherwise, why do you want to work there? But it's rarely a good idea to offer uncritical praise. You might sound too desperate. Constructive criticism is usually the best course, focusing on story treatments rather than personalities.

Story ideas

You should enter any journalism interview with at least three story ideas. There is no excuse for not having knowledge of the station's transmission area. It's easy enough to research online. And better still, if you can find local contacts, call them and ask what's going on. Don't just think about blockbuster exclusives – you'll be lucky to find those. Think about areas of local activity that are under-reported. Ask community leaders what they think is missing in local coverage. Then ask for contact details of people you can use in your treatment of the story.

Treat stories you want to use at interview in the same way as stories you are researching in the newsroom. An interview panel will be impressed by comprehensive research.

Treatment

The treatment of stories can be as important as the story idea itself. Interviewers may ask you how you would treat themes, trends and issues in the news – or how you would deal with it on different platforms.

Personalising a story is always a good idea – find somebody affected by the issue. Reeling off a list of potential interviewees is not so good. Your idea has to be achievable within the organisation's deadlines and budgets.

You should also be aware of forthcoming stories in the diary and how you would deal with them.

Law and ethics

Most interview panels (at the BBC they're known as 'boards') will want to know you can operate within legal and ethical guidelines. Study the Ofcom Code and BBC Editorial Guidelines. Make sure you know about defamation and contempt of court. An employer does not want the nagging doubt that the person they have appointed could land them in legal trouble.

For more on journalistic ethics and the regulatory framework, read Chris Frost's book *Journalism Ethics and Regulation*, published by Pearson. It should help you answer the tricky ethical questions that interviewers love to ask.

Interview exercises

Many selection processes will include group exercises. These are designed to assess your leadership, teamwork and problem-solving qualities.

There may be personal tests too. It might be a live two-way exercise, in which you are briefed on a story and then expected to deliver a 'live' report. Or it may be a reporting exercise. A favourite on BBC reporter interviews has been to send people out with a digital recorder and expect them to come back with a story. A tip – if you are sent into an unfamiliar town to find a story, look for a market. Market traders and their customers often have extraordinary stories to tell.

Using notes

There is nothing to stop you taking notes into a job interview as a prompt in case you forget the points you wanted to make. It's always worth jotting down three or four main points you want to get across, no matter what you are asked. The main points should be about your personal qualities and how they will fit into the job description. You don't have to look at the notes, but they can be a confidence booster and help prevent you drying up.

Dummy interviews

Before an important job interview, you would probably like some sort of rehearsal. Try to get a couple of people with experience of interviewing for journalism jobs to form a mock panel. Journalism tutors, or people you know from work experience, are the best option.

They should enter into role play and assume they have not met you before. After the interview, they should give you honest feedback. We regularly carry out these mock interviews, and students have benefited by getting the job.

Remember

- Know the organisation's output
- Prepare story ideas and treatments
- Take brief notes into the interview if it boosts your confidence
- Set up a dummy interview
- You can never prepare too much for an interview – more knowledge gives you more confidence

WEB LINKS

www.bbc.co.uk/journalism includes a 'tips for landing a job' section.

THE LAW AND BROADCAST JOURNALISTS

Broadcast journalists operate within a legal framework, regulated by the statutory bodies that govern broadcasting (in the UK, Ofcom) and the laws of the land (which differ in Scotland from the rest of the UK).

This is a guide to the areas of law and court practice of which journalists have to be aware. It is not a substitute for the law modules run within accredited broadcast journalism courses, or the information found in specialist books (*McNae's Essential Law for Journalists*, a core text, runs to over 500 pages).

Law comes from a variety of sources:

- custom – established practice (known as common law)
- precedent – the application of earlier decisions to a current case (case law)
- statute – Acts of Parliament (statutory instruments)
- European Union regulations
- the European Convention on Human Rights

In Scotland, there are also 'writers', institutional texts from respected writers on Scots law, mostly from the seventeenth, eighteenth and nineteenth centuries. Equity, the concept of natural justice and fairness, informs all the UK's legal systems.

DEFAMATION

Defamation is probably the biggest risk faced by working journalists. Whenever you write about someone, there is a danger you will damage their reputation, sometimes unwittingly. A spoken defamatory statement is slander, except where it is spoken in a broadcast (or in a public performance of a play). Then it has the same status as a statement in print and is defined as libel.

Civil actions for libel in pursuit of damages may be taken out against a broadcaster by anyone who considers they have been defamed. There is also, much more rarely, a risk of criminal libel, where the publication might lead to a breach of the peace.

Juries have to decide if reasonable men and women would consider a statement defamatory. Does it:

1 expose the person to hatred, ridicule or contempt?
2 cause him (or her) to be shunned or avoided?
3 lower him in the estimation of right-thinking members of society generally? *Or*
4 disparage him in his business, trade or profession?

A corporation (usually a business whose trading reputation has been damaged) can sue for libel, but most frequently actions are taken by individuals. A claimant has to prove the statement is defamatory, that it refers to him and that it has been published to a third party. He does not have to prove the statement is false. It is up to the defendant (the journalist) to prove it is true, or offer another defence.

Defences against libel

Knowing the defences available in a defamation case helps you decide what can and cannot be broadcast. The defences are:

- **Justification** – meaning that the words complained of are true. This is a difficult defence to sustain because you have to be able to prove facts are true. Unless you have proof to hand when you broadcast, this can involve a costly investigation to collect evidence. (The *Guardian* newspaper's investigation to successfully defend a libel action by the former Cabinet minister Jonathan Aitken took four years.)

  You also have to be able to prove not only the literal truth of a statement but also any inference or innuendo behind the words. For example, calling somebody 'a thief' might imply somebody is an habitual thief. If the claimant had a conviction for shoplifting the words would be literally true, but the defence might fail if it were proved the offence was a one-off lapse by an otherwise honest person. Sticking to a defence of justification and failing can result in the courts imposing higher penalties.

  Under section 5 of the 1952 Defamation Act, it is not necessary to prove every fact in a defamatory report. The Act says: 'a defence of justification shall not fail by reason only that the truth of every charge is not proved, if the words not proved to be true do not materially injure the claimant's reputation'.

  The exceptions to truth being a defence in a libel action are references to convictions covered by the Rehabilitation of Offenders Act 1974. It allows people with minor convictions (anything less than two-and-a-half years in prison) to live down their past. So, after ten years, sentences between six months and two-and-a-half years become 'spent' and cannot be referred to. A sentence of less than six months (or dismissal from the armed services) is spent after seven years, and a fine or other sentence is spent after five years. These periods are halved for offenders under 18.

- **Fair comment** – means comment made honestly on a matter of public interest. The comment has to be based on provable facts, or on privileged material.

- **Privilege** – usually laid out in Acts of Parliament – is a legal understanding that in some instances freedom of speech is more important than protection against defamation and untruths. Courts are covered by Absolute Privilege; a fair and accurate, contemporaneous report of proceedings in open court will not be the subject of a successful libel action. This is so that the media can report the often highly defamatory content of court cases. The law applies to UK courts, and to the European Courts of Justice and Human Rights and international criminal tribunals established by the Security Council of the United Nations or by an international agreement to which the UK is party.

  Qualified Privilege is a more limited defence, but applies to more than just courts. Qualified Privilege covers a wide range of matters of public concern, provided they are published or broadcast without malice (i.e., ill will, spite or an improper motive). It applies to reports of legislative bodies, courts, public inquiries and meetings of international organisations anywhere in the world, and to extracts from their official publications.

  Some statements only have Qualified Privilege 'subject to explanation or contradiction'. In other words, if a defamatory statement has been broadcast, 'a reasonable letter or statement by way of explanation or contradiction' must also be broadcast. This condition covers notices issued for the information of the public by a legislature in any member state of the European Parliament, by the government of any member state and by any authority performing governmental functions. This last category includes the police, so official police statements are covered by Qualified Privilege. Statements that are privileged subject to explanation also include reports of the meetings of local authorities, statutory tribunals, public companies in the UK (including documents circulated to their members) and also 'public meetings'.

A 'public meeting' is defined as 'a meeting bona fide and lawfully held for a lawful purpose and for the furtherance or discussion of a matter of public concern, whether admission to the meeting is general or restricted'. *So, a public meeting does not have to be open to all of the public.* The full list of statements covered by Qualified Privilege is contained in the Schedule to the Defamation Act 1996.

Another public interest defence is the Reynolds Defence, which recognises for the first time in law the importance of matters of public interest being broadcast, whether or not they can be proved to be true. It arises from a 1998 case when the former Irish Prime Minister, Albert Reynolds, sued the *Sunday Times* over allegations that he misled the Irish Parliament. The newspaper lost, because they'd failed to represent Reynolds' side of the story properly. The Reynolds Defence relies on a series of tests, which challenge the rigour of the journalistic process, including the reliability of sources, the steps taken to verify the information and whether comment was sought from the claimant.

- Accord and satisfaction – is a plea that the matter has already been dealt with, by the broadcast of a correction or apology, for example, which has been accepted by the claimant. If the claimant does not accept an apology, publishing a correction *may* make matters worse because it acknowledges a mistake was made. A broadcaster may make a payment into court – a sum of money the claimant can accept instead of pursuing the action. If the eventual damages prove to be less than or the same as the amount paid into court, the claimant will usually be expected to pay both sides' costs in the case.
- Offer of amends – is a written offer to pay damages and make a suitable apology and correction. This defence can only be used where someone has been accidentally defamed. If it is rejected it is up to the claimant to prove the defamation was not 'innocent'.

COURT REPORTING

It is a general principle of the law that courts should administer justice in public. There are exceptions, including matters of national security and where the welfare of children is concerned. Usually, though, the press are admitted to courts. But that does not mean you can report everything that is said. It is important to understand the functions of different courts and the restrictions on reporting from them.

Civil courts deal with the rights and duties of individuals towards each other. In a civil case a claimant sues a defendant who might be held liable. The civil courts include tribunals, and county and High Courts.

Criminal law deals with crimes against the state. A defendant is prosecuted by the state and will be found guilty or not guilty. In Scotland (where the law developed separately prior to the Act of Union in 1707 and has continued to be separate), a third verdict of 'not proven' is available. The state enforces law and order through the magistrates' courts, youth courts, and crown courts in England, Wales and Northern Ireland. In Scotland, the courts are the district court (presided over by a Justice of the Peace or magistrate), the sheriff court and the High Court of Justiciary.

The decisions of the lower courts can be overruled or reversed by the Court of Appeal, and after that the Supreme Court.

Courts can refer cases to the European Court of Justice, although this is not a formal stage in the appeal procedure. The European Court of Human Rights in Strasbourg hears allegations of breaches of the European Convention on Human Rights. The convention is incorporated into British law under the Human Rights Act 1998. Of particular importance to journalists are Article 10, Freedom of Expression, and Article 8, the Right to Respect for Privacy.

Since the Human Rights Act came into force in 2000, the extent of the right to privacy has been further defined in case law. It is now clear that a public place can be considered private if someone is there with a 'reasonable expectation of privacy'. This impacts on your ability to film public figures – unless you have a strong public interest justification and even that may not stand up in court.

Another legal trend involving privacy emerged in 2011 with celebrities taking out so-called superinjunctions to prevent stories about them being reported. These injunctions not only banned the reporting, but also banned mention of the injunctions themselves. A campaign on Twitter undermined the anonymity of the celebrities involved but the law remains in force.

Ninety-seven per cent of criminal cases are heard by magistrates (also known as Justices of the Peace or JPs). They do not have to be legally qualified. The maximum sentence they can give is 12 months in prison for a single offence or a fine of £5000, except in cases of customs and tax evasion. Sentences can be suspended for a length of time – the guilty party does not have to go to prison unless they re-offend within that time. It is wrong to say someone given a suspended sentence has been jailed.

Outside Scotland, there are three types of criminal offence:

1 those which can be tried only on indictment at crown court (e.g. serious offences such as murder, rape and robbery);
2 'either-way' cases which can be tried at crown or magistrates' court (e.g. theft, indecent assault);
3 summary offences (including motoring offences and drunkenness) which are usually only tried by magistrates.

The Crown Prosecution Service (CPS), not the police, is responsible for criminal prosecutions in England, Wales and Northern Ireland. In Scotland, the Crown Office and the Procurator Fiscal Service perform the same function (the Lord Advocate or an Advocate Depute presents the case in the High Court against the accused). Lawyers can represent people in court. Solicitors deal with members of the public and brief barristers ('advocates' in Scotland). Solicitors serve as advocates in the lower courts and in some higher court cases, but usually they 'solicit' the services of a barrister to put the case in higher courts.

Magistrates can send people to the crown court for sentencing if they think their own powers of sentencing are not harsh enough. They also commit people on serious offences for trial at the crown court.

There are restrictions on reporting committal proceedings, to prevent a potential juror being influenced. The Magistrates Court Act 1980 limits reports of preliminary hearings on offences triable by jury to 10 points, which include a summary of the offences and the names, ages and addresses of the accused and witnesses, but no details of the alleged crime beyond what is on the charge sheet. In Scotland there are no committal proceedings, but once a person has appeared before a sheriff on petition for judicial examination, they cannot be detained for longer than 110 days or, if given bail, they must be tried within 12 months.

What the English call 'indictable' cases are known as 'solemn' cases in Scotland. In England (and Wales and Northern Ireland) a judge sits with a jury of 12 people, and will usually prefer a unanimous verdict (all 12 people agreed). In Scotland, a judge or sheriff sits with a 15-strong jury, and will expect a majority verdict.

Contempt of court

Even if you are not attending court to report on proceedings, you need to be aware of the dangers of contempt of court.

The contempt law is designed to ensure trials are conducted fairly. You should not broadcast any material that might influence a potential juror, unless it has been presented before the jury in court. This means you have to be especially careful before a trial has started.

Under section 2 of the Contempt of Court Act 1981, strict liability contempt applies where:

1 the publication creates a substantial risk of serious prejudice or impediment to particular proceedings; and
2 proceedings are active.

So, you need to know whether criminal proceedings are 'active' or not. According to the Act, proceedings are active if a person has been arrested, a warrant for an arrest has been issued, a summons has been issued or a person has been charged orally. If you are not certain any of these things have taken place, you should be very cautious. Be wary of the phrase 'helping the police with their inquiries'. If someone is at a police station against their will, they are under arrest.

Proceedings cease to be active when:

1 a person is released without charge (except on police bail);
2 no arrest is made within 12 months of the issue of a warrant;
3 a case is discontinued;
4 a defendant is acquitted or sentenced; or
5 a defendant is found unfit to be tried, unfit to plead or the court orders the charge to lie on the file.

The proceedings remain active until sentencing, not just until a guilty verdict. After sentencing, even if a lawyer says his client will appeal, there is a so-called 'free-for-all' time before proceedings become active again when the appeal is formally lodged.

The court has powers to limit reporting under the Contempt of Court Act 1981. Under section 4, a court can order postponement of the reporting of a case, but only if there is a substantial risk to a fair trial. Under section 11, a court can order a name and address to be withheld; usually this is to protect a blackmail victim or a member of the security services. Both types of order can be challenged in court by the media.

This type of challenge happened in September 2006 in a high-profile and highly unusual case involving two immigration judges who had been lovers. A Brazilian cleaner was accused of blackmailing them by threatening to make public a video of them having sex. The cleaner, Roselane Driza, was found guilty of blackmailing the female judge, but not the male (she *was* found guilty of stealing two tapes from him). The media argued that, as there was no blackmail involved in his case, the male judge should be named. The Recorder of London, Judge Peter Beaumont, agreed. He said: 'The finding of the jury in respect of the allegation of the theft of his property does not in my judgement entitle the court to continue the protection over his identity. I can find no justification in doing so in light of the evidence given in this trial.' So, Mohammed Ilyas Khan was photographed and named across the media while his former lover remained anonymous.

Sometimes, a warrant for an arrest will be issued, but the police will still want help with a case and they will issue an appeal for information. To publish that information would be a contempt of court. But the Attorney General made it clear in 1981 that the press have nothing to fear from publishing such information, and there has never been a prosecution.

An area where broadcasters in particular run a risk of contempt is the definition of the precincts of the court. You will want to take pictures of people involved in a case arriving at and leaving court, but it is an offence to take pictures within a court's precincts. The definition of 'precincts' is left to the discretion of the court. So, it is worth checking with the court officers what is allowed. Incidentally, photographing jurors could be contempt, even when they are outside the court visiting a crime scene.

The decision to allow limited use of live text communication (Twitter) from some courts in 2010 was followed by a consultation exercise in 2011. If you want to use your phone in court to tweet reports of a case, the court has to agree it is in the interests of justice for you to do so.

YOUNG PEOPLE AND THE LAW

Youth courts deal with people under 18. In law, a child is anyone under 14 and a young person is a 14–18-year-old. A child under ten (under eight in Scotland) cannot be charged with a criminal offence.

Under the Children and Young Persons Act 1933, *you cannot identify a person under 18 who is a defendant or witness in a youth court*, although the court may lift that anonymity in the public interest or the interests of justice.

There is no automatic ban on naming a minor in an adult court. Under section 39 of the 1933 Act, the court can make an order preventing identification of a child involved in the case, but the judge or magistrate must have good reason and these orders can be challenged. The court has no power to prevent the naming of dead children.

According to the 1933 Act, a child or young person can be identified by their name, address, school or any other particulars. So, you need to be particularly careful. In a small village, for example, there would be comparatively few 12-year-olds. Obviously, recognisable photographs or moving pictures of children in court are forbidden, though pixelated images obscuring the face can usually be used (although there have been cases in Scotland where 'no picture' means literally that).

When a child is subject to a section 39 order, there is a danger of 'jigsaw identification' – where one news organisation names a defendant without giving their relationship to a child and another gives the relationship but not the name. The pieces of information fit together like a jigsaw to identify the child. The Code of Practice adopted by the Press Complaints Commission is also followed by broadcasters. Adults should be named but their relationship to a child should not be given (the word 'incest' should be avoided if it would identify a child victim).

Often ASBOs (anti-social behaviour orders) are granted by magistrates against young people. These are civil proceedings (although breach of an ASBO is a criminal offence) and there is no automatic ban on naming the defendant. Similarly, there is no automatic ban on naming the defendant in an ASBO application before a youth court.

You cannot identify a child as a ward of court (i.e., a minor who is under the care of the court), and it is contempt of court to publish information about court proceedings in private relating to children.

SEX OFFENCES

Victims of most sexual offences are granted lifetime anonymity by the law. As soon as an allegation has been made you cannot name or show pictures of the alleged victim. You must also avoid mentioning their place of work or any educational establishment they attend. The only exceptions are if the mention of a sexual offence comes in a report of a trial other than for a sex offence; if the judge or magistrates remove the anonymity because it imposes an unreasonable restriction on the reporting of the case; or, on the application of the defence, anonymity is lifted to bring witnesses forward.

Because the anonymity applies during the victim's *lifetime*, you *can* name a victim of rape who has been murdered.

Victims over 16 can agree to be identified. They need to give consent in writing, and the court needs to be satisfied no one 'interfered unreasonably with his or her peace or comfort to obtain that consent'. There is no anonymity for those accused of sex offences and the courts have no power to prevent their being named.

BREACH OF CONFIDENCE

Journalists often deal with leaked documents or information from whistle-blowers – people disclosing information about their employer or workplace. So, it is important you understand the principle in law that a person given information in confidence should not take unfair advantage of it.

The laws on breach of confidence are used by individuals and governments to try to keep information secret and to preserve their privacy. There is also a right to privacy under the Human Rights Act. Courts nowadays may be asked to weigh privacy against the public interest and the right to freedom of expression.

Breach of contract also covers the image rights of personalities. 'Snatched' wedding pictures of Michael Douglas and Catherine Zeta-Jones in *Hello!* resulted in *OK!* magazine being awarded more than £1 million in damages.

There are three elements to breach of confidence:

1 The information must have the necessary 'quality of confidence'.
2 It must have been imparted in circumstances imposing an obligation of confidence.
3 There must be unauthorised use of the information to the detriment of the party communicating it.

The law is often enforced by applications before judges to impose interim injunctions preventing the publication or broadcast of confidential information.

COPYRIGHT

Every broadcaster must understand the law of copyright, because every time you use a photograph, video clip or piece of music that is not your own, you risk breaking the law.

Copyright is a branch of intellectual property law designed to protect the products of people's work and time. Facts, ideas and information (the 'news', for example) cannot be copyrighted. Copyright exists after someone has put time and original effort into presenting the information.

Copyright in a written work lasts till 70 years after the author's death; copyright in a broadcast lasts 50 years.

Copyright belongs to the 'author' of the work (e.g. the photographer if it is a photograph) unless the work is carried out in the course of employment, when the employer owns copyright. Freelance work belongs to the author unless there is agreement to the contrary.

A person who commissions a photograph for private purposes has a right not to have it made public under the Copyright, Designs and Patents Act 1988. Reporters should be wary if borrowing a wedding photograph (taken since 1988) from a relative of someone in the news.

Copyright work (apart from a photograph) can be used for the purpose of reporting current events, as long as it has been made public and the author is acknowledged. This is known as 'fair dealing'. It also applies to review or criticism of a work. The courts decide if the dealing is fair, based on whether the use competes with the commercial interest of the copyright owner.

A broadcast work can have a number of 'authors'. The broadcast organisation transmitting it and the company that produced it will have copyright in the whole of a programme, while it may contain elements with different authors.

Copyright can be wholly or partly assigned to a third party, usually in the form of a licence. An exclusive licence would limit the material to one outlet. An 'all rights' agreement would mean the licensee could do what they wanted with the material, and the owner has effectively lost control of it. Whenever you use third-party material, you should be clear of the terms under which it is used.

THE REGULATORS

Broadcasting in the UK is regulated by Ofcom. The Ofcom Broadcasting Code can be found at **www.ofcom.org.uk/tv/ifi/codes/bcode**.

The BBC Editorial Guidelines, which perform a similar function within the BBC, are available at **www.bbc.co.uk/guidelines/editorialguidelines/edguide**.

FURTHER READING

Banks, David and Hanna, Mark (2012) *McNae's Essential Law for Journalists*, Oxford: Oxford University Press.

Bonnington, Alistair J., McInnes, Rosalind, McKain, Bruce and Clive, Eric M. (2000) *Scots Law for Journalists*, Edinburgh: W. Green.

Frost, Chris (2007) *Journalism Ethics and Regulation*, Harlow: Pearson.

Quinn, Frances (2011) *Law for Journalists*, Harlow: Pearson.

The most popular way to enter broadcast journalism as a career is by studying it at university. It's not the only way, and you might be lucky or talented enough to be taken onto a training scheme by a major broadcaster without any formal journalism training. But for most people entering the broadcast news business it will be skills learned at university that help them get their first job.

There are three-year undergraduate courses – and, increasingly, two-year, fast-track versions of the same thing – which teach broadcast journalism or journalism with strong broadcast elements. There are also postgraduate one-year degrees. You may want (and be able to afford) to study an academic subject at undergraduate level and then take your postgraduate or Masters in broadcast journalism.

If you choose the postgraduate route, your undergraduate qualification – politics or a science, say – might be a useful specialism for you as a journalist, or it could just be a subject at which you excel and want to study for its own sake. Many employers are impressed by the intellectual rigour required to achieve a good degree classification in an academic subject.

ACCREDITATION

When choosing a journalism degree – and there are dozens – you should look for accreditation, the benchmark of quality that shows the course meets industry standards of vocational training. The established accrediting body for broadcast courses is the Broadcast Journalism Training Council (BJTC). It is part funded by major broadcasters, including the BBC, ITV News and Sky News.

If you are on a BJTC course, it will help you get work placements with the BBC and other organisations, and will guarantee that you get plenty of experience of industry practice on 'newsdays', where you replicate professional newsgathering for a whole day at a time in the college environment. The BJTC also requires courses to provide a few consecutive newsdays, which teach the importance of forward planning and following up stories from day to day. These consecutive days are often the time when students realise just how much of a treadmill the news operation can be: it never stops.

Journalism courses are also accredited by the National Council for the Training of Journalists (NCTJ). Some of these are broadly based journalism courses, teaching core skills in the first year and allowing you to specialise in a broadcast pathway later. Historically, the NCTJ is the newspaper training body, but since the convergence of print and broadcast skills online, it has broadened its reach to include some elements of broadcasting. Unlike the BJTC, the NCTJ sets exams that test your skills. Their Diploma programme, which includes traditional journalism skills such as shorthand and media law, has extended to include a broadcast journalism module. There is also a 'video journalism for the web' exam, which requires a lower level of video production expertise than is taught on most broadcast courses.

The NCTJ's broadcast module has four methods of assessment: coursework, two practical timed tests and an exam on broadcast regulation. The course work can be a TV report of up to three minutes, two radio packages of no more than three minutes or one TV and one radio report. There's a TV exam involving scripting, editing and voicing a news package, and a radio exam involving producing and recording a short news bulletin. The broadcast regulation exam is designed to test knowledge of the Ofcom Broadcasting Code and BBC Editorial Guidelines.

It's not essential to have studied broadcast journalism to become a broadcast journalist, although it certainly helps. If you are going to engage in formal study, we strongly recommend you look for an accredited course.

PARTTHREE WORKSHOPS AND EXERCISES

CHAPTER ONE: INTRODUCTION

- Track the progress of a news story on different platforms from the same news organisation (the BBC and Sky News offer TV, radio, online and mobile phone services). How do the length and treatment of the story differ on:

  1 Terrestrial television news

  2 Rolling news

  3 Radio bulletins

  4 The website

  5 The iPad app

  6 Mobile phones?

- Visit the website of a major news provider. How many different types of job do they offer in broadcast journalism? Find out the roles of:

  1 A field producer in TV

  2 A foreign news editor

  3 A TV researcher

  4 A regional TV programme producer

  5 A reporter in commercial radio.

- Prepare a background file on a running story – e.g. conflict in the Middle East, the next US presidential election, the Olympics. Select stories that are new developments or related to the same issue. Order them in a folder (preferably as downloads or weblinks, or, if not, collect newspaper cuttings). Whenever there is a new angle on the story, consult your files and see how that helps your understanding of the story.

CHAPTER TWO: WHAT'S THE STORY?

- Who do you think is the typical listener to the radio station nearest to your home? Now do a bit of research into the profile – average age and social background.

- Ask somebody at the station if they have an imaginary listener in mind when they broadcast.

- Imagine a commercial radio station playing your favourite music. What might be the profile of the imaginary listener?

  Now think of a station playing your parents' favourite songs. Would the target audience just consist of older

people? Or would they have to broaden the appeal to attract advertisers?

- Think back over your lifetime. Can you recall five big stories and remember where you were when you first heard the news? How did you receive the news? Were you on your own or in company? How did you react?

- Look at the table on *Theories of News Production* and decide which model most closely represents the way news is produced on:

  1 BBC News Channel

  2 Sky News

  3 Your local commercial radio station

  4 A tabloid newspaper

  5 A Sunday broadsheet newspaper.

- Consider the *news values*, as defined by Harcup and O'Neill. Watch a TV news bulletin, listen to news programmes on radio, or consider a half-hour segment of any rolling news programme – Radio Five Live or Sky News, for example. Now ask:

  - Did all the stories fit into the categories outlined by Harcup and O'Neill?

  - If not, what were the factors that made other stories newsworthy?

  - Does the requirement for balance and impartiality in broadcast news affect the news agenda?

  - Where does sport fit into this list?

  - Is broadcast news becoming more or less like newspaper news?

- How could you make the following stories relevant to the core audience for an independent local radio station in Scotland:

  1 House prices in the Home Counties are rising by 10 per cent a year.

  2 London's congestion charge is going up again.

  3 A budget airline has announced more flights from Edinburgh airport.

  4 Andy Murray is promoting tennis for young people at a photo-call in a central London car park.

  5 Firemen in Cardiff have rescued an iguana from a chimney.

- Consider whether you would want to use any of these stories at all. Then imagine it is a slow news day – and you *have* to use them. How would you treat them? And what order would you put them in?

- Look at the ingredients that made some of the biggest stories of recent years so important to audiences worldwide:

  1 The death of Princess Diana – royalty, celebrity, death, sex, intrigue.

  2 The events of 11 September 2001 – high death toll, terrorism, religion, world-famous landmarks, global politics, dramatic TV pictures.

  3 The 2004 Tsunami – huge death toll, shock, natural disaster, holiday destinations affected, charity, global politics, dramatic TV pictures.

  4 Michael Jackson's death – celebrity, pop music, suspicious death, courtroom drama.

  5 Hurricane Katrina – natural disaster, high death toll, tourist destination, political bungling, allegations of racism, environmental problems, dramatic TV pictures.

- Watch a TV news programme or listen to the radio news. List the factors that made each item in the bulletin newsworthy. Now compare it with another programme or bulletin. Does your research suggest that different organisations have different news values?

- Next time you meet up with your friends, analyse the conversation: do you discuss the news at all? If you do, what are the news stories that you talk about? Do the same exercise with your family. Are the types of stories you discuss with them different? Why? Have you ever discussed a news story with a complete stranger, maybe someone you've sat next to on a bus or train? What was the story? What was it about the story that you felt able to discuss with a stranger?

- Call the local police, fire service and ambulance services and ask for their voice-bank numbers. Check the *voice-banks* regularly and see how many possible news stories they contain. Is there enough information on the voice-bank to write a convincing version of the story? What extra information do you need?

- Visit your local magistrates' or sheriff court. Look at the court list. Which cases appear to offer interesting copy? Sit in court (you may be allowed on to the press bench; otherwise use the public gallery). Pick the most interesting case and write about it. Did you manage to get down all the relevant facts? Have you been able to check names, addresses and their spellings?

- Make an application (in writing) to your local council under the *Freedom of Information Act* (FoI). Pick a subject you have heard people complaining about – waste collection services, for example, or the state of local parks. Ask for statistical information that should be easy to provide. Analyse the response. Do the figures suggest a story?

- See how many factual *inaccuracies* you can spot in established news outlets over the period of one week. This may involve comparing the same story in different newspapers, websites or radio and TV programmes. Do they all contain the same facts? What does this tell you about the journalistic process?

- Prepare a *diary of forthcoming events* you would want covered if you were the editor of a local radio station. See if you can find enough future events to fill bulletins for a period of three successive days, without resorting to new or breaking events.

- Listen to a radio news programme or watch the TV news and try to work out which stories are diary stories.

CHAPTER THREE: FINDING THE NEWS

- Start your own *contacts book*. Buy a small notebook with an alphabetical index. Begin by listing public and private bodies likely to figure in news stories (courts, councils, the emergency services, hospitals, airports, rail companies, major employers, chambers of commerce, trade unions, community groups, sports clubs). Find their numbers and email addresses from the Web or the phone book. Ring the switchboard of larger bodies and ask for the press officer. Then ask the press office for the names of contacts and their direct line numbers.

  Add friends and family to your contacts book if you think they have specialist knowledge or personal experience that might come in handy. Transfer numbers from your mobile phone. Cross-reference your entries so that people are found under their name and the subject heading (e.g. a friend who works on the railways might offer useful background to stories about train delays or a rail crash).

CHAPTER FOUR: THE INTERVIEW

How would you go about controlling your nerves before an important interview? Do you have your own relaxation techniques to cope with stress at work? Do you think you would be able to control your opinions?

- Take another look at Jeremy Paxman's interview with George Galloway and consider these questions:

  - *What does the interview tell you about George Galloway's relationship with the media?*

  - *Did Paxman achieve anything by being so adversarial?*

  - *What does it say about Paxman's attitude to politicians?*

- Watch any TV interview or listen to an interview on radio. Has the interviewer prepared well? How would you have prepared differently? Draw up a list of questions you would have asked if you had been the interviewer.

- Record and listen to an extended interview on the radio or a television chat show. Note any *soundbites* that could be used in a short news bulletin. What are the in and out points of the clips? What is the story?

- Carefully watch or listen to a *political interview*. Who is in control of the interview – the interviewer or the interviewee? Have ground rules been agreed beforehand? Are there any no-go areas? Does the interviewer give the interviewee a hard time or an easy time?

- Watch or listen to a news programme and study how *vox pops* are used. Are they predictable? What do they add to the story?

- Watch a current affairs programme such as *The Politics Show*, *Newsnight* or *Channel 4 News* and analyse the choice of guests interviewed. Are they all treated in the same way? If not, why not? Are guests in the studio given an easier ride than someone who is in a remote studio?

CHAPTER FIVE: NEWS WRITING

Here's some sound advice and an exercise in concise writing. It is worth trying because using words accurately and not vaguely is a vital discipline. It is tempting to use words that make a story sound important but which have no exact meaning. The BBC correspondent Allan Little, in an online guide to writing for radio, says: 'Choose words whose meaning you know. Don't use words like "substantial" or "considerable". These seem to me to be meaningless and their frequent use always suggests to me a writer who isn't sure what he means to say, and is therefore choosing a word which leaves the meaning of the sentence vague or obscure.'

Little suggests a lesson in news writing. *Try writing a news story in words of one syllable.* 'It's hard,' he says. 'But it makes you think about the way you're using the language.'

- Try writing a story in words of no more than two syllables – this is arguably more realistic, and an easier exercise to do.

- Research and collect different companies' *style guides* – compare them to see how they differ.

- Listen to news reports on Radio Four. Do they differ from reports on Radio Five Live? List the differences.

- Just after eight o'clock in the morning retune your radio (without looking) and try to decide what station you are listening to from the style of the writing, the running order and sound clips used. Rapidly repeat the exercise a number of times within the first couple of minutes after the hour. How many did you get right?

- Take a story from a newspaper. Assume the interview quotes are available as audio clips. Write the story (including a cue) in the style of:
  1 A BBC Radio Four 1.15 package
  2 A 40″ wrap for commercial radio

  3 A 20″ copy story
  4 A two-minute network television report for Sky News.

- Pick a story from the front page of a newspaper. Now write the following *headlines* for the story:
  1 A two-sentence programme opener (e.g. BBC or ITV News at Ten)
  2 A five-second headline for use in a menu (second or third story)
  3 A tease (for use before a commercial break)
  4 A closing head.

- Pick a page lead story from a newspaper. Write a cue or link for broadcast in the following styles:
  1 Hard news formula – the most important facts first
  2 Soft feature-style introduction
  3 Drop intro – saving the key facts for impact.

- Listen to the output of one day on radio. Listen to a range of output – a local commercial station, Five Live, a local BBC station, Radio Four, Radio One – and analyse what stories each station covers. Are they the same? Have they been treated the same? How does the writing change? Is audio used? Is music used? Are headlines used?

- Listen to radio news reports and see if you can apply the Christmas Tree theory to them.

CHAPTER SIX: LOCATION REPORTING AND PRODUCTION

- Try watching a TV news programme and working out whether a story was pre-planned or one that broke on the day. How did you tell? What proportion of stories in the bulletin were planned in advance? Does the proportion surprise you? What does that tell you about whether it is a slow news day?

- Visit a location where you know broadcast journalists work (e.g. you will have seen TV reporters outside courts, football grounds, in local shopping centres). Do a *recce* by making notes about the location under the following headings:
  1 Health and safety – What are the risks to safe operation of broadcasting equipment?
  2 Permissions – Can you work here without permission from the landowner or other authority? If not, find out who you need to ask and whether they are likely to agree.
  3 Interview locations – Is the environment suitable for conducting interviews? What are the background noise levels? Can they be reduced if necessary? Are there backgrounds useful for a TV interview?

CHAPTER SEVEN: LOCATION VIDEO AND SOUND

- Take a portable sound recorder and microphone on location with a friend to act as an interviewee. Pay particular attention to setting your levels and the distance you hold the mic from the speaker's mouth. Using headphones to monitor the results, compare the sound recorded in the following environments:

  1 A field or park

  2 A shopping centre

  3 A car park

  4 A crowded café or bar.

- Repeat the above exercise using a camera. Pay particular attention to what your shots look like. Does a tree appear to be growing out of the top of your interviewee's head? Can you see your reflection in a shop window? Is the background too distracting?

CHAPTER EIGHT: SPORTS REPORTING AND COMMENTARY

- Call a local sports club. See what criteria they apply to offering access to the media. What *accreditation* is needed? Are there sports rights agreements in place? What facilities do they have for the media? Is the venue divided into different levels of access for different media representatives? Do they accommodate student journalists or beginners?

- Study the sports pages of a newspaper. With a marker pen highlight all the examples of cliché and journalese (all the phrases you have seen many times before). Rewrite two or three stories without using the clichés.

- Research a televised sporting event using newspapers and the Web. Prepare lists of key facts about the fixture and the competitors. Turn the sound down on the broadcast and deliver your own *commentary*. Start with television commentary for ten minutes at a time. Build up to longer stretches. Then try radio commentary.

CHAPTER NINE: FOREIGN REPORTING

- Visit the FCO (Foreign and Commonwealth Office) website, follow the links, and find out what special preparations or permissions you would need to work as a broadcast journalist in the following countries:

  1 USA

  2 Turkey

  3 Israel

  4 Iraq

  5 Kazakhstan.

- Watch a TV news report from a foreign conflict. Apply a risk assessment to what you see on screen. What *health and safety* issues are there? Were the reporter and camera crew in danger? Did the report use agency material, user-generated content, pictures from YouTube, or was it all shot by the TV channel's own crew?

CHAPTER TEN: GOING LIVE

- Take a newspaper story that has few interviews in it and is unlikely to offer picture opportunities. Now rewrite the story as a series of questions and answers for a *two-way*. Practise answering by consulting notes (as if for radio) and then without notes, speaking for up to 30 seconds at a time. Start with two questions, and build up to five or six.

- Practise *talking to time*. Try talking on a topic of your choice, but preferably something in the news – for exactly 20 seconds. Now try 30 seconds. Now repeat the exercise on a topic you know little about and have researched in the past hour.

CHAPTER ELEVEN: THE PACKAGE

- Listen to reports on Radio Four (World at One and PM) and identify the techniques used in their reporters' packages. How have they used the sights and smells of a story in the audio? Have they painted pictures with the words that have been used? Which specific words and phrases worked well?

- Watch the television news with the sound turned down. See if you can tell what the story is about without hearing any speech. This is a very useful way to analyse how a story is told visually.

- Pick a story from a newspaper and work out what audio and interviews you would need for:

  1 A two-minute radio package

  2 A 40″ wrap

  3 A five-minute feature.

Would the piece be enhanced by archive sound or music? What would you use? How would you order the material for maximum impact?

- Listen to coverage of a personality-based political story on BBC Radio Four or another speech-based radio station. How would you tell the story in an engaging and entertaining way for television? Can you think of a *visual metaphor* or motif to explain the story to as wide an audience as possible?

- Watch a feature package on a television news programme and study the use of *music*. Why was it used? How was it used? Was the choice predictable? Did it add to your understanding and enjoyment of the package?

CHAPTER TWELVE: EDITING

- Listen to a news package on BBC Radio Four and analyse the pace and structure. How many audio clips have been used? How have they been combined or separated? Is the piece strong on actuality, or is it mainly the reporter's voice? Can you work out how many different audio channels were used in the edit?

- Record a short interview in a dead acoustic – such as a studio. Then record an interview in a live acoustic – such as a corridor or a room with background noise – and also record wildtrack at the second location. Now edit the first interview. Try adding some of the wildtrack to your studio recording. Does it match the sound of the second interview? Are the sound levels the same? What are the differences?

- Watch a TV news programme and see how often the reporter packages include *layered video* (split-screens or pictures within a picture). Are they successful in helping tell the story? If you have access to editing software, try replicating the effects.

CHAPTER THIRTEEN: GRAPHICS

- Count the number of characters (letters and spaces) in the on-screen graphics of a rolling news channel. Then pick a newspaper story and write it in the style of:
  1 A ticker-tape streamer
  2 A breaking news bar.

- Find a story with a series of statistics in it. Decide which are the most important facts and figures. Now script them to be accompanied by a *graphics sequence*. Write the sequence as a series of reveals or separate pages disclosing fresh information. What background images would you use behind your graphic?

- Imagine you have access to 3-D graphics in a *virtual reality* studio. Devise and sketch out a graphics sequence for each of the following stories:
  1 A national housing shortage
  2 Global warming

3 The widening of the motorway between Birmingham and Manchester.

CHAPTER FOURTEEN: PRESENTATION

- There is no substitute for practising reading aloud. When you have got used to writing and reading your own bulletins, add the following factors:
  1 Practise reading exactly to time – a three-minute bulletin should be three minutes long to the exact second, not five seconds over or seven seconds under.
  2 To replicate an unexpected change to your programme timings, set an alarm clock to ring towards the end of your bulletin – at that point you have ten seconds left to wrap up and end.
  3 Pick up a newspaper story that you have not read before halfway through your bulletin. Try to present it in a broadcast style.

- Practise *ad libbing* by adding extra information and your own comments at the end of each story. The ad lib should be unscripted and should always be relevant to the story that preceded it. Set yourself target times to fill: 5 seconds, 10 seconds and so on up to 30 seconds.

- Even if you do not have access to a professional studio, you can replicate working with talkback by practising reading a bulletin while you have the radio on. Keep it loud enough so that you can hear everything that is being said. Try to recall what was said on the radio at the end of your read. To replicate switch talkback, try turning the radio on for up to 10 seconds at a time (until you can understand the sense of what's being said) and then off again.

CHAPTER FIFTEEN: THE PROGRAMME

- Watch an hour of rolling news on TV. Make a note of the main headlines, the packages, interviews and two-ways. Draw up a running order for a half-hour *appointment-to-view* programme based on these elements.

- Using the *programme template* prepare a TV bulletin based on the content of a local radio station's news output. Now do the same with stories from a newspaper.

- Compare two news programmes on rival channels (TV or radio). Which stories, if any, could be described as exclusive? Were there elements of the same story that were exclusive to one channel or the other? What does this tell you about the nature of news gathering?

GLOSSARY

Accreditation Clearance to attend and cover an event. May involve special passes.

Recognition of a training course by an industry-approved body.

Actuality Sounds recorded as they happen – sometimes used to refer to interviews (aka wildtrack, atmos).

Ad Advertisement or commercial.

Ad lib Unscripted, improvised speech.

Adobe Audition A digital radio editing system (trade name).

Agency copy Story that has come from a news agency.

ALC Automatic level control. Electronic device to reduce or boost the incoming sound signal automatically.

A-listers Top celebrity guests.

AM Radio frequency on the AM waveband.

Ambush interview American term for forcing someone to speak with you on camera against their will. (Editorial guidance needed.)

Analogue A signal that has a continuous wave form.

Analogue recording Recording that is not digital – normally used when referring to magnetic tape.

Anchor American term for main news presenter.

And finally Item (often off-beat) at the very end of a bulletin.

Angle The point in a story that the journalist wants to emphasise. The new angle would be the latest development in a story and the local angle would be pointing up the relevance to the local audience.

AP Associated Press, one of the major wire services in America.

Appointment to view The decision to make a mental note to watch a particular programme at a particular time.

Archive Previously broadcast material.

ASBO Anti-social behaviour order – a civil order by magistrates (or in Scotland the sheriff court) to stop someone causing alarm, harassment or distress to others.

As-live Recorded inserts that look/sound live. (Remember, never claim that a recorded report or interview is live.)

Assault In legal language, assault is a hostile act that threatens an attack on another person.

Assignment editor Journalist who assigns stories to reporters and camera crews.

Aston Brand name for electronic caption on TV (aka super).

Atmos Atmosphere. Background noise that provides a sense of location to interviews or voice pieces (aka wildtrack).

Audacity A digital audio editing system (available as free shareware).

Audio Sound.

Audio feed Sound sent to other studios and stations.

Audio mixer Control desk (or control panel) for mixing sound sources.

Autocue TV prompting device that allows the presenter to read a script while looking at the camera. Autocue is a trade name – like 'Hoover' it is often used as a generic term (aka teleprompter, Portaprompt).

Avid Digital video editing system (trade name).

Back anno Back announcement. A final piece of script giving extra information (usually read by the presenter at the end of an item).

Back light The light used behind an interviewee or presenter to pick them out from the background. It adds depth, softens shadows and highlights the hair.

Back projection Pictures projected on to a screen behind the newsreader.

Band A separate piece of quarter-inch audio tape used on a reel-to-reel player.

Barn door Adjustable flaps on a studio or location light used to direct the beam.

BBC British Broadcasting Corporation.

BCU Big close-up.

Bed A music bed or a sound bed is audio played underneath a voice or actuality.

Berliner A newspaper size used by the *Guardian* in the UK, smaller than a broadsheet.

Bi-directional mic A mic (microphone) that will pick up sound from the front and from the back.

Biff To drop an item (aka spike).

Bi-media TV and radio operation.

BJ Broadcast journalist.

BJTC Broadcast Journalism Training Council. An accrediting body providing guidelines for university and college broadcast journalism courses.

Black Control track on a videotape. Also, a complete fade from a TV picture – 'fade to black'.

Blind lead-in A general lead-in to a report from location, used when you do not know what the reporter will say at the top of the report.

B-listers Celebrity guests who are not as well known as those on the A-list.

Blog A regularly updated website. A blog can be a personal diary, a political soapbox, a breaking-news outlet, opinion articles, private thoughts, memos to the world.

Blogger Someone who writes blogs on the Internet.

Bongs The headlines at the top of the ITV News.

Boom A long telescopic pole for holding a microphone.

Boom mic Microphone held on a pole or boom.

Box Used to indicate that a picture, freeze-frame video or graphic will appear in a box on screen.

Breaking news A news story that is happening now and developing throughout the day (aka a spot story in America).

Bridge Words that connect one piece of narration or soundbite to another (aka link).

Brief Instructions given to a reporter on how to cover a story.

British Broadcasting Company What the BBC was called before it became a public corporation in 1927.

Broadsheet A newspaper format that is the larger of the two standard UK newspaper sizes, characterised by long vertical pages. Broadsheet newspapers are usually more serious in content than tabloid newspapers.

B-roll A film term often used to describe the use of video to cover narration or an interview.

Bug An on-screen graphic.

Bulk eraser Powerful electromagnet used for erasing tapes for reuse.

Bulletin A report providing the latest information on a topic such as news, weather or travel.

Bumper The short sting before and after the commercial break (aka bump).

Bumper tease A short headline with video, used before commercials in a TV newscast, to hold the audience's attention (aka bump tease).

Camcorder Handheld video camera with a built-in recorder.

Camera desk The desk in a newsroom that assigns camera crews.

Calls see check calls.

Cans Headphones.

Capacitor mic Small battery-operated mic.

Caption A graphic with written information (aka Aston, super).

Carrier wave A frequency modulated to carry a video or audio signal.

Cart Cartridge used for recording and playing inserts into TV and radio programmes.

Catchline A one- or two-word name used to identify a story (aka slug).

CCD Charge-coupled device. A solid-state sensor used instead of tubes in cameras.

CCTV Closed circuit television.

Ceefax BBC's Text pages on TV.

Character generator Electronic caption machine.

Check calls Regular calls from the newsroom to the emergency services.

Chequebook journalism The form of journalism where a news organisation pays a subject money for the exclusive right to publish their story, often outbidding other organisations.

Child The legal term for a person under 14 years old.

Chroma key See CSO.

Citizen journalists Members of the public who send in pictures from their mobile phones or video recorders of a news event they've witnessed, or who contribute news content to Internet sites.

Claimant The person who takes an action to enforce a claim in the civil court (previously known as plaintiff).

Clean feed A special feed of the programme output that lets a remote contributor hear the presenters and other guests, without being distracted by hearing a delayed version of their own voice off air (aka mix-minus in America).

Cliché A hackneyed and over-used expression.

Clip Insert. Short extract (aka cut or grab).

COI Central Office of Information.

College Green The stretch of lawn opposite the public entrance to the House of Commons, often used for interviews with politicians.

Commentary booth Small studio in which a journalist records script or broadcasts live.

Contact Source of news information.

Contacts book Usually laid out alphabetically, a book containing names, addresses, phone numbers (particularly mobiles) and email addresses of anyone who might be a source of news.

Contemporaneous Originating, existing or occurring at the same time. To attract absolute privilege a court report must be contemporaneous, usually meaning at the earliest opportunity.

Continuity Network presentation studio – the place/person introducing programmes on a large network such as Channel 4 or BBC Radio 4.

Maintaining the appearance of continuous action in a recorded item.

Contribution circuit Network of linking landlines along which news material is sent and received.

Contribution studio Small studio used for sending material down-the-line (DTL) or for DTL interviews.

Cool Edit Pro Digital audio editing software (renamed Adobe Audition in May 2003).

Copy Material written for broadcast.

Copy story News story that is just script, with no accompanying audio or pictures.

Copytaster Journalist who sifts incoming stories to select items worth running.

Coroner An official responsible for investigating sudden or unusual deaths (and also treasure trove).

Cover footage Pictures shot at the scene of a news story, used for the reporter's V-O.

Crash Colloquialism for serious problems in a broadcast.

Crawler Ticker-tape graphic across the bottom of a TV screen.

Cross-fade Mixing or overlapping of one sound with another.

Crowd sourcing Using groups of people (usually online) to assist research.

CSO Colour separation overlay. Method of electronically replacing a single colour with a second image or graphic (aka chroma key).

CU Close-up.

Cubicle Control room for radio programmes.

Cue Written introduction to a report either live or recorded (aka in-cue).

The instruction/signal given to a presenter to start or stop speaking, either visual (hand or light) or verbal.

Sound of continuity or the programme played into a person's headphones to introduce or indicate when they should start broadcasting (e.g. in a live studio, on an outside broadcast or on a telephone).

Cue (feed) Cue, as opposed to clean feed, sends output down the line to the remote guest. When the remote guest talks, they will hear themselves as part of the full programme mix. There may be audible delay, especially if the contributor is on a satellite link.

Cue-light Light on top of a studio camera indicating the camera is live. In radio the cue-light is a small, normally green, light that sits on the studio table and lights when the presenter is cued to speak.

Cut Short extract of an interview to illustrate a story (aka grab or insert).

The term used to signal the end of filming a shot.

An edit which joins two shots together without a mix or other video transition.

Cutaway A shot used in TV to cover a jump-cut edit.

DAB Digital audio broadcasting. It uses a sound signal made up of discrete electronic units, rather than an analogue signal, which has a continuous wave form.

DAT Digital audio tape.

DB Decibel – unit of loudness.

Death-knock Calling on the recently bereaved to request an interview or pictures.

Delay A recorded delay of several seconds in playing back a 'live' phone-in programme to prevent defamation or obscenities being broadcast.

Delayed lead Keeping the most important information in a story until the middle or end to create suspense (aka drop intro).

Demographic The profile of a station's listeners based on age, gender, income, profession, race etc. Important to advertisers who target particular audiences.

Demos Demonstrations.

Desk The control panel in a studio that mixes sounds and/or pictures for transmission.

An operational unit in a newsroom (e.g., newsdesk, home desk, foreign desk, camera desk).

Diary Usually electronic – the future story file in a newsroom. A breaking story may be off-diary.

Digital radio Radio transmission system offering high-quality sound requiring a special receiver (aka DAB).

Digital recording The storage of sound and/or pictures digitally (as a series of noughts and ones in computer systems). Copies of digital recordings can be made with no loss of quality.

Digitising The process of playing tape into a digital editing system.

Directivity pattern Area over which a mic can pick up sound (aka pickup).

Dissolve A video effect that mixes from one image on the screen to another (aka mix).

DOA Dead on arrival. Term used by the emergency services for a victim who has died either before help could arrive or before the ambulance could reach the hospital.

Dog Digital on-screen graphic.

Dolby A system that reduces audio noise.

Doorstep To knock on a person's door unannounced or approach them in the street for an interview. Normally used when someone has refused to be interviewed previously; this is subject to editorial approval.

Double-header Item or programme presented by two people.

Down-the-line (DTL) An interview or report from a location conducted via an electronic link.

DR Dispatch rider.

Drive To drive a desk is to operate a radio studio desk.

Drive-time The time of day when much of the radio audience is driving. Usually the late afternoon/early evening.

DTL Down-the-line.

Dubbing Duplication of a recording from one recorder to another.

Laying a voice down over pictures, or mixing sound on to a TV programme (aka dub).

Dubbing theatre The studio where presenters record their voice-overs for television and audio dubbing takes place.

Dumbing down Oversimplification. The theory that media audiences are being fed an increasingly mass-produced, poor-quality and populist diet leading to an ever-decreasing audience attention span.

Duration The length to the nearest second of an item or programme (aka dur).

Earpiece Small device worn in the ear that enables a presenter or reporter to listen to talkback from the studio gallery.

Edit To prepare an item or programme for transmission by cutting out unwanted material.

Editor The person who edits audio or video. A senior journalist in charge of output.

Embargo Request not to release information until a specified date or time. Used to control the publication date and time of a news item.

ENG Electronic news gathering with portable video cameras.

ENPS Electronic News Production System (trade name). Networked newsroom computer system used worldwide.

EPK Electronic press kit.

EQ Equalisation. Improving audio quality by altering the frequency characteristics.

Establishing shot A wide shot to set a scene.

Evergreen An American term for a story that is timeless and can be used at any time (aka shelf item).

Executive producer A senior figure who oversees producers.

Face to face When two people are facing each other.

Fade out Used in TV when a picture fades to black. In radio when the volume of an audio signal is reduced until it disappears.

Fader Slide mechanism on a studio desk that opens an audio channel and controls its volume.

Feature An edited item for a programme. Also used to describe softer news stories.

Feature opener An introduction to a soft news story, designed more to arouse curiosity and to entertain than to inform (American term).

Feed A supply of audio or video from an outside source.

Programme output to a contributor at a location other than the programme's originating studio (e.g. a phone call or an interview down-the-line from a remote studio). Most studios offer a choice of cue (programme output) or clean feed.

Feedback The effect produced when the signal from a mic is transmitted through a nearby speaker. The mic picks up the speaker sound producing a high-pitched howling sound. It can also be caused by a phone-in contributor having their radio on, tuned into the same programme, too near to the phone (aka howl-round).

Fibre-optic Cable system composed of hollow fibres that carry light. Fibre-optic cables are used for telephone calls, computer data and TV signals.

Fill Lamp casting a soft light to fill in shadows.

Fillers Items of secondary importance (often without a peg) used to fill out a programme.

Final Cut Pro A digital editing system for TV (trade name).

Fish eye A special camera lens that gives an extremely wide angle (nearly 180 degrees), like the eye of a fish.

Fishpole Handheld sound boom.

Fixed spot An item that is regularly in a programme at a particular time, such as the weather, or travel news on a drive-time programme.

Fixer Someone (often a local person in a foreign country) who uses their contacts and local knowledge to 'fix' and organise filming and recording schedules.

Flash A graphics editing package (trade name).

FlashMic Trade name for an all-in-one microphone and digital recorder.

Flats Boards used as a backdrop to the studio set.

Fly-on-the-wall A documentary style. In television the camera watches the action apparently unnoticed; in radio the mic eavesdrops on the action, like a fly on the wall.

FM Radio frequency on the frequency modulation waveband.

FO The Foreign and Commonwealth Office, more commonly known as the Foreign Office. British government department responsible for overseas relations and foreign affairs (aka FCO).

FOI Freedom of Information Act. Act that enables anyone to have access to information held by public authorities.

Format The structure and presentation of programmes in an agreed style. The format will dictate how often time checks are given or station idents used.

Freelance Self-employed journalist who works for more than one employer and gets paid for the job or for the day.

Freeze-frame A still video image.

Frequency Rate at which a sound or light wave or an electronic impulse passes a given point over a specific time. A station's frequency denotes its position on the dial. Frequencies on the AM waveband (amplitude modulation) are expressed in kilohertz (KHz) including medium- and long-wave transmissions, and on the FM waveband (frequency modulation) in megahertz (MHz).

Front projection Pictures projected from in front of the newsreader on to a screen alongside.

Futures file File in which stories and news events that are known to be happening on a certain date are placed, so that coverage may be planned in advance (aka diary).

FX An abbreviation for sound or video effects.

GFX Graphics.

Glitch Technical error.

GNS General News Service. The BBC service to all its news outlets.

Google A widely used search engine (trade name). To 'Google' means to look something up on the Internet.

Grab Soundbite. Bit of an interview or a piece of actuality sound.

Graphics Graphs, photos, maps and other images used in a TV news story or online.

GTS Greenwich Time Signal. Now no longer from Greenwich but generated by the BBC. Six pips broadcast at the top of the hour to give an accurate time check.

Gun mic Directional microphone for picking up sound at a distance (aka rifle mic).

GV General view.

Handling noise Unwanted clicks and bumps picked up by a mic as a result of handling and moving the mic.

Hard disk Computer disk for the permanent storage of material.

Hard lead A lead that places the most important information at the top of a story.

Hard news Information of importance about events of significance.

Hard news formula A hard news story will cover most of the basic facts by answering the questions: Who? What? Where? When? Why? And How?

Head The moving top of a tripod.

Headlines or Heads Short summary of the main news stories.

Hertz (Hz) Frequency of sound measured in cycles per second.

HD High-definition TV system of more than a thousand lines resulting in excellent picture quality.

Holding copy The first version of a story left by a reporter to be run in their absence while they collect more information.

Hot desking Practice of workers not having their own desk, but logging onto work stations as needed.

Human interest Soft news item. Of interest to the audience, but often of no great news significance. Background stories after major news events can be human-interest stories; also stories about animals and celebrities.

Ident Piece of recorded music, or a simple announcement by the presenter, used to identify a particular programme (aka stab, sting, jingle).

ILR Independent local radio.

In-cue The first few words of a report.

Information overload Putting too much information in a story.

Ingest The input of video and audio material from external sources.

Input The news-gathering operation of a newsroom.

Inquest Formal process of investigation. An official inquiry (presided over by a coroner) into the cause of a death.

Insert Item inserted into a bulletin or programme.

Internet Global network of computers.

In the field On location.

Intro Introduction. The first paragraph of a script written to grab the audience's attention. It gives the main angle of the story and the main facts.

The cue into a report.

Investigative reporting News reports in depth. Investigation by a reporter usually about something that someone is trying to hide.

IPCC Independent Police Complaints Commission.

ips Inches per second. Refers to the speed of tape going past the recording head of an analogue tape machine. Rarely used today. The two most common speeds were 7.5 ips and 15 ips (faster speeds mean a higher recording quality) (aka inps).

IR Independent Radio – all non-BBC radio covering national, local and regional stations in the UK.

IRN Independent Radio News. Company that supplies national and international news to many independent radio stations in the UK.

ISDN Integrated Services Digital Network. High-quality digital audio signal sent through telephone lines.

ITC Independent Television Commission. It used to regulate independent TV in the UK. It ceased functioning in December 2003 and its duties have been assumed by Ofcom.

ITN Independent Television News. Company supplying news to networks including ITV and Channel 4, now known at ITV News.

IV In vision. Instruction on a script to indicate a TV presenter should be on camera.

Jack plug A connecting plug used to route or reroute sources.

Jigsaw identification Identification of a person who should not be named in court proceedings, by combining details from different sources. For example, one station broadcasts a person's name; another suppresses his name but gives details of his relationship to a child. If the two reports are heard, together they form a jigsaw identifying the child.

Jingle Piece of music used to identify a programme (aka ident, sting).

Journalese The jargon of bad journalism.

Judicial review Review by the Queen's Bench Divisional Court of decisions taken by a lower court, tribunal, public body or public official.

Jump cut An edit in a sequence of video, where the subject appears to jump from one position to another.

Juvenile A young person below the age of 18.

Key Main lamp providing a hard light.

To impose one image over another electronically (see Chroma key, CSO).

Key words One or two words that sum up the most important part of a news story. Used by search engines to search for information.

Kicker American term for a light story used at the end of a bulletin.

Landline Cable transmission for audio and/or video. The cables are capable of carrying a high-quality signal (used for radio outside broadcast before the introduction of ISDN).

Lead First and most important item in a news programme.

The written cue to a news report (US).

An electrical cable from one piece of equipment to another.

Leader Leader tape is coloured tape used to show the start and end of a piece of audio on analogue reel-to-reel tape. The leader tape cannot be recorded upon and the correct colours must be used: yellow for the start and linking bands and red for the end. Rarely used today, but useful if listening to archive tapes.

Leading question A question during an interview that tries to elicit information the reporter wants to hear.

LED Light emitting diode. Low-powered light used for electronic displays. Used on desks and other equipment for on/off indicators, level meters etc.

Level The volume of recorded or broadcast sound as registered on a meter.

Level check Pre-recording check on the volume of a speaker's voice.

Lighting grid Construction suspended from the studio ceiling to support lights.

Linear editing Editing where sounds and/or pictures have to be assembled in order.

Line-up The arrangement of stories in a bulletin (aka running order or rundown).

Link Any speech between items that introduces or sets up an item. Narrative linking or bridging interviews in a report.

Links vehicle Motor vehicle used as a platform for a microwave transmitter or satellite dish.

Live Broadcast in real time.

A live report from the scene of a story.

Local news Stories relevant to a local community.

Log A recording of all of a radio station's output on slow-speed audio, video or computer.

A register of music played so that royalties can be paid.

To note down the content of recordings in preparation for an edit, usually involving logging timecode.

Lower third The bottom third of a TV screen. This is where most Astons and name supers appear.

LS Long shot. Usually showing somebody full length.

Man-in-the-street American term for vox pops.

Marantz A portable recording machine (trade name). The make was popular for audio cassette machines, and more recently solid-state audio recorders.

Marking up Marking a story with important details: the catchline, who wrote it, and when it was written.

Masthead The front page title logo of a newspaper.

MCPS The Mechanical-Copyright Protection Society collects and distributes royalties for the use of recorded music.

MCU Medium close-up. The standard interview shot in television.

MD MiniDisc. Digital audio recording medium using small discs. Popular during the bridge between analogue tape and solid-state recorders.

Media Channels of communication for transmitting information to the public (e.g. the 'mass media' – newspapers, television, radio and the Internet).

Recorded data (e.g. audio files, video files).

Media conference A stage-managed event designed to impart information to journalists (aka news conference, press conference, presser).

Menu Script explaining what is coming up later in the bulletin or programme, including sound or video clips.

Meter Device for measuring audio level. The VU (volume unit) meter gives an average reading of the audio; the PPM (peak programme meter) measures the peaks of audio.

Mic Microphone (aka mike).

Mic rattle The noise caused when a mic cable is moved during recording.

Microwave System for relaying audio and video signals on very short wavelengths.

Minicam A lightweight video camera.

Mini DV A digital video tape format.

MiniDisc Digital audio recording medium using small (miniature) compact discs (aka MD).

Mini-jack Jack plug with a small connection.

Mini-wrap Brief package.

Misper Missing person.

Mix Transition from one audio source to another or from one picture to another (aka dissolve).

Mixing Combining two or more audio or picture sources. Used in making packages when interviews and/or links are played over music or special effects.

Mix-minus A special feed of the programme output that lets a remote contributor hear the presenters and other guests, without being distracted by hearing a delayed version of their own voice (aka clean feed).

MS Medium shot or mid-shot. Usually showing the head and upper body.

Multi-media Working across multiple media (usually TV, radio and Internet).

Multi-track Laying down several audio or video tracks on top of each other. The level of each track is adjusted for the finished project.

Recording technique in a music studio to record different voices and instruments on different tracks to mix later.

Nagra A portable recording machine (trade name).

Natural sound Location sound.

NCTJ The National Council for the Training of Journalists.

Needletime The amount of time a station may use to play commercially produced music.

Network A national broadcast channel.

Networked journalism Participatory journalism bringing together traditional journalists and the public using Web-based technologies.

News agency An organisation that provides news stories on a commercial basis for use by other news media.

News bed Music played under the reading of news.

News booth Small studio where bulletins are presented on air or recorded.

Newsclip Short extract of an interview to illustrate a story (aka cut, insert, grab, soundbite).

News conference A stage-managed media event designed to impart information to journalists (aka press conference, presser, media conference).

News copy News story.

Item in radio news with no audio, or TV with no pictures.

Newsflash Interruption of normal programming to give brief details of an urgent breaking news story.

News judgement Ability to recognise the relative importance of news.

Newsmix A mixture of different types of news in a summary (e.g. national and local, hard and soft).

News release Publicity handout from an organisation or PR company informing the newsroom about a possible news item. Traditionally these were received through the post but increasingly newsrooms receive them via email (aka press release or media release).

Newsroom conference Discussion between journalists about what stories to run and how they should be covered.

Newsroom diary A diary, usually electronic, in the newsroom listing all the known stories and news events by date (aka prospects).

Newsworthiness The qualities that make a story worth telling.

NIB News in brief.

Noddies Shots of the reporter nodding or listening, recorded separately from a television interview to be cut in later to cover edits.

Noise reduction The electronic reduction of interference induced by the transmission system.

Network A national broadcast channel.

Non-linear editing Editing out of sequence using digital storage of audio and video data.

Nose Angle. A journalist asked to give a story a new nose is expected to give it a new angle.

NUJ National Union of Journalists.

OB Outside broadcast.

Obscenity button Switch used for taking a programme instantly out of delay to prevent an obscene caller from being heard on air (aka profanity button).

O/C On camera.

Ofcom Office of Communications. A statutory body that sets standards for the content of TV and radio broadcasting in the UK.

Ofcom Code The Ofcom Broadcasting Code came into effect on 25 July 2005. It is available in printed form or online from the Ofcom website www.ofcom.org.uk.

Off-diary Off-diary stories are stories that break during the day, or exclusives uncovered by correspondents.

Officialese The use of official jargon (often from government offices), which is difficult for the public to understand.

Off-mic Noise not fed directly through the microphone but audible in the broadcast. If someone does not speak directly into the pick-up area of the mic, they may sound 'off-mic' and their sound will not be as crisp and clear as when they are 'on-mic'.

Off-the-record A term used when talking with sources. There are varying interpretations:

1 The informant does not mind the information being broadcast as long as they are not identified as the source.
2 The story can only run if it can be confirmed by somebody else.
3 The information should merely be guidance to the reporter in the pursuit of a story.

It must be made clear to the informant exactly what 'off-the-record' means.

OMB One-man band. Single-person camera crews – a single operator works the camera and monitors the sound levels.

Omni-directional Term used for a mic with a circular pick-up pattern.

One-to-one A one-to-one interview is when a reporter or presenter speaks to one interviewee.

On-mic When someone is positioned correctly and speaking into the pick-up area of the mic.

On-screen streamer Text that scrolls from right to left across the lower third of a TV screen (aka ticker-tape).

Open talkback When the presenter can hear everything that is going on in the studio gallery through an earpiece.

Opt-in The process of switching between local and network transmissions. Opting-in occurs when a local station goes over to a live network programme.

Opt-out To return to a local programme from a network.

An early point at which a report may be brought to an end (aka pot cut, early out).

A regional TV programme that opts out of a network.

OOV Out of vision. Instruction on a TV script to show the narrator is not to appear in vision while reading the script (aka voice-over, VO, underlay).

Out cue Last words in a sound bite (aka out).

Out of sync If video is 'out of sync', the sound and video do not match. People's mouths do not move in time with what they are saying.

Output The sound that is heard by radio listeners.

The programme-making operation of a newsroom.

Out-take Part of any recorded media that is not used.

PA Press Association. The UK's biggest news agency.

Package An edited report.

Padding Items used as fillers. Non-essential stories (aka pad copy, fill copy).

Paintbox Electronic graphics machine (trade name).

Pan A horizontal camera move.

Pan handle Handle on the camera to turn the head (aka panning handle).

P as B Programme as broadcast. A written record of everything used in a programme, including music, ads, jingles (aka log).

Pay-off The last words of a programme or item.

Peg A reason (date, anniversary, event) for using a story.

Phone-in Programme where listeners ring in with their comments.

Phono Report or interview made by telephone (aka phoner).

Phono lead A lead used to connect one piece of equipment to another.

Photo-calls Stage-managed media events similar to news conferences with the emphasis on the picture opportunities they offer the media.

Picture store Device for electronically storing pictures.

Piece-to-camera Reporter talking to camera on location (aka stand-upper, stand-up).

Pixel Single dot of information on a video screen. They combine to form a picture. The more pixels on a screen the higher the quality.

Pixelate To distort part of a TV picture to obscure the identity of something, such as a face or a car number plate.

Planning board Large board in a newsroom to show the stories that are being covered and which reporters and crews have been assigned to them.

Popping Harsh sound distortion during speech when saying the letters 'p' and 'b', usually caused by the speaker being too close to the mic.

Portable hard drive Portable computer hard drives used for storing digital audio and/or video clips for editing.

Portaprompt Electronic prompting equipment (trade name) (see Autocue).

Pot cut A rapid fade-out of a radio programme.

PPM Peak programme meter. Meter for measuring peak audio signal level.

PR Public relations/press relations.

Precincts Area around a court. Defined by the court, not by reporters. No photography (including moving pictures) is permitted within the precincts of a court.

Pre-fade Facility on a sound desk that enables you to listen to a source, without transmitting it. Used to check levels and in-cues.

Press conference A stage-managed event designed to impart information to journalists (aka presser, news conference, media conference).

Press pass A special pass for media representatives issued by the organisers of an event.

Press release Publicity handout from an organisation or PR company (aka news release).

Presser Press conference.

Pressure group An organisation that campaigns for change, usually on a political issue.

Prima facie At first sight (legal).

Primary source The initial source of a story.

Primetime The time when radio and TV have their highest audiences.

Producer A person in charge of a production – either a programme or an item within a programme.

Profanity button Switch used for taking a programme instantly out of delay to prevent an obscene caller from being heard on air (aka obscenity button).

Promo Promotional trail (aka trail).

Prompter Electronic device that projects scripts onto a screen in front of the camera lens so they can be read by presenters (aka teleprompter, teleprompt, Autocue, Portaprompt).

Prospects The stories from the newsroom diary likely to be covered.

Proximity Closeness to home. A concept defined by people's perception of themselves and how they fit into the world around them.

PRS Performing Rights Society. Collects and distributes licence fees for public performances and broadcasts of musical works.

PSC Portable single camera.

PTC Piece-to-camera. Reporter talking to camera on location (aka stand-upper, stand-up).

Q & A Question and answer. Often used for reporter two-ways.

Quango Quasi-autonomous non-governmental organisations – loosely used to describe non-elected public bodies that operate outside the Civil Service and are funded by the taxpayer.

Quantel A company producing TV transmission systems.

RadioMan A digital editing software program for audio (trade name).

RAJAR Radio Joint Audience Research. The body that measures audiences for all radio stations in the UK.

Reach The percentage of total listeners in the TSA (Total Survey Area) who tune in during a specified period.

Recordist Member of camera crew who operates sound and/or video recording equipment.

Red tops Populist tabloid newspapers usually identified by a red title or masthead.

Reel-to-reel A tape recorder that uses quarter-inch magnetic tape.

Remote studio Small, unmanned studio where guests can be interviewed.

Reithian Values ascribed to Lord John Reith, the first Director-General of the BBC (he had strong Scots Presbyterian values). Associated with the mission to 'inform, educate and entertain'.

Reuters An international news agency.

Reverse A shot of the reporter looking at the person being interviewed (to be used in the editing process).

Reverse question Shot of the reporter repeating questions asked during the interview.

Reverse two-shot Shot of two people with the interviewee's back to camera.

Ribbon mic Sensitive directional microphone, frequently used in recording studios.

Rifle mic Directional microphone for picking up sound at a distance (aka gun mic).

Rip and read Radio wire copy written for broadcast without any rewrite.

ROT Record Off Transmission. A recording of the output.

RSL Restricted Service Licence.

RSS Really Simple Syndication is the system that allows web users to choose topics they want to know about and be alerted when stories on those topics are available to view or hear.

Running order The arrangement of stories for a bulletin. The order the stories will run in (aka lineup, rundown).

Running story A story that develops and is repeatedly reported over a period of time.

Rushes Raw shots prior to editing.

SADiE A digital radio editing software system (trade name).

Safe area Central area of the TV screen where pictures and captions will not be cut off on domestic television sets.

Satellite phone A telephone using satellite technology rather than the phone networks.

Scanner An OB vehicle.

Telecine machine.

Caption scanner.

Device that copies pictures into a computer.

A radio that automatically tunes in to broadcasts by the emergency services.

Schedule A sequence of radio or TV programmes.

Scoop An exclusive story.

Scrambler Device for scrambling satellite TV signals so only authorised viewers can view them.

Segue A sequence of two or more pieces of music broadcast without interruption (aka seg).

Self-op Self-operation – a presenter operates without technical assistance.

Sexy story A story with instant audience appeal – not necessarily about sex.

Share A radio station's audience measured as a percentage of the total amount of time spent by people listening to radio in the survey area.

Shelf item A story that is timeless and can be used at any time (aka evergreen in America).

Signposting Headlining and trailing within a programme to keep the audience interested.

Simulcasting Broadcasting the same output on different services (e.g. radio and TV, or two radio channels).

Single-header Item or programme presented by one person.

Skeleton Incomplete programme script with gaps.

Sky News A 24-hour rolling news channel.

Sky News Radio A national and international radio news service for independent stations.

Slug Catchline. A word or two written at the top of the script to identify the story.

SMS Telephone text messaging.

SOC Standard out cue. An agreed form of words used by a reporter at the end of a story: e.g. 'Gary Hudson, *Midlands Today*, at Stafford Crown Court'.

Social media Interactive, web-based and mobile communication platforms, linking groups of users, such as Facebook, Twitter, etc.

SOF Sound on film.

Soft news Feature-type stories, as opposed to hard news.

SOT Sound-on-tape. Actuality (aka SOF, sync).

SOTUP Upsound – short for 'sound on tape up'.

Sound bed Natural sound played under voice or other sound.

Soundbite Usable part of an interview or snatch of actuality sound (aka grab, cut).

Sounder Ident, jingle.

Sound under Keeping the natural sound low under the voice of a reporter or newscaster.

Source Someone who provides information used in a news story.

The source of a line feed.

Spent conviction A conviction that can no longer be reported safely after a specified time.

Spike A metal prong on which unused or old copy and other pieces of paper are kept. To 'spike' a story is to drop it and not run it (aka biff).

Spin In PR, spin is giving a heavily biased portrayal of an event.

Spin doctors PR people who apply spin to stories.

Splicer Device for manually joining pieces of film or quarter-inch audio tape (aka editing block).

Splicing tape Sticky tape used to join edits on film or audio tape. Seldom used today.

Split page The standard layout of a TV news script. The left side of the page is used for video directions and the right side is for the script.

Split-screen Showing more than one moving image on the television screen at the same time.

Spoilers Stories designed to spoil the impact of a rival's scoop.

Spot story American term for an item of breaking news.

Stab Short jingle used for emphasis.

Staging Unethical practice in which a reporter asks people to behave in a contrived way on camera.

Standbys Items available for use if others are lost.

Stand-up A report on camera on location (aka PTC, piece-to-camera, stand-upper).

Stereo A recording using left and right channels to separate and spread the sound.

Sting Short jingle.

Stills Still images (such as photographs) used in TV programmes.

Stills store System for storing stills.

Strap Caption or Aston.

Streamer Text that scrolls from right to left across the lower third of the TV screen (aka ticker-tape, crawler).

Stringer Freelance reporter covering an area where there is no staff reporter available. Term often used for overseas freelance reporters.

Subpoena A court order compelling a person to attend court or submission of evidence.

Sub judice Literally 'under law'. Often applied to the risk that may arise in reporting forthcoming legal proceedings. Frequently and incorrectly used by authority as a reason for not disclosing information.

Summary Round-up of the most important news.

Summons An order issued by a magistrate to attend court at a stated time and date to answer a charge.

Super Title or caption mechanically superimposed or electronically generated on a TV picture. Used mostly for the names and titles of people being identified in a news package (aka Aston).

Switching pause Short pause in transmission before and after the network bulletin to permit local stations to opt in and out clearly.

Switch talkback Talkback limited by the use of a switch so the presenter can only hear instructions intended for them.

Sync Interview clips and featured sound (aka actuality, SOF, SOT).

Syndicated material Recordings sent out to radio stations by PR and advertising agencies to promote a company or product.

Tabloid A newspaper format that is the smaller of the two common formats in the UK.

Tabloid press Newspapers focusing on less 'serious' content, especially celebrities, sports and sex.

Tailpiece Light-hearted story at the end of a bulletin (aka And finally, kicker).

Talkback Off-air communication system linking studios, control rooms and OB locations. Commonly used for presenter, producer and technical staff to talk between studio and control cubicle.

Talking head A single shot of someone speaking on camera.

Taster Snappy, one-line headline that may include a snatch of actuality. Often used before a commercial break (aka teaser, bump tease).

TBU Telephone balance unit. Device used when recording telephone interviews. Permits the interviewer to use a studio mic and balance the levels of the two voices.

Teaser See Taster.

Tech op Technical operator. Someone who drives a radio programme from outside the studio.

Teleprompter Electronic device that projects scripts on to a screen in front of the camera lens so they can be read by presenters (aka teleprompt, prompter, Autocue, Portaprompt).

Teletext A text and graphic information service on TV.

3G phone Third-generation mobile phone.

Throw To link to a reporter, who picks up the story and runs with it, without relying on questions from the studio.

Ticker-tape Text that scrolls from right to left across the lower third of the TV screen (aka on-screen streamer, crawler).

Tilt A vertical camera move.

Time code A numerical code recorded as video is shot, used in editing. Shows on edit monitor but not on the finished story.

Tip-off Call from a stringer or member of the public about a story.

Tone A constant sound signal used by audio engineers to check sound levels are the same on recording and playback machines.

Top and tail To edit a piece to ensure a clean start and end.

Top line The first line or main point of a story. A new top line would be the latest development in a story.

Touchscreen Equipment controlled electronically by touching part of the screen.

Trail To tell the audience about items coming up.

A promotional item for a forthcoming programme (aka promo).

Transmission area The geographical area served by a station.

Tribunal A special court or committee appointed to deal with particular problems.

Tripod Portable, collapsible, three-legged stand used for mounting a camera.

TSA Total Survey Area – the area surveyed by RAJAR.

Two-shot Camera shot of two people.

Two-way An interview between a presenter and a reporter to provide information and analysis of an event or story (aka Q&A).

TX Transmission.

UCAS University and College Admissions Service. The university applications body.

UGC User-generated content. Content supplied by the public to broadcasters and websites.

U-lay Underlay. Pictures laid under a voice (aka OOV).

Umbrella story A single story incorporating a number of similar items under one link.

Underlay See U-lay.

Uni-directional mic Microphone that responds mainly to sounds directly in front of it.

UPI United Press International – a news agency.

Update New information in a news story that requires a rewrite.

VCR Videocassette recorder.

VJ Video-journalist. Journalist who reports with a videocamera and shoots and edits on their own.

Video phone A phone that transmits video.

Vision mixer Operator in a studio gallery who cuts between pictures.

The equipment a vision mixer uses.

Visuals The visual element of a TV report: stills, film or video and graphics.

Vlog A blog using video content.

V-O Voice-over. Commentary over pictures by an unseen speaker.

Voice-bank Recorded information from the emergency services accessed by journalists by phone.

Voice-over V-O.

Voice-piece Voicer.

Voicer Voice-only report (with no soundbites).

Vox pops Street interviews with members of the public. From the Latin *vox populi* or voice of the people (aka voxes).

VTR Videotape recorder or videotape recording.

VU meter Volume unit meter. Meter for monitoring recording and playback levels.

Wallpaper Derogatory term for TV pictures that are used simply to cover the narrator's words.

Waveform Digital image for audio displayed on a computer in the form of zig-zag waves. These can be edited on screen.

WHAT formula A formula for story construction: What has happened? How did it happen? Amplification. Tie up loose ends.

Wildtrack Recording of ambient sound for dubbing later as background to the report or to cover edits (aka atmos).

Windshield A foam 'sock' used over a mic to prevent wind noise.

Wipe Crossing from one picture to another, giving the impression that one is wiping the other off the screen.

Wire copy Material written for broadcast distributed by wire services such as AP and Reuters.

Wire service News agency that sends copy to newsrooms along landlines (wires). News agencies increasingly send copy online or via satellite, but are still known as 'the wires'.

WPB Waste paper bin.

Wrap To wrap is to end a shoot (according to film buffs the term is short for 'wind reel and print').

A radio news item including an interview clip: the reporter 'wraps' their voice around a soundbite. In some newsrooms a 'wrap' is interchangeable with a package, but it is usually shorter and only features one clip.

WS Wide camera shot.

WTN Worldwide Television News.

WWW World Wide Web. Graphical interface of the global network of digitised information stored on the Internet.

Young person In law, a person 14 years of age or above, but below 18.

INDEX